Ableism

Contemporary Social Issues

Contemporary Social Issues, a book series authored by leading experts in the field, focuses on psychological inquiry and research relevant to social issues facing individuals, groups, communities, and society at large. Each volume is written for scholars, students, practitioners, and policy-makers.

Series Editor: Daniel Perlman

Ableism

The Causes and Consequences of Disability Prejudice

Michelle R. Nario-Redmond

WILEY Blackwell

This edition first published 2020

© 2020 John Wiley & Sons, Inc.

The right of Michelle R. Nario-Redmond to be identified as the author of this work has been asserted in accordance with law.

Registered Office
John Wiley & Sons, Inc., 111 River Street, Hoboken, NJ 07030, USA

Editorial Office
111 River Street, Hoboken, NJ 07030, USA

For details of our global editorial offices, customer services, and more information about Wiley products visit us at www.wiley.com.

Wiley also publishes its books in a variety of electronic formats and by print-on-demand. Some content that appears in standard print versions of this book may not be available in other formats.

Library of Congress Cataloging-in-Publication data applied for
9781119142072 (Paper back), 9781119142126 (ePDF), 9781119142133 (epub)

Cover Design: Wiley
Cover Image: © Colin Anderson Productions pty ltd/Getty Images

Set in 10/12pt Galliard by SPi Global, Pondicherry, India

10 9 8 7 6 5 4 3 2 1

For Ceara Grace whose name means woman wielding a sword. *You are the reason I came to disability studies and became a warrior for disability culture and justice. I love you my girl.*

For Peter James, my rock who envisioned this long before I did. Thank you for your music, meals, and for nurturing these pursuits.

For Ethan Joseph – steadfast and loyal ally. Thank you for coming to our family and for your deep well of empathy for others.

For my parents' never-ending love and support and for all the Beachwood kids who gave me kisses as I worked.

For Dr. Arielle Silverman. Your collaboration on insider perspectives has been invaluable. And to the best developmental editor a gal could ever ask for. I am so grateful to Dr. Dan Perlman.

Finally, to my disabled students and allies: Alexia Kemerling, Nina Lester, and Zoe Sajen. I am especially thankful to you and to the many students who contributed to the Activist pages with news, scholarship, theme analyses, and polling data. Thank you for making sure I did not miss key implications for social change: Brianne Goodrich, Angela Cobb-Munez, Megan Schaefer, Vaal Ngalla, and Jacob Marvin. I appreciate your dedication to changing the world.

Contents

Foreword

Think for a moment: how many immediate family members, relatives, friends, and/or other significant people in your life – including yourself – have a disability; that is, who "happen to be blind, deaf, or living with chronic physical, intellectual, or mental health conditions"? How many close friends and relatives with such conditions can you think of? One, two, three, four, five …?

Given that a Gallup poll found most Americans have nine close friends, not counting relatives, let us say there are 20 people with whom you interact in important ways – working with them, attending parties with them, helping or being helped by them, etc. According to the US census, 19% of Americans or 56.7 of roughly 322 million are identified as disabled. Approximately one in five Americans have a disability; in your network of your 20 most important relationships, four members are likely to have a disability. Can you think of those members? I can.

In my own family network, three members have disabilities (autism, manic depression, and dementia) such that they need assisted living or social benefits for individuals with disabilities. One of my most important former mentors has congestive heart disease. I myself am sufficiently hearing impaired that I often ask my wife and others "What did you say?" and use various strategies at work and in noisy social situations to hear people. My point is that most of us, ourselves, have – or at some point in our lives will have – a disability.

Michelle Nario-Redmond's tour de force book is about ableism, aka disability prejudice, and the experiences of individuals with disability. It builds on decades of social science literature, integrating it in a comprehensive, fresh way. In addition to considering how individuals and macro forces contribute to ableism, Michelle emphasizes a previously neglected intergroup perspective. She writes: "An intergroup perspective on ableism recognizes that while prejudice often occurs between individuals interacting at the interpersonal level, prejudice also represents beliefs and motivations that derive from belonging to particular groups – groups of "us" and "them" – groups often motivated to maintain their status differences."

The book progresses in three logically organized sections. The first section examines the causes of disability prejudice, starting with evolutionary explanations.

Is prejudice against disabled individuals something innate in human nature designed to foster reproduction and the species' successful perpetuation? Another explanation for disability prejudice is rooted in our ideologies such as individualism or the Protestant ethic that get transmitted to us through social influences (e.g. the media, the stories we tell). An analysis of how stereotypes, the thoughts we have in our heads, contribute to our disability prejudices rounds out this section of the book.

The middle section of the book deals with the consequences of disability prejudice. One focus in this section is the emotional reactions, attitudes, and interaction patterns others have with and toward people with disabilities. These can be benevolent and caring, paternalistic, pitying, or hostile. Often they are an ambivalent mixture. Michelle illuminates when various reactions are most likely. The second focus of this section, written with disabled social scientist Arielle Silverman, is how people with disabilities respond, either individually or collectively, to the ableism they experience. Possible reactions include trying to conceal one's disability or endeavoring to improve the status of disabled people. Both approaches have risks and rewards.

The final section of the book introduces interventions to reduce ableism and promote social change. This section opens with three common approaches: encouraging contact between disabled and nondisabled people, various types of training, and the problem with simulations (e.g. using a wheelchair) designed to create aspects of the experience of having a disability. Contact under the right conditions arguably has the strongest record of effectiveness. The final segment of the book considers evidence on the success of the disability rights movement. Michelle writes that "Arguably, among the most enduring, positive impacts on ableist practices have been policy-based, including structural changes for inclusive integration at school and work, access to the built environment, and anti-discrimination legislation." Allies and group coalitions are helpful in bringing about these impacts.

There are many features that make this book special for me, among them are the following:

- It captures the complexity of disability: its varieties, causes, its challenges, the responses it elicits, and how society might combat ableism (aka disability prejudice).
- The attention to both disabled and nondisabled people in the analysis.
- The multiple conceptual perspectives including one's crossing disciplinary boundaries and the impressive body of evidence the author brings to bear on ableism.
- The author's bringing to the fore an intergroup perspective.
- The rich set of research ideas for scholars and students to pursue.

My favorite, reader-friendly feature is Michelle's including a set of Activist pages in the book. As their name implies, they offer ideas about ways people can address and resist ableism. They provide concrete cases and problems found in everyday life, fascinating topics (e.g. inspirational porn), getting below the surface (implicit ableism), cartoons, the views of individuals with disabilities, informational leads on disability resources and advocacy bodies, and so on. They add richness and immediacy to the phenomena of ableism.

It is the Society for the Psychological Study of Social Issues' (SPSSI's) honor and privilege to sponsor this volume as part of the Society's Contemporary Social Issues series. Reflecting the Society's traditions and values as a social justice organization, the series consists of authored books addressing a diverse array of social concerns that are amenable to psychological analysis. Grounded in its author's expertise, each volume focuses on an area of psychological inquiry relevant to social issues facing individuals, groups, communities, and/or society at large. Each volume is written for a diverse audience of scholars, students, practitioners, and policy-makers. Without any doubt, anyone who wants a scholarly informed analysis of a social issue in which they are interested should find the books in this series of interest. This volume will be of particular value to social science and disability scholars as well as professionals occupying various roles. Indeed, despite the sometimes distant or contentious relations between psychologists and disability study scholars, one of the Michelle's goals is to encourage more multidisciplinary cross-fertilization between camps and within the subdisciplines of social, rehabilitation, and community psychology. I am rooting that it will!

I started with a question. I will end with one. Do you want your family members or friends to be the targets of ableism – a phenomena that assumes the superiority of nondisabled individuals and perpetuates false perceptions of people with disabilities and discrimination against them? My answer is "No!" In its place, I want a socially just society that respects and fosters the well-being of all its members.

Dan Perlman
Editor (2013–2019)
SPSSI's Contemporary Social Issues Series

Further Reading

Carroll, J. (2004). *Americans satisfied with number of friends, closeness of friendships.* Gallup News Service. Retrieved from https://news.gallup.com/poll/10891/americans-satisfied-number-friends-closeness-friendships.aspx.

Erickson, W., Lee, C., and von Schrader, S. (2017). Disability Statistics from the American Community Survey (ACS). Ithaca, NY: Cornell University Yang-Tan Institute (YTI). Retrieved from Cornell University Disability Statistics website: www.disabilitystatistics.org.

1

Introduction: Defining Ableism

Ableism is when you say that I don't act disabled and expect me to take that as a compliment …

Ableism is when "whole" is a word reserved for the able-bodied, or when you say that I'm beautiful despite my differences, and fail to recognize that I'm beautiful because of them …

Ableism is when you leave us to ripen and rot hanging from the vine because you refuse to bite into our fruit. Ableism is the fruit of your fears …

Ableism is when you assume I'm single … when you assume I'm a virgin, when you assume I hate my body because in your narrow mind how could I not? …

Ableism is when parents yank their kids away and tell them not to stare, automatically teaching them that disability is a dirty word …

Ableism is when you make plans that do not include accessible venues, accessible spaces, so it becomes easier to erase me from your list …

Ableism is when disabled parents are told they should not be parents …

Ableism is making heroes out of people who take disabled kids to the prom and never talk to them again because that one "good deed" is good for at least 10 years, if not a lifetime …

Ableism is a lifetime of isolation, a lifetime of segregation, a lifetime of untold stories of "Once upon a time there was a cripple who could" and for every cripple that could there was and is an able-bodied person who should but doesn't …

Ableism is the fact that we can embarrass you just by sitting in the same room and breathing the same air …

Ableism is the way media portrays us as either objects of pity or inspiration …

Ableism: The Causes and Consequences of Disability Prejudice, First Edition.
Michelle R. Nario-Redmond.
© 2020 John Wiley & Sons, Inc. Published 2020 by John Wiley & Sons, Inc.

Ableism is how you want to lock us in the closet and how you believe that giving us new labels like physically challenged and differently abled is no longer labeling us …

Ableism is making buses accessible but not the streets leading to the bus stop …

Ableism is when you say that if God hasn't healed me, it is only because I don't have enough faith …

Ableism is how your faith considers me a punishment from God, or how you try to pray my differences away as if they were demons …

Ableism is your ability to find reasons to push us aside to keeps us in cages, leave our struggles out of the history pages … pretend we never existed …

Ableism is when you think I don't have a disability because you can't see it …

Ableism is asking my friends what I would like to order because you fear not being able to communicate with me. Ableism is the fact that you don't even try …

Ableism is calling my needs "special" and then ignoring them …

Ableism is believing I need to be fixed. Ableism is you refusing to fix what's really broken …

Ableism is painting our lives like a tragic story …

Ableism is our story told by nondisabled voices captured through a nondisabled lens …

Ableism is you feeling like I should be grateful for the ramps and the parking spaces as if access was not a basic right …

Ableism is when you force unsolicited help upon me because, to you, it seemed like I needed it …

Ableism is you thinking that my asking for help gives you the right to decide for me …

Ableism is when you wish for a world without disabled people, and you say that to me and expect me to agree with you …

Ableism is when you say that if you became disabled, you would want to die …

Ableism is wishing you could help us die, or wishing you didn't have to help us live …

Ableism is believing disabled people are better off dead …

(Selections from "Naming Ableism" by
Maria Palacios 2017. Full poem on pp. 34–36)

While research on ageism, heterosexism, and anti-fat attitudes has been steadily increasing, the study of ableism or disability prejudice is still in its infancy (Corrigan 2014). First referenced over 35 years ago in the women's news journal *Off Our Backs* (House 1981), ableism is an uncomfortable subject, a difficult dialogue, and not just because people feel bad for those who happen to be blind, deaf, or living with chronic physical, intellectual, or mental health conditions.

Disappointment, disregard, discomfort, and distain are provoked, in part, because disability is a group that anyone can join – at any time. This can be scary, especially for those less familiar with diverse disabled people.

However, this book was designed to provoke difficult dialogues about disability – a social status that incites both hostile and benevolent forms of prejudice – and a group that provokes stereotypes of incompetence and dependency, and behaviors that range from staring and unwanted assistance to abandonment, dehumanization, and hate crimes. As illustrated in the opening poem by educator, author, and activist Maria Palacios, sometimes these prejudices are motivated by fear and contempt – at other times pity, inspiration, and compassion are involved as well. Extending the multitude of volumes on racism, sexism, and intergroup prejudice more generally, this book is among the first to integrate the social scientific literature on the origins and manifestations of prejudice against disabled people as a social group writ large – a group that confronts pervasive discrimination for the right to live independently, to work, and to parent.

More than one billion people in the world live with some form of disability, of whom nearly 200 million experience considerable difficulties in functioning. In the years ahead, disability will be an even greater concern because its prevalence is on the rise. This is due to ageing populations and the higher risk of disability in older people as well as the global increase in chronic health conditions such as diabetes, cardiovascular disease, cancer and mental health disorders. World Health Organization (WHO 2011, p. 5)

The Largest Minority Group: Who Qualifies?

Disability is a membership status on the rise both globally and in the United States (WHO 2011). One in five people currently qualify as living with disability,[1] and many more will acquire the status on either a permanent or temporary basis, the longer they live (Fujiura and Rutkowski-Kmitta 2001). Yet, for reasons this book will tackle head on, disability is a status that seems avoidable – even preventable – unlike old age and the inevitability of death. People don't like to think about disability. Some even characterize it as a fate worse than death: "I'd rather be dead than disabled," is a comment that continues to resonate in popular discourse (Reynolds 2017).

Though surprising to some, disabled people make up the largest minority group in the United States, with 19% of the population or 56.7 million disabled people identified by the US Census (Brault 2012). But the census underestimates the population since it does not count institutionalized people with disabilities incarcerated in prisons or in nursing homes.[2] Some people are born into disability with conditions like Down syndrome, dwarfism, or other congenital impairments.[3] The vast majority of impairments, however (e.g. cerebral palsy, amputation, brain injury, multiple sclerosis), occur after birth, through accidental injury or the progression of disease (Vos et al. 2016). Furthermore, fractured limbs, concussions, low vision, hearing loss, and depression are quite common throughout the lifecycle, and many people experience multiple disabling conditions that vary in appearance and severity (Centers for Disease Control and Prevention 2013). According to US projections, given a 75-year life expectancy, newborns will average 11 years with disabilities that limit their activities, and those who live past 75 can expect an additional four to five years of disability (Melzer et al. 2000; Zola 1993). When it comes to disability – it's more a question of when it will happen – not if. I've often wondered whether the open-enrollment nature of disability is part of the reason ableism has been such a contentious topic, even among the experts who study stereotyping and prejudice.

> In 2003, there were no fewer than 67 US federal statutory definitions of disability. (Krahn et al. 2015, p. S199)

The concept of disability itself is highly contested (McDermott and Turk 2011). Who qualifies as disabled (and who doesn't) continues to be a moving target since defining characteristics change depending on the source, setting, and historical time period. For example, the same person who is considered disabled at school may not qualify as disabled at work. Different organizations have different inclusion criteria. Some people qualify as disabled if diagnosed with a specific impairment (e.g. autism, spina bifida, depression). Yet, a diagnosis alone does not predict a person's ability to function in different settings or with particular accommodations. People with the same exact diagnoses can differ widely in terms of their functional abilities, prognosis, and predictability of symptoms.

Not only can the same impairment result in very different limitations for different people, but very different impairments can produce similar limitations: both heart and back problems can reduce mobility. For this reason, many definitions of disability focus on age-specific activity restrictions related to self-care (e.g. bathing, dressing) and other activities of daily living (e.g. managing money, shopping). Questions about activity restrictions typically focus on what people *cannot* do (e.g. "Can you get outside the home?"), which fail to account for the use of technologies and other modifications like the availability of ramps to and from a wheelchair user's destination. Finally, some disabling conditions like facial scars, HIV/AIDS, or a record of "mental illness" are not associated with any physical limitations; yet, people still experience barriers that restrict their participation in a variety of settings. To address these complexities, the International Classification of Functioning, Disability and Health (ICF) defines disability as an umbrella term that incorporates impairments, activity limitations, and participation restrictions (Jelsma 2009).

The Americans with Disabilities Act (ADA 1990) also includes a three-pronged definition of disability to protect citizens against discrimination or unfair treatment on the basis of disability: "A person with a disability is defined as a person with a physical or mental impairment that substantially limits one or more major life activities; or a person with a record of such a physical or mental impairment; or a person who is regarded as having such an impairment." However, before the 2008 amendments, the ADA excluded protection for those with medically correctable conditions (e.g. hearing aids) and those treatable with drugs (e.g. bipolar disorder, epilepsy). This lack of consensus about disability status is also reflected in recent public opinion polls.

According to nationally representative surveys, Americans still do not agree on what conditions should qualify as disabilities, particularly when it comes to mental "illnesses" like schizophrenia, depression, and addiction (Shannon-Missal 2015). Agreement is even lower among older adults, Republicans, and those without disabled people in their household. In 2015, less than 58% of Americans believed that speech, language, and learning disabilities should qualify as disabilities under the ADA. Yet, in 2015, most (39%) students (ages 6–21) receiving special education services in the United States experienced specific learning disabilities, followed by those with speech-language disabilities (17%) (Lauer and Houtenville 2018). The disconnect between public perceptions and reality makes the study of disability and disability prejudice ripe for investigation.

> As I see it, the theoretical framework and analytical lens of Ableism is a gift from the disabled people rights movement [sic] and disability studies to the social sciences and humanities. (Wolbring 2012)

Ableism Defined

The term ableism emerged out of the disability rights movements in the United States and Britain to serve as an analytical parallel to sexism and racism for those studying disability as social creation (Wolbring 2012). With interdisciplinary origins, ableism has been defined as "ideas, practices, institutions, and social relations that presume able-bodiedness, and by so doing, construct persons with disabilities as marginalized ... and largely invisible 'others'" (Chouinard 1997, p. 380). Yet ableism affects the "able-bodied" too, as many impairments are not physically apparent in, or on, the body. Alternative definitions describe ableism as "a doctrine that falsely treats impairments as inherently and naturally horrible and blames the impairments themselves for the problems experienced by the people who have them" (Amundson and Taira 2005, p. 54). According to Hehir (2002), ableism is "the devaluation of disability that results in societal attitudes that uncritically assert that it is better for a child to walk than roll, speak than sign, read print than read Braille, spell independently than use a spell-check, and hang out with nondisabled kids as opposed to other disabled kids" (p. 2). Sometimes referred to as disablism (Miller et al. 2004) or disability oppression, ableism privileges a nondisabled perspective and promotes the inferior and unequal treatment of disabled people (Campbell 2009).

While multiple definitions help frame the scope of the concept, in the present volume, ableism is simply defined as prejudice and discrimination toward individuals simply because they are classified as disabled – regardless of whether their impairments are physical or mental, visible or invisible. In the field of social psychology, prejudice is traditionally conceptualized in terms of three related components. These are the A, B, Cs of ableism:

- Affective emotions or attitudinal reactions,
- Behavioral actions/practices, and
- Cognitive beliefs/stereotypes that go beyond general negativity.

To illustrate how this works at the interpersonal level, imagine meeting someone with a disability: if feelings of disgust or pity emerge (affect), one may offer to help or simply avoid interacting (behavior) – especially if one believes the person with a disability needs assistance or can't think clearly (cognition). Ableism can operate at multiple levels affecting personal self-perceptions, interpersonal interactions, and intergroup relations. Like other prejudices, there are both individual and institutionalized forms of ableism and discrimination as well.

Ongoing Disparities: Institutionalized Ableism

Based on the most recent US Census and nationally representative surveys, large disparities remain between disabled and nondisabled people in terms of educational attainment, employment status, healthcare, and other indicators of societal participation (Erickson et al. 2017; Kraus et al. 2018). In terms of educational attainment, in 2015, students with disabilities were twice as likely to have earned *less than a high school* education by age 25 compared to nondisabled peers. Furthermore, by age 25, only 10.3% of disabled students had earned a four-year college degree compared to 21.4% of nondisabled students, who were twice as likely to have achieved more than a four-year degree (Lauer and Houtenville 2018). Although the percentage of students with disabilities who pursue higher education has steadily increased (National Council on Disability 2014), some argue that the special education system itself contributes directly to the problem of underachievement. Special education, as a segregated system, can become a dumping ground for students with disabilities, especially for those with multiple minority statutes (Ferri and Connor 2005). In the United States, Black students make up 17% of total school enrollments but 33% of those labeled "mentally retarded," which is nearly three times higher than the figure for white children. Black students are also twice as likely to be labeled emotionally disturbed compared to White students (Macedo and Marti 2010). In fact, a disability diagnosis has been deployed as a nonracial basis for expulsion from school – contributing to the school-to-prison pipeline (Reid and Knight 2006; Redfield and Nance 2016).

The legacy of marginalization and segregation is not limited to the special education "short bus," as ableism is reflected in employment and healthcare disparities as well. For example, based on representative survey samples, compared to nondisabled people (12%) more than twice as many people with disabilities (27%) said they needed to see a doctor but did not because of cost (Krahn et al. 2015); and inadequate transportation was cited as a significant barrier to healthcare twice as often by people with disabilities compared to those without.

> Accessible transportation is a basic necessity for many Americans to secure and maintain employment. Regardless of the number or effectiveness of programs and incentives designed to promote job opportunities for people with disabilities, in most instances, workers cannot secure and maintain a job if they do not have accessible transportation to get to it. (National Council on Disability 2014, p. 28)

In 2016, 76.8% of people (18–64 years old) without disabilities were employed compared to only 35.9% of people with disabilities; and only 23% of these disabled people worked full-time, year round (Lauer and Houtenville 2018). This 40% employment gap has remained constant for the past 10 years across economic downturn and recovery (Kraus et al. 2018). In 2016, median work earnings were over $10 000 lower for those with disabilities while their poverty rate was more than twice as high (26.7%) as those without disabilities (11.6%).[4]

Moreover, ableism pervades many other "major life activities" including participation in political, parental, and romantic arenas. Disabled people are less likely to marry, and if they do are more likely to get divorced. The rate for first marriages for people from 18 to 49 years of age is 71.8 per 1000 but only 41.1 per 1000 for people with disabilities – significantly lower than the general population (Cohen 2014). These rates vary widely for different ethnic groups: African Americans with disabilities have among the lowest marriage rates. Furthermore, while divorce rates in the United States have increased in general over the past 25 years, if a spouse becomes disabled, the likelihood of divorce is much higher, particularly among young, educated men with acquired disabilities that prevent them from working (Singleton 2012). Based on analyses of the American Community Survey, Cohen (2014) found that people with disabilities are up to twice as likely to get divorced compared to those without disabilities. Similarly, parents with disabled children are also up to two times more likely to divorce than those in the general population (Hartley et al. 2010; Wymbs et al. 2008).

Finally, disabled people are at much higher risk for secondary health conditions like obesity and heart disease, and are at greater risk of both unintentional injury and intentional victimization and violent crime (see Chapter 2). Specifically, disabled people are "more than twice as likely to report rape or sexual assault compared to people without disability. Women are victimized more often than men … [and] both men and women with disabilities are at significantly increased risk for intimate partner violence" (Krahn et al. 2015, p. S201–S202).

Historical Approaches to the Study of Disability Prejudice

Since its inception in the mid-1980s, the field of Disability Studies, like Black Studies and Women's Studies, has underscored the importance of disability as a social construction – a concept created to provide some basis for shared ideas about reality. In the case of concepts like race, gender, and disability, the reality that is created (and perpetuated) is often hierarchical: Some groups are positioned with more privilege and power over other groups who remain disadvantaged. Because they are social creations, these concepts mean different things in different places, and change with time as societies evolve and regress. For example, some still consider homosexuality a lifestyle choice; yet, increasingly science has documented its biological bases (Mustanski et al. 2002). Likewise, disability has seen many alternative constructions throughout history, equating it with the supernatural, the animalistic, the biological, and most recently, the socio-political (Burch and Rembis 2014; Wendell 1996).

Some scholars who have taken up the issue of ableism focus on large-scale political, economic, and structural issues that systematically oppress those who differ from the norm (Charlton 1998; Hollomotz 2013). Others have written from a humanities perspective to theorize the philosophical contours of ableism, and challenge the concept of normalcy (Campbell 2009; Scuro 2017). Within the field of psychology, psychoanalytic critiques have been applied to explain how ableist beliefs can affect the socialization of self through discourses about trauma and control, projection, and the rationalization of bias (Goodley 2011; Watermeyer 2012). Rehabilitation psychologists have also expanded their research on personal adaptation to disability to examine the interpersonal and environmental factors affecting the attitudes of nondisabled people toward disabled people – a topic that has dominated the study of disability prejudice for many years (Dunn 2010).

A review of textbooks on the psychology of prejudice and discrimination, however, revealed very few, and mostly brief, sections on disability prejudice as a category of study (Chin 2010; Nelson 2006; Whitley and Kite 2009). As a consequence, most students of psychology, like the public more generally, continue to assume that disability has more to do with people's biological impairments (e.g. blindness, deafness, or spinal cord injury) than with their socially disadvantaged status, and they are not alone. My own field of social psychology has been slow to recognize disabled people as a social group (see Nario-Redmond 2010). This is unfortunate considering that the study of disability as a social creation began in the 1940s with Beatrice Wright, an early pioneer of disability studies and a student of Kurt Lewin. Lewin is recognized as the founder of social psychology, the man who championed the idea of: "No action without research. No research without action" (Adelman 1993, p. 8). Lewin's work inspired one of the most influential papers in my development as a social psychologist doing disability studies: "Disability Beyond Stigma: Social Interaction, Discrimination, and Activism." In this paper, Fine and Asch (1988) called for a return to Lewinian principles and a *minority-group approach* to disability prejudice. This was 30 years ago when these authors challenged the individualistic assumptions driving the study of disability in social psychology; yet, few have taken up that call for intergroup theorizing and action-based research, until recently (see Dirth and Branscombe 2018).

Instead, social psychological research has focused almost exclusively on the stigma and anxiety associated with specific impairment conditions like paralysis, autism, and schizophrenia. In fact, this focus on the stigma of individual impairments has influenced the questions researchers have asked, and the methods they have used for the past five decades. To illustrate, one very popular method for assessing disability attitudes asks people about the closest relationships they are willing to have with those who experienced any number of conditions, including mental illnesses, blindness, deafness, dwarfism, missing limbs, etc. The approach resulted in a rank ordering of those impairment groups that people would: institutionalize, live next to, or accept as co-workers, friends, or romantic partners (see Chapter 5). Studies using these "preference hierarchies" proliferated, although some have called for the permanent halting of this approach to measuring disability prejudice which can neither explain why some conditions rank higher than others nor predict prejudicial treatment more broadly (Olkin and Howson 1994).

By failing to conceptualize disability as a social category, a group membership, questions about ableism as a more global set of reactions toward disabled people as a whole (regardless of impairment) cannot be considered. This is changing as scholars begin to recognize that the study of stigma and attitudes is incomplete without an analysis of the experiences of disabled people as a group in order to uncover the broader social and political implications of ableism and its effects on the participation and well-being of current and future citizens with disabilities.

The subject of ableism is now being explored descriptively through personal narratives, and discourse analyses, at both micro and macro levels. What remains lacking is a distinctly *intergroup* perspective that incorporates contemporary theory and research on the psychology of prejudice, mindful of recent critiques and new interdisciplinary approaches (Dixon and Levine 2012). An intergroup perspective on ableism recognizes that while prejudice often occurs between individuals interacting at the interpersonal level, prejudice also represents beliefs and motivations that derive from belonging to particular groups – groups of "us" and "them" – groups often motivated to maintain their status differences (Tajfel and Turner 1979). Until very recently, the discipline of social psychology had not articulated disability as a socially contingent category, a disadvantaged minority status influenced by intergroup power dynamics and the material environment in ways that shape ableist attitudes, stereotypic beliefs, and discriminatory behaviors (Nario-Redmond 2010).

Therefore, the ground is extremely fertile for new research at the intersections of disability studies, social, and community psychology. There has been growing recognition that traditional approaches focused only on "what's wrong" with the individual are not sufficient because they don't account for persistent inequalities, prejudice, and discrimination experienced by this marginalized group. A social psychology of disability is needed to explore the mechanisms, myths, values, attributions, and emotional reactions that lead to biased intergroup judgments, group identify formation, self-stereotyping, and the tensions between interpersonal liking and collective action for change.

Among contemporary prejudice researchers, a self-critical approach has been gaining traction that recognizes how changing historical policies (e.g. ADA) have shifted the dynamics between disabled and nondisabled groups, altering the forms that ableism can take. Increasingly, prejudice is recognized as a complex manifestation of beliefs, mixed emotions, and behaviors that transcend expressions of general negativity (Glick and Fiske 2001). Prejudice, and disability prejudice in particular, can be benevolent and kind, paternalistic, pitying, and inspired by charitable intentions that nevertheless allow for the justification of control, restricted rights, and dehumanizing actions. For example, as more disabled people are gaining employment and access to higher education, ableism in the form of jealousy can emerge, especially when accommodations are framed as "special privileges," like extra time on tests, books on tape, and the ever coveted disability parking placard.

The changing socio-political landscape is also directing the focus of scholarly research to explore the shifting power dynamics of interpersonal and intergroup life for disabled and nondisabled people alike. This emerging multi-disciplinary scholarship remains somewhat marginalized itself as it is fragmented across many fields of study, appearing in the journals of psychology, sociology, rehabilitation medicine, social work, political science, and disability studies. One of the goals of the present volume is to translate across these disparate literatures on disability attitudes, stigma, stereotypes, prejudice, and discrimination to uncover convergent trends and theoretical advancements, and to call for future research on a myriad of questions yet unanswered. This volume aims to address five key questions:

- What does ableism look like? What are its common manifestations?
- What are the causes of ableism against disabled people, and how are these perpetuated?
- How do disabled people respond to ableism, and how do responses affect well-being?
- What works to reduce ableism, promote understanding, and increase equality?
- What research questions remain unanswered for a future research agenda?

The following section summarizes each of the chapters to follow, which are based on a thorough review of the contemporary and classic research on disability prejudice, and critiques of the prejudice problematic – the approaches that have driven research on stereotyping, prejudice, and stigma for the past 50 years. Each chapter situates findings within the context of intergroup relations theories, identifying methodological limits, and suggesting contingent interpretations along with next steps. The chapters are organized into three parts: the origins of ableism (Chapters 2, 3, and 4); its consequences for targets' interpersonal and social relationships (Chapters 5 and 6); and advances from interventions to reduce ableism and activism to promote equality and social change (Chapters 7 and 8).

Specifically, following this introductory chapter, I review research testing the various theoretical origins associated with disability prejudice, beginning with the most distal or remote explanations about our evolutionary predispositions and universal motives. This is followed by more midrange explanations focused on ideologies, media portrayals, and language. I then review the more proximal explanations for ableism and its impact on disabled people, including the cognitive-affective mechanisms and contextual factors that sustain, qualify, and alter its expression. The final chapters examine the impact of interventions that have been effective in reducing prejudice and ableism more specifically, and the disability rights advocacy and collective action efforts that have resulted in specific social changes, followed by an agenda for future research.

Chapter 2. The Evolutionary and Existential Origins of Ableism

The evolutionary and existential origins of ableism are among the more distal explanations for prejudice, less accessible to awareness. They focus on the relatively universal and unconscious tendencies that humans from around the world demonstrate, revealing some of our most basic needs for safety, belonging, and significance. This chapter first describes the basic premises of evolutionary theory, and its implications for disability prejudice. According to evolutionary theory, one of the root causes of prejudice derives from biological predispositions that were adaptive in early hunter-gatherer societies – where communal living offered safety, and attention to potential threats helped protect the group (Kurzban and Leary 2001). The idea is that human ancestors who inherited the tendency to be watchful and wary of danger were more likely to survive, reproduce, and pass on these same traits to their children. This evolved capacity for watchfulness is considered to be threat specific, which may help to explain why prejudice comes in a variety of forms. For example, if a stranger acted in ways that signaled competition, the most adaptive response might be anger (and beliefs that justified retaliation). However, if a stranger or even someone from within the group acted in ways suggestive of illness or disease, the most adaptive response might be avoidance (and beliefs that justified the elimination of this threat).

Some disability prejudice, therefore, might be an evolutionary holdover from those who inherited a disease-avoidance system that became overly sensitive to people whose appearance or behavior signaled poor health – even if they were not infectious. If some people inherited an overactive disease-detection mechanism, they might stare and respond fearfully to others with disease cues like open sores, spasms, or missing limbs, which tend to characterize some of the world's deadliest infections (Oaten et al. 2011). As a consequence, those who limp, tremor, or have uneven arms or eyes may trigger a false alarm in people who express discomfort and avoid contact even with objects touched by people with certain disabilities (Maguire and Haddad 1990). Some evidence in support of these ideas comes from tests of the disease-avoidance model of disability prejudice. Park et al. (2003) found that some people do overgeneralize their adaptive fear and disgust toward pathogens by avoiding those with disabilities who are not contagious. These evolved tendencies are even more likely when people feel vulnerable to disease, like when pregnant or in hospital settings.

People don't usually catch disability like the flu despite that fact that around the world disabled people provoke repulsion and are treated *as if* they are contagious. They are isolated and shunned from public venues. People with cancer, cleft palates, birthmarks, and burns report being treated as if they were contagious, and responded to with gestures of disgust. Such "germaphobic" tendencies have important implications for interventions designed to promote inclusion and physical connection. If some people have a predisposition to avoid those who trigger contagion fears, interventions that put people into close contact to reduce disability prejudice might actually increase anxiety. Alternatively, with increasing exposure, such fears might become obsolete over time. Unfortunately, by assuming prejudice is primarily learned (and therefore can be unlearned), prejudice researchers have focused less on the challenges from evolutionary (Neuberg and Cottrell 2006) and existential psychology (Pyszczynski et al. 2015), which both focus on more deep-seated and unconscious fears.

The second half of Chapter 2 summarizes theory and research on the existential fears associated with disability prejudice, dehumanization, and hate crimes. According to Terror Management Theory (TMT), some people are avoided because they remind others of their vulnerability to deterioration and death. Disability prejudice therefore, may be used as a way to escape awareness of our own frailty, which can be threatening to those who would rather not think about the prospect of acquiring a disability (or a disabled family member). Disability reminds people that strength, intellect, and language are neither guaranteed nor permanent. Like all animals, humans break. We all have accidents, and someday we will die. Research in over 25 countries has shown that fears of death are linked to prejudice against Jews, Muslims, immigrants, and disabled people (Pyszczynski et al. 2015). Although many cultures promote the superiority of humankind, evidence shows that viewing humans as superior to animals is another strong predictor of intergroup prejudice. If disabled people serve as unwanted reminders that life is not predictable, they may not only be excluded, they may also become the targets of violent crimes.

Ableism may also stem, in part, from a need to feel distinct from other animals. TMT lays the groundwork to examine how fears of death and the need for a meaningful, uniquely human existence can underlie prejudicial reactions – especially toward those who threaten beliefs about what it means to be human (Goldenberg et al. 2000). People work very hard to keep reminders of their animal natures at bay: we cover up blemishes, perfume body odors, and make private and sanitary the elimination of wastes. Enter people with disabilities who may crawl, shake, and drool. They can be blatant reminders that we, as animals, are made of flesh and blood. Research has yet to test whether making people aware of their animal natures increases ableist attitudes, but evidence shows these reminders do increase thoughts of death. Perhaps this is why birth control regulations are imposed on those whose human status continues to be questioned. People with disabilities are frequently denied personhood, and have a long history of dehumanizing treatments (Braddock and Parish 2001). People whose bodies or bodily fluids signal our essential creatureliness (and vulnerability to disability) may become targets of condescending but taming forms of social control, or animalistic hate crimes involving urination and defecation (Haslam and Loughnan 2012). Others, whose prosthetics and assistive devices appear machine-like, may become the targets of mechanistic forms of dehumanization: disabled residents in institutional settings have been deprived of medication and heat in the winter justified on the basis that they are unfeeling machines that do not feel pain (Bryen et al. 2003).

Critiques of both evolutionary and existential approaches, alternative interpretations, and next steps needed to corroborate the evidence to date will also be discussed. As long as disabled people are conceptualized as less than fully human, they will be treated in ways that benefit those whose lives are considered more valuable.

Chapter 3. Justifying Ableism: Ideologies and Language

Where else do such ideas about disability as a fate worse than death originate? From childhood on, people are exposed to many stories about human variability, the causes of disability, and why some people are more deserving of opportunity than others. In contrast to the universal origins of prejudice, this chapter focuses on the intermediate origins of ableism reflected in the complex belief systems used to justify and perpetuate both privilege and oppression. The chapter begins with a review of how ideologies like Social Darwinism, Individualism, Meritocracy, and the Protestant Work Ethic provide handy explanations that can be used to make sense of status differences and discriminatory practices.

Disabled people have endured a long history of persecution, from institutionalization and forced sterilization to medical experimentation and systematic extermination (Morris 1991). How are such practices that result in persecution, economic exploitation, and hate crimes justified? Across most forms of victimization, ideological beliefs about disabled people's deservingness of specific treatments can be found (Sherry 2016). Few people know that before World War II, over 240 000 disabled people were starved, gassed, and poisoned. Yet, these actions were not considered war crimes. Instead, they were rationalized as mercy killings intended to free families from "a lifetime of sacrifice"

(Gallagher 1990). Ableist beliefs that cast disability as burdensome may be even more common when resources are scarce, or when disabled people are described as taking opportunities away from those benefiting from the way things are (Sidanius et al. 1994). Idealistic beliefs about improving society through human enhancements, designer babies, and selective abortions in the case of disability still persist today as part of the New Eugenics movement (Allen 2001).

Several contemporary and clashing ideologies underscore competing definitions of disability itself, which have significant consequences for social policy. The moral, medical, and social models of disability are analyzed in relation to theories of system justification and social dominance. This work examines how different explanatory frameworks about disability can either fortify or weaken unequal status relationships that keep some groups at the top of the social hierarchy and others at the bottom. The disability models provide for very different explanations about where the problems of disability are located, and therefore dictate very different ideas about where solutions should be sought (Altman 2001). For example, when disability is attributed to supernatural forces, people may be more likely to endorse the need for divine intervention. Whether exorcism or other religious rituals are sought may depend on whether disability is attributed to demon possession or to the workings of a merciful God whose power is revealed through prayer (Braddock and Parish 2001).

Ideological beliefs are often transmitted through popular discourse and other forms of social influence. Chapter 3 goes on to review how language and media portrayals are both used to maintain social inequalities and to challenge the status quo. For example, talk is a form of action that both reflects and creates reality. The phrase "wheelchair bound" is a violation of journalistic guidelines that caution against describing disabled people as passive and imprisoned when mobility devices could also be described as liberating. Unwanted forms of helping can result from repeatedly hearing that people are "confined to wheelchairs" (Linton 1998). Simply overhearing someone use derogatory slurs leads people to devalue those described (Blanchard et al. 1994). Similarly, if the media consistently describes people as "suffering from" disability, viewers are more likely to reflect these restricted accounts. For example, those labeled as a danger to themselves are still forcibly medicated and committed to institutions in the name of protection; an entire "tragic persons' industry" exists for those with "special needs." When ramps and audio captions are characterized as "special needs," people may not identify them as civil rights. It wasn't until disabled people started describing their problems in terms of discrimination that disability rights activism became possible (Chapter 8).

Finally, Chapter 3 highlights the shifting nature of disability descriptions and media portrayals, particularly in everyday conversations where people often gesture toward prejudice through jokes, memes, and other humorous quips. What qualifies as ableist speech is hotly debated and changes with the times. What was previously considered acceptable may later be contested as prejudicial and vice versa. For example, previously stigmatized terms like freak, gimp, mad, and crip have been reclaimed as positive expressions of pride within the disability community. Furthermore, public expressions are not always managed to avoid prejudicial talk, especially when people are motivated to verify their biased allegiances. Many people remain unclear about what counts as offensive or funny when it comes to disability, but as minority groups gain power, humor may be used to relieve tension and help people process new social arrangements. The power of disability humor can also raise awareness of the everyday insults and microaggressions disabled people confront (e.g. the YouTube trend "Sh*t people say to ... disabled people"). Bridging the gulf between curious inquiry and offensive probes is a topic in desperate need of research informed by the experiences of disabled people who should not have to conform to normal standards or disclose their conditions just to put nondisabled people at ease. Future research is also suggested on the process by which popular discourse shifts between what was formerly considered acceptable, and what is increasingly recognized as ableist.

Chapter 4. Cultural and Impairment-Specific Stereotypes

When language and media portrayals consistently associate certain characteristics with disability (e.g. helplessness, dependence, asexuality) while failing to link the group with other roles and capabilities (parenthood, independence, competence), cultural stereotypes become engrained in memory, shaping what people notice and fail to notice about others. Novels, movies, and cartoons are full of examples that perpetuate stereotypes by portraying disabled people as tragic victims, angry villains, and incompetent dupes (Haller 2010). Even contemporary, award-winning films (e.g. *Million Dollar Baby, Me Before You*) reinforce stereotypes whenever the disabled character chooses to die so as not to be a burden to loved ones (Dolmage and DeGenaro 2005). As noted in Chapter 3, the removal of life-sustaining food and breathing tubes can be justified as mercy killing as long as disabled people are characterized as suffering burdens.

Chapter 4 summarizes key lessons on the content, functions, and use of disability stereotypes as the more proximal, cognitive components of disability prejudice. In general, a stereotype is defined as a set of attributes used to characterize a group and its members (Ashmore and Del Boca 1981). Although faulty and incomplete, stereotypes are not uniformly negative. They serve important psychological functions that allow perceivers to go beyond what is directly observable, and to predict how people are likely to behave. For example, if teachers expect to have a student with a disability in their classroom, they may anticipate needing to accommodate the student's perceived "special needs" or to help them overcome presumed dependence.

To date, most studies regarding disability stereotypes have focused on specific impairments such as physical, sensory, learning, or psychiatric conditions; yet, research examining the stereotypes of disabled people as a whole have been less common as psychology has been slow to conceptualize disabled people as a minority group (Nario-Redmond 2010). In reality, disabled people share many experiences with discrimination and restricted social status that are often reflected in stereotypic beliefs about the group. This chapter also summarizes research on the cultural stereotypes of disabled people which may not be personally endorsed, but can nevertheless impact judgments, interpretations, and decisions that influence policies. My own research team found strong consensus for cross-impairment cultural stereotypes generated spontaneously by both disabled and nondisabled people. These global or cross-impairment stereotypes characterize disabled people as dependent, incompetent, asexual, weak, passive, unattractive, and heroic (Nario-Redmond 2010). Such work directly contradicts previous assumptions that broad-based, consensually shared stereotypes about disabled people are unlikely due to the diversity of impairments that exist (Biernat and Dovidio 2000).

Disability stereotypes serve many of the same functions as do other minority stereotypes. They are used to define people in ways that best distinguish one group from another (Schaller and Conway III 2001). For example, if the cultural stereotype of disabled people includes traits diametrically opposed to sexuality and nurturance, this can influence opinions about their suitability as partners and parents. Moreover, these representations can impact plans for public facilities that might include accessible bathrooms without the provision of accessible changing tables (Anderson and Kitchin 2000). Stereotype contents influence stereotype use, and when shared across many perceivers, these consequences can be far-reaching. Furthermore, because stereotypes are often activated automatically, they influence people unconsciously. Without any awareness that one's perceptions are being influenced by disability stereotypes, some have questioned whether people can be held accountable for their biased judgments and decision making (Fiske 1989).

Other researchers have speculated that the stereotypes considered most diagnostic of group membership may help to maintain clear intergroup boundaries (Linton 1998; Tajfel and Turner 1979). By defining disabled people as incompetent and dependent, nondisabled people can define themselves as knowledgeable and self-reliant. Stereotypes also function to impose restrictive roles that rationalize discriminatory treatment: when an entire group is defined as incapable and incompetent, it is easier to justify special protections and joblessness. According to the Stereotype Content Model, stereotypes can be predicted as a function of structural variables related to a group's current status in society and competitive (or cooperative) orientation (Fiske et al. 2002). Specifically, people with disabilities (e.g. blind, intellectually and physically disabled) are thought to be stereotyped as "incompetent" because of their low status, but "warm" because of their noncompetitive social position. The implications of the work for prejudicial attitudes and behaviors is elaborated in Chapter 5.

Much more work is needed to examine how ableist stereotypes affect medical decision making and policies governing the allocation of resources. For example, pregnant women are often advised to abort if they test positive for Down syndrome, dwarfism, webbed fingers, and even conditions that may develop later in life like Alzheimer's (Allott and Neumayr 2013; Hubbard 2006). It is the deselection of only certain types of embryos that is problematic if based on assumptions that life with disability is a fate worse than not living at all.

Although stereotypes are resistant to change, they can be altered, especially when individuals are sufficiently motivated to update their current understandings. Cultural stereotypes also change over time in response to changing social circumstances (Haslam et al. 1999). Future research is needed to investigate the extent to which deeply engrained automatic biases change in response to updated representations of disabled people. Chapter 4 concludes with suggestions for studies that identify the boundary conditions of competency and other stereotypic evaluations: are people more likely to express bias toward disabled people when they appear consistent with disability stereotypes or when they violate stereotypic expectations; and how do disability stereotypes affect the judgments of those who appear less stereotypically impaired (e.g. with less visible, more fluid or temporary conditions)? If not readily categorized as disabled, some stereotypes may not be readily invoked, until disability is disclosed.

Chapter 5. Hostile, Ambivalent, and Paternalistic Attitudes and Interactions

Moving from the origins of ableism to its consequences, the next two chapters focus on the distinct evaluative or attitudinal components of disability prejudice (Chapter 5), and how these impact disabled people (Chapter 6). Prejudicial attitudes include the emotional reactions aroused in response to disability, but also reflect cognitive beliefs which often motivate discriminatory behaviors (Esses and Beaufoy 1994). Attitudes are defined as relatively enduring, global evaluations about a person, group, idea, or issue (Eagly and Chaiken 1993). The expression of attitudes are the effects – the consequences of deep-seated universal fears, learned ideologies, and culturally bound stereotypes – but they can also be a source of prejudice when they contribute to restricted access, increased surveillance, and exploitation. Chapter 5 begins with key lessons from the large body of research on when negative (e.g. hostile, aversive) disability attitudes are most prevalent, and when more positive (compassionate, enviable) and mixed (pitiable, inspirational) or ambivalent reactions should emerge.

Research is contextualized according to the traditional methods popular in the quest to understand variations in attitudes toward disability, disabled people, and different impairments. Theory-driven perspectives are emphasized throughout, including approaches that examine when disability attitudes include both positive and negative evaluations at the same time, and how these ideas have been advanced by modern scholarship. For example, theories of ambivalent prejudice predict that when disabled people are assumed to be incompetent but warm, they are also the targets of disrespectful, condescending attitudes, and infantilizing actions.

Consistent with this reasoning, pity and sympathy are the typical emotional responses to low-status, noncompetitive groups like the elderly and disabled (Fiske et al. 2002). Other evidence testing theories of ambivalent prejudice (Katz et al. 1988; Glick and Fiske 2001) shows that positive or negative expressions of prejudice depend on whether disabled people behave in ways that are consistent or inconsistent with expectations. Disabled people who take on the "sick role" or are assumed to be dependent and incompetent are treated with benevolence and charitable concern while those who violate stereotypical expectations (e.g. participate in work, sex) are treated as threatening and receive more hostile reactions. Paternalistic attitudes and beliefs have been used to reward disabled people for their subordination, docility, and gratitude with supportive services and care, which then justifies the use of exploitation and control under the guise of protection. More hostile and aggressive forms of prejudice are more likely to emerge in response to those who challenge the status quo.

Conversely, feelings of contempt, jealously, and a sense of begrudging admiration may be aroused when minority groups are perceived as cold, competitive, and capable, which may drive more actively harmful behaviors including aggression (Cuddy et al. 2007). Active harm can also result from feelings of envy toward groups – especially when envy arouses anger. The Stereotype Content Model helps to explain how envied groups can go from being tolerated to being attacked when intergroup circumstances change. For example, when privileged groups lose status to those considered inferior, envy may give way to anger and backlash against those viewed as encroaching on the privileges of the dominant group (Cuddy et al. 2007). During economic crises, envied groups are more likely blamed for widespread social problems (Glick 2005). Envious blame toward certain disability subgroups (e.g. ambitious, educated, or activist) is expected – especially when higher taxes and dwindling social security benefits are attributed to government-sponsored programs earmarked just for them. Resentment toward students with disabilities who receive extra time on tests or other "special" privileges (e.g. note takers, larger bathrooms) is also common (Harris 1991). This section concludes with a discussion of how kind or benevolent intergroup emotions work to maintain systems of inequality (Jackman 1994). Feelings of admiration and even inspiration may emerge along with narratives of disabled people as brave and heroic – especially those who "courageously overcome their limitations."

Disabled people have increasingly reported on how condescending it feels to be told by strangers "you are so inspirational." Like other forms of pornography, "inspiration porn" objectifies people and assumes incapacity. It also shames those without disabilities (e.g. "you have no excuse to complain, look at this disabled person who has it so much worse"). The more dangerous message is that if all it takes is a little hard work, perhaps disabled people don't really need accommodations or legal protections: *if one disabled person can overcome their limitations, so should everyone else.* The implication is that those who fail to "overcome" depression, addiction, stuttering, or dyslexia must not be trying hard enough. When disabled people are called inspirational, what is it that they inspire others to do? Will others take action to improve disability rights? These and many other questions remain unanswered.

Chapter 5 also reviews some of the more modern approaches to attitude measurement, including the novel Implicit Associations Test (IAT) that uses reaction times to capture unconsciously held associations. For example, people associate more negative terms (e.g. sad, awful, failure, war) with disability than with nondisability, and preferences favoring nondisabled over disabled people are among the strongest implicit biases documented (Robey et al. 2006). The IAT test was developed in response to critiques that the field needed alternative methods to capture the subtle, less controllable forms of prejudice (Dovidio et al. 2011). I discuss the small but growing number of studies on implicit disability prejudice, and the extent to which implicit forms of ableism correspond to explicit attitudes and behaviors. Several studies now corroborate the pervasiveness of implicit negative attitudes toward disabled people among professional caregivers (Enea-Drapeau et al. 2012), nurse educators (Aaberg 2012), special educators (Hein et al. 2011), and rehabilitation professionals (Pruett and Chan 2006).

Finally, Chapter 5 synthesizes studies on the implications of ableist attitudes for dynamic social interactions, including nonverbal behaviors like staring, exchange duration, and other more intentional forms of interpersonal discrimination (Langer et al. 1976). This work captures how the attitudes of both disabled and nondisabled people influence their reactions to one another. According to the social psychological literature, interactions between disabled and nondisabled people are typically characterized as awkward (Hebl et al. 2000). People unfamiliar with disability don't seem to know what to do, and may say things that are well-intended but come across as rude, intrusive, and just plain ignorant. Expecting to be treated badly, people with disabilities may also be reluctant to initiate interactions (Frable et al. 1998). Yet, both disabled and nondisabled people seem largely unaware of the discrepancies between their actions and intentions, and how inconsistent verbal and nonverbal behaviors contribute to distorted understandings. Classic interaction studies will be integrated to examine when expectations result in self-fulfilling prophecies (Kleck and Strenta 1980; Santuzzi and Ruscher 2002), and the factors that moderate both overt (explicit) and covert (implicit) attitudes, and ableist behaviors including race, gender, and disability status differences.

Chapter 6. Contending with Ableism from Internalized Ableism to Collective Action

Although narratives and perspectives of disabled people are integrated throughout this volume, Chapter 6 is devoted to research documenting insider reactions to ableist treatments ranging from the subtle gestures of disgust, objectifying stares, and invasive questions to the more insidious forms of exploitation, harassment, and harm. Co-authored with Dr. Arielle Silverman, this chapter provides several personal accounts to give readers a firm sense of the many ways ableism is manifested at the interpersonal, intergroup, and institutional levels. Chapter 6 first describes research on how disabled people have coped with stigma and social disadvantage, and then addresses the consequences of these coping strategies for health, self-advocacy, and collective actions for social change.

People with disabilities have choices when it comes to how they respond to ableist treatment – usually with the goal of protecting a positive sense of self or identity. While individual reactions to ableism are as diverse as the people reacting, research reveals some common response patterns. When people feel stressed or threatened by the possibility of being the target of stereotypes and prejudice, their well-being and achievement can be undermined (Chapter 6). One way to cope is through individualistic strategies that attempt to escape ableism by distancing from disability or hiding it from others. This can help people feel a sense of control and avoid discrimination. Yet, deliberately concealing a major aspect of the self-concept or refusing accommodations and other assistive devices can also contribute to self-blame, the internalization of hate, and a sense of hopelessness (Chapter 6). Denial of disability and strategic concealment can also backfire when one's impairment is not easily escapable. Furthermore, these individual coping strategies do nothing to confront social inequality and injustice. An alternative approach to coping with prejudice involves group-level strategies that focus on improving the status of disabled people as a group. Under certain conditions, pervasive experiences with prejudice trigger stronger identification with the disability community, feelings of pride and a sense of empowerment to advocate for disability rights. There are also risks to those who challenge the status quo as dominant groups in society are reluctant to share power, and push back against those who demand equality – dismissing them as rude, angry, and ungrateful, especially those who reject unwanted "help." Disabled people have also been punished (e.g. denied benefits; abused verbally and physically) for challenging the status quo while being rewarded with social services for "staying in their place" (Kteily et al. 2011).

Chapter 6 introduces Social Identity Theory (SIT) as generative framework (Tajfel and Turner 1979) for testing both individual and group-level responses to ableism, and the central role of group identity in explaining intergroup behaviors. According to this perspective, both perceivers and targets are recognized as members of social groups that exist in power and status relationships to one another, shaping the dynamics by which people come to understand their disadvantaged (and advantaged) statuses. Recent research documents that people with disabilities deploy both individualistic and collective strategies in response to ableist treatment. For example, those who self-identify as members of the disability community are much more likely to recognize discrimination, to affiliate with other disabled people, and to become involved in disability advocacy (Nario-Redmond et al. 2013; Nario-Redmond and Oleson 2016). Chapter 6 also reviews the conditions that facilitate both individual and collective responses to prejudice, including when members of disadvantaged groups are more and less likely to question the legitimacy of their social position and become politically active.

Chapter 7. Interventions to Reduce Prejudice

Over the past 30 years, there have been numerous approaches to reducing prejudice toward disabled people. Some have had minimal effects while others have worsened stigma and discrimination. Chapter 7 provides a comprehensive review of interventions designed to improve understanding or reduce negative disability attitudes and other misinformed reactions. Much anti-prejudice research has focused on interventions to increase contact with minority groups under the assumption that friendly interactions will produce more equitable outcomes. Chapter 7 describes the considerable evidence from longitudinal, experimental, and field studies showing when intergroup contact is most effective, and how interactions depend on institutionally supported, cooperative, and equal status exchanges (Pettigrew and Tropp 2008). Longitudinal studies have found that nondisabled children who participate in cooperative exchange programs with disabled peers form more complex impressions about disability, and rate peers as more attractive than those who were not part of the inclusion program (Maras and Brown 1996). Nevertheless, increased access to higher education, employment, and public spaces may be more important than friendship when it comes to creating the optimal conditions for contact between groups on an equal status basis (Chapter 8).

Other approaches to prejudice reduction include diversity training and programs that de-emphasize disability or treat it as but one, value-neutral aspect of human diversity (Björk 2009). Unfortunately, many of these interventions have time-limited effects and fail to generalize beyond the specific intervention context (Brown 2011), particularly if focused on de-categorizing individuals (e.g. "I don't even think of you as disabled"). Thus, students may learn to like disabled peers at school but this may not translate to inviting them to the house or to gathering with other disabled people with whom they have never met. This chapter also summarizes the factors that contribute to generalization of respectful attitudes beyond the intervention setting, and identifies the benefits and limitations of different program types, comparing the effectiveness of initiatives that minimize disability status (colorblind approaches) to those that keep disability-categorization salient (multicultural approaches).

Finally, interventions designed to induce empathy and perspective taking by attempting to simulate the disability experience are also described. These popular interventions include wearing blindfolds or ear plugs to simulate sensory impairments or using wheelchairs to enable a "more direct understanding" of physical disabilities. Yet, such programs consistently fail to improve disability attitudes, and can make people feel helpless, confused, and more vulnerable to disability themselves (Nario-Redmond et al. 2017); some even became less willing to volunteer for a campus accessibility project. Finally, evaluations comparing between interventions are described along with suggestions for future research designed to promote more egalitarian outcomes, including how increased awareness of pervasive discrimination impacts behavior change.

Chapter 8. Beyond Contact: Promoting Social Change and Disability Justice

Historically, prejudice-reduction interventions have failed to evaluate the perspectives of those targeted – members of minority groups (cf. Makas 1988). Furthermore, many interventions detract attention away from group-based disparities or minimize the importance of cultural identities (Wright and Lubensky 2009). Others have been criticized as promoting assimilative forms of inclusion which perpetuate minority disadvantage (Saguy et al. 2009). The final chapter of this volume addresses these limitations and provides an agenda for future research and sustainable social change.

To date, prejudice-reduction programs have not been in the service of challenging intergroup inequalities. Instead, they focus more on increasing interpersonal liking and tolerance. It has been assumed that once advantaged group members change their attitudes, they will stop discriminating and open the doors of opportunity to the passive disadvantaged. To address these assumptions, lessons from the literature on collective action and the work of disabled people in changing ableist practices is reviewed. Specifically, this chapter synthesizes research on the outcomes of the disability rights movement, and the role of disability advocacy in addressing ableism and disability discrimination (Barnartt et al. 2001). Consistent with the social justice orientation of disability studies, an approach that applies the study of ableism for social change requires the integration of research about why stereotypes and cultural beliefs allow for ableist behaviors, how group identities influence feelings of threat and empathy, and how these reactions facilitate or impede self-advocacy and allyship.

Arguably, among the most enduring, positive impacts on ableist practices have been policy-based, including structural changes for inclusive integration at school and work, access to the built environment, and anti-discrimination legislation. This final chapter describes some of the latest research on the role of nondisabled allies (Ostrove et al. 2009), and the utility of coalition building across multiple minority groups. Finally, an agenda for future research is suggested that focuses on perceptions of intergroup injustice and behavioral change (e.g. volunteering, donating, protesting), including a clearer specification on what is meant by social change and the need to differentiate between compensatory, preferential, and mutually beneficial strategies for transformation.

Identifying Assumptions and Calling for Action

As you, the reader, approach the following chapters – which begin with the indirect sources of prejudice, more removed from conscious awareness, and proceed to those that are more accessible to contemplation – consider how the research to date has been limited by yet untested assumptions. Empirically driven research is often based on the scientific understandings of the day. For many years, disability has been most typically and unquestionably framed as an *abnormal* condition – no different from the underlying impairment itself. Therefore, most research on disability in the social sciences has followed a biomedical approach that locates the primary problems of disability as residing within the disabled body and/or mind. Yet, when disabled people are consulted as expert knowers, in study after study, the most persistent difficulties disabled people face are *not* those associated with their biological conditions but stem directly from the damaging policies and practices that fail to include them as equal citizens (Linton 1998; Dirth and Nario-Redmond 2019). Similar to sexism, racism, and ageism, ableism is full of assumptions about what it means to be normal, whose lives are worth living, and why certain types of minds and bodies need to be controlled, protected, or improved.

> What keeps a poor child in Appalachia poor is not what keeps a poor child in Chicago poor – even if from a distance, the outcomes look the same. And what keeps an able-bodied black woman poor is not what keeps a disabled white man poor, even if the outcomes look the same. (Ijeoma Oluo 2018)

Disability also differs from other minority-group experiences of prejudice, and disability status intersects these as well. Biases toward someone who is Black, female, and queer may interact in ways that manifest quite differently, and create distinct impacts, than biases toward those experienced by white heterosexual males – even if both share similar impairments. Throughout this volume, ableism is therefore distinguished from other forms of minority-group prejudice as certain dimensions of disability may qualify generalizations from studies of sexism, racism, and ageism. For example, similar to transgender and sexual minorities, people with disabilities are often (but not always) the only member of the family with a disability. This means they may grow up more isolated from a cultural community of disabled role models who could offer coping strategies for the prejudice they confront. Without exposure to alternative narratives about disability as a positive cultural identity or a common human condition, individuals with disabilities are at the mercy of dominant cultural beliefs (Chapter 3), and may come to accept that disability is a tragic abnormality or defect that must be cured, overcome, or otherwise eliminated. Such pathologized worldviews have broad implications for psychological well-being (Chapter 6), self-advocacy, and social change for disability rights (Chapter 8).

Furthermore, some disabled people face unique impairment-related concerns including unpredictable pain and fatigue, especially when their participation is restricted to nondisabled ways of moving and learning that offer few alternatives for communicating or that block access altogether. How can people recognize the capabilities of disabled peers whose voices are silent, not because they have nothing to say but because they are not in the room or are denied the means to contribute? In addition, because disability is an open-enrollment group, ableism may involve some unique threats to people who would rather not think about this prospect, and who manage to do so by controlling their exposure to disabled people (Chapter 2). Old age is another category that most people eventually join, and both disability and aging can instigate existential fears of social death and abandonment common to both ableism and ageism; yet, expectations related to achieving the wisdom of old age, and the benefits of retirement and grandparent-hood, may also produce reactions that distinguish ageism from some forms of disability prejudice.

Despite different histories of oppression, the origins and consequences of ableism also mirror other minority group prejudices: A shared sense of social devaluation, exclusion, and inferiority are common across stigmatized groups, whether based on sexuality, gender, race, or age. Like other disadvantaged minorities, disabled people are frequently stereotyped (Nario-Redmond 2010), and at greater risk of negative outcomes including underemployment, inferior housing, poverty (Krahn et al. 2015), and abuse (Sherry 2016). Moreover, across groups, people who experience more discrimination in their daily lives report more physical and mental health problems, including higher blood pressure and stress hormones, higher rates of depression and suicidal thinking, and lower quality of life (Chapter 6). When people internalize ableist beliefs about themselves, lower self-esteem can follow. Nevertheless, the relationship between prejudice and self-worth critically depends on how people *interpret* the reasons for their marginalization. While some accept inferior treatment as inevitable and deserved, others come to recognize such treatment as unnecessary and unjust (Chapter 8).

A detailed comparison of the similarities and differences between ableism and related prejudices is beyond the scope of the present volume, which concentrates on studies that describe and explain disability prejudice. However, where research on disability is lacking, each chapter incorporates well-established theory and evidence from other types of intergroup prejudice. The reader is cautioned to recognize the limitations involved when generalizing from other disadvantaged group studies. Nevertheless, such studies are highly instructive for establishing a future research agenda that empirically confirms the extent to which previous theory and research apply to this diverse population. For example, meta-analytic studies testing theories of ambivalent racism and sexism offer guidance in how to test the factors that influence when, where, and for whom hostile forms of prejudice are predicted and when more benevolent or paternalistic prejudices are more likely on the basis of intergroup status and competitive relationships (Glick and Fiske 2001).

Social psychologists and disability studies scholars alike have called for increased transparency about the assumptions that have driven these fields for the past several decades. Ableism may not even be limited to prejudice against traditional impairment groups (e.g. blind, deaf, paralyzed), especially as technological advancements promote biases toward those who choose bionic limbs, prosthetic implants, and other supplements to enhance their abilities beyond what is considered typical for the human species (Wolbring 2012). The present volume articulates these assumptions while attempting to synthesize the evolutionary, ideological, and cognitive-affective sources of disability prejudice and its impacts on the lives of real people through personal accounts and interventions for social change and increased equality.

Ableism can be both blatant and unintentional, involving both hostile and compassionate reactions and practices that compromise the participation and equality of people with disabilities. In order to identify which solutions work, when, and for whom, much more work is needed to disentangle the origins that motivate prejudice and discrimination against those with disabilities. This work must include the perspectives of people living with a variety of impairments. The scientific study of ableism and its undoing will continue to be limited if the voices of those inside the disability experience remain underrepresented. This volume is designed to mitigate against this criticism by incorporating multiple perspectives and commentary from those with insider expertise. For example, Chapter 6 was written in collaboration Dr. Arielle Silverman, a fellow social psychologist who has been blind since birth; and most members of my student research team have been members of the disability community.

From an early age, students need to be educated about how ableism operates and can be changed. It is my hope that this volume will stimulate many new educational conversations and curricular reforms. The term ableism itself helps clarify the notion that anyone can be impacted by ability-related discrimination if denied rights based on their physical, mental, and sensory differences. Disability is part of the multicultural landscape – a group many belong to or will join, and a major aspect of human diversity. Responding to ableism is everyone's responsibility.

Notes

1 Global Burden of Disease as cited by the World Health Organization (2011) estimates 975 million (19.4%) persons live with a disability.
2 The prevalence of disability is much higher among prisoners compared to noninstitutionalized adults. According to the 2004 Survey of Inmates in State and Federal Correctional Facilities, 41% of prisoners reported a disability, particularly learning disabilities (Reingle Gonzalez et al. 2016). This reality is foreshadowed by the nearly one in three youth entering the juvenile justice system having a disability (Mader and Butrymowicz 2014).

3 Impairments are defined as problems in body function or alterations in body structure (e.g. paralysis or blindness; WHO 2011). While sometimes used interchangeably in the literature, according to the ICF, disability is an umbrella term that includes bodily impairments, activity limitations, and participation restrictions.

4 According to the 2017 Disability Statistics Annual Report, this earning gap has continued to increase since 2008 (Kraus et al. 2018).

References

Aaberg, V.A. (2012). A path to greater inclusivity through understanding implicit attitudes toward disability. *Journal of Nursing Education* 51 (9): 505–510.

Adelman, C. (1993). Kurt Lewin and the origins of action research. *Educational Action Research* 1 (1): 7–24.

Allen, G.E. (2001). Is a new eugenics afoot? *Science* 294 (5540): 59–61.

Allott, D., & Neumayr, G. (2013). Eugenic abortion 2.0. *American Spectator* (23 May). https://spectator.org/55745_eugenic-abortion-20/ (accessed 21 February 2019).

Altman, B.M. (2001). Disability definitions, models, classification schemes, and applications. In: *Handbook of Disability Studies* (ed. G.L. Albrecht, K.D. Seelman and M. Bury), 97–122. London: Sage.

Amundson, R. and Taira, G. (2005). Our lives and ideologies: the effect of life experience on the perceived morality of the policy of physician-assisted suicide. *Journal of Disability Policy Studies* 16 (1): 53–57.

Anderson, P. and Kitchin, R. (2000). Disability, space and sexuality: access to family planning services. *Social Science & Medicine* 51 (8): 1163–1173.

Ashmore, R.D. and Del Boca, F.K. (1981). Conceptual approaches to stereotypes and stereotyping. In: *Cognitive Processes in Stereotyping and Intergroup Behavior* (ed. D.L. Hamilton), 1–35. Hillsdale, NJ: Lawrence Erlbaum.

Barnartt, S., Schriner, K., and Scotch, R. (2001). Advocacy and political action. In: *Handbook of Disability Studies* (ed. G.L. Albrecht, K.D. Seelman and M. Bury), 430–449. Thousand Oaks, CA: Sage.

Biernat, M. and Dovidio, J.F. (2000). Stigma and stereotypes. In: *The Social Psychology of Stigma* (ed. T.F. Heatherton, R.E. Kleck, M.R. Hebl and J.G. Hull), 88–125. New York: Guilford Press.

Björk, E. (2009). Many become losers when the universal design perspective is neglected: exploring the true cost of ignoring universal design principles. *Technology and Disability* 21 (4): 117–125.

Blanchard, F.A., Crandall, C.S., Brigham, J.C., and Vaughn, L.A. (1994). Condemning and condoning racism: a social context approach to interracial settings. *Journal of Applied Psychology* 79 (6): 993–997.

Braddock, D.L. and Parish, S.L. (2001). An institutional history of disability. In: *Handbook of Disability Studies* (ed. G.L. Albrecht, K.D. Seelman and M. Bury), 11–68. Thousand Oaks, CA: Sage.

Brault, M. W. (2012). Americans with Disabilities: 2010. Current Population Reports, P70–131. Washington, DC: US Census Bureau. https://www.census.gov/prod/2012pubs/p70-131.pdf (accessed 21 February 2019).

Brown, R. (2011). *Prejudice: Its Social Psychology*. Malden, MA: Wiley-Blackwell.

Bryen, N., Carey, A., and Frantz, B. (2003). Ending the silence: adults who use augmentative communication and their experiences as victims of crimes. *Augmentative and Alternative Communication* 19 (2): 125–134.

Burch, S. and Rembis, M. (eds.) (2014). *Disability Histories*. Champaign, IL: University of Illinois Press.

Campbell, F.K. (2009). *Contours of Ableism*. New York: Palgrave Macmillan.

Centers for Disease Control and Prevention (2013). CDC grand rounds: public health practices to include persons with disabilities. *Morbidity and Mortality Weekly Report* 62 (34): 697–701.

Charlton, J.I. (1998). *Nothing About Us Without Us: Disability Oppression and Empowerment*. Berkeley, CA: University of California Press.

Chin, J.L. (2010). *The Psychology of Prejudice and Discrimination: A Revised and Condensed Edition*. Santa Barbara, CA: Praeger.

Chouinard, V. (1997). E&P search results: making space for disabling differences: challenging ableist geographies. *Environment and Planning D* 15 (4): 379–387.

Cohen, P. (2014). Marriage rates among people with disabilities (save the data edition). Council on Contemporary Families. https://thesocietypages.org/ccf/2014/11/24/marriage-rates-among-people-with-disabilities-save-the-data-edition (accessed 21 February 2019).

Corrigan, P.W. (2014). *The Stigma of Disease and Disability: Understanding the Causes and Overcoming Injustices*. Washington, DC: APA.

Cuddy, A.J., Fiske, S.T., and Glick, P. (2007). The BIAS map: behaviors from intergroup affect and stereotypes. *Journal of Personality and Social Psychology* 92 (4): 631–648.

Dirth, T. and Branscombe, N.R. (2018). The social identity approach to disability: bridging disability studies and psychological science. *Psychological Bulletin* 144 (12): 1300–1324.

Dirth, T. and Nario-Redmond, M.R. (2019). Disability advocacy for a new era: leveraging social psychology and a sociopolitical approach to change. In: *Disability: Social Psychological Perspectives*, Academy of Rehabilitation Psychology Series (ed. D. Dunn). Oxford: Oxford University Press.

Dixon, J. and Levine, M. (2012). *Beyond Prejudice: Extending the Social Psychology of Conflict, Inequality and Social Change*. Cambridge: Cambridge University Press.

Dolmage, J. and DeGenaro, W. (2005). "I cannot be like this Frankie": disability, social class, and gender in *Million Dollar Baby*. *Disability Studies Quarterly* 25 (2): http://dx.doi.org/10.18061/dsq.v25i2.555.

Dovidio, J.F., Pagotto, L., and Hebl, M.R. (2011). Implicit attitudes and discrimination against people with physical disabilities. In: *Disability and Aging Discrimination: Perspectives in Law and Psychology* (ed. R.L. Wiener and S.L. Willborn), 157–183. New York: Springer.

Dunn, D.S. (2010). The social psychology of disability. In: *Handbook of Rehabilitation Psychology*, 2e (ed. R.G. Frank, M. Rosenthal and B. Caplan), 379–390. Washington, DC: APA.

Eagly, A.H. and Chaiken, S. (1993). *The Psychology of Attitudes*. Orlando, FL: Harcourt Brace Jovanovich College Publishers.

Enea-Drapeau, C., Carlier, M., and Huguet, P. (2012). Tracking subtle stereotypes of children with trisomy 21: from facial-feature-based to implicit stereotyping. *PLoS One* 7 (4): e34369.

Erickson, W., Lee, C., and von Schrader, S. (2017). *Disability statistics from the American Community Survey (ACS)*. Ithaca, NY: Cornell University Yang-Tan Institute.

Esses, V.M. and Beaufoy, S.L. (1994). Determinants of attitudes toward people with dis-abilities. *Journal of Social Behavior and Personality* 9 (5): 43–64.

Ferri, B.A. and Connor, D.J. (2005). In the shadow of Brown: special education and over-representation of students of color. *Remedial and Special Education* 26 (2): 93–100.

Fine, M. and Asch, A. (1988). Disability beyond stigma: social interaction, discrimination, and activism. *Journal of Social Issues* 44 (1): 3–21.

Fiske, S.T. (1989). Examining the role of intent: toward understanding its role in stereo-typing and prejudice. In: *Unintended Thought* (ed. J.S. Uleman and J.A. Bargh), 253–283. New York: Guilford Press.

Fiske, S.T., Cuddy, A.J.C., Glick, P., and Xu, J. (2002). A model of (often mixed) stereo-type content: competence and warmth respectively follow from perceived status and competition. *Journal of Personality and Social Psychology* 82 (6): 878–902.

Frable, D.E., Platt, L., and Hoey, S. (1998). Concealable stigmas and positive self-perceptions: feeling better around similar others. *Journal of Personality and Social Psychology* 74 (4): 909–922.

Fujiura, G.T. and Rutkowski-Kmitta, V. (2001). Counting disability. In: *Handbook of Disability Studies* (ed. G.L. Albrecht, K.D. Seelman and M. Bury), 69–96. Thousand Oaks, CA: Sage.

Gallagher, H. (1990). *By Trust Betrayed: Patients, Physicians, and the License to Kill in the Third Reich*. New York: Henry Holt.

Glick, P. (2005). Choice of scapegoats. In: *Reflecting on the Nature of Prejudice* (ed. J.F. Dovidio, P. Glick and L. Rudman), 244–261. Malden, MA: Blackwell.

Glick, P. and Fiske, S.T. (2001). An ambivalent alliance: hostile and benevolent sexism as com-plementary justifications for gender inequality. *American Psychologist* 56 (2): 109–118.

Goldenberg, J.L., Pyszczynski, T., Greenberg, J., and Solomon, S. (2000). Fleeing the body: a terror management perspective on the problem of human corporeality. *Personality and Social Psychology Review* 4 (3): 200–218.

Goodley, D. (2011). Social psychoanalytic disability studies. *Disability & Society* 26 (6): 715–728.

Haller, B.A. (2010). *Representing Disability in an Ableist World: Essays on Mass Media*. Louisville, KY: Advocado Press.

Harris, L. and Associates (1991). *Public Attitudes Toward People with Disabilities*. Washington, DC: National Organization on Disability.

Hartley, S.L., Barker, E.T., Seltzer, M.M. et al. (2010). The relative risk and timing of divorce in families of children with an autism spectrum disorder. *Journal of Family Psychology* 24 (4): 449–457.

Haslam, N. and Loughnan, S. (2012). Prejudice and dehumanization. In: *Beyond Prejudice: Extending the Social Psychology of Conflict, Inequality and Social Change* (ed. J. Dixon and M. Levine), 89–104. Cambridge: Cambridge University Press.

Haslam, S.A., Oakes, P.J., Reynolds, K.J., and Turner, J.C. (1999). Social identity salience and the emergence of stereotype consensus. *Personality and Social Psychology Bulletin* 25 (7): 809–818.

Hebl, M.R., Tickle, J., and Heatherton, T.F. (2000). Awkward moments in interactions between nonstigmatized and stigmatized individuals. In: *The Social Psychology of Stigma* (ed. T.F. Heatherton, R.E. Kleck, M.R. Hebl and J.G. Hull), 273–306. New York: Guilford Press.

Hehir, T. (2002). Eliminating ableism in education. *Harvard Educational Review* 72 (1): 1–33.

Hein, S., Grumm, M., and Fingerle, M. (2011). Is contact with people with disabilities a guarantee for positive implicit and explicit attitudes? *European Journal of Special Needs Education* 26 (4): 509–522.

Hollomotz, A. (2013). Disability, oppression and violence: towards a sociological explanation. *Sociology* 47 (3): 477–493.

House, S. (1981). A radical feminist model of psychological disability. *Off Our Backs* 11 (5): 34–35.

Hubbard, R. (2006). Abortion and disability: who should and who should not inhabit the world. In: *The Disability Studies Reader*, 2e (ed. L.J. Davis), 93–103. New York: Routledge.

Jackman, M.R. (1994). *The Velvet Glove. Paternalism and Conflict in Gender, Class, and Race Relations*. Berkeley, CA: University of California Press.

Jelsma, J. (2009). Use of the International Classification of Functioning, Disability and Health: a literature survey. *Journal of Rehabilitation Medicine* 41 (1): 1–12.

Katz, I., Hass, R.G., and Bailey, J. (1988). Attitudinal ambivalence and behavior toward people with disabilities. In: *Attitudes Toward Persons with Disabilities* (ed. H.E. Yuker), 47–57. New York: Springer.

Kleck, R.E. and Strenta, A. (1980). Perceptions of the impact of negatively valued physical characteristics on social interaction. *Journal of Personality and Social Psychology* 39 (5): 861–873.

Krahn, G.L., Walker, D.K., and Correa-De-Araujo, R. (2015). Persons with disabilities as an unrecognized health disparity population. *American Journal of Public Health* 105 (S2): S198–S206.

Kraus, L., Lauer, E., Coleman, R., and Houtenville, A. (2018). *2017 Disability Statistics Annual Report*. Durham, NH: University of New Hampshire.

Kteily, N.S., Sidanius, J., and Levin, S. (2011). Social dominance orientation: cause or "mere effect"?: evidence for SDO as a causal predictor of prejudice and discrimination against ethnic and racial outgroups. *Journal of Experimental Social Psychology* 47 (1): 208–214.

Kurzban, R. and Leary, M.R. (2001). Evolutionary origins of stigmatization: the functions of social exclusion. *Psychological Bulletin* 127 (2): 187–208.

Langer, E.J., Fiske, S., Taylor, S.E., and Chanowitz, B. (1976). Stigma, staring, and discomfort: a novel-stimulus hypothesis. *Journal of Experimental Social Psychology* 12 (5): 451–463.

Lauer, E.A. and Houtenville, A.J. (2018). *Annual Disability Statistics Compendium: 2017*. Durham, NH: University of New Hampshire, Institute on Disability.

Linton, S. (1998). *Claiming Disability: Knowledge and Identity*. New York: New York University Press.

Macedo, D. and Marti, T.S. (2010). Situating labeling within an ideological framework. In: *The Myth of the Normal Curve* (ed. C. Dudley-Marling and A. Gurn), 53–70. New York: Peter Lang.

Mader, J., & Butrymowicz, S. (2014). Pipeline to prison: special education too often leads to jail for thousands of American children. *The Hechinger Report* (26 October). https://hechingerreport.org/pipeline-prison-special-education-often-leads-jail-thousands-american-children/ (accessed 21 February 2019).

Maguire, P. and Haddad, P. (1990). Psychological reactions to physical illness. In: *Seminars in Liaison Psychiatry: College Seminar Series*, 2e (ed. E. Guthrie and F. Creed), 157–191. London: Royal College of Psychiatrists.

Makas, E. (1988). Positive attitudes toward disabled people: disabled and nondisabled persons' perspectives. *Journal of Social Issues* 44 (1): 49–61.

Maras, P. and Brown, R. (1996). Effects of contact on children's attitudes toward disability: a longitudinal study. *Journal of Applied Social Psychology* 26 (23): 2113–2134.

McDermott, S. and Turk, M.A. (2011). The myth and reality of disability prevalence: measuring disability for research and service. *Disability and Health Journal* 4 (1): 1–5.

Melzer, D., McWilliams, B., Brayne, C. et al. (2000). Socioeconomic status and the expectation of disability in old age: estimates for England. *Journal of Epidemiology & Community Health* 54 (4): 286–292.

Miller, P., Parker, S., and Gillinson, S. (2004). *Disablism: How to Tackle the Last Prejudice*. London: Demos.

Morris, J. (1991). *Pride against Prejudice: Transforming Attitudes to Disability*. London: New Society.

Mustanski, B.S., Chivers, M.L., and Bailey, J.M. (2002). A critical review of recent biological research on human sexual orientation. *Annual Review of Sex Research* 13 (1): 89–140.

Nario-Redmond, M.R. (2010). Cultural stereotypes of disabled and non-disabled men and women: consensus for global category representations and diagnostic domains. *British Journal of Social Psychology* 49 (3): 471–488.

Nario-Redmond, M.R. and Oleson, K.C. (2016). Disability group identification and disability-rights advocacy: contingencies among emerging and other adults. *Emerging Adulthood* 4 (3): 207–218.

Nario-Redmond, M.R., Noel, J.G., and Fern, E. (2013). Redefining disability, re-imagining the self: disability identification predicts self-esteem and strategic responses to stigma. *Self and Identity* 12 (5): 468–488.

Nario-Redmond, M.R., Gospodinov, D., and Cobb, A. (2017). Crip for a day: the unintended negative consequences of disability simulations. *Rehabilitation Psychology* 62 (3): 324–333.

National Council on Disability (2014). *A Progress Report*. Washington, DC: National Council on Disability https://ncd.gov/progress_reports/10312014 (accessed 21 February 2019.

Nelson, T.D. (2006). *The Psychology of Prejudice*, 2e. New York: Pearson.

Neuberg, S.L. and Cottrell, C.A. (2006). Evolutionary bases of prejudices. In: *Evolution and Social Psychology* (ed. M. Schaller, J.A. Simpson and D.T. Kenrick), 163–187. Madison, CT: Psychosocial Press.

Oaten, M., Stevenson, R.J., and Case, T.I. (2011). Disease avoidance as a functional basis for stigmatization. *Philosophical Transactions of the Royal Society, B: Biological Sciences* 366 (1583): 3433–3452.

Olkin, R. and Howson, L.J. (1994). Attitudes toward and images of physical disability. *Journal of Social Behavior and Personality* 9 (5): 81–96.

Oluo, I. (2018). *So You Want to Talk About Race*. New York: Seal Press.

Ostrove, J.M., Cole, E.R., and Oliva, G.A. (2009). Toward a feminist liberation psychology of alliances. *Feminism & Psychology* 19 (3): 381–386.

Palacios M. G. (2017). "Naming Ableism". CripStory. https://cripstory.wordpress.com/2017/04/01/naming-ableism (accessed 21 February 2019).

Park, J.H., Faulkner, J., and Schaller, M. (2003). Evolved disease-avoidance processes and contemporary anti-social behavior: prejudicial attitudes and avoidance of people with physical disabilities. *Journal of Nonverbal Behavior* 27 (2): 65–87.

Pettigrew, T.F. and Tropp, L.R. (2008). How does intergroup contact reduce prejudice? Meta-analytic tests of three mediators. *European Journal of Social Psychology* 38 (6): 922–934.

Pruett, S.R. and Chan, F. (2006). The development and psychometric validation of the Disability Attitude Implicit Association Test. *Rehabilitation Psychology* 51 (3): 202–213.

Pyszczynski, T., Solomon, S., and Greenberg, J. (2015). Thirty years of terror management theory: from genesis to revelation. *Advances in Experimental Social Psychology* 52: 1–70.

Redfield, S. E., & Nance, J. P. (2016). School-to-Prison Pipeline. Preliminary report. Prepared by the American Bar Association Joint Task Force on Reversing the School-to-Prison Pipeline. https://www.americanbar.org/content/dam/aba/publications/criminaljustice/ school_to_prison_pipeline_report.authcheckdam.pdf (accessed 21 February 2019).

Reid, D.K. and Knight, M.G. (2006). Disability justifies exclusion of minority students: a critical history grounded in disability studies. *Educational Researcher* 35 (6): 18–23.

Reingle Gonzalez, J.M., Cannell, M.B., Jetelina, K.K., and Froehlich-Grobe, K. (2016). Disproportionate prevalence rate of prisoners with disabilities: evidence from a nationally representative sample. *Journal of Disability Policy Studies* 27 (2): 106–115.

Reynolds, J.M. (2017). "I'd rather be dead than disabled" – the ableist conflation and the meanings of disability. *Review of Communication* 17 (3): 149–163.

Robey, K.L., Beckley, L., and Kirschner, M. (2006). Implicit infantilizing attitudes about disability. *Journal of Developmental and Physical Disabilities* 18 (4): 441–453.

Saguy, T., Tausch, N., Dovidio, J.F., and Pratto, F. (2009). The irony of harmony: intergroup contact can produce false expectations for equality. *Psychological Science* 20 (1): 114–121.

Santuzzi, A.M. and Ruscher, J.B. (2002). Stigma salience and paranoid social cognition: understanding variability in metaperceptions among individuals with recently-acquired stigma. *Social Cognition* 20 (3): 171–197.

Schaller, M. and Conway, L.G. III (2001). From cognition to culture: the origins of stereotypes that really matter. In: *Cognitive Social Psychology: The Princeton Symposium on the Legacy and Future of Social Cognition* (ed. G.B. Moskowitz), 163–176. Mahwah, NJ: Lawrence Erlbaum.

Scuro, J. (2017). *Addressing Ableism: Philosophical Questions Via Disability Studies.* Lexington, MA: Lexington Books.

Shannon-Missal, L. (2015). Overwhelming public support for the Americans with Disabilities Act, but disagreements exist on what should qualify as a disability. The Harris Poll, 43 (24 June). https://theharrispoll.com/this-coming-sunday-will-mark-25-years-to-the-day-since-president-george-h-w-bush-signed-the-americans-with-disabilities-act-ada-into-law-and-americans-are-clearly-still-behind-the-legislation-with/ (accessed 21 February 2019).

Sherry, M. (2016). *Disability Hate Crimes: Does Anyone Really Hate Disabled People?* New York: Routledge.

Sidanius, J., Liu, J.H., Shaw, J.S., and Pratto, F. (1994). Social dominance orientation, hierarchy attenuators and hierarchy enhancers: social dominance theory and the criminal justice system. *Journal of Applied Social Psychology* 24: 338–366.

Singleton, P. (2012). Insult to injury disability, earnings, and divorce. *Journal of Human Resources* 47 (4): 972–990.

Tajfel, H. and Turner, J.C. (1979). An integrative theory of intergroup conflict. In: *The Social Psychology of Intergroup Relations* (ed. W.G. Austin and S. Worchel), 33–48. Monterey, CA: Brooks/Cole.

The Americans with Disabilities Act (ADA). (1990). Pub. L. No. 101-336, 104 Stat. 328.

Vos, T., Allen, C., Arora, M. et al. (2016). Global, regional, and national incidence, prevalence, and years lived with disability for 310 diseases and injuries, 1990–2015: a systematic analysis for the Global Burden of Disease Study 2015. *The Lancet* 388 (10053): 1545–1602.

Watermeyer, B. (2012). *Towards a Contextual Psychology of Disablism*. Abingdon: Routledge.

Wendell, S. (1996). *The Rejected Body*. New York: Routledge.

Whitley, B. and Kite, M. (2009). *The Psychology of Prejudice and Discrimination*. Boston, MA: Cengage Learning.

Wolbring, G. (2012). Expanding ableism: taking down the ghettoization of impact of disability studies scholars. *Societies* 2 (3): 75–83.

World Health Organization. (2011). World Report on Disability. World Health Organization and World Bank. http://www.who.int/disabilities/world_report/2011/report.pdf (accessed 21 February 2019).

Wright, S.C. and Lubensky, M.E. (2009). The struggle for social equality: collective action versus prejudice reduction. In: *Intergroup Misunderstandings: Impact of Divergent Social Realities* (ed. S. Demoulin, J.P. Leyens and J.F. Dovidio), 291–310. Hove: Psychology Press.

Wymbs, B.T., Pelham, W.E. Jr., Molina, B.S. et al. (2008). Rate and predictors of divorce among parents of youths with ADHD. *Journal of Consulting and Clinical Psychology* 76 (5): 735–744.

Zola, I.K. (1993). Disability statistics, what we count and what it tells us: a personal and political analysis. *Journal of Disability Policy Studies* 4 (2): 9–39.

Ableism ~ A Poem By Maria Palacios (2017)

https://commons.m.wikimedia.org/wiki/
File:Circular_staircase_of_the_Vatican_
Museums.jpg

Ableism is when you say that I don't act disabled and expect me to take that as a compliment. Ableism is when you assume that I'm automatically strong and courageous simply because I'm disabled. Ableism is when my blindness becomes your darkness … when you wear my scars in your sleeve and pretend to understand my truths. Ableism is when you try to heal me, and fix me and promise me that I will walk, or see, or hear or that I will be everything I was really meant to be … one day in heaven. Ableism is believing that heaven is an able-bodied place where broken bodies finally become whole. Ableism is when "whole" is a word reserved for the able-bodied, or when you say that I'm beautiful despite my differences, and fail to recognize that I'm beautiful because of them. Ableism is when you leave us to ripen and rot hanging from the vine because you refuse to bite into our fruit. Ableism is the fruit of your fears. Ableism is when you think "sexy" is not a word that applies to me. Ableism is you bragging about your independence while you watch me struggle to get free. Ableism is how free you feel to assume. Ableism is when you assume I'm single … when you assume I'm a virgin, when you assume I hate my body because in your narrow mind how could I not? Ableism is when your discomfort becomes a bigger barrier than a flight of stairs. Ableism is when parents yank their kids away and tell them not to stare automatically teaching them that disability is a dirty word. Ableism is when you tell me how inspiring it is to watch me work or watch me cook. Ableism is when you can't look at my scars without cringing or feeling like you have to say you're sorry … or like you owe me an apology for *my* body because I'm such a monster, and your able-bodiedness almost makes you feel guilty, and I say almost because if it had, you would not be so quick to push me out of your mind with a "Thank God it's not me" curling under your tongue like a snake. Ableism is when you make plans that do not include accessible venues, accessible spaces so it becomes easier to erase me from your list. Ableism is when you can pretend disabled people don't exist. Ableism is not being able to join your schoolmates in the class picture or school play because there is no ramp to the stage. Ableism is our disabled lives played by nondisabled actors. Ableism is nondisabled actors who think they totally understand our struggles because they got to play our role. Ableism is having to roll on inaccessible sidewalks because I have no choice. Ableism is the fact that I have no choice, but you do. Ableism is when disabled parents are told they should not be parents. Ableism is when you feel that your baby is not safe with me, or when you pat me on the head as if I were a kid and call me cute. Ableism is when my service dog gets kicked off the plane because nondisabled passengers complained. Ableism is when I ask you for help and you feel entitled to choose for me. Ableism is nodding your head in understanding instead of admitting that you don't have a clue what I said. Ableism is the fact that you're afraid to tell the truth. Ableism is making heroes out of people who take disabled kids to the prom and never talk to them again because that one "good deed" is good for at least ten years if not a lifetime. Ableism is a lifetime of isolation, a lifetime of segregation a lifetime of untold stories of "Once upon a time there was a cripple who could" and for every cripple that *could* there was and is an able-bodied person who should but doesn't. Ableism is the fact that it doesn't matter because unless you're the one being oppressed, unless it's YOUR body that fails, it's not YOUR problem and you can push it away. Out of sight, out of mind. Ableism is leaving behind the imperfect ones, the ones that slow you down, the ones that embarrass you. Ableism is the fact that we can embarrass you just by sitting in the same room and breathing the same air. Ableism is when you say it's not fair that I don't have to wait in line. Ableism is thinking that I'm out of line for demanding human rights. Ableism is when you say how lucky I am that I get to sit all the time while your poor able-bodied feet get tired. Ableism is you saying that, but deep down feeling grateful you're not me. Ableism is the way media portrays us as either objects of pity or inspiration. Ableism is inspiration porn. Ableism is when you say disabled people should not do porn because our bodies are not something anyone would want to see naked. Ableism is your naked bigotry, peeking through the keyhole of your closet. Ableism is how you want to lock us in the closet and how you believe that giving us new labels like physically challenged and differently abled is no longer labeling us. Ableism is making buses accessible but not the streets leading to the bus stop. Ableism is how the bus stop becomes like a *Forrest Gimp* story always waiting to be told. Ableism is when not even the back of the bus was available to us in the unwritten pages of our history and how we have to become our own crip version of Rosa Parks every single day to this day. Ableism is when you say that if God hasn't healed me, it is only because I don't have enough faith. Ableism is how your faith considers me a punishment from God, or how you try to pray my differences away as if they were demons. Ableism is the demons of your ignorance. Ableism is having accessible parking, but denying us access to the door. Ableism is how the Real Estate industry continues building inaccessible homes and acting as if eliminating a step would be an eyesore, an offence, a code violation. Ableism is the violation of our rights done so quietly and shoving us under the rug. Ableism is when you tell ableist jokes and expect me to think they're funny. Ableism is how your version of funny becomes my version of painful. Ableism is how the rich play monopoly with real properties and make none of them affordable or accessible. Ableism is when words like affordable and accessible are too good to be true. Ableism is saying there are no qualified disabled applicants. What you mean to say is: Disabled people who can pass as nondisabled are hard to find. Ableism is your ability to find reasons to push us aside to keeps us in cages, leave our struggles out of the history pages ... pretend we never existed. Ableism is when you say I'm the only disabled friend you've ever had. Ableism is when you say that and still don't understand why we feel invisible. Ableism is when you think I don't have a disability because you can't see it. Ableism is expecting me to always be brave like Pollyanna. Ableism is thinking that if I'm in a bad mood, it must be because I'm disabled, and I must have a "chip on my shoulder." Ableism is expecting me to shoulder your ableist beliefs because the weight of my differences are too heavy for you to carry. Ableism is me having to carry the guilt you force upon me. Ableism is when you think Autism equals stupid, and when stupid becomes just another word to describe those like me. Ableism is when you use my hearing child to interpret for you. Ableism is when I find myself forced to use my hearing child to interpret for me. Ableism is when you say it's not your fault that I'm disabled, but act as if it were mine. Ableism is always having to blame someone. Ableism is asking my friends what I would like to order because you fear not being able to communicate with me. Ableism is the fact that you don't even try. Ableism is when your disabled child is the only one that didn't get invited to the party. Ableism is when a political party treats disability as a mockery of our struggles. Ableism is when cops see my disability as a threat. Ableism is when it's dangerous just to be out while cripple. Ableism is calling my needs "special" and then ignoring them. Ableism is believing I need to be fixed. Ableism is you refusing to fix what's really broken. Ableism is painting our lives like a tragic story. Ableism is our story told by nondisabled voices captured through a nondisabled lens. Ableism is you feeling like I should be grateful for the ramps and the parking spaces as if access was not a basic right. Ableism is when my basic rights are considered a burden. Ableism is when you force unsolicited help upon me because, to you, it seemed like I needed it. Ableism is you thinking that my asking for help gives you the right to decide for me. Ableism is when a relationship with me is something you keep from your friends. Ableism is when you have sex with me out of curiosity. Ableism is when your curiosity invades my space ... when your curiosity hurts when your curiosity kills *my* cat and leaves *me* wounded. Ableism is making those things essential to my survival out of my financial reach, but call yourself [an] ally if I qualify for the financial aid, or the loan or the insurance premium that would make you my friend. Ableism is when you pretend to care because you're paid to care but deep down you don't give a shit. Ableism is when you wish for a world without disabled people and you say that to me, and expect me to agree with you. Ableism is when you say that if you became disabled, you would want to die. Ableism is wishing you could help us die, or wishing you didn't have to help us live. Ableism is believing disabled people are better off dead. Ableism is when you turn your head the other way and say that your able-bodied privilege is not privilege and refuse to see that *your* privilege is the face of *my* oppression.

2

The Evolutionary and Existential Origins of Ableism

The attitude of "I don't see how you can live with that" – sometimes expressed more dramatically as "I'd rather be dead than have [X disability] – is one that people still shockingly profess openly in encounters with people with disabilities. National Council on Disability (2015)

The following quotes from our international survey of disabled people bear this out:

When I was a child, people used to cross the street when they saw me or told their children to get away from me. I cried. ~ Person with a physical disability, 2015

People have said "I could never live like you" to my face. ~ Person with multiple disabilities, 2015

Had someone tell me they would rather be dead then disabled. ~ Person with multiple disabilities, 2015

I have had people tell that if they ever become as ill and disabled as I am, they would probably kill themselves and kudos to me for not killing myself. ~ Person with multiple disabilities, 2015

Among the root causes or "distal" origins of prejudice are those that focus on the relatively universal and unconscious tendencies that reveal some of our most basic needs for safety, belonging, and significance. By assuming prejudice is primarily learned (and therefore can be unlearned), most prejudice researchers have not focused on challenges from evolutionary (Neuberg and Cottrell 2006) and existential psychology (Greenberg et al. 1997). This chapter begins with a discussion of how some forms of disability prejudice may reflect fears of contamination and the

Ableism: The Causes and Consequences of Disability Prejudice, First Edition.
Michelle R. Nario-Redmond.
© 2020 John Wiley & Sons, Inc. Published 2020 by John Wiley & Sons, Inc.

conditions most likely to contribute to expressions of disease avoidance. Extending the idea of disability as a threat to survival, the chapter examines how and when disability threatens beliefs about the meaning and purpose of life – reminding people of their vulnerability to death, dismemberment, and incapacitation. The chapter goes on to describe some implications for access to healthcare and anti-hate crime legislation when evolved and existential fears are operating, including flaws with approaches that assume the inevitability of fear.

> A blind friend told me that she once tried to sit next to someone on a bus and the person screamed, "Don't sit next to me, I don't want to catch it." ~ Person with a sensory disability, 2015

> When my step mom married my father, her mother was against the marriage because she was afraid that their subsequent children would be disabled or catch my (non-contagious) disability. I was 7 years old and have never forgotten that. Person with a physical disability, 2015

People don't usually catch a disability like they can catch the flu, chicken pox, or even sexually transmitted diseases. However, as these examples show, people from around the world often respond to disabled people as if they were contagious (e.g. acting repulsed or shunning them through forced public exclusion or isolating them as if to quarantine). Why does this happen to those who pose no risk of infecting others? Does the tendency to avoid those who appear "sick" serve some adaptive function? Did it ever? And can fear of contagious illness explain why disabled people are often treated as if they were diseased? This section describes one of the most basic origins of disability prejudice based on evolutionary arguments, and provides evidence about when, where, and with whom this more unconscious form of prejudice is most likely to emerge.

The Basics of Evolutionary Theory

Evolutionary psychology has a lot to say about why common behavioral reactions like prejudice and fear may have been beneficial to a species' survival at one time in the distant past – yet still show up today. According to the principle of natural selection, the surroundings of our early hominid ancestors placed certain demands on their survival, making some of their characteristics more adaptive to living in particular environments. The argument goes like this: All species, including humans, have members born with different characteristics and behavioral tendencies. Some of these characteristics, like the fear of dangerous plants and animals, made it more likely for some to survive into adulthood than others. For example, those inherently warier of poisonous foods or dangerous people were more likely to stay alive long enough to pass on their cautious tendencies to offspring. On the other hand, those who could not readily detect dangers would be less likely to survive, mate, and pass on their less-guarded orientations.

Over long periods of evolutionary history, therefore, threat detection should become more common in the population, making our predecessors quite good at responding to various kinds of survival threats. While some "lessons" about surviving in early hunter-gatherer societies were surely learned through experience (e.g. fire can burn), other capacities like attentiveness to signs of potential danger may have been more instinctual or genetically based – although most are some combination of both.

Evolutionary explanations of prejudice focus on the genetic predispositions considered *adaptive* to the extent that they contributed to survival, and were passed on to future generations through reproduction. Other examples of biologically inherited traits that would have been adaptive in protecting early hunter-gatherers involve tendencies toward reciprocation and cooperation within the group, a wariness of strangers from competing groups, and avoidance of the dangers posed by infectious disease. The evolved capacity for attentiveness to dangerous threats is considered to be somewhat threat specific, which may explain why prejudice can be expressed in so many different ways through different emotions and actions (Kurzban and Leary 2001). According to the functional-specificity hypothesis (Neuberg et al. 2011), if a stranger or outside threat behaves in ways that signal competition, the most adaptive response would be anger and beliefs that justify aggressive reactions. However, if a stranger or even someone from within the group acts or appears in ways that suggest illness or contamination, the most adaptive response might be avoidance and disgust, perhaps accompanied by beliefs that justify the containment or elimination of the threat (Oaten et al. 2009).

Most evolutionary explanations for stigma focus on the functional advantages of avoiding danger, disease, and related threats to survival. Similar arguments have been developed to explain racism and anti-immigrant and anti-gay attitudes (Cottrell and Neuberg 2005). Stangor and Crandall (2000) also proposed that stigmas associated with different nationalities, criminality, mental illness, and disfigurement may have all originated from an evolved motivation to avoid threats to individual health and societal well-being (for other evolutionary accounts of stigma see Kurzban and Leary 2001).

Evolutionary Origins of Prejudice: Disease Avoidance

One functionally specific mechanism gaining increased attention focuses on an evolved predisposition to avoid disease as a root cause of prejudicial responses toward chronic illness and disability/impairment groups, even those who do not carry infectious diseases. Specifically, people who have cancer (Chapple et al. 2004), missing limbs (Kleck 1968; Kouznetsova et al. 2012), cleft palates, burns, and birthmarks (Clarke 1999) are all frequently treated *as if* they are contagious. They are shunned, avoided, kept at a distance, and responded to with various gestures of disgust (e.g. sticking the tongue out; scrunching the nose up; pulling head back; saying "ewww"). If it was adaptive to avoid disease-causing agents (e.g. pathogens like germs and viruses) then our early hominid ancestors would have needed a way to detect cues in the ancestral environment that signaled the presence of potentially dangerous pathogens.

What kinds of clues signal disease? Are we talking about open sores, rashes, and discharges from coughing and sneezing? What about swollen glands, facial discolorations, fevers, spasms, seizures, and other behaviors associated with discomfort like fatigue, weakness, and irregular postures or pace? As it turns out, one or more of these symptoms characterize the majority of the world's deadliest infections – including the measles, mumps, and influenza (Oaten et al. 2011). Even though vaccinations have eliminated many of these from *recent* history, in ancient times, it would have been beneficial to survival if animals could protect themselves by avoiding anything that indicated the *potential* for a deadly disease. In fact, infectious agents have been linked to more chronic conditions than previously acknowledged, including certain cancers, auto-immune syndromes, and neurodevelopmental disorders (O'Connor et al. 2006).

Unfortunately, clues to disease are not always visible or even detectable through bad smells or squelching sounds. Furthermore, not all observable "signs" of disease are accurate. So early hominids would have had to figure out a way to detect dangerous diseases using less than perfect cues – like visible signs of bodily weakness, deformity, and disfigurement (Faulkner et al. 2004; Park et al. 2003). These less than perfect disease cues may have led to a disease-avoidance mechanism that evolved to be bit too risk-averse – too hyper-sensitive to cues that signaled vulnerability to disease (Oaten et al. 2011). If applied indiscriminately to any unusual characteristic or body type, the protective mechanism becomes over-inclusive. That is, people start responding to *anyone* who looks or behaves unusually with an overgeneralized fear response – a fear of catching a condition that not only isn't contagious but that may not even be a disease! For example, people who walk with a limp or who have uneven arms or eyes might all trigger the same alarm. According to evolutionary logic, it's better to err on the side of caution to avoid those who aren't contagious than to fail to avoid those who potentially are. As a consequence, people are more likely to react to false alarms by avoiding those with any characteristic that automatically triggers the disease avoidance mechanism – characteristics like facial scars, missing limbs, spastic muscles, and other visible conditions including unequal facial features and irregular body shapes – characteristics that are sometimes associated with disability.

To summarize, evolutionary sources of disability prejudice propose that our avoidance of certain people reflects an unconscious bias that overreacts by automatically triggering fears of contagion when faced with certain observable impairments. Contagion fears may even be triggered by cues that *anticipate* interactions with disabled people. According to the theory, both humans and animals around the world should demonstrate evidence of this universal tendency to avoid those with visible disabilities and other features perceived to be contagious. Why?

Because this biased tendency was designed through natural selection to protect against the more serious problem of missing real-disease carriers. Clearly, an over-generalized reaction to physical difference poses a signal-detection problem if interpersonal avoidance and social policies that exclude disabled people are due, at least in part, to some overactive, precautionary system wired deeply into the evolved brain.

Evidence of Disease Avoidance as a Primary Determinant of Disability Prejudice

Despite the fact that disability prejudice is driven by multiple causes, we can examine when an overgeneralized fear of disease seems to be operating based on research that supports the basic premises of this theory. First, if prejudice is driven by unconscious fears of contagion, people should be more likely to demonstrate avoidance behaviors and disgust reactions (Kurzban and Leary 2001) as opposed to angry reactions, pity, or undeserved praise. Second, if based on more "instinc-tual" tendencies to self-protect, we should see similar disease-avoidance patterns in nonhuman animals. Third, evolutionary sources of prejudice should be rela-tively universal – people from across the world should show similar patterns of stigmatizing those with characteristics that trigger contamination fears, even if cultural beliefs about disease and disability exist to counter these reactions (Oaten et al. 2011).

Consistent with a disease-avoidant account, many studies have documented pervasive patterns of social and physical distancing from disabled people. For example, Rumsey and colleagues found that pedestrians stood further away from those with both permanent birthmarks and temporary scars and bruises (Rumsey et al. 1982). On commuter trains, people avoided sitting next to fellow passen-gers with facial birthmarks (Rumsey and Bull 1986) compared to those without facial "disfigurements." In an airport study, people stayed twice as far away from a person seated in a wheelchair who asked for directions compared to when that same person was seated in an ordinary chair; however, the time spent giving direc-tions did not differ (Worthington 1974).

In addition to these field studies, lab experiments, which attempt to keep eve-rything the same except the disability status of those being studied, have shown that people keep more personal distance between themselves and those using wheelchairs (Kleck 1969), those with facial scars (Rumsey et al. 1982), and those described with the seizure disorder, epilepsy (Kleck et al. 1968). Looking more closely at these "classic" studies from the 1960s, many of Kleck's carefully con-trolled experiments used a special wheelchair that made the user appear to have an amputated leg. Specifically, nondisabled high school and college students engaged in short face-to-face interactions with trained research assistants who used these wheelchairs to simulate physical disability. They found that students in the 1960s stood at a greater distance from the "disabled" actor compared to when the same actor was not seated in a wheelchair (Kleck 1969). However, this same pattern of avoidance was not found when students were asked to have a second encounter with the same disabled actor. Compared to nondisabled encounters, students in one study spent more time talking to the disabled actor but in another study spent less time with him (Kleck et al. 1966). In addition, students made twice as much eye contact and had fewer eye and body movements when listening to the disabled actor when he was seated in a wheelchair compared to when he was not (Kleck 1968). Atypical bodies tend to capture and hold people's attention (Ackerman et al. 2009), but are findings of increased eye contact and stillness consistent with a motivation to avoid disease? Perhaps – if we assume that people were standing still and staring in order to stay on high alert. However, it should also be noted that distancing from disabled actors seems much more likely upon first encounters, which is all that many studies have examined.

Nevertheless, physical distancing is not only observed with those who have visible disabilities. Some studies have shown that people refuse to shake hands with those who have cancer and avoid using their kitchen utensils as well (Maguire and Haddad 1990). Others have avoided swimming in the same pool as those labeled mentally ill (Wheeler et al. 1983). Crandall and Moriarty (1995) found that both contagious (measles, herpes, head lice) and noncontagious conditions (blindness, paralysis, cerebral palsy) were socially rejected, particularly the more severe and transmittable they were *perceived* to be.

Some evidence has documented that such avoidance patterns are accompanied by disgust reactions and/or avoidance of objects considered "contaminated" through simple contact with a disabled person. Stangor and Crandall (2000) note that gut-level aversion and disgust often occur when in contact with those who exhibit distorted physical features, including obesity (Park et al. 2007). For example, Oaten et al. (2011) described grimacing and other nonverbal disgust displays as common among those confronting people with facial deformities including burns (Knudson-Cooper 1981) and face transplants (Soni et al. 2010). Others have found that people demonstrate disgust reactions in response to photos of bodily disfigurement (Park et al. 2012; Ryan et al. 2012; Shanmugarajah et al. 2012). Sometimes these disgust reactions are also associated with contamination *behaviors*. That is, people are less willing to wear the clothing previously worn by someone with AIDS, tuberculosis, or even someone injured in an auto accident (Rozin et al. 1994). Case et al. (2010) also found evidence of contamination fear and an unwillingness to wear clothing if it had been *touched* by people described as obese, mentally ill, brain injured, old, or as having amputated limbs, birthmarks, or cancer. In fact, those disabled by obesity not only arouse disgust, but are considered social parasites (Dijker and Koomen 2003). Disgust reactions and behaviors that seek to avoid objects considered contaminated through contact with disability and noncontagious illnesses are all consistent with the idea that prejudice sometimes reflects an overgeneralized fear of contagion.

The seeming irrationality of avoiding individuals with non-contagious medical conditions has been noted by the very people who engage in this behaviour (Rachman 2004), and even by the victims themselves, who may harbour implicit biases against people with the same condition (Teachman et al. 2006). (Kouznetsova et al. 2012, p. 492)

Under what conditions are contagion fears most likely to be expressed and by whom?

While considered universal and quite common, avoidance and disgust reactions are also more likely to be engaged under certain conditions and with certain types of people (Hodson et al. 2013). This means evolved reactions are not inevitable but instead can be more flexibly applied (Neuberg et al. 2011). People are more likely to express avoidant forms of prejudice when they are in situations that make them feel more vulnerable to disease, like when pregnant (Fessler et al. 2005), visiting healthcare settings (Weir 2004), or perhaps traveling to foreign lands. Studies have confirmed that after reading a news story about contagious hepatitis, some people were much more likely to link ideas about disease with disability compared to those who read a story about noncontagious diabetes (Park et al. 2003). In fact, whenever the context highlights the idea of disease or someone just mentions a disease label (e.g. HIV, measles), avoidance can follow (Bishop et al. 1991; Fernandes et al. 2007). For example, after viewing photos of dirty kitchen sponges (a context that signaled the possibility of contamination), people were more likely to associate older adults with disease concepts – but this occurred only among those who were particularly worried about germs (Duncan and Schaller 2009).

As this result suggests, people who have more intense contagion fears may be more likely to demonstrate disability avoidance across contexts. Previous research has shown that people consistently worried about their personal vulnerability to disease react prejudicially not only toward those with AIDS (Crandall et al. 1997; Herek and Capitaniato 1998), but also toward those with noncontagious physical differences, including immigrants (Faulkner et al. 2004), obese people (Park et al. 2007), and older adults. People who feel particularly susceptible to infections like the flu also report having less contact with disabled people (Park et al. 2003). Specifically, those who score high on measures of perceived vulnerability to disease (PVD) are more likely to automatically associate physical disability with disease, and report having fewer friends and family members with disabilities. By contrast, people who have more friends and family with disabilities report feeling less vulnerable to disease and are less germaphobic as well (Park et al. 2003). Evolutionary psychologists would argue that this means that people who are more fearful of disease to begin with will actively avoid disabled others who seem infectious, even if this is illogical. However, another interpretation of these findings is that those who regularly encounter people with disabilities actually become less concerned about disease! The direction of these findings remains uncertain, but in Chapter 7, the causal effects of having increased contact with disabled people for prejudice reduction will be reviewed.

Are Contagion Fears More Likely to Be Expressed Toward Particular Disabled People?

Thus far, I have reviewed research showing that overgeneralized avoidance applies to many different stigmatized groups with visible and less visible conditions, including people with colostomy bags (Smith et al. 2006), cancer (Peters-Golden 1982), and psychiatric diagnoses once discovered (Corrigan et al. 2001). However, some disability groups are much more likely to trigger contagion fears than others. Studies have found that students preferred more social distance from those with visible (e.g. leg amputation) compared to less visible (e.g. blindness in one eye) conditions; and both students and healthcare professionals preferred more social distance from those with disabilities caused by illnesses compared to those with disabilities caused by injuries (Shiloh et al. 2011). Furthermore, those with facial disfigurements and skin conditions seem to be among the most consistently avoided (Oaten et al. 2011). Gangestad and Thornhill (1998) argued that faces that are not equal on each side (asymmetrical) may signal poor health or a lack of reproductive fitness. Down syndrome is a developmental disability associated with baby-face features (round faces, large eyes, small noses and chins), which are typically considered likeable and nonthreatening (Kenny et al. 1992). Yet, people with Down syndrome (a common form of intellectual disability) are also the targets of prejudice and discrimination. Pregnancies are frequently terminated following the prenatal diagnosis of this condition. For example, population-based studies conducted between 1995 and 2011 have documented rates of abortion ranging from 61 to 93%, with an average termination rate of 67% of those diagnosed prenatally with Down syndrome (Natoli et al. 2012; Shaffer et al. 2006). Similarly, high rates of pregnancy termination (63%) have been documented cross-culturally for other prenatally diagnosed physical disabilities (e.g. spina bifida) as well (Johnson et al. 2012). Therefore, while overgeneralized, contagion fears may be more likely to drive prejudice and discrimination toward those with visible conditions, particularly those affecting the face, and/or when the disability is assumed to be the result of some illness as opposed to an injury (e.g. from an accident or war).

In one of the first studies to directly test the hypothesis that fear of physical contagion causes avoidance of disabled people, Park et al. (2013) found that across three studies, people from various ethnic backgrounds reported the most extreme discomfort levels over the idea of touching those with real contagious conditions (e.g. HIV and skin rash), but were similarly uncomfortable with the idea of touching those with amputated limbs, facial birthmarks, and obese bodies. In addition, people expressed more than twice the amount of discomfort about physically shaking hands with those who had amputations, birthmarks, or obese bodies compared to having a nonphysical phone conversation with these same people. In other words, it was the idea of physically touching them that caused the discomfort and not the idea of interacting in general, by phone. By contrast, people reported the same level of comfort about physically touching *and* talking with an ex-convict – indicating they were not concerned about contagion in this case. This discrepancy between not wanting to touch but not minding to talk to those stigmatized by *physical* disability supports the overgeneralized disease-avoidance explanation of disability prejudice. This is among the first studies to document that one reason for discomfort about those with unusual bodies seems to be driven by a desire to avoid contagion through physical contact; this reason is considered distinct from other reasons for avoiding stigmatized groups that may operate in addition to or instead of irrational contagion fears.

Critique of Evolutionary Accounts of Disability Prejudice

Evolutionary accounts have described disability prejudice as serving an adaptive survival function, and therefore it should be relatively universal. If universal, this means that this cause of prejudice should not be unique to humans, should not be unique to time periods or specific cultures, and should be more "instinctually" triggered, unconscious, and automatic. This, however, does not mean that any evolved sources of prejudice cannot change, or are not nurtured and shaped by social influences. But if we are to take seriously that distant evolutionary origins can explain some of the prejudices against disabled people (e.g. disgust and avoidance), then the evolutionary account should make certain predictions that are distinct from other explanatory models of prejudice – explanations based on learned beliefs, for example. Prejudices that depend on other motives, shared values, and cultural stereotypes will be reviewed in subsequent chapters that describe both avoidance and approach reactions to disabled people, including curiosity, sympathy, and inspirational responses.

One prediction that a disease-avoidance account for prejudice requires is that avoidance should be relatively universal. To the extent that nonhuman animals also avoid things like pathogens and parasites, an evolved disease-avoidance account would be supported. By the same token, if over time and cross-culturally people exhibit similar reactions toward those with differing body types and disabilities, again, support for this universal explanation gains credibility. Evidence for universality, however, is mixed. For example, many evolutionary psychologists have argued that avoidance behaviors among animals are common (Dugatkin et al. 1994; Freeland 1981; Hart 1990). However, a review of the literature shows that this depends on how avoidance is defined (Oaten et al. 2011). Relevant to the analysis of disability prejudice, several authors cite the Jane Goodall (1986) studies about a troop of chimpanzees in Gombe who were observed sleeping at a distance and failing to groom two members of their troop whose legs were paralyzed from polio. Interestingly, over half the group was seen approaching one of the disabled males, although less than one third approached closely. He was touched by four fellow chimps but was also attacked twice. By contrast, Goodall (1971) also described how family members (e.g. mothers and siblings) of these chimps provided them with care and companionship. Other researchers have found that rhesus monkeys born with shorter arms, and macaques who were either blind (Berkson 1970, 1973, 1977) or had weak legs (Fedigan and Fedigan 1977) sometimes received additional care – not only from family but from the entire troop. These approach-oriented interest and caregiving behaviors seem inconsistent with disease avoidance explanations (see Dijker 2013).

In addition, anthropological research has documented the skeletal remains of prehuman Neanderthals with head injuries, amputated limbs, and other physical disabilities as regularly living among several prehistoric human populations around the world – again inconsistent with a strict disease-avoidance account where social exclusion is expected.

> When we estimate the number of impaired individuals from the skeletal record alone, we necessarily underestimate the number of impaired individuals since many impairments such as deafness, blindness, epilepsy, mental retardation, and psychiatric disorders, are impossible to identify through skeletal remains. (Scheer and Groce 1988, p. 26)

Less evidence of disease avoidance is noted among animals with more limited mental capacities, but some species of fish (Dugatkin et al. 1994), frog (Behringer et al. 2006), and lobster (Kiesecker et al. 1999) do avoid contact with members infected by parasites; and some mice avoid mating with diseased members as well (Able 1996; Kavliers et al. 2003). Clearly more research is needed to clarify the prevalence of disease-avoidance in the animal kingdom.

In terms of cross-cultural research, again if disease-avoidance is a primary driver of disability prejudice, we should see evidence across time and place of similar avoidance patterns toward those with characteristics that trigger contagion fears – even if particular cultural beliefs and experiences with human differences work against these fears. Although a historical review is beyond the scope of this chapter, there have been many examples of institutionalized avoidance prohibiting disabled people from appearing in public spaces including restaurants and religious services (Braddock and Parish 2001; Plous 2003). Disabled people were among the first to be exterminated in the holocaust (Morris 1991), and, like the Jews, were characterized as "parasitic vermin" and "useless eaters" (Gallagher 1990).

Furthermore, several well-established texts have claimed that in most societies, people with physical disabilities are similarly stigmatized (Murphy 1995; Ustun 2001). Indeed, studies show that those with conditions that affect the face and skin are often excluded from communal events and participation in key social roles (e.g. marriage) in Indian (Chaturvedi et al. 2005; Dogra and Kanwar 2002; Papadopoulos et al. 2000), African (Weiss 2008), and Southeast Asian societies (Walkser et al. 2008). Ingstad and Whyte (1995) found that in several East African settings those with epilepsy were required to sleep apart or were cast out and cut off from the family inheritance. Furthermore, those with physical disabilities like paralysis, swollen, spastic, or amputated limbs, and epilepsy have also been formally rejected or shunned in West African, Portuguese, and Caribbean countries (Boutté 1987; Goerdt 1986; Hunter 1992; Person et al. 2008). On the other hand, in some Central African countries, facial scars are created intentionally and considered attractive (Liggett 1974). Furthermore, much of the evidence cited in support of cross-cultural disability avoidance does not measure avoidant behaviors at all, but instead asks people to self-report on how much social distance they prefer to keep between themselves and various impairment groups (see Chapter 5). Self-reported descriptions of what people *think* they would do are not nearly as convincing as observations of actual behavioral avoidance, which seem to better capture the impact of contagion fears. In addition, several studies point to an extremely diverse set of reactions toward the disabled members of any given society that critically depend on the cultural values of each group (Albrecht 2005; Groce 1999; Ustun 2001). Even US ethnic groups have diverse reactions toward people with disabilities that reflect traditional beliefs, religious views, and broader ideologies of worth (Groce and Zola 1993) – a topic taken up in Chapter 3. To illustrate, in recent studies testing the evolved disease-avoidance model, unlike Europeans, East Asians did not associate disability (or older age) with disease concepts (Duncan and Schaller 2009; Park et al. 2003). The authors explained these findings as due to the cultural influence of beliefs about the source and transmission of disease in East Asian countries, where Chinese medicine is practiced and internal causes for disease are emphasized (Pachuta 1996).

In response to criticisms around cultural inconsistencies, some argue that the tendencies people evolved to adapt to particular environments in the ancient past are still subject to dynamic social pressures like differing exposures or cultural experiences with disease cues (Downes 2016). Thus, while different cultures may share a common reaction to visible signs of disease, their beliefs about contamination may vary widely (Oaten et al. 2011). Furthermore, people also vary in their sensitivity to disgust or reactivity to certain external cues, suggesting that the disease avoidance mechanism may not be universally distributed in all humans – some may have cultivated higher and lower thresholds for disease avoidance. According to Downes (2016) it is false to assume that adaptations cannot be subject to variation.

> Parents help contagious children, superordinate goals unify rival groups, and political institutions emerge to enforce egalitarian ideals. Any given cognitive system's operation is subject to the countervailing forces of other mechanisms. Of course, some systems might be more easily deactivated than others. (Kurzban and Leary 2001, p. 200)

Perhaps more problematic for a disease-avoidance account of disability prejudice has been its near exclusive emphasis on threat detection and avoidance at the expense of other functionally adaptive motives that may have also evolved to promote survival – motives associated with tolerance, forgiveness, and help. Dijker (2013) found that instead of stigmatizing those who are deviant, groups may have also evolved more benevolent forms of social control that operate through sympathy, caregiving, and guilt to help to return deviant individuals, who later conform, to the group. This may be particularly likely among kin who, perhaps because of disability or illness, violate ingroup norms or standards of behavior. Instead of stigmatizing and excluding these individuals, it may be advantageous for the group to offer "healing" treatments or therapies designed to restore those who are motivated and able to return to normative group standards. Interestingly, those who reform themselves through rehabilitation efforts to overcome their deviance may gain more acceptance and encouragement for acquiescing to ingroup expectations (e.g. losing weight, surgically removing blemishes; wearing painful prosthetics that look like "real" limbs; investing in bionic limbs to walk instead of using assistive devices). Future research is needed to investigate alternative responses to ostracism and avoidance, eliminating the need for the costly exclusion of valued members, and the shame that may implicate relatives through stigma by association. By reserving social exclusion and more aggressive responses to those who fail to change or adapt to important ingroup values, the group may gain advantages that maintain its social status (Dijker 2013).

Clearly, multiple factors from distantly inherited mechanisms to more recently learned responses interact to influence reactions to disabled people. To accommodate the influences of both evolved contagion fears and culturally specific beliefs, Oaten et al. (2011) developed a model that suggests three causal pathways through which disease avoidance contributes to prejudice. The first and most direct pathway is when a visible cue triggers disgust automatically – without our awareness or control – resulting in avoidance. The second pathway is when unconscious beliefs or labels (e.g. HIV) about disease are automatically activated in memory leading to avoidance behavior. And the third pathway is when fear is triggered indirectly through the images and interpretations evoked when people consciously think about labels and beliefs (e.g. imagining how germs are left on doorknobs; how people can contaminate the objects that they touch). This model makes some interesting predictions that have yet to be tested about when disease avoidance should be more or less likely, and how we might reduce this bias by thinking critically about the irrationality of these fears. Some of these ideas appear at the end of this chapter in the section on future research.

In summary, an evolutionary, disease-avoidance explanation of disability prejudice suggests that unconscious fears of contagion are considered to be an underlying or "distal" cause of avoidance behaviors – behaviors that are often knee-jerk reactions, applied even when contagion is not possible, and especially toward those with visible conditions of unknown origin or when people are particularly worried about germs. Evolutionary origins of prejudice are not inevitable nor are they the *only* causes of ableism in societies. Distal causes of prejudice are further removed from more immediate or "proximal" causes of prejudice which may conflict or reinforce each other. For example, humans may have evolved a tendency to pay special attention to dangerous disease signals to better avoid them, but if first allowed to stare prior to meeting with someone who experiences a disability, people actually stand closer and spend more time interacting than those without the opportunity to stare first (Langer et al. 1976). If disease avoidance is a "hard-wired" evolved reaction, why does staring at disabled people sometimes *reduce* avoidance? Does the satisfaction of curiosity about people with novel or unusual characteristics reduce contagion fears or does experience with disabled people or differences of any kind simply reduce anxieties about the unknown? Furthermore, when do fears of the unknown or fears about the likelihood of becoming disabled in the future, not through contagion, but through traumatic injury and old age, contribute to prejudicial reactions? I turn next to some of these questions.

Existential Fears of Becoming Disabled

It is well documented that the disfigured person makes others feel anxious and he becomes an object to be warded off. He is viewed as simultaneously inferior and threatening. He becomes associated with the special class of monster images that haunt each culture. (Fisher 1973, p. 73)

The fact that anyone can become disabled at any time is a very intimidating idea for most people, who prefer not to think about such possibilities, at least not for themselves. Instead, most people work hard to avoid things that seem to take away the prospect of a meaningful life, including other people who contradict their beliefs about the absolute importance of physical and intellectual capabilities. In fact, what it means to be fully human is often described in terms of *abilities* – language, self-reflection, and independence – abilities that distinguish humans as unique from other animals (Goldenberg et al. 2000). Furthermore, many psychology textbooks define the essence of human nature as requiring a capacity for rationality, self-awareness, and language – begging the question: Are people with intellectual disabilities or those who do not speak or use language not fully human?

Some of the earliest ideas about the origins of disability prejudice focus on these so called "existential" concerns about the *frailty* of life, the purpose of living, and what a quality life requires. For example, Siller et al. (1967) proposed that negative attitudes toward disabled people were the result of a distressed identification with their circumstances. Elaborating on this, Jones et al. (1984) proposed that disabled people actually remind us of death, which is the primary reason they are so uniformly avoided. More recently, contemporary psychoanalytic theories have resurrected these same ideas in calling for a more contextual psychology of disability (Watermeyer 2013).

What many of these explanations have in common is the critical role of the unconscious in helping to keep worries about our vulnerability to death and/or disability out of mind. People can use a number of unconscious strategies or "defenses" to help escape awareness of their own frailty, deny their limitations (Katz et al. 1970), and avoid reminders that disability is a fate that could, and most likely will, happen to them (Janoff-Bulman and Yopyk 2004; Livneh 1985). This functional view of disability prejudice as a way to reduce anxiety about one's one mortality and impermanence is described in the pages that follow. Following this, I present evidence supporting how and when such unconscious mechanisms lead to ableism and support for policies that keep disabled people trapped in separate facilities, subordinate positions, and at risk for dehumanizing treatments.

When confronted with ideas about disability, how do people make sense of it? Does it really threaten the meaning of their own lives? What forms of prejudice allow people to reaffirm threatened beliefs about what matters in life and the values associated with health, beauty, and hard work? And how are disabled people exploited and used to make others feel better about themselves and their privileges? The focus here is on *observers* (whether disabled or not) and their use of specific strategies driven by unconscious motives. Chapter 6 will then focus more on the ways people with disabilities have coped with their experiences of stigma, and consequences for well-being.

According to existential theories of prejudice, the existence of disability serves as an unwanted reminder that life is not predictable, and that people can and do exist outside of the boundaries of what many consider to be a purposeful, quality, human life. In response to such unwanted reminders, people may ignore and exclude disabled people, mock or lash out in violent contempt, or project those characteristics that they refuse to acknowledge in themselves onto disabled others. According to psychoanalytic approaches to disability prejudice, all of these defenses or strategies function to help protect people from the conscious consideration of disability as a fate worse than death (Marks 1999; Morris 1991).

> I have learned that the cripple must be careful not to act differently from what people expect him to do. Above all they expect the cripple to be crippled; to be disabled and helpless; to be inferior to themselves, and they will become suspicious and insecure if the cripple falls short of these expectations. (Carling 1962, p. 54)

Consider the strategy of projection. Here people who do not want to consider themselves weak, angry, or unattractive, for example, locate others to represent these characteristics in order to deflect attention away from the possibility that they themselves possess these features. Sampson (1993) describes a related strategy where people use certain groups to function as "serviceable others." That is, if nondisabled people want to think of themselves as smart, strong, and valid, then it serves them well to characterize disabled people as stupid and weak – as invalids. Chapter 4 provides evidence supporting this idea that the stereotypes we use to define disabled people communicate traits used to maintain the boundary between normalcy and its absence (Nario-Redmond 2010).

Disabled People Violate Dominant Cultural Beliefs

In addition to threatening important ideas that people hold about themselves, disabled people can also threaten a number of other cultural values. For example, in Western countries, many people value freedom, independence, intellect, and productivity. We hear parents praise children by saying, "You accomplished that *all by yourself*," whether or not the child had help from others. Adults also seem to care a lot about what others do for a living, and may express disapproval of those who choose not to work outside of the home. Many privileges are given to those with superior intelligence, including higher wages and membership into exclusive professional and social organizations (Mayer 2007). Contrast these values against those whose competencies do not include a high IQ, or who live interdependently with a personal care attendant or receive funding through social security benefits.

Beyond intelligence and productivity, many cultures value rationality, morality, and language as uniquely human characteristics. Some believe that in order to have a good life, people need companionship, good health, and a purpose for living. Others insist that humans have a higher calling and are superior to animals. Disability reminds that strength, intellect, and language are neither guaranteed nor permanent. Disabled people can also remind that humans are not necessarily unique from animals: we are all mortal and frail. We break, we decline and have accidents that result in spinal cord and traumatic brain injuries. These reminders threaten the stability of beliefs about who we are, what we think we deserve, and what those that don't conform to "normal" standards deserve. Some people have impairments that appear discrepant from current standards of beauty or "species typicality"; they arouse comparisons to one's own body image, physicality, and assumed autonomy. Furthermore, when asked to imagine what disability is like, people tend to assume the worst: that disabled lives are tragic and that they would never be able to cope or adjust to this eventuality (Nario-Redmond et al. 2017). In fact, studies on adaptation to disability and chronic illness show that people consistently underestimate their own and others' ability to bounce back from difficult circumstances (Gilbert et al. 1998). Instead, they tend to believe that their own well-being would be compromised by disability. In general, people are very poor predictors of their own capacity for adjustment following a serious health condition (Riis et al. 2005). Therefore, it makes sense that they would project these biases onto disabled people, treating them as though their lives are both tragic and long suffering; this can also result in expressions of unwanted help and pity in addition to fear and avoidance.

The problem with many of these psychodynamic approaches to explaining disability prejudice is that they have not been well tested to identify when different forms of prejudice are more or less likely to be expressed. Clearly, disability can be threatening on a number of existential grounds: Disabled people can remind us of our own mortality and vulnerability to deterioration, physical damage, and traumatic injury. In addition, disabled people may also violate several cultural values about human superiority over other animals (e.g. what capabilities are needed for quality life?), ideals related to physical appearance standards (e.g. what is beautiful?), and beliefs about justice (e.g. do people get what they deserve?). One prominent theory that has formally tested these psychodynamic ideas identifies the uniquely human fear of death as an instigator of several forms of prejudicial attitudes, beliefs, and behaviors toward a variety of stigmatized and other minority groups.

Terror Management Theory

Terror Management Theory (TMT) explains prejudice as a defensive strategy used to protect the human psyche from existential fears about the frailty of life and the inevitability of death. Developed in 1986 based on insights from scholars across the disciplines of anthropology (Ernest Becker), philosophy (Frederick Nietzsche), sociology (Erving Goffman; George Herbert Mead), and psychology (Sigmund Freud, Otto Rank), TMT is one of the few unifying theories that identifies the mechanisms thought to give rise to several human behaviors – both prosocial (e.g. helping) and antisocial (e.g. aggression) (Greenberg et al. 1997).

Over the past 30 years, TMT has been systematically tested and refined with studies conducted in over 25 countries (for a recent review see Pyszczynski et al. 2015). The theory argues that in addition to survival needs, humans also evolved both conscious and unconscious capacities to protect themselves from various threats to well-being. Unlike other animals, humans are aware that someday they will die, and this awareness can be terrifying. One way to manage this terror, to keep these worrisome thoughts about mortality out of mind, is by creating and engaging in elaborate cultural activities that give life meaning. So, people go to school, work, many get married, have children, and play multiple roles that allow them to contribute to society. It is through a deep involvement with all of these cultural practices that humans are able to transform themselves from mere mortal creatures that breathe, eat, poop, and procreate into superior "souls" with the capacity for immortality through beliefs in an afterlife and the legacies we leave behind (e.g. offspring, photographs, this book). People who live up to culturally defined standards of value – the beautiful, intelligent, and productive people – get to feel good about themselves. According to the theory, this is how people derive self-esteem (Greenberg et al. 1986; Solomon et al. 1991). On the other hand, those who deviate from cultural standards are often devalued and should not feel so great about themselves. In fact, those who depart from the characteristics and beliefs that a culture considers worthwhile are at risk for many negative outcomes, from ostracism and incarceration to depression and suicidal tendencies (Pyszczynski et al. 2015). It is this group of cultural "deviants" for whom existential anxiety (terror) is said to be poorly managed due primarily to their exclusion from opportunities to contribute to the primary cultural avenues of value.

According to TMT, an important function of any culture is to provide its members with coherent views about reality. These "worldviews" include ideologies, religious and secular beliefs about what should be valued, how to behave, and how people can find purpose by contributing to specific social roles – parent, student, teacher, worker are all important roles in many parts of the world. Although different cultures and subcultures endorse different values and views about life's purpose and what is considered "normal," the point is that all cultures have belief systems that dictate how to be successful, and what happens to people who violate important standards of behavior. While recognition and rewards are given to those who meet and exceed culturally shared values, penalties and punishments often accumulate for those who do not. Unfortunately, these worldviews require constant validation and affirmation from others, particularly when confronted with ideas that compete or conflict with one's own important beliefs. Therefore, people have a lot invested in their cultural worldviews, which are said to function like a buffer – a protective barrier – that distracts them from dwelling on their own mortality (Pyszczynski et al. 2015).

A substantial body of research has put these ideas to the empirical test. If our important beliefs about the world (and our place in it) help distract us from being preoccupied with our own demise, then when people are deliberately made to consider their own death, they should defend and cling to those beliefs. This is called the mortality salience (MS) hypothesis. TMT predicts that after becoming aware of one's own death (mortality is made salient), people are more likely to condemn, ridicule, or punish those who violate their cherished beliefs, and to praise, admire, or reward those who support them.

Much evidence has accumulated testing these ideas as explanations for different forms of prejudice, including positively biased evaluations toward those who support our central beliefs (Greenberg et al. 1990), and preferential treatment for members of our own ingroups (e.g. Castano et al. 2002; Harmon-Jones et al. 1996). Similarly, mortality salience has also been found to increase prejudice toward Jews (Greenberg et al. 1990), Muslims (Das et al. 2009), and most recently, disabled people (Hirschberger et al. 2005). Some have even shown that aggressive acts (McGregor et al. 1998) and support for violent solutions (Pyszczynski et al. 2006) increase following mortality salience.

TMT and Disability Prejudice

A few cross-cultural studies have directly assessed the extent to which responses to disabled people are driven by underlying fears of death. In 2005 and 2008, Hirschberger and colleagues conducted several experiments finding support for TMT that reactions to disability are due, at least in part, to mortality fears. To test the death-disability-rejection hypothesis (Ben-Naim et al. 2008), these researchers have taken two approaches. In the first, reactions to disabled people are measured after people are asked to think about their own death. In the second, this order is reversed to see if thoughts about death are more likely after exposure to disabled people. To illustrate how MS works, some people are asked to write an open-ended response to the question, "What do you think happens to you as you physically die and once you are physically dead?" For comparison purposes, a control group is asked to write about another aversive experience like going to the dentist and experiencing severe pain. Findings have shown that compared to control conditions, after writing about their own death, people give more negative evaluations (Ben-Naim et al. 2008), and are less willing to help a female wheelchair user with a simple request (Hirschberger et al. 2008). Furthermore, after being reminded of their own death, people are more likely to blame both males and females with physical disabilities (e.g. spinal cord injuries) for their disabling circumstances (Hirschberger 2006). In fact, when people are made to consider their own death, they assign more blame to those who became paralyzed due to no fault of their own than they do to those who became paralyzed due to their own recklessness. This finding may seem surprising, but it is consistent with the idea that disability is particularly threatening when people are reminded of their own vulnerability to random accidents, which also undermines beliefs about the world being a fair place where only those deserving of negative consequences (e.g. reckless people) get punished. The topics of blame and responsibility for one's disability are taken up in greater detail in Chapter 3.

In another series of studies (Hirschberger et al. 2005), students were asked to write about what happens when they either physically die, or when they fail an important exam or watch television (control conditions); then they read about a day in the life of a *same-sex peer* with a physical disability. Results showed that overall compassion toward the disabled peer was lower for men (but not women) who first wrote about their own death compared to the control conditions. A follow-up study replicated this finding: death awareness reduced compassion among men toward a fellow male with a disability; women, however, showed the opposite pattern, expressing more compassion toward a fellow female with a disability. Conceivably, death awareness may have led to increased gender-role conformity in terms of how men and women are taught to respond to people in need since men became less compassionate and women more compassionate toward disabled peers following mortality salience. Future research is needed to disentangle same and opposite sex reactions to disabled peers.

Studies have also examined disability prejudice using the second approach to see if the presence of disabled people actually provokes death-related thoughts. According to TMT, if our cultural beliefs really protect us from reminders of our own death, then when confronted with people who violate those beliefs, thoughts of death should become even more accessible in memory than before. To capture whether people were thinking more about their own death or not, Hirschberger (2006) asked a group of Jewish-Israeli students to complete words that were missing a few letters after reading about a peer who either broke his leg or became paralyzed after a car accident. The study used Hebrew word fragments that could be completed in several different ways – some that related to death and some that did not. To provide some examples in English: the incomplete word: G R ___ V E can either be completed with an O to make the word GROVE or with an A to make the word GRAVE; similarly the incomplete word D E ___ D can be completed with an E to make the word DEED or with an A to make the word DEAD. This research found that students generated more death-related words after reading about a paralyzed person compared to reading about someone who just broke their leg; and they generated the most death-related words when the driver was described as careful as opposed to being described as reckless. Similar results were found in an earlier study among male students who read about a same-sex peer (Hirschberger et al. 2005). These findings suggest that people think more about death when threatened by permanent disability (paralysis) and when they learn that disability can happen even when drivers are careful – which is far more threatening than when the outcomes can be blamed on the recklessness of the driver. These studies provide clear evidence for the idea some forms of disability prejudice may be due to feelings of threat regarding our own vulnerability to death. Yet, the research did not isolate the specific reasons why disabled people may be threatening. That is, disabled people may remind us of our death but they may also remind us of other vulnerabilities as well, including the frailty of the human body, and its similarity to other nonhuman creatures.

I am not an animal! I am a human being! I … am … a … man! (John Merrick, *The Elephant Man*, Lynch 1980)

Although values and views about the world differ from culture to culture, many cultures around the world seem to share the belief that humans are elevated above, and distinct from, other animals (Goldenberg et al. 2000). For example, some consider humans to be the only species with a soul – the only species capable of language, sentiments, and advanced reasoning (Leyens et al. 2000). While science has now documented that other animals may also have some language and other cognitive capacities, many still maintain that the human race is far superior (Chandler and Dreger 1993; Snodgrass and Gates 1998). According to the TM theorists, this belief in the supreme status of humankind goes a long way in protecting people from feeling anxious about death, the purpose of their lives, and their place in the universe (Goldenberg et al. 2000). As a consequence, any reminders that we are not so very different from other animals have the potential of making us feel more vulnerable to death.

Enter people with disabilities who have sustained traumatic injuries that sometimes leave them drooling and incontinent. Those paralyzed by accidents and war who no longer walk upright, and people who are chronically or mentally "ill" who may rock, shake, and moan – all serve as blatant reminders that we, like animals, are made of flesh and blood with bodies that decline, deteriorate, and die. Studies show that people strive to distance themselves from any reminders of their more animalistic natures after being made aware of their own death (as opposed to going to the dentist or watching television). Specifically, thoughts of death lead people to prefer stories that focus on how humans are unique from other animals, and increase their disgust toward animals and bodily products (e.g. the smell of urine, the presence of excrement, and the sound of mucus) – all reminders of our essential creatureliness (Goldenberg et al. 2001).

> So powerful is the desire to cordon ourselves off from our animality that we often don't stop at feces, cockroaches, and slimy animals. We need a group of humans to bound ourselves against, who will come to exemplify the boundary line between the truly human and the basely animal. If those quasi-animals stand between us and our own animality, then we are one step further away from being animal and mortal ourselves. (Nussbaum 2009, p. 107)

Other studies have made people aware of their animal natures using images and descriptions of urination, nose mucus, and blood which result in increased thoughts of death (Cox et al. 2007a). Similarly, when reminded of a woman's menstruation, people are more likely to avoid her and consider her incompetent, compared to those without this reminder (Roberts et al. 2002). Negative evaluations have also been assigned to breastfeeding (Cox et al. 2007b) and pregnant women (Goldenberg et al. 2007) following reminders of humans' similarity to animals. The argument is that we work very hard to keep these reminders of our animal natures at bay by covering up blemishes (Goldenberg et al. 2001), perfuming body odors, and making private and sanitary the elimination of wastes. Cross-culturally, people develop purification and other rituals to transform the natural body into something more symbolic. Consequently, when confronted with those who leave hints of menstruation on wheelchair cushions or who leak urine and other bodily fluids (Rozin et al. 1999), it becomes harder to deny our animalistic natures, which may explain why disabled people have historically been shunned from many public venues (Jones et al. 1984; Katz 1981).

> No person who is diseased, maimed, mutilated or in any way deformed so as to be an unsightly or disgusting object or improper person to be allowed in or on the public ways or other places in this city, shall therein or thereon expose himself to public view. (Chicago Municipal Code, Sec. 36034, 1966, as cited in Plous 2003)

It wasn't that long ago that several US cities, including San Francisco, Columbus, and Omaha, had "ugly laws" prohibiting disabled people from frequenting restaurants and other public spaces (Schweik 2009). In fact, when it comes to eating behavior, many cultures prescribe appropriate standards for chewing, burping, and the use of utensils that are not to be violated without penalty. Those who eat from the floor, with assistive devices, or who have personal care attendants to wipe their mouths and feeding tubes may provoke images of animal behaviors considered inappropriate to "civilized" company.

Caregivers also expend much effort to regulate the behavior of those who fail to control their bodily impulses. Children are punished for soiling the bed, disabled people are shamed for crawling on the floor; those "sheltered" in group homes are sometimes prevented from engaging in intimate relationships (Swango-Wilson

2008), and sex is even more highly regulated in nursing homes and other "care" facilities (O'Callaghan and Murphy 2007). According to Goldenberg et al. (2000), one of the reasons sex is so highly controlled in many cultures is because it is so suggestive of our animal roots. This may also be why marital and birth control regulations (Kerr and Shakespeare 2002) seem more justifiable when imposed upon those whose human status continues to be questioned.

Dehumanization and Disability Hate Crimes

I was traveling abroad and felt as if I was treated like baggage at the airport. When I checked in, employees asked my companions questions about me and did not speak to me. They refused to allow me to take my own wheelchair to the plane and had me transfer to a chair someone else would push. The man pushing me spoke to my companions but not to me other than to tell me no when I put my hands on the wheels. I felt powerless, as if I were just an object that needed to be moved from one place to another. ~ Person with a physical disability, 2015

I am often touched, patted, grabbed or pulled by random strangers who seem to have no idea that their behavior is inappropriate. Such actions could be considered either dehumanizing (treating me like an animal or a piece of luggage) or condescending (treating me like a child). I also often hear the phrase 'I'll put you over there' when somebody is guiding me. That also comes across as objectifying. ~ Person with a sensory disability, 2015

Research on dehumanization or the denial of humanity has found that perceiving others to be less than human allows people to deem them "unworthy" of assistance, and justify their exclusion (Costello and Hodson 2011). Dehumanization of outgroups is also associated with support for violence (Goff et al. 2008) and animalistic characterizations of African Americans as apes, Jews as vermin (Livingstone-Smith 2011), and disabled people as dogs, seals, and "useless eaters" (Burleigh 1994; Sherry 2010; Gallagher 1990).

People are dehumanized when denied traits used to distinguish them from other animals; these "uniquely" human attributes emphasize characteristics exclusively associated with humans, such as rationality, civility, and morality (Haslam and Loughnan 2012). However, dehumanization can also refer to the denial of traits considered more universal and "essential" to human nature, including emotionality, openness, and warmth. According to this approach, those denied uniquely human traits are more likely to be viewed as animalistic (e.g. people with paraplegia or cerebral palsy), while those denied human nature traits are more likely to be viewed as non-feeling machines or robots (e.g. people on the autistic spectrum) (Loughnan et al. 2009). One implication of this distinction is that prejudice may differ depending on which form of dehumanization is primary, although both may operate simultaneously. In one particularly insidious form of discrimination, computer hackers used cyber technology to attack the website of the Epilepsy Foundation where members were redirected to a page designed to trigger seizures by embedding messages with flashing computer animation (Sherry 2010).

In an attempt to identify which dimensions of humanness were more commonly associated with particular social groups, Bastian et al. (2011), asked people to rate 24 different groups (ethnic, religious, age, occupation, and impairment groups) on dimensions related to both human uniqueness and human nature. While the groups varied on how much each was thought to possess the human nature traits of emotional responsiveness and warmth, disability groups scored lowest on traits that distinguished humans as unique from other animals. Specifically, "the disabled," "mentally ill," and "retarded" were all rated in the very bottom quartile of all groups for lacking rationality, cultural refinement, and self-restraint; and those labeled "retarded" were assigned the very lowest of these uniquely human qualities. This may explain why so many cases of violence against intellectually disabled people involve insults that refer to them as bestial and immoral creatures (Sherry 2010). In philosophical debates, there remains disagreement about whether those with severe intellectual disabilities should even qualify as persons (Kittay and Carlson 2010). Such rhetoric is still used to justify subhuman treatment in various residential settings where "fight clubs" have been documented in Texas in 2009 and again in New York in 2014. In these cases, developmentally disabled residents were coerced by group home employees to hit one another other while the employees videotaped them (Hill et al. 2009; Thomas 2014).

Throughout the twentieth century there have been enumerable atrocities against intellectually disabled people, particularly in institutional settings, where residents have been starved or routinely fed bird-like while lying down, left alone stewing in their own wastes (Keith and Keith 2013); some were denied heat in the wintertime on the basis of beliefs that institutional inmates were not sensitive to the cold (Carlson 2010).

Future research is needed to examine whether other impairment groups, stereotyped as "stony and emotionless" (e.g. schizophrenic and autistic people or those who use assistive technologies like bionic limbs or computers that voice) experience more objectifying forms of dehumanization reserved for those assumed to be unfeeling machines (e.g. the denial of pain medicine; the stealing or destruction of equipment or assault with prosthetic devices) (Bryen et al. 2003; McKinney 2018).

> Virtually every study of disability and abuse in the last 30 years has found that disabled people are victimized and abused at much higher rates than nondisabled people. (Sherry 2010, p. 75)

Documenting the pervasiveness of disability hate crimes in the Unites States and elsewhere, Sherry (2010) recounts numerous cases of contemporary dehumanization where perpetrators deliberately target disabled individuals because of their disability status to exploit, humiliate, and violently attack their persons. Disability hate crimes have been described as particularly sadistic, involving sustained attacks, humiliation, degradation, and torture (Sherry 2014). Reports include cases where people urinated on targeted individuals from a position of dominance, rubbing or dumping feces in their hair (e.g. WKYC Staff 2014). According to the US Bureau of Justice Statistics, disabled people are 1.5 times more likely to be victimized by violent crimes than nondisabled people, and are more than twice as likely to be raped or sexually assaulted. Rates of sexual victimization are even higher among women with severe disabilities (Casteel et al. 2008). An analysis of Federal Bureau of Investigation (FBI) data from 1997 to 2007 revealed that rape was over 30 times more likely to occur in disability hate crimes compared to other hate crimes (Sherry 2010) – a finding that seems inconsistent with an evolved disease-avoidance account of ableism. Furthermore, hate crimes motivated by disability were much more likely to be perpetrated by people *known* to the victim and in the victim's own home. Currently, anti-disability hate groups are said to be rapidly increasing on the internet (Sherry 2014), and these do not include the countless examples of biased language that pervades the media (see Chapter 3). Many of these crimes not only escape prosecution, they are rarely reported in the media (Findlay 2016). In 2016, for example, 19 people were brutally murdered and 26 more were injured in a home for disabled people near Tokyo, Japan. The murderer, who turned himself in, was quoted saying, "It is better that disabled disappear. I envision a world where a person with multiple disabilities can be euthanized" (McCurry 2016). Despite the violence of this massacre, it received very little attention in the media. According to disability activist Carly Findlay, "There was no hashtag. No public outcry. Not even prayers" (Adams 2016).

Beliefs in human superiority have long been used to justify various forms of exploitation, genocide, and the "oppression of humans alleged to be in an animal condition" (Patterson 2002, p. 25). There is a growing body of research on dehumanization finding that viewing humans as superior to animals is a strong predictor of intergroup prejudice (Costello and Hodson 2014; Leyens et al. 2000). Future research is needed to identify the parameters of this and other dehumanizing biases that may be based on characteristics considered essential to a quality life, which are then used to justify decisions about sterilization, abortion, physician-assisted suicide, and life-sustaining treatments solely on the basis of one's disability status (Marks 1999; Morris 1991).

When Are Existential Sources of Prejudice Most Likely?

Although fears about human vulnerability and the ways we manage these fears are considered universal, the specific content of the worldviews that give our lives meaning vary widely across cultures. Even within a culture, the extent to which people endorse specific values or consider certain standards to be important will also differ; and some contexts and particular people are also more likely to threaten these beliefs. For example, the death anxiety of the United States was raised after September 11, 2001, when people collectively came to appreciate human vulnerability to mass devastation. Many Americans responded by reaffirming their patriotic and conservative values – American flags were everywhere, and church attendance increased while anger and prejudice toward those with darker skin was frequently a topic in the news (Neimeyer et al. 2004). Prejudice toward other cultural "deviants," including religious minorities, following the 9/11 attacks has also been documented (Pyszczynski et al. 2003).

Another context likely to arouse fears of death and disability confronts those working in medical settings and nursing homes, who not only have more death-related concerns (Bennett 2002) but are also more likely to devalue older people (Eakes 1985; Vickio and Cavanaugh 1985). Ageist attitudes are particularly likely among those whose fears stem from what happens to the body after death (Depaola et al. 1994). People are also more likely to dehumanize others in places where they experience disgust (e.g. hospitals, nursing homes, and unclean eating establishments) (Buckels and Trapnell 2013). The emotion of disgust seems to shift perceptions of the human–animal boundary in ways that facilitate dehumanizing beliefs by blocking the brain's ability to perceive another's humanity (Harris and Fiske 2006). Even educational exercises where people are asked to use wheelchairs, ear plugs, and dark glasses to simulate paralysis, deafness, and blindness can be threatening reminders of one's personal vulnerability to disability (Nario-Redmond et al. 2017; Silverman et al. 2015). Some of the unintended consequences of disability simulations that attempt to reduce prejudice by increasing empathy are described in Chapter 7.

In addition to threat-specific contexts, certain people are more likely to respond prejudicially when their own mortality has been threatened, including those who live with more fear about their own demise (Florian and Mikulincer 1997), and those with low feelings of self-worth (Harmon-Jones et al. 1996, 1997). Several TMT studies confirm that those with low self-esteem are much more likely than those with high self-esteem to express prejudice against people who violate their cherished beliefs (Pyszczynski et al. 2004). Similarly, for people whose self-worth is strongly tied to their physical bodies, thoughts of death can increase the value of bodily appearance even more (Goldenberg et al. 2000). For example, those who care more about "appearances" and the "ideal body" – as thin, muscular, "upright," and attractive – should feel more threatened by disabled bodies, especially in situations when they are feeling insecure or temporarily less attractive themselves. Interestingly, one study found that when made to think about their own death and similarity to other creatures (e.g. chimps), people expressed more negative attitudes toward animals in general, but only when they were low in self-esteem (Beatson and Halloran 2007). Those who felt more secure in their self-worth demonstrated much more positive attitudes toward animals, even when thinking about their own similarity to these creatures. Furthermore, compared to those with less power (e.g. assistants), people with more power (e.g. managers) are more likely to animalistically dehumanize peers (Gwinn et al. 2013). This has implications for disability prejudice to the extent that some view disabled people as threatening the importance they place on human superiority. These ideas remain to be tested.

> The development of a stigmatized condition in a loved one or in oneself represents a major breach of trust – a destruction of the belief that life is predictable. In a sense, stigma represents a kind of death – a social death. Nonstigmatized people, through avoidance and social rejection, often treat stigmatized people as if they were invisible, nonexistent, or dead. (Coleman-Brown 2016, p. 155)

Feeling personally vulnerable to disability and/or death also depends on what people fear most. Disability has often been characterized as a fate worse than death – perhaps because it has historically resulted in extreme marginalization akin to social death. Consistent with this idea, Hirschberger et al. 2005 found that after being exposed to a disabled peer, both male and female students expressed more anxiety about the *interpersonal* or social losses associated with their own death (e.g. worried that their absence would not be felt, and that they would not be able to contribute to their families). However, following mortality salience, these students did not express more fear about the *personal* aspects of dying (e.g. failure to complete important tasks).

Few published studies have directly compared the effects of making death salient to the effects of making disability salient, although some have suggested that both can remind people of the frailty of the human body. In a study designed to examine attitudes toward college disability policies, Brough (2005) found that students were significantly less supportive of providing alternative formats for disabled students when they were first asked to consider becoming physically disabled compared to those first asked to consider their own death; however, this effect was limited to those who strongly valued the physical appearance aspects of their body image. Those who strongly valued their physical appearance were also less supportive of a tuition increase to recruit underrepresented groups to the college when first asked to consider becoming disabled compared to those asked to consider their own death. In addition, those who considered their own disability status were less supportive of accessible library resources compared to those primed with death, but only when they scored high on a measure of disability prejudice. Much more work is needed to disentangle the circumstances under which particular types of people will express different forms of disability prejudice when made to feel personally vulnerable. It may be that while people work to manage their fears of both physical and social death (e.g. ostracism), fears about becoming socially irrelevant through disability may be particularly threatening to some.

Finally, certain impairment groups may be targeted more than others in situations where their particular features or other characteristics trigger fear and animosity in others. For example, successful disabled people may threaten the identities of certain caregivers or those who have used the inferiority of disabled people to justify their own positions of authority and worth. In a classic study, Katz et al. (1978) found that students were less willing to be interviewed by an outgoing and achievement-oriented person using a wheelchair than by the same outgoing and achievement-oriented person not using a wheelchair. In fact, when outgoing, the wheelchair user aroused more anger in students compared to when not using a wheelchair. The authors argued that people who strongly believe that disability must cause suffering or that only nondisabled people can live successful, happy lives, might feel challenged by those who violate these beliefs. Consistent with this idea, this study found that students were more willing to be interviewed when the person using a wheelchair acted frustrated and unfriendly compared to the same frustrated and unfriendly person who did not use a wheelchair.

Other studies have found that people are more likely to distance themselves from those who possess the very characteristics that they considered undesirable about themselves (Schimel et al. 2000). In some cases, acts of violence and hate have been documented toward those who may remind people of their own limitations or repudiated identities (e.g. anti-gay violence). Hate crimes, which often involve dehumanizing treatments, frequently target those with intellectual disabilities, often characterized as animalistic and in need of taming. On one internet discussion board, a child with Down syndrome was described as *"something walking around pretending to be human that's no more than a living mannequin; a facsimile of human life, no more real than a dummy"* (Sherry 2010, p. 41). Although anti-disability hate crimes have been documented against nearly every type of impairment, the FBI classification system, which currently divides crimes into those perpetrated against people with mental or physical disabilities, complicates conclusions for people with more than one impairment and for those who have conditions that do not easily fit into either category (e.g. those with blindness or HIV/AIDS). Nevertheless, the data clearly demonstrate that rates of anti-mental disability crimes were three times higher than those classified as anti-physical disability crimes during the 10-year period between 1997 and 2007. Disability hate crimes have been increasing every year since 2011 (Ryan 2015); and the number of prosecutions for disability hate crimes showed an increase of over 200% in the United Kingdom since 2007 (Wheeler 2015).

Summary

In summary, both contagion-based and existential sources of disability prejudice involve fears that operate at the more distal and unconscious level. Both forms seem to defy rational understandings about the nature of contamination, and the inevitability of disability and death as part of the life course. Yet, both may represent the vestiges of evolutionary adaptations and strategies that developed to protect the human species from perceived threats to well-being – even if neither seem relevant to modern-day living.

We know that most people do not "catch" disability, so why do some persist in avoiding disabled people as if they were contagious, isolating them from society, and treating them with disgust and contempt? Following evolutionary logic, people have long been motivated by safety concerns to self-protect; they will, however, respond differently depending on the nature of the perceived threat.

If disability prejudice is driven in part by exaggerated tendencies to avoid contamination and disease, people should be more likely to react with disgust and avoid disabled people than to react with anger, pity, or exaggerated praise. Furthermore, these reactions should be relatively universal (observed in multiple cultures), and consistent with animal studies. While many studies have documented patterns of social and physical distancing in response to disability, evidence for the universality of the disease-avoidance model is mixed. A general consensus among studies is that the more visible impairments and those that signal contagion are consistently avoided, especially those that affect the face and skin; distancing reactions are also more likely to be expressed when people are feeling particularly vulnerable to disease (such as while pregnant, in a hospital, or while traveling abroad). Interestingly, however, studies that examine interactions beyond the first encounter find that upon subsequent exposure to disability, patterns of avoidance are less likely to continue. Similarly, people with disabled friends and family members report feeling *less* vulnerable to disease – which seems to reflect the critical role of learning and social contact in overriding initial fear-based reactions. Furthermore, evidence for disease avoidance in the animal kingdom is also mixed, and in some cultures, bodily disfigurement is both sought after and considered attractive. Today, some nondisabled people even seek to transition into disability status by removing limbs or seeking to blind or paralyze themselves as part of the transability movement (for more information see Baril 2015; Stevens 2011) – a phenomenon that seems hard to reconcile with the disease-avoidance model. Much more research is needed to examine the conditions under which fears of contagion as distinct from other fears that are learned or develop over time predict specific forms of ableism. For example, fears about becoming disabled are not the same as fears of catching it from contact with others.

Existential fears about the meaning of human life (and why certain people are disabled while others are not) also play a role in disability prejudice. Specifically, some forms of ableism seem to be driven by perceived threats to beliefs about the nature of humanness itself, and the importance of language, physicality, beauty, and intellect in defining human nature. In such cases, prejudicial reactions may reflect defensive projections, condemnations, and dehumanizing treatments of those that violate cherished values in an effort to justify the validity of threatened beliefs. Disabled bodies remind people about their own mortality, frailty, and the significance of certain human characteristics and abilities considered "essential" to quality living. Disabled people can and do exist outside of what many consider to be "normal living" or "species typicality," and this can be frightening to some – causing them to ignore, exclude, and lash out against disabled people, often in violent ways.

In fact, people who view humans as superior to animals may be more likely to condone dehumanizing treatments as appropriate for those who appear "uncivilized" or "animalistic" – who represent unwanted reminders of our essential creatureliness as beings who leak bodily fluids and expel wastes. For example, autistic people have been treated as non-feeling robots; those who don't communicate verbally have been caged as if they are animals; and those who have less control over bodily functions are increasingly the targets of abuse and neglect. The US Bureau of Justice reports that disabled people are 1.5 times more likely to be a victim of a violent crime and twice as likely to be raped or sexually assaulted.

A psychoanalytic approach to prejudice suggests that people may view disability as a "fate worse than death," and do not like to be reminded that such a fate could be their own. For example, TMT views prejudice as a defensive strategy used to protect the human psyche from existential fears about vulnerability to death (and disability). One way to manage these fears is to participate in the cultural activities and social roles that give life meaning – to endorse beliefs that set the standards for what a society considers a "normal," "human," or "worthy" life. Research shows that those who do not meet the valued standards of a culture are often invalidated, ostracized, and discriminated against, particularly when people are reminded of their own mortality. While much evidence has accumulated in support of TMT, fewer studies have tested its implications for disability prejudice. In general, however, when people are made aware of their own death, they are more likely to condemn, ridicule, and punish those who violate important norms and expectations. People reminded of their own death are also more likely to blame disabled people for their disabling conditions. This may be why people defensively project their fears about disability onto those who threaten their beliefs about which lives are of most value, who is more deserving of rewards and punishments, and how disability is something that only happens to people who break "the rules" – a topic elaborated on in the next chapter.

It is important to remember that disability prejudice and the fears that motivate it have real-world consequences, even when unintentional and unconscious. They manifest in hate crimes and in public policies that segregate and differentially incarcerate disabled people. Several US cities, including San Francisco and Columbus, once had laws prohibiting disabled people from entering public spaces; these laws have since been overturned. Thus, while many prejudices reflect underlying fears and unconscious motivations, they can and do change. New beliefs and behaviors can be learned; however, the ideological frameworks that underlie prejudicial beliefs are often deeply engrained in societal practices and must first be uncovered before they can be dismantled.

References

Able, D.J. (1996). The contagion indicator hypothesis for parasite-mediated sexual selection. *Proceedings of the National Academy of Sciences* 93 (5): 2229–2233.

Ackerman, J.M., Becker, D.V., Mortensen, C.R. et al. (2009). A pox on the mind: disjunction of attention and memory in the processing of physical disfigurement. *Journal of Experimental Social Psychology* 45 (3): 478–485.

Adams, R. (2016). Why has Japan's massacre of disabled people gone unnoticed? *The Independent* (31 August). www.independent.co.uk/voices/japan-disability-rights-massacre-tsukui-yamayuriena-gone-unnoticed-a7217661.html#commentsDiv (accessed 26 February 2019).

Albrecht, G.L. (ed.) (2005). *Encyclopedia of Disability*. London: Sage.

Baril, A. (2015). Needing to acquire a physical impairment/disability: (re)thinking the connections between trans and disability studies through transability. *Hypatia* 30 (1): 30–48.

Bastian, B., Laham, S.M., Wilson, S. et al. (2011). Blaming, praising, and protecting our humanity: the implications of everyday dehumanization for judgments of moral status. *British Journal of Social Psychology* 50 (3): 469–483.

Beatson, R.M. and Halloran, M.J. (2007). Humans rule! The effects of creatureliness reminders, mortality salience and self-esteem on attitudes towards animals. *British Journal of Social Psychology* 46 (3): 619–632.

Behringer, D.C., Butler, M.J., and Shields, J.D. (2006). Avoidance of disease by social lobsters. *Nature* 441 (7092): 421.

Ben-Naim, S., Aviv, G., and Hirschberger, G. (2008). Strained interaction: evidence that interpersonal contact moderates the death-disability rejection link. *Rehabilitation Psychology* 53 (4): 464–470.

Bennett, M.A. (2002). The therapist's transference: younger therapists working with older adults. *Dissertation Abstracts International* 63 (5-B): 2573.

Berkson, G. (1970). Defective infants in a feral monkey group. *Folia Primatology* 12 (4): 284–289.

Berkson, G. (1973). Social responses to abnormal infant monkeys. *American Journal of Physical Anthropology* 38 (2): 583–586.

Berkson, G. (1977). Rejection of abnormal strangers from macaque monkey groups. *Journal of Abnormal Psychology* 86 (6): 659–661.

Bishop, G.D., Alva, A.L., Cantu, L., and Rittiman, T.K. (1991). Responses to persons with AIDS: fear of contagion or stigma? *Journal of Applied Social Psychology* 21 (23): 1877–1888.

Boutté, M.I. (1987). "The stumbling disease": a case study of stigma among Azorean-Portuguese. *Social Science & Medicine* 24 (3): 209–217.

Braddock, D.L. and Parish, S.L. (2001). An institutional history of disability. In: *Handbook of Disability Studies* (ed. G.L. Albrecht, K.D. Seelman and M. Bury), 11–68. Thousand Oaks, CA: Sage.

Brough, K. M. (2005). Disability prejudice from a terror management perspective. Undergraduate thesis. Reed College, Portland, OR.

Bryen, D.N., Carey, A., and Frantz, B. (2003). Ending the silence: adults who use augmentative communication and their experiences as victims of crimes. *Augmentative and Alternative Communication* 19 (2): 125–134.

Buckels, E.E. and Trapnell, P.D. (2013). Disgust facilitates outgroup dehumanization. *Group Processes & Intergroup Relations* 16 (6): 771–780.

Burleigh, M. (1994). Return to the planet of the apes? *History Today* 44 (10): 6–8.

Carling, F. (1962). *And Yet We Are Human*. North Stratford, NH: Ayer.

Carlson, L. (2010). Who's the expert? Rethinking authority in the face of intellectual disability. *Journal of Intellectual Disability Research* 54 (S1): 58–65.

Case, T. I., Stevenson, R. J., and Oaten, M. (2010). Disease avoidance and false alarms. *22nd Annual Conference of the Human Behavior and Evolution Society, Eugene, OR, 16 June 2010*. Los Angeles, CA: Human Behavior and Evolution Society.

Castano, E., Yzerbyt, V., Paladino, M., and Sacchi, S. (2002). I belong, therefore, I exist: ingroup identification, ingroup entitativity, and ingroup bias. *Personality and Social Psychology Bulletin* 28: 135–143.

Casteel, C., Martin, S.L., Smith, J.B. et al. (2008). National study of physical and sexual assault among women with disabilities. *Injury Prevention* 14 (2): 87–90.

Chandler, E.W. and Dreger, R.M. (1993). Anthropocentrism: construct validity and measurement. *Journal of Social Behavior & Personality* 8 (2): 169–188.

Chapple, A., Ziebland, S., and McPherson, A. (2004). Stigma, shame and blame experienced by patients with lung cancer: a qualitative study. *British Medical Journal* 328: 1470–1473.

Chaturvedi, S.K., Singh, G., and Gupta, N. (2005). Stigma experience in skin disorders: an Indian perspective. *Dermatologic Clinics* 23 (4): 635–642.

Clarke, A. (1999). Psychosocial aspects of facial disfigurement: problems, management and the role of a lay-led organization. *Psychology, Health & Medicine* 4 (2): 127–142.

Coleman-Brown, L. (2016). Stigma: an enigma demystified. In: *The Disability Studies Reader* (ed. L. Davis), 145–159. New York: Routledge.

Corrigan, P., Edwards, A.B., Green, A. et al. (2001). Prejudice, social distance, and familiarity with mental illness. *Schizophrenia Bulletin* 27 (2): 219–225.

Costello, K. and Hodson, G. (2011). Social dominance-based threat reactions to immigrants in need of assistance. *European Journal of Social Psychology* 41 (2): 220–231.

Costello, K. and Hodson, G. (2014). Explaining dehumanization among children: the interspecies model of prejudice. *British Journal of Social Psychology* 53 (1): 175–197.

Cottrell, C.A. and Neuberg, S.L. (2005). Different emotional reactions to different groups: a sociofunctional threat-based approach to "prejudice". *Journal of Personality and Social Psychology* 88 (5): 770–789.

Cox, C.R., Goldenberg, J.L., Arndt, J., and Pyszczynski, T. (2007a). Mother's milk: an existential perspective on negative reactions to breastfeeding. *Personality and Social Psychology Bulletin* 33 (1): 110–122.

Cox, C.R., Goldenberg, J.L., Pyszczynski, T., and Weise, D. (2007b). Disgust, creatureliness, and the accessibility of death-related thoughts. *European Journal of Social Psychology* 37 (3): 494–507.

Crandall, C.S. and Moriarty, D. (1995). Physical illness stigma and social rejection. *British Journal of Social Psychology* 34: 67–83.

Crandall, C.S., Glor, J., and Britt, T.W. (1997). AIDS-related stigmatization: instrumental and symbolic attitudes. *Journal of Applied Social Psychology* 27 (2): 95–123.

Das, E., Bushman, B.J., Bezemer, M.D. et al. (2009). How terrorism news reports increase prejudice against outgroups: a terror management account. *Journal of Experimental Social Psychology* 45 (3): 453–459.

Depaola, S.J., Neimeyer, R., and Ross, S.K. (1994). Death concern and attitudes toward the elderly in nursing home personnel as a function of training. *OMEGA – Journal of Death and Dying* 29 (3): 231–248.

Dijker, A.J.M. (2013). Stigmatization, repair, or undesirable side effect of tolerance? Being clear about what we study and target for intervention. *Basic and Applied Social Psychology* 35 (1): 22–30.

Dijker, A.J.M. and Koomen, W. (2003). Extending Weiner's attribution-emotion model of stigmatization of ill persons. *Basic and Applied Social Psychology* 25 (1): 51–68.

Dogra, S. and Kanwar, A.J. (2002). Skin diseases: psychological and social consequences. *Indian Journal of Dermatology* 47 (4): 197–201.

Downes, S.M. (2016). Evolutionary psychology, adaptation and design. In: *Handbook of Evolutionary Thinking in the Sciences* (ed. P. Huneman, G. Lecointre and M. Silbersteintein), 659–673. Netherlands: Springer.

Drake, S. (2010). Connecting disability rights and animal rights – a really bad idea. Not Dead Yet. http://notdeadyet.org/2010/10/connecting-disability-rights-and-animal.html (1 March 2019).

Dugatkin, L.A., FitzGerald, G.J., and Lavoie, J. (1994). Juvenile three-spined sticklebacks avoid parasitized conspecifics. *Environmental Biology of Fishes* 39 (2): 215–218.

Duncan, L.A. and Schaller, M. (2009). Prejudicial attitudes toward older adults may be exaggerated when people feel vulnerable to infectious disease: evidence and implications. *Analyses of Social Issues and Public Policy* 9 (1): 97–115.

Eakes, G.G. (1985). The relationship between death anxiety and attitudes toward the elderly among nursing staff. *Death studies* 9 (2): 163–172.

Faulkner, J., Schaller, M., Park, J.H., and Duncan, L.A. (2004). Evolved disease-avoidance mechanisms and contemporary xenophobic attitudes. *Group Processes & Intergroup Relations* 7 (4): 333–353.

Fedigan, L.M. and Fedigan, L. (1977). The social development of a handicapped infant in a freeliving troop of Japanese monkeys. In: *Primate Bio-social Development: Biological, Social and Ecological Determinants* (ed. S. Chevalier-Skolnikoff and F.E. Poirier), 205–222. New York: Garland.

Fernandes, P., Salgado, P., Noronha, A. et al. (2007). Prejudice toward chronic diseases: comparison among epilepsy, AIDS and diabetes. *Seizure* 16 (4): 320–323.

Fessler, D.M.T., Eng, S.J., and Navarrete, C.D. (2005). Elevated disgust sensitivity in the first trimester of pregnancy: evidence supporting the compensatory prophylaxis hypothesis. *Evolution and Human Behavior* 26 (4): 344–351.

Findlay, C. (2016). Why did the mass murder of 19 disabled people in Japan barely rate? *The Sydney Morning Herald* (2 August). www.smh.com.au/lifestyle/why-did-the-mass-murder-of-19-disabled-people-in-japan-barely-rate-20160801-gqiphz.html (accessed 26 February 2019).

Fisher, S. (1973). *Body Consciousness: You Are What You Feel*. Englewood Cliffs, NJ: Prentice-Hall.

Florian, V. and Mikulincer, M. (1997). Fear of death and the judgment of social transgressions: a multidimensional test of terror management theory. *Journal of Personality and Social Psychology* 73 (2): 369–380.

Freeland, W.J. (1981). Parasitism and behavioural dominance among male mice. *Science* 213 (4506): 461–462.

Gallagher, H. (1990). *By Trust Betrayed: Patients, Physicians, and the License to Kill in the Third Reich*. New York: Henry Holt.

Gangestad, S.W. and Thornhill, R. (1998). Menstrual cycle variation in women's preferences for the scent of symmetrical men. *Proceedings of the Royal Society of London. Series B: Biological Sciences* 265 (1399): 927–933.

Gilbert, D.T., Pinel, E.C., Wilson, T.D. et al. (1998). Immune neglect: a source of durability bias in affective forecasting. *Journal of Personality and Social Psychology* 75: 617–638.

Goerdt, A. (1986). Social integration of the physically disabled in Barbados. *Social Science & Medicine* 22 (4): 459–466.

Goff, P.A., Eberhardt, J.L., Williams, M.J., and Jackson, M.C. (2008). Not yet human: implicit knowledge, historical dehumanization, and contemporary consequences. *Journal of Personality and Social Psychology* 94 (2): 292–306.

Goldenberg, J.L., Pyszczynski, T., Greenberg, J., and Solomon, S. (2000). Fleeing the body: a terror management perspective on the problem of human corporeality. *Personality and Social Psychology Review* 4 (3): 200–218.

Goldenberg, J.L., Pyszczynski, T., Greenberg, J. et al. (2001). I am not an animal: mortality salience, disgust, and the denial of human creatureliness. *Journal of Experimental Psychology: General* 130 (3): 427–435.

Goldenberg, J.L., Cox, C.R., Arndt, J., and Goplen, J. (2007). "Viewing" pregnancy as existential threat: the effects of creatureliness on reactions to media depictions of the pregnant body. *Media Psychology* 10 (2): 211–230.

Goodall, J. (1971). *In the Shadow of Man*. New York: Dell.

Goodall, J. (1986). Social rejection, exclusion, and shunning among the Gombe chimpanzees. *Evolution and Human Behavior* 7 (3): 227–236.

Greenberg, J., Pyszczynski, T., and Solomon, S. (1986). The causes and consequences of a need for self-esteem: a terror management theory. In: *Public Self and Private Self* (ed. R.F. Baumeister), 189–212. New York: Springer.

Greenberg, J., Pyszczynski, T., Solomon, S. et al. (1990). Evidence for terror management theory II: the effects of mortality salience on reactions to those who threaten or bolster the cultural worldview. *Journal of Personality and Social Psychology* 58 (2): 308–318.

Greenberg, J., Solomon, S., and Pyszczynski, T. (1997). Terror management theory of self-esteem and cultural worldviews: empirical assessments and conceptual refinements. *Advances in Experimental Social Psychology* 29: 61–139.

Groce, N.E. (1999). Disability in cross-cultural perspective: rethinking disability. *The Lancet* 354 (9180): 756–757.

Groce, N.E. and Zola, I.K. (1993). Multiculturalism, chronic illness, and disability. *Pediatrics* 91 (5): 1048–1055.

Gwinn, J.D., Judd, C.M., and Park, B. (2013). Less power = less human? Effects of power differentials on dehumanization. *Journal of Experimental Social Psychology* 49 (3): 464–470.

Harmon-Jones, E., Greenberg, J., Solomon, S., and Simon, L. (1996). The effects of mortality salience on intergroup bias between minimal groups. *European Journal of Social Psychology* 26 (4): 677–681.

Harmon-Jones, E., Simon, L., Greenberg, J. et al. (1997). Terror management theory and self-esteem: evidence that increased self-esteem reduces mortality salience effects. *Journal of Personality and Social Psychology* 72 (1): 24–36.

Harris, L. and Fiske, S. (2006). Dehumanizing the lowest of the low: neuroimaging responses to extreme out-groups. *Psychological Science* 17 (10): 847–853.

Hart, B.L. (1990). Behavioral adaptations to pathogens and parasites: five strategies. *Neuroscience & Biobehavioral Reviews* 14 (3): 273–294.

Haslam, N. and Loughnan, S. (2012). Prejudice and dehumanization. In: *Beyond Prejudice: Extending the Social Psychology of Conflict, Inequality and Social Change* (ed. J. Dixon and M. Levine), 89–104. Cambridge: Cambridge University Press.

Herek, G.M. and Capitaniato, J.P. (1998). Symbolic prejudice or fear of infection? A functional analysis of AIDS-related stigma among heterosexual adults. *Basic and Applied Social Psychology* 20 (3): 230–241.

Hill, A. M., Rhee, J., and Ross, B. (2009). Mentally disabled forced into "fight club" at Texas home. ABC News. https://abcnews.go.com/Blotter/mentally-disabled-forced-fight-club-texas-home/story?id=7556740 (accessed 26 February 2019).

Hirschberger, G. (2006). Terror management and attributions of blame to innocent victims: reconciling compassionate and defensive responses. *Journal of Personality and Social Psychology* 91 (5): 832–844.

Hirschberger, G., Florian, V., and Mikulincer, M. (2005). Fear and compassion: a terror management analysis of emotional reactions to physical disability. *Rehabilitation Psychology* 50 (3): 246–257.

Hirschberger, G., Ein-Dor, T., and Almakias, S. (2008). The self-protective altruist: terror management and the ambivalent nature of prosocial behavior. *Personality and Social Psychology Bulletin* 34 (5): 666–678.

Hodson, G., Choma, B.L., Boisvert, J. et al. (2013). The role of intergroup disgust in predicting negative outgroup evaluations. *Journal of Experimental Social Psychology* 49 (2): 195–205.

Huang, J.Y., Sedlovskaya, A., Ackerman, J.M. et al. (2011). Immunizing against prejudice: effects of disease protection on attitudes toward out-groups. *Psychological Science* 22 (12): 1550–1556.

Hunter, J.M. (1992). Elephantiasis: a disease of development in north east Ghana. *Social Science & Medicine* 35 (5): 627–645.

Ingstad, B. and Whyte, S.R. (1995). *Disability and Culture*. Berkeley, CA: University of California Press.

Janoff-Bulman, R. and Yopyk, D.J. (2004). Random outcomes and valued commitments. In: *Handbook of Experimental Existential Psychology* (ed. J. Greenberg, S.L. Koole and T.A. Pyszczynski), 122–138. New York: Guilford Press.

Johnson, C.Y., Honein, M.A., Dana Flanders, W. et al. (2012). Pregnancy termination following prenatal diagnosis of anencephaly or spina bifida: a systematic review of the literature. *Birth Defects Research Part A: Clinical and Molecular Teratology* 94 (11): 857–863.

Jones, E.E., Farina, A., Hastorf, A.H. et al. (1984). *Social Stigma: The Psychology of Marked Relationships*. New York: W. H. Freeman.

Katz, I. (1981). *Stigma: A Social Psychological Analysis*. Hillsdale, NJ: Lawrence Erlbaum.

Katz, J.L., Weiner, H., Gallagher, T.F., and Hellman, L. (1970). Stress, distress, and ego defenses: Psychoendocrine response to impending breast tumor biopsy. *Archives of General Psychiatry* 23 (2): 131–142.

Katz, I., Farber, J., Glass, D.C. et al. (1978). When courtesy offends: effects of positive and negative behavior by the physically disabled on altruism and anger in normals. *Journal of Personality* 46 (3): 506–518.

Kavliers, M., Colwell, D.D., Braun, W.J., and Cholersis, E. (2003). Brief exposure to the odour of a parasitized male alters the subsequent mate odour responses of female mice. *Animal Behaviour* 65 (1): 59–68.

Keith, H. and Keith, K.D. (2013). *Intellectual Disability: Ethics, Dehumanization and a New Moral Community*. Chichester: Wiley.

Kendrick, D. T. (2011). Can you immunize yourself against prejudice? Psychology Today. https://www.psychologytoday.com/us/blog/sex-murder-and-the-meaning-life/201111/can-you-immunize-yourself-against-prejudice (1 March 2019).

Kenny, D.A., Horner, C., Kashy, D.A., and Chu, L.C. (1992). Consensus at zero acquaintance: replication, behavioral cues, and stability. *Journal of Personality and Social Psychology* 62 (1): 88–97.

Kerr, A. and Shakespeare, T. (2002). *Genetic Politics: From Eugenics to Genome*. London: New Clarion Press.

Kiesecker, J.M., Skelly, D.K., Beard, K.H., and Preisser, E. (1999). Behavioral reduction of infection risk. *Proceedings of the National Academy of Sciences* 96 (16): 9165–9168.

Kittay, E. and Carlson, L. (2010). *Cognitive Disability and its Challenge to Moral Philosophy*. Oxford: Wiley Blackwell.

Kleck, R. (1968). Physical stigma and nonverbal cues emitted in face-to-face interaction. *Human Relations* 21 (1): 19–28.

Kleck, R. (1969). Physical stigma and task oriented interactions. *Human Relations* 22 (1): 53–60.

Kleck, R., Ono, H., and Hastorf, A.H. (1966). The effects of physical deviance upon face-to-face interaction. *Human Relations* 19 (4): 425–436.

Kleck, R., Buck, P.L., Goller, W.L. et al. (1968). Effect of stigmatizing conditions on the use of personal space. *Psychological Reports* 23 (1): 111–118.

Knudson-Cooper, M.S. (1981). Adjustment to visible stigma: the case of the severely burned. *Social Science & Medicine. Part B: Medical Anthropology* 15 (1): 31–44.

Kouznetsova, D., Stevenson, R.J., Oaten, M.J., and Case, T.I. (2012). Disease-avoidant behaviour and its consequences. *Psychology & Health* 27 (4): 491–506.

Kurzban, R. and Leary, M.R. (2001). Evolutionary origins of stigmatization: the functions of social exclusion. *Psychological Bulletin* 127 (2): 187–208.

Langer, E.J., Fiske, S., Taylor, S.E., and Chanowitz, B. (1976). Stigma, staring, and discomfort: a novel-stimulus hypothesis. *Journal of Experimental Social Psychology* 12 (5): 451–463.

Leyens, J.P., Paladino, P.M., Rodriguez-Torres, R. et al. (2000). The emotional side of prejudice: the attribution of secondary emotions to ingroups and outgroups. *Personality and Social Psychology Review* 4 (2): 186–197.

Liggett, J. (1974). *The Human Face*. New York: Stein and Day.

Livingstone-Smith, D. (2011). *Less than Human: Why We Demean, Enslave, and Exterminate Others*. New York: St. Matrin's Press.

Livneh, H. (1985). Death attitudes and their relationship to perceptions of physically disabled persons. *Journal of Rehabilitation* 51 (1): 38–80.

Loughnan, S., Haslam, N., and Kashima, Y. (2009). Understanding the relationship between attribute-based and metaphor-based dehumanization. *Group Processes & Intergroup Relations* 12 (6): 747–762.

Lynch, D (Dir.) (1980). *The Elephant Man*. Hollywood, CA: Paramount Pictures.

Maguire, P. and Haddad, P. (1990). Psychological reactions to physical illness. In: *Seminars in Liaison Psychiatry: College Seminar Series* (ed. E. Guthrie and F. Creed), 157–191. London: Royal College of Psychiatrists.

Marks, D. (1999). *Disability: Controversial Debates and Psychosocial Perspectives*. London: Routledge.

Mayer, J.D. (2007). *Personality: A Systems Approach*. Boston, MA: Allyn & Bacon.

McCurry, J. (2016). Japan care home attack: picture emerges of modest man with horrifying vision. *The Guardian* (26 July). https://www.theguardian.com/world/2016/jul/26/japan-care-home-attack-satoshi-uematsu-horrifying-vision-disabled-people (accessed 26 February 2019).

McGregor, H.A., Lieberman, J.D., Greenberg, J. et al. (1998). Terror management and aggression: evidence that mortality salience motivates aggression against worldview-threatening others. *Journal of Personality and Social Psychology* 74 (3): 590–605.

McKinney, D. (2018). The invisible hate crime. In: *Intelligence Report: Confronting Hate*. *The Southern Poverty Law Center*. https://www.splcenter.org/fighting-hate/intelligence-report/2018/invisible-hate-crime (accessed 26 February 2019).

Morris, J. (1991). *Pride Against Prejudice: Transforming Attitudes to Disability*. London: New Society.

Murphy, J.S. (1995). *The Constructed Body: AIDS, Reproductive Technology and Ethics*. Albany, NY: State University of New York Press.

Nario-Redmond, M.R. (2010). Cultural stereotypes of disabled and non-disabled men and women: consensus for global category representations and diagnostic domains. *British Journal of Social Psychology* 49 (3): 471–488.

Nario-Redmond, M.R., Gospodinov, D., and Cobb, A. (2017). Crip for a day: the unintended negative consequences of disability simulations. *Rehabilitation Psychology* 62 (3): 324–333.

National Council on Disability. (2015). NCD response to controversial Peter Singer interview advocating the killing of disabled infants: "Professor, Do Your Homework." https://ncd.gov/newsroom/04232015 (accessed 26 February 2019).

Natoli, J.L., Ackerman, D.L., McDermott, S., and Edwards, J.G. (2012). Prenatal diagnosis of Down syndrome: a systematic review of termination rates (1995–2011). *Prenatal Diagnosis* 32 (2): 142–153.

Neimeyer, R.A., Wittkowski, J., and Moser, R.P. (2004). Psychological research on death attitudes: an overview and evaluation. *Death Studies* 28 (4): 309–340.

Neuberg, S.L. and Cottrell, C.A. (2006). Evolutionary bases of prejudices. In: *Evolution and Social Psychology* (ed. M. Schaller, J.A. Simpson and D.T. Kenrick), 163–187. Madison, CT: Psychosocial Press.

Neuberg, S.L., Kenrick, D.T., and Schaller, M. (2011). Human threat management systems: self-protection and disease avoidance. *Neuroscience & Biobehavioral Reviews* 35 (4): 1042–1051.

Nussbaum, M.C. (2009). *Hiding from Humanity: Disgust, Shame, and the Law*. Princeton, NJ: Princeton University Press.

Oaten, M., Stevenson, R.J., and Case, T.I. (2009). Disgust as a disease-avoidance mechanism. *Psychological Bulletin* 135 (2): 303–321.

Oaten, M., Stevenson, R.J., and Case, T.I. (2011). Disease avoidance as a functional basis for stigmatization. *Philosophical Transactions of the Royal Society B: Biological Sciences* 366 (1583): 3433–3452.

O'Callaghan, A.C. and Murphy, G.H. (2007). Sexual relationships in adults with intellectual disabilities: understanding the law. *Journal of Intellectual Disability Research* 51 (3): 197–206.

O'Connor, S.M., Taylor, C.E., and Hughes, J.M. (2006). Emerging infectious determinants of chronic diseases. *Emerging infectious diseases* 12 (7): 1051–1058.

O'Toole, J. J. (2016). Listening to Ghosts: Making Art About Disabled People Killed By Their Families. http://www.twothirdsoftheplanet.com/listening-ghosts-making-art-disabled-people-killed-families/ (1 March 2019).

Pachuta, D.M. (1996). Chinese medicine: the law of five elements. In: *Healing East & West* (ed. A.A. Sheikh and K.S. Sheikh), 64–90. New York: Wiley.

Papadopoulos, L., Walker, C., Aitken, D., and Bor, R. (2000). The relationship between body location and psychological morbidity in individuals with acne vulgaris. *Psychology, Health & Medicine* 5 (4): 431–438.

Park, J.H., Faulkner, J., and Schaller, M. (2003). Evolved disease-avoidance processes and contemporary anti-social behavior: prejudicial attitudes and avoidance of people with physical disabilities. *Journal of Nonverbal Behavior* 27 (2): 65–87.

Park, J.H., Schaller, M., and Crandall, C.S. (2007). Pathogen-avoidance mechanisms and the stigmatization of obese people. *Evolution and Human Behavior* 28 (6): 410–414.

Park, J.H., Van Leeuwen, F., and Stephen, I.D. (2012). Homeliness is in the disgust sensitivity of the beholder: relatively unattractive faces appear especially unattractive to individuals higher in pathogen disgust. *Evolution and Human Behavior* 33 (5): 569–577.

Park, J.H., Van Leeuwen, F., and Chochorelou, Y. (2013). Disease-avoidance processes and stigmatization: cues of substandard health arouse heightened discomfort with physical contact. *The Journal of Social Psychology* 153 (2): 212–228.

Patterson, C. (2002). *Eternal Treblinka: Our Treatment of Animals and the Holocaust.* New York: Lantern Books.

Perry, D. M., and Carter-Long, L. (2016). The Ruderman white paper on media coverage of law enforcement use of force and disability: a media study (2013–2015) and overview. Ruderman Family Foundation. https://rudermanfoundation.org/white_papers/media-coverage-of-law-enforcement-use-of-force-and-disability/ (1 March 2019).

Person, B., Bartholomew, L.K., Gyapong, M. et al. (2008). Health-related stigma among women with lymphatic filariasis from the Dominican Republic and Ghana. *Social Science & Medicine* 68: 30–38.

Peters-Golden, H. (1982). Breast cancer: varied perceptions of social support in the illness experience. *Social Science & Medicine* 16 (4): 483–491.

Plous, S.E. (2003). *Understanding Prejudice and Discrimination.* New York: McGraw-Hill.

Pyszczynski, T., Solomon, S., and Greenberg, J. (2003). *In the Wake of 9/11: The Psychology of Terror.* New York: American Psychological Association.

Pyszczynski, T., Greenberg, J., Solomon, S. et al. (2004). Why do people need self-esteem? A theoretical and empirical review. *Psychological Bulletin* 130 (3): 435–468.

Pyszczynski, T., Abdollahi, A., Solomon, S. et al. (2006). Mortality salience, martyrdom, and military might: the great Satan versus the axis of evil. *Personality and Social Psychology Bulletin* 32 (4): 525–537.

Pyszczynski, T., Solomon, S., and Greenberg, J. (2015). Thirty years of terror management theory: from genesis to revelation. In: *Advances in Experimental Social Psychology*, vol. 52, 1–70. San Diego, CA: Academic Press.

Rachman, S. (2004). Fear of contamination. *Behaviour Research and Therapy* 42 (11): 1227–1255.

Riis, J., Loewenstein, G., Baron, J. et al. (2005). Ignorance of hedonic adaptation to hemodialysis: a study using ecological momentary assessment. *Journal of Experimental Psychology: General* 134 (1): 3–9.

Roberts, T.A., Goldenberg, J.L., Power, C., and Pyszczynski, T. (2002). "Feminine protection": the effects of menstruation on attitudes toward women. *Psychology of Women Quarterly* 26 (2): 131–139.

Rothman, J. (2017). Are disability rights and animal rights connected? *The New Yorker* (5 June). https://www.newyorker.com/culture/persons-of-interest/are-disability-rights-and-animal-rights-connected (1 March 2019).

Rozin, P., Markwith, M., and McCauley, C. (1994). Sensitivity to indirect contacts with other persons: AIDS aversion as a composite of aversion to strangers, infection, moral taint, and misfortune. *Journal of Abnormal Psychology* 103 (3): 495–504.

Rozin, P., Haidt, J., McCauley, C. et al. (1999). Individual differences in disgust sensitivity: comparisons and evaluations of paper-and-pencil versus behavioral measures. *Journal of Research in Personality* 33 (3): 330–351.

Rumsey, N. and Bull, R. (1986). The effects of facial disfigurement on social interaction. *Human Learning* 5: 203–208.

Rumsey, N., Bull, R., and Gahagan, D. (1982). The effect of facial disfigurement on the proxemic behaviour of the general public. *Journal of Applied Social Psychology* 12 (2): 137–150.

Ryan, F. (2015). Lee Irving's murder is a chilling reminder that disability hate crime is rising. *The Guardian* (10 June). https://www.theguardian.com/commentisfree/2015/jun/10/lee-irving-murder-disability-hate-crime-increase (accessed 26 February 2019).

Ryan, S., Oaten, M., Stevenson, R.J., and Case, T.I. (2012). Facial disfigurement is treated like an infectious disease. *Evolution and Human Behavior* 33 (6): 639–646.

Sampson, E.E. (1993). Identity politics: challenges to psychology's understanding. *American Psychologist* 48 (12): 1219–1230.

Scheer, J. and Groce, N. (1988). Impairment as a human constant. *Journal of Social Issues* 44 (1): 23–27.

Schimel, J., Pyszczynski, T., Greenberg, J. et al. (2000). Running from the shadow: psychological distancing from others to deny characteristics people fear in themselves. *Journal of Personality and Social Psychology* 78 (3): 446–462.

Schweik, S.M. (2009). *The Ugly Laws: Disability in Public*. New York: New York University Press.

Shaffer, B.L., Caughey, A.B., and Norton, M.E. (2006). Variation in the decision to terminate pregnancy in the setting of fetal aneuploidy. *Prenatal Diagnosis* 26 (8): 667–671.

Shanmugarajah, K., Gaind, S., Clarke, A., and Butler, P.E. (2012). The role of disgust emotions in the observer response to facial disfigurement. *Body Image* 9 (4): 455–461.

Sherry, M. (2010). *Disability Hate Crimes: Does Anyone Really Hate Disabled People?* Farnham: Ashgate.

Sherry, M. (2014). Exploring disability hate crimes. *Review of Disability Studies: An International Journal* 1 (1).

Shiloh, S., Heruti, I., and Berkovitz, T. (2011). Attitudes toward people with disabilities caused by illness or injury: beyond physical impairment. *International Journal of Rehabilitation Research* 34 (4): 321–329.

Siller, J., Chipman, A., Ferguson, L., and Vann, D.H. (1967). *Studies in Reactions to Disability. XI: Attitudes of the Non-disabled Towards the Physically Disabled*. New York: New York University, School of Education.

Silverman, A.M., Gwinn, J.D., and Van Boven, L. (2015). Stumbling in their shoes: disability simulations reduce judged capabilities of disabled people. *Social Psychological and Personality Science* 6 (4): 464–471.

Smith, D.M., Loewenstein, G., Rozin, P. et al. (2006). Sensitivity to disgust, stigma, and adjustment to life with a colostomy. *Journal of Research in Personality* 41 (4): 787–803.

Snodgrass, C.E. and Gates, L. (1998). Doctrinal orthodoxy, religious orientation, and anthropocentrism. *Current Psychology* 17 (2–3): 222–236.

Solomon, S., Greenberg, J., and Pyszczynski, T. (1991). A terror management theory of social behavior: the psychological functions of self-esteem and cultural worldviews. *Advances in Experimental Social Psychology* 24: 93–159.

Soni, C.V., Barker, J.H., Pushpakumar, S.B. et al. (2010). Psychosocial considerations in facial transplantation. *Burns* 36 (7): 959–964.

Stangor, C. and Crandall, C.S. (2000). Threat and the social construction of stigma. In: *The Social Psychology of Stigma* (ed. T.F. Heatherton, R.E. Kleck, M.R. Hebl and J.G. Hull), 62–87. New York: Guilford Press.

Stevens, B. (2011). Interrogating transability: a catalyst to view disability as body art. *Disability Studies Quarterly* 31 (4).

Swango-Wilson, A. (2008). Caregiver perception of sexual behaviors of individuals with intellectual disabilities. *Sex & Disabilities* 26 (2): 75–81.

Teachman, B.A., Wilson, J.G., and Komarovskaya, L. (2006). Implicit and explicit stigma of mental illness in diagnosed and healthy samples. *Journal of Social and Clinical Psychology* 25 (1): 75–95.

Thomas, E. (2014). "Developmentally disabled fight club" busted. *Huffington Post* (2 July). https://www.huffingtonpost.com/2014/02/07/developmentally-disabled-fight-club_n_4747937.html (accessed 26 February 2019).

Ustun, T.B. (2001). *Disability and Culture: Universalism and Diversity*. Seattle: Hogrefe & Huber.

Vickio, C.J. and Cavanaugh, J.C. (1985). Relationships among death anxiety, attitudes toward aging, and experience with death in nursing home employees. *Journal of Gerontology* 40 (3): 347–349.

Walkser, S.L., Shah, M., Hubbard, V.G. et al. (2008). Skin disease is common in rural Nepal: results of a point prevalence study. *British Journal of Dermatology* 158 (2): 334–338.

Watermeyer, B. (2013). *Towards a Contextual Psychology of Disablism*. New York: Routledge.

Weir, E.C. (2004). Identifying and preventing ageism among health-care professionals. *International Journal of Therapy and Rehabilitation* 11 (2): 56–63.

Weiss, M.G. (2008). Stigma and the social burden of neglected tropical diseases. *PLoS Neglected Tropical Diseases* 2 (5): e237.

Wheeler, C. (2015). Hate crimes on disabled people up by 213%. *Express* (11 January). https://www.express.co.uk/news/uk/551327/EXCLUSIVE-Hate-crimes-on-disabled-rise-by-213 (accessed 26 February 2019).

Wheeler, D.S., Farina, A., and Stern, J. (1983). Dimensions of peril in the stigmatization of the mentally ill. *Academic Psychology Bulletin* 5: 397–430.

WKYC Staff. (2014). Bay Village cops seek charges in revolting ALS "ice bucket" prank. WKYC-TV. https://www.wkyc.com/article/news/local/cuyahoga-county/bay-village-cops-seek-charges-in-revolting-als-ice-bucket-prank/95-242033849 (accessed 26 February 2019).

Worthington, M.E. (1974). Personal space as a function of the stigma effect. *Environment and Behavior* 6 (3): 289–294.

When Prejudice Rears Its Ugly Head...

Fears of catching or becoming disabled often manifest in subtle ways – choosing to sit far away from a disabled person, reluctance to share personal items. Yet sometimes the prejudice is more obvious, uncomfortably obvious. **What can you do if you're a target?**

https://crippencartoons.wordpress.com/

1. Assess the situation to make sure that you are safe. You do not always need to respond.

2. You might respond with humor to highlight the ridiculousness of bias, like this Crippen cartoon which shows a mother of a family in front of a house for sale pointing to a nearby psychiatric hospital saying: "But what if the wind changes and my kids all catch schizophrenia?!"

3. You could also take the time to educate people about ableism.

What Do Psychologists Say About Contagion Fears?

A recent study by Huang et al. (2011) investigated the links between prejudice and the behavioral immune system. They essentially found that people who had been vaccinated or who had recently washed their hands were less fearful of disease, and were less prejudiced toward people who were not members of their groups.

https://c1.staticflickr.com/3/2715/431453 0838_65c57bb85f_z.jpg?zz=1

Image of hand washing

This study illustrates how people may engage in avoidance behaviors because of an internalized fear of contagion and a need to self-protect. Even if unintentional, avoidance patterns can still harm relationships. Better understanding where such fears come from can inform more considered responses. See also Kendrick (2011) "Can You Immunize Yourself Against Prejudice?".

Hidden Headlines and Police Brutality

According to research conducted by David M. Perry and Lawrence Carter-Long (2016), here's what the news isn't telling you: **Half of people killed by police in the United States may have a disability.**

https://www.hbo.com/documentaries/say-her-name-the-life-and-death-of-sandra-bland

Image of Sandra Bland

In 2015, Sandra Bland was arrested after being pulled over for a traffic violation; three days later she committed suicide. Her controversial arrest made headlines but many reports failed to note that Bland was epileptic and jailed without medication. Could the side effects of not having her medicine have contributed to her suicide?

In 2016, after being pulled over for speeding, Daniel Kevin Harris, a 26-year-old Deaf man, was shot and killed by an officer. Harris was unarmed and had been trying to communicate.

In 2017, an Arizona officer pinned a 14-year-old autistic boy to the ground. The officer had mistaken the teen's stimming as drug-related behavior.

What Can We Do About This?

- Support increasing the funding for Crisis Intervention Teams and the Justice and Mental Health Collaboration Act.
- Advocate for better training of police officers in de-escalating situations and recognizing disabilities.
- Continue to speak out about wrongful deaths and ask questions about the handling of these situations.

Varying Perspectives: Comparing Disability Rights and Animal Rights

Disabled people are sometimes seen as less than human or as exhibiting "animalistic behaviors." Here are two different perspectives on the utility of comparing disability rights to animal rights:

Stephen Drake of Not Dead Yet, a disability rights organization, argues against linking these two movements (2010). Here's why:

- People seem to be okay with "putting down" old, sick, or disabled animals that are in pain as "mercy killings." If we connect disability rights to animal rights, this same logic can be used to justify the killing of disabled people. Peter Singer, the philosopher and champion of animal rights, has already deemed it morally acceptable to kill disabled people who don't fit his definition of "personhood."
- There are also differences in who speaks for each movement: In the animal rights movement, humans are deciding. In the disability rights movement, disabled people lead the charge.

Sunaura (Sunny) Taylor, a scholar, artist, vegan, and disabled woman, argues for linking the two movements (Rothman 2017). Here's why:

- Taylor, who has arthrogryposis, was often compared to an animal when she was a child. She says disabled people should be proud of this comparison because ableism oppresses both animals and humans. For her the comparison is one of connection not shame.
- Taylor argues that environmental circumstances are responsible for the creation of disability in both humans and animals.
- She explores this notion in her painting "Sunnys in Chicken Cages," which shows variable human bodies in a cage.

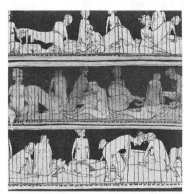

https://i.pinimg.com/originals/1a/0e /41/1a0e41edd4054d142f8b7389 fd345841.jpg

Responding to Hate

In 2015, 27 disabled children and 28 disabled adults were murdered by their families. These crimes are often portrayed as "mercy killings" in the news. Artist and activist Corbett Joan O'Toole responded to the problem by creating a quilt to memorialize the many lives lost.

"I wanted to make art that asked the viewer to examine their assumption that people are better off dead than disabled and specifically to ask people to question whether the killing of a disabled child is a 'mercy' or a murder," O'Toole (2016).

https://www.corbettotoole.com/

The quilt features the names and images of 14 children murdered in 2015.

Disability-memorial.org is dedicated to remembering these victims. They keep yearly records of the stories of those murdered by family.

March 1 is the International Day of Mourning dedicated to these victims.

3

Justifying Ableism: Ideologies and Language

The core theory of ABA [Applied Behavior Analysis] was that a therapist, "forcing a change in a child's outward behavior" would, "effect an inward psychological change." Lovaas feels that by 1) holding any mentally crippled child accountable for his behavior and 2) forcing him to act normal, he can push the child toward normality. (Dr. Ivar Lovaas as cited in Jones 2016)

Societies and scientists have historically made serious errors in determining which kinds of people are acceptable and which behaviors should be aggressively treated. People with differences have been ostracized then forced into mandatory treatments for their own good: left-handed people, and homosexuals, and many others. Where ABA needs scrutiny is when its power is used to remove odd behaviors which may be useful and necessary to the autistic (such as rocking, flapping, and analytical rather than social or "imaginative" play); and when typical, expected behaviors which may be stressful, painful, or useless to the autistic (such as pointing, joint attention, appropriate gaze, and eye contact) are imposed (Dawson 2004).

Disabled people have endured a long history of persecution, from trauma inducing therapies, sexual violence, and forced sterilization (e.g. removing sex organs to prevent offspring) to medical experimentation and extermination (Kerr and Shakespeare 2002; Morris 1991). Across most forms of victimization, long-standing beliefs about why certain people deserve specific treatments can be found (Sherry 2016). Historically, when people were believed to be cursed or demon possessed, divine interventions like exorcisms seemed reasonable. For those viewed as animals, captivity and behavioral training to tame them into "civility" made sense. Even today, those labeled as a danger to themselves and others can still be forcibly medicated or committed to institutions in the name of protection; and an entire "tragic-persons' industry" (Marks 1999) exists to care for those with "special needs." When a disabled life is characterized as full of

Ableism: The Causes and Consequences of Disability Prejudice, First Edition.
Michelle R. Nario-Redmond.
© 2020 John Wiley & Sons, Inc. Published 2020 by John Wiley & Sons, Inc.

suffering – a tragic burden on the family – then the removal of life-sustaining food and breathing tubes may be justified as a "mercy" killing.

This chapter describes how complex belief systems or ideologies work to justify a variety of discriminatory practices, offering handy *explanations* for why some groups get treated differently than others. Starting with broad beliefs about human status hierarchies, the nature of justice, and how people get ahead in the world, the chapter goes on to examine how clashing explanations about the problems of disability completely alter the solutions considered appropriate. Finally, I consider how ideological beliefs are communicated through language and media in ways that perpetuate but sometimes challenge prejudicial understandings about the disability experience. While Chapter 2 described some of the more distant origins of disability prejudice that arise from fears about death and frailty, this chapter considers how ideological beliefs operate at a more intermediate level to influence how disabled people are positioned and how policies that determine life outcomes are justified.

Justification Ideologies

Cultural ideologies involve a set of interrelated, shared beliefs about how society works, including the values and standards expected of people encouraged to participate. The influence of such beliefs on policy decisions and individual behaviors often, but not always, operates at an unconscious level. That is, people may recognize they support the idea that some groups make superior leaders while others are destined to be led (or that anyone can succeed if they work hard enough), but they take for granted how these beliefs affect everyday attitudes and actions. For example, some people support the idea that society benefits from competition where those who are most skilled assume positions of power and dominance over those better suited for subordinate roles. In fact, social hierarchies have pervaded both ancient and modern societies across many different political regimes (Sidanius et al. 2001). Status differences can even seem rational and useful to the operation of corporations, governments, and educational institutions. However, they also function to justify and legitimize many discriminatory and oppressive practices while suppressing intergroup conflict. Justification ideologies, in particular, include "any set of beliefs, attitudes, values, or group stereotypes which provide the moral and intellectual support for group-based inequality" (Sidanius et al. 2001, p. 310). These beliefs explain why dominant groups tend to have more power, wealth, and access to better education and healthcare while subordinate groups are more likely to be poor, in prison, and without resources to foster achievement.

> Tyrants always justify their oppression of groups by claiming that their victims are inferior people, all defective, and all deserving their fate. (Albee 1996, p. 13)

Social Darwinism and the American Eugenics Movement

One of the most pervasive ideologies justifying the need for social hierarchy is known as Social Darwinism. Emerging in the late 1800s, and based on evolutionary ideas about "survival of the fittest," social Darwinists argued that humans, like animals, are naturally competitive; therefore, those with certain advantages have an obligation to dominate those with inferior or disadvantaged traits (Herbert Spencer, 1964, as cited in Stucke 2008). According to Social Darwinism, because the weak (and/or unintelligent) would not survive otherwise, they did not deserve expensive educational or medical interventions that would keep them alive long enough to procreate and further erode the gene pool (Morris 1991). Social Darwinism made group inequalities seem both inevitable and morally defensible (Crandall 2000).

Although largely discredited, the idea that societies evolve to reflect the natural superiority of some groups over others has influenced many laws and social policies that persist today (Bowler 2003). Such policies often take the form of discriminatory treatments resulting in the control, segregation, and murder of people from a variety of stigmatized groups, including Blacks, immigrants, and disabled people (Pfeiffer 1994).

> It is better for all the world, if instead of waiting to execute degenerate offspring for crime, or to let them starve for their imbecility, society can prevent those who are manifestly unfit from continuing their kind. The principle that sustains compulsory vaccination is broad enough to cover cutting the fallopian tubes. Three generations of imbeciles are enough (Supreme Court Justice, Oliver Wendall Homes, 1927, in *Buck vs. Bell*, 274 US 200).

The social Darwinian principles of racial "hygiene" to improve society were applied extensively, via the Eugenics Movement, throughout the United States and Europe, where funds and laws were dedicated to selective breeding and birth control policies designed to "purify" the human race (Burke and Castaneda 2007). The word eugenic means "well-born," and by the turn of the twentieth century, many methods were put in place to increase the number of people with superior talents and strengths while reducing the number of people considered physically or morally inferior or weak. Policies were adopted to encourage healthy, smart, upper-class people to marry and multiply, offering them financial incentives through better-baby contests designed to promote procreation among the most fit. At the same time, laws were also enacted to limit the expansion of "unhealthy" and "incompetent" people through sexual segregation, institutionalization, and forced sterilization – removing "defectives" from public sight and preventing them from reproducing more of "their kind" (Kliewer and Drake 1998). Many early eugenicists were psychologists, statisticians, and other progressive leaders with a grand utopian vision based on a very limited understanding of genetics (Morris 1991). It was assumed that societal problems – alcoholism, criminality, chronic illness, mental and physical disability, unemployment, poverty, and prostitution – all involved traits that could be inherited and passed down to subsequent generations of "degenerates" who would take up valuable resources and limit social progress. Genetics had not yet been well established as a field of study to resist the idea that social problems could be inherited, although it should have been obvious – even if all genetically acquired conditions could be eliminated, people would still become physically and mentally impaired through accidents, traumas, and other environmental insults.

The Eugenics Movement was popular worldwide and legitimately practiced well into the mid-twentieth century until recognition of its corrupt scientific bases became increasingly apparent (although many US states retained eugenics laws through the 1970s or later). The horrors of the Eugenics Movement are beyond the scope of this chapter, but several facts are worth noting as they have implications for contemporary eugenic practices that have emerged since. Eugenic ideologies were developed in the United States, Canada, and Britain long before being practiced by the Nazis in Germany. During World War II, over 240 000 disabled children and adults were among the first to be rounded up by medical personnel before being starved, poisoned, or gassed between 1940 and 1945 (Burleigh 1994). Few are aware of the history of disabled lives massacred – because these actions were rationalized not as war crimes, but as medical mercy killings done "out of pity for the victim and out of a desire to free the family and loved ones from a lifetime of needless sacrifice" (Gallagher 1990, p. 257).

What nature does blindly, slowly, and ruthlessly, man may do providently, quickly, and kindly. (Galton 1904 as cited in Darwin 1914, p. 15)

Meanwhile in 1938, 33 US states had laws authorizing the forced sterilization of those considered genetically inferior or insane (Pfeiffer 1994). By 1964, over 65 000 Americans had been involuntarily sterilized (Ferster 1966; Hubbard 2006). Even in states without these laws, directors of asylums could still request a court order as long as sterilization was said to be in the best interest of the patient or the public (Pfeiffer 1994). As late as 1968, 27 states still had laws allowing the sterilization of those deemed "mentally deficient" (Ghent 1973 as cited in Miller and Levine 2013). To date, the Supreme Court precedent for involuntary sterilization of developmentally disabled people has never been formally overturned. For more on the history of involuntary confinement, mass incarceration, and compulsory sterilization of disabled people see Bashford and Levine (2010), Ben-Moshe (2014a), and Morris (1991).

The feebleminded are a parasitic, predatory class, never capable of self-support or managing their own affairs ... It has been truly said that feeblemindedness is the mother of crime, pauperism and degeneracy ... No feebleminded person should be allowed to marry or become a parent ... Certain families should become extinct. Parenthood is not for all. (Fernald 1912, p. 92)[1]

Consequences of Social Darwinism and the New Eugenics

Since 2002, several state governors have issued formal apologies for violating the fundamental rights of those living with cognitive impairments, particularly their right to bear children (Burke and Castaneda 2007). Despite public recognition of this institutionalized form of ableism, the right to marry remains restricted or banned for disabled people in more than 30 states (Miller and Levine 2013). The right to parent is not guaranteed either, as the children of disabled people can be removed on the basis of child health, safety, or parental IQ – even though IQ is not predictive of parental capacity (Pfeiffer 1994), particularly when parents have social support (Starke 2011). Parental and adoption restrictions also apply to those with physical disabilities. In one California case, parental restriction was based on the assumption that good parents should be able to "play catch" with their kids (Pfeiffer 1994).

In addition to compulsory sterilization, Social Darwinism continues to be used to justify involuntary confinement for those diagnosed as psychiatrically or intellectually disabled (Kliewer and Fitzgerald 2001). Several books have documented survivors' accounts of the cruel and inhumane conditions witnessed during custodial incarceration, including extensive periods of isolation, starvation, and experimentation (Ben-Moshe et al. 2014a,b). For example, institutionalized inmates with disabilities have been deliberately exposed to diseases like hepatitis and shingles for vaccine trials (Kliewer and Drake 1998); others were exploited as human guinea pigs to test the effects of radiation (D'Antonio 2005) and other experimental treatments (e.g. electroshock therapy). As long as disabled people were considered unfeeling, inferior, and otherwise useless, it was easy to justify treating them in ways that protected or benefited those whose lives were considered more valuable.

> The professions fear the idea that the community, family, friends, neighbors and inclusive schools may provide a more meaningful life experience for people with disabilities than do clinically generated segregated contexts built on psychological theories of deviance originating with eugenics. (Kliewer and Drake 1998, p. 108)

The legacy of eugenic ideologies is also found in criticisms against desegregation policies for greater inclusion of disabled people in communities and classrooms (see MacMillan et al. 1996; Schopler 1995). Specifically, some who profit from the disability helping professions have insisted that changes to the status quo (e.g. deinstitutionalization) are anti-scientific fads, but this implies that science has conclusively demonstrated the benefits associated with confinement to nursing homes, special education classrooms, and other sheltered facilities. Instead, most studies demonstrate that institutional placements stunt human development, and contribute to maladaptive behaviors (Dudley-Marling and Gurn 2010). Countering these claims, disability studies scholars argue that special education is a one-way road leading to "successful institutionalization," where, instead of achievement, kids learn to submit to a curriculum of control

(Ben-Moshe et al. 2014a). These "special" placements are justified using the language of protection for those described as "at risk if placed in typical classrooms," or who require behavioral modification "in order to function" (e.g. make eye contact, avoid hand flapping or rocking back and forth) (Dawson 2004).

> Soon it will be a sin for parents to have a child that carries the heavy burden of genetic disease. We are entering a world where we have to consider the quality of our children. (Robert Edwards, 2010 Nobel Prizewinner and creator of the first test-tube baby, as cited in Obasogie 2013)

Finally, euthanasia – the practice of withholding life-saving treatments or intentionally ending someone's life in order to "relieve pain and suffering" has long been rationalized with ideologies of Social Darwinism and eugenics (Marks 1999; Morris 1991). Modern-day examples include physician-assisted suicide, and selective (eugenic) abortion in the case of disabilities like Down syndrome, spina bifida, dwarfism, deafness, muscular dystrophy, and webbed fingers – to name just a few of the over 900 conditions currently identifiable through prenatal testing (Collins 2003; Hubbard 2006). Some prenatal tests can even detect conditions that may not develop until later in life, like Alzheimer's and breast cancer (Allott and Neumayr 2013). While these issues are controversial and complex, they are noted here because they represent a new wave of ableist practices selectively applied to people with disabilities that continue to be justified as "mercy" killings. Today, medical personnel routinely counsel parents to consider an abortion if the mother is discovered to be carrying a disabled fetus (Parens and Asch 2000; Miringoff 1991). Selective abortion is often framed as part of prenatal health or to reduce "wrongful births" and the incidence of children born with disabilities (Blumberg 1994; Brown 2018). Famous animal rights philosopher Peter Singer has repeatedly said that, "Killing a disabled infant is not morally equivalent to killing a person. Very often it is not wrong at all" (Singer 1993, p. 191). In 2012, during a BBC interview, he said, "It would be morally wrong to choose to have a child with a disability" (National Council on Disability 2015).

According to recent US and European data tracking eugenic abortion, the number of children born with Down syndrome has plummeted in recent years, and so has federal funding research and treatments for those living with Down syndrome (Allott and Neumayr 2013). These trends have clear implications for those advocating for disability and human rights. In fact, many disability studies scholars and activists have publicized their concerns about anti-disability bias in contemporary debates including cases where physician-assisted suicide was justified only for those with disabilities based on assumptions that their quality of life was worse than not living at all (Morris 1991).

Such practices trouble those concerned about selective termination and the deselection of only certain types of embryos, not to mention the genetic engineering of designer babies though sperm/egg banks that allow wealthy people to pick from a menu of valued traits and characteristics (Wolbring 2003).

> I think it's irresponsible not to try and direct evolution to produce a human being who will be an asset to the world ... Those parents who enhance their children, then their children are going to be the ones who dominate the world ... I only hope that the many biologists who share my opinion will stand tall in the debates to come and not be intimidated by the inevitable criticism ... If such work be called eugenics, then I am a eugenicist. (James Watson, Nobel Prize Winner for discovering the double helix, as cited in Center for Eugenics and Society 2007)

These reproductive technologies reflect modern eugenic strivings toward continuous improvement of the human genome without considering the ideological underpinnings and negative social consequences that may follow, including the loss of human biodiversity and an ever widening gap between the classes (Miller and Levine 2013).

Despite warnings about the dangers of such ideologies, including liberal ideals about self-determination and choice (Amundson and Taira 2005), beliefs about inherent superiority are more likely among the politically conservative, who also tend to support the idea that people succeed on the basis of their own merits and abilities (Crandall 2000). For example, studies have found that those who strongly believe in the value of unequal status between groups were much more likely to support the death penalty and the torture of prisoners (Sidanius et al. 2006). In one study, those most supportive of the death penalty were people with the highest social status (e.g. income, education), particularly among the most politically conservative (Mitchell and Sidanius 1993).

Social Dominance and System Justification Theories

Two theories that have tested how specific ideological beliefs are used to justify contemporary status relations are social dominance theory (SDT) and system justification theory (SJT). Drawing from political science, the social dominance approach describes how many forms of oppression, whether based on class, race, gender, or other stigmas, are maintained through beliefs that rationalize the social positions of both dominant and subordinate groups. For this reason, such beliefs are called "legitimizing myths" because they help people make sense of group inequalities that would otherwise seem unfair if based only on race, gender, or disability status. To illustrate, if people believe in the paternalistic ideology that some groups (children, females, and disabled people) need protection because they are "naturally" more innocent and vulnerable, then practices around their supervision and control make sense. Stereotypes also serve as legitimizing myths: if disabled people are only imagined as the helpless recipients of others' care and unqualified for caregiving, then restricted parental rights are easier to justify (see Chapter 4).

Research testing SDT has used an individual differences approach to capture the extent to which people prefer unequal relationships between groups (hierarchy enhancers) or more equitable intergroup relations (hierarchy attenuators). Specifically, the social dominance orientation scale (SDO; Sidanius and Pratto

1999) was designed to measure support for social hierarchies with items like: "to get ahead in life it is sometimes necessary to step on other groups," and "inferior groups should stay in their place" (Kteily et al. 2011). Based on research over the last 20 years, SDO is associated with several ideologies that reinforce the current system or status quo, including political conservatism and social Darwinist beliefs (Pratto et al. 1994). A strong orientation toward social dominance predicts ableism (Brandes and Crowson 2009), racism, and classism: blaming poverty on the personal characteristics of the poor. (Sidanius and Pratto 1999). Over time, SDO has led to increased sexism (Sibley et al. 2007) and prejudice toward Latinos, Asians, and African Americans (Duckitt 2001; Kteily et al. 2011). Furthermore, people who score high on the social dominance scale (high social dominators) more strongly support policies that restrict the redistribution of resources to people with disabilities (Duckitt 2006), and immigrants (Esses et al. 2001). High social dominators also oppose policies designed to include disabled students in general education classes (Brandes and Crowson 2009). In fact, high social dominators are more likely believe that groups compete for scarce resources (Sidanius et al. 1994); and feelings of threat are especially likely when material (e.g. financial or human) resources provided to one group are believed to be at the expense of another. For example, if schools have a limited amount of money for student tutors, and the disabled students have access to them first, then those without documented disabilities may be left out in the cold.

Bustillos and Silván-Ferrero (2013) tested these ideas among high school students in Spain and found that attitudes toward students with physical disabilities were much more negative among students with strong SDOs. Furthermore, intergroup anxiety and beliefs about school resources going to disabled instead of nondisabled students were the main reasons behind the negative attitudes of high social dominators. In other words, those who believed most in their group's superiority, felt most threatened about disabled students "taking advantage" of resources, which explained why they were less positive about peers with disabilities. In another study, people who scored highest in social dominance not only opposed, but sought to restrict the human and civil rights of those they considered inferior – people with either intellectual or physical disabilities (Crowson et al. 2013). Similarly, Duckitt (2006) found that the disrespect and dislike of disabled people among high social dominators was completely driven by the perception that disabled people were competing for resources that would be "taken away from people like me." Thus, anxiety over competition for resources seems to motivate negative attitudes about disability, at least among those who prefer their group to dominate over others. These results suggest that ableism may be inflamed whenever disabled people are characterized as being a "burden" to others, when opportunities are limited or policies for advancing disability rights seem to encroach on the privileges of those benefiting from the way things are.

Religious, scientific, and other ideological beliefs are powerful tools in maintaining the social order and minimizing social unrest. To the extent that both dominant and subordinate groups buy into ideologies that morally and intellectually justify social inequalities, the use of force becomes less necessary as people fail to perceive group-based differences as unjust. Ideologies help ensure the stability of the system where the privileged maintain their positions of power, and the likelihood of social change is minimized (Sidanius et al. 2001). According to SJT, people are motivated to defend existing social, political, and economic arrangements which are both familiar and understandable (Jost and Hunyady 2005). This tends to be true not only among the privileged classes – who benefit most from the way things currently are – but also among those from lower status groups:

> For many people, the devil they know seems less threatening and more legitimate than the devil they don't ... In general, threats to the system – as long as they fall short of toppling the status quo – lead people to bolster existing arrangements by endorsing system-justifying ideologies. [but] ... when regime change seems inevitable, people will begin to rationalize the new arrangements almost immediately. (Jost and Hunyady 2005, p. 262)

Chapters 6 and 8 examine when subordinate groups do rise up to question the system, assert radically alternative and more egalitarian ideologies, and/or revolt against the established social order to address their disadvantaged status.

There are certain conditions that increase the likelihood that people will support justification ideologies, and certain individuals more consistently espouse these beliefs than others. As previously noted, people are more likely to cling to cherished beliefs whenever the validity of those beliefs is challenged (Jost and Hunyady 2005). For example, when disabled people proudly display their crooked limbs, scars, or flapping behaviors, this may threaten those who believe that "imperfections" should be covered, concealed, or cured (Murphy 1995). Furthermore, under conditions of uncertainty, natural disaster (Skitka 1999), or temporary threat, people are more likely to support conservative, system-justifying beliefs (Duckitt 2006; Jost et al. 2003). For example, when asked to think about one's own death, people are more likely to blame "careful" drivers who became paralyzed from a car accident than they are those described as "reckless" (Hirschberger 2006). These results run counter to findings where those judged responsible for their disability are typically blamed more (Weiner et al. 1988). This reversal reflects the idea that sometimes it is more threatening to consider how car accidents happen – even to careful drivers; blaming them, therefore, restores faith that the world is not unfair but remains a just place. In addition, some people are particularly prone to holding strong system-justifying beliefs, including those with a strong need for order; those less open to new experiences or less flexible to change; those more sensitive to danger; and those with a strong fear of their own mortality (Jost and Hunyady 2005). It should also be noted that while research on system-justifying beliefs has focused on Western capitalist ideologies, the process of using ideologies to legitimize political and economic structures should be similar even if the ideological content differs dramatically (see Slorach 2011 for a discussion of disability under Marxism).

Political Conservatism, Protestant Work Ethic, Meritocracy, and Individualism

> Political conservatives locate causes of mental conditions inside the victims, not in social injustice, thereby precluding any need for social changes. The dominant ideas of a society are those that support the ruling class! (Albee 1996, p. 6)

Different ideologies often even work together in ways that help maintain the status quo. For example, conservative principles focus on the preservation of traditional family values, limited government, and resistance to change (Batavia 1997). The Protestant work ethic promotes the traditional American ideal that hard work is a moral responsibility, and that self-control and self-determination are virtues necessary for success. Similarly, believing that society is a meritocracy means that anyone can get ahead on the basis of their merits; therefore, success comes from individual talents and abilities and not from "special" treatment that favors some groups over others (Jost et al. 2003). The ideology of rugged individualism – common among Western capitalist countries – takes these ideas one step further, valuing not only hard work, but the hard work of individuals who *independently* achieved success without the cooperation or help of others. If widespread and deeply engrained, these beliefs become quite useful in explaining why some people deserve their positions of power since they must have worked hard enough or had the right combination of independent abilities. Such beliefs have also been used to justify the disadvantaged status of other groups whose laziness or lack of abilities has been blamed for their failure to succeed (Rosenthal et al. 2011).

> Most handicapped people, myself included, sense that others resent them for this reason: we are subverters of the American Ideal, just as the poor betray the American Dream. (Murphy 1995, p. 143)

Support for the Protestant work ethic is associated with negative attitudes toward the poor, homeless, and unemployed, and the disapproval of public assistance polities (Rosenthal et al. 2011). This may be particularly true in cultures that value individualism, where social inequalities are frequently described in terms of a failure to work hard enough to overcome challenges. Meritocratic beliefs – insisting that anyone can achieve great fame and fortune regardless of their gender, race, sexuality, or disability status – are also used to undermine support for policies that protect certain groups from discrimination, like affirmative action (Jost and Hunyady 2005). According to these views, there is no need for government remedies if achievement is completely due to individual effort. That is, the only reason people fail to self-improve (e.g. lose weight, overcome depression, addiction, stuttering, or dyslexia) is because they didn't do enough personally. And if people don't work hard enough to earn it, they don't deserve "special" treatment, or so the argument goes. Socio-political conservatism also predicts prejudice toward a variety of stigmatized groups, including immigrants, Jews, Blacks, gays/lesbians, fat (Crandall 2000), and disabled people (Crowson and Brandes 2008). Among conservatives, public assistance to the "needy" is often withheld as punishment for those viewed as causing their own disadvantaged circumstances, even when there are plenty of resources to go around (Skitka and Tetlock 1993). The lesson is: if you want access to expensive medical procedures or equipment, you need to take personal responsibility and strive for independent living (Batavia 1997; Vade and Solovay 2009).

Sidanius and Pratto (1999) tested several ideologies to identify which of them best predicted the justification of policies related to government assistance and the protection of minority groups. They found that political conservatism was among the most powerful ideologies used to legitimize opposition to government subsidies for social welfare and fair treatment of minority groups. One study found that the more people supported the legitimacy of the existing system, the more politically conservative they were, and the more they identified with being White (Levin et al. 1998). Underscoring the importance of preserving the status quo, another component of conservative ideology focuses on believing in a just world (Crandall and Biernat 1990).

> The realization that one is susceptible to severe misfortune as a result of random, meaningless causes over which one has little or no control can be extremely troubling ... intolerable, and observers are compelled to believe that the victim has somehow merited his or her fate. (Hirschberger 2006, p. 841)

Just-World Beliefs and Attributions of Blame, Responsibility, and Cause

One of the most well-research theories on the power of ideologies to influence perceptions and behaviors focuses on the idea of a just world: a world where people get what they deserve and deserve what they get. If people believe that the world is a fair and just place, they can rest assured that good things will come to those who are good, while those who are bad will be punished. These beliefs offer a sense of control in an uncertain future (Furnham 2003), and delude people into thinking that they are not at risk for negative outcomes – as long as they behave (Lambert et al. 1999). In Western cultures, research testing Just World Theory (Lerner 1980) demonstrates that some people will go to great lengths to distort their perceptions in ways that allow them to preserve beliefs about world justice. For example, people will actively seek out information that blames others for their own victimization following car accidents and rape (Herbert and Dunkel-Schetter 1992; Struckman-Johnson and Struckman-Johnson 1992). The idea is if negative outcomes like disability can be blamed on someone's own negligence, as long as I'm not negligent or don't make bad decisions, such things can't happen to me. Research shows that those who hold strong just-world beliefs have more negative attitudes toward the poor (Cozzarelli et al. 2001), people with disabilities (Furnham 1995), mental illness (Bizer et al. 2012), AIDS (Anderson 1992), cancer (Montada 1998), and those considered obese (Crandall 1994).

It can be difficult, however, to maintain beliefs about fairness when confronted with innocent victims who seem to have done nothing to deserve their "misfortune," like those born blind, paralyzed, or otherwise impaired. In fact, people with disabilities can trigger a lot of insecurity among those with strong just-world beliefs, which may underlie ableist attitudes (Furnham 1995). People who care deeply about the idea that bad things should only happen to bad people may even feel justified believing that certain people suffer because they have somehow earned their fate. Several lines of research have revealed when just-world beliefs influence who is blamed for their disadvantaged status, and how blame is then used to justify prejudice. (Crandall 2000). Blame depends not only on the type of disability (Robbennolt 2000), but on how it was acquired, and how permanent or controllable it seems to be (Corrigan and Kosyluk 2014; Weiner et al. 1988).

Initially, it was assumed that people with physical conditions (e.g. blindness and paralysis) were much less likely to be blamed for their circumstances than those with psychiatric or mental-behavioral conditions (e.g. drug abuse, schizophrenia) (Saetermoe et al. 2001). However, Weiner et al. (1988) found that those with mental illnesses described as "war syndromes" (e.g. post-traumatic stress disorder, or PTSD) were not blamed any more than those with paralysis. Furthermore, several studies have found that those with the physical conditions of HIV/AIDS or obesity were not only considered responsible for their fate (Hafer and Begue 2005), but were blamed just as much as those who had committed child abuse (Weiner et al. 1988). Similarly, Crandall and Martinez (1996) found rejection was more likely toward people with stigmas believed to be personally controllable (e.g. obesity), especially among conservatives with strong just-world beliefs.

Beliefs about controllability – how reversible or permanent a disabling condition is thought to be – are also related to policy attitudes, including eligibility for health insurance, personal care attendants, and other accommodations. Weiner et al. (1988) found that while blindness, paralysis, and AIDS were considered equally permanent and unchangeable, people were much more willing to support job training for blind and paralyzed people than for those with AIDS – a condition for which people are held more personally responsible. Medical treatments are also more likely to be supported for conditions thought to be temporary or reversible (Weiner et al. 1988). Such results have implications for disabled people who may be expected (or perhaps mandated) to pursue medical treatments considered curative (e.g. surgical procedures to correct blindness; cochlear implants to eliminate deafness; and gastric bypass to remove fat) (Wolbring 2003). Indeed, medical solutions to treat obesity are more likely to be endorsed if caused by a glandular problem instead of excessive eating (Weiner et al. 1988). If drivers who fail to wear corrective glasses are held liable for car accidents, some deaf people worry that they may not be eligible for sign language interpreters once deafness can be "cured" with sophisticated hearing aids (Crouch 1997).

One key distinction seems to be whether or not a person is perceived to have caused his/her disability or not (Hebl and Kleck 2000). When people are believed to have caused the onset of their own disabilities, others express more anger and are less willing to help them compared to when impairments are thought to be caused by factors beyond their control (Weiner et al. 1988). Specifically, if people became blind (or paralyzed or obese) due to their own carelessness, they were blamed more, held more responsible, and considered less worthy of personal assistance than when these same conditions were described as due to the careless actions of another person. Even for less visible conditions like drug addiction (and PTSD), when described as originating from a prescribed pain medication (or the war draft), people were blamed less than when disability onset was due to the use of recreational drugs (or volunteering for a second tour of duty).

Explanations about the origin and meaning of disability extend far beyond attributions about the onset of any particular impairment. From ancient times to the present day, people have been trying make sense of why some people are born with particular impairments and why others become disabled later in life. Is disability an act of God or the devil? Is there something wrong in the body or the mind; or are different abilities just another aspect of human diversity? Ideologies related to the origins of disability are often described as *models of disability* (Low 2006). There have been many models and alternative frameworks that attempt to explain disability (Pfeiffer 2001) because like race, gender, and homosexuality, disability is a contested concept, a socially created phenomenon.

The Ideological Construction of Disability

Like many stigmatizing conditions, disability is a *social construction* – a human creation or way of looking at reality (Smart 2009). Even the definition of disability depends on the historical time period and cultural context. To some people, disability is synonymous with disease, for others it is not an illness at all. For some, disability is a temporary state of being; for others it's a more permanent status related to unemployment. Sometimes a person who qualifies as disabled in one state or agency might not be considered disabled in another. To illustrate, in some states parents may qualify for respite care on the basis of a child's impairment diagnosis (e.g. cerebral palsy) while this diagnosis is insufficient for other services unless major life activities are restricted, or there is some kind of achievement gap (Wolanin and Steele 2004).

Disability is a moving target: how people make sense of the "problems of disability" lead them to consider particular solutions and to ignore others. Consider how the Nuer tribe in Central Africa made sense of babies born with physical disabilities (Scheer and Groce 1988). Based on widely shared beliefs, those born with physical impairments were culturally understood to be baby hippopotamuses. Therefore, it was not surprising to locals when these baby hippos were brought to the river and released in an act that would *not* have been considered infanticide based on *this* interpretation. If a disabled newborn is understood to be a baby hippo, the solution of returning it to water makes sense.

Explanations for, and responses to sexual orientation, have changed over time and place as well. Prior to the 1970s, many Americans considered homosexuality to be a "mental illness" that could be cured with certain types of therapy. In fact, it was listed as a psychopathology until 1973 when it was finally removed from the Diagnostic and Statistical Manual (DSM) in response to growing awareness that sexual orientation did not meet the criteria for a disorder at all (Eyler and Levin 2014). Instead, many began discussing gay and lesbian "lifestyles" as a personal choice, and today more recognize the strong biological bases of both sexual orientation and gender identification (Garnets and Kimmel 2003). Similarly, alcoholism was once considered to be a moral failing, a choice associated with weak will and poor upbringing. Yet, today practitioners emphasize a disease model which influences treatment options and understandings about substance abuse and alcohol dependence (Young 2011). Obesity too is socially constructed: once a sign of health and abundance, it later became associated with gluttony and a lack of personal control or willpower (Crandall 1994); however, obesity is increasingly being described today as a disease that should be treated medically, and covered by insurance – some even consider it a disability (Ells et al. 2006).

Explanations for stigmatizing conditions matter because they affect how people react to them. Medical explanations for stigma sometimes help to reduce the blame associated with more "sinful" explanations of alcoholism (and obesity), especially when constructed as less controllable diseases amenable to therapy and cure (Teachman et al. 2003; Young 2011). However, other conditions like homosexuality, if considered a disease of the mind, may lead to views that something is inherently "wrong" and needs to be fixed. Disability too has had a number of ideological explanations that have influenced popular understandings about the problems disabled people face, and where solutions can be found. Three of the most pervasive models for explaining disability are the moral model, the biomedical model, and the socio-political model.

> If you do not carefully follow His commands ... The Lord will afflict you with madness, blindness and confusion of the mind. (Deuteronomy 28:15, 28–29)

The Moral Model of Disability

Many cultures and world religions share a version of the ideology that disability is the result of some divine intervention: whether inspired by God, spirits, or demon possession (Braddock and Parish 2001). Disability is often viewed as a curse or punishment for sins or other evils committed either by the disabled person, by their parents, or by other ancestors (Groce and Zola 1993). Some scholars have argued that many of those persecuted as witches in colonial New England may have had misdiagnosed psychiatric conditions (Braddock and Parish 2001). These ideas persist today as manifested in literary and news stories that link mental "illnesses," autism, and schizophrenia to criminality and evildoing (Kearney 2005).

In some cases, however, disability is viewed as a gift or transfer of magical powers (Ingstad 2001; Perry 2016). For example, some people believe that God chose them to be the parents of a disabled child (Mardiros 1989), and this belief may underlie the common response, "God only gives people what they can handle." Some consider disability to be an opportunity to reveal God's mercy through the miracle of healing for those who have strong faith (Olkin 1999). Still today, many disabled people lament being approached in public by strangers who offer to pray for their healing.

> Any time I go to church, multiple people tell me how they are "praying for me to walk again" or how much they "hate to see me in a wheelchair." This always feels condescending because I don't want them to do that but if I try to explain this to them, they act like they have a better idea of what my life should be like regardless of the journey I've taken to be cool with how I am now. ~ Person with multiple disabilities, 2015

According to Florian (1982), the prescientific origins of the moral model of disability date back to biblical ideas about divine retribution. Independent of any physical manifestations, impairments were thought to originate in the spirit or soul (Mackelprang and Salsgiver 1999). Furthermore, when disability is attributed to the divine, only certain solutions are considered appropriate. For example, if psychiatric or other types of disability represent demon possession, then prayers of exorcism make more sense. Similarly, those who espouse certain religious beliefs about disability may believe it is their moral obligation to contribute to charities that serve "the needy."

> The whole medical and rehabilitation enterprise is founded upon an ideology of normality, and this has far reaching implications for rehabilitation and treatment. (Oliver 1996, p. 36)

The Biomedical or Individual Model of Disability

Once scientific breakthroughs identified the various biomedical origins of conditions like blindness, dyslexia, and muscular dystrophy, a new ideological construction emerged to explain disability as an abnormality, a deviation from normal functioning (Altman 2001). Today, the biomedical or individual model of disability remains deeply entrenched as the predominant way of viewing the problems of disability – problems assumed to be located inside the brains and bodies of people characterized as sick, diseased, and otherwise malformed (Smart 2009). With internal pathology as the starting point for making sense of disability as a neurochemical or physiological "defect," the biomedical model promotes an understanding of *physical* causes, and the use of diagnostic tools to prevent impairments, reduce symptoms, and ideally eradicate individual abnormalities (Marks 1999). According to a biomedical model, disability is no different than one's specific impairment or diagnosis. The term disability is in fact used interchangeably with specific impairments like blindness, deafness, and schizophrenia.

From this perspective, the only appropriate solutions to the problems of disability are those provided by medical experts using medical tools – drugs, therapies, surgeries – to eliminate individual "deficits," to rehabilitate what's broken, and if possible, to cure what is defective (Conrad 2004). People with disabilities are expected to comply with medical authorities as good patients even if that means enduring aversive "therapies" like electroshock, mind-altering drugs, and painful prosthetic devices used to normalize their appearance and behavior. Compared to conceptions of disability as a moral failing, this more medicalized explanation of disability emphasizes physical and mental *loss* and *limitation*. Furthermore, limitations are presumed to derive directly from particular impairments without considering environmental barriers. For example, people who view disability exclusively as an internal condition of the body may assume that a child with a physical disability is not participating on the playground because her legs are paralyzed – failing to consider that the playground surface (e.g. bark chips or gravel) prevents her wheelchair from accessing the swings.

The biomedical model of disability is not opposed to the discipline of medicine, which has saved and improved the quality of many lives. However, as an ideology for understanding the complex problems of those who experience disability, this model is, at best, incomplete. Some disability studies scholars claim that the biomedical model is responsible for creating many forms of disability prejudice while precluding recognition of institutionalized ableism (Hahn 1993). Disability has even been invoked to justify discrimination against other social groups, including women, Blacks, and immigrants denied citizenship rights on the basis of certain psychological, intellectual, and physical deficits like emotionality, incompetence, and weakness (Baynton 2013).

> To treat the emotionally distressed victims of discrimination, of exploitation, of impoverishment, as if their problems are the result of biological/genetic defect is clearly a form of blatant Social Darwinism. To drug them into silent passivity rather than to fight for social justice is to join the powerful exploiters. (Albee 1996, p. 15)

Consistent with ideologies that legitimize ableist practices, the biomedical model, "allows others in the broader culture to view their prejudicial and discriminating treatment of people with disabilities as somehow justified because, after all, the prestigious, authoritative, scientific medical profession has labeled people with disabilities as biologically inferior, or 'special,' or abnormal, ... thus relieving the public of any need to provide access to services and civil rights" (Smart 2009, p. 3). When the problem is located in the individual, it becomes the individual's responsibility to fix that problem – usually through treatments designed to restore the individual's body and mind to as near "normal" as possible so the person can better fit in and function as nondisabled people do. Although the biomedical model equates disability with impairment, this is not the definition of disability according to many in the disability rights movement – where disability is equated with discrimination imposed on people with impairments.

> While some people are physically, intellectually, or psychologically different from the norm, their primary "problems" stem not from their appearance or other eccentricities but from being in a society that fails to include them as other citizens. ~ Author unknown

Socio-Political/Minority Model of Disability

In stark contrast to the biomedical model of disability is the civil rights framework that identifies disability as an exclusively social phenomenon. According to the socio-political or minority model of disability, it is society that disables certain people who are excluded from participating as equals due to environmental, political, and attitudinal barriers. Emerging from disability activists and scholars in the 1970s and 1980s (Finkelstein 1980; Oliver 1996), this model reframes disability as something imposed *on top* of any impairment-related concerns, including the many architectural, educational, and economic restrictions that are neither natural nor inevitable consequences of mind-body differences (Linton 1998). In a world designed for a much narrower range of human variability than currently exists, if some groups are systematically denied access to community events, voting, school, and work, this can be understood as discrimination (Scotch 2000).

Distinct from models explaining disability as a problem of the individual, the socio-political model locates the problems of disability at the societal level, and simultaneously acknowledges the status of disabled people as a minority group. Although previously fragmented and divided into separate, often rival impairment camps (Altman 2001), in sharing their collective concerns, disabled people began to identify a cohesive set of interests and experiences with oppression. These included segregated schools and living arrangements, social and recreational marginalization, economic exploitation, and misrepresentation in the media (Marks 1999; McCarthy 2003). Following other civil rights movements, the socio-political model of disability frames disabled people not as a collection of individuals with special needs but as a disadvantaged social group. Like other minorities, disabled people are assumed to be inferior, are pressured to assimilate, and confront pervasive discrimination including organized brutality (e.g. hate crimes); inferior housing, education, and insurance which places them at much higher risk for substance abuse; failure to graduate; under-employment; and incarceration (Ben-Moshe et al. 2014a; Olkin 1999). The disproportionate rates of physical and mental impairments among the poor (see Morris 2017), who face chronic unemployment, malnutrition, and inadequate healthcare in addition to hazardous neighborhood and working conditions (Smart 2009), provide further evidence that disability is a socially created phenomenon. The socio-political model both politicized and empowered disabled people, providing them with a sense of belonging and fostering identification with a broader disability community, a topic to be explored further in Chapters 6 and 8.

> I think I went through an almost evangelical conversion as I realised that my disability was not, in fact, the epilepsy, but the toxic drugs with their denied side-effects; the medical regime with its blaming of the victim; the judgement though distance and silence of bus-stop crowds, bar-room crowds, and dinner-table friends; the fear and, not least, the employment problems. All this was the oppression, not the epileptic seizure at which I was hardly (consciously) present. (Hevey 1992 as cited in Oliver 1996, p. 42)

More recent versions of the socio-political model of disability do not deny the presence of physiological issues (e.g. pain) related to certain impairments, but instead acknowledge that these are not within the scope of what the model was designed to articulate. The socio-political model of disability focuses on identifying problems related to discrimination and exclusion as the ultimate factors determining who is disabled by society. Therefore, solutions to disabling conditions aim to both protect and defend civil rights through collective action for social change (Hahn 1985). The benefits of this approach have been many: instead of seeking charity, welfare, or "special privileges," disabled people have fought for equal access and responsible citizenship leading to legislation supporting independent living, inclusive education, the Disability Discrimination Act, and the Americans with Disabilities Act (ADA). Legal reforms now require access to buildings and public transportation. Anti-discrimination policies mandate equal opportunities in employment; and educational campaigns raise awareness of media underrepresentation and bias. Similar efforts in community psychology have called for societal changes to reduce environmental stressors that contribute to the development of psychiatric disabilities, including prevention programs through the National Institutes of Mental Health (NIMH) (Albee 1996).

In terms of reducing interpersonal prejudice, the socio-political model of disability may be limited as laws cannot legislate tolerance and understanding. Yet, structural and policy changes that bring people into greater contact on equal status terms are a step in the right direction as people become more familiar with diversity and difference with more exposure and intergroup cooperation (see Chapter 7).

> Disability is finally whatever public officials say it is. (Hahn 1985, p. 102)

Disability Model Comparisons and Implications

The implication of these models is revealed through human decisions that create the laws and social policies that affect people's lives. For example, decisions inform the location and width of building entrances, the presence or absence of ramps, elevators, and signage, and the spacing of public and private arenas. Yet, often these decisions have failed to take certain types of people into account

(Marks 1999), which is why we still see disabled people conspicuously absent from many public and private venues. Human decision makers are also responsible for the layout of college campuses, the content of the curriculum, and the choice of delivery options including print-only, books on tape, and interactive formats that may privilege certain ways of learning and being in the world. If professors or campus administrators are more likely to endorse a biomedical model explanation of disability, they may very well assume that unless students can adjust themselves to fit into existing facilities and formats provided, they don't belong in college – unless or until they seek remediation to overcome their biological limitations (Molloy and Nario-Redmond 2007). By contrast, to the extent educators recognize the socio-political aspects of disability, they may be more apt to comply with federal regulations and ensure reasonable accommodations for members of the disability community. The reality, however, is that compliance (and best practices) when it comes to access and inclusion is highly variable across college campuses (Dolmage 2017; for top disability-friendly colleges see College Choice 2018). This means that the model of disability endorsed will still influence decisions ranging from where to hold campus-wide events to the provisioning of educational resources in time for class.

To illustrate, Dr. Bruce Pomero, former President of the Association for Higher Education and Disability (AHEAD), shared how college students with vision impairments often have to wait weeks for course materials to be provided in digital or electronic formats, and these often exclude descriptions of important graphs and tables or include transcription errors (e.g. eliminating the word "not" which significantly alters the meaning of a text); this undermines student achievement and puts them at a significant disadvantage from peers (personal communication, February 11, 2015). If more people recognize such practices as discriminatory – in violation of disabled students' civil rights – they may become more proactive in preparing to accommodate a fuller range of qualified students, faculty, and staff (see Dolmage 2017). Every day decisions are influenced by the model of disability espoused, with major implications for participation and advancement in society.

The usefulness of alternative frameworks or models for understanding disability lies in their ability to predict how people think and behave toward disability issues. Yet research testing the impact of these models on attitudes and actions is conspicuously absent. We also know very little about the characteristics of those who are more or less likely to endorse different model explanations. In one of the few studies examining predictors of model endorsement, Darling and Heckert (2010) found that disabled people were more likely to support a biomedical model explanation of disability if they were retired, unmarried, or less involved in disability activism. Those more involved in disability activism or who had physical-mobility impairments themselves were more supportive of the socio-political model. Consistent with this finding, another study found that those with physical conditions were less likely to endorse the biomedical model compared to those with learning disabilities (Goodrich and Ramsey 2013). Clearly more research is needed on the factors influencing how people shift between alternative explanations, and who will be most resistant or receptive to interventions that reframe disability as discrimination against a minority group.

In summary, as these disparate models for understanding disability illustrate, the solutions to the persistent problems that disabled people face critically depend on the ideological orientations used to explain these circumstances. Moral explanations that blame social disadvantage and ostracism on divine punishment for sins are not focused on solutions to repair the physical body or a discriminating society, although they may encourage charitable giving (Miller et al. 1993). Biomedical approaches move away from supernatural explanations of disability but still pathologize disabled people – solving impairment problems with treatments that make people fit into the existing environment. By contrast, the sociopolitical model emphasizes disabling aspects of the physical and policy environment that must be changed to ensure equal rights. Each of these models fails to fully account for the full range of issues facing people with disabilities. However, when asked, most disabled people say that their most pressing concerns are not about the body or the soul but about a society that systematically excludes them (Florian 1982; Smart 2009).

> Discovering this way of thinking about my experiences was the proverbial raft in stormy seas. It gave me an understanding of my experiences, shared with thousands, even millions, of other people in the world, and I clung to it … I don't think it is an exaggeration to say that the social model has saved lives. (Crow 1996 cited in Morris 2001, p. 6)

Language: Communicating and Maintaining System-Justifying Ideologies

As should be clear by now, system justification ideologies benefit the current social order by providing ready-made explanations of why some groups find themselves at the bottom of the social hierarchy while others have advanced. Both the moral and the biomedical models of disability are ideologies that maintain the status quo. They legitimize social inequality as medically or supernaturally deserved. Furthermore, if widespread, such belief systems can suppress a drive for social change: why fix a system that isn't broken? Although research on the impact of disability-specific ideologies on attitudes and behavior is limited, there is a literature on how broad values and ideas are learned and reinforced through particular forms of communication – the specific words, labels, and descriptions chosen to represent social groups and characterize their life circumstances.

Ideological belief systems are communicated both formally and informally. Some are codified into legal rulings, policies, and procedures, and also spread through conversations, jokes, and media portrayals. Everyday terms used to describe disability in the news and on social media are not just reflections of reality, they are actively deployed to preserve existing inequalities. On the other hand, language can also sway public opinions and initiate social change. This section highlights a few communication and media studies to illustrate how ideological beliefs about disability become engrained as part of the collective consciousness.

> No human group has been forced to change its name so frequently. The sick and the poor are always with us, in physical presence and in verbal terms, but not the handicapped. (Sinason 1992, p. 40)

Disability Markers, Labels, and Metaphors

Are they handicapped, challenged, or people with special needs? Are they people with disabilities, disabled people, or differently abled? Which terms are currently in favor, and who are the language police always ready with political corrections for those who aren't keeping up with what is considered offensive? Given an ever-changing landscape of alternatives, why do words matter in shaping public attitudes and policies, and what do those who experience disability have to say about their identity preferences and representations? Language is not just about communicating a message – language influences what people think, and what they fail to consider as well (Schaller and Conway III 2001). For example, when ramps, elevators, and video captioning are described as "special needs," people may not consider these as civil rights. Similarly, the term "handicapped" may call to mind an image of disabled people begging for charity, a cap in hand, especially when linked to messages that guilt people into helping those characterized as needing a handout (Barnes 1992).

Several books exist on the historical evolution of terms used to describe disability as a tragic, pitiable, or burdensome condition – a stigma that produces suffering, weakness, and loss (Devlieger 1999; Haller and Zhang 2013). However, many terms that now seem offensive were not always considered derogatory. Even the "r-word" (retard), which derives from mental retardation, was once an improvement to previous terms (e.g. idiot, feebleminded, imbecile, moron) for those now labeled as intellectually disabled (Siperstein et al. 2010). In fact, updating language or "linguistic inflation" is one way in which those in the professional fields can distinguish themselves from previous service-providers associated with outdated approaches and terms.

> Politically correct language can be seen as just another device with which to reinforce hierarchy between professional groups. Some professionals may use the most up-to-date language in order to compete with other professionals and appear "more politically correct than thou." (Marks 1999, p. 150)

Over time, and just like terms that came before, the word "retard" came to be seen as an insult used to demean those with lower than average intelligence

(Siperstein et al. 2010). And the term has continued to evolve as slang for general disapproval. "Retard" can refer to almost anyone or anything, much like the term "gay" has been applied to anything not considered "cool" (Thurlow 2001).

Stigmatized identity markers can divide those who are "in the know" and up to date from those who are not. In this way, stigmatized identity terms are used to regulate others' behaviors, to shame them into conforming to ingroup standards based on their association with lower status groups (de Klerk 2005). For example, a national sample of students ages 8 to 18, found that most considered the r-word acceptable, as long as it was not directed toward a person with a disability (Siperstein et al. 2010). In fact, students were twice as likely to say they would do nothing to deter others from using the r-word compared to when the r-word was used to describe a person with a disability. Furthermore, they were five times more likely to join in and laugh when hearing the r-word if directed toward someone *without* a disability, and 10 times more likely to join in and laugh when a friend said the word compared to when a stranger did so. Finally, while 40% of elementary school students were actively opposed to using the r-word, this declined to only 26% by high school. Other research demonstrates that even when used as a metaphor, the r-word is still painful to those in the intellectually disabled community who have advocated against its continued use (see R-Word: Spread the Word to End the Word 2017). According to neuroimaging studies, the pain of social rejection activates the same areas of the brain as physical pain (Eisenberger 2012). Clearly, wounds are often inflicted without sticks and stones.

Studies of physicians in training found a history of demeaning terms used to describe disabled and other undesirable patients in healthcare settings. Terms of derision like "crock" describe patients with psychiatric disabilities believed to be faking symptoms that medical students cannot readily diagnose (Coombs et al. 1993). The term "gomer" is reserved for patients considered unintelligent, senile, or of lower social status; those in a coma are called "Gomertose" or "GORK," which stands for God Only Really Knows. Medical students also use acronyms to describe those with lower intelligence as "LMCs" (low marble count), and those with low income/status are "SHPOSs" (a subhuman piece of shit). The use of such demeaning slang may help new medical students cope with the stress of managing life and death, creating a sense of belonging to a very exclusive group. As medical students move up the social ladder, their use of these terms *increases* particularly during hospital internships, but declines somewhat among practicing physicians (Coombs et al. 1993). Similar findings have been documented among nursing students along with calls for reform in order to "Disabled labels that disable" (Alex and Whitty-Rogers 2012).

Metaphors about people with disabilities are deeply engrained in everyday language, news, and literature although many remain oblivious to their impact. For example, people often say, "blind to" to signify lack of awareness. Politicians in their last year of office are called "lame ducks"; and to experience terror is said to be "crippled or paralyzed by fear." In addition to expressing ideas about ignorance, ineligibility, and motionlessness, these terms help maintain the inferior position of people with disabilities. Simply overhearing someone use hate speech leads people to devalue those targeted (Greenberg and Pyszczynski 1985; Simon and Greenberg 1996).

> When we use terms like "retarded," "lame," or "blind" – even if we are referring to acts or ideas and not to people at all – we perpetuate the stigma associated with disability. By using a label, which is commonly associated with disabled people to denote deficiency, a lack, or an ill-conceived notion, we reproduce the oppression of people with disabilities. (Ben-Moshe 2005, p. 108–109)

Contemporary and Clashing Ideologies: The Language of Media Portrayals

It wasn't until people with disabilities started describing their problems in terms of oppression, using the language of civil rights, that collective action for social change became possible (Shapiro 1993). Media studies scholar John Clogston (1990) found that prior to landmark legislation like the ADA, US news stories about disability focused almost exclusively on medical and social welfare topics; and people with disabilities were consistently characterized as helpless victims – a burden on the family and a drain on government resources. Prior to the ADA, disabled people were commonly portrayed as "unfortunates who were sad but apologetic for their fate; this made them appear more deserving of pity and charitable assistance from those in positions to provide it (Haller and Zhang 2013). Consistent with social dominance views, such news stories help rationalize why those who are "inherently weak" require the kindness and support of people from higher status groups.

Since talk is a form of action used to transmit ideologies (Haller and Zhang 2013), many social movements have attempted to introduce new terminology to disrupt and replace dominant discourses with more contemporary viewpoints. For example, the disability rights movement was central to advocating for more accurate reporting and updated terminology across news media and research professions (Barnartt et al. 2001). In response, the ADA introduced language to advance the civil rights of a genuine minority group (Fleischer and Zames 2011), insisting they be called "people with" disabilities. This person-first language was intentionally selected to acknowledge the humanity and individuality of people as more than their collective impairments (Carlson 2010). Examining the impact of such legislated changes, Haller et al. (2006) analyzed disability terms used in the *Washington Post* and the *New York Times* in 1990 (the year the ADA passed) and again in 2000. They found that use of the term "handicapped" decreased over the 10-year period while "people/persons with disabilities" increased. However, both newspapers increased use of the terms "wheelchair bound" and "confined to a wheelchair," *despite* professional journalistic guidelines that advised against characterizing wheelchair users as passive and their equipment as imprisoning (Burns 2014; Goldstein 2002). Not only are these terms inaccurate – most people transfer in an out of wheelchairs, in which they are not trapped – but these phrases are irrelevant to the story at hand (Haller et al. 2006). Unwanted forms of helping may even result from repeatedly hearing that people are "confined to wheelchairs" instead of feeling liberated by them (Linton 1998).

> I received some unwanted help on the subway last week that resulted in me failing in jumping the gap. Consequently, my front wheelchair casters got stuck in the gap and I had to jump out of my chair to safety. It was a scary situation. I have modified my DME as much as possible to avoid unwanted help (no more push handles on the back of my wheelchair, for example), but that didn't stop this occurrence. ~ Person with a physical disability, 2015

Media scholars acknowledge that news outlets proactively seek out stories that reinforce existing ideologies, like the meritocracy belief that anyone can get ahead with enough hard work. One of the most popular news stories is the type that spotlights disabled people who have worked hard to overcome their personal limitations or to achieve an important goal or milestone (Haller and Zhang 2013). These stories are known as "supercrip" features, which follow a common formula describing disabled individuals as inspiring to others because they have achieved success against all odds (or above what most expect from them). The odds that have been overcome, however, rarely focus on architectural or attitudinal barriers that systematically exclude. Instead, these stories highlight how everyday accomplishments like participating in a sport, graduating from high school, or getting married were somehow managed *despite* not being able to walk, see, hear, or talk. Not only does this message reinforce biomedical ideas that the problems disabled people face are really all about their impairments, but the subtler message implies that if *this* person can overcome his/her limitations, so should everyone else. Even more problematic, if these messages convince people that all it takes is a little hard work for anyone to get ahead, is that some people may assume that disabled people don't really need accommodations to address environmental barriers, or that discrimination isn't keeping people from improving their social status. It is this interpretation that many disability studies scholars find dangerous to public opinion (Zola 1991). In fact, the more people think about arguments in support of "hard-work to success" ideologies, the less money they are willing to donate to shelters for the homeless (Levy et al. 2006).

There are at least two variations on the "supercrip" feature that have been around since the mid-1800s (Covington 1988). The first type portrays the disabled person as superhuman for accomplishing some extraordinary feat (e.g. a blind person climbing Mt. Everest or an amputee sculpting with his toes). The other, more typical, variety highlights the apparent courageousness involved in an activity that most people find ordinary (e.g. taking public transportation, going to the prom). The activity is often described as an accomplishment managed "in spite of" an impairment, playing on the assumption that the audience's stereotypical expectations will be exceeded. Mary Duffy, disabled artist and activist, describes a common refrain she has heard:

> Isn't it marvelous what they can train you to do nowadays? (Vital Signs: Crip Culture Talks Back, Snyder and Mitchell 1996)

These objectifying and condescending portrayals conflict with the messages the disability rights movement seeks to advance related to persistent discrimination, unemployment, and inaccessibility (Birenbaum 2000; Shapiro 1993). Yet, to this day, inspirational supercrip stories permeate both traditional and social media because this is what audiences seem to want (Haller and Zhang 2013). Editors and media executives still control much of what is considered publishable or newsworthy, and serve as gatekeepers to public consumption, filtering through what should be included and omitted along the way (Jones 2012).

In response, more contemporary news outlets, including blogs from disability rights activists, are promoting alternative narratives and critiquing stories that continue to misrepresent disabled people as either tragic or heroic (Clogston 1990). Activists have even adopted a new term, "inspiration porn," to call attention to the perpetuation of the supercrip narrative (Young 2016). Chapter 5 elaborates on this paternalistic form of prejudice in terms of the attitudes and motivations that drive a desire to exploit disabled people as inspirational role models, including research on the extent to which such narratives inspire actual achievement in others or not.

> If you do not name that which has to be defeated, it will not be beaten. (Miller et al. 2004, p. 5)

Resistance, Backlash and Humor in Disrupting the Status Quo

Language change and the reclaiming of labels have been central to shifting explanations for social disadvantage away from physical and mental impairments to expose the social practices that unfairly restrict certain types of people from participating as equals. By recognizing and labeling status differences as discriminatory, people with disabilities have transformed the debate into one that requires changing policies instead of fixing people (Nario-Redmond and Oleson 2016). People on the inside of the disability experience have argued that they are the ones who should get to decide what they are called instead of those in government and healthcare bureaucracies designated to speak on their behalf (Dunn and Andrews 2015). For example, many activists and disability studies scholars now prefer to be called Disabled People – privileging disability identity first (Linton 1998; Shapiro 2011). This phrasing is consistent with much scholarship examining the growth of disability as a proud cultural heritage similar to ethnicity and sexuality (Brown 2002; Brueggemann 2013). Putting identity first reflects a socio-political orientation that society is what "disables people." The person-first approach, "people with disabilities" (PWD), has been criticized for equating disability with impairments and ignoring discrimination (Oliver and Barnes 1998).

> Disabled person seems less pejorative than PWD, at least from the point of self-determination and self-naming … I think Disabled person is important because PWD can be construed negatively. Like it is something I have, and I'd get rid of if I could. "Person with a" makes me feel like disability is a suit that I wear … I liken it to Physically Challenged, Handicapper, Handicapable, etc. and those other terms. Those attempt, in part, to make my disability "cute" and palatable to a nondisabled population. (Cheu 2002)

Some in the disability community consider person-first language to be euphemistic – a softer substitute for words that seem too blunt like "oppression" or "homeless." By contrast, euphemistic words like "differently abled" or "street person" are used to disguise the oppressive and abusive realities of a group disabled by society (Dunn and Andrews 2015; Marks 1999). For this disability activist Lawrence Carter-Long initiated the Say the Word Campaign arguing, "If you 'see the person not the disability' you're only getting half the picture. Broaden your perspective. You might be surprised by everything you've missed. DISABLED. #SayTheWord" (King 2016). Research on preferred identity markers among those in the disability community, and the implications of disability identification for well-being, perceptions of discrimination, and advocacy for change is covered in Chapter 6.

Debates over what is regarded as appropriate and respectful language are frequently met with resistance (Marks 1999). Few people appreciate constraints on their freedoms of speech and press, much less being shamed into compliance. Backlash against new terminology is often expressed as irritation over external pressures to comply with norms about "political correctness" (Haller et al. 2006). People who feel that their language use is already acceptable may even resent having to behave and speak in ways that others consider nonprejudicial (Crandall et al. 2013). Some argue that language restrictions are all a waste of time since new terms of derision will just replace those that have changed (Salvador-Carulla and Bertelli 2008) – a position used to justify inaction (Haller et al. 2006). Ironically, those who are externally motivated to suppress their prejudices may actually express *more* prejudice in reaction to new norms of political correctness (Plant and Devine 1998), a topic discussed further in Chapter 7. Norms about speech and behavior are constantly fluctuating, which can also result in clashes over what is considered acceptable and what is not.

Crandall et al. (2013) describe the "normative window" as a unique period of time where contested ideologies begin to shift between what was once considered acceptable in popular discourse, and what has become increasingly recognized as prejudicial. Prior to this shift, some terms may have been considered offensive in some communities while other terms were being reclaimed as signifiers of pride (e.g. we're here, we're queer, get used to it). However, the dynamic nature of language can give way to more widespread public recognition of a new "normal" as the window of change is pulled open, and metaphors previously considered neutral become less publically tolerated, and more readily acknowledged as hate or dehumanizing speech (Sherry 2016). For example, prior to Native American protests about their representation in professional sports, which still includes racist mascots (Chief Wahoo, Chief Illiniwek), few people questioned the legitimacy of terms like "Injun," "Scalper," or "Redskin," much less the harm they inflicted on a living people (Phillips and Stegman 2014). Similarly, what is recognized today as destructive to members of the disability community is only now gaining attention thanks to those raising awareness of the power of language to promote ideologies that sustain social inequality. As one sign of progress, recent legislation has been introduced to remove the term "retarded" from professional practices (Schalock et al. 2007). Chapter 6 will include additional examples of how language is used strategically to alter the normative environment, reclaim previously stigmatized terms, and challenge prejudicial representations.

It is commonly assumed that people spend a lot of effort dodging the identity of prejudice. Few people want to be identified as a bigot, and often preface insensitive comments by saying, "I'm not prejudiced but ..." or add "Just joking; I didn't mean to offend." However, while people often seek to avoid appearing prejudiced, public expressions about minority groups are not always managed to avoid prejudicial talk. When people are motivated to have their prejudicial views verified, they may actively communicate their beliefs through humor and other gestures to signal like-minded others with an implicit message: "Hey, I still think they are inferior, how about you?" Sherif and Sherif (1967) described this as a "psycho-logic" to prejudice where people often intentionally work to transmit a shared understanding of their ideological allegiances.

Ideologies that justify existing status relations are only effective to the extent that they are shared through repeated communication, and exposure to messages that reinforce these teachings. Few studies have examined the degree of consensus on these issues, and people remain unclear about what counts as offensive or humorous when it comes to disability (e.g. *Assisted Suicide: The Musical*). Research on minority humor suggests that as groups gain increasing independence, jokes are often used to alleviate tension, and help people process new social arrangements (Dundes 1987; Haller 2010). According to Barrick (1980), a joke in bad taste (a sick joke) "has had the cathartic effect of erasing the pity normally felt toward the disabled, so the joke teller and his listener now accept these people on equal terms ... How can you hate someone who makes you laugh?" (p. 449). There's an empirical question.

On the other hand, people may also find it difficult to take seriously the progress of the disability rights movement if their gains are considered laughable. Future research is critically needed to examine the impact of disability humor which has itself evolved from sick jokes that make fun of specific impairments, to jokes written by disabled people themselves poking fun at societal ignorance and their mistreatment. Consider the following version of this joke: "How many disabled people does it take to screw in a lightbulb?" Answer: "One to screw it in and five able-bodied people to say, 'You are such an inspiration'" (Nina G. 2014). Similarly, on the animated TV show *South Park*, the character Timmy, who uses a wheelchair, is asked, "You know what you call an able-bodied guy on the doorstep?" Answer: "Whatever his name is."

One place to examine shifting ideologies is within academic discourse. How are psychologists and other social scientists talking about disability prejudice? Within the past 10–15 years, there has been debate about the terms and methods used to study disability stigma and prejudice (see Biernat and Dovidio 2000; Phelan et al. 2008). In 2000, leading social psychologists argued that disability stereotypes were not common, and until 2010, little research investigated consensus for broad-based beliefs about this group (Nario-Redmond 2010). Even then, the term ableism was not yet circulating in the social sciences as a construct to be studied. According to Harpur (2012), the next step in the struggle against oppression requires harnessing the power of the term ableism to signify disability-based prejudice and discrimination. Just as ageism, racism, sexism, sizeism, and heterosexism have been used to legitimize and organize prejudice and discrimination scholarship about these groups, ableism is gaining traction in the field of disability studies and beyond. Only recently has the term ableism emerged as part of psychological discourse (Dunn and Andrews 2015; Marshak et al. 2009; Wolbring 2012). In fact, the knowledge base in psychology is only now advancing to include studies of prejudice against disabled people. For many years, the field focused only on stigmas related to particular types of impairment (Phelan et al. 2008). The term ableism also has the potential to apply more broadly to discrimination on the basis of any differing ability – regardless of whether or not one qualifies or even identifies as disabled. For example, people without a diagnosed impairment or documented activity restriction can still be denied rights based on their physical, cognitive, or sensory abilities (Harpur 2012). Abilities are fluid and change with the context and over the life course. Some conditions are chronic, some unpredictable, and some temporary – the term ableism clarifies the notion that anyone can be impacted by ability discrimination, and therefore may appeal to a wider base of support in an increasingly diverse and global world.

Summary

The prejudice and discrimination disabled people (and other minorities) face reflect a complex system of ideological beliefs that are widely shared and actively maintained through various practices and institutionalized policies. Justification ideologies, in particular, are those used to rationalize the status quo and justify group inequalities. For example, both old and newer forms of Social Darwinism champion improvements to the human species to eradicate disease and disability and to perfect the world of the future. This ideology is reflected in the practices of the Eugenics Movement: forced sterilizations, involuntary confinement, and school segregation, and in the rationales for selective abortion and assisted suicide on the basis of disability. These utopian ideals of societal reform that continue to seek human betterment through the elimination of disability ignore the value that disabled people bring to a multicultural world, and fail to recognize that disability defies genetic inheritance. Other justification ideologies operate in subtler ways to reinforce hierarchical arrangements where some groups are positioned to dominate over others who are described as "better suited" for subordinate roles. Justifications for inequalities can also be found in the ways in which disabled people defy American ideals. The concepts of the Protestant work ethic, rugged individualism, and the value of meritocracy all place expectations on the individual as responsible for their own fate. For example, beliefs that anyone can get ahead with enough hard work put the onus on disabled individuals to overcome their bodily limitations to achieve independence, which undermines the recognition of socially created barriers that limit access to participation in the existing environment. When ideologies frame individual participation as an accommodation of "special needs," people fail to recognize the problem as discrimination or the violation of a minority group's civil rights. Ideologies about the nature of justice influence how people come to understand who is the blame for poverty, accidents of birth, or acquired injuries: those who endorse the workings of a "just world" may view disability as punishment against those who fail to meet societal standards of morality, productivity, and achievement. In fact, explanations of disability itself influence beliefs about how the problems of disability should be solved – depending on where they are located. Looking at disability through a moral lens (model) suggests that disability can be understood as a divine intervention: a gift, a punishment, or perhaps a test of faith designed to reveal God's mercy through prayer. Those who view disability through a biomedical lens (the predominant viewpoint), understand it to be an abnormality, something that went "wrong" that requires a "cure" or at least some remediation so the individual can be restored to some approximation of "normality." Increasingly, a socio-political alternative is gaining traction that recognizes disabled people as a disadvantaged minority group. This model works to uncover the influence of human decisions that have privileged the participation of certain bodies and minds while systematically excluding others, who are then disabled from participating as fellow citizens with consequences that result in persistent economic, educational, and health disparities.

Justification ideologies do not exist in a vacuum but are actively perpetuated (and disrupted) in the way that we communicate about disability (and in what we fail to communicate as well). Everyday language and media portrayals that pathologize disabled lives as "burdensome," "suffering," and "wheelchair bound" work to validate ideological beliefs. The portrayals of disabled people as tragic victims or inspirational heroes in television, movies, and books often misrepresent the lived disability experience, and are a source of ongoing tensions about who is allowed to speak for whom and to what end. However, just as language can reinforce harmful beliefs, it can also challenge them. There is power in the voices of disabled people who challenge system-justifying ideologies, and replace them with their own stories – stories that disrupt ableist assumptions. Though change happens slowly, both mainstream and academic worlds are beginning to include these complex narratives, and to recognize their effects on disability stereotypes, ambivalent attitudes, and internalized experiences of ableism. As these changes happen, more research is needed to understand the dynamics involved in shifting the "normative window" – the process by which ideas and language go from being considered acceptable to being widely recognized as ableist. Chapter 4 begins to articulate the psychological processes involved in the formation, perpetuation, and disruption of disability stereotypes as cognitive representations of beliefs about specific social groups, and offers strategies for understanding the motives behind these stereotypes and under what conditions they change.

Note

1 The Fernald State School ran until the 1970s as an institution for the feebleminded, housing over 250 000 boys many of whom were not intellectually disabled. Their story of abuse, drugging, sterilization, and experimentation appears in D'Antonio (2005).

References

Albee, G.W. (1996). Introduction to the special issue on Social Darwinism. *The Journal of Primary Prevention* 17 (1): 3–16.

Alex, M. and Whitty-Rogers, J. (2012). Time to disable the labels that disable: the power of words in nursing and health care with women, children, and families. *Advances in Nursing Science* 35 (2): 113–126.

Allott, D. and Neumayr, G. (2013). Eugenic Abortion 2.0. A new blood test could zero out the disabled unborn in the 21st century. *American Spectator* 46 (4): https:// spectator.org/55745_eugenic-abortion-20/ (accessed 26 February 2019).

Altman, B.M. (2001). Disability definitions, models, classification schemes, and applications. In: *Handbook of Disability Studies* (ed. G.L. Albrecht, K.D. Seelman and M. Bury), 97–122. London: Sage.

Amundson, R. and Taira, G. (2005). Our lives and ideologies: the effect of life experience on the perceived morality of the policy of physician-assisted suicide. *Journal of Disability Policy Studies* 16 (1): 53–57.

Anderson, V.N. (1992). For whom is this world just? Sexual orientation and AIDS. *Journal of Applied Social Psychology* 22 (3): 248–259.

Barnartt, S., Schriner, K., and Scotch, R. (2001). Advocacy and political action. In: *Handbook of Disability Studies* (ed. G.L. Albrecht, K.D. Seelman and M. Bury), 430–467. London: Sage.

Barnes, C. (1992). *Disabling Imagery and the Media: An Exploration of Media Representations of Disabled People*. Belper: British Council of Organizations of Disabled People.

Barrick, M.E. (1980). The Helen Keller joke cycle. *The Journal of American Folklore* 93 (370): 441–449.

Bashford, A. and Levine, P. (eds.) (2010). *The Oxford Handbook of the History of Eugenics*. New York: Oxford University Press.

Batavia, A.I. (1997). Ideology and independent living: will conservatism harm people with disabilities? *The Annals of the American Academy of Political and Social Science* 549 (1): 10–23.

Baynton, D.C. (2013). Disability and the justification of inequality in American history. *The Disability Studies Reader* 17: 37–57.

Ben-Moshe, L. (ed.) (2005). *Building Pedagogical Curb Cuts: Incorporating Disability in the University Classroom and Curriculum*. Syracuse: Syracuse University Press.

Ben-Moshe, L., Carey, A.C., and Chapman, C. (eds.) (2014a). *Disability Incarcerated: Imprisonment and Disability in the United States and Canada*. New York: Palgrave Macmillan.

Ben-Moshe, L., Davis, A.Y., Chapman, C. et al. (2014b). *Disability Incarcerated: Imprisonment and Disability in the United States and Canada*. New York: Palgrave Macmillan.

Biernat, M. and Dovidio, J.F. (2000). Stigma and stereotypes. In: *The Social Psychology of Stigma* (ed. T.F. Heatherton, R.E. Kleck, M.R. Hebl and J.G. Hull), 88–125. New York: Guilford Press.

Birenbaum, A. (2000). Once again, for the first time, people with disabilities are recruited into the workforce. *Ragged Edge* 21 (4): http://www.raggededgemagazine. com/0700/0700medge1.htm (accessed 26 February 2019).

Bizer, G.Y., Hart, J., and Jekogian, A.M. (2012). Belief in a just world and social dominance orientation: evidence for a mediational pathway predicting negative attitudes and discrimination against individuals with mental illness. *Personality and Individual Differences* 52 (3): 428–432.

Blumberg, L. (1994). Eugenics and reproductive choice. In: *The Ragged Edge: The Disability Experience From the Pages of the First Fifteen Years of "The Disability Rag"* (ed. B. Shaw), 228–239. Louisville, KY: Advocado Press.

Bowler, P. (2003). *Evolution: The History of an Idea*. Berkeley: University of California Press.

Braddock, D.L. and Parish, S.L. (2001). History of disability. In: *Handbook of Disability Studies* (ed. G.L. Albrecht, K.D. Seelman and M. Bury), 11–68. London: Sage.

Brandes, J.A. and Crowson, H.M. (2009). Predicting dispositions toward inclusion of students with disabilities: the role of conservative ideology and discomfort with disability. *Social Psychology of Education* 12 (2): 271–289.

Brown, S. (2002). What is disability culture? *Disability Studies Quarterly* 22 (2): 34–50.

Brown, L.X. (2018). Legal ableism, interrupted: developing tort law & policy alternatives to wrongful birth & wrongful life claims. *Disability Studies Quarterly* 38 (2): http:// dsq-sds.org/article/view/6207/4903 (accessed 26 February 2019).

Brueggemann, B.J. (2013). Disability studies/disability culture. In: *Oxford Handbook of Positive Psychology and Disability* (ed. M.L. Wehmeyer), 279–299. New York: Oxford University Press.

Buck vs. Bell, 274 US 200 (1927).

Burke, C.S. and Castaneda, C.J. (2007). The public and private history of eugenics: an introduction. *The Public Historian* 29 (3): 5–17.

Burleigh, M. (1994). Return to the planet of the apes? *History Today* 44 (10): 6–8.

Burns, S. (2014). How editors and journalists can produce better and fairer reporting on people with disability. *World News Publishing Focus* (8 September). https://blog.wan-ifra.org/2014/09/08/how-editors-and-journalists-can-produce-better-and-fairer-reporting-on-people-with-disabi (accessed 26 February 2019).

Bustillos, A. and Silván-Ferrero, M.D.P. (2013). Attitudes toward peers with physical disabilities at high school: applying the integrated threat theory. *Rehabilitation Counseling Bulletin* 56 (2): 108–119.

Carlson, L. (2010). Who's the expert? Rethinking authority in the face of intellectual disability. *Journal of Intellectual Disability Research* 54 (S1): 58–65.

Center for Eugenics and Society. 2007. James Watson's legacy. https://www.geneticsandsociety.org/biopolitical-times/james-watsons-legacy (accessed 26 February 2019).

Cheu, J. (2002). *Language and labels*. DISABILITY-RESEARCH@http://JISCMAIL.AC.UK

Clogston, J.S. (1990). *Disability Coverage in 16 Newspapers*. Louisville, KY: Advocado Press.

College Choice. (2018). 50 best disability friendly colleges and universities. http://www.collegechoice.net/50-best-disability-friendly-colleges-and-universities (accessed 26 February 2019).

Collins, F. S. (2003) A brief primer on genetic testing. World Economic Forum (24 January). http://www.genome.gov/10506784 (accessed 26 February 2019).

Conrad, P. (2004). The discovery of hyperkinesis: notes on the medicalization of deviant behavior. In: *Crucial Readings in Special Education* (ed. S. Danforth and S.D. Taff), 18–24. Upper Saddle River, NJ: Pearson-Merrill, Prentice-Hall.

Coombs, R.H., Chopra, S., Schenk, D.R., and Yutan, E. (1993). Medical slang and its functions. *Social Science & Medicine* 36 (8): 987–998.

Corrigan, P.W. and Kosyluk, K.A. (2014). Mental illness stigma: types, constructs, and vehicles for change. In: *Understanding Causes and Overcoming Injustices* (ed. P.W. Corrigan), 35–56. Washington, DC: American Psychological Association.

Covington, G. (1988). The stereotypes, the myths and the media. *Washington, D.C., The News Media and Disability Issues*. Washington, DC: National Institute on Disability and Rehabilitation Research, 1–2.

Cozzarelli, C., Wilkinson, A.V., and Tagler, M.J. (2001). Attitudes toward the poor and attributions for poverty. *Journal of Social Issues* 57 (2): 207–227.

Crandall, C.S. (1994). Prejudice against fat people: ideology and self-interest. *Journal of Personality and Social Psychology* 66 (5): 882–894.

Crandall, C.S. (2000). Ideology and lay theories of stigma: the justification of stigmatization. In: *The Social Psychology of Stigma* (ed. T.F. Heatherton, R.E. Kleck, M. Hebl and J. Hull), 126–150. New York: Guilford Press.

Crandall, C.S. and Biernat, M. (1990). The ideology of anti-fat attitudes. *Journal of Applied Social Psychology* 20 (3): 227–243.

Crandall, C.S. and Martinez, R. (1996). Culture, ideology, and anti-fat attitudes. *Personality and Social Psychology Bulletin* 22 (11): 1165–1176.

Crandall, C.S., Ferguson, M.A., and Bahns, A.J. (2013). When we see prejudice: the normative window and social change. In: *Stereotyping and Prejudice* (ed. C. Stangor and C.S. Crandall), 65–82. New York: Psychology Press.

Crouch, R.A. (1997). Letting the deaf be deaf: reconsidering the use of cochlear implants in prelingually deaf children. *Hastings Center Report* 27 (4): 14–21.

Crowson, H.M. and Brandes, J.A. (2008). Explaining opposition to rights for individuals with disabilities: the roles of cultural conservatism, religious openness (versus closedness), and dangerous world beliefs. In: *Human Rights in the 21st Century* (ed. M.S. Becker and J.N. Schneider), 151–166. Hauppauge, NY: Nova.

Crowson, H.M., Brandes, J.A., and Hurst, R.J. (2013). Who opposes rights for persons with physical and intellectual disabilities? *Journal of Applied Social Psychology* 43 (S2): E307–E318.

D'Antonio, M. (2005). *The State Boys Rebellion*. New York: Simon and Schuster.

Darling, R.B. and Heckert, D.A. (2010). Orientations toward disability: Differences over the lifecourse. *International Journal of Disability, Development and Education* 57 (2): 131–143.

Darwin, F. (1914). Francis Galton. *The Eugenics Review* 6 (1): 1–17.

Dawson, M. (2004). The misbehavior of behaviourists. http://www.sentex.net/~nexus23/naa_aba.html (accessed 26 February 2019).

Devlieger, P.J. (1999). From handicap to disability: language use and cultural meaning in the United States. *Disability and Rehabilitation* 21 (7): 346–354.

Dolmage, J.T. (2017). *Academic Ableism: Disability and Higher Education*. Ann Arbor, MI: University of Michigan Press.

Duckitt, J. (2001). A dual-process cognitive-motivational theory of ideology and prejudice. *Advances in Experimental Social Psychology* 33: 41–113.

Duckitt, J. (2006). Differential effects of right-wing authoritarianism and social dominance orientation on outgroup attitudes and their mediation by threat from and competitiveness to outgroups. *Personality and Social Psychology Bulletin* 32 (5): 684–696.

Dudley-Marling, C. and Gurn, A. (2010). Troubling the foundations of special education: examining the myth of the normal curve. In: *The Myth of the Normal Curve* (ed. C. Dudley-Marling and A. Gurn), 9–23. New York: Peter Lang.

Dundes, A. (1987). At ease, disease – AIDS jokes as sick humor. *American Behavioral Scientist* 30 (3): 72–81.

Dunn, D.S. and Andrews, E.E. (2015). Person-first and identity-first language: developing psychologists' cultural competence using disability language. *American Psychologist* 70 (3): 255–264.

Eisenberger, N.I. (2012). The pain of social disconnection: examining the shared neural underpinnings of physical and social pain. *Nature Reviews Neuroscience* 13 (6): 421–434.

Ells, L.J., Lang, R., Shield, J.P. et al. (2006). Obesity and disability – a short review. *Obesity Reviews* 7 (4): 341–345.

Esses, V.M., Dovidio, J.F., Jackson, L.M., and Armstrong, T.L. (2001). The immigration dilemma: the role of perceived group competition, ethnic prejudice, and national identity. *Journal of Social Issues* 57 (3): 389–412.

Eyler, A.E. and Levin, S. (2014). Interview with Saul Levin, MD, MPA, CEO/Medical Director of the American Psychiatric Association on the 40th anniversary of the decision to remove homosexuality from the DSM. *LGBT Health* 1 (2): 70–74.

Fernald, W. (1912). The burden of feeblemindedness. *Journal of Psychoasthenics* 18: 90–98.

Ferster, E.Z. (1966). Eliminating the unfit – is sterilization the answer? *Ohio State Law Journal* 27 (4): 591–633.

Finkelstein, V. (1980). *Attitudes and Disabled People: Issues for Discussion*. London: Royal Association for Disability and Rehabilitation.

Fleischer, D.Z. and Zames, F. (2011). Disability and the media in the 21st century. *Human Rights and Media* 6: 181–218.

Florian, V. (1982). Cross-cultural differences in attitudes towards disabled persons: a study of Jewish and Arab youth in Israel. *International Journal of Intercultural Relations* 6 (3): 291–299.

Furnham, A. (1995). The just world, charitable giving and attitudes to disability. *Personality and individual differences* 19 (4): 577–583.

Furnham, A. (2003). Belief in a just world: research progress over the past decade. *Personality and Individual Differences* 34 (5): 795–817.

Gallagher, H. (1990). *By Trust Betrayed: Patients, Physicians, and the License to Kill in the Third Reich.* New York: Henry Holt.

Garnets, L. and Kimmel, D. (eds.) (2003). *Psychological Perspectives on Lesbian, Gay, and Bisexual Experiences.* New York: Columbia University Press.

Goldstein, N. (ed.) (2002). *The Associated Press Stylebook and Briefing on Media Law.* Cambridge, MA: Perseus.

Goodrich, K. and Ramsey, R. (2013). Do people with disabilities feel excluded? Comparison of learning and physical disabilities. *Journal of Community Positive Practices* 13 (3): 74–87.

Greenberg, J. and Pyszczynski, T. (1985). The effect of an overheard ethnic slur on evaluations of the target: how to spread a social disease. *Journal of Experimental Social Psychology* 21 (1): 61–72.

Groce, N.E. and Zola, I.K. (1993). Multiculturalism, chronic illness, and disability. *Pediatrics* 91 (5): 1048–1055.

Hafer, C.L. and Begue, L. (2005). Experimental research on just-world theory: problems, developments, and future challenges. *Psychological Bulletin* 131 (1): 128–167.

Hahn, H.D. (1985). Toward a politics of disability: definitions, disciplines, and policies. *The Social Science Journal* 22 (4): 87–105.

Hahn, H.D. (1993). The political implications of disability definitions and data. *Journal of Disability Policy Studies* 4 (2): 41–52.

Haller, B. (2010). *Representing Disability in an Ableist World: Essays on Mass Media.* Louisville, KY: Advocado Press.

Haller, B. and Zhang, L. (2013). Stigma or empowerment? What do disabled people say about their representation in news and entertainment media? *Review of Disability Studies: An International Journal* 9 (4): 19–33.

Haller, B., Dorries, B., and Rahn, J. (2006). Media labeling versus the US disability community identity: a study of shifting cultural language. *Disability & Society* 21 (1): 61–75.

Harpur, P. (2012). From disability to ability: changing the phrasing of the debate. *Disability & Society* 27 (3): 325–337.

Hebl, M.R. and Kleck, R.E. (2000). The social consequences of physical disability. In: *The Social Psychology of Stigma* (ed. T.F. Heatherton, R.E. Kleck, M.R. Hebl and J.G. Hull), 419–440. New York: Guilford Press.

Herbert, T.B. and Dunkel-Schetter, C. (1992). Negative social reactions to victims: an overview of responses and their determinants. In: *Life Crises and Experiences of Loss in Adulthood* (ed. L. Montada, S.H. Filipp and M.J. Lerner), 497–518. Hillsdale, NJ: Lawrence Erlbaum.

Hirschberger, G. (2006). Terror management and attributions of blame to innocent victims: reconciling compassionate and defensive responses. *Journal of Personality and Social Psychology* 91 (5): 832–844.

Hitselberger, K. (2016). Five questions to stop asking wheelchair users immediately (and what to ask instead). *Huffington Post* (29 October). https://www.huffingtonpost.com/karin-hitselberger/5-questions-to-stop-asking-wheelchair-users-immediately_b_8385954.html (accessed 28 February 2019).

Hubbard, R. (2006). Abortion and disability: who should and who should not inhabit the world. In: *The Disability Studies Reader*, 2e (ed. L.J. Davis), 93–103. New York: Routledge.

Ingstad, B. (2001). Disability in the developing world. In: *Handbook of Disability Studies* (ed. G.L. Albrecht, K.D. Seelman and M. Bury), 772–792. London: Sage.

Jones, C. (2012). Literature review: journalism and disability from a Canadian perspective. *Canadian Journal of Disability Studies* 1 (2): 75–108.

Jones, S. R. (2016). ABA. *Unstrange mind.* http://unstrangemind.com/?s=ABA (accessed 26 February 2019).

Jost, J.T. and Hunyady, O. (2005). Antecedents and consequences of system-justifying ideologies. *Current Directions in Psychological Science* 14 (5): 260–265.

Jost, J.T., Glaser, J., Kruglanski, A.W., and Sulloway, F.J. (2003). Political conservatism as motivated social cognition. *Psychological Bulletin* 129 (3): 339–375.

Kearney, R. (2005). *Strangers, Gods and Monsters: Interpreting Otherness.* New York: Routledge.

Kerr, A. and Shakespeare, T. (2002). *Genetic Politics: From Genetics to Genome.* London: New Clarion Press.

King, B. J. (2016). "Disabled": Just #SayTheWord. NPR. https://www.npr.org/sections/13.7/2016/02/25/468073722/disabled-just-saytheword (accessed 26 February 2019).

de Klerk, V. (2005). Slang and swearing as markers of inclusion and exclusion in adolescence. In: *Talking Adolescence: Perspectives on Communication in the Teenage Years* (ed. A. Williams and C. Thurlow), 111–127. New York: Peter Lang.

Kliewer, C. and Drake, S. (1998). Disability, eugenics, and the current ideology of segregation: a modern moral tale. *Disability & Society* 13 (1): 95–111.

Kliewer, C. and Fitzgerald, L.M. (2001). Disability, schooling, and the artifacts of colonialism. *Teachers College Record* 103 (3): 450–470.

Kteily, N.S., Sidanius, J., and Levin, S. (2011). Social dominance orientation: cause or "mere effect"?: evidence for SDO as a causal predictor of prejudice and discrimination against ethnic and racial outgroups. *Journal of Experimental Social Psychology* 47 (1): 208–214.

Ladau, E. (2015). *Four disability-euphemisms that need to bite the dust.* Center for Disability Rights: http://cdrnys.org/blog/disability-dialogue/the-disability-dialogue-4-disability-euphemisms-that-need-to-bite-the-dust/ (accessed 28 February 2019).

Lambert, A.J., Burroughs, T., and Nguyen, T. (1999). Perceptions of risk and the buffering hypothesis: the role of just world beliefs and right-wing authoritarianism. *Personality and Social Psychology Bulletin* 25 (6): 643–656.

Lerner, M.J. (1980). The belief in a just world. In: *The Belief in a Just World*, 9–30. Boston, MA: Springer.

Levin, S., Sidanius, J., Rabinowitz, J.L., and Federico, C. (1998). Ethnic identity, legitimizing ideologies, and social status: a matter of ideological asymmetry. *Political Psychology* 19 (2): 373–404.

Levy, S.R., West, T., Ramírez, L., and Karafantis, D.M. (2006). The Protestant work ethic: a lay theory with dual intergroup implications. *Group Processes & Intergroup Relations* 9 (1): 95–115.

Linton, S. (1998). *Claiming Disability: Knowledge and Identity.* New York: New York University Press.

Low, C. (2006). Some ideologies of disability. *Journal of Research in Special Educational Needs* 6 (2): 108–111.

Mackelprang, R. and Salsgiver, R. (1999). *Disability: A Diversity Model Approach in Human Service Practice.* New York: Brooks/Cole.

MacMillan, D.L., Gresham, F.M., and Forness, S.R. (1996). Full inclusion: an empirical perspective. *Behavioral Disorders* 21 (2): 145–159.

Mardiros, M. (1989). Conception of childhood disability among Mexican-American parents. *Medical Anthropology* 12 (1): 55–68.

Marks, D. (1999). *Disability: Controversial Debates and Psychosocial Perspectives*. London: Routledge.

Marshak, L.E., Dandeneau, C.J., and Prezant, F.P. (2009). *The School Counselor's Guide to Helping Students with Disabilities*. Hoboken, NJ: Wiley.

McCarthy, H. (2003). The disability rights movement: experiences and perspectives of selected leaders in the disability community. *Rehabilitation Counseling Bulletin* 46 (4): 209–223.

Miller, P.S. and Levine, R.L. (2013). Avoiding genetic genocide: understanding good intentions and eugenics in the complex dialogue between the medical and disability communities. *Genetics in Medicine* 15 (2): 95–102.

Miller, B., Jones, R., and Ellis, N. (1993). Group differences in response to charity images of children with Down syndrome. *Down Syndrome Research and Practice* 1 (3): 118–122.

Miller, P., Parker, S., and Gillinson, S. (2004). *Disablism: How to Tackle the Last Prejudice*. London: Demos.

Miringoff, M.L. (1991). *Social Costs of Genetic Welfare*. New Brunswick, NJ: Rutgers University Press.

Mitchell, M. and Sidanius, J. (1993). Group status and ideological asymmetry: the case of capital punishment, political conservatism and social dominance orientation. *National Journal of Sociology* 7: 67–93.

Molloy, E. and Nario-Redmond, M.R. (2007). College faculty perceptions of learning disabled students: stereotypes, group identity and bias. In: *Disabled Faculty and Staff in a Disabling Society: Multiple Identities in Higher Education* (ed. M. Vance). Huntersville, NC: Association on Higher Education and Disability.

Montada, L. (1998). Justice: just a rational choice. *Social Justice Research* 11 (2): 81–101.

Morris, J. (1991). *Pride Against Prejudice: Transforming Attitudes to Disability*. London: New Society.

Morris, J. (2001). Impairment and disability: constructing an ethics of care that promotes human rights. *Hypatia* 16 (4): 1–16.

Morris, M. (2017). National Disability Institute launches DISABLE POVERTY campaign. *Huffington Post* (6 December). https://www.huffingtonpost.com/michael-morris/national-disability-insti_b_11187834.html (accessed 26 February 2019).

Murphy, J.S. (1995). *The Constructed Body: AIDS, Reproductive Technology and Ethics*. Albany, NY: State University of New York Press.

Nario-Redmond, M.R. (2010). Cultural stereotypes of disabled and non-disabled men and women: consensus for global category representations and diagnostic domains. *British Journal of Social Psychology* 49 (3): 471–488.

Nario-Redmond, M.R. and Oleson, K.C. (2016). Disability group identification and disability-rights advocacy: contingencies among emerging and other adults. *Emerging Adulthood* 4 (3): 207–218.

National Council on Disability. (2015). NCD response to controversial Peter Singer interview advocating the killing of disabled infants: "Professor, Do Your Homework." https://ncd.gov/newsroom/04232015 (accessed 26 February 2019).

Nina G. (2014). How many disabled people does it take to screw in a lightbulb? https://www.youtube.com/watch?v=zak5Aq1m_xg (accessed 26 February 2019).

Obasogie, O. K. (2013). Commentary: The eugenics legacy of the nobelist who fathered IVF. *Scientific American* (4 October). https://www.scientificamerican.com/article/eugenic-legacy-nobel-ivf (accessed 26 February 2019).

Oliver, M. (1996). *Understanding Disability: From Theory to Practice*. New York: St. Martin's Press.

Oliver, M. and Barnes, C. (1998). *Disabled People and Social Policy: From Exclusion to Inclusion*. Boston, MA: Addison Wesley Longman.

Olkin, R. (1999). *What Psychotherapists Should Know About Disability*. New York: Guilford Press.

Parens, E. and Asch, A. (eds.) (2000). *Prenatal Testing and Disability Rights*. Washington, DC: Georgetown University Press.

Perry, D. (2016). "Amoris Laetitia" reflects narrow view of disabled persons. *Crux* (12 April). https://cruxnow.com/church/2016/04/12/amoris-laetitia-reflects-narrow-view-of-disabled-persons (accessed 26 February 2019).

Pfeiffer, D. (1994). Eugenics and disability discrimination. *Disability & Society* 9 (4): 481–499.

Pfeiffer, D. (2001). The conceptualization of disability. In: *Exploring Theories and Expanding Methodologies: Where We Are and Where We Need to Go* (ed. S.N. Barnartt and B.M. Altman), 29–52. Bingley: Emerald Group Publishing Limited.

Phelan, J.C., Link, B.G., and Dovidio, J.F. (2008). Stigma and prejudice: one animal or two? *Social Science & Medicine* 67 (3): 358–367.

Phillips, V. and Stegman, E. (2014). *Missing the Point: The Real Impact of Native Mascots and Team Names on American Indian and Alaska Native Youth*. Center for American Progress https://digitalcommons.wcl.american.edu/cgi/viewcontent.cgi?article=1003&context=fasch_rpt (accessed 26 February 2019).

Plant, E.A. and Devine, P.G. (1998). Internal and external motivation to respond without prejudice. *Journal of Personality and Social Psychology* 75 (3): 811–832.

Pratto, F., Sidanius, J., Stallworth, L.M., and Malle, B.F. (1994). Social dominance orientation: a personality variable predicting social and political attitudes. *Journal of Personality and Social Psychology* 67 (4): 741–763.

Robbennolt, J.K. (2000). Outcome severity and judgments of "responsibility": a meta-analytic review. *Journal of Applied Social Psychology* 30 (12): 2575–2609.

Rosenthal, L., Levy, S.R., and Moyer, A. (2011). Protestant work ethic's relation to intergroup and policy attitudes: a meta-analytic review. *European Journal of Social Psychology* 41 (7): 874–885.

R-Word: Spread the Word to End the Word. (2017). https://www.r-word.org (accessed 26 February 2019).

Saetermoe, C.L., Scattone, D., and Kim, K.H. (2001). Ethnicity and the stigma of disabilities. *Psychology & Health* 16 (6): 699–713.

Salvador-Carulla, L. and Bertelli, M. (2008). "Mental retardation" or "intellectual disability": time for a conceptual change. *Psychopathology* 41 (1): 10–16.

Schaller, M. and Conway, L.G. III (2001). From cognition to culture: the origins of stereotypes that really matter. In: *Cognitive Social Psychology: The Princeton Symposium on the Legacy and Future of Social Cognition* (ed. G.B. Moskowitz), 163–176. Mahwah, NJ: Lawrence Erlbaum.

Schalock, R.L., Luckasson, R.A., and Shogren, K.A. (2007). The renaming of mental retardation: understanding the change to the term intellectual disability. *Intellectual and Developmental Disabilities* 45 (2): 116–124.

Scheer, J. and Groce, N. (1988). Impairment as a human constant: cross-cultural and historical perspectives on variation. *Journal of Social Issues* 44 (1): 23–37.

Schopler, E. (ed.) (1995). *Parent Survival Manual: A Guide to Crisis Resolution in Autism and Related Developmental Disorders*. New York: Plenum Press.

Scotch, R.K. (2000). Models of disability and the Americans with Disabilities Act. *Berkeley Journal of Employment and Labor Law* 21 (1): 213–222.

Shapiro, J.P. (1993). *No Pity*. New York: Times Books.

Shapiro, J.P. (2011). *No Pity: People with Disabilities Forging a New Civil Rights Movement*. New York: Broadway Books.

Sherif, C.W. and Sherif, M. (eds.) (1967). *Attitude, Ego-involvement, and Change*. Hoboken, NJ: Wiley.

Sherry, M. (2016). *Disability Hate Crimes: Does Anyone Really Hate Disabled People?* New York: Routledge.

Sibley, C.G., Wilson, M., and Duckitt, J. (2007). Antecedents of men's hostile and benevolent sexism: the dual roles of social dominance orientation and right-wing authoritarianism. *Personality and Social Psychology Bulletin* 33 (2): 160–172.

Sidanius, J. and Pratto, F. (1999). *Social Dominance: An Intergroup Theory of Social Hierarchy and Oppression*. New York: Cambridge University Press.

Sidanius, J., Liu, J.H., Shaw, J.S., and Pratto, F. (1994). Social dominance orientation, hierarchy attenuators and hierarchy enhancers: social dominance theory and the criminal justice system. *Journal of Applied Social Psychology* 24 (4): 338–366.

Sidanius, J., Levin, S., Federico, C.M., and Pratto, F. (2001). Legitimizing ideologies: the social dominance approach. In: *The Psychology of Legitimacy: Emerging Perspectives on Ideology, Justice, and Intergroup Relations* (ed. J.T. Jost and B. Major), 307–331. New York: Cambridge University Press.

Sidanius, J., Mitchell, M., Haley, H., and Navarrete, C.D. (2006). Support for harsh criminal sanctions and criminal justice beliefs: a social dominance perspective. *Social Justice Research* 19 (4): 433–449.

Simon, L. and Greenberg, J. (1996). Further progress in understanding the effects of derogatory ethnic labels: the role of preexisting attitudes toward the targeted group. *Personality and Social Psychology Bulletin* 22 (12): 1195–1204.

Sinason, V. (1992). *Mental Handicap and the Human Condition*, vol. 38. London: Free Association Books.

Singer, P. (1993). *Practical Ethics*, 2e. New York: Cambridge University Press.

Siperstein, G.N., Pociask, S.E., and Collins, M.A. (2010). Sticks, stones, and stigma: a study of students' use of the derogatory term "retard". *Intellectual and Developmental Disabilities* 48 (2): 126–134.

Skitka, L.J. (1999). Ideological and attributional boundaries on public compassion: reactions to individuals and communities affected by a natural disaster. *Personality and Social Psychology Bulletin* 25 (7): 793–808.

Skitka, L.J. and Tetlock, P.E. (1993). Providing public assistance: cognitive and motivational processes underlying liberal and conservative policy preferences. *Journal of Personality and Social Psychology* 65 (6): 1205–1223.

Slorach, R. (2011). Marxism and disability. *International Socialism* 129: 111–136.

Smart, J.F. (2009). The power of models of disability. *Journal of Rehabilitation* 75 (2): 3–11.

Snyder, S.L. and Mitchell, D.T. (Dirs.) (1996). *Vital Signs: Crip Culture Talks Back*. Boston, MA: Fanlight Distributors.

Starke, M. (2011). Supporting families with parents with intellectual disability: views and experiences of professionals in the field. *Journal of Policy and Practice in Intellectual Disabilities* 8 (3): 163–171.

Struckman-Johnson, C. and Struckman-Johnson, D. (1992). Acceptance of male rape myths among college men and women. *Sex Roles* 27 (3–4): 85–100.

Stucke, M.E. (2008). Better competition advocacy. *St. John's Law Review* 82 (3): 951–1036.

Teachman, B.A., Gapinski, K.D., Brownell, K.D. et al. (2003). Demonstrations of implicit anti-fat bias: the impact of providing causal information and evoking empathy. *Health Psychology* 22 (1): 68–78.

Thurlow, C. (2001). Naming the "outsider within": homophobic pejoratives and the verbal abuse of lesbian, gay and bisexual high-school pupils. *Journal of Adolescence* 24 (1): 25–38.

Vade, D. and Solovay, S. (2009). No apology. In: *The Fat Studies Reader* (ed. E. Rothblum and S. Solovay), 167–175. New York: New York University Press.

Weiner, B., Perry, R.P., and Magnusson, J. (1988). An attributional analysis of reactions to stigmas. *Journal of Personality and Social Psychology* 55 (5): 738–748.

Wolanin, T.R. and Steele, P.E. (2004). *Higher Education Opportunities for Students with Disabilities: A Primer for Policymakers*. Washington, DC: Institute for Higher Education Policy. https://files.eric.ed.gov/fulltext/ED485430.pdf (accessed 26 February 2019).

Wolbring, G. (2003). Disability rights approach toward bioethics? *Journal of Disability Policy Studies* 14 (3): 174–180.

Wolbring, G. (2012). Expanding ableism: taking down the ghettoization of impact of disability studies scholars. *Societies* 2 (3): 75–83.

Young, L.B. (2011). Joe Sixpack: normality, deviance, and the disease model of alcoholism. *Culture & Psychology* 17 (3): 378–397.

Young, S. (2016). I'm not your inspiration. Thank you very much. TED talk by disabled activist, comedian, and journalist on the topic of inspiration porn. https://www.ted.com/talks/stella_young_i_m_not_your_inspiration_thank_you_very_much (accessed 26 February 2019).

Zola, I.K. (1991). Bringing our bodies and ourselves back in: reflections on a past, present, and future medical sociology. *Journal of Health and Social Behavior* 32 (1): 1–16.

Talk About Disability Identity

What is the difference between saying a "disabled person" or a "person with a disability"? The first example, "disabled person," is described as identity-first language. "Person with a disability" is an example of person-first language. People have different identity preferences, but increasingly, many disabled people argue that identity-first language is most appropriate in writing.

 Lawrence Carter-Long @LCarterLong · Jul 19
Preferences (& reasons for 'em) are important to discuss. Whether person-first or prefix first 'tis most important to #SayTheWord #DISABLED
twitter.com/GaelynnLea/sta...

Lawrence Carter-Long is a disability rights activist who started the #SayTheWord campaign.

https://disabledspectator.com/saytheword-power-language-disability/
https://twitter.com/hashtag/saytheword?lang=en

Carter-Long says:
"If you 'see the person not the disability' you're only getting half the picture. Broaden your perspective. You might be surprised by everything you've missed. DISABLED. **#SayTheWord**"

"To suggest disability is simply a 'difference' and has no impact on a person's life is a very privileged position to take." Amy Sequenzia, a non-speaking multiply-disabled activist and writer who blogs about neurodiversity says, "Use Identity First Language for the things you consider positive. Disability, to you, is negative. This is ableism."

https://ollibean.com/autistic-autism/

She gives the example, you don't say "Amy is a person with awesomeness," you say "Amy is awesome." This photo says: My name is Amy, I am a writer, a poet, an activist, a self-advocate. I am HAPPY, I am PROUD. I am AUTISTIC.

https://psychologybenefits.
org/2015/07/28/parental-
rights-include-disability-equality/

Adaptive Parenting

https://www.disabledparenting.com

Time and time again disability communities prove that they should not be under-estimated. They are creative and capable, resisting myths and fighting for the right to parent. Dr. Alette Coble-Temple started P.R.I.D.E. (Parental Rights Include Disability Equality) to raise awareness about parents with disabilities. The disabled parenting project also provides a forum for parents who experience disability to share their stories, and find adaptive products.

http://disabledparent.com/pedialift-crib/

This image shows the PediaLift Crib, which opens from the side to support parents who need alternative access to manage baby care, like the woman shown lifting her infant from the side of the crib.

The image above shows the Balance Buddy Bike Handle, which shows how a parent can use the handle to guide a child on their bike without having to bend over.

Recognize Ableism in Pop Culture Portrayals

1. Notice how often people with disabilities are *not* represented in movies, TV shows, and news.
2. Critically analyze portrayals of disability in both fictional and nonfictional outlets:
   - Is the story presenting disabled lives as tragic?
   - Is the disability shown as something to be overcome or solved rather than accommodated and accepted?
   - Consider why misrepresentations are problematic.
3. Send feedback or comment on any biased language used:
   - Phrases like "suffers from" and "wheelchair bound" both have negative connotations.
   - Share tips for effective media and advocacy writing. Tips on euphemisms to avoid by Emily Ladau (2015), and tips on asking questions by Karin Hitselberger (2016).
   - Confront people who use offensive terms: "What did you say?" "Why would you say that when so many people find that expression hurtful?"

Resources for evaluating disability portrayals in journalism and children's literature:

http://ncdj.org/

http://disabilityinkidlit.com/

The National Center for Disability and Journalism offers a variety of resources, including a list of terms to use and avoid when writing or talking about disability, and links to promoting accurate disability news articles. Disability in Kidlit is a blog where kids with disabilities review books about disability.

Lives Worth Living

Not Dead Yet is an advocacy group that protests assisted suicide and euthanasia, combating the myth that disabled lives are not worth living. They have groups all over the world.

http://notdeadyet.org/

Below are photos from a demonstration in March 2017 by Not Dead Yet UK protesting an assisted suicide bill. The empty wheelchairs signify what happens when people are not given access to better care. The signs on the chairs say "I was coerced," "I had no support," "I wasn't valued," and "I will be next."

The cartoon below illustrates the message to disabled people with the passing of an assisted suicide bill. It shows a power chair user between an inaccessible stair-

case with a sign reading "Suicide Prevention Program" and a ramp with a sign reading "Assisted Suicide."

http://alexschadenberg.blogspot.
com/2015/02/assisted-suicide-is-dis-
criminatory.html

4

Cultural and Impairment-Specific Stereotypes

Most people seem reluctant to talk of group stereotypes as if acknowledging them admits to some mistaken understanding about their own system of beliefs. In fact, college students enrolled in first year sociology and psychology courses have been heard gasping at the introduction of the term "stereotype" as part of the curriculum – as if to say, "Oh no, those are just wrong – why would we want to learn how to stereotype, professor?" However, stereotypes serve many useful purposes. They help *explain* social roles like which gender is best suited to take care of children – the one stereotyped as more sensitive and nurturing, of course. Stereotypes help *simplify* complex social information and help make sense of confusing interactions (e.g. "oh, he's autistic; that must explain the constant rocking"). Stereotypes are also used to *predict* what to expect from individuals and groups, as in, "what are Vegans most likely to say?" As described in Chapter 3, stereotypes can also be used to *justify* inequalities, *prescribe* who is eligible for certain roles, and perpetuate the status quo.

Simply defined, a stereotype is a set of attributes used to characterize a group and its members (Ashmore and Del Boca 1981). Although faulty and incomplete, stereotypes are not always negative. Some are quite positive and many are ambivalent – a blend of both positive and negative beliefs. For example, men are often stereotyped as breadwinners, strong but insensitive, whereas women are stereotyped as nurturing, weak but sensitive (Nario-Redmond 2010) – consistent with traditional gender roles (Eagly 1987). In this way, stereotypes also *differentiate* between groups, and they serve other psychological functions as well. Stereotypes allow people to go beyond what they observe to predict how others (including themselves) are likely to behave. If teachers expect students with disabilities to join their classes, they may anticipate accommodating their "special needs," and try to help them "overcome" presumed dependence.

This chapter focuses on disability stereotypes as one of the more proximal[1] causes of prejudice: the group-specific beliefs that provoke and maintain ableist

Ableism: The Causes and Consequences of Disability Prejudice, First Edition.
Michelle R. Nario-Redmond.
© 2020 John Wiley & Sons, Inc. Published 2020 by John Wiley & Sons, Inc.

judgments and other forms of differential treatment. Distinguishing between stereotypes that are culturally shared and individually endorsed, impairment-specific or cross-impairment, this chapter emphasizes how disability stereotypes are distinct from broader concepts of stigma and ideological beliefs. Contemporary research supporting when stereotypes are most likely to exert their influence on judgments and behavior is also reviewed, in addition to studies on the purposes stereotypes serve in maintaining status differences. Finally, new directions on the shifting nature of disability stereotypes, how they are communicated, and suggestions for stereotype change will also be described.

Two distinctions are worth mentioning early. First, some stereotypes describe beliefs about specific impairment groups like those used to characterize "the blind," "the deaf," and "autistic people." Other stereotypes are applied to disabled people in general, regardless of impairment type. These are often referred to as global or cross-impairment stereotypes. In addition to level of analysis, a second distinction relates to how much agreement or consensus there is about the *contents* of a stereotype within the culture or society. Cultural stereotypes are more widely recognized understandings about how different groups are represented; however, this doesn't mean that individuals all personally endorse these stereotypes as truthful. People vary in how much they personally accept stereotypic beliefs – whether these beliefs are about specific disabilities or about disability in general. For example, people may hold personal beliefs about social groups that they do consider to be true: beliefs that some racial groups are inherently more athletic than others or that jocks aren't as smart as nerds. Others recognize that such simplistic overgeneralizations hide the fact that differences within groups are greater than the differences between them (Tajfel and Turner 1979). Yet, even when people dispute the validity of others' stereotypic beliefs, they may still be familiar with the contents of those beliefs (e.g. blondes are stereotyped as dumb; lawyers as manipulative; gay men as effeminate, etc.). It bears repeating: whether people believe a stereotype is true or not, as part of the knowledge base, stereotypes can still automatically influence what is noticed and ignored about others, resulting in biased impressions, emotions, and behaviors (Fiske and Neuberg 1990).

Impairment-Specific Stereotypes

In contrast to disability as a global categorization, most psychological research on disability stereotypes has focused on impairment-related stigmas – physical or mental attributes that spoil identity (Goffman 1963). A construct that is both negative and idiosyncratic, disability *stigma* typically comes in two varieties: the more visible "abominations of the body" and the "blemishes of character." Chapter 5 reviews research on stigma and attitudinal constructs – both of which invoke an evaluative component as disability prejudice frequently involves emotional reactions like fear, anxiety, and pity. The present chapter focuses more on the content and judgment implications of group-specific beliefs – those associated with disability overall, and with particular impairment classifications such as blindness, deafness, learning, physical, and psychiatric conditions. A summary of this work reveals a few distinctions between the characteristics associated with different impairment groups, and some intriguing commonalities as well. In fact, the majority of studies have focused on *physical* impairments (e.g. paralysis, wheelchair users), which some have speculated to be the default or prototypical idea evoked from the category of disability in general (Ben-Moshe and Powell 2007; McCaughey and Strohmer 2005).

Physical Impairments

According to a recent summary of the literature on physical impairment stereotypes, 10 characteristics are most prominently associated with physically disabled people as a group. They are stereotyped as isolated, lonely, dependent or helpless, asexual, unemployable, entitled, unattractive, weak, passive, and incompetent (Stern et al. 2010). For example, using a checklist of 85 positive and 85 negative adjectives,[2] Fichten and Amsel (1986) found that the top seven stereotypes most commonly held about physically disabled people described them as isolated, lonely, helpless, silent, depressed, unpopular, and quiet. Furthermore, this study demonstrated how groups are often defined in opposition to one another: physically disabled people were stereotyped as submissive, unassuming, and introverted while able-bodied people were stereotyped as dominant, arrogant, and extraverted. In another study, using multiple pairs of bipolar adjectives (e.g. strong – weak) to capture stereotypic impressions, wheelchair-using job applicants were considered more dependent, passive, weak, cowardly, subdued, and self-pitying than able-bodied applicants, who were judged more well-adjusted, both socially and psychologically (Gething 1992).

Sensory Impairments

Other studies using bipolar adjective ratings have compared stereotypes about physical impairment to those associated with speech and sensory conditions (e.g. vision or hearing impairments). For example, Stern et al. (2010) found that compared to no disability, those pictured with a physical disability (wheelchair user) or a speech impairment (text-to-speech keyboard user) were both stereotyped as isolated, dependent, unemployable, unattractive, and entitled; however, unemployable and unattractive stereotypes were more prominent for physical disability whereas dependent, entitled, and isolated stereotypes were more prominent for speech impairment. Therefore, some evidence supports distinctions between the stereotypes used to characterize particular impairments.

Using an open-ended format, Kiger (1997) found the most common stereotypes linked to "typical members" of the deaf community characterized them as happy, alone, angry, and friendly – reflecting both positive and negative beliefs. Similarly, stereotypes about blind people have also included uniquely positive features including docility and mystical visionary powers that seem to differentiate this group from other impairment categories (Gowman 1957). For example, in one study, 75% of students agreed with the statement: People with visual impairments can hear and feel things that no one else can; they seem to have a "sixth sense" (Patterson and Witten 1987). Most research on the stereotypes of blind people contrast their assumed incapacities with super-human powers in other senses (Courington et al. 1983; Marsh and Friedman 1972).

In a study comparing blind to deaf stereotypes using a list of 31 adjectives, only 10 distinguished between these two social groups (Cambra 1996). Blind people were characterized as needing more assistance but as more hard-working and attentive than deaf people. By contrast, deaf people were stereotyped as more reserved, solitary but quicker, more impulsive, unsure, nervous, and imprudent. However, in comparison to people without sensory impairments – blind and deaf stereotypes were substantially similar. Both groups were equally characterized as more dependent, passive, boring, unpleasant, and rude compared to people without a disability. Furthermore, comparisons between visually and physically disabled groups revealed no differences on traits related to dependence, unhappiness, insecurity, or honesty (Fichten et al. 1989).

Learning, Developmental, and Intellectual Impairments

Most stereotypes about those with developmental or learning disabilities (LDs) have focused on negative cognitive characteristics, including incompetence, lower intelligence, laziness, lack of motivation, and poor social skills (Riddick 1995). For example, undergraduates consider LD students to be less desirable (Bryan and Perlmutter 1979), less adaptable, and more hostile (Bryan et al. 1982) than peers without LDs. Teachers have harbored similar stereotypic beliefs, characterizing LD students as angry, hostile, and hyperactive but less responsible, less socially acceptable, and less able to cope with new situations than typical peers (Algozzine 1979). In another study, both students and teachers similarly stereotyped LD students as dumb, lazy, spoiled, and less intelligent (Shapiro and Margolis 1988).

Fewer studies have systematically investigated the content of stereotypes about people with intellectual disabilities (IDs) (Werner and Roth 2014). Some find this group can be characterized as aggressive, threatening, and violent (Slevin and Sines 1996; van Alphen et al. 2012). Others have documented stereotypes related to their unemployment (Shaw et al. 2004). However, typically, people with ID are portrayed as happy and loving, dependent, and eternally childlike (Gilmore et al. 2003; McCaughey and Strohmer 2005). Stereotypes of permanent immaturity have also been linked to assumptions that people with IDs are incapable of raising dependent children (Hayman 1990;

McConnell and Llewellyn 2002). Furthermore, studies on the stereotypes associated with "mental retardation" consistently rate this group low in competence but high in warmth (Cuddy et al. 2008) – similar to those with Alzheimer's disease (Sadler et al. 2012). The co-existence of these two dimensions – warmth and incompetence – as part of the same ambivalent stereotype will be discussed more fully in the sections on stereotype change, and again in Chapter 5 on the factors predicting ambivalent attitudes.

Research on autism stereotypes is even less extensive, but common stereotypic themes include: a lack of empathy and social skills, restricted or "machine-like" emotions, learning difficulties alongside savant capabilities, and violent tendencies (e.g. Yergeau 2009). Currently, autism spectrum "disorders" are classified among the psychiatric conditions listed in the Diagnostic and Statistical Manual (DSM-5) of "mental illnesses." A recent study found that international media portrayals of autistic characters on television and film largely coincided with the DSM-5 criteria (Nordahl-Hansen et al. 2018) – criteria which have come under much scrutiny by autistic advocates.

> It's as though we're labeling some autistics as gaming PCs with a few missing processor chips, and we're labeling other autistics as ribbonless, keyless, cordless typewriters circa 1883. [High Functioning Autism] HFA and [Low Functioning Autism] LFA are attempts to technologize autism – and not positively, either. This machine metaphor is horrid and inaccurate, and it perpetuates division upon division, stereotype upon stereotype. (Yergeau 2009)

Psychiatric Conditions

More studies have been conducted on the broader category of "mental illness" stereotypes, which corroborate the pervasiveness of beliefs associating this group with dangerousness, (Martin et al. 2000; Phelan et al. 2000), unpredictability, and immorality (Angermeyer et al. 2003; Read and Harre 2001). In open-ended assessments, violence emerges as a centrally defining characteristic of the category "mental disorders" (Phelan et al. 1997) – a perception that has increased over time. Nationally representative surveys have found that people were more than twice as likely to link mental illness with violent psychosis in 1996 than they were in 1950 (Phelan et al. 2000).

Recent evidence further differentiates between the stereotypes associated with psychiatric disabilities where people with schizophrenia are assumed to be more dependent than those with major depression (Angermeyer and Matschinger 2003), who, in turn, are stereotyped as less competent than those with anorexia or bulimia (Roehrig and McLean, 2010). Sadler et al. (2012) found that while several psychiatric conditions were stereotyped as incompetent, only those with sociopathy, schizophrenia, and multiple personality disorder were stereotyped as cold and unfriendly compared to those with depression and anxiety, who scored in the midrange on both competence and warmth.

Impairment Group Comparisons

In summary, while review studies are rare, certain commonalities are clearly shared across physical, sensory, and cognitive disabilities where expectations of dependence, incompetence, and unemployment frequently recur. Other studies have failed to find *any* differences between impairment groups (e.g. Abrams et al. 1990; Fiske et al. 2002). Nevertheless, social scientists have been reluctant to view disabled people as a minority group bound together by common experiences with discrimination, restricted roles, and marginalized status (Linton 1998). To illustrate, in the 2011 edited volume on disability and discrimination, Selmi argued:

> It is impossible to talk with any meaning about the stigma of disability but instead we need to consider what I refer to as the stigma of disabilities. A point that has been made many times bears repeating – disability is a heterogeneous condition that lacks a unifying theme and which makes the concept of disability quite different from other antidiscrimination categories. (p. 125)

In fact, most of the psychological research to date has ignored the consensually shared aspects of disability as a social category in favor of a more differentiated approach to studying disability prejudice and its potential solutions (Gervais 2011). If there were consensually shared ideas or cultural stereotypes about disabled people, they should be an inescapable part of the cultural landscape – familiar to those who experience disability and those who do not.

The Origins of Cultural Stereotypes About Disability

Cultural stereotypes are simply the community-wide beliefs about different groups of people learned as part of the socialization process among people living in the same culture (Ashmore and Del Boca 1981). They are communicated through books, television, and interpersonal conversations, often becoming engrained in memory (Schneider 2004). Consider children's animated cartoons and movies. Through the years, several have represented disabled people as tragic but heroic victims (e.g. Quasimodo as the Hunchback of Notre Dame, Nemo), angry villains (e.g. Captain Hook, Elmer Fudd), and incompetent dupes (e.g. Mr. Magoo, Dopey from *Snow White*); for reviews see Cheu (2013) and Kirkpatrick (2009). Such portrayals instill and perpetuate cultural stereotypes, especially when they systematically associate only certain traits with the group – such as helplessness, dependence, and asexuality – while failing to link disability to other characteristics – such as parenthood, independence, and competence. Among the most common portrayals in film, television (Wolfson and Norden 2000), and the news media (Haller 2000), disabled people are represented as courageous heroes, evil avengers, or tragic victims. Even in radio broadcasts, disabled people recognize their group to be represented as helpless, sexless, bitter, but brave (Ross 2001).

To date, however, there have been very few studies examining the consensually shared contents of global disability stereotypes as distinct from stigma-specific, personal beliefs and other forms of disability prejudice (Gervais 2011). Just 15 years ago, researchers in social psychology considered cultural stereotypes about disability unlikely given the diversity of impairments that seem to resist unified classification (Biernat and Dovidio 2000). Stereotypes are more likely to develop for visibly identifiable social categories, and those that seem stable or unchanging, such as race and gender (Yzerbyt et al. 1997). Yet, disability has long been considered a master status (Frable et al. 1990), a superordinate attribute (Rohmer and Louvet 2009), regardless of the fluid and temporary nature of some impairments. These seemingly "essential" or "natural" categories encourage people to draw inferences about a broad range of attributes thought to derive from group membership.

Several studies have found that disability is also considered an essential element of the person, a relatively uncontrollable and immutable fate (Yuker 1988). Related to these notions, early attribution theorists documented the phenomena of "spread" whereby disability serves as a primary cue used to infer information about a person (Wright 1983). Specifically, assumptions about disability *spread* to all aspects of a person's identity, and are used to explain personality, motives, and behaviors. "Why does he appear shy? It must have something to do with his disability?" "Why did she choose that major? It must be related to her disability." This kind of categorical processing may account for what Gowman (1957) described as the "gestalt of disability, so that the individual shouts at the blind as if they were deaf or attempts to lift them as if they were crippled" (p. 198). These experiences are not exclusive to the blind community, but are consistently reported from people with cognitive and physical impairments as well (Sutherland 1981).

> If a person with a disability has a problem with employment, it is almost always the result of the disability. (Patterson and Witten 1987, p. 43)

Stereotypes are also more likely to develop for groups found disproportionately in certain societal roles, as is the case with men and women. Furthermore, when certain group memberships overlap (e.g. women, wives, mothers), stereotypic beliefs often confuse group status with role expectations (Eagly 1987). Consistent with this theorizing, disability stereotypes often reflect overgeneralized assumptions about "the essential" characteristics that define disabled men and women. Throughout history, disabled people have been assigned to particular social roles (e.g. sick patient, unemployed beggar) and excluded from others (e.g. parent, partner, executive) (Asch et al. 2001). Therefore, both theoretical and empirical research suggest that global and undifferentiated disability representations may operate in ways that predict category-based responding.

Preliminary Evidence for Global Disability Stereotypes

Of the few studies suggestive of consensually held global stereotypes about disabled people, most have used a comparative approach to examine impairment-specific beliefs about those with paralysis or blindness, as described in the previous section. However, these between-group comparisons reveal several commonalities suggestive of a global disability stereotype. Weinberg (1976) found that those with sensory and physical disabilities were similarly characterized as less intelligent, more courageous, and less aggressive than the average able-bodied person. On 27 of the 29 traits evaluated, no differences were found between ratings of blind, deaf, or wheelchair-using targets – supporting the notion of a generalized stereotype. Other studies have found that school-aged children failed to differentiate between people labeled as physically or mentally "handicapped," and considered both to be equally friendly, stupid, speech impaired, and to have trouble walking (Abrams et al. 1990). Prior to students' participation in an integrated educational program, Maras and Brown (1996) found no differences in the running, hearing, or thinking abilities ascribed to those identified as hearing-impaired, physically disabled, or learning disabled. Additionally, by the end of the program, nondisabled students had improved attitudes that *generalized* across impairment groups – even though their interactions were limited to peers with learning disabilities. Finally, students continued to use disability as an umbrella category to organize these groups. More recently, Fiske et al. (2002) found that blind, disabled, elderly, and "retarded" people were all conceptualized similarly as having lower competence but higher warmth compared to other nondisabled groups.

All of these studies support the hypothesis that an overarching cross-impairment stereotype may be associated with disabled people as a social group, especially when classified in terms of some normal–abnormal binary that positions disabled people as interchangeable category members. The empirical evidence corroborates what disability studies scholars and personal accounts have argued for a long time: disabled people are stereotyped in pervasive and consistent ways:

> We are held to be visually repulsive; helpless; pathetic; dependent; too independent; plucky, brave and courageous; bitter, with chips on our shoulders; evil (the twisted mind in a twisted body); mentally retarded ... and much else. (Sutherland 1981, p. 58)

Evidence for Cross-Impairment/Global Disability Stereotypes

In 2010, a team of student researchers with disabilities in my lab were among the first to quantify the global, cultural stereotypes of disabled men and women in terms of their consensually shared dimensions, using participants with and without disabilities (Nario-Redmond 2010). Approximately 100 college undergraduates and community participants were recruited though disability service offices, independent living centers, and national disability organizations. The first part of the study used an open-ended format to capture the spontaneous thoughts generated when people are simply asked to think about the characteristics of a group. Specifically, participants were asked to think about the "traits, dispositions, or other descriptive features considered by society to be stereotypical" of each of four target groups: disabled men (DM), disabled women (DW), nondisabled men (NM), and nondisabled women (NW). Everyone had a chance to provide responses about all four groups, presented one at a time in random order. It was emphasized that the research was aimed only at their awareness of the stereotypical characteristics assumed to represent these groups, and not whether they believed these to be true.

Following an established methodology (Nieman et al. 1994), open-ended responses were limited to five numbered lines per page for each of the four target groups. This produced 1679 free responses which were organized into themes without reference to target sex or disability status. After extensive review, 50 mutually exclusive themes were identified to represent the universe of culturally stereotypic responses. Some themes focused on dispositional traits (e.g. nurturing, ambitious, passive), others on states (e.g. independent, incompetent, active), societal roles (hero, homeless, married), and appearance cues (attractive, feminine, sexual). Separate themes were generated for positive and negative domains (e.g. independence and dependence, competence and incompetence, weakness and strength). Two independent judges coded each of the 1679 responses into one of the 50 empirically derived themes, without knowing which groups were described. To illustrate, free responses that related to motherhood, caregiving, and parenting skills were all coded as instances of the "nurturing" theme while responses related to bravery, inspiration, and overcoming hardships were coded as instances of the "heroic-survivor" theme. Interrater agreement was 76%, and discrepancies were resolved through a team-wide discussion.

Comparing Stereotypes About Disabled Men and Disabled Women

Table 4.1 shows the 10 most frequently generated cultural stereotypes for the four groups (reprinted from Nario-Redmond 2010). The top three stereotypes associated with both DM and DW described them as similarly dependent, incompetent, and asexual. Both DM and DW were also equally stereotyped as unattractive and weak, passive and heroic. That is, 7 of the top 10 stereotypes used to describe DM were the same ones used to describe DW – revealing substantial agreement about the traits that characterized disabled people – regardless of gender or assumed impairment. The fact that participants came up with so many of the same open-ended descriptions for both DM and DW provides evidence that this knowledge is widely shared – part of a collective consciousness stored in memory.

Table 4.1 Frequencies and percentages of the top 10 themes used for each target group.

Target group and theme	Total uses	Uses per group	% of theme attributed to group	Target group and theme	Total uses	Uses per group	% of theme attributed to group
Disabled men				Disabled women			
Dependent	147	56	38.10	Dependent	147	78	53.06
Incompetent$_a$	93	32	34.41	Incompetent$_a$	93	31	33.33
Asexual$_b$	61	30	49.18	Asexual$_b$	61	29	47.54
Angry	42	29	69.05	Unattractive$_f$	48	28	58.33
Heroic survivor$_c$	44	23	52.27	Weak$_d$	61	23	37.70
Weak$_d$	61	19	31.15	Passive$_e$	56	21	37.50
Inferior	31	19	61.29	Societally excluded	29	16	55.17
Passive$_e$	56	18	32.14	Heroic survivor$_c$	44	15	34.09
Unattractive$_f$	48	18	37.50	Vulnerable	18	14	77.78
Lazy	30	17	56.67	Poor homeless	25	13	52.00
Nondisabled men				Nondisabled women			
Ambitious	87	48	55.17	Nurturing	63	53	84.13
Strong	50	44	88.00	Sensitive	71	40	56.34
Domineering	63	34	53.97	Attractive	39	32	82.05
Employed	43	33	76.74	Emotional	47	29	61.70
Independent$_g$	59	32	54.24	Ambitious	87	25	28.74
Active	49	32	65.31	Independent$_g$	59	23	38.98
Macho	29	28	96.55	Incompetent$_a$	93	23	24.73
Insensitive	41	28	68.29	Weak$_d$	61	19	31.15
Competent	44	27	61.36	Domineering	63	18	28.57
Aggressive	30	26	86.67	Feminine	17	17	100.00

Note. Frequency attributions sharing a common subscript are not significantly different at the $p < 0.05$ level.

Comparing Stereotypes About Nondisabled Men and Nondisabled Women

Interestingly, the stereotypes of the two nondisabled genders were much less overlapping than their disabled counterparts – only 3 of the top 10 were shared. Both NM and NW were stereotyped as ambitious, independent, and domineering. However, NM were more often characterized as physically strong, macho, and employed, while NW had the corner on nurturance, femininity, and attractiveness (see also Hanna and Rogovsky, 1993). Consistent with early scientific discourses that cast savage societies, Africans, and homosexuals as primitive, inferior, and undifferentiated by gender – we only observed gender-specific stereotypes to characterize the nondisabled targets. Perhaps gender stereotypes continue to serve as signifiers of a more "civilized" status reserved for the "normative" class (Somerville 1994; White 2001). According to Shields (1982), male–female role differences reflect a discourse about evolutionary progress that positions sexual inequality as a hallmark of *civilization*, where women are assigned to the "special" sphere of nurturance labor. In our study, the absence of gender differentiation is consistent with the historic portrayal of other marginalized groups as "animalistic throwbacks" (Somerville 1994), and the widespread assumption that disabled people are somehow less-than-human perversions of the human form (Morris 1991).

Disability Stereotypes as Diagnostic Tools

Because cultural stereotypes function in part to help people distinguish between social groups (McCauley and Stitt 1978), we also examined which stereotypes emerged as most diagnostic or *defining* of disability and gender groups uniquely. We found the most commonly generated stereotype overall had to do with dependence – 91% of the time participants mentioned dependency, they did so to stereotype DW, who were characterized as dependent even more often than DM. The remaining uses of dependence were reserved for stereotyping NW. On several dimensions, there were no differences between disabled men and either of the two female groups. That is, all three groups – DM, DW, and NW – were equally likely to be stereotyped as incompetent and weak compared to NM, who were rarely assigned these traits. Consistent with the writings of Asch et al. (2001), a redundant intersection exists between disability and femininity. Both imply childlike dependency and weakness, making them interchangeable, and in opposition to the normatively valued nondisabled male (see also Garland-Thomson 1997).

   In contrast to dependence, the theme of independence only discriminated between disabled and nondisabled groups – irrespective of gender. NM and NW were just as likely to be considered independent while DM and DW were equally *unlikely* to be considered independent. Similarly, DM and DW were rarely stereotyped as intellectually competent while NW were more often considered competent – but only half as often as NM.

Additionally, certain stereotypes differentiated between groups better than others. DM were more likely to be stereotyped as angry, inferior, and lazy, while DW were more often characterized as vulnerable, socially excluded, and poor. There was even less overlap between the two female groups. Consistent with previous research (Kite et al. 2008), both disabled and nondisabled women were characterized as weak and incompetent. However, disabled women were never described as feminine, were rarely considered nurturing, and were nearly the universal recipients of the "unfit parent" designation. These results support disability studies' critiques of discourses that position DW as asexual, unfeminine, and de-gendered (Garland-Thomson 1997; Milligan and Neufeldt 2001; Morris 1991). No overlap was observed among the top 10 stereotypes describing the two male groups.

Perhaps most intriguing are the stereotypic dimensions that most clearly distinguished between the four target groups. One of the most fundamental features of stereotypes is that they make clear how groups are defined in ways that highlight their intergroup distinctions (Ford and Stangor 1992). Figure 4.1 illustrates the stereotypes most "diagnostic" or defining of group membership (reprinted from Nario-Redmond 2010). The first graph shows that not only was "anger" among the top four most frequently occurring stereotypes for DM, it was rarely used to characterize any of the other groups. That is, nearly 70% of anger-related responses in our study were used to describe DM. By contrast, DW were best distinguished from the others as being "vulnerable victims" with nearly 80% of the vulnerable-victim responses used to stereotype DW. DW were also much more likely to be excluded from the role of parent than any other group. Participants specifically noted that DW: "should not have children" or "should not have children because they would be bad mothers." The availability of this expectation may explain why people often react with surprise when they encounter women with disabilities who actually are parents. In fact, when asked to think about the category "mother," images of disabled women may not readily come to mind. This remains an area for future research, particularly given recent campaigns designed to raise awareness about the parental rights of disabled people (Coble-Temple 2015; Powell et al. 2012).

> People are often surprised to hear that I work, am married and have six children … as if I shouldn't have these opportunities. ~ Person with multiple disabilities, 2015

Convergent evidence for parental and gender-role restrictiveness also comes from the stereotypes considered most diagnostic of the two nondisabled groups. Consistent with the traditional role of maternal caregiver, nurturance was not only the most frequent stereotype used to characterize NW, it was the most defining trait distinguishing NW from the other groups. Similarly, NM were best distinguished from all others as being employed – 77% of all descriptions to employment were made with reference to NM. Furthermore, employment is one of those stereotypes that reflect a social reality. According to the 2014 American Community

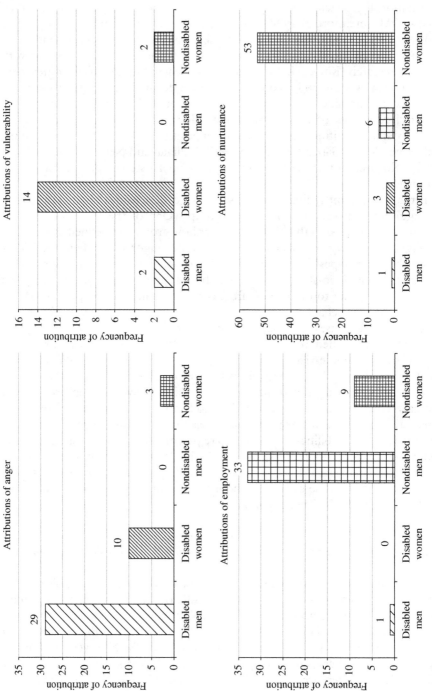

Figure 4.1 Frequencies by target group of the themes diagnostic of each group.

Survey, 84% of nondisabled men are employed compared to less than 35% of disabled people (Erickson et al. 2015). Marginalized economically, disabled people continue to have high rates of unemployment and poverty, and are less likely to marry or matriculate from college as well (Asch et al. 2001; Brault 2012).

In sum, these four stereotypic domains – *angry, vulnerable, nurturing, and employed* – were the most diagnostic or exclusively defining of group membership for disabled men, disabled women, nondisabled women and nondisabled men, respectively (Nario-Redmond 2010). Within an intergroup context, they are the dimensions on which these groups seem to differ most from one another according to culturally prescribed stereotypes. But why are these traits so uniquely defining? The next section explores the judgment implications related to how disability stereotypes are used.

Implications for the Use of Disability Stereotypes

Identifying the specific and unique contents of consensual stereotypes is important because stereotype contents influence stereotype use, and when shared across a variety of perceivers, these consequences can be far reaching (Sechrist and Stangor 2001). Certain stereotypical characteristics may become group defining because they can be deployed strategically to explain the social roles particular groups have occupied, and to *assign* roles on the basis of stereotypical expectations (Glick and Fiske 2001; Schaller and Conway III 2001). For example, the role of breadwinner for nondisabled men and caregiver for nondisabled women consistently emerge as central to traditional gender stereotypes (Koenig and Eagly 2014). There is a substantial body of research describing how gender stereotypes contribute to exaggerated differences about the abilities of men and women, sexist attitudes, and restricted job opportunities (for a review see Kite et al. 2008). On the other hand, minimal evidence exists about the outcomes attributable to the stereotypes of disabled men and women.

However, if disabled men are best distinguished from other groups as angry (hostile, bitter, frustrated, and cranky), to what extent does this characterization contribute to justifications for their unemployment, physical restraint, and incarceration? Although research has yet to test these ideas, it is worth noting that in 2016, less than 35.9% of the noninstitutionalized population of people with disabilities were employed (Lauer and Houtenville 2018). And based on data from the Department of Justice, in 2006, one out of every three people incarcerated in federal and state prisons had documented disabilities – three times the prevalence rate of disability in the general population of working age adults (She and Stapleton 2006). Since this time, rates of incarceration – particularly among those with psychiatric, intellectual, and learning disabilities – have only increased (Reingle Gonzalez et al. 2016).[3]

By contrast, the cultural stereotype of disabled women focuses on their vulnerability, and includes traits diametrically opposed to sexuality and nurturance.

Such expectations have significant implications for perceptions about their eligibility as prospective partners and mothers (Killoran 1994). When describing the stereotypes of disabled women, our 2010 participants wrote: *[They] can't cook, clean or take care of basic needs; [they are] not able to take care of children. [they are] taken care of rather than being the caretaker. Society doesn't want them to bear/produce disabled kids. [They are] not capable of being mothers.*

Stereotypic assumptions that preclude disabled women from the role of parent and partner can impact public policies and organizational plans for public facilities – for example when accessible bathrooms are provisioned without accessible baby-changing tables (Anderson and Kitchin 2000). Furthermore, if doctors do not expect their disabled patients to be sexual beings, they may fail to screen for pregnancies and sexually transmitted diseases (STDs) (Kirshbaum and Olkin 2002; Powell et al. 2012). Several studies document inadequate sexual health services, abuse prevention, and fertility support for disabled women, who are frequently encouraged to remain celibate or be sterilized (O'Toole 2002; Reis et al. 2004).

Stereotypical expectations can also directly impact legislative decisions related to child custody (Powell et al. 2012). In 37 US states, disability status alone is sufficient grounds for the legal termination of parental rights (Frederick 2014). Disabled mothers, in particular, are more likely to experience heightened scrutiny, unwarranted social service investigations, and the removal of their children on the basis of overgeneralized stereotypes about their fitness (Powell et al. 2012). Yet, disability status alone does not constitute a safety risk, and fails to predict child maltreatment (Preston 2012). According to a leading advocacy agency for parents with disabilities, "Securing the rights of disabled Americans to parent without unreasonable interference is the 'last frontier in disability rights'" (Frederick 2014, p. 32).

In summary, the defining stereotypes that characterize disabled men as angry, disabled women as vulnerable, and both as incompetent, dependent, and asexual may have some bearing in realistically describing their restricted social circumstances. Perhaps there is a reason for anger and frustration – an accuracy about being vulnerable to segregation and abuse, irrational fears, and misguided assumptions. Some argue stereotypes are like stories that emerge to explain why certain groups of people are more likely to be found in particular social positions. Stereotypes are also used as everyday shortcuts to simplify social judgments by filling in what people can expect beyond what they actually observe. This can lead to biased evaluations and erroneous decisions.

Disability Stereotypic Judgments

Much research has demonstrated that the simple *knowledge* of cultural stereotypes can lead to stereotype-congruent judgments and behaviors (Bargh et al. 1996). Stereotypes related to incompetence can even produce lower performance expectations despite evidence to the contrary. For example, college professors considered a student to have significantly less academic potential when labeled with a disability compared to a nondisabled student – even when the disabled student was described as having above-average grades, no social problems, and career goals. Instead, faculty expectations were highest for nondisabled students, even those characterized as having mediocre grades, poor social skills, and few career aspirations. As a consequence of globalized stereotypes, college professors may discourage disabled students from higher education pursuits (Molloy and Nario-Redmond 2007).

Faculty members are not just educational mentors, they are also guardians of an academic system, and strive to maintain the quality and status of their professional affiliations. In this way they serve as gatekeepers, acting on behalf of their disciplines and institutions to maintain academic standards and preserve the status quo (Barga 1996). Faculty may even guard against students they perceive to be unfit by discouraging them from majoring in their fields, refusing to write letters of recommendation, or voting for dismissal at grade reviews. Professors who view their students as protégés may be particularly invested in which students come to represent their particular fields. Students who experience disability can threaten those who highly identify as academics because of stereotypes that violate the characteristics they value most: independence and intellectual prowess. Consistent with this idea, one study found that professors who strongly identified as members of the academic community were more likely to dismiss disabled students as better suited for other majors, and more likely to drop out (Molloy and Nario-Redmond 2007). Furthermore, if disability status instantiates a set of overgeneralized beliefs about intellectual capability, these may be used to establish low competency standards against which disabled students are constantly compared – across academic domains (Wright 1983). The prevalence of incompetence, dependency, and other stereotypes may also explain disabled students' hesitancy toward self-disclosure, underutilization of resources, and lower graduation rates (Wolanin and Steele 2004) – a topic discussed further in Chapter 6.

Future research is needed to identify the boundary conditions of competency and other stereotypic evaluations, and the extent to which biased judgments depend on additional information provided. For example, are people more likely to express bias toward disabled people when they appear more consistent with disability stereotypes or when they violate stereotypic expectations (Stern et al. 2010)? The evidence to date is mixed. Fichten et al. (1991) found that nondisabled students had more negative thoughts, and were less comfortable to date a person with disability – even when that person was described in nonstereotypic terms (e.g. as independent, capable, and self-assured). On the other hand, Fox and Giles (1996) found that when a female wheelchair user was treated in a patronizing matter at a restaurant (e.g. the waitress spoke to her in baby talk as opposed to like an adult), people judged the disabled woman to be more passive – consistent with the disability stereotype. However, patronizing speech did *not* affect the disabled woman's perceived competence: she was judged to be equally competent whether treated like a baby or not.[4] Thus, the influence of disability stereotypes on evaluations may depend on the particular judgment context. Furthermore, we know little about how stereotypes impact the judgments of those who appear *less* stereotypically impaired (e.g. those with less visible, more fluid, or temporary conditions). If not readily categorized as disabled, some stereotypes may not be readily invoked, unless disability is disclosed.

Other forms of bias confront those whose disability status is frequently questioned or invalidated as illegitimate (Selmi 2011). For example, those with psychiatric disabilities are sometimes considered not impaired enough to be disabled (Blanck 2011). When circumstances are particularly ambiguous, impairment-specific and other personal characteristics may alter the form that ableism takes (LaChapelle et al. 2014). For example, someone with a minor limp or spasticity may be treated as drunk or refused accommodations at work for chronic pain or environmental sensitivities unless medical documentation proving disability status is provided.

> I'm told on a very regular basis that I can't have a TBI [traumatic brain injury] because I appear so normal. One person told me it was impossible because I was (and he paused here) "lucid." ~ Person with multiple disabilities, 2015

Alternatively, those who appear to have more stereotypic features may be more easily categorized as disabled and, once categorized, may be treated as interchangeable with other members of the disability community. Despite objective differences, once categorized as belonging to a group, individual members are more likely to be perceived as acting and appearing more alike (Park and Rothbart 1982). One of the most pervasive features of categorical processing relates to the exaggeration of perceived similarities within groups as well as the accentuation of differences between them (Tajfel and Turner 1979). Exaggerated estimates of group member similarities is even more pervasive when evaluating outgroups – or groups to which one does not belong. Furthermore, much research confirms that people are more likely to rely on stereotypes to inform them when uncertain about what is expected, or when the social category is highly salient (Schneider 2004). This is often the case upon initial encounters with people marked with visibly identifiable conditions or equipment, or in disability-relevant spaces.

Disability Stereotypic Behaviors

Fewer studies to date have tested the extent to which disability stereotypes lead to stereotype-consistent behaviors. However, in a classic study on the behavioral effects of the elderly stereotype, students actually walked slower after first solving a puzzle with words associated with older adults (e.g. Florida, retired, Bingo) compared to words unrelated to the elderly stereotype (e.g. thirsty, clean, private) (Bargh et al. 1996). In a similar study, students exposed to the elderly stereotype performed more poorly on a memory test compared to controls. Ironically, it was students who had the most contact with elderly people that most strongly associated older adults with forgetfulness (Dijksterhuis et al. 2000).

Extending these behavioral effects to disability stereotypes, Ginsberg et al. (2012) found that nondisabled people took longer and performed more poorly on a manual dexterity task after solving a puzzle of words associated with disability (e.g. dependent, deficient, wheelchair) compared to those who did not; those exposed to words associated with older adults also took longer than controls. In addition, Giotta (2006) found that after writing about perceptions of "the learning disabled," nondisabled students reported feeling less smart after a reading comprehension test, and rated the test as harder than those who did not first write about this group. Moreover, female students who first considered the LD stereotype actually took longer to complete the exam compared to controls. Similar experimental results of the impact of broader disability stereotypes on performance have yet to emerge in the published literature, although some dissertations have examined stereotype threat among particular impairment groups (May and Stone 2014; Fields 2012).

Research documents the clear negative effects of age stereotypes on the cognitive, memory, and intellectual performance of older adults (for a review see Lamont et al. 2015). Similar stereotype-driven performance declines have not been consistently found among those with specific disabilities. For example, when students with reading disabilities were made to consider the stereotypes of their group, they read more slowly but answered more questions correctly on a reading test compared those who did not consider these stereotypes (Powner 2015). However, Silverman and Cohen (2014) found that the more blind students worried about being stereotyped negatively, the more stress they experienced, and the lower their life satisfaction. In fact, the more concern these students had about confirming blind stereotypes, the less often they engaged with others publically and the more likely they were unemployed, suggesting that over time stereotype threat can promote underachievement as a way to protect self-worth – a topic explored further in Chapter 6.

Much more scholarship is needed on the impact of disability stereotypes for hiring and performance evaluations, college admission, and support/service determinations – all of which should depend on context, how strongly stereotypes are endorsed, and actual experiences with disabled people. To the extent that the disability representations stored in memory include both group-specific and individuated information about specific people and their unique circumstances, the impact of stereotypical expectations may be lessened.

Stereotypes also operate when people are not consciously aware of their influence. To understand how stereotypes become activated for use, it is helpful to consider how psychologists conceptualize the way stereotypes are processed mentally, and how categorical beliefs combine with other information to affect unconscious and automatic reactions to members of stereotyped groups.

Implicit Stereotyping: The Automatic Operation of Disability Stereotypes

Contemporary psychological theory conceptualizes the stereotype in terms of an associative network that links a group label to a particular set of traits, attributes, and images in memory (see Schneider 2004 for a review). To illustrate, Figure 4.2

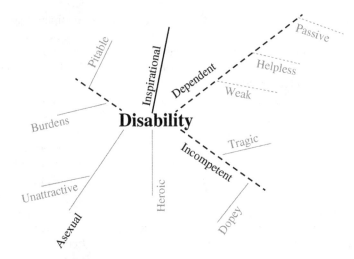

Figure 4.2 Conceptual depiction of the disability stereotype as an associative network.

depicts the category label "disability" as linked to various descriptors that may have become associated with this social group. Psychologists often describe these associations as a web of interconnected neural pathways that signify ideas, images, and even behavioral inclinations connected to particular concepts (e.g. dependency) or groups (e.g. disabled people). According to the logic of associative networks, whenever a concept is activated in memory, other closely related concepts become temporarily accessible for use through the process of spreading neural activation (Collins and Loftus 1975). Although people remain unaware of their own spontaneous mental images or beliefs as they become activated, the information processed can still influence their judgments and reactions. To the extent that people *differentially* process stereotypical information while considering certain groups, prejudicial bias may be indicated. For example, when a wheelchair user comes in for an interview, if disability stereotypes about dependence or incompetence are automatically triggered, credentials may be filtered through these expectations – compromising the likelihood of hiring.

Even when not asked to provide a formal evaluation of others, there are ways to measure the automatic or implicit biases that people have when thinking about or meeting people with disabilities. Some of the most innovative techniques to measure the underlying thoughts (and feelings) associated with different groups use brain activity, heart rates, and nonverbal behaviors including reaction times (for a review see Fazio and Olson 2003). Reaction time measures capitalize on the assumption that people should respond faster to concepts that are closely related in memory compared to concepts that are more distantly related (Nelson 2006). That is, it should take less time to identify that walking canes are more often associated with older adults than are skateboards. Similarly, thoughts of disability may be automatically linked to the international symbol of the wheelchair;

people may also connect the concept of disability with particular disabled people they know, and with stereotypes that characterize the group as dependent, incompetent, and asexual.

To test the operation of implicit disability stereotypes, Rohmer and Louvet (2012; see also Rohmer and Louvet 2018) presented people with a subliminal image of the international disability symbol (a stick figure seated in wheelchair), the international pedestrian symbol (a stick figure walking), or a neutral (baseline) square for less than 20 milliseconds (ms) on a computer screen. Extensive previous research has established this to be sufficient time for an image to be perceptually registered, but not enough time for it to be consciously detected (Nosek et al. 2011). After the extremely brief presentation of one of these images, a set of letters appeared on the screen (e.g. "warm" or "ramw") for 250 ms. People were then asked to classify each letter string as either a "word" or a "nonword" using one of two computer keys. The letters either formed words that were stereotypically related to nondisabled people (e.g. warm, competent, capable), or were scrambled anagrams of the same words. As predicted, relative to baseline responses, people were much faster at identifying words related to both competence and warmth when those words were preceded by the *nondisabled* pedestrian image compared to the disability image. In other words, seeing an image of a nondisabled pedestrian sped up responses to positive characteristics while an image of a wheelchair user slowed down responses to the same positive traits. These results suggest that when it comes to implicit stereotyping measures, disabled people are thought to be both less competent and less warm compared to people without disabilities (although other interpretations are discussed in the implicit attitudes section of Chapter 5). Similar implicit stereotyping results have found that "fat people" are automatically associated with laziness, particularly among fitness professionals who had never been overweight themselves (Robertson and Vohora 2008).

Another implicit stereotyping study found that caregivers at an institution for people with multiple impairments were more likely to associate disability with infantilizing words like "child," "infant," and "young" than they were to associate non-disability with these same childlike words (Robey et al. 2006). Consistent with these findings, Proctor (2011) found that child-protection workers were more likely to assume that children would be at higher risk for neglect if parents were said to have "mild mental retardation" compared to parents described as having "average intelligence." Finally, although the general public was faster to identify words like "helpless," "incompetent," "childish," "unpredictable," and "dangerous" when first presented with the label "crazy," those actually diagnosed with psychiatric conditions (e.g. schizophrenia, bipolar and unipolar depression) demonstrated less implicit stereotyping (Rüsch et al. 2011). Others, however, have found similar levels of implicit stereotyping regardless of participants' mental health status (Teachman et al. 2006). Future research is needed to investigate the extent to which deeply engrained automatic biases change in response to updated representations of disabled people as a group, or information about their changing social circumstances.

Stereotype Preservation: Biases that Maintain Overgeneralized Beliefs

There is reason to be pessimistic about stereotype change, however, as several studies of other marginalized groups document the many forces that contribute to the preservation of stereotypic beliefs. Over 25 years ago, disability activist Paul Hunt (1991) described 10 of the most common stereotypes of disabled people portrayed in the media. These included traits that characterized them as sinister, burdensome, nonsexual, and pitiable, or as laughable, self-defeating, and objects of both violence and inspiration. Many of these stereotypic representations have persisted over time. In 2010, our research found substantial consensus about the top 10 stereotypes ascribed to disabled people, regardless of their gender or presumed impairment (Nario-Redmond 2010). If there was little agreement over the descriptive contents of this cultural stereotype, freely generated responses would not have been so uniformly similar. Yet, the same most frequently occurring traits emerged independently for our disabled and nondisabled participants alike – documenting the ubiquity of global disability stereotypes as a cultural phenomenon.

If both disabled and nondisabled people are socialized or exposed to similar messages about gender and disability, it isn't surprising that dominant cultural narratives influence how information is organized in memory. Our results conceptually replicated findings from 30 years ago (Fichten et al. 1989), showing that our disabled and nondisabled participations shared 17 of the top 20 disability stereotypes generated. While these were not necessarily stereotypes that participants personally endorsed as true, they were similarly recognized as part of the cultural stereotype defining disabled people.

Despite this considerable overlap, our nondisabled participants were more likely to stereotype DM as passive and sensitive while our disabled participants were more likely to mention laziness, inferiority, and low socio-economic status, which may reflect more of an insider's perspective about how society positions disabled men as a group. Similarly, nondisabled participants were more likely to stereotype DW as sensitive but plucky while disabled participants were more likely to stereotype DW as vulnerable, impoverished, and unfit mothers. Perhaps, the rejection of disabled women as caregivers has increased saliency among those who have experienced negative reactions in response to their actual parenting of children (Asch et al. 2001; Kirshbaum and Olkin 2002).

Although some media representations about disabled people have changed through the years (see Chapter 3), others continue to communicate persistent stereotypic assumptions. Furthermore, stereotypes are much more likely to be perpetuated over time the more often they are communicated through everyday conversations and dialogues. Schaller and Conway III (2001) argue that most people are motivated to achieve consensus by selectively communicating only certain information about groups while failing to repeat or elaborate on other things.

This suggests that the dimensions that become part of consensually shared cultural stereotypes are not random, but involve deliberate consensus goals – goals designed to establish some agreement about what constitutes reality, who belongs where, and why. According to the social identity perspective, a stereotype's defining characteristics often reflect important group identity concerns that help people maintain a sense of positive distinctiveness about the groups they belong to relative to those to which they do not (see Chapter 6). Consensus goals, driven by needs for belonging, validation, and shared understanding, allow people to establish their value though group stereotypes that clearly distinguish them from other groups – groups defined by traits they may not want or apply to themselves (Schaller and Conway III 2001). By stereotyping disabled people as dependent and weak, nondisabled people can consider themselves as helpful and strong. Similar contrasts have been made between the normal and the abnormal, the free and the enslaved.

> Africanism is the vehicle by which the American self knows itself as not enslaved, but free; not repulsive, but desirable; not helpless, but licensed and powerful; not history-less, but historical; not damned, but innocent; not a blind accident of evolution, but a progressive fulfillment of destiny. (Morrison 1992, p. 52)

In line with Sampson's (1993) idea of the serviceable other, in order for a group to self-define as competent, another group must be defined as incompetent to establish the comparison. Indeed, our research found that disabled and nondisabled target groups were most clearly distinguishable on traits related to independence and autonomy (Nario-Redmond 2010). In this way, the stereotypes of disabled people shore up the boundaries of what it means to be nondisabled or normal (Linton 1998).

> The natural and the normal ... Both are constituted in large part by being set in opposition to culturally variable notices of disability – just as the natural was meaningful in relation to the monstrous and the deformed, so are the cultural meanings of normal produced in tandem with disability. (Baynton 2013, p 35)

Several disability studies scholars have written on the origins of the terms normal or normality as a tool, historically deployed to demarcate, measure, and manage deviant populations considered less than human, animalistic, or impediments to human progress (e.g. Longmore and Umansky 2001; Michalko and Titchkosky, 2009). Historians of disability have also documented how other disadvantaged groups have used the strategy of defining themselves in opposition to disability in their movements' struggle for equality (Baynton 2013). Interestingly, when fighting for the civil rights of women, Blacks, and immigrants, disability stereotypes were invoked to distance one's group from accusations that they share the same deficits (e.g. irrationality, physical and emotional weaknesses; White 2001). That is, stereotypical ideas, considered sexist and racist, were still presumed to be *inherent* to disabled bodies – bodies for whom inferiority had yet been challenged (Hahn 1996).

This essentialist notion that group differences can be explained in terms of the biological characteristics inherent to particular groups is a key ingredient of stereotypic thinking (Yzerbyt et al. 1997). Take the stereotype that disabled people are unemployed. The reason for this has more to do with discriminatory policies affecting education levels and biased hiring practices than with individuals' physical or mental capacities (Lengnick-Hall et al. 2001). Yet, unemployment is often falsely attributed to the mind and/or body of the disabled individual – their internal disposition or impairment-related features – while less attention is paid to situational constraints. In fact, it is quite common for people to underestimate the power of the situation – the external environment and other socially created barriers that restrict certain people from participating in the workforce (Patterson and Witten 1987). This fundamental attribution error (Ross 1977) is one reason stereotypes are difficult to change. Fixing disabled people instead of altering the environment is the grand fallacy of the biomedical model that presumes costly technology (appropriate for very few) will eventually make disability obsolete:

> People love the stair climbing wheelchair and the standing scooter because they think it fixes the accessibility issue caused by a lack of ramps or elevators without actually having to install ramps and elevators. The perception is that the problem is solved without any change to society or the environment … It assumes that it is ok to always put the burden of change on disabled people rather than deal with the reasons that accessibility isn't already the norm … people ignore the universal benefits of an accessible environment. (crippledscholar 2015)

Compounding this tendency to focus on individuals' internal dispositions – to the exclusion of other influences on behavior – are biases that involve selective information processing. People selectively attend to and remember information that fits their stereotypical expectations; they are less likely to notice and remember information that does not fit, or that clearly violates group expectations (Fiske and Neuberg 1990). Such biases also contribute to the perpetuation of stereotypical beliefs. For example, when a disabled person appears or acts in a way that confirms a stereotype (e.g. is not employed), people may readily assume this is because of something internal to his or her specific impairment. Yet, when a disabled person acts in way that is inconsistent or disconfirming of a stereotype (e.g. is employed), people may dismiss this as a fluke, as temporary, or as somehow situational (Nelson 2006). If stereotype disconfirming information receives less attention, it is less likely to produce changes in the way groups are represented in memory.

Even when group members are recognized as appearing inconsistent with group stereotypes, they are often viewed as exceptions to the rule – part of a "sub-type" that doesn't really represent the broader group. This dismissal of information about people who violate stereotypical expectations works to maintain global stereotypes which can then still be applied to the majority of others in the group (Kunda and Oleson 1995). For this reason, research has investigated whether stereotypes are more likely to change when observers are confronted with several counter-stereotypical examples of a social group, or whether stereotype-inconsistent behaviors are more memorable if performed by people that seem more typical of the social category (Rothbart and Lewis 1988). In other words, how many *employed* disabled people does one have to meet to revise one's stereotypic expectations? Furthermore, do these counter-stereotypical examples have to really look disabled for people to take notice, and update their representations in memory?

Clearly, changing cultural and individual stereotypes depends on a variety of factors beyond just the stereotypicality of individual group members. Context matters, and so do perceiver goals, and the relationship between those perceiving and those being perceived: the judges and the judged. In summary, not only do stereotypes help define groups in ways that distinguish them from one another, they are also maintained in ways that are mutually accepted as understandable while preserving the distinctiveness of ingroups relative to outgroups. Similar to ideologies, cultural stereotypes are shared realities that must be negotiated (Stangor and Crandall 2000). How is it that those who are members of both dominant and subordinate groups come to agree on, accept, or at least recognize the stereotypes that define them? When are these resisted and renegotiated? This topic is explored in the final chapters on prejudice reduction and social change.

The Stereotype Content Model and Changing Representations

We know that the contents of various group stereotypes are not fixed. Instead, they adjust to reflect certain social realities, even if the causal attributions or reasons for those realities are misinformed (Oakes et al. 1994). Consider the stereotypical expectation that disabled people – as a group – are more likely to be impoverished. While overgeneralized and attributable to many factors, this stereotype is nevertheless an accurate one. Stereotypes would no longer be functional if they completely failed to fit the available evidence, manage expectations, and predict how people are likely to behave. In addition, stereotypic descriptions about group characteristics and outcomes are meaningful to the extent that they convey information about how groups differ – whether those differences are claimed, imposed, or contested. Thus, another reason stereotypes are so resistant to change is that they remain predictive of the social positions many stereotyped groups occupy (or are *expected* to occupy). In this way, stereotypes contribute to maintaining group inequalities that perpetuate the status quo (Jost and Major 2001). There is often a tension between the current contents of cultural stereotypes and the dynamic socio-structural relationships between various majority and minority groups whose relative positions in society evolve with the changing economic, political, and legislative landscape.

> If we want to predict which particular traits are likely to become central to the stereotype of some group, we would be advised to identify those traits that describe that group's physical and social environment. (Schaller and Conway III 2001, p. 166)

The stereotype content model (SCM) explains how the specific contents of ingroup and outgroup stereotypes are often predictable on the basis of two dimensions critical to intergroup perception – the group's status and its intention to compete, instead of cooperate (Glick and Fiske 2001). People want to know (i) whether a group is generally cooperative (warm) or competitive (cold), and (ii) whether it has the power (status) to carry out goals and intentions. According to the SCM, stereotypes are useful because they provide information to make inferences about both – group intentions and group status. Stereotypes about a group's warmth signal whether its members are likely to be cooperative: the colder the group, the less cooperative and more competitive they are expected to be. Stereotypes about a group's competence signal information about its social status: the more incompetent, the lower the group's status in society, and the less likely they are to achieve certain goals.

Stereotypes related to warmth and incompetence are common among certain types of subordinate (low-status) groups that typically do not compete for resources – groups like children, the elderly, housewives, and the disabled (Glick and Fiske 2001). These groups are the targets of ambivalent stereotypes that include both positive (warmth) and negative (incompetent) elements. Evidence testing the SCM has found that across multiple studies in several nations, the elderly and the intellectually and physically disabled were all rated well below average on the dimension of competence (Cuddy et al. 2008). According to the model, the main reason these groups are considered incompetent (e.g. unintelligent, incapable) is because they have occupied inferior, non-powerful positions in society (Cuddy et al. 2008). However, the SCM also predicts that disabled people will be stereotyped as warmer (e.g. more likeable and trustworthy) than many other social groups. The reason the SCM proposes that disabled people score above average on warmth is because in general they are perceived to be a cooperative and (inter)dependent outgroup. Some even argue that "the disabled" as a group are stereotypically "compliant" – considered among society's legitimate dependents, like children and the elderly (Glick and Fiske 2001). Several studies testing the SCM have found that "disabled," "blind," "retarded," and "elderly" people were all stereotyped as having lower competence but higher warmth compared to other social groups (Fiske et al. 2002). These observations are consistent with research on consensual cultural beliefs that characterize the entire group as helpless and dependent (Nario-Redmond 2010). According to the SCM, negative intentions are not expected of stereotypically warm (noncompetitive) groups (Cuddy et al. 2008). In our 2010 research, warmth was not among the 10 most frequent stereotypes used to describe disabled people – although it was among the top 20.

> Disabled people and housewives, groups that are not viewed as competing for economic and educational resources, are rated warmer than virtually all other groups, including most majority groups. (Cuddy et al. 2008, p. 95)

In Chapter 5 on disability attitudes, the SCM is further described as it relates to the emotional and behavioral reactions that correspond to groups ambivalently stereotyped as both low in competence and high in warmth. These groups tend to garner more paternalistic forms of prejudice, including pity and protective intentions. Disrespectful, condescending, and infantilizing actions are common toward those stereotyped as incompetent but warm. By contrast, other beliefs, feelings, and behaviors are expected toward those stereotyped as incompetent but cold (e.g. competitive). For example, low-status groups, including the homeless, drug addicts, immigrants, and welfare recipients, are often characterized as manipulative, freeloading parasites, and exploiters who compete for social resources (Cuddy et al. 2008). According to the SCM, it is these groups – the incompetent but cold – who are the targets of more resentful and hostile forms of prejudice. In Chapter 5, these ambivalent, negative, and benevolent forms of prejudice are all reviewed along with the behavioral manifestations of prejudice that coincide with different combinations of warm/cold and competent/incompetent stereotypes.

Importantly, the SCM makes room for the idea that disabled people may not always be stereotyped as warm and incompetent – especially if they are thought to be intentionally competing for resources and/or occupying roles associated with higher social statuses. As the social position of disabled people changes, so should the stereotypes that come to dominate the cultural imagination. During historical periods, when new policies were enacted to extend financial supports, benefits, and civil rights to disabled people as a group, *resentful* attitudes tended to increase in public discourse (Blanck 2011). Yet, few psychologists have studied the extent to which stereotypes related to this group's perceived competitiveness emerge as a function of advancements in disability rights and the more equitable distribution or redistribution of resources (but see Dorfman forthcoming).

When it comes to challenging stereotypic assumptions about the cooperative dependence (warmth) of disabled people, it may not take many (cold) acts of defiance to question their competitive intentions. Perceived competitiveness is more likely to the extent that groups appear to be getting "special breaks" or taking resources away from the rest of society (Cuddy et al. 2008). To illustrate, legal scholars have described forms of "disability backlash" in judicial decisions involving certain protected-status impairments, or following increases in disability-benefit determinations, and advancements in disability rights (Colker 2005; Travis, 2011). Even in the latest national opinion polls, 45% of Americans surveyed still believe that the Americans with Disabilities Act (ADA) which requires disability accommodations at work, puts too much of a burden on small companies – an attitude that increases to 60% among older Americans (Shannon-Missal 2015). Although Europeans are often ahead of the United States in terms of disability reform, in an Irish national survey, over a third of respondents (36%) said employers should *not* make special allowances for people with disabilities (Office of the First Minister and Deputy First Minister 2003). An often cited critique of the ADA describes it as creating, "a lifelong buffet of perks, special breaks and procedural protections, a web of entitlement that extends from cradle to grave" (Shalit 1997, p. 21). Such opinions may die hard, even if they are no longer normative or considered politically correct. Although limited research has investigated these issues, resentment over disability parking places may be chief among contemporary manifestations of changing stereotypic beliefs (Dorfman forthcoming).

> I hate handicapped parking places. I hate the idea of them. I see them as punishment for being healthy ... every mall in America is expecting Cripple-Fest 2000 to visit them and they need to hold parking spots for all of the tour members. (online hate group cited in Sherry 2016, p. 37)

More research is needed to examine whether eligibility determinations for accessible technologies, new programs, scholarships, and other limited funding opportunities are contingent on perceptions of disabled people as cooperative dependents, interdependent, or independent agents. If portrayed as "fighting" for access to limited resources, or as qualified for high-status positions, to what extent will stereotypes about the group's warmth diminish or competence improve?

Some of the research on changing older adult stereotypes is relevant here. Specifically, changing overgeneralized assumptions about the positive trait of warmth may be easier than changing stereotypes about the negative trait of incompetence, which may be more resistant to change. For example, research has found that when people were provided with positive information about the competence of an older adult, his low competence ratings did not improve – although his ratings of warmth decreased (Cuddy et al. 2008). Therefore, even when behavioral demonstrations of competence fail to update this stereotype domain, they can still undermine perceptions of warmth, suggesting a wariness about those seen as capable of competing. By contrast, when an elderly adult behaved in a stereotypically incompetent way, he was rated higher in warmth – suggesting that people may reward those who conform to stereotypical beliefs by liking them more. Similar results have been found in sexism studies of women who either violate or conform to gender stereotypes. When women behave competently, sexists consider them to be cold and less likeable, but when they appear incompetent, they are viewed as warm and worthy of praise (Glick and Fiske 1996).

These speculations related to stereotype change are based on research in person-perception that shows that when evaluating another person's competence, people pay more attention to intelligent than unintelligent behaviors (Singh and Teoh 2000). By contrast, when evaluating others' warmth (or likeability), people are more sensitive to untrustworthy than trustworthy behavior – since dishonesty is more informative of presumed intentions (Tausch et al. 2007). For example, when individuals with disabilities clearly demonstrate their competence and capabilities in educational or occupational settings, they may directly challenge the presumed competence of other (perhaps more dominant) groups. This may explain why disabled people are sometimes accused of malingering or faking their conditions when they appear so capable in particular domains (Cook et al. 2000). Studies on the costs of feigned disability for the purposes of compensation have estimated that as many as 60% of adult social security cases may be fraudulent.

When such claims frequently make headlines, stereotypes about the competitiveness of disabled people are likely to increase, stimulating calls for the importance of stricter testing to validate disability status (Chafetz and Underhill 2013).

Shared realities in the form of stereotypes are constantly being renegotiated (Stangor and Crandall 2000) as social circumstances change. Much work has yet to be done on the mechanisms involved in stereotype change as it pertains to individual impairments and more globalized culturally shared beliefs. This work includes measuring the impact of the increased visibility and participation of disabled people in public life, and challenging the distorted and limiting representations that disability stereotypes embody (Hevey 1993). Additional research should address the extent to which individuals personally endorse specific aspects of the cultural stereotype, and the conditions that contribute to their use and modification.

Summary

While some students fear that learning about stereotypes contributes to their perpetuation, social psychologists point out that stereotypes serve many useful functions, and do change with the times. Studying these overgeneralized belief systems can help explain social roles, differentiate between groups, and predict group behavior. Defined as a set of attributes used to characterize a group and its members, stereotypes are often faulty and incomplete but can be positive, negative, or ambivalent; they are among the more proximal origins of prejudice, and in the case of disability, also function to maintain ableist judgments and treatments. Regardless of whether people personally endorse stereotypical beliefs as true, their simple awareness of a stereotype's contents can influence perceptions and bias impressions, emotions and behavior.

The vast majority of studies on disability stereotypes have focused on the characteristics of those with specific impairments – the blind sage, the autistic savant, for example. Stereotypes regarding sensory impairments, such as blind and D/deaf people, are often ambivalent (see Chapter 6 for discussion of Deaf identity and deafness as an impairment). Both can be seen as happy or alone, angry or friendly, as well as dependent, passive, boring, unpleasant, or rude. Ambivalent stereotypes are often seen in learning and developmental disabilities as well, with common stereotypes characterizing this group as dumb, lazy, and violent but also happy, loving, and childlike. The stereotyping of physically disabled people as submissive, unassuming, and introverted also allows the able-bodied to be defined as dominant, arrogant, and extroverted by contrast. Studies examining the stereotypes about disabled people as a whole across impairment types are less common, though much needed. In reality, disabled people share many experiences with discrimination, access limitations, and restricted social statuses, regardless of the impairments they experience.

People vary in terms of their awareness of various group stereotypes; cultural stereotypes capture the more widely recognized understandings about how different groups are represented. Learned as part of the socialization process, cultural stereotypes are often spread through everyday conversation, as well as through representations in books, television, and social media. For example, disabled people are often seen in fictional works as tragic but heroic victims without much agency or capacity as professionals or as care-*givers*. Although studies are few, our research documents that consensually based, cross-impairment stereotypes consistently characterize disabled people as dependent, asexual, incompetent, and not differentiated by gender. These global stereotypes demonstrate that disabled people are represented in memory as a broader social classification category, rather than only by impairment type.

The real world consequences of these disability stereotypes are far reaching. They can result in restricted job opportunities, higher incarceration rates, and discriminatory public policies related to education, parenting, and child custody. They also affect employment practices and the design of public spaces. For example, if disabled women are seen as "unfit" parents, accessible bathrooms may not include baby-changing tables; if disabled men are viewed as "angry," they may be subject to harsher punishments and more physical restraints. The consequences of stereotypes also manifest in subtler ways: influencing teacher expectations, lowering disabled students' retention rates, and undermining higher education pursuits. Contemporary psychological theory has demonstrated that while a person may be unaware that they hold stereotypical beliefs, it's the simple knowledge of these beliefs that can still affect impressions and decisions to recruit, admit, hire, and promote.

As this chapter helps to articulate the complex and persistent qualities of disability stereotypes, we begin to understand what it will take to challenge and change these perceptions. Due to selective information processing, when people do encounter someone who defies a stereotype, they are less likely to remember these qualities, and more likely to remember information that fits their expectations. Outliers may not be seen as disproving a stereotype but rather as an exception to the rule; yet as social circumstances change, stereotype contents should change along with them – in predictable ways. Groups that were once thought to be among the lowest on the totem pole may be perceived as more competent as they gain social status through upward mobility. Similarly, those once thought to be cooperative, warm, and compliant – society's legitimate dependents – may be recast as more competitive and cold as they compete for jobs and other resources on their way to securing civil rights.

In the next chapter, the discussion of changing beliefs and disability attitudes continues along with considerations about when ambivalent beliefs that incorporate both positive and negative components give way to hostile and more benevolent behaviors and emotions.

Notes

1 In contrast to the more distal origins of prejudice that tend to be removed from conscious awareness, proximal origins refer to the more immediate, cognitively accessible influences that contribute to the expression of prejudicial reactions; however, stereotypes

can function both as causes and as effects of differential treatment, and are often mutually reinforcing. For example, a stereotypic belief that disabled people are "dependent" can instigate unwanted helping behaviors just as observing people receiving help may reinforce stereotypes about dependency.

2 Most stereotyping studies rely on an empirically derived system for classifying the valence (positivity/negativity) of the trait terms examined, based on previously published work that systematically established each word's relative positivity/negativity according to pre-classified ratings or rankings. For example, Fichten and Amsel (1986) used 170 trait words pre-classified on the basis of their social desirability from Anderson's (1968), Wiggins's (1979), and Conte and Plutchik's (1981) lists and taxonomies.

3 According to the 2004 nationally representative Survey of Inmates in State and Federal Correctional Facilities, 41% of inmates reported a disability – most were cognitive (Reingle Gonzalez et al. 2016).

4 This was inconsistent with predictions as other research has shown that patronizing speech can reduce competency (intelligence) ratings of older adults who are treated like babies (Giles et al. 1993; Ryan et al. 1991).

References

Abrams, D., Jackson, D., and St. Claire, L. (1990). Social identity and the handicapping functions of stereotypes: Children's understanding of mental and physical handicap. *Human Relations* 43 (11): 1085–1098.

Algozzine, B. (1979). *The Disturbing Child: A Validation Report*. Minneapolis Institute for Research on Learning Disabilities. Washington DC: Bureau of Education for the Handicapped.

van Alphen, L.M., Dijker, A.J.M., Bos, A.E.R. et al. (2012). The influence of group size and stigma severity on social acceptance: the case of people with intellectual disability moving into neighbourhoods. *Journal of Community & Applied Social Psychology* 22 (1): 38–49.

Anderson, N. (1968). Likableness ratings of 555 personality trait words. *Journal of Personality and Social Psychology* 9 (3): 272–279.

Anderson, P. and Kitchin, R. (2000). Disability, space and sexuality: access to family planning services. *Social Science & Medicine* 51 (8): 1163–1173.

Angermeyer, M.C. and Matschinger, H. (2003). The stigma of mental illness: effects of labeling on public attitudes towards people with mental disorder. *Acta Psychiatrica Scandinavica* 108 (4): 304–309.

Angermeyer, M.C., Beck, M., and Matschinger, H. (2003). Determinants of the public's preference for social distance from people with schizophrenia. *Canadian Journal of Psychiatry* 48 (10): 663–668.

Asch, A., Rousso, H., and Jefferies, T. (2001). Beyond pedestals: the lives of girls and women with disabilities. In: *Double Jeopardy: Addressing Gender Equity in Special Education* (ed. H. Rousso and M.L. Wehmeyer), 13–41. Albany, NY: SUNY Press.

Ashmore, R.D. and Del Boca, F.K. (1981). Conceptual approaches to stereotypes and stereotyping. In: *Cognitive Processes in Stereotyping and Intergroup Behavior* (ed. D.L. Hamilton), 1–35. Hillsdale, NJ: Lawrence Erlbaum.

Barga, N.K. (1996). Students with learning disabilities in education: managing a disability. *Journal of Learning Disabilities* 29 (4): 413–421.

Bargh, J.A., Chen, M., and Burrows, L. (1996). Automaticity of social behavior: direct effects of trait construct and stereotype activation on action. *Journal of Personality and Social Psychology* 71 (2): 230–244.

Baynton, D.C. (2013). Disability and the justification of inequality in American history. In: *The Disability Studies Reader*, 4e (ed. L.J. Davis), 17–33. New York: Routledge.

Ben-Moshe, L. and Powell, J.J. (2007). Sign of our times? Revis(it)ing the International Symbol of Access. *Disability & Society* 22 (5): 489–505.

Biernat, M. and Dovidio, J.F. (2000). Stigma and stereotypes. In: *The Social Psychology of Stigma* (ed. T.F. Heatherton and R.E. Kleck), 88–125. New York: Guilford Press.

Blanck, P. (2011). Disability and aging: historical and contemporary views. In: *Disability and Aging Discrimination: Perspectives in Law and Psychology* (ed. R.L. Wiener and S.L. Willborn), 49–70. New York: Springer.

Brault, M.W. (2012). *Americans with Disabilities: 2010*. Current Population Reports, P70-131. Washington, DC: US Census Bureau. https://www.census.gov/prod/2012pubs/p70-131.pdf (accessed 26 February 2019).

Bryan, J.H. and Perlmutter, B. (1979). Immediate impressions of LD children by female adults. *Learning Disability Quarterly* 2 (1): 80–88.

Bryan, J.H., Bryan, T.H., and Sonnefeld, L.J. (1982). Being known by the company we keep: the contagion of first impressions. *Learning Disability Quarterly* 5 (3): 288–294.

Cambra, C. (1996). A comparative study of personality descriptors attributed to the deaf, the blind, and individuals with no sensory disability. *American Annals of the Deaf* 141 (1): 24–28.

Chafetz, M. and Underhill, J. (2013). Estimated costs of malingered disability. *Archives of Clinical Neuropsychology* 28 (7): 633–639.

Cheu, J. (2013). *Diversity in Disney Films: Critical Essays on Race, Ethnicity, Gender, Sexuality and Disability*. Jefferson, NC: McFarland.

Coble-Temple. (2015). Parental rights include disability equality: a call to action for psychology. Psychology Benefits Society. https://psychologybenefits.org/2015/07/28/parental-rights-include-disability-equality (accessed 26 February 2019).

Colker, R. (2005). *The Disability Pendulum: The First Decade of the Americans with Disabilities Act*. New York: New York University Press.

Collins, A.M. and Loftus, E.F. (1975). A spreading-activation theory of semantic processing. *Psychological Review* 82 (6): 407–428.

Conte, H.R. and Plutchik, R. (1981). A circumplex model for interpersonal and personality traits. *Journal of Personality and Social Psychology* 40 (4): 701–711.

Cook, B.G., Gerber, M.M., and Murphy, J. (2000). Backlash against the inclusion of students with learning disabilities in higher education: implications for transition from post-secondary environments to work. *Work* 14 (1): 31–40.

Courington, S.M., Lambert, R.W., Becker, S. et al. (1983). The measurement of attitudes toward blindness and its importance for rehabilitation. *International Journal of Rehabilitation Research* 6 (1): 67–72.

crippledscholar. (2015). When celebrating accessible technology is just reinforcing ableism. https://crippledscholar.com/2015/07/04/when-celebrating-accessible-technology-is-just-reinforcing-ableism (accessed 26 February 2019).

Cuddy, A.J., Fiske, S.T., and Glick, P. (2008). Warmth and competence as universal dimensions of social perception: the stereotype content model and the BIAS map. *Advances in Experimental Social Psychology* 40: 61–149.

Dijksterhuis, A., Aarts, H., Bargh, J.A., and Van Knippenberg, A. (2000). On the relation between associative strength and automatic behavior. *Journal of Experimental Social Psychology* 36 (5): 531–544.

Dorfman, D. (forthcoming). The fear of disability con. *Law and Society Review*.

Eagly, A.H. (1987). *Sex Differences in Social Behavior: A Social-Role Interpretation*. Hillsdale, NJ: Lawrence Erlbaum.

Erickson, W., Lee, C., and von Schrader, S. (2015). *Disability Statistics from the 2014 American Community Survey (ACS)*. Ithaca, NY: Cornell University Employment and Disability Institute (EDI). www.disabilitystatistics.org (accessed 26 February 2019).

Fazio, R.H. and Olson, M.A. (2003). Implicit measures in social cognition research: their meaning and uses. *Annual Review of Psychology* 54: 297–327.

Fichten, C.S. and Amsel, R. (1986). Trait attributions about college students with a physical disability: circumplex analyses and methodological issues. *Journal of Applied Social Psychology* 16 (5): 410–427.

Fichten, C.S., Robillard, K., Judd, D., and Amsel, R. (1989). College students with physical disabilities: myths and realities. *Rehabilitation Psychology* 34 (4): 243–257.

Fichten, C.S., Goodrick, G., Amsel, R., and McKenzie, S.W. (1991). Reactions toward dating peers with visual impairments. *Rehabilitation Psychology* 36 (3): 163–178.

Fields, T.M. (2012). California high school exit exam for students with disabilities: the impact of setting, anxiety, and stereotype threat on students' math performance. *Dissertation Abstracts International Section A* 72: 3218. https://repository.usfca.edu/diss/282 (accessed 26 February 2019).

Fiske, S.T. and Neuberg, S.L. (1990). A continuum of impression formation from category-based to individuating processes: influences of information and motivation on attention and interpretation. In: *Advances in Experimental Social Psychology*, vol. 23 (ed. M.P. Zanna), 1–108. San Diego, CA: Academic Press.

Fiske, S.T., Cuddy, A.J.C., Glick, P., and Xu, J. (2002). A model of (often mixed) stereotype content: competence and warmth respectively follow from perceived status and competition. *Journal of Personality and Social Psychology* 82 (6): 878–902.

Ford, T.E. and Stangor, C. (1992). The role of diagnosticity in stereotype formation: perceiving group means and variances. *Journal of Personality and Social Psychology* 63 (3): 356–367.

Fox, S.A. and Giles, H. (1996). Inter-ability communication: evaluating patronizing encounters. *Journal of Language and Social Psychology* 15 (3): 265–290.

Frable, D.E., Blackstone, T., and Scherbaum, C. (1990). Marginal and mindful: deviants in social interactions. *Journal of Personality and Social Psychology* 59 (1): 140–149.

Frederick, A. (2014). Mothering while disabled. *Contexts* 13 (4): 30–35.

Garland-Thomson, R. (1997). Feminist theory, the body, and the disabled figure. In: *The Disability Studies Reader* (ed. L.J. Davis), 279–292. New York: Routledge.

Gervais, S.J. (2011). A social psychological perspective of disability prejudice. In: *Disability and Aging Discrimination: Perspectives in Law and Psychology* (ed. R.L. Wiener and S.L. Willborn), 249–262. New York: Springer.

Gething, L. (1992). Judgements by health professionals of personal characteristics of people with a visible physical disability. *Social Science & Medicine* 34 (7): 809–815.

Giles, H., Fox, S.A., and Smith, E. (1993). Patronizing the elderly: intergenerational evaluations. *Research in Language and Social Interaction* 26 (2): 129–150.

Gilmore, L., Campbell, J., and Cuskelly, M. (2003). Developmental expectations, personality stereotypes, and attitudes towards inclusive education: community and teacher views of Down syndrome. *International Journal of Disability, Development and Education* 50 (1): 65–76.

Ginsberg, F., Rohmer, O., and Louvet, E. (2012). Priming of disability and elderly stereotype in motor performance: similar or specific effects? *Perceptual and Motor skills* 114 (2): 397–406.

Giotta, T.D. (2006). The effects of stereotype priming in an academic setting. Undergraduate thesis. Reed College, Portland, OR.

Glick, P. and Fiske, S.T. (1996). The ambivalent sexism inventory: differentiating hostile and benevolent sexism. *Journal of Personality and Social psychology* 70 (3): 491–512.

Glick, P. and Fiske, S.T. (2001). An ambivalent alliance: hostile and benevolent sexism as complementary justifications for gender inequality. *American Psychologist* 56 (2): 109–118.

Goffman, E. (1963). *Stigma: Notes on the Management of Spoiled Identity*. Englewood Cliffs, NJ: Prentice-Hall.

Gowman, A.G. (1957). *The War Blind in American Social Structure*. New York: American Foundation for the Blind.

Hahn, H. (1996). Antidiscrimination laws and social research on disability: the minority group perspective. *Behavioral Sciences & the Law* 14 (1): 41–59.

Haller, B. (2000). If they limp, they lead? News representations and the hierarchy of disability images. In: *Handbook of Communication and People with Disabilities: Research and Application* (ed. D.O. Braithwaite and T.L. Thompson), 273–288. New York: Routledge.

Hanna, W.J. and Rogovsky, B. (1993). Women with disabilities: two handicaps plus. In: *Perspectives on Disability* (ed. M. Nagler), 109–120. Palo Alto, CA: Health Markets Research.

Hayman, R.L. Jr. (1990). Presumptions of justice: law, politics, and the mentally retarded parent. *Harvard Law Review* 103 (6): 1201–1271.

Hevey, D. (1993). From self-love to the picket line: strategies for change in disability representation. *Disability, Handicap & Society* 8 (4): 423–429.

Hunt, P. (1991). Discrimination: disabled people and the media. *Contact* 70: 45–48.

Jost, J.T. and Major, B. (eds.) (2001). *The Psychology of Legitimacy: Emerging Perspectives on Ideology, Justice, and Intergroup Relations*. Cambridge: Cambridge University Press.

Kiger, G. (1997). The structure of attitudes toward persons who are deaf: emotions, values, and stereotypes. *The Journal of Psychology: Interdisciplinary and Applied* 131 (5): 554–560.

Killoran, C. (1994). Women with disabilities having children: it's our right too. *Sexuality and Disability* 12 (2): 121–126.

Kirkpatrick, S.R. (2009). The Disney-fication of disability: The perpetuation of hollywood stereotypes of disability in Disney's animated films. Doctoral dissertation. University of Akron.

Kirshbaum, M. and Olkin, R. (2002). Parents with physical, systemic, or visual disabilities. *Sexuality and Disability* 20 (1): 65–80.

Kite, M.E., Deaux, K., and Haines, E.L. (2008). Gender stereotypes. In: *Psychology of Women: A Handbook of Issues and Theories* (ed. F.L. Denmark and M.A. Paludi), 205–236. Westport, CT: Greenwood Press.

Koenig, A.M. and Eagly, A.H. (2014). Evidence for the social role theory of stereotype content: observations of groups' roles shape stereotypes. *Journal of Personality and Social Psychology* 107 (3): 371–392.

Kunda, Z. and Oleson, K.C. (1995). Maintaining stereotypes in the face of disconfirmation: constructing grounds for subtyping deviants. *Journal of Personality and Social Psychology* 68 (4): 565–579.

LaChapelle, D.L., Lavoie, S., Higgins, N.C., and Hadjistavropoulos, T. (2014). Attractiveness, diagnostic ambiguity, and disability cues impact perceptions of women with pain. *Rehabilitation Psychology* 59 (2): 162–170.

Lamont, R.A., Swift, H.J., and Abrams, D. (2015). A review and meta-analysis of age-based stereotype threat: negative stereotypes, not facts, do the damage. *Psychology and Aging* 30 (1): 1–14.

Lauer, E.A. and Houtenville, A.J. (2018). *Annual Disability Statistics Compendium: 2017.* Durham, NH: University of New Hampshire, Institute on Disability.

Lengnick-Hall, M.L., Gaunt, P.M., and Brooks, A.A. (2001). *Why Employers Don't Hire People with Disabilities: A Survey of the Literature.* San Antonio: College of Business, University of Texas at San Antonio.

Linton, S. (1998). *Claiming Disability: Knowledge and Identity.* New York: New York University Press.

Longmore, P.K. and Umansky, L. (2001). *The New Disability History: American Perspectives.* New York: New York University Press.

Maras, P. and Brown, R. (1996). Effects of contact on children's attitudes toward disability: a longitudinal study. *Journal of Applied Social Psychology* 26 (23): 2113–2134.

Marsh, V. and Friedman, R. (1972). Changing public attitudes toward blindness. *Exceptional Children* 38 (5): 426–428.

Martin, J.K., Pescosolido, B.A., and Tuch, S.A. (2000). Of fear and loathing: the role of "disturbing behavior," labels, and causal attributions in shaping public attitudes toward people with mental illness. *Journal of Health and Social Behavior* 41 (2): 208–223.

May, A.L. and Stone, C.A. (2014). An initial investigation into the role of stereotype threat in the test performance of college students with learning disabilities. *Journal of Postsecondary Education and Disability* 27 (1): 89–106.

McCaughey, T.J. and Strohmer, D.C. (2005). Prototypes as an indirect measure of attitudes toward disability groups. *Rehabilitation Counseling Bulletin* 48 (2): 89–99.

McCauley, C. and Stitt, C.L. (1978). An individual and quantitative measure of stereotypes. *Journal of Personality and Social Psychology* 36 (9): 929–940.

McConnell, D. and Llewellyn, G. (2002). Stereotypes, parents with intellectual disability and child protection. *Journal of Social Welfare and Family Law* 24 (3): 297–317.

Michalko, R. and Titchkosky, T. (eds.) (2009). *Rethinking Normalcy: A Disability Studies Reader.* Toronto: Canadian Scholars' Press.

Milligan, M.S. and Neufeldt, A.H. (2001). The myth of asexuality: a survey of social and empirical evidence. *Sexuality and Disability* 19 (2): 91–109.

Molloy, E. and Nario-Redmond, M.R. (2007). College faculty perceptions of learning disabled students: stereotypes, group identity and bias. In: *Disabled Faculty and Staff in a Disabling Society: Multiple Identities in Higher Education* (ed. M. Vance). Association on Higher Education and Disability: Huntersville, NC.

Morris, J. (1991). *Pride Against Prejudice: Transforming Attitudes to Disability.* London: New Society.

Morrison, T. (1992). *Playing in the Dark: Whiteness and the Literary Imagination,* vol. 6. Cambridge, MA: Harvard University Press.

Nario-Redmond, M. (2010). Cultural stereotypes of disabled and non-disabled men and women: consensus for global category representations and diagnostic domains. *British Journal of Social Psychology* 49 (3): 471–488.

Nelson, T.D. (2006). *The Psychology of Prejudice,* 2e. Boston, MA: Pearson Allyn and Bacon.

Nieman, Y.F., Jennings, L., Rozelle, R.M. et al. (1994). Use of free responses and cluster analysis to determine stereotypes of eight groups. *Personality and Social Psychology Bulletin* 20 (4): 379–390.

Nordahl-Hansen, A., Tøndevold, M., and Fletcher-Watson, S. (2018). Mental health on screen: a DSM-5 dissection of portrayals of autism spectrum disorders in film and TV. *Psychiatry Research* 262: 351–353.

Nosek, B.A., Hawkins, C.B., and Frazier, R.S. (2011). Implicit social cognition: from measures to mechanisms. *Trends in Cognitive Sciences* 15 (4): 152–159.

Oakes, P.J., Haslam, S.A., and Turner, J.C. (1994). *Stereotyping and Social Reality*. Oxford: Blackwell.

Office of the First Minister and Deputy First Minister (2003). Northern Ireland Life and Times Survey on Public Attitudes to Disability. Economic and Social Research Council (ESRC), Northern Ireland, the Social and Political Archive (ARK), and the University of Ulster.

O'Toole, C. (2002). Sex, disability and motherhood: access to sexuality for disabled mothers. *Disability Studies Quarterly* 22 (4): 80–101. http://www.dsq-sds.org/article/view/374/495 (accessed 26 February 2019).

Park, B. and Rothbart, M. (1982). Perception of out-group homogeneity and levels of social categorization: memory for the subordinate attributes of in-group and out-group members. *Journal of Personality and Social Psychology* 42 (6): 1051–1068.

Patterson, J.B. and Witten, B.J. (1987). Myths concerning persons with disabilities. *Journal of Applied Rehabilitation Counseling* 18 (3): 42–44.

Phelan, J.C., Link, B.G., Moore, R., and Stueve, A. (1997). The stigma of homelessness: the impact of the label "homeless" on attitudes toward poor persons. *Social Psychology Quarterly* 60 (4): 323–337.

Phelan, J.C., Link, B.G., Stueve, A., and Pescosolido, B.A. (2000). Public conceptions of mental illness in 1950 and 1996: what is mental illness and is it to be feared? *Journal of Health and Social Behavior* 41 (2): 188–207.

Powell, R., Callow, E., Kirshbaum, M., Preston, P., and Coffey, L. (2012). Rocking the cradle: ensuring the rights of parents with disabilities and their children. National Council on Disability. https://www.ncd.gov/sites/default/files/Documents/NCD_Parenting_508_0.pdf (accessed 26 February 2019).

Powner, S.J. (2015). Stereotype threat in college age students with reading disabilities: does it exist? *Dissertation Abstracts International* 76: 3-B(E).

Preston, P. (2012). Parents with disabilities. In: *International Encyclopedia of Rehabilitation* (ed. J.H. Stone and M. Blouin), 1–20. Buffalo, NY: Center for International Rehabilitation Research Information and Exchange (CIRRIE).

Proctor, S. (2011). Implicit bias, attributions, and emotions in decisions about parents with intellectual disabilities by child protection workers. Doctoral dissertation. Pennsylvania State University. https://etda.libraries.psu.edu/files/final_submissions/5719 (accessed 26 February 2019).

Read, J. and Harre, N. (2001). The role of biological and genetic causal beliefs in the stigmatization of "mental patients.". *Journal of Mental Health UK* 10 (2): 223–235.

Reingle Gonzalez, J.M., Cannell, M.B., Jetelina, K.K., and Froehlich-Grobe, K. (2016). Disproportionate prevalence rate of prisoners with disabilities: evidence from a nationally representative sample. *Journal of Disability Policy Studies* 27 (2): 106–115.

Reis, J.P., Breslin, M.L., Iezzoni, L.I., and Kirschner, K.L. (2004). *It Takes More than Ramps to Solve the Crisis of Healthcare for People with Disabilities*. Chicago: The Rehabilitation

Institute of Chicago. http://www.tvworldwide.com/events/hhs/041206/PPT/RIC_whitepaperfinal82704.pdf (accessed 26 February 2019).

Riddick, B. (1995). Dyslexia: dispelling the myths. *Disability & Society* 10 (4): 457–473.

Robertson, N. and Vohora, R. (2008). Fitness vs. fatness: implicit bias towards obesity among fitness professionals and regular exercisers. *Psychology of Sport and Exercise* 9 (4): 547–557.

Robey, K.L., Beckley, L., and Kirschner, M. (2006). Implicit infantilizing attitudes about disability. *Journal of Developmental and Physical Disabilities* 18 (4): 441–453.

Roehrig, J.P. and McLean, C.P. (2010). A comparison of stigma toward eating disorders versus depression. *International Journal of Eating Disorders* 43 (7): 671–674.

Rohmer, O. and Louvet, E. (2009). Describing persons with disability: salience of disability, gender and ethnicity. *Rehabilitation Psychology* 54 (1): 76–82.

Rohmer, O. and Louvet, E. (2012). Implicit measures of the stereotype content associated with disability. *British Journal of Social Psychology* 51 (4): 732–740.

Rohmer, O. and Louvet, E. (2018). Implicit stereotyping against people with disability. *Group Processes & Intergroup Relations* 21 (1): 127–140.

Ross, L. (1977). The intuitive psychologist and his shortcomings: distortions in the attribution process. In: *Advances in Experimental Social Psychology*, vol. 10, 173–220. Cambridge, MA: Academic Press.

Ross, K. (2001). All ears: radio; reception, and discourses of disability. *Media, Culture and Society* 23 (4): 423–436.

Rothbart, M. and Lewis, S. (1988). Inferring category attributes from exemplar attributes. *Journal of Personality and Social Psychology* 55 (6): 861–872.

Rüsch, N., Corrigan, P.W., Todd, A.R., and Bodenhausen, G.V. (2011). Automatic stereotyping against people with schizophrenia, schizoaffective and affective disorders. *Psychiatry Research* 186 (1): 34–39.

Ryan, E.B., Bourhis, R.Y., and Knops, U. (1991). Evaluating perceptions of patronizing speech addressed to elders. *Psychology and Aging* 6 (3): 442–450.

Sadler, M.S., Meagor, E.L., and Kaye, K.E. (2012). Stereotypes of mental disorders differ in competence and warmth. *Social Science & Medicine* 74 (6): 915–922.

Sampson, E.E. (1993). Identity politics: challenges to psychology's understanding. *American Psychologist* 48 (12): 1219–1230.

Schaller, M. and Conway, L.G. III (2001). From cognition to culture: the origins of stereotypes that really matter. In: *Cognitive Social Psychology: The Princeton Symposium on the Legacy and Future of Social Cognition* (ed. G.B. Moskowitz), 163–176. Mahwah, NJ: Lawrence Erlbaum.

Schneider, D.J. (2004). *The Psychology of Stereotyping*. New York: Guilford Press.

Sechrist, G.B. and Stangor, C. (2001). Perceived consensus influences intergroup behavior and stereotype accessibility. *Journal of Personality and Social Psychology* 80 (4): 645–654.

Selmi, M. (2011). The stigma of disabilities and the Americans with Disabilities Act. In: *Disability and Aging Discrimination: Perspectives in Law and Psychology* (ed. R.L. Wiener and S.L. Willborn), 123–143. New York: Springer.

Shalit, R. (1997). Defining disability down. *The New Republic* 40: 16–27.

Shannon-Missal, L. (2015). Overwhelming public support for the Americans with Disabilities Act, but disagreements exist on what should qualify as a disability. The Harris Poll, 43(24 June). https://theharrispoll.com/this-coming-sunday-will-mark-25-

years-to-the-day-since-president-george-h-w-bush-signed-the-americans-with-
disabilities-act-ada-into-law-and-americans-are-clearly-still-behind-the-legislation-with/
(accessed 26 February 2019).

Shapiro, A. and Margolis, H. (1988). Changing negative peer attitudes toward students
with learning disabilities. *Journal of Reading, Writing, and Learning Disabilities
International* 4 (2): 133–146.

Shaw, L., MacKinnon, J., McWilliam, C., and Sumsion, T. (2004). Consumer participation in the employment rehabilitation process: contextual factors and implications for
practice. *Work* 23 (3): 181–192.

She, P. and Stapleton, D.C. (2006). An Inventory of Disability Information for the
Population Living in Institutions. Ithaca, NY: Rehabilitation Research and Training
Center on Disability Demographics and Statistics, Cornell University. https://digitalcommons.
ilr.cornell.edu/cgi/viewcontent.cgi?referer=https://scholar.google.com/&httpsredir=1&arti
cle=1205&context=edicollect (accessed 26 February 2019).

Sherry, M. (2016). *Disability Hate Crimes: Does Anyone Really Hate Disabled People*. New
York: Routledge.

Shields, S.A. (1982). The variability hypothesis: the history of a biological model of sex
differences in intelligence. *Signs* 7 (4): 769–797.

Silverman, A.M. and Cohen, G.L. (2014). Stereotypes as stumbling-blocks: how coping
with stereotype threat affects life outcomes for people with physical disabilities.
Personality and Social Psychology Bulletin 40 (10): 1330–1340.

Singh, R. and Teoh, J.B.P. (2000). Impression formation from intellectual and social traits:
evidence for behavioural adaptation and cognitive processing. *British Journal of Social
Psychology* 39 (4): 537–554.

Slevin, E. and Sines, D. (1996). Attitudes of nurses in general hospitals towards people
with learning disabilities: influences of contact, and graduate-non-graduate status, a
comparative study. *Journal of Advanced Nursing* 24 (6): 1116–1126.

Somerville, S. (1994). Scientific racism and the emergence of the homosexual body.
Journal of the History of Sexuality 5 (2): 243–266.

Stangor, C. and Crandall, C.S. (2000). Threat and the social construction of stigma. In:
The Social Psychology of Stigma (ed. T.F. Heatherton, R.E. Kleck, M.R. Hebl and J.G.
Hull), 62–87. New York: Guilford Press.

Stern, S., Mullennix, J.W., Fortier, A.W., and Steinhauser, E. (2010). Stereotypes of people with physical disabilities and speech impairments as detected by partially structured
attitude measures. In: *Computer Synthesized Speech Technologies: Tools for Aiding
Impairment* (ed. J.W. Mullennix and S. Stern), 219–233. Hershey, PA: IGI Global.

Sutherland, A.T. (1981). *Disabled We Stand*. London: Souvenir.

Tajfel, H. and Turner, J.C. (1979). An integrative theory of intergroup conflict. In: *The
Social Psychology of Intergroup Relations* (ed. W.G. Austin and S. Worchel), 33–48.
Monterey, CA: Brooks/Cole.

Tausch, N., Hewstone, M., Kenworthy, J. et al. (2007). Cross-community contact, perceived status differences, and intergroup attitudes in Northern Ireland: the mediating
roles of individual-level versus group-level threats and the moderating role of social
identification. *Political Psychology* 28 (1): 53–68.

Teachman, B.A., Wilson, J.G., and Komarovskaya, I. (2006). Implicit and explicit stigma
of mental illness in diagnosed and healthy samples. *Journal of Social and Clinical
Psychology* 25 (1): 75–95.

Travis, M.A. (2011). Impairment as protected status: a new universality for disability rights. *Georgia Law Review* 46 (4): 937–1002.

Weinberg, N. (1976). Social stereotyping of the physically handicapped. *Rehabilitation Psychology* 23 (4): 115–124.

Werner, S. and Roth, D. (2014). Stigma in the field of intellectual disabilities: impact and initiatives for change. In: *The Stigma of Disease and Disability: Understanding Causes and Overcoming Injustices* (ed. P.W. Corrigan), 73–91. Washington, DC: American Psychological Association.

White, E.F. (2001). *Dark Continent of our Bodies: Black Feminism and the Politics of Respectability*. Philadelphia, PA: Temple University Press.

Wiggins, J. (1979). A psychological taxonomy of trait-descriptive terms: the interpersonal domain. *Journal of Personality and Social Psychology* 37 (3): 395–412.

Wolanin, T.R. and Steele, P.E. (2004). *Higher Education Opportunities for Students with Disabilities: A Primer for Policymakers*. Washington, DC: Institute for Higher Education Policy.

Wolfson, K. and Norden, M.F. (2000). Film images of people with disabilities. In: *Handbook of Communication and People with Disabilities: Research and Application* (ed. D.O. Braithwaite and T.L. Thompson), 289–305. Mahwah, NJ: Lawrence Erlbaum.

Wright, B.A. (1983). *Physical Disability: A Psychosocial Approach*, 2e. New York: Harper & Row.

Yergeau, M. (2009). Circle wars: reshaping the typical autism essay. *Disability Studies Quarterly* 30 (1). http://dsq-sds.org/article/view/1063/1222 (accessed 26 February 2019).

Yuker, H.E. (ed.) (1988). *Attitudes Toward Persons With Disabilities*. New York: Springer.

Yzerbyt, V., Rocher, S., and Schadron, G. (1997). Stereotypes as explanations: a subjective essentialistic view of group perception. In: *The Social Psychology of Stereotyping and Group Life* (ed. R. Spears, P.J. Oakes, N. Ellemers and S.A. Haslam), 20–50. Oxford: Blackwell.

Fighting Pop Culture Stereotypes

Many harmful stereotypes are reflected in the media and pop culture. The 2016 movie *Me Before You* is a romance between a quadriplegic man and his caregiver. Despite the film tagline "Live Boldly" the man ultimately opts to end his life, which is portrayed as burdensome, dependent, and asexual.

Image of Actors from *Me Before You* holding a DVD of the film.

How Does This Film Perpetuate Ableism?

It depicts disabled lives as not worth living, and relies on the common tropes of fear and pity, perpetuating stereotypes.

How Are Activists Responding?

Activists flooded social media with #MeBeforeAbleism and #MeBeforeEuthanasia. *BuzzFeed* called the sheer volume and traction of the protest "unprecedented," showing that Disability voices were heard and CAN make a difference!

Image of protestors holding signs in front of theaters showing the film.

The Dangers of Inspiration Porn

What is Inspiration Porn?

Social media memes and ads often portray disabled people as extraordinarily brave and heroic simply for living their lives. When disabled people are out shopping, working, or dating, it can be condescending to be approached by strangers and told "you are so inspirational." Like other forms of pornography, inspiration porn objectifies people, assumes incapacity, and is used to shame those without disabilities (e.g. *you have no excuse to complain, look at this disabled person who has it so much worse yet seems to have overcome his/her limitations*).

Why Is It Offensive to Be Called Inspirational?

Viewing a disabled person as inspirational for doing everyday tasks is patronizing and perpetuates misunderstandings. Inspiration porn contributes to an assumption that all disabled people can (and should) overcome challenges by trying harder, which may undermine the importance of removing access barriers.

https://tldegray.wordpress.com/2012/04/18/
the-only-disability-in-life-is-what/

Image of paralympic athlete Oscar Pistorius running next to a little girl in pig tails. Both have blade leg prosthetics. The quote by Scott Hamilton reads, "The only disability in life is a bad attitude."

What's Wrong With This Headline?

Star Athlete and Prom King Asks Girl in Wheelchair to Dance

Articles like these focus on the nondisabled person in the story; the disabled person is rarely given a chance to speak for themselves. While interactions between different social groups are positive, drawing attention to the power difference between them is not, especially when at the expense of the person with a disability to make the audience feel good.

No More Pity for Disability

Many disability stereotypes reinforce pity. Here are some examples:

> Disabled people are assumed to be: helpless, asexual, incompetent, passive, weak and unattractive.

These stereotypes are not only harmful but false. As ordinary people demonstrate on a daily basis, having a disability is not the problem – the problem is misrepresentation, and ableist attitudes and behaviors.

Activists Show Disability Is Not Inherently Negative

https://www.youtube.com/
watch?v=JGlUjcou6_E

In her 2015 TEDTalk, designer Elsie Roy, a Deaf woman, declared that "when you design for disability everyone benefits." For example, text messaging was originally a program to benefit the Deaf that has since been adopted worldwide.

https://twitter.com/iamnormcampaign?lang=en

"I am Norm" is a campaign aimed at middle school and high school students with the goals of redefining what it means to "be normal," uniting disabled and nondisabled students, and promoting inclusion. You can find resources on how to "Take Action" in your community, make videos and blogposts to share your identity, and declare that you are part of the norm.

Accommodations ... Envy?

Sometimes when people learn about accommodations like disability parking, extra time, or flexible work schedules, they can become jealous. Some feel as if accommodations give disabled peers an unfair advantage. *This is not the case.* Accommodations afford disabled people access to their rights to school and work. The barriers to access are illustrated in the Crippen cartoon that shows a man with a cane questioning his decision to accept a job offer when confronted with barriers like: delays in transferring his support, inaccessible housing, the lack of accommodations, and people asking if he is sure he will be able to cope.

https://crippencartoons.wordpress.com/

Ways to support accessibility in your community:

1. Per the Americans with Disabilities Act (ADA), disability and accommodations are private in the workplace. Co-workers do not need to know why they are needed.
2. Organizations like DREAM (Disability Rights, Education, Activism, and Mentoring) connect disabled and nondisabled students, and help with accommodations in higher education.
3. Volunteer at local independent living centers (CILS), disability rights groups, university centers on disability, and ally networks, or contribute to organizations doing important advocacy work.
4. Do not wait until there's a complaint or negative press, be proactive and then get your business onto AXS Map or AccessNow – apps that lets customers know where to go for accessible goods and services, locally, nationally, and worldwide.

5

Hostile, Ambivalent, and Paternalistic Attitudes and Interactions

These people say that I have a special aura and that I radiate happiness that I am blessed and want to touch me. They may act disappointed or irritated if I shy away from their touch and get away as fast as possible (which is not as fast as I would like I cannot run). Religious people do not always respond pleasantly when I reject their offer of healing through prayer. ~ Person with a physical disability, 2015

If I tell someone I don't like their pitying behavior or point out that their kind intent had a harmful impact, they become hostile, usually accusing me of being ungrateful or disabled people like me as "too sensitive." ~ Person with multiple disabilities, 2015

People go from pity party, you're so inspirational to you're an ungrateful bitch really fast when I turn down help. ~ Person with multiple disabilities, 2015

Moving from a focus on the origins and antecedents of disability prejudice, this chapter illustrates the multiple manifestations or forms that prejudicial attitudes can take. Attitudes toward disability are often described as negative, provoking aversion, hostility, and contempt, or alternatively, distress, guilt, and pity (Antonak and Livneh 2000). On the other hand, disability attitudes can also seem positive, evoking feelings of compassion, inspiration, even envy (Brown 1997). Attitudes comprise the "A" in the A, B, Cs of ableism – they are the affective or emotional reactions aroused in response to disability. Although primarily evaluative, attitudes also reflect underlying Cognitive beliefs, and can certainly trigger discriminatory Behaviors (Fishbein and Ajzen 2011). They are the *effects*, the consequences of deep-seated universal fears, learned ideologies, and culturally bound stereotypes. However, attitudes are also a source of prejudice when they trigger additional reactions that result in restricted access to employment and education, and increased surveillance and exploitation. Broadly speaking,

Ableism: The Causes and Consequences of Disability Prejudice, First Edition.
Michelle R. Nario-Redmond.
© 2020 John Wiley & Sons, Inc. Published 2020 by John Wiley & Sons, Inc.

attitudes are defined as relatively enduring, global evaluations about a person, group, idea, or issue (Eagly and Chaiken 1993). People may not form attitudes about everything, but when they do, their attitudes are often ambivalent – a mixture of positive and negative sentiments that lie dormant until triggered by some attitude "object." For example, people may hold a positive attitude about a wheelchair that looks like a futuristic space machine, a negative attitude toward the metal variety found in hospitals, and have no opinion about less familiar mobility devices. Furthermore, what may seem like a positive attitude about an innovative wheelchair may turn negative when a child is seen using it, or when people are asked to try it out themselves.

This chapter focuses on the key lessons and converging evidence from years of research about when negative attitudes are most prevalent, and when positive or mixed reactions are more likely to emerge. Emphasis is given to contemporary theories used to predict which attitudes are most common, when, and toward whom. Specific types of attitudes may also trigger specific behavioral consequences. Therefore, understanding the circumstances that contribute to the expression of particular attitudes is important to those interested in anticipating bias, and promoting more equitable interactions and inclusive social policies.

Historical Approaches to Capturing Attitudes about Disability

Social psychologists have long been interested in the study of attitudes toward disability and disabled people (Dunn 2015). Beginning with Strong (1931), much of this research has been descriptive and atheoretical, which means that traditional scholarship has lacked a guiding framework to explain the multidimensional nature of attitudes, or to make useful predictions about when and how they affect behavior (Yuker 1994). Importantly, the vast majority of this work has been based on assumptions that disability is a wholly negative experience that resides *inside* bodies and minds of those from impairment groups that can be ranked from bad to worse. As a result, the vast majority of studies on disability attitudes have selectively employed questions and formats that ignore the impact of institutional and environmental barriers, while reinforcing stereotypes about loss, limitation, and tragedy (Stone and Priestly 1996). For example, Yuker and Block (1986) asked people for their attitudes using these statements: "Most disabled people feel sorry for themselves," and "Disabled people are often grouchy." In fact, most traditional research on disability attitudes has used one of two approaches that directly ask people to self-report how they feel and think about various aspects of disability. The first focuses on the entire social group "disabled people," often using agreement scales to capture global evaluations, whereas the second requires rating a variety of specific impairments in an attempt to rank order which are more or less "preferred."

Traditional Disability Attitude Scales

Among the most established and widely used instruments to measure explicit attitudes toward disabled people is the Attitudes Toward Disabled Persons (ATDP) scale (Yuker and Block 1986), which has generated the largest body of research, spanning over 50 years. Although easy to administer and generally consistent in its findings, the scale has been strongly criticized because of its one-dimensionality and vulnerability to self-presentational biases – where people try to answer in socially desirable ways or mask their true feelings and beliefs (Antonak and Livneh 2000). Others have developed more multidimensional tools to distinguish between specific beliefs, emotions, and attributions about disability onset (Findler et al. 2007; Siller et al. 1967), or to capture specific attitudes toward disabled people at work, or in romantic relationships (Esses and Beaufoy 1994). One of these more well-established instruments is the Interaction with Disabled Person's Scale (IDPS; Gething 1994). The IDPS measures relative discomfort when interacting with people with disabilities (PWDs) based on previous theorizing (Antonak and Livneh 2000; Wright 1983) about the multiple antecedents of disability prejudice, including: fear of the unknown and ignorance about how to behave; aversion to weakness; and feelings of pity and vulnerability about becoming disabled oneself.

According to multiple review articles across years of data collection with these and related instruments, a few central lessons have consistently emerged. One of the best predictors of disability attitudes relates to the experiences people have with disabled people (Gething 1994; Hernandez et al. 1998; Yuker 1994). Not surprisingly, frequent contact, interpersonal interactions, and personal relationships with real disabled people positively influence attitudes in a variety of ways (Wallymahmed et al. 2007). In fact, many contact-based interventions designed to increase tolerance and understanding have resulted from this work, and are described in Chapter 7 on prejudice reduction. Similarly, people who take an insider's perspective, and recognize that disability is neither tragic nor overwhelming, express much more favorable disability attitudes (Gething 1994). Those with more education also consistently report more positive attitudes toward PWDs (Scior 2011).

Not all types of education result in more positive evaluations however. According to Dunn, "Much of the rehabilitation literature suggests that predominant attitudes toward PWDs are explicit and negative" (2015, p. 60), which is consistent with previous reviews (Cook 1998; Brodwin and Orange 2002; Chan et al. 2009; Vilchinsky et al. 2010; Yuker 1994). These findings carry serious implications as prejudicial attitudes can result in negative rehabilitation outcomes, including biased diagnoses, more restrictive interventions, and unfair service eligibility decisions for disabled clients, particularly ethnic minorities (Capella 2002; Toriello et al. 2003). This negativity bias may be a function of working in healthcare settings where disabled people are considered "patients" seeking help from those trained to rehabilitate what's "wrong" with them instead of considering their strengths (Wright 1983). Healthcare practitioners are typically trained to blame the person's impairment for their problems, ignoring the impact of environmental barriers (Olkin 1999). These attitudes are consistent with the biomedical model of disability where medical "experts" tend to value clients who are obedient and responsive to "treatment" over those with more stable and "incurable" conditions (Marks 1999). Changes have been called for to update biomedical training programs with coursework on the social model of disability to address how functional capacities critically depend on physical and attitudinal environments (Tregaskis 2000). For example, programs that include training in empathetic listening in contrast to objective distancing are gaining traction, particularly graduate programs with a disability studies focus (Wallace et al. 2000).

> Let us stop studying the presumably horrible negative effects of a child with a disability on parents and siblings. (Yuker 1994, p.12)

Several recent reviews (e.g. Dunn 2015) note that certain types of people have more favorable attitudes toward PWDs than others. For example, women typically report more positive feelings toward disabled people than do men (Antonak and Livneh 2000; Yuker and Block 1986) – except when it comes to dating and marriage, where nondisabled men are more likely to partner with a disabled person of the opposite sex (Chen et al. 2002). Some cultural differences have also been documented, with Asian Americans revealing more unfavorable attitudes toward various disability groups (Saetermore et al. 2001) compared to other American minorities, particularly African Americans, who tend to be *less* biased toward disabled and overweight individuals (Harris et al. 1991). Finally, favorable attitudes toward disabled people are more likely among open-minded personalities who are more tolerant of uncertainty (Galbreath and Feinberg 1973), and those with higher self-worth (Findler et al. 2007). What most of this research has in common is a preoccupation with comparing the attitudes of different occupational groups, students, and family members to see if mothers differ from fathers, nurses from doctors etc., without recognizing how much variation exists within these groups (Yuker 1994). Several researchers have called for a halt to any more studies investigating personality and demographic variables, which are less modifiable and have contributed little to understanding the causes and consequence of ableism (Olkin 1999).

Impairment-Specific Hierarchies

The second, more controversial, attitude methodology focuses on specific impairment groups to determine a hierarchy of which conditions are more or less stigmatized than others. Similar to the popular inquiry, "Would you rather be blind or deaf," the approach asks students, rehabilitation, and other occupational groups to indicate how much distance or intimacy they would prefer to keep between themselves and those who experience one of several different impairments. A ranking is then produced that orders the impairments according to their social "acceptability," alongside other stigmatized statuses (e.g. cancer, ex-convict). For example, people are often asked to indicate the closest relationship they are willing to have with someone who is: an amputee, paraplegic, blind, deaf, mentally ill, and mentally retarded. Using a social distance scale, a number is then assigned to each condition ranging from: (1) would marry to (9) would put to death – although some versions alter the end point to: (8) would send out of my country. The middle options typically include: (2) would accept as a close kin by marriage; (3) would have as a next-door neighbor; (4) would accept as a casual friend; (5) would accept as a fellow employee; (6) would keep away from; (7) would keep in an institution. Rankings are then calculated based on the average social distance score for each condition (Tringo 1970).

Of the multitude of studies conducted using this approach, a few consistent findings along with several criticisms have emerged (Deal 2007; Olkin and Howson 1994). While individual ratings may shift, the order of preference that typically emerges positions those with physical impairments (arthritis, amputation) as more preferred than those with sensory impairments (blindness, deafness), who are more preferred to those with cognitive (intellectual disabilities) or psychological conditions ("mental illness") (Albrecht et al. 1982; Esses and Beaufoy 1994; Westbrook et al. 1993).

Thirty years after the original study (Tringo 1970), this same pattern has replicated, although cancer has become less stigmatized (Thomas 2000), and several have concluded that the stigma hierarchy has remained relatively stable through the years (Chan et al. 2009). The consistent preference against those with cognitive and psychiatric conditions relative to those with physical impairments has been replicated in employment (e.g. Miller and Werner 2005), and rehabilitation settings as well (e.g. Tsang et al. 2004). Not only do health professionals indicate a preference for working with those with physical over mental disabilities, but disabled people themselves demonstrate a hierarchy of preference that favors those with fewer functional limitations (Deal 2007; Mastro et al. 1996). In terms of individual differences, women tend to express more acceptance than men, but most demographic variables, including ethnicity, fail to alter the relative position of impairment types in the hierarchy (Jaques et al. 1970); Saetermore et al. 2001; Westbrook et al. 1993). Interestingly, across 14 countries, Room et al. (2001) found higher approval ratings for wheelchair users compared to those with addictions, HIV, or a criminal record, even though paralysis was thought to be among the most disabling in all cultures.

What few of these ranking studies mention, however, is that the overall social distance scores – even back in the 1970s – were quite low for all conditions, ranging from "a willingness to accept as close kin" (e.g. people with arthritis and asthma) to somewhere between "acceptance as a fellow employee" and "would keep away from" (e.g. mental retardation, mental illness) (Tringo 1970). In 2000, even the lowest ranked category, alcoholic, was accepted as more than "a fellow employee," but less than "a casual friend" (Thomas 2000; Saetermore et al. 2001). By 2015, while allied-health students still differentiated between impairments, the most social distance preferred across all impairment groups – including people with "full-blown AIDS," "paranoid schizophrenia," "crack or heroin addictions" – was that of a casual friend. Among studies that have focused exclusively on visible, physical disabilities, the vast majority say they would befriend all impairment types; and as intimacy increases, there is more variation, but people are less likely to agree about those they would marry (e.g. Olkin and Howson 1994).

Many researchers have speculated on why some conditions are thought to be more acceptable than others, presumably to inform intervention efforts. Yet attempts to explain the organization of the hierarchy have been mixed. Severity or degree of functional ability fails to explain findings across studies (Abroms and Kodera 1978). Impairments considered more permanent, severe, or contagious are sometimes viewed more negatively than impairments that are curable, less severe, and noncontagious (Saetermore et al. 2001; Weiserbs and Gottlieb 2000). However, this is not always the case, as perceptions depend on role relationships (Barr and Bracchitta 2012), experience (Furnham and Pendred 1983), and context (Yuker 1994). For example, while initial attitudes toward a newly disabled family member may be negative, with familiarity, accurate information, and resources, most families report enhanced appreciation and value disabled family members (Wright 1983). Some authors suggest an aesthetic bias exists against those who deviate most from a "total gestalt of a whole and beautiful body," but this explanation seems more relevant to studies of "classic" disability groups (Antonak and Livneh 2000). Others have suggested that those with more obvious conditions, who are more likely to be unemployed, are less preferred than those with hidden conditions (Martz 2003). Yet, this doesn't account for the lower acceptability rankings of those with non-apparent psychological conditions (Thomas 2000). According to Jutel and Conrad (2014), people often question the legitimacy of conditions that are "less physical" as if they are "less real."

> A majority of the bottom rated conditions are associated with credibility issues, both in regard to the reliability of patients with these conditions and the epistemological status of the conditions themselves. (Grue et al. 2015, p. 184)

In studies that include both visible and less apparent conditions, research has found that psychiatric disabilities, AIDS, and addictions are ranked less acceptable, in part, because individuals are considered responsible for their onset (Corrigan et al. 2001). In addition, preferred social distance *increases* for conditions perceived as more threatening and unpredictable. Mental conditions are often considered more threatening than physical conditions, especially those associated with the dangerousness stereotype of psychiatric disabilities (Lauber et al. 2004). Attempting to integrate conflicting explanations, Toriello et al. (2007) found that allied-health students preferred more distance from groups classified as threatening to others' physical safety regardless of how visible the condition was (e.g. AIDS, paranoid schizophrenia, and addictions) – consistent with evolutionary and stereotypical explanations of ableism. For less threatening conditions, more distance was preferred from those with more obvious (e.g. cerebral palsy, obesity, and paraplegia) compared to less obvious (e.g. cancer, asthma, depression) disabilities – consistent with existential fears and aesthetic anxieties (Hahn 1988).

Among the most innovative advancements in this research come from a 2015 Norwegian study that articulated key socio-structural variables to explain persistent stigma against particular impairment groups. Disability service specialists representing over 365 000 disabled people were asked to rate 38 diseases (e.g. AIDS, asthma, psoriasis, and several specific cancers) and specific disabilities (e.g. ADHD, anorexia, autism, blindness, cerebral palsy, deafness, depression, Down syndrome, dyslexia, fibromyalgia, schizophrenia) according to how much *prestige* (how highly regarded) each had among professionals in the disability field (Grue et al. 2015). Findings revealed that the highest prestige ratings went to the most clearly defined biomedical conditions, and those representing the largest, most affluent disability service organizations – heart attacks, leukemia, brain tumors, and specific cancers. By contrast, the least prestigious impairments – depression, schizophrenia, anxiety, chronic fatigue, fibromyalgia, and cirrhosis of the liver – were either those less easily verified, "medically unexplained," or psychiatric conditions. Furthermore, the most "prestigious" conditions were also among the most life-threatening but medically *treatable* diseases, while lower prestige scores went to the more permanent, psychological, and prototypical disabilities. These findings are consistent with scholarship showing that higher salaries and more prestige is often associated with medical specialties that deal with curable, acute conditions, or those that affect the young; the opposite is true for fields that serve more chronic, self-imposed impairments, and those that serve older populations (Album and Westin 2008). In the United States, a similar pattern may apply to explain why blindness and deafness are consistently ranked higher than conditions such as paralysis and facial disfigurement, given that organizations serving these constituencies are among the most established and well-funded in the nation. Future research is needed to examine whether accusations of faking one's disability status and victim blaming are more common among those with less well-established conditions that have yet to be medically legitimized (Grue et al. 2015).

Although abundant, stigma hierarchies are among the most criticized of the disability attitude approaches. According to Olkin and Howson (1994), few studies have used the same list of impairment classifications, and many use different response options to capture intimacy levels. Furthermore, all but one (Would marry) of the social distance options assume intolerance (Would accept), marginalization (Would institutionalize), and hostility (Would put to death) – which clearly seem to prime negativity. These scales also mix questions about how disabled people should be treated in society with personal reactions which may reflect different kinds of attitudes (e.g. Disabled people should have access to employment, but I personally don't prefer to work beside them) (Leonard and Crawford 1989). Some have argued that the structure of disability attitudes is less organized by impairment type than by attitude-specific dimension (Rosenthal et al. 2006; Siller et al. 1967). This is consistent with work showing that attitudes are only good predictors of behaviors that fall within the same topic or domain (Fishbein and Ajzen 2011). For example, attitudes toward personally employing disabled people should be much better at predicting actual hiring practices than attitudes about disabled people working in general.

Subtle bias among coworkers was cited as a leading reason for job change and voluntary layoff, particularly among people of color, affecting an estimated 2 million workers in the United States annually at an estimated cost of $64 billion in wages. (Corporate Leavers Survey 2007 as cited in Pearson et al. 2009, p. 325)

Attitudes Toward Disability Rights and Employment

To illustrate how more narrowly defined disability attitudes are better predictors of behaviors in specific domains, researchers have examined attitudes toward disability rights and policies related to the Americans with Disabilities Act (ADA) (Hernandez et al. 1998; Moore and Crimando 1995). Prior to its passage, the ADA was described as "the most disruptive piece of civil rights legislation in our history" (Mandel 1989 as cited in Hernandez et al. 1998, p. 204). Given its controversial status in trying to remove barriers to employment, education, and civic participation, early research investigated the relationship between policy attitudes and actual practices. For example, the Disability Rights Attitude Scale (DRAS) measures the extent to which disabled people are considered equal members of society (Hernandez et al. 1998), asking participants to indicate how much they agree with statements about employment barriers, government services, and specific accommodations. Examples include: "Providing supports for persons with disabilities costs more than its worth"; "State unemployment forms should be available in Braille, large print, and alternative forms for persons with disabilities"; and "It's better for businesses to hire people without disabilities." Limited research using the DRAS has found that unlike other attitude measures, people seem less concerned with responding in socially desirable ways. Brough (2005) found that support for disability rights does predict endorsement of campus-specific accessibility policies. Moreover, the strongest support for disability rights comes from those who have had the most contact with disabled people (Hernandez et al. 1998).

The unemployment rate among blind people is between sixty and seventy percent, depending on the estimate you consult. This isn't because blind people can't work or don't wish to do so. It is because people do not know, and cannot imagine, how we can perform most jobs, even though many of us are already doing them. (Riccobono 2016)

Several review articles on disability employment describe a common paradox where employers consistently express positive global attitudes toward workers with disabilities, but are less supportive of hiring them relative to workers without disabilities (Fraser et al. 2011; Siperstein et al. 2006). This expressed willingness to hire disabled workers also exceeds actual hiring practices (Hernandez et al. 2000). In national surveys of diverse executives and personnel managers from Fortune 500 companies, positive evaluations toward workers with many types of impairments are common, including those with developmental disabilities (Levy et al. 1992). Other Fortune 500 studies reveal negative attitudes when asked about promoting these workers and the costs associated with accommodations. Specifically, employers are less willing to hire disabled people if they believe accommodations will be expensive or if they assume disabled people are less productive or have high turnover rates (McFarlin et al. 1991). Hiring biases are less likely on objective indicators of job performance – where prejudice would appear obvious – but bias does emerge in the form of lowered expectations for future success, and fewer recommendations for professional development and training (Colella and Varma 1999).

While the cost of accommodations is often cited as a reason not to hire a person with a disability, in reality the cost is usually very minimal. (Siperstein et al. 2006 p. 4)

Still, misconceptions about the costs of reasonable accommodations persist, and may contribute to ongoing disparities (Peck and Kirkbride 2001). When employers are informed of the specific benefits relative to costs associated with access, they are more positive about hiring people with disabilities (Hill et al. 1987). Furthermore, research consistently demonstrates that once hired, employees with disabilities are considered more reliable, and have better attendance than nondisabled employees (Graffam et al. 2002). In fact, companies with previous experience hiring disabled people (e.g. through supportive employment and other vocational programs) are more likely to value their contributions, and recommend these programs to others (Hernandez et al. 2000). Attitudes toward accommodating the needs of those with psychiatric conditions are also more positive among those who actually employ them (Cook et al. 1994); and the vast majority of employers of those with intellectual disabilities said they would hire more people from this group in the future (Morgan and Alexander 2005). Unfortunately, nationally representative surveys show that less than half (40%) of US employers provide training related to the inclusion of PWDs in the workplace (Dixon et al. 2003). To the extent that corporations value consumer feedback, they may need to rethink these practices. A recent national poll on corporate social justice revealed that 90% of consumers favored companies that hired PWDs, and 87% preferred to do business with them. The favorability ratings of corporations employing disabled people were second only to those companies who provided health insurance and protected the environment (Siperstein et al. 2006).

Benevolent or Positive Disability Attitudes

In stark contrast to the often cited negative attitudes toward disability and disabled people, several studies have demonstrated the opposite – a substantial positivity bias favoring people with disabilities (Carver et al. 1977; Carver et al. 1978; Pruett and Chan 2006). This "sympathy effect" was demonstrated in several early experiments where student transcripts for college were evaluated much more positively when a student was said to be "handicapped" compared to when no disability information was provided (Carver et al. 1977). This benevolent reaction favoring disabled over nondisabled college applicants occurred whether their applications were equally positive or equally negative. That is, even when negative information was included in their applications (e.g. students had no future plans, few interests or friends), disabled students were evaluated more positively than nondisabled students (but see Gibbons et al. 1980). According to a comprehensive review, given comparable information, people consistently rate the achievements of disabled people more highly than nondisabled people (Dovidio et al. 2011). There are strong social pressures to "be kind and avoid criticizing" disabled people, which may drive some people – particularly those motivated to appear non-prejudiced – to exaggerate their positive attitudes and charitable concerns. To illustrate, in a shopping mall study, wheelchair users requesting some loose change from strangers were successful 72% of the time compared to 46% for those who did not use wheelchairs (Taylor 1998). Others have replicated this sympathy or compassion effect, showing a positivity bias for disabled over nondisabled interviewees whether seen on video, in person (Gibbons et al. 1980), or during interactions (Ben-Naim et al. 2008). Positive disability biases persisted even when researchers told people that they can detect their "true" feelings through elaborate machines that supposedly distinguish between emotional states. That is, attitude ratings were just as positive about the disabled candidate whether evaluators were hooked up to a bogus pipeline or not (Carver et al. 1978).

Why do people sometimes bend over backwards to exaggerate the favorability of disabled compared to nondisabled candidates, even when both have equally unimpressive credentials? There are several possible explanations: people often take pity on disabled people or think they have "overcome" more challenges; they may try to overcorrect or suppress their negative feelings in some situations (Crandall and Eshleman 2003). Alternatively, some people may be genuinely impressed, given their lowered expectations for the group (Nario-Redmond 2010). While early studies were not able to isolate the reasons for sympathetic attitudes, these alternative explanations were examined in later, more theory-driven research using more modern measurement techniques.

Theoretical Approaches to Ambivalent or Mixed Attitudes About Disability

Some of the earliest pioneers of disability prejudice research recognized that attitudes toward disabled people are neither wholly positive nor wholly negative, but are typically ambivalent or mixed (Katz et al. 1988; Siller et al. 1967). Ambivalent attitudes are assumed to reflect both positive and negative components – often at the same time. Whether the positive or negative form of the attitude finds expression depends on a number of factors, including the demands of the situation and the goals, needs, and characteristics of those involved. For example, during public or face-to-face encounters, people may exhibit more favorable or caring responses toward disabled people while privately ridiculing and rejecting them.

According to ambivalence amplification theory (Katz et al. 1988), people simultaneously hold competing attitudes about people with disabilities. They recognize it is socially acceptable to treat members of this group with kindness and compassion, yet may feel uncomfortable and anxious in their presence. As a consequence, people may unknowingly display nervousness (e.g. sweat, twitch, or use more vocal fillers like "um"). However, if the goal is to present oneself as friendly and helpful, positive reactions can be exaggerated, and include patronizing, unwanted forms of assistance (Wang et al. 2015).

Given conflicting feelings, which reaction surfaces should depend, in part, on what people are being asked to do in a given situation: are they being asked to privately evaluate or to publically interact with another person? Participant goals also matter: are people motivated to appear non-prejudiced or to fit in with ableist peers? Both positive (e.g. affirming, empathetic) and negative (insensitive, cruel) reactions should also depend on the characteristics of those involved as well: Is the disabled person confirming stereotypical expectations or violating them; are qualifications clear or ambiguous; and are they considered equal or subordinate to a nondisabled peer?

Ambivalence: Situational Factors Affect the Direction of Reactions

To illustrate the power of the situation on the expression of ambivalent reactions, a classic field study from 1979 found that people voluntarily chose to sit next to a physically disabled person – a considerate reaction – if two televisions on opposite sides of a waiting room were playing the same movie. However, when a different movie was playing on each television, people were avoidant, and consistently chose to sit across the room, away from the disabled person. Presumably, people chose to sit further away (but closer to the distant television) because their choice could not be attributed to disability prejudice since a different movie was playing on each television. Perhaps completely unaware of their bias, people could easily rationalize their actions on the basis of a preference for the other movie (Snyder et al. 1979). Similar results were found across over 30 studies on differences in giving help to members of a minority group (Blacks) (Saucier et al. 2005). Helping stigmatized minorities is socially expected, but may make people uncomfortable. Therefore, whenever people can rationalize that helping is too risky, too difficult, or takes too much time, they actually help minorities less than dominant group members (Saucier et al. 2005). In this case, failing to help minorities can be blamed on some aspect of situation instead of acknowledging the possibility of prejudice.

What about situations where people believe that they have caused harm to another person: are they more or less likely to help if the person has a disability? Katz et al. (1979) found that after blasting a loud noise believed to cause harm, people were willing to provide three times as much assistance to a wheelchair user compared to an able-bodied person – even though both were exposed to the same loud noise. However, when not given the chance to help people previously blasted with a loud noise, negative disability attitudes were found as the wheelchair user was devalued more than the able-bodied person (Katz et al. 1977). The authors speculated that positive attitudes will be exaggerated when people can compensate for harming members of a stigmatized group. On the other hand, negative attitudes will be exaggerated – perhaps as a way to reduce guilt – when people are not able to compensate or help a stigmatized other. Ultimately, many situational and personal factors can shift the balance and influence how mixed feelings about disability are revealed, including the motivations and expectations of those involved.

Ambivalence: Perceiver Expectations and Motives Affect the Direction of Reactions

In addition to situational influences, the goals and expectations of perceivers matter to the expression of positive or negative attitudes. Extending early studies of attitudinal ambivalence, Dovidio and Gaertner (2004) recognized that certain *people* are highly motivated to view themselves as non-prejudiced, even if they harbor subtle forms of aversion and hostility toward minorities beneath the surface. Such individuals work hard to exhibit positive attitudes toward stigmatized groups, especially when to do otherwise might make them look biased. Nevertheless, in private, some do discriminate against minorities – as long as any evidence of bias can be disguised or otherwise justified. In this way, people can maintain the belief that discrimination is wrong while denying their own prejudices (Dovidio and Gaertner 2004). This "aversive" form of prejudice characterizes those who genuinely espouse more tolerant and egalitarian attitudes toward minority groups while failing to acknowledge any underlying feelings of hostility and discomfort (Pearson et al. 2009). As a consequence, expressions of aversive prejudice are often inconsistent. When norms are clearly supportive of equality, and discrimination appears both wrong and obvious, these individuals strive for fairness; but when expectations are unclear, or guidelines for appropriate behavior are vague, prejudice emerges, often unnoticed or deniable.

Testing these ideas, studies of stigmatized minority groups (e.g. African Americans or Blacks) have found that when candidates are equally qualified – and it is clear that all groups *should* be treated equally – people tend to favor the minority over the majority candidate as a reflection of their nondiscriminatory beliefs (for a review see Aberson and Ettlin 2004). Sometimes, even when clearly unqualified, minorities are given the benefit of the doubt. For example, feedback on a poorly worded essay was less critical when the writer was thought to be Black compared to White (Hodson et al. 2002). However, when the evidence is mixed or ambiguous with respect to qualifications, people are much more likely to discount a minority in favor of a majority candidate – even when both have identical profiles with the same mix of positive and negative characteristics. It is as if people selectively emphasize different aspects of the mixed evidence to appear nonbiased: "I'm not prejudiced, I picked the White person because of *these* qualities ..." or "I didn't pick the Black person because of *those* qualities." In a fascinating study of patients applying for healthcare, when described as gainfully employed, Black patients were considered more eligible for insurance than Whites, but when described as unemployed, the opposite was found (Murphy-Berman et al. 1998). Apparently, although being unemployed suggests a greater need for healthcare, it can also be used to justify exclusion for medical assistance without appearing prejudiced.

In summary, whether evaluating job or college applicants (Dovidio and Gaertner 2004), support for affirmative action (Murrell et al. 1994), or child-welfare decisions (Hill 2004), research has consistently found more prejudice against minorities when normative expectations are unclear, or when mixed evidence can be used to discriminate without appearing biased.

To date, few have tested these ideas as they apply to disability prejudice. However, Deal (2007) argued that aversive forms of ableism are not hard to imagine from those conflicted about the value of social integration, and the impulse to protect disabled people from unnecessary risks or hardships. Such "good intentions" may limit opportunities for career and educational advancement if support for segregated schooling, sheltered work, and residential placements (nursing homes) are easily justified as "in the best interests" of disabled students and workers. For example, given the tension between feelings of discomfort and compassion toward disabled people, ableism in the form of exclusion may be more likely when people are less clear about expectations for inclusion or risks associated with certain opportunities; but when normative expectations about the benefits of equal access are clearly articulated, people may be more inclined to express positivity toward inclusion policies. Consistent with Dovidio's aversive prejudice ideas, those most motivated to appear non-prejudiced may still waver about including disabled peers when norms about disability rights are not salient – as long as decisions that fail to consider disabled peers do not make them look ableist.

Ambivalence: Disability Characteristics Affect the Direction of Reactions

The specific characteristics and behaviors of disabled people can also impact the direction of ambivalent reactions. For example, in one study Katz et al. (1978) showed that attitudes can change dramatically if interacting with a disabled person who is outgoing (friendly and achievement-oriented) compared to bad-tempered (sarcastic and annoyed). Ironically, college students were three times *more* willing to help a woman in a wheelchair who acted angry and aloof – consistent with disability stereotypes – than when she acted friendly and outgoing. This finding stands in stark contrast to how students reacted to an able-bodied person scripted to behave in the same way – they were three times *less* likely to offer help to a nondisabled woman who acted angry and aloof than when she was friendly and polite. Specifically, students were much more willing to volunteer their time for a friendly able-bodied person and for an *unfriendly* person in wheelchair – both of whom behaved consistent with stereotypical expectations about their groups.

> Normal people tend to (1) insist that the disabled person is suffering, even when there is no evidence of suffering, or (2) devaluate the unfortunate person because he or she ought to suffer and does not. (Katz et al. 1978, p. 53)

According to several early theorists (Goffman 1963; Katz et al. 1988), non-disabled people seem to need disabled people to suffer to remind themselves that their own physical abilities are essential to well-being. When disabled people appear to be suffering, others are more likely to feel pity, and to want to help them – particularly when they are portrayed as stereotypically vulnerable (Dijker 2001). On the other hand, when disabled people appear well adjusted and achievement oriented, they may incite anger among those who need or expect them to be miserable! Consistent with these ideas, Katz et al. (1978) found that students showed more covert anger toward a wheelchair user when she acted friendly and outgoing compared to when she appeared angry and aloof. This research was conducted over 40 years ago; replication of these results today would demonstrate the extent to which these biases persist.

> Pity is a deceptive emotion. When people pity a person or a group of people, it may seem like they care about them and are interested in improving their lives. But beneath this seeming benevolence actually lies rejection, fear, discomfort, and a strong sense of the inferiority of the person who is pitied. (Presley 2008)

When it comes to perceiver motives, both pity and anger can be aroused when someone behaves in a way that subverts another person's needs (Dijker 2001). Which emotion wins out may depend on where blame is placed (e.g. who or what is responsible for causing the frustration). If a disabled person is seen as capable instead of vulnerable, the need to protect them should be undermined, which may trigger frustration in some. Furthermore, pity over a disabled person's suffering does not always contribute to a strong need to comfort them, especially if associated with feelings of personal distress (Dijker 2001).

In addition to expectations of suffering and bitterness, other cultural stereotypes characterize both disabled men and disabled women as incompetent and unattractive (Nario-Redmond 2010) – traits that can also influence ambivalent reactions to those applying for certain jobs. One study found that applicants described as wheelchair users were considered less qualified than nondisabled applicants, but only for jobs requiring significant public contact (sales), and not for more solitary positions (accounting) (Louvet 2007). Furthermore, disabled applicants were only discounted on traits related to their competence and not on traits having to do with their warmth, agreeableness, or personal qualities. This sentiment is illustrated in the following quote that was repeated by several of our survey participants, "It's too bad, you have such a pretty face. Maybe it would be easier for you if you weren't smart" (Person with multiple disabilities, 2015).

In summary, it seems that people are more negatively biased against disabled people when expectations are unclear, stereotypes are violated, and important needs are thwarted. Unfortunately, these are common circumstances as most situations are not clear cut, most evidence is mixed, and disabled people are increasingly more visible in public. Given the diversity of human needs and capabilities, which are not always the same (e.g. sometimes a wheelchair user chooses to use crutches; chemical sensitivities depend on the environment), contradictory reactions may contribute to ongoing misunderstandings and perpetuate inequality. More recent theorizing has attempted to articulate the circumstances most likely to produce particular forms of prejudice, even when reactions are mixed.

The Stereotype Content Model: Implications of Competency and Warmth

The stereotype content model (SCM) reviewed in Chapter 4 is extended here as it has implications for how stereotypes impact disability attitudes, emotional reactions, and discriminatory behaviors. According to the model, the emotions people feel toward ambivalent groups like disabled people are more volatile than for groups stereotyped as more uniformly negative (or positive) (Fiske et al. 2002; Glick and Fiske 2001). However, it also makes specific predictions about how people will feel and behave toward these groups in different situations (see Figure 5.1). The model is very clear on when people can expect to feel pity, contempt, envy, and admiration toward other groups depending on the group's social position and perceived intentions to cooperate or compete (Fiske et al. 2007; Fiske et al. 2002). In contrast to the primary emotions of anger and fear found in a number of species, these four secondary emotions – pity, contempt, envy, and admiration – are considered uniquely human (Demoulin et al. 2004).

Stereotype Content Model (SCM)

	Status lower	**Status higher**
Competitive lower	**ST:** Warm AND incompetent **FEEL:** Pity, sympathy **WHO:** *Disabled, older,* *"legitimate dependents"* **BEH:** Protect, subordinate	**ST:** Warm AND competent **FEEL:** Pride, admiration **WHO:** *Allies, students,* *"reference ingroups"* **BEH:** Deference, respect
Competitive higher	**ST:** Cold AND incompetent **FEEL:** Disgust, contempt **WHO:** *Poor, immigrants,* *"illegitimate dependents"* **BEH:** Objectify, segregate	**ST:** Cold AND competent **FEEL:** Envy, resentment **WHO:** *Rich, jews,* *"aspirational groups"* **BEH:** Scapegoat, harass

Figure 5.1 The Stereotype Content Model (SCM). Status and competitiveness dimensions are represented by the columns and rows, respectively. Within each quadrant, warmth and competence stereotypes are indicated by the initials ST, emotions by FEEL, and behavioral tendencies by BEH, along with example target groups, WHO.

Low competence, high warmth people are viewed as deserving pity and sympathy for uncontrollable negative outcomes that occur despite their best intentions. (Cuddy et al. 2008, p. 103)

Pity And Paternalistic Prejudice

Research testing SCM predictions has found that groups that are ambivalently stereotyped as both incompetent and warm elicit feelings of pity, sympathy, and other forms of paternalistic prejudice (Cuddy et al. 2008). Pity has been described as an altruistic emotion that often motivates the alleviation of another person's suffering (Batson 1987) – an approach reaction. Feelings of pity are directly linked to active helping behaviors including volunteering time and donating to charitable causes (Cuddy et al. 2008; Cooper et al. 2003). However, pity is not just one emotion but is a mixture of both tenderness and distress – feelings that are often in conflict, which may undercut inclinations to help (Dijker 2001). People who feel sorry for others may even try to avoid or distance themselves from their suffering (Schimel et al. 2000). However, at lower levels of suffering, pity may trigger a desire to protect those perceived as vulnerable to harm – especially those with characteristics that signal dependency or lack of control. For example, limited muscles, impaired senses, and unstable movements are characteristics often associated with toddlers, older adults, and people with disabilities who also generate pity and motivate a tendency to protect (Dijker 2001).

When asked to describe times when they have felt pity toward others, people most often refer to those with physical disabilities, victims of catastrophes, and those living in poverty through no fault of their own (Weiner, et al. 1982). In studies comparing up to 25 different social groups, pity ratings were consistently highest for "disabled," "blind," "retarded," and "elderly" people (Cuddy et al. 2008; Fiske et al. 2002). Pity is also more likely to be evoked for people with impairments caused by undeserved circumstances (Weiner et al. 1982). Those considered responsible for their fate (e.g. people with psychiatric impairments, HIV/AIDS) are pitied less (Weiner 1995). Pity increases toward those with uncontrollable conditions considered more permanent (stable and internal) compared to the more temporary variety (Weiner et al. 1982). When people are pitied for permanent conditions, "they are pitied for something that will not change. To be pitied for a permanent condition is to become permanently pitiful. In these cases, pity conveys the judgment of unchanging tragedy" (Boleyn-Fitzgerald 2003, p. 14).

In general, pity and sympathetic concern seem to be reserved for disabled people who "can't seem to help it," who are otherwise submissive, and who *would* overcome their condition if only they could. This may have implications for denying sympathetic care (and services) to those perceived as not doing enough to overcome their limitations. In fact, healthcare professionals have been distinguished in terms of those who exhibit genuine compassion, and those who seem more fearful, pitying, and aloof (Boleyn-Fitzgerald 2003). Unlike compassion, pity seems more emotionally distant, especially if it motivates alleviating another person's discomfort in order to relieve one's own. Pity occurs when people feel sorry for someone, while compassion is more about feeling sorry with another. Similar arguments have been made among disability rights activists who remind that no one wants to hire or befriend someone they pity. Adopting the slogan, "Piss On Pity," many disability advocates condemn using people with disabilities as pitiable objects in order to raise money for charitable campaigns (Cole and Johnson 1994; Finger 1994).

> Pity is an ambivalent emotion – comprising both compassion, but also sadness and an implicit sense of superiority over the other. Pity implicitly involves condescension (i.e. disrespect) and can therefore lead to dismissive behaviors, such as patronizing speech and poor medical treatment. (Cuddy et al. 2008, p. 111)

Behavioral Manifestations of Pity and Other Ambivalent Emotions

In addition to ambivalent feelings, pity is also associated with patronizing verbal and nonverbal behaviors, which are often disrespectful and condescending (e.g. the head tilts, eyes wince, and someone says, "poor sweet baby"). Studies of patronizing speech have shown that students used a much higher pitched voice when speaking to adults they assumed to be disabled professionals than they used for adults without disabilities. The same high-pitched voice was also used to address a 12-year-old child (Liesener and Mills 1999). Similar infantilizing, repetitive speech patterns have been observed in naturalistic settings on college campuses (Gouvier et al. 1994), and among medical students when interacting with visibly impaired others (Eddey et al. 1998). Such patronizing forms of prejudice are sometimes difficult to recognize, perhaps because they so often appear to be expressions of care and concern. In fact, good intentions may or may not be what motivates benevolent treatment when it comes to subordinate groups. People with disabilities consistently report being the targets of unsolicited, inappropriate, and unwanted assistance for which they are expected to be grateful (Braithwaite and Eckstein 2003). These experiences occur on a daily basis for some people, and are discussed further in Chapter 6.

> Strangers bend down to speak to me and address me in saccharine tones. I am often referred to as "sweetie" or "hon" even by people significantly younger than me. Sales clerks will address my teenager rather than me despite my being the one who requested assistance. ~ Person with a visible disability, 2015

Importantly, patronizing forms of help may only *appear* to be prosocial. When help is unsolicited, overbearing, or imposed, recipients are presumed to be inferior (Steele 1992), and incompetent (Becker et al. 2011). Some argue that those who provide unwanted help may do so deliberately as a way to reinforce dependency and maintain the subordinate position of certain groups (Gilbert and Silvera 1996; Nadler 2002). To explain some of these behavioral manifestations of ambivalent prejudice, the SCM proposes a behavioral map that follows from intergroup emotions and stereotypes of warmth and incompetence (Cuddy et al. 2008). The "Behavior from Intergroup Affect and Stereotypes" or BIAS map makes the prediction that helping behaviors are more actively imposed on those groups stereotyped as warm (i.e. those that are cooperative and don't compete). Certainly, both disabled people and older adults tend to receive a lot of unwanted help, imposed overprotection, patronizing speech, and charitable handouts (Ryan et al. 2006). However, because these groups are simultaneously stereotyped as incompetent subordinates, they are also more likely to be passively neglected and ignored. This can translate into friends not inviting them to parties, employers dismissing the legitimacy of requests, and student life staff failing to plan for access. At an institutional level, warehousing people in nursing homes and other segregated facilities combines both active helping and passive neglect, consistent with SCM predictions.

More recently my research team has questioned whether disabled people are consistently perceived as warm (e.g. kind and cooperative), because the existing evidence is mixed. For example, blind, "retarded," and elderly people were rated significantly higher in warmth than the broader category of "disabled people" in several SCM studies (Cuddy et al. 2008; Fiske et al. 2002). It may be that disabled people, as an overarching group, are considered more *lukewarm* – particularly if cooperative or submissive to the authority and control of others. To the extent that they are sometimes thought to be *competing* for societal resources in the form of accommodations or financial or government assistance, disabled people may also be viewed as cold and potentially exploitive. Thus, depending on whether disabled people are seen as warm and obliging or cold and manipulative, ableist attitudes and emotional reactions should differ markedly.

The Implications of Being Incompetent and Cold

Remember the SCM suggests that different stereotypes produce distinct emotions driving specific behavioral reactions (Cuddy et al. 2008). When a group is assumed to have goals incompatible with another group, anger is likely to fuel aggression toward those considered weaker and less capable of goal achievement (Mackie et al. 2000). For example, having access to the best parking spaces may be a goal that both nondisabled and disabled people want. If nondisabled people feel angry or resentful about this, they may deliberately choose to park in spaces designated only for people with disabilities. The SCM model predicts that groups stereotyped as incompetent (low status) and cold (competitive) will elicit contempt in the form of anger, bitterness, and resentment – emotions that reflect moral outrage toward exploitive behaviors. Among those groups stereotyped as both incompetent and cold are the homeless, drug addicts, and those receiving government assistance (including those with various impairments) – who are often characterized as "free-loading" at the expense of others. Even people with conditions like blindness, cancer, and obesity can elicit anger when described as responsible for causing their own less fortunate circumstances (Rush 1998).

More actively harmful behaviors are also expected toward those groups stereotyped as cold, illegitimate dependents. People who are poor, homeless, or on welfare are more likely to be intimidated, victimized, robbed, and even raped. Institutionally, these groups are also more likely to be imprisoned and brutalized through hate crimes (Sherry 2016). Furthermore, because of their perceived incompetence, these groups are also the targets of passive forms of harm – neglect, exclusion, and withdrawal of social support (Cuddy et al. 2008). At the institutional level, passive harm may also come from policies that restrict access to housing, healthcare, and educational benefits. To date, very few studies have examined resentment toward, and active harassment of, disabled people due to their low status and perceived competition for resources. However, in nationally representative surveys, 16% of those polled admitted to being angry when inconvenienced by another's disability, and 9% said they resented those assumed to be getting special privileges (Harris and Associates 1991).

Consequences of Other Stereotype Combinations

Envy and jealousy are the prejudicial emotions associated with groups stereotyped as cold but *competent* (e.g. Jews and Asians) (Cuddy et al. 2008). Studies have found that envy itself is an ambivalent emotion that reflects a sense of begrudging admiration for another group's achievements or superior outcomes

(Smith et al. 1994). Feelings of envy or jealousy contribute to behaviors that reflect passive tolerance, or that "go along to get along" when interacting with competent outgroups. However, because these groups are considered competitors and therefore cold, they are also the targets of active harm and harassment. During economic crises, envied groups, stereotyped as competent but cold competitors, are more likely to be treated as scapegoats and blamed for widespread social problems (Glick 2005). When might disabled people and older adults be scapegoated? Envious blame toward certain disability subgroups (e.g. ambitious, educated activists) is plausible – especially if higher taxes and dwindling social security benefits are attributed to government-sponsored programs earmarked just for them. Backlash against the progress of successful minority groups often takes the form of restricting affirmative action-like policies designed to rectify their underrepresentation (Cook et al. 2000). It can also take the form of violence.

> In a culture that dehumanizes disabled people by portraying them as benefit fraudsters, liars and leeches, it's little wonder they are targets of abuse … Research shows that disabled people are more likely to experience "particularly sadistic" treatment: sustained attacks that involve dehumanising humiliation, torture, and degradation. Listen to disabled people describing the everyday abuse they face in public and it becomes difficult to tell them it is not because of their disability: be it a woman who had her crutches pushed from under her in a supermarket as she was called a "scrounger," … this focus on alleged fraud and "overclaiming" of disability benefits was causing an increase in abuse directed at disabled people. (Ryan 2015)

Thus far, little research has examined conditions where disabled people might elicit envy, resentful admiration, and distain. However, there have been reports of resentment toward students with disabilities who receive extra time on tests or other "special" privileges (e.g. note takers, larger bathrooms) that nondisabled people would like access to as well. In a novel attempt to capitalize on the shorter waiting times offered to those with disabilities at Disney World, some have resorted to hiring a disabled "companion" for the day, or rented a wheelchair for a nondisabled family member to use (Thompson 2013). It is this kind of deceitful practice that contributes to exaggerated perceptions of disability fraud and fakery (Bekhour 2016). Some impairment groups are more likely to be falsely accused of faking disability than others, particularly those with less visible or psychiatric conditions, whose legitimacy is often questioned if they don't appear "disabled enough" to qualify for support (Fitzgerald and Patterson 1995). There have been reports of skeptical accusations and misplaced aggravation by those who fail to understand how physically disabled people sometimes stand up from their mobility devices to reach something or walk a short distance: "Hey! I saw you move your legs; you're not really disabled!" Several accusations of fakery followed a popular meme circulating on social media that pictured a little person from behind, standing on her wheelchair to reach something on a higher grocery shelf with the caption, "There has been a miracle in the alcohol isle [sic]" (Haller and Preston 2016; Patston 2014).

> Wow oh wow, you're such an inspiration; if someone like you, who's unstable and stuff can do this, then I need to up my game, because if I can't at least do what you do, then I should be ashamed. After all, I have nothing holding me back so therefore I should be surpassing you at every level and if I'm not, then I'm just wasting my life. ~ Said to a person with a psychiatric disability, 2015

Finally, a few studies have examined when disabled people are admired – an emotion associated with groups considered warm and competent. Interestingly, the vast majority of people responding to national surveys (92%) said they feel admiration when they encounter a person with a serious disability whereas 74% said they feel pity (Harris and Associates 1991). One recent video study we conducted found that positive portrayals of disabled people achieving success at work and school were judged to be inspirational role models, stirring feelings of surprise and awe. Specifically, after viewing a video of young adults with physical and sensory impairments shown working and going to college, other college students reported feeling more interested, ambitious, and personally inspired compared to baseline levels. Not only did students report feeling more positive overall, but feelings of fear, frustration, and hostility were significantly reduced. Following the video, people with disabilities were considered less scary, tragic, or complaining. However, paternalistic attitudes increased post video as disabled people were considered even more heroic, and able to overcome most odds. What did not change were perceptions of ableism or disability discrimination. Critics of the objectification of disabled people in the media argue that disabled people are portrayed as extraordinary objects (or inspiration porn) for the gratification of the nondisabled (Haller and Preston 2016; Pulrang 2013). We wanted to test this idea by examining the consequences of inspiration-based portrayals on disability attitudes and behavioral intentions. If such images were truly inspiring – an emotion described as motivating self-improvement and stimulating personal strivings (Thrash et al. 2010) – people should demonstrate signs of goal setting or approach behaviors. Consistent with this prediction, the most frequently generated responses students gave following the inspiring disabled people video related to striving for self-improvement, making a difference in the world, and helping others. However, these spontaneous descriptions of awe, contentment, and gratitude were not accompanied by similar behavioral inclinations. That is, self-reported feelings of inspiration did not translate into a greater willingness to volunteer to help make the college campus more accessible. Future research is needed to extend these preliminary results.

In summary, research testing the SCM has shown that emotions are often the vehicle through which cognitive beliefs or stereotypes effect certain behaviors (Mackie et al. 2000). In general, emotions are better at predicting behaviors than stereotypes alone (Dovidio et al. 2002). Extending Figure 5.1, feelings of pity aroused from perceiving a group as incompetent drive passively neglectful behaviors (e.g. exclusion). By contrast, feelings of contempt aroused from perceiving a group as competitive (cold) drive more actively harmful behaviors, including aggression (Cuddy et al. 2008). Active harm can also result from feelings of envy toward groups – especially when envy arouses anger. Therefore, the SCM helps explain how envied groups can go from being tolerated to being attacked when intergroup circumstances change. For example, when privileged groups lose status to those considered inferior, envy may give way to anger and backlash against those seen as encroaching on the privileges of the dominant group (Cuddy et al. 2008; Glick and Fiske 2001).

Much more research is needed to examine which circumstances matter most to the expression of ambivalent attitudes. For example, status decisions involving job hiring or promotions may trigger stereotypes related to competency, while the dimension of warmth might be more salient when decisions involve cooperative relationships and personal care resources. Intergroup contexts that emphasize competition or heighten perceived threat should also impact ambivalent reactions in different ways compared to situations or goals that emphasize inclusivity. In addition, the specific characteristics of stereotyped individuals should influence how ambivalent attitudes are expressed. Research with other minority groups shows that attitudes are more negative toward Blacks who demonstrate more stereotypic features compared to those who appear less stereotypical (Livingston and Brewer 2002). By contrast, research on ambivalent sexism shows that women receive more *benevolent* treatment when they act in accordance with gender stereotypes, but more hostile reactions when they violate gender expectations (Glick and Fiske 2001), consistent with Katz et al. (1978) and the quotes opening this chapter.

Questions that remain untested include: How are ambivalent attitudes toward disabled people used to justify inequalities? Do healthcare professionals respond with more compassion toward those who gratefully submit to the sick role, while withholding care as punishment from those who refuse to comply or get well? If some disabled people are less easily categorized or appear less stereotypical, will attitudes depend more on context and behavior? Are certain rights more likely to be denied when group membership is less obvious, and which forms of prejudice are more common when disability stereotypes are activated? Some have called for more research on how manifestations of ambivalent prejudice depend on impairment type and severity (Gervais 2011). However, it may be that prejudice depends less on impairment types than on the specific threats aroused in others: fear of contamination, competition for scarce resources, or perceived exploitation of benefits.

Modern Approaches to Measuring Disability Prejudice

Since the 1960s civil rights movements, public attitudes toward a variety of minority and stigmatized groups have become much more positive. Explicit forms of racial and gender prejudice are no longer considered acceptable, and many people endorse the values of diversity while denouncing bigotry and prejudice. According to the national polls, public opinions about disabled people have also shifted to become more positive and inclusive over time (Harris and Associates 1991; Katz and DeRose 2010). Thus, explicit attitudes *do* evolve with the times. However, other, even more subtle forms of bias may continue to lurk below the surface, persisting "underground," as people seek to avoid public expressions of their more deeply rooted and less conscious feelings (Monteith et al. 2001).

> Because many people are often oblivious to their own biases, it is quite likely that implicit cognitive and affective processes, and their neurological underpinnings, are part of the problem of the perpetuation of prejudice, discrimination, and inequality. (Jackson 2011, p. 128)

Contemporary approaches to the study of social attitudes differentiate between the more explicit and controllable forms and those that are more implicit and unconscious. That is, people can hold dual attitudes about groups that often involve competing evaluations. At the conscious level people may claim that they enjoy working with disabled individuals – yet, without much self-awareness – they demonstrate avoidance and fear (Guglielmi 1999). One of the strongest criticisms about explicit attitude research is the lack of consistency between what people say their attitudes are and how they actually behave. If attitudes are to be useful, researchers need a better way to capture what people actually feel when evaluating different groups. One problem with people self-reporting their attitudes toward stigmatized others is that verbal and written descriptions are often inaccurate. People generally don't want to admit they could be prejudiced, so they may lie when asked about their feelings. They may be able to describe how they *think* they feel or how they think they *should* feel, especially if they want to present themselves in socially desirable ways. Furthermore, people may not be fully *aware* of their true feelings toward certain groups. That is, they may not have introspective access to describe their attitudes on paper. Therefore, verbal self-reports and other explicit attitude measures are often unreliable when it comes to sensitive subjects since people can exert considerable effort to control their responses (Dovidio et al. 2001).

Today several novel approaches have been developed to measure what researchers call implicit attitudes or attitudes so subtle they often go unrecognized. Implicit attitudes are defined as "introspectively unidentified (or inaccurately identified) traces of past experience that mediate favorable or unfavorable feeling, thought, or action toward social objects" (Greenwald and Banaji 1995). Recall that attitudes are simply the learned associations people have stored in memory of the ideas and feelings they connect with particular concepts (Nelson 2006). Implicit associations reflect early and repeated experiences learned from family, media, and the broader culture that remain unconscious until activated when meeting or imagining people with disabilities.

The Implicit Associations Test (IAT)

One of the most widely used methods to capture implicit forms of prejudice uses reaction time tasks that assume people respond faster when reacting to ideas that are closely related in memory compared to ideas that are more distantly related (Nelson 2006). That is, it should take *less* time to classify a negative word linked to a negative category (e.g. sad and disabled) than to classify a positive word with a negative category (e.g. love and disabled) – assuming that a given individual considers disability a negative classification (Rojahn et al. 2008). A few studies have tested these ideas as they relate to disability prejudice using the IAT (Wilson and Scior 2014). The test is usually administered through a computer, and a person is asked to respond as fast as possible to categorize a series of words (or photos, symbols, or images) using one of two computer keys. The images and words presented on the screen belong to one of four categories – two are social categories (e.g. Disabled and Able-bodied), and two are attribute categories that include positive (e.g. good, pleasant) and negative (e.g. bad, unpleasant) words. People are then instructed to press one key (e.g. the letter "e") anytime they see an able-bodied image *or* anytime they see a positive attribute, but to press another key (e.g. the letter "i") anytime they see a disabled image *or* a negative attribute. The classification procedure is then reversed and people are instructed to press the opposite, "e" key anytime they see a disabled image *or* a positive attribute, but to press the "i" key whenever they see an able-bodied image *or* negative attribute. The test proceeds for about 15 to 20 minutes, carefully balancing the presentations and keys used to account for differences in hand preferences, practice, and order effects. What matters is how people respond when presented with evaluatively congruent pairs: two positive (or two negative) concepts compared to evaluatively incongruent pairs: one positive and one negative concept. People are expected to respond much faster when categorizing concepts that are both considered positive – like when "able-bodied" and "good" share the same response key – and slower when categorizing incongruent concepts like when "able-bodied" and "bad" share a key. Similarly, it should be easier to classify concepts when both are considered negative – like when "disability" and "bad" share a response key – but more difficult to classify "disability" with terms considered "good." The speed of responses is then used to infer the strength of the association between pairings and the extent to which implicit biases are present. At the end of the test, an overall score is calculated that reveals whether one has demonstrated a slight, moderate, or strong preference for one category over another. The question that many continue to ask, however, is whether or not the strength of one's attitudinal associations with a particular social group actually indicates prejudice (Nelson 2006).

Evidence of Implicit Attitudes Toward Disabled People

Since 1998, over 5 million IATs have been completed testing implicit attitudes and stereotypes associated with a multitude of social groups in over 20 countries, translated into 16 languages (Nosek et al. 2007). Several reviews and meta-analyses have documented a dominant pattern of implicit preferences for whites compared to blacks, younger compared to older adults, lighter compared to darker skin tones, straight compared to gay people, thin compared to fat people, and other people compared to Arab/Muslims (Nosek et al. 2007). Although widespread, implicit biases vary systematically depending on race, gender, and other characteristics of the test takers and the target groups presented. For example, many studies find that people have stronger implicit preferences for their own ingroups over outgroups, to which they do not belong; however, this is not always the case, particularly among lower status groups that have internalized the stigma associated with their memberships (Nosek et al. 2007). Chapter 6 describes the implications of internalized stigma for well-being, and the conditions that facilitate the reappraisal of stigma as ingroup pride.

A recent 10-year review of the literature summarized several implicit attitude studies to compare the strength of attitudes toward people with physical and intellectual impairments and toward disabled people in general (Wilson and Scior 2014). Across all 18 studies reviewed, whether using words, photographs, or images associated with disability status, negative implicit attitudes were at moderate to strong levels. To illustrate, Robey et al. (2006) found people were faster to respond to positive words (e.g. happy, joy, love, peach) when paired with the words "nondisabled," "able-bodied," "non-handicapped," and "normal" compared to when these same positive words were paired with the terms "disabled," "palsy," "handicapped," and "impaired." People also associated more negative terms (e.g. sad, awful, failure, war) with disability than with non-disability. Moreover, these implicit biases were found among those who worked at a facility for people with multiple impairments. Several studies now corroborate the pervasiveness of implicit negative attitudes toward disabled people among professional caregivers (Enea-Drapeau et al. 2012), nurse educators (Aaberg 2012), special needs instructors (Federici and Meloni 2008), and students studying to be physician assistants (Archambault et al. 2008), special educators (Hein et al. 2011), and rehabilitation professionals (Pruett and Chan 2006). While some studies reported that implicit attitudes were less negative among those with more years of caregiving experience (Enea-Drapeau et al. 2012; Pruett and Chan 2006), others found that neither the frequency nor the quality of contact with disabled people predicted *implicit* preferences (Hein et al. 2011; Thurneck 2008).

Reviewing over 38 000 disability IATs conducted between 2003 and 2006, Nosek et al. (2007) reported that preferences favoring nondisabled over disabled people are among the *strongest* implicit biases across all 17 social groups studied – second only to an even stronger implicit preference for younger compared to older people. In fact, a full 76% of the sample demonstrated an anti-disability or "pro able-bodied" implicit bias, which was higher among men, African Americans, and political conservatives. Disability bias also increased with age, with those over 60 showing the strongest association favoring people *without* disabilities. An implicit preference for able-bodied over disabled people was even found among the 3000 people who reported having a disability themselves

(Nosek et al. 2007); however, this bias was weaker than for people who did not experience disability. Thus, while racial, sexuality, and religious groups typically have implicit preferences that *favor* their own groups, an "outgroup bias" is more common among overweight people who prefer the thin (Teachman and Brownell 2001), older adults who prefer the young, and disabled people who prefer the able-bodied (Nosek et al. 2007). Those with and without psychiatric diagnoses show similar negative implicit attitudes about people with "mental illnesses" (Teachman et al. 2006). For lower status groups to show a preference for the ingroup may require the rejection of culturally prescribed attitudes stigmatizing the group as unworthy (see Chapter 6).

Implicit attitudes also depend on the type of disability assessed. Stone and Wright (2012) found that implicit attitudes were more negative toward people with facial disfigurements than wheelchair users, whereas Thomas et al. (2007) found stronger implicit bias against those with paraplegia, followed by those with cancer, alcoholism, and mental illness. Implicit attitudes toward physical disability were also more negative among those with heightened fears of disease (Park et al. 2003), but were more positive among those who believe they had personal control over the future (e.g. less fear of uncertainty). Replicating these results, Dionne et al. (2013) demonstrated a positive preference for active disability images associated with sports (e.g. Paralympic pictures of wheelchair tennis, basketball, and rugby) compared to disability images of inactivity (wheelchair user pictured watching television, on the phone, or on a laptop). The increasing prevalence of implicit association tests to identify subtler forms of bias has led to a number of critiques about what implicit associations actually represent and predict.

The Pros and Cons of Implicit Prejudice Research

Many have questioned what is really being measured in the milliseconds of reaction-time responses to words and images presented on a screen. Isolated from the complexities of the social situation, these tests do not address the intergroup dynamics, contextual constraints, and power differentials involved in actual social interactions. The idea that the speed of retrieving negative (or positive) associations reflects prejudice seems to contradict the importance of what people actually think, say, and do with respect to various groups. Can people be held responsible for unconscious feelings and thoughts they don't acknowledge? If people fail to acknowledge any kind of endorsement of their implied attitudes, implicit associations may simply reflect an awareness of stereotypical portrayals and other culturally learned evaluations. They may also reflect general discomfort, guilt, or lack of familiarity, which usually does not qualify as discriminatory treatment (Banks et al. 2006).

Others have praised implicit stereotyping and prejudice research as an ingenious approach to capturing mental associations and feeling states while avoiding the response biases involved with explicit self-reports. Several studies provide strong evidence showing the IAT to be a valid and reliable measure, resistant to faking and other self-presentational concerns (Cunningham et al. 2001). Whereas voluntary behaviors (e.g. verbal comments, jury deliberations, and intentional actions) correspond more with explicit attitudes (Dovidio et al. 2001), automatic or implicit evaluations are better at predicting *spontaneous* behaviors, particularly nonverbal behaviors. Nonverbal facial expressions and other gestures can be much more difficult to control, and are more likely to reveal hidden biases that operate without awareness. For example, negative implicit attitudes toward African Americans are associated with more blinking and less eye contact (Dovidio et al. 1997), less smiling, and more tentative, abrupt conversations (McConnell and Leibold 2001). Similarly, implicit anti-fat attitudes predicted how far away people sat from a larger woman (Bessenoff and Sherman 2000).

Studies that compare explicit with implicit attitudes about racial minorities and other stigmatized groups typically find only weak correlations between the two, and implicit attitudes are consistently more negative (Dovidio et al. 2001; Hofmann et al. 2005; Nosek et al. 2007). Even studies that show no evidence of bias toward disabled people on explicit scales, show a substantial bias when implicit measures are included (Pruett and Chan 2006; Rojahn et al. 2008). Explicit attitudes that are well rehearsed and repeatedly applied can also *develop* into implicit attitudes that become automated over time (Dovidio et al. 2001) – even in a climate of increased tolerance and acceptance of intergroup differences. If certain attitudes are no longer considered normative but instead are viewed as ignorant and outdated, some people may go out of their way to appear non-prejudiced, and support the values of equality and diversity. Deep inside, however, some may resent having to conform to be "politically correct," while still harboring prejudicial attitudes, whether or not acknowledged.

Future research is needed to validate how implicit attitudes are enacted behaviorally during interactions with others. What do people do when first primed with disability imagery or stereotypes before meeting with peers, disabled or not? When do such associations and automatic feelings manifest as behavioral avoidance, rejection, unwanted helping, or aggression? Research should also be expanded to include other implicit measures that operate through speech forms like conversational contradictions that shape actual policy decisions. Students and researchers can access materials to replicate and extend previous findings through the Project Implicit website (http://www.projectimplicit.net/stimuli.html) among other places.

Implications for Social Interaction: Manifestations of Ableism

> Attitudes do not exist in isolation, but are created, altered, and maintained by a wide range of external material and cultural factors, as well as psychological ones ... it is indeed possible to re-situate the "attitude problem" where I believe it belongs – both in the interface between individual disabled people and non-disabled people, and in the positioning of those individual relationships within a wider social context of political, economic and administration inclusionary/exclusionary influences. (Tregaskis 2000, p. 348)

Because studies have focused almost exclusively on nondisabled perceivers' attitudes about disability, many have called for more research from the perspective of disabled people, and about how differing viewpoints can affect the dynamics of interaction (Makas 1988). This section describes work designed to capture how the attitudes of disabled and nondisabled people influence their behavioral reactions to one another, and how reactions can then influence subsequent perceptions and behaviors in ways that can confirm biased expectations. According to the social psychological literature, interactions between disabled and nondisabled people are typically characterized as awkward (Hebl et al. 2000). People unfamiliar with disability don't seem to know what to do or say, and often say things that are well-intended but come across as rude, intrusive, and just plain ignorant. Expecting to be treated badly, people with disabilities may also be reluctant to initiate interactions (Frable et al. 1998). Yet both disabled and nondisabled people seem largely unaware of the discrepancies between their actions and intentions, and how inconsistent verbal and nonverbal behaviors contribute to distorted understandings.

> I'm often touched without consent by people/strangers. I have an arm that is smaller and looks different to others. People that I have just met in public sometimes grab or touch it and talk about it. They often try to say how "cool" it is, but they don't realize how dehumanizing it is to have your difference highlighted in that way and to have people think that it is ok to touch you without asking. I usually don't do anything and let it happen. I usually don't realize until afterwards how and why I was uncomfortable during the interaction. ~ Person with multiple disabilities, 2015

Those who study "mixed interactions" between disabled and nondisabled people consistently describe them as strained and socially disruptive (Jaques et al. 1970). For example, studies have found that in more intimate situations, nondisabled people display more anxiety, avoidance, and even hostility toward disabled people (e.g. Berry and Meyer 1995). Feelings of nervousness, uncertainty, and embarrassment are commonly observed, whether anticipating future interactions (Fichten et al. 1991) or reporting on them after the fact (for a review see Hebl et al. 2000). Even in national surveys, a majority of the population admits to feeling awkward and uncomfortable when meeting people with disabilities (Harris and Associates 1991). Although more people report having disabled friends, co-workers, and acquaintances today than ever before, uncertainties prevail particularly among those for whom exposure to disability has been limited (Hebl et al. 2000).

It should be noted that much of this mixed interaction research has focused on the uncomfortable feelings and behaviors of those without disabilities (Albrecht et al. 1982). Less typical are studies that examine feelings of intrigue, inspiration, and respect (but see Langer et al. 1976; Sigelman et al 1986). Traditionally, studies of "interaction pathology" are often premised on the assumption that mixed interactions are awkward because of some feature "inherent" to a particular stigma or impairment (Hebl et al. 2000). Something about the stigma itself is assumed to be disruptive to having a smooth social exchange – inevitably provoking anxiety, avoidance, and strained communication (Goffman 1963). However, this is a rather narrow – some might say, ableist – interpretation that fails to consider what both parties bring or fail to bring to the interaction context. For example, is the strain associated with communication between deaf and hearing people attributed to hearing loss or to the language barrier present when not all parties communicate in sign language? Similarly, is the frustration associated when conversing with someone who stutters attributed to the speech impairment or to the lack of patience on the part of certain listeners? Even those with visible burns, facial scars, or missing limbs may only provoke discomfort among people unfamiliar with these conditions – just as visible piercings, tattoos, or other body modifications are relative to cultural expectations of attractiveness. According to Hebl et al. (2000), the various dimensions of stigma (e.g. visibility, origin, disruptiveness) are theoretically arbitrary, and inconsistently predict interaction outcomes which vary widely depending on personal experience. Those with less exposure to human diversity and people from different impairment groups may indeed display more hesitancy due to uncertainty about how to respond, especially those who fear embarrassing themselves or offending others. This lack of know-how is why so many programs have been developed to teach "disability etiquette" to the uninformed, with suggestions that include: addressing the disabled person directly instead of his/her companion or interpreter, and asking, when unsure, how people prefer to be addressed or assisted, if at all (Jain et al. 2013).

Furthermore, fewer studies have investigated the feelings of disabled people. Yet, those who experience disability report similar feelings of discomfort, annoyance, and aggravation. One of the first studies to examine how disabled insiders feel found that wheelchair users smiled less, were more inhibited, and ended an interview sooner when the interviewer was nondisabled compared to when the interviewer was also a wheelchair user (Comer and Piliavin 1972). These results suggest that the anxiety commonly reported in mixed-ability interactions is not exclusive to nondisabled people. Those who experience disability display similar avoidance patterns which are less likely to be present when interacting with a fellow disabled person (see also Frable et al. 1998). If anticipating rejection and misunderstanding, it is not surprising that people with disabilities approach interactions with caution (Oyserman et al. 2007).

In studies of other stigmatized groups, Dovidio et al. (2002) found that racial minorities often report feeling suspicious about the intentions and true feelings of others, and this mistrust contributes to increased alertness and sensitivity in anticipation of negative reactions. Testing the idea that anticipated rejection alone can affect perceptions, Kleck and Strenta (1980) found that people led to believe that they had facial scars cosmetically applied to their faces perceived their interaction partners to be tenser – even though the scars had been removed without their knowledge prior to the interaction. In other words, when people expect to be stigmatized or treated unfairly, they may interpret the behavior of others as confirming their expectations even when it does not; in fact, independent judges found no evidence of differential treatment in this study. Such is the power of expectation on perception. These results were replicated among separate disabled and nondisabled samples: whenever people believed they were observing an inter-action between a nondisabled person and a wheelchair user, they perceived the nondisabled partner to be more on edge, tense, and patronizing, even when the interaction they observed was actually between two nondisabled people only vis-ible from the waist up (Strenta and Kleck 1985).

The sensitivity to unwanted awkward interactions on the part of both disabled and nondisabled people has led some to research how mixed-ability relations are negotiated with strategies to compensate for inexperience and uncertainty. Several studies have found that attitudes are more positive toward disabled people who are themselves positive about their disability experiences (Hebl et al. 2000; Wright 1983). The advantages to portraying self-acceptance are associated with more positive social evaluations, longer conversations, and increased eye contact (Elliott et al. 1991). Another strategy that has received a lot of empirical attention relates to the "acknowledgement tactic" where disabled people are encouraged to spe-cifically mention their disability status – even if already visible and irrelevant to the conversation – as a way to signal their openness about the topic (Hebl and Kleck 2002). The idea is that by acknowledging the "elephant in the room," disabled people communicate self-acceptance, which puts others at ease, reducing inhibi-tions and encouraging dialogue. Studies have found that those willing to acknowl-edge their disability (e.g. "I should let you know that I stutter"; "I have had this scar on my face since birth"; "Well, people notice that I use a wheelchair") are treated more positively during interactions (Collins and Blood 1990). Compared to those who did not acknowledge an observable impairment, those who did were considered more open and well-adjusted (Hastorf et al. 1979), were more preferred as work partners (Collins and Miller 1994), and were considered more hirable for professional jobs (Hebl and Kleck 2002).

Clearly, the acknowledgement strategy should depend on the context, timing, and the form disclosures can take, and may even be a liability for job applicants whose disabilities are considered preventable (e.g. those deemed "overweight" or who choose not to wear hearing aids). Sometimes acknowledgement makes no difference in disabled job applicants' evaluative ratings (Healey et al. 2007); and when disclosed at the end of an interview, disability status may even be viewed more negatively than not acknowledging it at all (Hebl and Skorinko 2005).

As a result of some of this research, rehabilitation, mental health, and other professionals often make the recommendation that disabled people verbally acknowledge their already observable conditions in order to pave the way for smoother interactions (Goldberg et al. 2005). The strategy is assumed to work by "straightforwardly addressing the source of the tension underlying a social inter-action and allowing interactants to get beyond it sooner than might otherwise occur without the acknowledgement" (Hebl et al. 2000, p. 430). But this is problematic for a number of reasons, as it assumes disability is something that must be "gotten beyond," which undermines the recognition of disability as a positive cultural identity. Furthermore, it puts the onus on the disabled person as the one responsible for creating a smoother interaction and relieving anxieties assumed to be inevitable among nondisabled peers. For example, disabled people who anticipate discomfort are advised to first disclose their impairment and its cause, or to make a joke about it so that interaction partners can feel free to ask follow-up questions before moving on to other topics and tasks.

Sometimes these follow-up questions reflect sincere interest in learning more about what disabled life is like, but at other times they are insensitive and intrusive inquiries about how one goes to the bathroom to eliminate waste, or manages to get up in the morning without wanting to kill oneself. Some people have even created video parodies to illustrate the most repeated insults imposed upon people with disabilities as they go about their daily lives. For example, there is a video campaign on YouTube called, "Sh*t People Say to"... people with disabilities, ... autistics, ... stutterers, ... little people, ... blind people – the list goes on. Some are produced by disabled people (LaRoy 2016; Reynolds 2012), and some by people without identifiable disabilities (StanfordPushProject 2012)

As these videos illustrate, bridging the gulf between inquisitive interest and offensive probes that would be considered inappropriate in most other circumstances is a topic in desperate need of research informed by the experiences of disabled people, and evaluated for effectiveness. The emerging literature on microaggressions is just beginning to examine ableist forms of subtle but demeaning put-downs, dismissive glances, and identity-denying behaviors so common that they are often overlooked (Gonzales et al. 2015; Sue 2010). Ironically, many of these seemingly automatic micro-assaults still appear acceptable to some – even courteous and complementary: "Let me get that door for you," "You're so inspirational to me," "I don't even think of you as disabled." As such, scholars have investigated the extent to which people agree on the difference between paternalistic prejudice and truly positive attitudes, and whether these depend on disability status.

Divergent Perspectives

In a unique dual perspectives approach to identify what qualifies as a "positive disability attitude," Makas (1988) found significant discrepancies between disabled and nondisabled people's views. Nondisabled people were much more likely to assume that disabled people should be given special considerations, including leniency in punishment for breaking the law, exemption from income tax, and acquiescence in the form of "not trying to win" during competitions. These attitudes in support of "giving disabled people a break" and "treating them as saintly" were endorsed as even more appropriate among those instructed to respond in a way they thought would really impress people with disabilities! By contrast, disabled participants were much less likely to agree that such patronizing concessions reflected positive attitudes; similarly, they were less likely to consider fellow disabled people as more easy going and courageous than their nondisabled counterparts. As this study demonstrates, the paradox of well-intentioned kindness seems to reflect pervasive misunderstandings that what disabled people really want is admiration, special treatment, and charitable protection instead of human recognition, respect, and equal rights.

Several reasons have been cited to explain why perceivers and the targets of their perception have such divergent perspectives about each other. For one, each actor has access to different kinds of information during interpersonal exchanges. Neither side may be fully aware of what gestures and expressions are visible to their interaction partners (Pearson et al. 2009). For example, when in the role of actor or speaker, people may focus more on their own deliberate words, explicit attitudes, and behaviors while attending less to their partners' reactions (Pronin et al. 2004). However, while listening, interaction partners may be more sensitive not only to what is being said but to the speaker's nonverbal reactions as well. These actor–observer differences are particularly likely for those who are members of majority groups interacting with people from minority communities (Shelton 2003). Studies of interracial interactions show that Whites' perceptions of their own friendliness are more related to their explicit attitudes toward Blacks, while Blacks' perceptions of their White partners are more related to the nonverbal cues that Whites express (Dovidio et al. 2002). If such encounters are fraught with implicit biases that only minority members detect, very different impressions may result from the same encounter – Black partners may leave feeling slighted while White partners remain oblivious to offending.

Verbal and Nonverbal Mismatches and Mixed Messages

Extending these results to mixed-ability interactions, if nondisabled people consistently display more rigid or closed postures, avoid eye contact, or stare from a distance (Perlman and Routh 1980), but in the next moment express their admiration using higher-pitched simplistic language while asking highly personal questions (Robey et al. 2006), what is a disabled person to think? People sometimes say things that do not match their body language (e.g. exaggerating compliments from a distance or with arms folded). Sometimes verbal–nonverbal contradictions take the opposite form, like when nondisabled people smile during interactions while later reporting they disliked their disabled partners (Frable et al. 1990).

I would say the patronization and condescension comes from people I know, or acquaintances, who show through facial expressions, gestures, words, and speech, verbal and nonverbal and body language, that they feel bad and sorry and uncomfortable at my pain or having symptoms or having experienced something difficult.
~ Person with multiple disabilities, 2015

More often, however, it is the verbal, intentional, and public behaviors that reflect a positivity bias, whereas facial expressions and bodily gestures are more apt to reveal negativity and aversion (Hebl et al. 2000). In general, people are less able to regulate their nonverbal expressions compared to what they say out loud when trying to "be kind" and courteous. Our nonverbal channels of communication are just more likely to betray genuine feelings because they are more difficult to control. Evidence supporting this nonverbal behavioral leakage of "true attitudes" comes from several studies documenting the relationships between implicit attitudes and various forms of nonverbal bias (Dovidio et al. 2002).

Some speculate that awkward interactions reflect conflicting feelings about not wanting to offend or violate social norms (e.g. by staring or invading someone's privacy) while simultaneously being curious and interested in the disability experience (Sigelman et al. 1986). In a classic study investigating the consequences of wanting to stare at people with novel bodies, but not wanting to violate the social rule against staring, Langer et al. (1976) found that when prohibited from staring before interacting with a physically disabled woman, people chose to sit almost two feet further away from her than those allowed to stare for three minutes prior to interacting. The implication of this work is that lack of exposure drives avoidance of those to whom people have limited access. Once familiar with novel impairments, interaction strain in the form of social distancing should be eliminated without the need for acknowledgement or personal disclosures.

> You can imagine how many times each of these men and women have heard a parent tell their child, "Don't look. Don't stare at him. That's rude." I take these pictures so that we can look; we can see what we're not supposed to see. And we need to see them because we created them. (Blair 2015 citing David Jay, photographer of injured war veterans)

When uncertain about how to behave, those with the least amount of experience interacting with disabled people put more effort into monitoring themselves (Hebl et al. 2000). Research has shown that when people try too hard to control their verbal expressions, they have fewer attentional resources to manage their nonverbal reactions (DePaulo and Friedman 1998). As a consequence of exerting extra effort – trying not to appear ignorant or prejudiced – some people actually slip up when it comes to reactions that are more difficult to control (Gilbert and Hixon 1991). People are also more likely to put "their foot in their mouth," and inadvertently blurt out exactly what they are trying to suppress. For example, if trying hard not to stare at someone's missing leg, people might nervously cross their own legs repeatedly or randomly mention how they once broke an ankle. Studies on the rebound effect have found that ironically, when people exert a lot of effort to suppress unwanted thoughts and feelings, their intentions can backfire – bottled-up feelings slip out in the form of inappropriate comments, intrusive inquiries, or overzealous aid (Macrae et al. 1994). Several reviews document the difficulties associated with deliberate attempts to regulate and suppress the nonverbal expression of emotions (DePaulo and Friedman 1998). Conversational delays, where interaction partners slow down their pace of speech or hesitate – even for one brief second – can also increase anxiety, reducing interest in becoming acquainted (Pearson et al. 2009).

One does not have to be a rocket scientist to detect ambivalent disinterest and dislike. Disabled people can, and do, perceive discrepancies between verbal and nonverbal messages signaling that others are not comfortable in their presence. In fact, the more minority members expect to be treated prejudicially, the more negative they feel during mixed interactions (Shelton et al. 2005), reinforcing beliefs that majority members are indeed prejudiced. Furthermore, when people give off the subtle impression that they are anxious and uncomfortable, those on the receiving end – who interpret these behaviors as evidence of rejection – often even respond in kind, whether they are aware of this or not. Specifically, nonverbal biases can become socially "contagious" whenever the recipient of a negative bodily reaction (e.g. frown, yawn) adopts the same expression once exposed to this expression in others. The phenomenon is known as the chameleon effect (Chartrand and Bargh 1999).

Tiedens and Fragale (2003) found that discomfort and dislike were highest during interactions where partners mimicked each other's *constricted* behaviors (e.g. legs together, hands in lap, slouched) compared to when these nonverbal behaviors were not mimicked. Automatic mimicry is even more likely among people from lower social status groups when interacting with higher status individuals (Gregory and Webster 1996). Consistent with this idea, Frable et al. (1990) found that members of various stigmatized groups were more "mindful" and attentive of their nondisabled interaction partners than these partners were of them. Nonconscious mimicry may be responsible for why negative expectations resulting in prejudicial treatment often produce similarly negative reactions from an interaction partner. For example, job applicants performed worse when responding to interview questions delivered in a negative, unenthusiastic tone of voice compared to those responding to the same questions delivered in a more neutral tone (Smith-Genthôs et al. 2015). Furthermore, the reason applicants' performance was considered less qualified was due to the fact that these applicants inadvertently shifted their own tone of voice to mimic the less enthusiastic tone of the interviewer – which ultimately impacted the content of their answers.

Self-Fulfilling Prophecies

Research on behavioral confirmation or self-fulfilling prophecy effects demonstrates how under some conditions, biased expectations not only affect how one person treats another, but can actually provoke the very behaviors expected – confirming perceivers' original (often biased) beliefs (Hilton and Darley 1991; Miller and Turnbull 1986; Word et al. 1974). If disabled (or elderly) people are expected to be incompetent and helpless, others may talk to them as if they are children and impose unwanted assistance which, if passively accepted, may contribute to the impression that disabled people are less capable and more dependent (see Nadler 2002). Over time, some disabled people may even develop learned helplessness, internalizing stereotypes and tolerating invasions of privacy that render them vulnerable to abuse – even by medical and service professionals designated to support their independence (Mikulincer 2013).

Although few studies have tested these ideas in the context of disability, Harris et al. (1994) did find support for self-fulfilling expectations related to the competency of older adults. They found that those who expected to teach a 61-year-old retiree behaved differently compared to those expecting to teach a 19-year-old college student – even though both groups were trying to maximize the number of correct answers they could get. Specifically, videotaped observations of the student "teachers" described them as more nervous and less friendly when they thought they were teaching an older adult than when they thought they were teaching a college student (although there were no differences in the number of concepts actually taught). More importantly, when these videos were subsequently used to teach other college students, those who viewed the video with the *expectation* of an older adult actually answered fewer questions correctly than those who viewed the tape expecting a college student. More recently, Hornstra et al. (2010) found a similar confirmation bias in teachers who assigned lower scores in writing achievement to their learning disabled students the more negative their implicit attitudes were toward students with dyslexia. Moreover, these students scored lower on an independently scored, standardized spelling test, when their teachers had more negative implicit attitudes.

Extending these results to peer interactions, Harris et al. (1992) found that when school-aged boys expected to interact with a boy diagnosed with attention deficit hyperactivity disorder (ADHD), they behaved less friendly, spent less time talking, and gave their partners less credit for a Lego task compared to those who did not expect their interaction partner to have ADHD. As a direct consequence of these negative expectations, boys labeled with ADHD – who neither had the disorder nor were aware that others thought they did – rated the interaction as more unpleasant, and took less credit for the task than boys who were not labeled with ADHD. Interestingly, this study also found that boys who actually *did* have an ADHD diagnosis liked the interaction better, and were judged more friendly than those who did not have this diagnosis – even though nondisabled peers were more likely to reject those with ADHD compared to those without the condition. The authors of this study concluded that the effects of an ADHD expectation did not make those labeled more active or disruptive. Instead, it made their interaction partners more unfriendly and withdrawn, which reduced the enjoyment of those labeled – independent of whether they had ADHD or not.

Many mechanisms can contribute to these attitude-behavioral confirmation effects, including nonverbal expressions of less warmth, more interpersonal distance, or less time and effort spent during verbal interactions. Future research is needed to better understand when self-fulfilling effects are most likely to undermine mixed-ability interactions with severe consequences for employment, educational, and other outcomes. Again, disabled people do perceive discrepancies between verbal and nonverbal messages that signal that others are not comfortable in their presence. How are people to understand one another when interactions are fraught with misconceptions about disability, its relevance to the conversation, and the responsibility of each person in the communication process? <u>Disabled people should not have to become comedians nor disclose intimate details in order to put the nondisabled at ease</u>. It can be exhausting to navigate the biased expectations and inconsistent communication patterns of many mixed-ability interactions (Oyserman et al. 2007). The implications of such differential treatment for disabled people's coping responses and well-being, including disengagement from interactions anticipated to be prejudicial or unfair, are reviewed in Chapter 6.

Summary

The literature on disability attitudes spans several decades of investigations dating back to the 1930s. Many of these studies reflect researcher assumptions that disability is a wholly negative experience, and fail to consider the impact of institutional and environmental barriers. This large body of research illustrates multiple manifestations of ableist evaluations ranging from aversion and contempt to a mixture of compassion, sympathetic pity, and even inspiration. While much of this work has been atheoretical, research has converged on some important lessons about when prejudicial reactions are most likely to occur, which can inform advocacy efforts designed to mitigate biases, and promote more accurate understandings and interactions. Based on multiple review articles using a variety of measurement tools, we know that women, those with more education, and those with personal relationships with real disabled people report the most positive and accurate attitudes – particularly when education moves beyond a biomedical approach that assumes disability must be cured or somehow fixed. Graduate programs in healthcare are beginning to incorporate training that recognizes the multidimensional issues disabled people face.

Traditionally, most research has relied on self-reported attitudes with tools that have been criticized as one-dimensional, and subject to responses that showcase what people think they're supposed to feel rather than their actual feelings. One of the most enduring but controversial of these methodologies measures attitudes according to how close or intimate people are willing to become with different impairment groups. These so-called disability preference hierarchies rank impairment types as more or less stigmatized depending on the social distance people prefer to keep between themselves and those who experience physical, sensory, and various other conditions. International findings consistently reveal that people tend to prefer or find "acceptable" those with physical and sensory impairments over those with cognitive and psychological conditions. However, these preferences may not be reflected in the workplace, where those with more visible or obvious conditions are more likely not to be employed. Some argue that greater social distance is "preferred" for groups considered more threatening, unpredictable, and responsible for their fates. More recent evidence suggests that rankings reflect the societal prestige associated with conditions that are more well-funded, and medically treatable – the curable, acute conditions, and those that affect the young; conditions that are more chronic, self-imposed, or that affect older populations may be preferred less, in part because they are simply less medically prestigious.

Taking a more policy-relevant focus, several have investigated attitudes in relation to the ADA. The Disability Rights Attitude Scale (DRAS) measures support for policies designed to remove discriminatory barriers and accommodate disabled people as equal citizens. Unfortunately, positive attitudes on this scale do not always translate to real-life situations. While an employer may say they support the hiring of disabled people, fears about the expense of accommodations and stereotypes of disabled people as less productive still undermine their actual hiring. Employers clearly need more education based on research showing that once hired, disabled people are considered highly reliable and valued and are recommended to other employers.

Although not necessarily positive or progressive, research has also documented what are deemed to be benevolent attitudes about disability. Perhaps a function of lowered expectations, the "sympathy effect" describes how the achievements of disabled people are consistently inflated relative to their nondisabled counterparts – a response akin to an act of charity. There are strong social pressures about how society's "legitimate dependents" (e.g. children, elderly, disabled) should be treated that regulate the expression of disability attitudes. People not only avoid criticizing this group but frequently report feeling inspired whenever they appear to be overcoming daily challenges. Very few studies have investigated the nature of these inspired reactions or their consequences. However, when attitudes are examined at the unconscious level, people do not seem to automatically associate positive attributes with disability – particularly people working in medical and special education fields. In fact, strong preferences for nondisabled over disabled people are pervasive in the literature on implicit bias, as people spontaneously link disability with negative feelings and infantilizing, stereotypical traits.

More often than not, disability attitudes are found to be ambivalent: a competing combination of positive and negative reactions. Whether the positive (I must be kind; I don't want to seem prejudiced) or negative (I'm uncomfortable, annoyed, and want to leave) form surfaces depends on the situation, along with the goals and characteristics of those involved. In general, when people have conflicting attitudes, research shows that positive, prosocial reactions are more likely in public; when people want to compensate or demonstrate their egalitarian values; when their involvement is not too time-consuming or difficult; and when the disabled person behaves in expected ways. By contrast, negative, antisocial reactions are more likely when the situation is unclear; when there is confusion about what is socially acceptable; or when the disabled person violates stereotypical expectations. In ambiguous situations, when uncertainty is high, people are more apt to ignore or devalue disabled people – especially if this rejection can be attributed to something besides ableism (e.g. It's not that we deliberately left her out, we just didn't know what to do).

In an effort to systematically predict the form ambivalent reactions will take, the SCM proposes that people use information about a group's social status and perceived competitiveness to derive their stereotypic beliefs, emotional reactions, and behaviors. Consistent with the model, research finds that groups with lower social status, such as older and disabled people, incite feelings of pity and intentions to protect – as long as they are not perceived to be competing for resources. As soon as low-status groups are perceived to be competitive, freeloading, or defrauding the system, they are more likely to incite disgust, contempt, and possible hostility. Furthermore, groups that gain social status but who are perceived to be competing for limited resources or receiving "special" privileges (e.g. parking, extra time on tests, or supplemental income) can also become targets of envy, jealousy, and active harm. Inspiration and admiration are predicted for group members that exceed stereotypical expectations of incompetence while remaining cooperative and nonthreatening. To date, research testing the SCM has found that disabled people are often considered incompetent but relatively warm and deserving of protection; however, as their social circumstances change, ableism in the form of resentment, accusations of fraud, physical abuse, and hate crimes may emerge. Resentment toward ADA accommodations seems to demonstrate a real misunderstanding about how access enables *equal* rights, and often improves participation for the majority who benefit from ramps, elevators, and various digital technologies.

Some of the more nuanced applications of this large body of research come from studies that examine the impact of attitudes on interactions. Both disabled and nondisabled people say that these interactions can be awkward, although those who experience disability seem particularly sensitive to microaggressions, gestures and speech patterns that signal discomfort and ignorance. Unfortunately, most studies have focused on the reactions of the nondisabled. Yet, those with disabilities can inform efforts to improve interactions in ways that don't perpetuate invasive and unwanted forms of helping, inappropriate questions, or unnecessary disclosures, but instead promote active listening and interest in disability as a positive identity. When a disabled person (or any minority) expects to be treated unfairly, they may be reluctant to interact or misinterpret curiosity as discriminatory. These fears stem from very real experiences that are not without reason, which is why disabled activists have been leveraging social media to educate the public through humor, performance, and insider blogs designed to bridge the gap. Outlets like the Disability Visibility Project work to create disabled media from oral histories through tweets, podcasts, and critiques on ableism such as how to distinguish between offensive probes and informative parody or how become a better ally by learning how to confront misinformation (a topic discussed in Chapter 7).

When mixed interactions fail due to mismatched expectations about what constitutes a positive, affirming attitude about disability, the consequences for both parties can be devastating. More significantly, when disabled people internalize negative attitudes, a self-fulfilling cycle can result whereby expectations of incompetence and helplessness are inadvertently confirmed. There are many ways disabled people have learned to cope with ableism, and some are more effective than others. Chapter 6 turns to these divergent strategies and the effects of ableism on individuals' physical and mental health, achievement, and the upward mobility of the group overall.

References

Aaberg, V.A. (2012). A path to greater inclusivity through understanding implicit attitudes toward disability. *Journal of Nursing Education* 51 (9): 505–510.

Aberson, C.L. and Ettlin, T.E. (2004). The aversive racism paradigm and responses favoring African Americans: meta-analytic evidence of two types of favoritism. *Social Justice Research* 17 (1): 25–46.

Abroms, K. and Kodera, T.L. (1978). Expectancies underlying the acceptability of handicaps: the pervasiveness of the medical model. *Southern Journal of Educational Research* 12 (1): 7–20.

Albrecht, G.L., Walker, V.G., and Levy, J.A. (1982). Social distance from the stigmatized: a test of two theories. *Social Science & Medicine* 16 (14): 1319–1327.

Album, D. and Westin, S. (2008). Do diseases have a prestige hierarchy? A survey among physicians and medical students. *Social Science & Medicine* 66 (1): 182–188.

Antonak, R.F. and Livneh, H. (2000). Measurement of attitudes towards persons with disabilities. *Disability and Rehabilitation* 22 (5): 211–224.

Archambault, M.E., Van Rhee, J.A., Marion, G.S., and Crandall, S.J. (2008). Utilizing implicit association testing to promote awareness of biases regarding age and disability. *Journal of Physician Assistant Education* 19 (4): 20–26.

Banks, R.R., Eberhardt, J.L., and Ross, L. (2006). Discrimination and implicit bias in a racially unequal society. *California Law Review* 94 (4): 1169–1190.

Barr, J.J. and Bracchitta, K. (2012). Attitudes toward individuals with disabilities: the effects of age, gender, and relationship. *Journal of Relationships Research* 3: 10–17.

Batson, C.D. (1987). Prosocial motivation: is it ever truly altruistic? In: *Advances in Experimental Social Psychology*, vol. 20 (ed. L. Berkowitz), 65–122. San Diego: Academic Press.

Becker, J.C., Glick, P., Ilic, M., and Bohner, G. (2011). Damned if she does, damned if she doesn't: consequences of accepting versus confronting patronizing help for the female target and male actor. *European Journal of Social Psychology* 41 (6): 761–773.

Bekhour, D. (2016). Anderson Cooper: What were you thinking? *Medium* (7 December). https://medium.com/@OptimisticGrin/anderson-cooper-what-were-you-thinking-425fa6a9932a (accessed 26 February 2019).

Ben-Naim, S., Aviv, G., and Hirschberger, G. (2008). Strained interaction: evidence that interpersonal contact moderates the death-disability rejection link. *Rehabilitation Psychology* 53 (4): 464–470.

Berry, J.O. and Meyer, J.A. (1995). Employing people with disabilities: impact of attitude and situation. *Rehabilitation Psychology* 40 (3): 211–222.

Bessenoff, G.R. and Sherman, J.W. (2000). Automatic and controlled components of prejudice toward fat people: evaluation versus stereotype activation. *Social Cognition* 18 (4): 329–353.

Blair, E. (2015). It's not rude: these portraits of wounded vets are meant to be stared at. National Public Radio (25 May). https://www.npr.org/templates/transcript/transcript.php?storyId=408505821v (accessed 26 February 2019).

Boleyn-Fitzgerald, P. (2003). Care and the problem of pity. *Bioethics* 17 (1): 1–20.

Braithwaite, D.O. and Eckstein, N.J. (2003). How people with disabilities communicatively manage assistance: helping as instrumental social support. *Journal of Applied Communication Research* 31 (1): 1–26.

Brodwin, M.G. and Orange, L.M. (2002). Attitudes toward disability. In: *Rehabilitation Services: An Introduction for the Human Service Professional* (ed. J.D. Andrew and C.W. Faubion), 145–173. Osage Beach, MO: Aspen Professional Services.

Brough, K.M. (2005). Disability prejudice from a terror management perspective. Undergraduate thesis. Reed College, Portland, OR.

Brown, S.E. (1997). "Oh, don't you envy us our privileged lives?" A review of the disability culture movement. *Disability and Rehabilitation* 19 (8): 339–349. http://www.independentliving.org/docs3/brown97c.pdf (accessed 26 February 2019.

Capella, M.E. (2002). Inequities in the VR system: do they still exist? *Rehabilitation Counseling Bulletin* 45 (3): 143–153.

Carver, C.S., Glass, D.C., Snyder, M.L., and Katz, I. (1977). Favorable evaluations of stigmatized others. *Personality and Social Psychology Bulletin* 3 (2): 232–235.

Carver, C.S., Glass, D.C., and Katz, I. (1978). Favorable evaluations of Blacks and the handicapped: positive prejudice, unconscious denial, or social desirability? *Journal of Applied Social Psychology* 8 (2): 97–106.

Chan, F., Livneh, H., Pruett, S.R. et al. (2009). Societal attitudes toward disability: concepts, measurements, and interventions. In: *Understanding Psychosocial Adjustment to Chronic Illness and Disability: A Handbook for Evidence-Based Practitioners in Rehabilitation* (ed. F. Chan, E. da Silva Cardoso and J.A. Chronister), 333–370. New York: Springer.

Chartrand, T.L. and Bargh, J.A. (1999). The chameleon effect: the perception–behavior link and social interaction. *Journal of Personality and Social Psychology* 76 (6): 893–910.

Chen, R.K., Brodwin, M.G., Cardoso, E., and Chan, F. (2002). Attitudes toward people with disabilities in the social context of dating and marriage: a comparison of American, Taiwanese, and Singaporean college students. *Journal of Rehabilitation* 68 (4): 5–11.

Cole, J.S. and Johnson, M. (1994). Time to grow up. In: *The Ragged Edge: The Disability Experience from the Pages of the First Fifteen Years of "The Disability Rag."* (ed. B. Shaw), 131–136. Louisville, KY: Advocado Press.

Colella, A. and Varma, A. (1999). Disability-job fit stereotypes and the evaluation of persons with disabilities at work. *Journal of Occupational Rehabilitation* 9 (2): 79–95.

Collins, C.R. and Blood, G.W. (1990). Acknowledgment and severity of stuttering as factors influencing nonstutterers' perceptions of stutterers. *Journal of Speech and Hearing Disorders* 55 (1): 75–81.

Collins, N.L. and Miller, L.C. (1994). Self-disclosure and liking: a meta-analytic review. *Psychological Bulletin* 116 (3): 457–475.

Comer, R.J. and Piliavin, J.A. (1972). The effects of physical deviance upon face-to-face interaction: the other side. *Journal of Personality and Social Psychology* 23 (1): 33–39.

Cook, D. (1998). Psychosocial impact of disability. In: *Rehabilitation Counseling: Basics and Beyond*, 3e (ed. R.M. Parker and E.M. Szymanski), 303–326. Austin, TX: Pro-Ed.

Cook, J.A., Razzano, L.A., Straiton, D.M., and Ross, Y. (1994). Cultivation and maintenance of relationships with employers of people with psychiatric disabilities. *Psychosocial Rehabilitation Journal* 17 (3): 103–116.

Cook, B.G., Gerber, M.M., and Murphy, J. (2000). Backlash against the inclusion of students with learning disabilities in higher education: implications for transition from post-secondary environments to work. *Work* 14 (1): 31–40.

Cooper, A.E., Corrigan, P.W., and Watson, A.C. (2003). Mental illness stigma and care seeking. *The Journal of Nervous and Mental Disease* 191 (5): 339–341.

Corrigan, P.W., Green, A., Lundin, R. et al. (2001). Familiarity with and social distance from people who have serious mental illness. *Psychiatric services* 52 (7): 953–958.

Crandall, C.S. and Eshleman, A. (2003). A justification-suppression model of the expression and experience of prejudice. *Psychological Bulletin* 129 (3): 414–446.

Cuddy, A.J., Fiske, S.T., and Glick, P. (2008). Warmth and competence as universal dimensions of social perception: the stereotype content model and the BIAS map. *Advances in Experimental Social Psychology* 40: 61–149.

Cunningham, W.A., Preacher, K.J., and Banaji, M.R. (2001). Implicit attitude measures: consistency, stability, and convergent validity. *Psychological Science* 12 (2): 163–170.

Deal, M. (2007). Aversive disablism: subtle prejudice toward disabled people. *Disability & Society* 22 (1): 93–107.

Demoulin, S., Rodríguez-Torres, R., Rodríguez-Pérez, A. et al. (2004). Emotional prejudice can lead to infrahumanization. *European Review of Social Psychology* 15 (1): 259–296.

DePaulo, B.M. and Friedman, H.S. (1998). Nonverbal communication. In: *The Handbook of Social Psychology* (ed. D.T. Gilbert, S.T. Fiske and G. Lindzey), 3–40. New York: McGraw-Hill.

Dijker, A.J. (2001). The influence of perceived suffering and vulnerability on the experience of pity. *European Journal of Social Psychology* 31 (6): 659–676.

Dionne, C.D., Gainforth, H.L., O'Malley, D.A., and Latimer-Cheung, A.E. (2013). Examining implicit attitudes towards exercisers with a physical disability. *The Scientific World Journal* 2013: 1–8.

Dixon, K.A., Kruse, D., and Van Horn, C.E. (2003). *Restricted Access: A Survey of Employers about People with Disabilities and Lowering Barriers to Work*. New Brunswick, NJ: John J. Heldrich Center for Workforce Development. http://dx.doi.org/10.1155/2013/621596.

Dolmage, J. and Kerschbaum, S. (2016). Wanted disabled faculty members. Inside Higher Education. https://www.insidehighered.com/advice/2016/10/31/advice-hiring-faculty-members-disabilities-essay (accessed 28 February 2019).

Dovidio, J.F. and Gaertner, S.L. (2004). Aversive racism. *Advances in Experimental Social Psychology* 36: 1–52.

Dovidio, J.F., Kawakami, K., Johnson, C. et al. (1997). On the nature of prejudice: automatic and controlled processes. *Journal of Experimental Social Psychology* 33 (5): 510–540.

Dovidio, J.F., Kawakami, K., and Beach, K.R. (2001). Implicit and explicit attitudes: examination of the relationship between measures of intergroup bias. *Blackwell handbook of social psychology: Intergroup processes* 4: 175–197.

Dovidio, J.F., Gaertner, S.E., Kawakami, K., and Hodson, G. (2002). Why can't we just get along? Interpersonal biases and interracial distrust. *Cultural Diversity and Ethnic Minority Psychology* 8 (2): 88–102.

Dovidio, J.F., Pagotto, L., and Hebl, M.R. (2011). Implicit attitudes and discrimination against people with disabilities. In: *Disability and Aging Discrimination* (ed. R.L. Wiener and S.L. Willborn), 157–183. New York: Springer.

Dunn, D.S. (2015). *The Social Psychology of Disability*. New York: Oxford University Press.

Eagly, A.H. and Chaiken, S. (1993). *The Psychology of Attitudes*. San Diego, CA: Harcourt Brace Jovanovich College Publishers.

Eddey, G.E., Robey, K.L., and McConnell, J.A. (1998). Increasing medical student's self-perceived skill and comfort in examining persons with severe developmental disabilities: the use of standardized patients who are nonverbal due to cerebral palsy. *Academic Medicine: Journal of the Association of American Medical Colleges* 73 (10 Suppl): S106–S108.

Elliott, T.R., MacNair, R.R., Herrick, S.M. et al. (1991). Interpersonal reactions to depression and physical disability in dyadic interactions. *Journal of Applied Social Psychology* 21 (16): 1293–1302.

Enea-Drapeau, C., Carlier, M., and Huguet, P. (2012). Tracking subtle stereotypes of children with trisomy 21: from facial-feature-based to implicit stereotyping. *PLoS ONE* 7 (4): e34369–e34369.

Esses, V.M. and Beaufoy, S.L. (1994). Determinants of attitudes toward people with disabilities. *Journal of Social Behavior and Personality* 9 (5): 43–64.

Federici, S. and Meloni, F. (2008). Making decisions and judgments on disability: the disability representation of parents, teachers, and special needs educators. *Journal of Education, Informatics and Cybernetics* 1 (3): 20–26.

Fichten, C.S., Robillard, K., Tagalakis, V. et al. (1991). Casual interaction between college students with various disabilities and their nondisabled peers: the internal dialogue. *Rehabilitation Psychology* 36 (1): 3–20.

Findler, L., Vilchinsky, N., and Werner, S. (2007). The multidimensional attitudes scale toward persons with disabilities (MAS) construction and validation. *Rehabilitation Counseling Bulletin* 50 (3): 166–176.

Finger, A. (1994). And the greatest of these is charity. In: *The Ragged Edge: The Disability Experience from the Pages of the First Fifteen Years of the Disability Rag* (ed. B. Shaw), 115–119. Louisville, KY: The Avocado Press.

Fishbein, M. and Ajzen, I. (2011). *Predicting and Changing Behavior: The Reasoned Action Approach*. Abingdon: Taylor & Francis.

Fiske, S.T., Cuddy, A.J., Glick, P., and Xu, J. (2002). A model of (often mixed) stereotype content: competence and warmth respectively follow from perceived status and competition. *Journal of Personality and Social Psychology* 82 (6): 878–902.

Fiske, S.T., Cuddy, A.J., and Glick, P. (2007). Universal dimensions of social cognition: warmth and competence. *Trends in Cognitive Sciences* 11 (2): 77–83.

Fitzgerald, M.H. and Paterson, K.A. (1995). The hidden disability dilemma for the preservation of self. *Journal of Occupational Science* 2 (1): 13–21.

Frable, D.E., Blackstone, T., and Scherbaum, C. (1990). Marginal and mindful: deviants in social interactions. *Journal of Personality and Social psychology* 59 (1): 140–149.

Frable, D.E., Platt, L., and Hoey, S. (1998). Concealable stigmas and positive self-perceptions: feeling better around similar others. *Journal of Personality and Social Psychology* 74 (4): 909–922.

Fraser, R., Ajzen, I., Johnson, K. et al. (2011). Understanding employers' hiring intention in relation to qualified workers with disabilities. *Journal of Vocational Rehabilitation* 35 (1): 1–11.

Furnham, A. and Pendred, J. (1983). Attitudes towards the mentally and physically disabled. *British Journal of Medical Psychology* 56 (2): 179–187.

Galbreath, J. and Feinberg, L.B. (1973). Ambiguity and attitudes toward employment of the disabled: a multidimensional study. *Rehabilitation Psychology* 20 (4): 165–174.

Gervais, S.J. (2011). A social psychological perspective of disability prejudice. In: *Disability and Aging Discrimination* (ed. R.L. Wiener and S.L. Willborn), 249–262. New York: Springer.

Gething, L. (1994). The Interaction with Disabled Persons Scale. *Journal of Social Behavior and Personality* 9 (5): 23–42.

Gibbons, F.X., Stephan, W.G., Stephenson, B., and Petty, C.R. (1980). Reactions to stigmatized others: response amplification vs sympathy. *Journal of Experimental Social Psychology* 16 (6): 591–605.

Gilbert, D.T. and Hixon, J.G. (1991). The trouble of thinking: activation and application of stereotypic beliefs. *Journal of Personality and social Psychology* 60 (4): 509–517.

Gilbert, D.T. and Silvera, D.H. (1996). Overhelping. *Journal of Personality and Social Psychology* 70 (4): 678–690.

Glick, P. (2005). Choice of scapegoats. In: *On the Nature of Prejudice: Fifty Years after Allport* (ed. J.F. Dovidio, P. Glick and L.A. Rudman), 244–261. Oxford: Blackwell.

Glick, P. and Fiske, S.T. (2001). An ambivalent alliance: hostile and benevolent sexism as complementary justifications for gender equality. *American Psychologist* 56 (2): 109–118.

Goffman, E. (1963). *Stigma: Notes on the Management of Spoiled Identity*. Englewood Cliffs, NJ: Prentice-Hall.

Goldberg, S.G., Killeen, M.B., and O'Day, B. (2005). The disclosure conundrum: how people with psychiatric disabilities navigate employment. *Psychology, Public Policy, and Law* 11 (3): 463–500.

Gonzales, L., Davidoff, K.C., Nadal, K.L., and Yanos, P.T. (2015). Microaggressions experienced by persons with mental illnesses: an exploratory study. *Psychiatric Rehabilitation Journal* 38 (3): 234–241.

Gouvier, W.D., Coon, R.C., Todd, M.E., and Fuller, K.H. (1994). Verbal interactions with individuals presenting with and without physical disability. *Rehabilitation Psychology* 39 (4): 263–268.

Graffam, J., Shinkfield, A., Smith, K., and Polzin, U. (2002). Factors that influence employer decisions in hiring and retaining an employee with a disability. *Journal of Vocational Rehabilitation* 17 (3): 175–181.

Greenwald, A.G. and Banaji, M.R. (1995). Implicit social cognition: attitudes, self-esteem, and stereotypes. *Psychological Review* 102 (1): 4–27.

Gregory, S.W. Jr. and Webster, S. (1996). A nonverbal signal in voices of interview partners effectively predicts communication accommodation and social status perceptions. *Journal of Personality and Social Psychology* 70 (6): 1231–1240.

Grue, J., Johannessen, L.E., and Rasmussen, E.F. (2015). Prestige rankings of chronic diseases and disabilities. A survey among professionals in the disability field. *Social Science & Medicine* 124: 180–186.

Guglielmi, R.S. (1999). Psychophysiological assessment of prejudice: past research, current status, and future directions. *Personality and Social Psychology Review* 3 (2): 123–157.

Hahn, H. (1988). The politics of physical differences: disability and discrimination. *Journal of Social Issues* 44 (1): 39–47.

Haller, B. and Preston, J. (2016). Confirming normalcy: "inspiration porn" and the construction of the disabled subject? In: *Disability and Social Media: Global Perspectives* (ed. K. Ellis and M. Kent). New York: Routledge.

Harris, L., and Associates. (1991). *Public Attitudes toward People with Disabilities*. Washington, DC: National Organization on Disability.

Harris, M.B., Walters, L.C., and Waschull, S. (1991). Altering attitudes and knowledge about obesity. *The Journal of Social Psychology* 131 (6): 881–884.

Harris, M.J., Milich, R., Corbitt, E.M. et al. (1992). Self-fulfilling effects of stigmatizing information on children's social interactions. *Journal of Personality and Social Psychology* 63 (1): 41–50.

Harris, M.J., Moniz, A.J., Sowards, B.A., and Krane, K. (1994). Mediation of interpersonal expectancy effects: expectancies about the elderly. *Social Psychology Quarterly* 57 (1): 36–48.

Hastorf, A.H., Wildfogel, J., and Cassman, T. (1979). Acknowledgement of handicap as a tactic in social interaction. *Journal of Personality and Social Psychology* 37 (10): 1790–1797.

Healey, E.C., Gabel, R.M., Daniels, D.E., and Kawai, N. (2007). The effects of self-disclosure and non self-disclosure of stuttering on listeners' perceptions of a person who stutters. *Journal of Fluency Disorders* 32 (1): 51–69.

Hebl, M.R. and Kleck, R.E. (2002). Acknowledging one's stigma in the interview setting: effective strategy or liability? *Journal of Applied Social Psychology* 32 (2): 223–249.

Hebl, M.R. and Skorinko, J.L. (2005). Acknowledging one's physical disability in the interview: does "when" make a difference? *Journal of Applied Social Psychology* 35 (12): 2477–2492.

Hebl, M.R., Tickle, J., and Heatherton, T.F. (2000). Awkward moments in interactions between nonstigmatized and stigmatized individuals. In: *The Social Psychology of Stigma* (ed. T.F. Heatherton, R.E. Kleck, M. Hebl and J. Hull), 275–306. New York: Guilford Press.

Hein, S., Grumm, M., and Fingerle, M. (2011). Is contact with people with disabilities a guarantee for positive implicit and explicit attitudes? *European Journal of Special Needs Education* 26 (4): 509–522.

Hernandez, B., Keys, C., Balcazar, F., and Drum, C. (1998). Construction and validation of the Disability Rights Attitude Scale: assessing attitudes toward the Americans with Disabilities Act (ADA). *Rehabilitation Psychology* 43 (3): 203–218.

Hernandez, B., Keys, C., and Balcazar, F. (2000). Employer attitudes toward workers with disabilities and their ADA employment rights: a literature review. *Journal of Rehabilitation* 66 (4): 4–16.

Hill, R.B. (2004). Institutional racism in child welfare. *Race and Society* 7 (1): 17–33.

Hill, M.L., Banks, P.D., Handrich, R.R. et al. (1987). Benefit-cost analysis of supported competitive employment for persons with mental retardation. *Research in Developmental Disabilities* 8 (1): 71–89.

Hilton, J.L. and Darley, J.M. (1991). The effects of interaction goals on person perception. *Advances in Experimental Social Psychology* 24: 235–267.

Hodson, G., Dovidio, J.F., and Gaertner, S.L. (2002). Processes in racial discrimination: differential weighting of conflicting information. *Personality and Social Psychology Bulletin* 28 (4): 460–471.

Hofmann, W., Gawronski, B., Gschwendner, T. et al. (2005). A meta-analysis on the correlation between the Implicit Association Test and explicit self-report measures. *Personality and Social Psychology Bulletin* 31 (10): 1369–1385.

Hornstra, L., Denessen, E., Bakker, J. et al. (2010). Teacher attitudes toward dyslexia: effects on teacher expectations and the academic achievement of students with dyslexia. *Journal of Learning Disabilities* 43 (6): 515–529.

Jackson, L.M. (2011). *The Psychology of Prejudice: From Attitude to Social Action.* Washington, DC: American Psychological Association.

Jain, S., Foster, E., Biery, N., and Boyle, V. (2013). Patients with disabilities as teachers. *Family Medicine* 45 (1): 37–39.

Jaques, M.E., Linkowski, D.C., and Sieka, F.L. (1970). Cultural attitudes toward disability: Denmark, Greece, and the United States. *International Journal of Social Psychiatry* 16 (1): 54–62.

Jutel, A.G. and Conrad, P. (2014). *Putting a Name to It: Diagnosis in Contemporary Society.* Baltimore, MD: Johns Hopkins University Press.

Katz, E. and DeRose, R. (2010). The ADA 20 years later: the 2010 survey of Americans with disabilities. *The Journal of Spinal Cord Medicine* 33 (4): 345.

Katz, I., Glass, D.C., Lucido, D.J., and Farber, J. (1977). Ambivalence, guilt, and the denigration of a physically handicapped victim. *Journal of Personality* 45 (3): 419–429.

Katz, I., Farber, J., Glass, D.C. et al. (1978). When courtesy offends: effects of positive and negative behavior by the physically disabled on altruism and anger in normals. *Journal of Personality* 46 (3): 506–518.

Katz, I., Glass, D.C., Lucido, D., and Farber, J. (1979). Harm-doing and victim's racial or orthopedic stigma as determinants of helping behavior. *Journal of Personality* 47 (2): 340–364.

Katz, I., Hass, R.G., and Bailey, J. (1988). Attitudinal ambivalence and behavior toward people with disabilities. In: *Attitudes toward Persons with Disabilities* (ed. H.E. Yuker), 47–57. New York: Springer.

Kleck, R.E. and Strenta, A. (1980). Perceptions of the impact of negatively valued physical characteristics on social interaction. *Journal of Personality and Social Psychology* 39 (5): 861–873.

Langer, E.J., Fiske, S., Taylor, S.E., and Chanowitz, B. (1976). Stigma, staring, and discomfort: a novel-stimulus hypothesis. *Journal of Experimental Social Psychology* 12 (5): 451–463.

LaRoy, C. (2016). Shit people say to disabled people. https://www.youtube.com/watch?v=Y69YYEmzztM (accessed 26 February 2019).

Lauber, C., Nordt, C., Falcato, L., and Rössler, W. (2004). Factors influencing social distance toward people with mental illness. *Community Mental Health Journal* 40 (3): 265–274.

Leonard, R. and Crawford, J. (1989). Two approaches to seeing people with disabilities. *Australian Journal of Social Issues* 24 (2): 112–125.

Levy, J.M., Jessop, D.J., Rimmerman, A., and Levy, P.H. (1992). Attitudes of Fortune 500 corporate executives toward the employability of persons with severe disabilities: a national study. *Mental Retardation* 30 (2): 67–75.

Liesener, J.J. and Mills, J. (1999). An experimental study of disability spread: talking to an adult in a wheelchair like a child. *Journal of Applied Social Psychology* 29 (10): 2083–2092.

Livingston, R.W. and Brewer, M.B. (2002). What are we really priming? Cue-based versus category-based processing of facial stimuli. *Journal of Personality and Social Psychology* 82 (1): 5–18.

Louvet, E. (2007). Social judgment toward job applicants with disabilities: perception of personal qualities and competences. *Rehabilitation Psychology* 52 (3): 297–303.

Mackie, D.M., Devos, T., and Smith, E.R. (2000). Intergroup emotions: explaining offensive action tendencies in an intergroup context. *Journal of Personality and Social Psychology* 79 (4): 602–616.

Macrae, C.N., Milne, A.B., and Bodenhausen, G.V. (1994). Stereotypes as energy-saving devices: a peek inside the cognitive toolbox. *Journal of Personality and Social Psychology* 66 (1): 37–45.

Makas, E. (1988). Positive attitudes toward disabled people: disabled and nondisabled persons' perspectives. *Journal of Social Issues* 44 (1): 49–61.

Marks, D. (1999). *Disability: Controversial Debates and Psychosocial Perspectives*. London: Routledge.

Martz, E. (2003). Invisibility of disability and work experience as predictors of employment among community college students with disabilities. *Journal of Vocational Rehabilitation* 18 (3): 153–161.

Mastro, J.V., Burton, A.W., Rosendahl, M., and Sherrill, C. (1996). Attitudes of elite athletes with impairments toward one another: a hierarchy of preference. *Adapted Physical Activity Quarterly* 13 (2): 197–210.

McConnell, A.R. and Leibold, J.M. (2001). Relations among the Implicit Association Test, discriminatory behavior, and explicit measures of racial attitudes. *Journal of Experimental Social Psychology* 37 (5): 435–442.

McFarlin, D.B., Song, J., and Sonntag, M. (1991). Integrating the disabled into the work force: a survey of Fortune 500 company attitudes and practices. *Employee Responsibilities and Rights Journal* 4 (2): 107–123.

Mikulincer, M. (2013). *Human Learned Helplessness: A Coping Perspective*. New York: Springer Science & Business Media.

Miller, D.T. and Turnbull, W. (1986). Expectancies and interpersonal processes. *Annual review of psychology* 37 (1): 233–256.

Miller, B.K. and Werner, S. (2005). Factors influencing the inflation of task performance ratings for workers with disabilities and contextual performance ratings for their coworkers. *Human Performance* 18 (3): 309–329.

Monteith, M.J., Voils, C.I., and Ashburn-Nardo, L. (2001). Taking a look underground: detecting, interpreting, and reacting to implicit racial biases. *Social Cognition* 19 (4): 395–417.

Moore, T.J. and Crimando, W. (1995). Attitudes toward Title I of the Americans with Disabilities Act. *Rehabilitation Counseling Bulletin* 38 (3): 232–247.

Morgan, R.L. and Alexander, M. (2005). The employer's perception: employment of individuals with developmental disabilities. *Journal of Vocational Rehabilitation* 23 (1): 39–49.

Murphy-Berman, V.A., Berman, J.J., and Campbell, E. (1998). Factors affecting healthcare allocation decisions: a case of aversive racism? *Journal of Applied Social Psychology* 28 (24): 2239–2253.

Murrell, A.J., Dietz-Uhler, B.L., Dovidio, J.F. et al. (1994). Aversive racism and resistance to affirmative action: perception of justice are not necessarily color blind. *Basic and Applied Social Psychology* 15 (1–2): 71–86.

Nadal, K.L. (2014). A guide to responding to microaggressions. *Cuny Forum* 2 (1): 71–76. https://advancingjustice-la.org/sites/default/files/ELAMICRO%20A_Guide_to_Responding_to_Microaggressions.pdf (accessed 28 February 2019.

Nadler, A. (2002). Inter-group helping relations as power relations: maintaining or challenging social dominance between groups through helping. *Journal of Social Issues* 58 (3): 487–502.

Nario-Redmond, M. (2010). Cultural stereotypes of disabled and non-disabled men and women: consensus for global category representations and diagnostic domains. *British Journal of Social Psychology* 49 (3): 471–488.

Nelson, T.D. (2006). *The Psychology of Prejudice*, 2e. New York: Pearson.

Nosek, B.A., Smyth, F.L., Hansen, J.J. et al. (2007). Pervasiveness and correlates of implicit attitudes and stereotypes. *European Review of Social Psychology* 18 (1): 36–88.

Olkin, R. (1999). *What Psychotherapists Should Know about Disability*. New York: Guilford Press.

Olkin, R. and Howson, L.J. (1994). Attitudes toward and images of physical disability. *Journal of Social Behavior and Personality* 9 (5): 81–96.

Oyserman, D., Uskul, A.K., Yoder, N. et al. (2007). Unfair treatment and self-regulatory focus. *Journal of Experimental Social Psychology* 43 (3): 505–512.

Park, J.H., Faulkner, J., and Schaller, M. (2003). Evolved disease-avoidance processes and contemporary anti-social behavior: prejudicial attitudes and avoidance of people with physical disabilities. *Journal of Nonverbal Behavior* 27 (2): 65–87.

Patston, P. (2014). The most offensive part of this meme is its spelling! http://www.philippatston.com/blog/the-most-offensive-part-of-this-meme-is-its-spelling (accessed 26 February 2019).

Pearson, A.R., Dovidio, J.F., and Gaertner, S.L. (2009). The nature of contemporary prejudice: insights from aversive racism. *Social and Personality Psychology Compass* 3 (3): 314–338.

Peck, B. and Kirkbride, L.T. (2001). Why businesses don't employ people with disabilities. *Journal of Vocational Rehabilitation* 16 (2): 71–75.

Perlman, J.L. and Routh, D.K. (1980). Stigmatizing effects of a child's wheelchair in successive and simultaneous interactions. *Journal of Pediatric Psychology* 5 (1): 43–55.

Presley, G. (2008). *Seven Wheelchairs: A Life Beyond Polio*. Iowa City, University of Iowa Press.

Pronin, E., Gilovich, T., and Ross, L. (2004). Objectivity in the eye of the beholder: divergent perceptions of bias in self versus others. *Psychological Review* 111 (3): 781–799.

Pruett, S.R. and Chan, F. (2006). The development and psychometric validation of the Disability Attitude Implicit Association Test. *Rehabilitation Psychology* 51 (3): 202–213.

Pulrang, A. (2013). Reconsidering "inspiration porn." Disability Thinking. http://disabilitythinking.com/disabilitythinking/2013/10/reconsidering-inspiration-porn.html (accessed 26 February 2019).

Reynolds, S. (2012). Shit people say to people with disabilities. https://www.youtube.com/watch?v=uVg8RVTzPps&feature=youtu.be (accessed 26 February 2019).

Riccobono, M.A. (2016). Blindfolding is not the way to educate the public about blindness and blind people. *Huffington Post* (4 October). https://www.huffingtonpost.com/entry/blindfolding-is-not-the-way-to-educate-the-public-about_us_57f3a70 3e4b0f482f8f0bd23 (accessed 26 February 2019).

Robey, K.L., Beckley, L., and Kirschner, M. (2006). Implicit infantilizing attitudes about disability. *Journal of Developmental and Physical Disabilities* 18 (4): 441–453.

Rojahn, J., Komelasky, K.G., and Man, M. (2008). Implicit attitudes and explicit ratings of romantic attraction of college students toward opposite-sex peers with physical disabilities. *Journal of Developmental and Physical Disabilities* 20 (4): 389–397.

Room, R., Rehm, J., Trotter, I.I. et al. (2001). Cross-cultural views on stigma, valuation, parity, and societal values towards disability. In: *Disability and Culture: Universalism and Diversity* (ed. T.B. Üstün), 247–297. Seattle: Hogrefe & Huber.

Rosenthal, D.A., Chan, F., and Livneh, H. (2006). Rehabilitation students' attitudes toward persons with disabilities in high- and low-stakes social contexts: a conjoint analysis. *Disability and Rehabilitation* 28 (24): 1517–1527.

Rush, L.L. (1998). Affective reactions to multiple social stigmas. *The Journal of Social Psychology* 138 (4): 421–430.

Ryan, F. (2015). Lee Irving's murder is a chilling reminder that disability hate crime is rising. *The Guardian* (10 June). https://www.theguardian.com/commentisfree/2015/jun/10/lee-irving-murder-disability-hate-crime-increase (accessed 26 February 2019).

Ryan, E.B., Anas, A.P., and Gruneir, A.J. (2006). Evaluations of overhelping and underhelping communication: do old age and physical disability matter? *Journal of Language and Social Psychology* 25 (1): 97–107.

Saetermore, C.L., Scattone, D., and Kim, K.H. (2001). Ethnicity and the stigma of disabilities. *Psychology & Health* 16 (6): 699–713.

Saucier, D.A., Miller, C.T., and Doucet, N. (2005). Differences in helping whites and blacks: a meta-analysis. *Personality and Social Psychology Review* 9 (1): 2–16.

Schimel, J., Pyszczynski, T., Greenberg, J. et al. (2000). Running from the shadow: psychological distancing from others to deny characteristics people fear in themselves. *Journal of Personality and Social Psychology* 78 (3): 446–462.

Scior, K. (2011). Public awareness, attitudes and beliefs regarding intellectual disability: a systematic review. *Research in Developmental Disabilities* 32 (6): 2164–2182.

Shelton, J.N. (2003). Interpersonal concerns in social encounters between majority and minority group members. *Group Processes & Intergroup Relations* 6 (2): 171–186.

Shelton, J.N., Richeson, J.A., and Salvatore, J. (2005). Expecting to be the target of prejudice: implications for interethnic interactions. *Personality and Social Psychology Bulletin* 31 (9): 1189–1202.

Sherry, M. (2016). *Disability Hate Crimes: Does Anyone Really Hate Disabled People?* New York: Routledge.

Sigelman, C.K., Adams, R.M., Meeks, S.R., and Purcell, M.A. (1986). Children's nonverbal responses to a physically disabled person. *Journal of Nonverbal Behavior* 10 (3): 173–186.

Siller, J., Chipman, A., Ferguson, L., and Vann, D.H. (1967). *Studies in Reactions to Disability: XI. Attitudes of the Nondisabled toward the Physically Disabled*. New York: New York University, School of Education.

Siperstein, G.N., Romano, N., Mohler, A., and Parker, R. (2006). A national survey of consumer attitudes towards companies that hire people with disabilities. *Journal of Vocational Rehabilitation* 24 (1): 3–9.

Small Business BC (2016). Get funding to make your workplace more accessible. https://smallbusinessbc.ca/article/get-funding-make-workplace-accessible/ (accessed 28 February 2019).

Smith, R.H., Parrott, W.G., Ozer, D., and Moniz, A. (1994). Subjective injustice and inferiority as predictors of hostile and depressive feelings in envy. *Personality and Social Psychology Bulletin* 20 (6): 705–711.

Smith-Genthôs, K.R., Reich, D.A., Lakin, J.L., and de Calvo, M.P.C. (2015). The tongue-tied chameleon: the role of nonconscious mimicry in the behavioral confirmation process. *Journal of Experimental Social Psychology* 56: 179–182.

Snyder, M.L., Kleck, R.E., Strenta, A., and Mentzer, S.J. (1979). Avoidance of the handicapped: an attributional ambiguity analysis. *Journal of Personality and Social Psychology* 37 (12): 2297–2306.

StanfordPushProject. (2012). Shit people say to people with disabilities. https://www.youtube.com/watch?v=DNoVSusaAVE&feature=youtu.be (accessed 26 February 2019).

Steele, C.M. (1992). Race and the schooling of Black Americans. *The Atlantic Monthly* 269 (4): 68–78.

Stone, E. and Priestley, M. (1996). Parasites, pawns and partners: disability research and the role of non-disabled researchers. *British Journal of Sociology* 47 (4): 699–716.

Stone, A. and Wright, T. (2012). Evaluations of people depicted with facial disfigurement compared to those with mobility impairment. *Basic and Applied Social Psychology* 34 (3): 212–225.

Strenta, A.C. and Kleck, R.E. (1985). Physical disability and the attribution dilemma: perceiving the causes of social behavior. *Journal of Social and Clinical Psychology* 3 (2): 129–142.

Strong, E.K. Jr. (1931). *Change of Interests with Age*. Palo Alto, CA: Stanford University Press.

Sue, D.W. (2010). *Microaggressions and Marginality: Manifestation, Dynamics, and Impact*. Chichester: Wiley.

Taylor, C.J. (1998). Factors affecting behavior toward people with disabilities. *The Journal of Social Psychology* 138 (6): 766–771.

Teachman, B.A. and Brownell, K.D. (2001). Implicit anti-fat bias among health professionals: is anyone immune? *International Journal of Obesity* 25 (10): 1525–1531.

Teachman, B.A., Wilson, J.G., and Komarovskaya, I. (2006). Implicit and explicit stigma of mental illness in diagnosed and healthy samples. *Journal of Social and Clinical Psychology* 25 (1): 75–95.

Thomas, A. (2000). Stability of Tringo's hierarchy of preference toward disability groups: 30 years later. *Psychological Reports* 86 (3): 1155–1156.

Thomas, A., Doyle, A., and Vaughn, D. (2007). Implementation of a computer based Implicit Association Test as a measure of attitudes toward individuals with disabilities. *The Journal of Rehabilitation* 73 (2): 3–14.

Thompson, D. (2013). Well, this is just awful: "renting" disabled people to skip lines at Disney World. *The Atlantic* (14 May). https://www.theatlantic.com/business/archive/2013/05/well-this-is-just-awful-renting-disabled-people-to-skip-lines-at-disney-world/275840 (accessed 26 February 2019).

Thrash, T.M., Elliot, A.J., Maruskin, L.A., and Cassidy, S.E. (2010). Inspiration and the promotion of well-being: tests of causality and mediation. *Journal of Personality and Social Psychology* 98 (3): 488–506.

Thurneck, D.A. (2008). The impact of inclusive education on the development of disability attitudes. Doctoral dissertation. James Madison University.

Tiedens, L.Z. and Fragale, A.R. (2003). Power moves: complementarity in dominant and submissive nonverbal behavior. *Journal of Personality and Social Psychology* 84 (3): 558–568.

Toriello, P.J., Leierer, S.J., and Keferl, J.E. (2003). The impact of race on the use of physical restraint with adolescent males with behavioral disabilities: an initial study. *Journal of Applied Rehabilitation Counseling* 34 (4): 38–43.

Toriello, P.J., Leierer, S.J., Sheaffer, B.L., and Cubero, C.G. (2007). Threat and visibility impact of disabilities and other conditions on social distance preferences. *Rehabilitation Education* 21 (3): 159–168.

Tregaskis, C. (2000). Interviewing non-disabled people about their disability-related attitudes: seeking methodologies. *Disability & Society* 15 (2): 343–353.

Tringo, J.L. (1970). The hierarchy of preference toward disability groups. *The Journal of Special Education* 4 (3): 295–306.

Tsang, H.W., Chan, F., and Chan, C.C. (2004). Factors influencing occupational therapy students' attitudes toward persons with disabilities: a conjoint analysis. *American Journal of Occupational Therapy* 58 (4): 426–434.

Vilchinsky, N., Findler, L., and Werner, S. (2010). Attitudes toward people with disabilities: The perspective of attachment theory. *Rehabilitation Psychology* 55 (3): 298–306.

Wallace, D., Abel, R., and Ropers-Huilman, B.R. (2000). Clearing a path for success: deconstructing borders through undergraduate mentoring. *The Review of Higher Education* 24 (1): 87–102.

Wallymahmed, A.H., McKay-Moffat, S.F., and Cunningham, C.C. (2007). The Interaction with Disabled Persons' scale: a validation with UK midwives. *Social Behavior and Personality* 35 (8): 1049–1060.

Wang, K., Silverman, A., Gwinn, J.D., and Dovidio, J.F. (2015). Independent or ungrateful? Consequences of confronting patronizing help for people with disabilities. *Group Processes & Intergroup Relations* 18 (4): 489–503.

Weiner, B. (1995). *Judgments of Responsibility: A Foundation for a Theory of Social Conduct.* New York: Guilford Press.

Weiner, B., Graham, S., and Chandler, C. (1982). Pity, anger, and guilt: an attributional analysis. *Personality and Social Psychology Bulletin* 8 (2): 226–232.

Weiserbs, B. and Gottlieb, J. (2000). The effect of perceived duration of physical disability on attitudes of school children toward friendship and helping. *The Journal of Psychology* 134 (3): 343–345.

Westbrook, M.T., Legge, V., and Pennay, M. (1993). Attitudes towards disabilities in a multicultural society. *Social Science & Medicine* 36 (5): 615–623.

Wilson, M.C. and Scior, K. (2014). Attitudes towards individuals with disabilities as measured by the Implicit Association Test: a literature review. *Research in Developmental Disabilities* 35 (2): 294–321.

Word, C.O., Zanna, M.P., and Cooper, J. (1974). The nonverbal mediation of self-fulfilling prophecies in interracial interaction. *Journal of Experimental Social Psychology* 10 (2): 109–120.

Wright, B.A. (1983). *Physical Disability: A Psychosocial Approach.* New York: Harper & Row.

Yuker, H.E. (1994). Variables that influence attitudes toward people with disabilities: conclusions from the data. *Journal of Social Behavior and Personality* 9 (5): 3–22.

Yuker, H.E. and Block, J.R. (1986). *Research with the Attitude toward Disabled Persons Scales (ATDP) 1960–1985.* Hempstead, NY: Hofstra University, Center for the Study of Attitudes toward Persons with Disabilities.

What to do if …

You commit a microaggression: Some people may be more offended than others. According to a guide to responding to microaggressions by Kevin L. Nadal (2014), the best thing you can do in any situation is:

1. *Listen.* Each and every human being is different, so while one person with autism may prefer person-first language, another person with autism may not. Ask them!
2. *Be respectful.* Some people may be more open to talking about their disability than others. Keep in mind that when talking with someone about their disability, open dialogue can be positive, but it should be a conversation not an interrogation.
3. *Be accepting.* If something you say offends someone and they correct you, accept the way that they wish to be treated. It is not up to you to decide what each person prefers. If you think that person-first language is the best response but the person you are talking to disagrees, listen to them.

https://crippencartoons.wordpress.com/

Image of a Crippen cartoon where one doctor says to another: "What do you think they want?" Behind them are several disabled people in chairs imagining responses like: "To make my own decisions," "To be asked," "Information I can access," and "To be treated with respect." Crippen – Disabled Cartoon: www.crippencartoons.co.uk

How to be aware of your attitudes

1. *Discover your implicit biases*
   Learn more about implicit bias by visiting https://implicit.harvard. edu/implicit/ and taking a quiz. Studies show that implicit bias can predict behaviors toward different groups of people. If you are aware of your implicit biases than you can become more critical of them, and make a conscious decision to treat others with respect.

2. *Learn how attitudes affect employment*
   - For tips on funding to make your workplace accessible, check out the article from Small Business BC (2016).
   - For tips on job searches and higher education interviews, visit Wanted: Disabled Faculty Members (Dolmage and Kerschbaum 2016).

3. *Avoid self-fulfilling prophesies*
   Over time, some disabled people may internalize ableist attitudes and stereotypes. For example, if a teacher expects a student with dyslexia to be slow, he/she might not perform to his/her potential. Consider how to avoid self-fulfilling prophesies by disrupting the cycle:

https://socialanxietyinstitute.org/self-fulfilling-prophecy-breaking-cycle

The image shows a feedback loop labelled Self-Fulfilling Prophecy, with arrows pointing clockwise around the circle. At the top is: "Our actions toward others" impacting "others' beliefs about us" causing "others' actions towards us" which then reinforces "our beliefs about ourselves" and ultimately influences our actions toward others.

What to do if ...

A microaggression is directed toward you:

1. First consider the consequences of responding or not responding, and ask yourself these questions:
   - If I respond, will my personal safety be at risk?
   - If I don't respond, will I be condoning the behavior and later regret not saying something?

2. If you decide that a response would be beneficial, here are some tips on responding:
   - Consider using "I" statements ("I felt hurt by that statement") instead of "You" statements ("You are ableist!")
   - Be clear about what specifically offended you and why.

Offer a suggestion on how the aggressor can better approach the situation in the future.

https://crippencartoons.wordpress.com/

In the first Crippen cartoon, a man uses sarcasm to respond to a woman telling him he doesn't "look mentally ill." The man says, "That's because I'm disguised as a human being today." In the second cartoon, a woman points to a sign that says, "Normality Training: How to stop upsetting people by looking disabled." One of two disabled people holding a crutch questions this by saying, "Be normal – but what makes you think we'd want to lower our standards?!" Crippen – Disabled Cartoon: www.crippencartoons.co.uk

Implicit Ableism in Action

You have probably heard the term "microaggression" related to race, gender, and sexuality. The disability community also deals with microaggressions quite regularly during casual conversations. Usually these comments are not intended to be offensive or discriminatory but reflect implicit biases to which the aggressor is often oblivious. Let's look at some examples of microaggressions:

Microaggression	Theme	Message
"Wow, I'd hate to be you." "I could never deal with that."	Disability is an unfortunate fact or even a curse.	This sends the message that disability is always a negative quality.
"Oh you look so normal." "Are you sure you aren't faking it?"	Deciding for others the severity of their disability based on preconceived ideas and appearance.	This perpetuates negative stereotypes of people with disabilities by expecting them to look/act a certain way.
"You are so inspirational." "You work? That is SO amazing."	Inspiration porn.	Making a big deal out of people with disabilities doing everyday things promotes the idea that they are lesser people.
"I'm really OCD today." "I misspelled something, I'm so dyslexic right now."	Disability is a minor or common experience that can be used as a punchline.	This belittles the seriousness of the conditions that disable people.
"She suffers from hearing loss." "He is wheelchair bound."	Disability is a tragic loss that limits or restricts.	Language assumes disability is a negative trait that needs to be fixed. In reality many people feel disability is a positive identity.
"You people in wheelchairs ..." "All disabled people ..."	Generalizations and blanket statements.	Implies that disabled people are all the same.

6

Contending with Ableism from Internalized Ableism to Collective Action

Co-authored with Arielle Silverman

In middle school I moved to a new town. Students didn't want to sit by me, they asked to be moved out of my class because they thought they could catch blindness. I hated this time of my life. I cried every day and wished I was dead. I begged my parents to switch me out of this school or to homeschool me. The school didn't help, they blamed me for not being more proactive. ~ Person with a sensory disability, 2015

I was putting my kids and groceries into the car and had a guy walk up to me and tell me I didn't look disabled enough to be in "one of those spots" (disabled parking). I was taken aback by his response and didn't say anything (which seems to be my reaction more often than not). I got in the car and cried hard for about 30 minutes before I calmed down enough to drive away. ~ Person with physical impairment, 2015

I've experienced being infantilized a lot like teachers trying to get me held back because of "emotional immaturity" which basically was just stuff related to my disabilities. And my parents often still talk to me like I'm a child. In school I didn't really do much but I can get angry at being infantilized or condescended to really easily, because of how it reminds me of my parents. And then I turn into a "bad disabled person" for being angry. ~ Person with multiple impairments, 2015

A newlywed couple sat next to me on the plane, and we chatted about a lot of different things … Toward the end of the conversation, he asked, genuinely kind, if they could pray for my healing. I shook my head, smiling. "I really appreciate you asking, but I like being who I am." They looked surprised and a little hurt, maybe, by my refusal, and I went on to say, "I figure that god made me the way I'm supposed to be, and I wouldn't be the person I am without the experiences I've had. Because of my disability I've gotten to see the world in a different way than a lot of people, and that's been good for me. I wasn't made wrong, I like me." ~ Person with multiple impairments, 2015

Ableism: The Causes and Consequences of Disability Prejudice, First Edition.
Michelle R. Nario-Redmond.
© 2020 John Wiley & Sons, Inc. Published 2020 by John Wiley & Sons, Inc.

Everybody just needs to chill and understand that disability is just a variable, like height or skin color or weight. We don't need to correct it, we need to correct society's response to it. ~ Person with a physical disability, 2015

In reading the quotes above, it is clear that ableism, in its many forms, has a powerful impact on the lives of disabled people. Disabled people react in a variety of ways, from tears and shock, to anger or shame, to pride and a drive for social change. These reactions, in turn, have varied consequences for well-being.

Up until now, the book chapters have explored the reasons for and factors contributing to disability prejudice: the fears people have (Chapter 2), the ideologies (Chapter 3), the stereotypic beliefs (Chapter 4), and attitudes (Chapter 5) about disabled people as a group. But prejudice is a two-way street. Chapter 5 concludes with how prejudice is really a dynamic mixed interaction process between those who level prejudice at disabled people and the disabled people who are the targets of this prejudice.

This chapter focuses on ableism's *effects* for disabled people, the "targets" of prejudice. We begin by describing research on stigmatized group members in general and how chronic discrimination, or episodes of discrimination, can be associated with negative health, achievement, and self-esteem patterns. We also describe some of the unique features of disability prejudice that differ from prejudices against other groups. Then we compare and contrast coping styles that disabled people might use to respond to prejudice. Specifically, social identity theory (SIT; Tajfel and Turner 1979) postulates that people may handle a devalued identity (such as having a disability) through either *individualistic* or *collectivistic* coping strategies. Both of these strategies have trade-offs for personal well-being and reactions to societal treatment. Individualistic strategies include minimizing, hiding, or otherwise distancing oneself from a disability identity. These strategies can help individuals escape stigma and discrimination at times, but if the disability cannot be easily hidden or escaped, these strategies can hurt well-being. Collectivistic strategies, on the other hand, include disability pride, affiliating with others who have disabilities, and engaging in collective action to redefine disability and counteract ableism. Such strategies can benefit both individual well-being and the standing of disabled people as a group, but in some cases, people who challenge ableism may risk punishment or sanctions by the larger society (see Chapter 3). We will describe what the current research tells us about when people might use individualistic or collectivistic coping, and the variety of consequences arising from each strategy. Finally, the chapter will end with a discussion of areas where more research is needed, and what SIT teaches us about ways to reduce ableism.

Discrimination's Toll on Well-Being

In recent decades, psychologists have turned their attention to understanding how day-to-day discrimination affects members of stigmatized groups. Most of the research has explored the experiences of ethnic minorities (e.g. African

Americans and Latino Americans), women in male-dominated settings, and sexual minorities (e.g. gay, lesbian, bisexual, and transgender) (Major and O'Brien 2005; Pascoe and Richman 2009). While this research is not specific to disabled people, it lays the conceptual groundwork for a deeper understanding of disabled people's varied responses to ableism.

Of course, being discriminated against has direct negative consequences, such as being denied opportunities for employment, education, housing, and other resources (for reviews see Major and O'Brien 2005; Sidanius and Pratto 1999). However, prejudice also affects people indirectly by presenting a "social identity threat" (Steele et al. 2002). SIT begins with the idea that people define themselves and others, in part, by the social groups to which they belong and the social roles they fulfill. Ethnicity, gender, sexual orientation, and disability status are all social groupings that make up part of a person's social identity. People are motivated to feel good about the groups to which they belong and to avoid situations in which those groups are devalued (Tajfel and Turner 1979).

Thus, when people encounter or anticipate prejudice against members of their group, they may experience mental and physical stress (Major and O'Brien 2005). This stress can be heightened in specific settings, such as when a woman is being interviewed by a group of men, or when a disabled person requests accommodations from an employer. In these situations, the fear of prejudice can become a "threat in the air" (Steele 1997). In other cases, the stress of worrying about possible discrimination becomes chronic and perpetual. People can become sensitized to the stress – vigilant to signs that others around them hold prejudices against members of their group. They may wonder if ambiguous actions against them, such as a bad grade or a negative performance review, are related to their group membership – a phenomenon known as attributional ambiguity (Crocker et al. 1998). For example, when not invited to a college party or hired for a job, people often wonder what reason to attribute this to. Was it an oversight or intentional, was it due to one's age, appearance, race, or disability status? Most often the evidence is ambiguous as to whether the outcome was due to prejudice against one's group or not. The chronic stress and effortful vigilance, in turn, can have consequences for health, achievement, and self-esteem. These consequences differ depending upon the strategies that people use to fend off social identity threat.

Health Effects

Across stigmatized groups, people who perceive more discrimination in their daily lives report more physical and mental health problems. Pascoe and Richman (2009) looked at 134 studies and found small but consistent correlations between perceived everyday discrimination and both mental and physical health problems. Mental health problems included higher rates of depression, anxiety, paranoia, and suicidal ideation, negative moods, and lower overall well-being. In one study, Black Americans who reported more experiences with racial discrimination were more likely to develop depression and psychological distress one year later (Brown et al. 2000). Another study, of gay and bisexual Latino men, found that one in six reported suicidal ideation, 80% experienced depression, and nearly half reported significant anxiety. Encounters with homophobia and racism were both strong predictors of mental health problems in these men (Diaz et al. 2001). It is clear that the stress and negative feelings associated with discrimination can directly undermine mental health and life expectancy (due to suicidal behavior).

People who experience chronic prejudice and discrimination are also at risk for physical health problems. Elevated blood pressure is one such problem that has been well documented. In African Americans, for example, perceived racism is associated with higher resting blood pressure during the day (Steffen et al. 2003), and less of a decrease during the night (Brondolo et al. 2008). Cole et al. (1997) found that HIV-positive gay men who were more sensitive to rejection based on sexual orientation showed more rapid disease progression than those who were less sensitive. The ever-present need to be alert to potential discrimination fosters patterns of increased stress reactivity in which blood pressure, heart rate, and stress hormones spike more than usual after a stressful experience (Guyll et al. 2001). If this happens frequently, it can increase the risk of serious health problems like heart disease and stroke.

Additionally, people who encounter frequent prejudice and discrimination may choose to cope in ways that actually compromise their health. One study of more than 2000 African American college students found that students who had been racially harassed were twice as likely to use tobacco daily as those who were not (Bennett et al. 2005). In another large study, Filipino Americans who perceived being treated unfairly were more likely to abuse alcohol and use illicit drugs than those who did not perceive such treatment (Gee et al. 2007). These studies and others suggest that perceptions of prejudice and discrimination can affect health – not only by causing stress, but by motivating people to manage stress in unhealthy ways. The threats associated with discriminatory treatment and stereotypic expectations also take a toll on personal achievement and performance behaviors.

Achievement Effects

Many minority groups are stereotyped as lacking competence in important achievement domains. African Americans have historically been stereotyped as lacking general intelligence (Steele 1997), and women have been stereotyped as lacking math ability (Spencer et al. 1999). Awareness of these stereotypes can spark a special kind of identity threat in achievement situations. This threat is known as stereotype threat (Steele 2010), and it constitutes a fear of being judged in stereotypic terms. For example, people may worry that their poor performance on a test could be attributed to their racial or gender identity, and that they would then confirm others' negative stereotypes about their groups. As a consequence, their performance can actually suffer.

Like social identity threat more generally, achievement-based stereotype threat can cause anxiety and stress (Blascovich et al. 2001; Steele 2010). It can also impair performance since worrying about performing badly can be distracting, deplete memory resources (Schmader et al. 2008), and make learning more difficult (Taylor and Walton 2011). As a result, people's attempts to try extra hard to perform well under stereotype threat can ironically undermine their achievement. Alternatively, some people may cope with these fears by putting in less effort or avoiding situations where they are likely to be stereotyped – again undermining their performance (Stone 2002).

This consequence was first demonstrated in a 1995 study where both Black and White students (matched for intellectual ability), answered a series of verbal test questions from the Graduate Record Exam (GRE) (Steele and Aronson 1995). All students took the same test, but half from each group were told that the exam tested their intelligence while the others were told that it was simply a problem-solving exercise with no bearing on intelligence. Compared to White students, Black students performed worse, but only when they thought they were taking an intelligence test; they performed equally well when the activity was presented as unrelated to intelligence. Stereotype threat effects have since been replicated in a variety of groups, such as women taking math tests (Spencer et al. 1999), older adults taking memory tests (Chasteen et al. 2005), and even White athletes performing tasks said to indicate athletic ability (Stone et al. 1997).

Notably, disabled people are also negatively stereotyped in terms of their competence and achievement abilities, as described in Chapter 4. Research on stereotype threat in disabled people is just beginning, but there is some evidence that they too encounter the same anxieties and resulting performance problems as other social groups. In one of the few published studies on this subject, May and Stone (2014) found that students with learning disabilities took longer to complete GRE problems if they thought the test was indicative of their ability – a sign that they were feeling the pressure of stereotype threat. Areas for future research on this topic will be discussed at the end of the chapter.

Self-Esteem Effects

It was once widely assumed that members of stigmatized groups would experience a hit to their self-esteem as a direct result of social devaluation (Crocker and Major 1989). Indeed, if people internalize and believe negative stereotypes about their group, lower self-esteem can result (Jones et al. 1984). However, empirical evidence suggests a more complex relationship between stigma and self-esteem. Stigmatized group members do not consistently report lower self-esteem, and in some cases their self-esteem is higher than that of their non-stigmatized counterparts (Crocker et al. 1994; Twenge and Crocker 2002). Critically, the relationship between stigma and self-esteem depends on how people *appraise*, and therefore react to, being socially devalued or stigmatized. What may be perceived as helpful and complimentary to some may be interpreted as patronizing and objectifying to others. What some accept as inevitable or deserved, others may view as changeable, unjust, and discriminatory. Furthermore, reactions to personal devaluation and social disadvantage also run the gamut – but certain reaction patterns can be predicted.

People engage a variety of strategies that, if successful, can buffer their sense of self-worth when confronted with social stigma and rejection. Self-esteem is often linked to the social comparisons people make between their own circumstances and those facing similar others. For example, when members of stigmatized minorities compare themselves to fellow ingroup members – rather than to relatively advantaged members of the majority group – they often experience benefits to their self-esteem (Festinger 1954; Wood 1989). This is particularly true when making self-comparisons to those who appear to be in even more disadvantaged circumstances (Wills 1981). Another way to protect self-esteem from the harmful consequences of stigma is to reappraise the cause for negative treatment as due to discrimination against one's group instead of blaming oneself for being rejected, criticized, or excluded (Major et al. 2003; Major et al. 2002). Finally, people can also protect their self-worth by placing less value on areas where their group is assumed to perform poorly, and instead focus on areas where they excel personally or their group is thought to excel (Crocker and Major 1989; Rosenberg 1979; Swain and French 2000). As we will see later in the chapter, disabled people who engage in any of these strategies often report healthy levels of self-esteem, life satisfaction, and well-being.

How Does Ableism Affect Disabled People?

Most of the research described above comes from work with other stigmatized groups. However, in many ways disabled people's experiences with stigma and discrimination resemble those of other disadvantaged minorities. For example, research on mental illness stigma suggests that individuals who internalize the negative beliefs about those with similar psychiatric conditions experience a variety of negative consequences, from decreased hope and lower self-esteem to increased psychiatric symptoms and poorer medication adherence (Corrigan and Watson 2002; Livingston and Boyd 2010). In individuals with neurological impairments, perceptions of greater stigma are associated with lower quality of life and depressed moods (Molina et al. 2013; Van der Beek et al. 2013).

Yet ableism also differs from stigmas against other minority groups, and can, at times, present unique challenges for its targets. One unique challenge stems from the fact that disabled people, as a group, are often widely dispersed and may have few opportunities to interact with similar others (Olkin 1999), although disability becomes less widely dispersed in older age (Silverman et al. 2017). The negative effects of stigma are enhanced when stigmatized group members become "tokens," being the only member of their group in a particular setting (Roberson et al. 2003; Steele 2010). While tokenism can be a problem common to many minority groups, certain minority group members often find settings in which they are not the only or token member of the group. For example, people who are ethnic minorities can escape tokenism by associating with family members and friends who share their ethnic identity, and often grow up immersed in subcultural communities. Women can befriend other women whose achievements defy gender stereotypes, and can follow their example. However, it can be more difficult for disabled people to find groups or communities in which they are not the only disabled member. Thus, they may not only suffer from the negative impact of token status, but also miss out on the benefits of affiliating with a community of similar others (Schachter, 1959).

Disability is often, though not always, a "horizontal identity," meaning that it is not shared with a person's parents, siblings, or children (Solomon 2012). Thus, one may be the only disabled person in one's entire family, neighborhood, school, or workplace, and may face ongoing prejudice even in "safe" settings such as one's own home environment. When prejudice-free environments are limited, we might expect the toll on health, achievement, and self-esteem to be magnified. Furthermore, ableism can potentially infiltrate even the most fundamental social relationships, such as the parent–child relationship, interfering with the social support that these relationships normally offer (Solomon 2012).

> As a child I experienced verbal abuse from a parent which I believe is a common experience as parents deal with their own feelings about having a disabled child. The destruction caused to one's self-esteem cannot be overstated. ~ Person with a visible physical disability, 2015

A second challenge stems from the benevolent, helpful intent behind many instances of prejudice, a problem particularly encountered by people with more visibly identifiable impairments. We, Nario-Redmond et al. (2019) found that people with more visibly identifiable conditions were more likely to confront paternalistic forms of ableism, including family overprotection, infantilization, and unwanted help, compared to those whose conditions were less readily apparent. By contrast, people with less visible impairments – described as hidden unless disclosed – were much more likely to report feeling invalidated by doctors, family, and friends who frequently questioned the legitimacy of their conditions:

> People frequently think they understand what I need better than I do. When they are unrelenting and rude I ask them exactly how many years they have spent in my body. I usually just ignore people as it takes a lot out of me to be intentionally rude. ~ Person with a visible physical disability, 2015

> In addition to having cerebral palsy as a result of premature birth, I began experiencing symptoms of fibromyalgia at age 20 and was diagnosed a year later. I've had the most issues with condescension from other women, and from so-called "radical" feminists in particular; a few of them have told me to my face that fibromyalgia is "an invention of patriarchy" to make women think they are sick. ~ Person with multiple disabilities, 2015

Invisible Disability: A Lonely Road

The isolation associated with horizontal identities or solo status can pose particular psychological problems for people with "invisible" or less apparent disabilities, for whom it may be even more difficult to find similar others. As discussed later in the chapter, people with invisible disabilities may not actively disclose their identity in many situations, or they may even take steps to intentionally hide it (Cook et al. 2016; Fitzgerald and Paterson 1995; Goldberg et al. 2005). Consequently, a person with less visible conditions may not know if others in their social environment share a group membership.

In one study, Frable et al. (1998) used experience sampling to examine whether people felt happier and better about themselves when they were around others who shared a stigmatized group membership than when they were around others who did not. They sampled Harvard undergraduates who had either a positively viewed characteristic (e.g. children of celebrities), a visible stigma (e.g. African American), or an invisible stigma (gay or lesbian, bulimic, or lower-income status). They asked the students to report their self-esteem and mood five times each day for 11 days, and to indicate who else was present in the social setting. Not surprisingly, students with invisible stigmas reported being around others with the same status less often than students with visible stigmas. Overall, the students with invisible stigmas also had lower self-esteem, and more negative mood states, than those with either visible stigmas or positively valued characteristics. Importantly, students with invisible stigmas reported a boost in their mood and self-esteem during the moments when they were around similar others. When around dissimilar others, however, their self-esteem was just as low as when they were alone. This suggests that people with invisible conditions may feel lonely even when they are around other people who don't share their particular stigma. Although this study did not look specifically at invisible disability, we might expect that people with hidden disabilities – similar to closeted gay people – might feel especially isolated in the absence of others who have a shared understanding of their circumstances.

The loneliness of invisible disability may have another unique consequence: Without similar others to validate their experiences, people with less visible disabilities may begin to doubt the legitimacy of their own disability status. In one study, Fitzgerald and Paterson (1995) interviewed people with temporomandibular joint syndrome (TMJ) and hidden multiple sclerosis (MS). Several interviewees described occasions when they began to doubt the reality of their symptoms. One woman with TMJ said, "What made it worse was when I didn't know what it was. And they keep telling me it's in my head, you really believe that you are going crazy" (Fitzgerald and Paterson 1995, p. 16).

> One doctor told my husband that my symptoms were "made up" and not real and a cry for attention. His cure was to tell my husband to pay more attention to me. Then, he dismissed me from his practice. ~ Person with multiple disabilities, 2015

People with invisible impairments frequently report that close others, strangers, and even some medical professionals invalidate their embodied experiences, and make assumptions that an impairment which cannot be seen cannot be real. Indeed, in our survey, 20% of participants who reported experiences with patronizing ableism also reported feelings of invalidation. Furthermore, these feelings of invalidation were more common for respondents with hidden disabilities (58%) than for those with visible disabilities (42%). Similarly, 16% of those describing examples of being shamed and dehumanized also reported that people questioned the validity of their impairments, and these invalidating experiences were more than twice as common among those with hidden impairments (Nario-Redmond et al. 2019).

> People saying victim blaming and shaming things about how I got my head injury TBI disability, like I was somehow negligent and it caused me to be attacked ... I felt ashamed, embarrassed, began/continued blaming myself and internalizing guilt and powerlessness and self-doubt and criticism. Outwards and directly I could not respond to that person. ~ Person with multiple impairments, 2015

Self-questioning attitudes and erasing accusations can become internalized over time, and coupled with a lack of similar others, can contribute to feelings of shame and self-blame. However, as discussed later in the chapter, people with both visible and less visible disabilities can obtain solace, empowerment, and fortification against pervasive prejudice by actively choosing to embrace their disability identity – a strategy gaining more traction as evidence accumulates in support of the psychological, health, and societal benefits associated with this most social of cures (Jetten et al. 2012).

> Often when I am going through a door, and am pushing the door open (I walk with crutches), people grab the door to open it for me, which sometimes throws my balance off. ~ Person with a visible physical disability, 2015

> Sometimes, when I objected, the other person would act as if I was unreasonably angry when they were "only trying to help" or "doing what was best" for me. ~ Person with multiple disabilities, 2015

Coping with Benevolent Ableism: Being a Visible Target for Others' Good Intentions

People with visible disabilities often encounter unsolicited offers of help, or in some cases, forced intervention (e.g. being grabbed or pushed without request or consent). Some researchers have even referred to visible disability markers, such as the presence of a white cane or a wheelchair, as "implied petitions for aid" (Cahill and Eggleston 1995). In our survey, the most common form of patronizing prejudice was unwanted help, which was reported six times more often among those with visible compared to less apparent disabilities (Nario-Redmond et al. 2019). Though well-intended, unsolicited or "assumptive help" can be psychologically threatening because it implies that the recipient lacks the competence or skills to complete the task independently (Gilbert and Silvera 1996). In one experiment, Black students who were helped by White students without requesting help showed temporary decreases in self-esteem and depressed moods after the helping interaction (Schneider et al. 1996).

In addition, condescending treatment constitutes a subtle form of dehumanization. Bastian and Haslam (2011) argued that condescension denies aspects of the recipient's humanity that distinguish him or her from animals, such as intelligence, ambition, and civility. In one study, they had participants recall times when they were treated "as if they were unintelligent, incompetent, unsophisticated, and uncivilized." After considering an experience like this, the participants reported feeling painfully self-conscious, and experiencing guilt and shame related to the loss of status implied by the dehumanizing experience (Bastian and Haslam 2011).

Self-conscious feelings have also been described by visibly disabled people encountering overzealous helping behavior (Braithwaite and Eckstein 2003; Cahill and Eggleston 1995). In our survey, 27% of respondents described experiences with being dehumanized, particularly being treated as an object and grabbed without consent – an experience that was three times more common among those with visible impairments (Nario-Redmond et al. 2019). In other qualitative studies, visibly disabled participants have described occasions when someone would interrupt what they were doing and rush over to offer help, drawing unwanted attention, and causing them embarrassment. One woman, who uses a wheelchair, described having five restaurant workers rush over to carry her up several steps so she could enter the restaurant. She said, "I get embarrassed when people make too much of a fuss over me" (Cahill and Eggleston 1995, p. 687). Even when assistance is needed and appreciated, accepting it can still foster feelings of "aversive self-awareness" (Bastian and Haslam 2011).

> I have had people move my chair with me in it to a place they feel is appropriate [and] they don't ask before. Pushing my chair fast on a sidewalk – that is not good without asking. ~ Person with multiple disabilities, 2015

In some cases, unsolicited helping can injure not only the ego, but the body (and assistive equipment) as well. People may be eager to help but lack the knowledge of how best to do so. If they are unwilling to follow instructions from the disabled person, their intervention could unwittingly cause harm. Several participants in Braithwaite and Eckstein's (2003) interviews, and in our own survey, described times when inappropriate forms of helping caused problems, ranging from inconveniences to equipment damage (e.g. having a van door broken) to physical harm from being knocked off balance. Because helping in the appropriate manner is so critically important, these participants emphasized that helpers should *ask for permission* before intervening: listen and follow the disabled person's instructions in providing the most appropriate form of help in the given situation.

Thus, although helping is usually well-intended, it can result in significant costs. For example, disabled recipients may reject unwanted assistance in order to protect their safety and their dignity. Refusing others' help can also have negative consequences, creating negative feelings for both the would-be helper and the recipient (Rosen et al. 1987). Disabled people often do recognize the benevolent intent behind unsolicited help, and may struggle to balance their desire for autonomy against their desire to get along with others – especially if they might someday need that person's help.

Wang et al. (2015) investigated the costly consequences of confronting unwanted help and other forms of prejudice for disabled people. In two studies they examined how benevolent, patronizing help was perceived in contrast to more overtly hostile prejudice using a scenario based largely on the two first authors' experiences as blind people navigating city streets. In the scenario, a blind woman asked a stranger for confirmation that she was near a bus stop. In response, the stranger either gave her a patronizing response: "Here. It's not safe for you to walk alone, let me take you" (while grabbing the woman's arm), or the stranger gave her a hostile response: "You shouldn't be out here. Go home." In Study 1, both blind and nondisabled people read the scenarios. Blind readers recognized both the benevolent and hostile responses as ableist and equally inappropriate, but nondisabled readers judged the benevolent response as more acceptable than the hostile response.

In Study 2, nondisabled participants read a variation where the blind target confronted the benevolent (or hostile) stranger saying, "I can handle myself just fine and was only asking for directions. Could you please just answer my question?" In this case, nondisabled readers judged the blind target as less warm and more rude when she verbally confronted the *patronizing* treatment than when she quietly accepted it. Interestingly, in these studies, the blind target who confronted *hostile* treatment was not penalized in this way – she was judged as equally warm whether she confronted or ignored the hostility (but see Katz et al. 1978). As these studies illustrate, nondisabled individuals often have difficulty recognizing patronizing behavior as prejudicial (Fehr and Sassenberg 2009). They may feel taken aback or even angered if their well-intended but inappropriate acts of helping are rebuffed or confronted by a disabled person. Disabled people, in turn, may worry about the interpersonal repercussions of rejecting inappropriate assistance, facing a kind of "damned if you do, damned if you don't" quandary similar to that faced by many women interacting with sexist men (Becker et al. 2011).

I've had reactions from caregivers or friends mostly because I was asserting some right to autonomy. I have felt at time[s] people want me to be dependent and then want to vent anger about helping. ~ Person with multiple disabilities, 2015

People with disabilities experience unique struggles when negotiating unsolicited help. At times, they may want or even require help from strangers. However, if help is unwanted or if what is offered doesn't match the recipient's needs, then one's sense of competence, control, and even physical safety can be threatened. Recipients must decide whether to assert themselves – and risk being judged as rude or ungrateful – or to accept the inappropriate help, sacrificing autonomy. They may also plan ahead to minimize their need for assistance from strangers. Sometimes, disabled people develop strategies to assert themselves while minimizing hurt feelings. These include making jokes or gently educating helpers about how to provide useful assistance. In our survey, the most common reaction to patronizing prejudice was to ignore it, followed by getting angry and declining impositions to help (Nario-Redmond et al. 2019). Though a balance can often be struck, negotiating these interactions constitutes a perpetual challenge for many people with visible disabilities.

In sum, ableism presents many of the same psychological challenges as other forms of stigma and prejudice, such as stress-related health problems or threats to self-esteem. However, it also presents some additional challenges that other stigmatized groups may not encounter, and disabled people can choose from a variety of strategies in response. We now turn to a discussion of the role of disability identity in determining which strategies people use to cope with ableism.

Coping with Ableism: The Central Role of Disability Identity

As described earlier, SIT posits that people carry several social identities based upon the groups they belong to and the roles they occupy (Tajfel and Turner 1979). A single individual may simultaneously identify as a student from a particular college, a woman, an African American, a Christian, a daughter, a girlfriend, and a person with a disability or disabled person. For any individual, some of these identities will be more central or important to self-definition than others. Furthermore, social identities can fluctuate in strength and centrality depending on the situation. That is, one may identify most strongly with school during a football game or with Christianity while attending church. One may also identify to a greater or lesser extent with one's disability status.

Research in the social identity tradition has shown that people are fundamentally motivated to feel positively, overall, about their network of identities. Early research by Tajfel et al. (1971) showed that people will work to enhance the standing of their own social identities even if these memberships are completely fictional. In their classic study, participants completed a bogus dot-counting task and were told, based on a coin flip, that they were either an "over-estimator" or an "under-estimator" – a completely arbitrary distinction. They were then asked to assign some hypothetical resources to other people classified as over-estimators and under-estimators. Consistently, participants gave more resources to whichever group they had been assigned to, despite having no previous contact or ties with either "over-estimators" or "under-estimators." This experimental paradigm has been called the "minimal group paradigm," and it demonstrates the basic human tendency to favor one's own social ingroups in comparison to outgroups.

In fact, people from both advantaged (e.g. majority) and disadvantaged (e.g. minority) groups work to elevate their social identity network in a variety of ways. One strategy is to simply identify most strongly with those social categories that others value most while minimizing identification with groups that are devalued. A simple but elegant illustration of this selective identification process comes from a study by Cialdini et al. (1976). They found that college students referred to their school's sports team as "we" when the team won a game, but referred to it as "they" when the team lost. Using the terms "we" or "us" implies identification with a group, while terms such as "they" imply distance between oneself and the group. Similarly, because disability is often a socially devalued membership, people may choose to disidentify with their disability status in a number of ways. We refer to these disidentification strategies as *social mobility strategies* since they involve the escaping or moving away from a disability identity (Dirth and Branscombe 2018). Social mobility strategies are individually-focused since they can protect individuals from social rejection and stigma without benefiting (and sometimes harming) the broader group (Kulich et al. 2015; Wright and Taylor 1998).

When it comes to deploying social mobility strategies, disability can be a difficult identity to deny or escape. If the disability is visible to others, or a person desires an accommodation (e.g. a modified schedule, quiet workspace, or sign language interpreters) for a less apparent disability, social mobility strategies may be ineffective or pose serious costs to quality of life. In these cases, people may choose a different tactic to feel good about themselves in lieu of distancing from disability status. In brief, they may either redefine disability as a positive asset (*social creativity strategies*), work to change social inequalities and disability injustice in society (*social change strategies*), or both. Together, social creativity and social change are considered "collective" coping strategies because they attempt to improve the social standing of disabled people as a group rather than merely advancing the status of the individual.

In the next sections, we detail some of the specific ways that people might use social mobility, creativity, and change to cope with or manage ableism (see Table 6.1 for a summary). We then discuss research on factors associated with which strategies a person might use, followed by research on the personal and collective consequences of using each type of strategy.

Social Mobility Strategies

Some people employ social mobility (sometimes called individual mobility) strategies to escape the mark of disability on their social identity. They may do so by seeking medical treatment to eliminate impairments, denying or concealing their disability status, or embracing an "overcoming" narrative (see Table 6.1) that also serves to distance them from the group.

Table 6.1 Strategies for maintaining positive social identities in the presence of ableism.

Strategy type	Strategy	Examples
Social mobility	Direct attempts to escape disability	Seeking medical treatments to cure or remove impairments (e.g. cosmetic surgery; bionic eyes)
Social mobility	Concealing disability	Medical treatment to change appearance (e.g. limb lengthening surgery); denying or actively hiding a disability from others; forgoing accommodations
Social mobility	Overcoming disability	Describing oneself as successful "in spite of" disability; "beating the odds"; trying harder to meet "normal" standards; minimizing or not referring to oneself as disabled
Social creativity	Revaluing disability as an asset	"Deaf people have beautiful sign language"; "blind people can echolocate and read in the dark"; "autistic people are direct and tell the truth"
Social creativity	Reclaiming disability labels as positive subcultural signifiers	Re-appropriating "crip," "freak," "gimp," and "mad" as terms of group pride
Social creativity	Comparing oneself to others perceived to be "worse off"	Some impairment groups distancing themselves from other impairment groups
Social creativity	Establishing new norms, values, or dimensions of comparison	"Who cares about walking, I've got wheel power"; "I don't want to drive because I prefer to be driven"
Social change	Challenging discrimination	Calling out instances of ableism or inaccessibility in social structures; raising awareness about disability rights
Social change	Disability affiliation	Forming advocacy groups tied by disability
Social change	Collective action	Lobbying, litigation, protests and collective efforts to counteract discrimination

Medical Treatment The most obvious way to escape disability is to seek an intervention that removes the impairment. People may seek medical treatments – approved or experimental – to improve limited sight, hearing, mobility, or mood, and to reduce physical symptoms that signal impairment. Obviously, this strategy is more feasible for some impairments than others. The medical treatment strategy may also involve decisions that parents make on behalf of their young or unborn children. Cochlear implants are one controversial medical treatment that parents choose for their deaf infants in some cases (Solomon 2012; Sparrow 2005).[1] Much of the controversy surrounds their incomplete efficacy, as cochlear implants often improve hearing to an extent, but not to the level of typically hearing people. Thus, cochlear implants raise interesting questions about the consequences of incomplete social mobility, in which people may transform severe impairments into milder but still present impairments. Some argue that these devices can actually marginalize users as members of neither the deaf nor the hearing communities (Crouch 1997), with implications for one's need for belonging, and acceptance as a peripheral, temporary, or liminal member of multiple groups.

Concealing Disability Even if a medical treatment to reverse impairment is not feasible, people may choose to conceal their impairments from others. Goffman (1963) frequently described the strategy of "passing," denying or pretending not to have a disability as a way to manage stigmatized social identities. Concealment may be active (e.g. having limb-lengthening surgery to hide the effects of dwarfism; lying about one's reason for wearing glasses) or passive (not divulging disability during a job interview, not requesting classroom accommodations). If a disability is less visible, it may remain concealed by default unless the disabled person actively discloses it to others or is otherwise discovered. People with more visible disabilities can also conceal their disability status in some settings, such as telephone or online conversations, but may be unable to conceal it in others (i.e. face-to-face meetings). Most disabled people wish to control when, and to whom, their disability is disclosed (Goldberg et al. 2005; Hyman 2008). These strategic choices to disclose or conceal disability can have important consequences both psychologically and practically.

Overcoming Disability Even if a disability cannot be directly reversed or hidden, people may frame their disability status in a way that divorces it from their identity. Popular cultural narratives often depict disability as a challenge to be overcome, and celebrate those who succeed "despite" their impairments as exceedingly brave and inspiring. People may embrace this overcoming narrative by minimizing or downplaying a disability's significance in their lives or attempting to compensate for the impairment's impact through increased effort, with a goal of meeting normative standards (McVittie et al. 2008; Watson 2002). While this strategy may constitute an individual's resistance to ableism, it still reflects social mobility in that it involves a distancing of self from the broader disability group. For example, students with learning disabilities may choose to forgo note takers and extra time on tests, or stay up long hours instead of requesting books on tape or other accommodations. These choices can compromise achievement (Wolanin and Steele 2004).

Social Creativity and Social Change Strategies

When simply escaping disability and its associated stigma is not a viable choice, people may instead cope with ableism through attempts to combat or confront disability stigma at the collective level. These collective strategies include redefining disability as a valued attribute (social creativity) or directly working to change systems that work to oppress disabled people's status (social change).

> What would happen if the autism gene was eliminated from the gene pool? You would have a bunch of people standing around in a cave, chatting and socializing and not getting anything done. (Temple Grandin, as cited in Baron-Cohen 2002, p. 190)

Social Creativity Instead of accepting society's devaluation of disability, sometimes people reappraise their disability as a valued characteristic (see Table 6.1). They may compare themselves (and others with their impairment) favorably to the general public, or focus on the unique strengths their impairments afford. In the above quotation, for example, Temple Grandin argues that her autism has allowed her to optimize her concrete thinking abilities. They may also celebrate the experience of disability in general as an asset that affords skill in adapting to challenges or empathizing with others who are socially disadvantaged. Generally, social creativity strategies frame the disability experience as a valued, positive, and life-enriching rather than negative or tragic (Linton 1998; Swain and French 2000).

One distinctive way people express social creativity is through language. Traditionally derogatory words such as "cripple," "gimpy," and "madness" have been rebranded, with the terms "crip," "gimp," and "mad" connoting disability pride and solidarity (Kafer 2013; McRuer 2006). Deaf people, likewise, use capitalization to subtly distinguish "deaf" (the medicalized impairment condition) from Deaf (the cultural marker):

> When capitalized, *Deaf* refers to a culture, as distinct from *deaf*, which is a pathological term; this distinction echoes that between *gay* and *homosexual*. An increasing number of deaf people maintain they would not choose to be hearing. To them, *cure* – deafness as pathology – is anathema; *accommodation* – deafness as disability – is more palatable; and *celebration* – Deafness as culture – trumps all. (Solomon 2012, p. 50)

While social creativity strategies can unify disabled people as a group, they can also divide. People may positively revalue their own impairment by comparing themselves favorably to people with different impairments – ranking some more negative or disabling than others (see Chapter 5 on stigma hierarchies). Tensions have been documented, for instance, when Deaf people seem to distance themselves from other impairment groups by claiming themselves not as people with disabilities but as a language minority (Lane 2002). Alternatively, some people use "intragroup" social comparisons within their impairment category to compare themselves to others with their condition who they perceive to be worse off. For example, people with learning disabilities have compared themselves to poorer-performing students in their classes (Finlay and Lyons 2000). Such social comparisons may effectively mitigate against perceived devaluation, but they do not address the social inequality that maintains ableist reactions. Furthermore, downward social comparisons that position one impairment group against another undermine solidarity and the cohesion needed to build cross-impairment coalitions (Anspach 1979). The other social creativity strategies involved in reclaiming former terms of disparagement, positive reappraisal, and promoting alternative standards of comparison, may be more strategically aligned with efforts toward social change.

> Most importantly, ADA is a landmark commandment of fundamental human morality. It is the world's first declaration of equality for people with disabilities by any nation. It will proclaim to America and to the world that people with disabilities are fully human; that paternalistic, discriminatory, segregationist attitudes are no longer acceptable; and that henceforth people with disabilities must be accorded the same personal respect and the same social and economic opportunities as other people. (Dart 1990)

Social Change Sometimes, disabled people may go beyond revaluing or redefining their interpretation of disability, and instead work actively to challenge stigma, elevate their group's social status, and fight for disability rights. For example, they may form political advocacy groups, either impairment-specific or cross-disability; petition lawmakers to support disability rights legislation; use litigation to challenge discriminatory policies and practices; or engage in public education campaigns to raise awareness of ableism and reduce stigma (see Chapter 8). As the above quote from a disability activist illustrates, disability rights laws like the Americans with Disabilities Act (ADA) were intended to improve the status of disabled people by promoting equal access and prohibiting discrimination in employment (and all places open to the general public) on the basis of disability (Brennan 2015).

As shown in Table 6.1, collective action begins with the belief that one's group is a target of discrimination, and that this discrimination is unjust and illegitimate (Branscombe and Ellemers 1998). In order to engage in collective action, people must also believe that their attempts to address discrimination will be effective (Mummendey et al. 1999). Further, collective action depends, by definition, on the existence of cohesive groups formed around a common purpose. In the case of disability, forming action groups can be challenging if people with similar disabilities are geographically or otherwise isolated. Despite this challenge, a variety of groups are working in disability rights advocacy, ranging from local independent living centers to national and international cross-disability coalitions. Some argue that disabled individuals acting on behalf of the group are also engaging in collective action as representatives (Wright and Taylor 1998) (e.g. Disability Visibility Project is spotlighted in the *Activist pages* of this chapter).

Who Uses Which Coping Strategies?

Researchers working at the intersections of social psychology and disability studies have begun to identify some of the factors associated with the tendency to use either individualistic coping strategies (social mobility) or collectivistic strategies

Table 6.2 Predictors of social mobility, social creativity, and social change strategies.

Factor	Social mobility	Social creativity	Social change
Impairment factors	Less severe, shorter-lived, or less visible impairments	More severe, longer-lived, or more visible impairments	More severe, longer-lived, or more visible impairments
Disability identification (DI)	Low DI; disability seen as less important and negative feelings about being disabled	High DI; disability seen as more important and positive feelings about being disabled	High DI; disability seen as important and positive feelings about being disabled
Beliefs about social change	Stigma seen as legitimate, justifiable, inevitable consequence of disability	Stigma seen as illegitimate, less justified, but inevitable consequence of disability	Stigma seen as illegitimate, unjustified, and modifiable

(social creativity or social change). Here we focus on three factors: impairment factors, disability identification, and beliefs about social change. Table 6.2 summarizes the conditions that are most likely to inspire each coping strategy.

Impairment Factors

If a person believes that their impairment is relatively easy to escape, conceal, or minimize, they may be more attracted to social mobility as a way to cope with ableism. Such a belief may depend, in part, on characteristics associated with particular impairments. For example, people with less severe, shorter-lived, or more fluctuating impairments may have a stronger connection to a nondisabled identity, or may be more likely to perceive a fluid boundary between disability and non-disability. By contrast, people who were born with more permanent impairment(s) may see disability as an inescapable part of themselves (Bogart 2014). People with invisible impairments or very mild impairments are also much more able to manage stigma through concealing their disability status in a broader range of situations (Rottenstein 2013), and therefore have more ready access to this strategy compared to those with more severe or visible conditions. Furthermore, when impairments require certain visible accommodations, concealment may not be a viable or desirable strategy. Whenever social mobility strategies of escape and concealment are foreclosed to certain impairment groups, collectivistic coping strategies are more likely to be considered. That doesn't mean that just because people with less apparent conditions can conceal their disability status that they will always choose to do so; nor does it imply that those with more visible conditions will necessarily engage in strategies designed to improve the overall status of the group. Nevertheless, impairment factors should directly influence the likelihood of strategies used for coping with ableism. They may also influence coping indirectly via a person's level of disability identification.

Psychological Identification

As described earlier, disability may be a stronger social identity for some people than for others. Psychologists typically measure identity strength as a combination of centrality (how much a person feels the identity is important to his or her self-definition) and evaluation (how positively or negatively the person feels about the identity or others with the identity). Generally, people who score high on measures of disability identification report that disability is an important part of who they are, that they don't regret having their disability, and a that they even feel pride about their disability. People who score low in disability identification, on the other hand, believe that disability is a relatively unimportant part of their self-image, deny pride in their disability status, and may express negative feelings about disability.

For people with weak disability identities, social mobility may be an attractive way of coping with disability stigma. These people have little to lose and, perhaps, some to gain psychologically by further distancing themselves from an identity that is already unimportant to them. People with stronger disability identities, however, may prefer to engage in social creativity or social change strategies in response to ableist treatment. These individuals are more invested in their disability identity, and may have more to gain by appraising disability in positive terms and/or working to elevate the status of disabled people as a group.

Supporting these ideas, Nario-Redmond et al. (2013) conducted two surveys asking people with a variety of impairments about their use of various coping strategies as well as their disability identification (see Table 6.3). In both surveys, people who reported that their disability was less central to their identity were more likely to report concealing, minimizing, or trying to overcome their disability than those with higher disability identification. Those who described their disability as a more central part of their identity were more likely to engage in both social creativity (e.g. valuing their disability experience) and social change (e.g. viewing themselves as "disability rights activists" and participating in advocacy).

Further, people who had less visible disabilities or who had spent less time living with impairment also reported lower disability identification. In another series of studies (Nario-Redmond and Oleson 2016), disabled college students with higher disability identification were more likely to participate in disability rights advocacy (Study 1); and both college students and adults with disabilities were more involved in organizations with other disabled people if they were more disability identified (Studies 2 and 3). Thus, self-identification with disability was related to promoting the advancement of disabled people as a group, and to preferences for affiliation and more solidarity with other disabled people – all important prerequisites for participation in collective action. Furthermore, those most highly identified with disability were also among the most likely to recognize ableism or disability discrimination in their own lives and in the lives of other disabled people.

In a different stigmatized group, fat[2] women who identified more strongly as members of a community of others who shared a similar body weight were more

Table 6.3 Index items and reliability coefficients for measures of disability identification and strategic coping strategies.

Disability identity α = 0.87–0.89	Community pride α = 0.73–0.76	Minimize deny α = 0.69–0.75	Group discrimination α = 0.71–0.76
Being a part of a group of people who have disabilities is important to me.	I have a lot of pride in the disability community.	Overall, my disability status has very little to do with how I feel about myself.	The biggest problem faced by people with disabilities is the attitudes of other people.
I'm glad to be a member of the disability community.	Disability culture is alive and well.	I don't think of myself as a disabled person.	People with disabilities are discriminated against in society.
Being a member of the disabled community is central to my identity.	It is important to build a cross-disability community.	Being a nondisabled person is important to who I am.	My disability is how society reacts to people with disabilities/impairments.
I want to remain a member of the disabled community.	I believe in "disability pride."	I am not disabled.	Lack of accessibility and discrimination by employers are the main reasons why people with disabilities are unemployed.
I want other people to know that I'm a person with a disability.	I like when people with disabilities use the words "crip" or "cripple" positively.		

Affiliation preferences $\alpha = 0.65–0.78$	Valuing disability experience $\alpha = 0.85–0.87$	Attempt to overcome $\alpha = 0.76–0.80$	Personal discrimination $\alpha = 0.72–0.73$
Most of my friends have disabilities.	My disability is a strength.	I identify with people who are trying to overcome their disabilities.	The problem is not my disability, but how people react to my disability.
I would rather associate with disabled people than nondisabled people.	My disability enriches my life.	I wish someone would find a cure for my disability.	I am often excluded from activities because of my disability.
I feel most comfortable around people with disabilities.	I am a better person because of my disability.	I try to overcome my disability.	I have been discriminated against because of my disability.
	I am proud to be disabled.	I would prefer not to have a disability.	If I am treated poorly at a store or restaurant, it is because I am a person with a disability.
	I would *not* change my disability status, even if I could.		Other people look down on me because I'm a person with a disability.

Ingroup solidarity $\alpha = 0.64–0.65$	Social change $\alpha = 0.75–0.82$	Attempt to conceal $\alpha = 0.74–0.80$
I have a lot in common with other people with disabilities.	I am a disability rights activist.	I try to hide my disability from others in certain situations.
People with disabilities of all kinds share similar experiences.	I advocate for the rights of other people with disabilities.	I frequently pass as a nondisabled person.
I feel strong ties to other disabled people.	I do not want to participate in protests for Disability Rights. (R)	I try to hide my disability whenever I can.

Note. Reliability coefficients for indices are based on national ($N = 93$) and international ($N = 268$) samples from Nario-Redmond et al. (2013) and Nario-Redmond and Oleson (2016).

likely to endorse social creativity statements such as "big is beautiful" and "my body size is sexy" than those who were less strongly fat identified. They were also more supportive of social change efforts (i.e. fat advocacy), and less supportive of individual change efforts (i.e. weight loss and dieting). Furthermore, those who endorsed dieting and gastric bypass as viable means of escaping the group were also among the least group-identified (Lindly et al. 2014). Interestingly, people identify less strongly with groups that seem more escapable. On average, "elderly people" tend to have stronger age identities than "young people" because the "young people" identity is temporary by definition, whereas "elderly people" will remain members of this group for the rest of their lives (Garstka et al. 2004). Similarly, disability identity is affected by factors that affect ease of escape. Rottenstein (2013) found that people with hidden or less severe impairments rarely self-identified as disabled, whereas those with visible or more severe impairments were more likely to identify as disabled all the time. Additionally, those who rarely identified as disabled also endorsed strategies of hiding or overcoming their disability, and were less active in disability organizations than those who identified as disabled all the time. This suggests that impairment characteristics can affect identification, which in turn can affect strategy use.

More than likely, the relationship between disability identification and strategy use is a reciprocal one. For example, people who conceal or minimize disability might come to disidentify with their disability status over a period of time. Conversely, those who value their disability (engaging in social creativity) or participate in collective action (engaging in social change) might find their disability identity growing stronger as a result of these activities, which can further reinforce the use of these collective coping strategies. This has important implications for creating opportunities for disabled people to meet one another, discuss common concerns, and foster a sense of community which can facilitate further engagement, disability identification, and contributions to social change (Little 2010).

> Until recently the blind and those interested in them have insisted that society revise and modify its attitude toward this specific group. Obviously, for many reasons, this is an impossibility, and effort spent on such a program is as futile as spitting into the wind. (Cutsforth, as cited in Zahl 1950, pp. 179)

> The assumption is that the blind are fit to participate in society on a basis of equality … And the corollary of this assumption is that there is nothing fixed and immutable about the obstacles encountered by the blind in their progress toward integration; that social attitudes and opinions are essentially on our side, and that where they appear otherwise they are based on ignorance and error and can be changed. (TenBroek 1951)

Beliefs About Social Change

The above quotes, both written by blind men, highlight the authors' contrasting beliefs about the efficacy of social change. Cutsforth's statement embodies a belief structure known as the biomedical model of disability (also described in Chapter 3).

He argues not only that social change is futile, but that the responsibility for coping with stigma lies with the blind person him or herself (see also Cutsforth 1933). In keeping with this philosophy, biomedical models present disability as a defect of body or mind that should be "fixed" by medical experts or mental health professionals. Discrimination against disabled people is perceived as unfortunate but inevitable (Darling and Heckert 2010; Shakespeare 1994). The biomedical model thus highlights social mobility as the optimal way to cope with stigma, while discounting the possibility of social change.

By contrast, the second quotation comes from the founder of one of the largest blindness advocacy groups in the United States, the National Federation of the Blind. Dr. TenBroek presents an optimistic belief in the efficacy of social change attempts. His view is consistent with a socio-political model of disability (Darling and Heckert 2010; Hahn 1985). Generally, the socio-political model presents disability stigma as a social construct rooted in discrimination and access barriers in the environment. The responsibility for removing these barriers is placed upon the larger society and not on disabled individuals (Davis 1995; Linton 1998). Socio-political models question the legitimacy of discrimination and call upon social change efforts as critical to disabled people's welfare. Thus, socio-political models foster belief structures that encourage people to engage in social creativity and social change strategies in response to ableist practices.

Generally, SIT predicts that people will use the coping strategy that they imagine will be most effective according to their social identity beliefs (Tajfel and Turner 1979). If people believe that escape or social mobility is both possible and desirable, they will tend to use that strategy by minimizing or concealing their disability status or seeking medical intervention. If people believe that social change is a viable way to enhance their own identities and advance the status of disabled people overall, they will be more likely to engage in social change strategies. And what of those people who believe that escape from the group is either impossible or undesirable, but who also doubt the efficacy of social change? These individuals will be most likely to make the best of their situation by using social creativity strategies. As the next section illustrates, social creativity can be a powerful means of bolstering self-worth even when it is impossible to escape from, or directly remove, a social identity threat.

Consequences of Coping Strategies

All of the coping strategies described above have trade-offs for well-being. Both individualistic coping (social mobility) and collectivistic coping (social creativity and social change) can benefit well-being in different ways, and can also pose different threats. On one hand, concealing or minimizing disability can directly protect the person from experiencing discrimination or stigmatization *in the short term*, but these strategies do nothing to change the material, economic, and political circumstances of the group. Moreover, hiding or devaluing a key part of oneself can become a significant source of stress, isolation, and self-esteem threat (Shakespeare 1996; see also Hahn and Belt 2004). Conversely, creatively redefining a disability as valued or participating in collective actions can foster belonging, self-worth, and buttress feelings of empowerment which may result in more intergroup equality. At the same time, actively promoting oneself as disabled and challenging the status quo can also threaten intergroup relations, and result in feelings of jealousy and backlash (Cook et al. 2000). The following sections summarize research on these trade-offs.

Consequences of Social Mobility

> One thing that's really interesting is that when I have my service dog with me I'm visibly disabled, but when I don't then I appear non-disabled. This changes my experience drastically. I don't get stopped going in to stores, I don't get asked personal questions by strangers, I'm not spoken down to. I don't have a spotlight on me. ~ Person with multiple invisible disabilities, 2015

Consequences for Individuals The above quote illustrates the appeal of concealing disability: in many cases others will not treat a person in ableist ways if they are unaware that the person has a disability. Passing as nondisabled may thus present a situational option for avoiding some forms of ableism and the resulting "spotlight" of identity threat. This largely explains why many people conceal disability at least some of the time (Goldberg et al. 2005). Disability nondisclosure can have significant practical benefits, such as shielding against employment discrimination (Rowe 2011) as well as the social psychological benefits of being able to "blend in" (Cook et al. 2016; Fitzgerald and Paterson 1995). In addition, choosing when and how to disclose (or conceal) a disability can offer a sense of control over the disability's framing and its role in the situation (Hyman 2008). Furthermore, psychologically minimizing the negative aspects of an impairment can sometimes benefit mood (e.g. for amputees; Dunn 1996).

On the flip side, hiding a disability can create its own set of stressors. Worries about lying to others, fears of being "found out," and difficulty explaining some of the effects of disability (e.g. resume gaps, work restrictions, or poor performance) can plague those who choose not to disclose a disability at work or school (Fitzgerald and Paterson 1995; Goldberg et al. 2005). People may feel an uncomfortable divide between their publicly and privately presented selves – an aversive situation that can lead to depression (Sedlovskaya et al. 2013). Moreover, disability disclosure can improve the quality of personal relationships (Chaudoir and Quinn 2010) – so nondisclosure may limit relationship closeness. Further, it is often difficult or impossible to receive disability accommodations on the job or at school without disclosing disability, and concealing disability may require a person to forgo using assistive devices that protect or facilitate participation in public. Thus, nondisclosure can pose threats to productivity or even physical safety.

More generally, attempts to escape a disability identity are usually imperfect and rarely completely successful. When people struggle to devalue an inescapable part of themselves, they often suffer significant internal self-threats (Gill 1997). Attempts at social mobility may set the stage for self-hate and internalized ableism, as people accept the legitimacy of their group's low status, perhaps thinking "If I am trying so hard to escape this group, it must be pretty bad." People may also come to blame the impairment itself for the challenges they face, embracing dangerous, painful, and uncertain outcomes when attempting full escape from disability as the only viable solution (Hahn and Belt 2004).

Together, the psychological consequences of social mobility can have a negative impact on multiple dimensions of well-being, including feelings of self-worth and satisfaction with life. In fact, several studies have found correlations between impairment factors and well-being, suggesting that people with *acquired* impairments have lower life satisfaction than those who were born with their impairments (Bogart 2014); people with *less visible* impairments have lower self-esteem than those with more visible impairments (Goodrich and Ramsey 2013); and people with *less severe* impairments have lower self-esteem and life satisfaction than those with more severe impairments (Jones et al. 2011; Roy and MacKay 2002; Silverman and Cohen 2012). Ironically, these findings indicate that people with impairments most conducive to social mobility experience a chronic self-esteem hit when compared to those for whom social mobility is not an option.

Further, self-esteem is positively related to disability identification. In the study by Nario-Redmond et al. (2013), higher disability identification was associated with higher self-esteem – both personal (global feelings of self-worth) and collective (feelings of worth as a member of the disability community). Participants who had higher disability identification were also less likely to conceal their disability from others, and attempts to conceal disability were independently predictive of lower personal and collective self-esteem. Together, these findings suggest that engaging in social mobility strategies (e.g. hiding, escaping, minimizing, or overcoming) as a way to cope with ableist treatment and disability stigma can result in significant costs for well-being.

Importantly, the consequences of using social mobility strategies to distance the self from disability status also depend on cultural norms and personal resources. In a cross-cultural study, Fernández et al. (2012) compared predictors of well-being for people with dwarfism in Spain and in the United States. In Spain, limb-lengthening surgery to reverse short stature (a social mobility strategy) is popular and culturally supported. In the United States, by contrast, there seems to be more of a normative preference to join support organizations like Little People of America (LPA), and to express disability pride. Fernández et al. (2012) found that for people with dwarfism living in Spain, having limb-lengthening surgery benefited well-being by protecting people from discrimination. In the United States by contrast, limb-lengthening surgery was rare in this study. The strongest predictor of well-being for US participants was making positive contact with other people with dwarfism – which buffered self-worth from the impact of discrimination. Therefore, social mobility strategies may be beneficial only to the extent that they are widely endorsed within the national culture as well as the disability subculture. Additionally, medical (bionic and other surgical) interventions are not equally distributed. People with more material and social resources will obviously be more successful in their social mobility attempts, particularly when it comes to accessing new technologies (e.g. stair-climbing wheelchairs, neuro-prosthetics, and memory implants) that facilitate concealing or minimizing certain impairments (Dunn and Brody 2008; Wolbring 2008).

Consequences for the Group Beyond individual costs, there is an even more insidious outcome associated with defection from a lower status group that can occur when those who escape undercut or deride their former group to justify the legitimacy of their own decision to escape (Ellemers 2001). For example, some who mobilize away from a stigmatized or disadvantaged group may find themselves taking personal credit for overcoming their former status and penetrating into a more privileged group (male, nondisabled, thin, or White). They may argue that if they can do it on their own merits, so should everyone else – implying that perhaps discrimination isn't as big of a problem as people claim. And if claims of discrimination are dismissed as a pervasive social problem, then there is room to argue against the need for legal protections, special accommodations, or laws to improve access because the exception proves the rule, and anyone can "pull themselves up by the bootstraps." As noted in Chapter 3, ideologies related to the Protestant Work Ethic and American Meritocracy all feed into just-world beliefs about the power of individual resilience in the face of challenge – women do break through the "glass ceiling," the United States had a Black president, and with the right attitude and enough willpower, disabled people can do anything they want, right? The danger is not so much in choosing to escape stigma or even in wanting to alter or "improve" oneself – the danger is what happens when a select few demonstrate that intergroup boundaries appear to be open, no longer caring about the rights of their former peers and diminishing the influence of privilege, connections, and other resources that may have supported their transition. This is not an inevitable consequence of social mobility; however, such patterns have has been documented with women (e.g. queen bee syndrome), ethnic minorities (i.e. Uncle Toms) (Kulich et al. 2015), and other disadvantaged groups (Jost et al. 2004; Wright 2001). More research is clearly needed on the personal and group consequences of disidentification for disabled people, including the growing influence of alternate identifications, transhumanism, and human enhancement on well-being, ableist attitudes, and intergroup outcomes (Wolbring 2008, 2009).

Consequences of Social Creativity and Social Change for Well-Being

> Why do people always feel the need to correct you when you self-identify as "disabled/have a disability?" It is *not* analogous with negativity. Please stop assuming that; you are choosing to see disability through the prism of limitations

and that is a fractured lens. Also "DIS" prefix is not only "un" and "not" but has a Latin and Greek derivative meaning "duo" and "two" hence *another* way of doing and being. Consider that and stand down your need to correct an experience that you don't own and negative worldview of being disabled/living with disabilities. (Watkins 2017)

I have been asked, mainly by the elderly, "What's wrong with you?" If I chose to reply, I would say something along the lines of, "there's nothing wrong with me, but there is with the environment around me" or "nothing's wrong with me, what's wrong with you?" With the second statement, they would just look at me without knowing what to say. I took this as a win for myself! ~ Person with a visible physical disability, 2015

Benefits of Social Creativity and Competition Several lines of convergent evidence support that both of the group advancement or collective strategies for coping with social devaluation (social creativity and social change) have clear benefits for well-being. Psychologists have long known that people can creatively reappraise aspects of themselves in positive terms to enhance their self-esteem (e.g. Dunning and Cohen 1992). In the case of stigma, Crocker and Major (1989) argued self-esteem is also protected when people either revalue formerly stigmatized traits, compare themselves to similarly stigmatized others, or shift blame away from internalized self-loathing and toward a recognition that *others* may be prejudiced against them. The first two of these responses constitute social creativity strategies, while the third (attributing negative outcomes to prejudice) also forms a basis for social change.

Our own empirical research confirms this connection between disability identification, social creativity, and well-being (Nario-Redmond et al. 2013). In our US and international studies, over and above the self-esteem benefits associated with identifying as a member of the disability community, the more people expressed value in the disability experience, the more personal and collective self-esteem increased. That is, the more people indicated that they appraised their disability as a strength, an experience that enriched their lives and made them better people, the more they felt a personal sense of self-worth and a collective sense of worth derived from the broader disability community. Other researchers have found similar connections where a positive disability identity was linked to lower levels of anxiety and depression in a sample of persons with multiple sclerosis (Bogart 2015). Jones et al. (2011) also found that the biggest predictor of life satisfaction after brain injury was the degree to which people positively self-identified as "survivors," followed by the number of new close relationships they formed post-injury. In fact, these two factors alone explained the counterintuitive positive relationship between more severe injury and higher life satisfaction in this sample.

Support groups, in particular, can help facilitate the benefits of social creativity and social change. Crabtree et al. (2010) found that members of a mental health support group expressed less internalized stigma and greater stereotype resistance to the extent that they identified strongly with their support group. Highly identified support group members were less likely to agree with statements like "mentally ill people shouldn't get married," and more likely to agree with statements like "I can have a good, fulfilling life." This stereotype resistance was associated with higher personal self-esteem.

Similarly, Mejias et al. (2014) interviewed nine young women with disabilities about their experiences as members of a disability empowerment group. The group included women aged 16–24 with a variety of disabilities. Group members participated in discussions of issues like disability pride, personal agency, and emerging womanhood. They also engaged in collective action efforts such as creating a documentary about sexuality and disability. In one group outing, support group members visited a sex shop in the community, thus rejecting stereotypes of themselves as asexual beings. The group thus merged social creativity strategies (cultivating disability pride, resisting stereotype internalization) with social change (attempting to educate the public about the woman's sexuality and autonomy).

Support group members also described several benefits of being in the group, including enhanced disability pride, a sense of belonging through meaningful connection with group members, protection from negative social messages about disability, and heightened self-confidence that translated to relationships outside the group. "I'm with my own people," one group member stated. Another said of the trip to the sex shop: "When we went to the sex shop, I think we influenced the community, it's all about eight to nine girls in wheelchairs coming through and holding up dildos, and we were, like, empowered for real, we were so empowered it was ridiculous" (p. 9).

The support group members learned not only to value themselves and feel that they belonged, but to assert their rights and those of other women with disabilities. Belonging is an essential component of well-being (Baumeister and Leary 1995), and disabled people may derive an especially strong sense of belonging from friendships with others who have disabilities. This may explain findings by Silverman and colleagues where disabled adults who reported more friends with disabilities had higher life satisfaction (Study 1) and overall quality of life (Study 2) than those without disabled friends (Silverman et al. 2017).

Although clear psychological and interpersonal benefits can emerge from redefining disability and joining with other disabled people in collective action, whenever a disadvantaged group challenges the status quo or seeks to advance the rights and privileges of its members, pushback often follows. That is, advantaged group members don't just step aside and make way for those who question the legitimacy of their social position – particularly when power and status implications are at stake. The costs associated with creative reclamation of the value of multicultural and minority perspectives, the recognition of discrimination, and the motivation to rectify the subordination and marginalization of one's group are topics well covered in the intergroup relations literature (Krieger 2010; Sidanius and Pratto 1999; Wright 2001). In fact, the social repercussions disabled people have encountered for challenging the status quo or failing to stay in their "place" are the multifaceted forms of ableism that fill the pages of this book. Below we focus on the more immediate costs associated with challenging the predominant view of disability as a stigmatized status, and disabled people as stereotypically tragic, inferior, and helpless beings who exploit the system designed for those considered more fully human and deserving.

Social and Interpersonal Costs Actively challenging disability stereotypes can have social repercussions. The most obvious of these are the institutional punishments for participating in civil disobedience, such as being arrested, or a loss of social services that can come from directly challenging an ableist disability support system – described by some as the tragic persons' industry (Marks 1999). Additionally, people may suffer consequences from confronting prejudice, particularly benevolent prejudice as described earlier (Wang et al. 2015). Disabled people who reject benevolent ableism may be labeled as ungrateful, rude, or angry, which can produce a shift in attitudes from benevolent to hostile ableism. That is, what was once offered as help or considered as caregiving might switch to abuse. The impact of such hostility may be compounded if the disabled person depends on the perpetrator of ableism for instrumental support:

> I am frequently lectured by [my] spouse on what I should eat, how I should sit, how I am holding my body improperly, etc. Generally, I understand that he is trying to help, though sometimes I do lose my temper. I feel as though I am not allowed to leave the house without permission, though there is not a threat of violence. Rather he will worry about me. Also, as I am dependent upon him for ADL [activities of daily living], I hesitate to assert myself. ~ Person with a visible physical disability

> On two occasions that I have had to terminate personal care assistants, they have retaliated with mean-spirited text messages that specifically targeted my disability needs saying things like, "Good luck finding someone to take time away from their family to take care of you." ~ Person with a visible physical disability, 2015

In our survey, hostile forms of ableism were reported by 27% of the sample, with verbal abuse constituting the most prevalent form, followed by physical or sexual assault, and threatening or exploitive harassment. While physical abuse was reported equally across those with visible and less apparent disabilities, verbal threats and other forms of harassment were more common among those with visible conditions.

People who use collective coping strategies are less likely to forgo disability accommodations needed to participate at work and school. However, an often unrecognized cost associated with accommodations is the jealous envy these can incite in others. One quarter of our survey respondents noted experiences of envious ableism. Most frequently, these jealousies pertained to nondisabled others' wanting what they perceived to be a "special privilege" or advantage, like extra time on tests, books on tape, and the ever coveted disability parking placard. Those with more visible impairments were much more likely to be the targets of accommodation envy compared to those whose impairments were hidden. Yet, people with less apparent disabilities often confronted a different form of jealous envy by those who considered them "lucky" that they could so easily get out of work and school; those with hidden impairments were also more likely to be berated for exploiting the system (Nario-Redmond et al. 2019).

> I have "invisible" disabilities. I have been told I am lazy, exploiting people, and even stealing from the government. Though none of these things are true, it is still painful to hear. ~ Person with multiple disabilities, 2015

People who employ collective coping strategies are also more likely to recognize discrimination, and to blame their negative experiences on prejudice against their group (Lindly et al. 2014; Nario-Redmond et al. 2013). Attributing negative outcomes to discrimination can certainly protect self-esteem (Major et al. 2003). However, it can also foster a mistrust of people or institutions seen as discriminating. For example, Yeager et al. (2013) described how ethnic minority students may assume that critical feedback they receive from White teachers is racist, and may begin to mistrust their teachers and the school system instead of building collaborative relationships or discerning the validity of feedback. Similarly, disabled people who attribute professional or social slights to ableism may have difficulty trusting others. It can often be tricky to accurately determine when an act of discrimination has occurred – for instance, to determine whether one has been passed up for a job because of disability or because an internal candidate was preferred. While correctly identifying discrimination can buttress self-esteem and motivate social change, seeing discrimination where there is none can undermine perceived control, and has other negative interpersonal effects (Schmitt et al. 2014).

Social services can also be constructed in ways that reward disabled people for conforming to stereotypic roles and, conversely, punish them for defying stereotypes. For example, government-sponsored disability insurance programs in the United States require potential recipients to essentially demonstrate that their disability has rendered them unemployable in order to begin receiving benefits. This process can act as a psychological disincentive to future employment efforts (Hyde and Stapleton 2015). Furthermore, such programs are often designed to suddenly cease providing benefits once recipients gain regular earnings, thereby discouraging the stereotype-defying act of employment.

Group-Based Social Identity Threat We have described how people experience social identity threat when they worry about being personally judged in light of a negative stereotype. Social creativity and competition approaches can help protect people from this individual-level threat. However, disadvantaged group members also worry about how their entire group is perceived by others. SIT predicts that those who are more strongly identified with a group will experience more group-based identity threat. Indeed, group identification is a predictor of stereotype threat in other stigmatized groups. That is, people who are more strongly identified with their race or gender worry more about confirming stereotypes relevant to that group (Aronson and McGlone 2009).

Shapiro and colleagues (2007; 2011) distinguished between "self-as-target" and "group-as-target" stereotype threats, arguing that people may worry either about how they are personally judged or about how their group is judged. She found that people who identify more strongly with their groups, including congenitally blind persons, tend to experience more "group-as-target" stereotype threat, worrying more about how their own actions might affect perceptions of their group (Shapiro 2011). Silverman and Cohen (2014, Study 1) asked a sample of blind people how much social identity threat they typically experience by measuring their agreement with four items: "In public places, I worry that people will expect less of me because I am blind"; "I often worry that sighted people will think I need help when I don't"; "In public places, I worry that sighted people will expect me to make a mistake"; and "If I make a mistake in public, I worry about making blind people look bad." Not surprisingly, blind participants who reported higher threat levels across the four items were more likely to report reduced life satisfaction and increased stress (Silverman and Cohen 2014, Study 1). Interestingly, only the final item ("I worry about making blind people look bad") was associated with stronger disability identification. Thus, people who identify more strongly with their disability may be better equipped to cope with personal instances of prejudice – but at the same time, they may be more concerned with how their actions reflect on their group, which could make them susceptible to stereotype threat in achievement settings (Steele 1997). Highly identified group members may also be more sensitive to stress and criticism about their group, even when not directly targeted at them personally. When one's sense of self is strongly linked to a group identity, membership in that group serves to regulate a variety of intergroup perceptions, emotions, and emotional reactions (Jetten et al. 2012).

Directions for Future Research

SIT gives us the explanatory power to better understand how disabled people respond in such varied ways to ableism, and the consequences, both good and bad, of those responses. Yet, the application of SIT to disability in particular is fairly new, and several questions still remain. Dirth and Branscombe (2018) identified four broad areas that a disability research agenda can address, with the social identity approach as a guiding framework: stereotypes, social identity threat, predictors of collective action, and able-bodied privilege.

First, SIT can enrich our understanding of disability stereotypes. As was described in Chapter 4, disability stereotypes go beyond impairment-specific depictions and represent disability as a broad social category (Nario-Redmond 2010). Instead of being rigid, irrational representations, SIT posits that stereotypes can be fluid, context-dependent, and representative of the social roles that the disabled have historically occupied. For example, the stereotype of disabled people as dependent may simply reflect the societal structures that place many disabled people in dependent roles (Nario-Redmond 2010). This has important implications for models of stereotype change. Future studies can examine how disability stereotypes have changed over time as disabled people make collective gains through social activism, legislative reforms, and the penetration of disability arts and culture into the social imagination.

Second, research on social identity threat in the context of disability is in its infancy. In particular, little is known about how disabled people respond to stereotype-specific threats – the fear of confirming group-based stereotypes discussed earlier in this chapter. Limited evidence suggests that the stereotype threat process may play out in the classroom for students with learning disabilities (May and Stone 2014), and it is possible that people with other disabilities also experience threats that impact their achievement (Silverman and Cohen 2014). Research is needed to identify the conditions that trigger stereotype threat and other forms of identity threat. For example, media depictions of disabled people as inspirational overcomers, tragic sufferers, or both, may trigger social identity threat, as such negative representations have been threatening for members of other minority groups (Davies et al. 2002; Fryberg et al. 2008). Research is also needed to develop institutional programs and policies that can counteract social identity threats for disabled people (Dirth and Branscombe 2018), and affirm a positive sense of belonging among those relatively isolated from other members of the disability community, or who grow up with little information about the history of disability rights, and the many contemporary figures working for change and increased disability visibility (e.g. https://disabilityvisibilityproject.com; http://www.disabilitymuseum.org/).

Third, there is a need to better predict who will participate in collective action in support of disability rights. In other groups, predictors of collective action include a belief that the group experiences discriminatory injustice, a belief that collective action will be effective, and social identification with the group (Klandermans 1997; Van Zomeren et al. 2008). Future research will be useful in identifying when disabled people perceive their group's status as both illegitimate and changeable. It may also be useful to study how the disability identities of members of political organizations might differ from other highly identified disabled people who are neither involved in such organizations nor participate in activism. Does a strong disability identity impel certain group-level behaviors (i.e. activism) motivating some to serve as core representatives? And can people who don't want to be politically active still strongly identify with a broader disability culture?

Fourth, the social identity approach could help to generate a better understanding of "able-bodied (on nondisabled) privilege" (Dirth and Branscombe 2018). We may not think of being able-bodied as a group identity, but such individuals may experience a kind of social identity threat when their group's superior status is challenged. This may motivate them to push back against social change efforts driven by disabled people and their allies. Social identity principles can be applied to better understand perceptions, emotions, and behaviors of disabled people from an intergroup perspective. Similarly, more work is needed on the consequences of social mobility strategies, not only for those who choose alternative identity constructions, but for ongoing status relations between former and current members of the group. When will those who escape disability, and advance individually, work on behalf of those still disabled by society, and when will they neglect former ingroups members or sabotage their progress?

Summary

Reactions to ableism are as diverse as the people reacting; yet, research has revealed some common response patterns. In many ways, responses to ableism are similar to responses of many other minority groups to prejudice: People feel stressed or threatened by the possibility of being the target of prejudice and discrimination, and their health, well-being, and achievement often suffer. The geographic isolation of some disabled people and the benevolent nature of much disability prejudice can complicate responses to ableism.

People respond to ableism in differing ways, but consistently with the goal of preserving a positive social identity. Sometimes, people cope by distancing themselves from a disability identity, concealing it from others, or even attempting to change the disability itself. These "social mobility" strategies can sometimes help the person avoid discrimination, but they can backfire when the disability is not easily escapable. Social mobility coping also does nothing to elevate the status of disabled people as a group.

For some people, though, prejudice can trigger a stronger identification with one's group, creative reframing of a previously negative identity, and engagement in collective efforts to reduce prejudice. The research discussed in this chapter has shown that disabled people, like other stigmatized groups, do engage in these positive reactions to prejudice – particularly when they acknowledge that their disability identity is permanent, incorporate it strongly into their network of self-definitions, and believe that social change is a possibility. People who use these strategies often report feeling better about themselves, and their work can motivate progress in the ways disabled people are perceived by society. On the flip side, however, people may have to overcome negative reactions from the broader society in order to effect change. The next chapter, discusses ableism reduction strategies that incorporate the complex interplay between perceivers and targets.

Note

1 Medical treatments serve multiple purposes, many of which can improve individual wellness or reduce pain. As a strategy to cope with stigma however, medical treatments are described here as one potential response to ableism.
2 The term fat is descriptively and non-pejoratively in concordance with similar research (Crandall 1994) and recommendations from the National Association to Advance Fat Acceptance (2010). The term fat has been positively reclaimed to describe individuals historically labeled as "overweight" or "obese" as part of the Fat Acceptance Movement that began in the 1960s.

References

Anspach, R.R. (1979). From stigma to identity politics: political activism among the physically disabled and former mental patients. *Social Science & Medicine* 13A (6): 765–773.

Aronson, J. and McGlone, M.S. (2009). Social identity and stereotype threat. In: *Handbook of Stereotyping, Prejudice, and Discrimination Research* (ed. T. Nelson), 153–178. New York: Psychology Press.

Baron-Cohen, S. (2002). Is Asperger syndrome necessarily viewed as a disability? *Focus on Autism and Other Developmental Disabilities* 17 (3): 186–191.

Bastian, B. and Haslam, N. (2011). Experiencing dehumanization: cognitive and emotional effects of everyday dehumanization. *Basic and Applied Social Psychology* 33 (4): 295–303.

Baumeister, R. and Leary, M. (1995). The need to belong: desire for interpersonal attachments as a fundamental human motivation. *Psychological Bulletin* 117 (3): 497–529.

Becker, J.C., Glick, P., Ilic, M., and Bohner, G. (2011). Damned if she does, damned if she doesn't: consequences of accepting versus confronting patronizing help for the female target and male actor. *European Journal of Social Psychology* 41 (6): 761–773.

Bennett, G.G., Wolin, K.Y., Robinson, E.L. et al. (2005). Racial/ethnic harassment and tobacco use among African American young adults. *American Journal of Public Health* 95 (2): 238–240.

Blascovich, J., Spencer, S.J., Quinn, D., and Steele, C. (2001). African Americans and high blood pressure: the role of stereotype threat. *Psychological Science* 12 (3): 225–229.

Bogart, K.R. (2014). The role of disability self-concept in adaptation to congenital or acquired disability. *Rehabilitation Psychology* 59 (1): 107–115.

Bogart, K.R. (2015). Disability identity predicts lower anxiety and depression in multiple sclerosis. *Rehabilitation Psychology* 60 (1): 105–109.

Braithwaite, D.O. and Eckstein, N.J. (2003). How people with disabilities communicatively manage assistance: helping as instrumental social support. *Journal of Applied Communication Research* 31 (1): 1–26.

Branscombe, N.R. and Ellemers, N. (1998). Coping with group-based discrimination: individualistic versus group-level strategies. In: *Prejudice: The Target's Perspective* (ed. J.K. Swim and C. Stangor), 243–266. New York: Academic Press.

Brennan, N. (2015). *The ADA National Network. Disability Law Handbook*. Houston, TX: Southwest ADA Center https://adata.org/publication/disability-law-handbook (accessed 26 February 2019).

Brondolo, E., Libby, D.J., Denton, E. et al. (2008). Racism and ambulatory blood pressure in a community sample. *Psychosomatic Medicine* 70 (1): 49–56.

Brown, T., Williams, D.R., Jackson, J.J. et al. (2000). "Being Black and feeling blue": the mental health consequences of racial discrimination. *Race and Society* 2 (2): 117–131.

Cahill, S.E. and Eggleston, R. (1995). Reconsidering the stigma of physical disability: wheelchair use and public kindness. *The Sociological Quarterly* 36 (4): 681–698.

Chasteen, A.L., Bhattacharyya, S., Horhota, M. et al. (2005). How feelings of stereotype threat influence older adults' memory performance. *Experimental Aging Research* 31 (3): 235–260.

Chaudoir, S.R. and Quinn, D.M. (2010). Revealing concealable stigmatized identities: the impact of disclosure motivations and positive first-disclosure experiences on fear of disclosure and well-being. *Journal of Social Issues* 66 (3): 570–584.

Cialdini, R.B., Borden, R.J., Thorn, A. et al. (1976). Basking in reflected glory: three (football) field studies. *Journal of Personality and Social Psychology* 34 (3): 366–375.

Cole, S.W., Kemeny, M.E., and Taylor, S.E. (1997). Social identity and physical health: accelerated HIV progression in rejection-sensitive gay men. *Journal of Personality and Social Psychology* 72 (2): 320–335.

Cook, B.G., Gerber, M.M., and Murphy, J. (2000). Backlash against the inclusion of students with learning disabilities in higher education: implications for transition from post-secondary environments to work. *Work* 14 (1): 31–40.

Cook, J.E., Germano, A.L., and Stadler, G. (2016). An exploratory investigation of social stigma and concealment in patients with multiple sclerosis. *International Journal of MS Care* 18 (2): 78–84.

Corrigan, P.W. and Watson, A.C. (2002). The paradox of self-stigma and mental illness. *Clinical Psychology: Science and Practice* 9 (1): 35–53.

Crabtree, J.W., Haslam, S.A., Postmes, T., and Haslam, C. (2010). Mental health support groups, stigma, and self-esteem: positive and negative implications of group identification. *Journal of Social Issues* 66 (3): 553–569.

Crandall, C.S. (1994). Prejudice against fat people: ideology and self-interest. *Journal of Personality and Social Psychology* 66 (5): 882–894.

Crocker, J. and Major, B. (1989). Social stigma and self-esteem: the self-protective properties of stigma. *Psychological Review* 96 (4): 608–630.

Crocker, J., Luhtanen, R., Blaine, B., and Broadnax, S. (1994). Collective self-esteem and psychological well-being among White, Black, and Asian college students. *Personality and Social Psychology Bulletin* 20 (5): 503–513.

Crocker, J., Major, B., and Steele, C. (1998). Social stigma. In: *The Handbook of Social Psychology*, vol. 2 (ed. D.T. Gilbert, S.T. Fiske and G. Lindzey), 504–553. New York: McGraw Hill.

Crouch, R.A. (1997). Letting the deaf be deaf: reconsidering the use of cochlear implants in prelingually deaf children. *Hastings Center Report* 27 (4): 14–21.

Cutsforth, T.D. (1933). *The Blind in School and Society: A Psychological Study*. New York: D. Appleton and Co.

Darling, R.B. and Heckert, D.A. (2010). Orientations toward disability: differences over the lifecourse. *International Journal of Disability, Development and Education* 57 (2): 131–143.

Dart, J. (1990). Justin Dart's 1990 ADA statement. Association of University Centers on Disabilities. https://www.aucd.org/template/news.cfm?news_id=1413&parent=&parent_title=News%20/%20Document%20Search%20Results&url=/template/news_mgt.cfm?start%3D9504%26sort%3Ddate%2520desc%2Ctitle (accessed 26 February 2019).

Davies, P.G., Spencer, S.J., Quinn, D.M., and Gerhardstein, R. (2002). Consuming images: how television commercials that elicit stereotype threat can restrain women academically and professionally. *Personality and Social Psychology Bulletin* 28 (12): 1615–1628.

Davis, L.J. (1995). *Enforcing Normalcy: Disability, Deafness, and the Body*. New York: Verso.

Diaz, R.M., Ayala, G., Bein, E. et al. (2001). The impact of homophobia, poverty, and racism on the mental health of gay and bisexual Latino gay men: findings from US cities. *American Journal of Public Health* 91 (6): 927–932.

DiLeo, D. (2015). Benevolent ableism: when help isn't helping. Training and Advocacy for the Inclusion of People with Disabilities. https://daledileo.com/benevolent-ableism-when-help-isnt-helping/ (accessed 28 February 2019).

Dirth, T. and Branscombe, N.R. (2018). The social identity approach to disability: bridging disability studies and psychological science. *Psychological Bulletin* 144 (12): 1300–1324.

Dunn, D.S. (1996). Well-being following amputation: salutary effects of positive meaning, optimism, and control. *Rehabilitation Psychology* 41 (4): 285–302.

Dunn, D.S. and Brody, C. (2008). Defining the good life following acquired physical disability. *Rehabilitation Psychology* 53 (4): 413–425.

Dunning, D. and Cohen, G.L. (1992). Egocentric definitions of traits and abilities in social judgment. *Journal of Personality and Social Psychology* 63 (3): 341–355.

Ellemers, N. (2001). Individual upward mobility and the perceived legitimacy of intergroup relations. In: *The Psychology of Legitimacy: Emerging Perspectives on Ideology, Justice and Intergroup Relations* (ed. J.T. Jost and B. Major), 205–222. Cambridge: Cambridge University Press.

Fehr, J. and Sassenberg, K. (2009). Intended and unintended consequences of internal motivation to behave nonprejudiced: the case of benevolent discrimination. *European Journal of Social Psychology* 39 (6): 1093–1108.

Fernández, S., Branscombe, N.R., Gómez, A., and Morales, J.F. (2012). Influence of the social context on use of surgical-lengthening and group-empowering coping strategies among people with dwarfism. *Rehabilitation Psychology* 57 (3): 224–235.

Festinger, L. (1954). A theory of social comparison processes. *Human Relations* 7 (2): 117–140.

Finlay, W.M. and Lyons, E. (2000). Social categorizations, social comparisons and stigma: presentations of self in people with learning difficulties. *British Journal of Social Psychology* 39 (1): 129–146.

Fitzgerald, M.H. and Paterson, K.A. (1995). The hidden disability dilemma for the preservation of self. *Journal of Occupational Science* 2 (1): 13–21.

Frable, D.E.S., Platt, L., and Hoey, S. (1998). Concealable stigmas and positive self-perceptions: feeling better around similar others. *Journal of Personality and Social Psychology* 74 (4): 909–922.

Fryberg, S.A., Markus, H.R., Oyserman, D., and Stone, J.M. (2008). Of warrior chiefs and Indian princesses: the psychological consequences of American Indian mascots. *Basic and Applied Social Psychology* 30 (3): 208–218.

Garstka, T.A., Schmitt, M.T., Branscombe, N.R., and Hummert, M.L. (2004). How young and older adults differ in their responses to perceived age discrimination. *Psychology and Aging* 19 (2): 326–335.

Gee, G.C., Delva, J., and Takeuchi, D.T. (2007). Relationships between self-reported unfair treatment and prescription medication use, illicit drug use, and alcohol dependence among Filipino Americans. *American Journal of Public Health* 97 (5): 933–940.

Gilbert, D.T. and Silvera, D.H. (1996). Overhelping. *Journal of Personality and Social Psychology* 70 (4): 678–690.

Gill, C.J. (1997). Four types of integration in disability identity development. *Journal of Vocational Rehabilitation* 9 (1): 39–46.

Goffman, E. (1963). *Stigma: Notes on the Management of Spoiled Identity*. New York: Simon & Shuster.

Goldberg, S.G., Killeen, M.B., and O'Day, B. (2005). The disclosure conundrum: how people with psychiatric disabilities navigate employment. *Psychology, Public Policy, and Law* 11 (3): 463–500.

Goodrich, K. and Ramsey, R. (2013). Do people with disabilities feel excluded? Comparison of learning and physical disabilities. *Journal of Community Positive Practices* 13 (3): 74–87.

Guyll, M., Matthews, K.A., and Bromberger, J.T. (2001). Discrimination and unfair treatment: relationship to cardiovascular reactivity among African American and European American women. *Health Psychology* 20 (5): 315–325.

Hahn, H.D. (1985). Toward a politics of disability: definitions, disciplines, and policies. *The Social Science Journal* 22 (4): 87–105.

Hahn, H.D. and Belt, T.L. (2004). Disability identity and attitudes toward cure in a sample of disabled activists. *Journal of Health and Social Behavior* 45 (4): 453–464.

Hyde, J.S. and Stapleton, D.C. (2015). Changes to the ticket to work regulations in 2008 attracted providers and participants, but impacts on work and benefits are unclear. *Social Security Bulletin* 75 (4): 15–33.

Hyman, I. (2008). Self-Disclosure and Its Impact on Individuals Who Receive Mental Health Services. HHS Pub. No. (SMA)-08-4337. Rockville, MD. Center for Mental Health Services, Substance Abuse and Mental Health Services Administration.

Jetten, J., Haslam, C., and Alexander, S.H. (eds.) (2012). *The Social Cure: Identity, Health and Well-Being*. New York: Psychology Press.

Jones, E.E., Farina, A., Hastorf, A.H. et al. (1984). *Social Stigma: The Psychology of Marked Relationships*. New York: Freeman.

Jones, J.M., Haslam, S.A., Jetten, J. et al. (2011). That which does not kill you can make you stronger (and more satisfied with life): the contribution of personal and social changes to well-being after brain injury. *Psychology & Health* 26 (3): 353–369.

Jost, J.T., Banaji, M.R., and Nosek, B.A. (2004). A decade of system justification theory: accumulated evidence of conscious and unconscious bolstering of the status quo. *Political Psychology* 25 (6): 881–919.

Kafer, A. (2013). *Feminist, Queer, Crip*. Bloomington, IN: Indiana University Press.

Katz, I., Farber, J., Glass, D.C. et al. (1978). When courtesy offends: effects of positive and negative behavior by the physically disabled on altruism and anger in normals. *Journal of Personality* 46 (3): 506–518.

Kemerling, A. A. (2018). What I wish I'd known about "deaf anxiety." The Mighty. https://themighty.com/2018/06/deaf-anxiety/ (accessed 28 February 2019).

Klandermans, B. (1997). *The Social Psychology of Protest*. Oxford: Blackwell.

Krieger, L.H. (2010). *Backlash against the ADA: Reinterpreting Disability Rights*. Ann Arbor, MI: University of Michigan Press.

Kulich, C., Lorenzi-Cioldi, F., and Iacoviello, V. (2015). Moving across status lines: low concern for the ingroup and group identification. *Journal of Social Issues* 71 (3): 453–475.

Lane, H.L. (2002). Do deaf people have a disability? *Sign Language Studies* 2 (4): 356–379.

Lester, N. (2017). *Intersectionality. Senior Capstone Project*. Hiram, OH: Hiram College.

Li, C., Zhang, X., Hoffman, H.J. et al. (2014). Hearing impairment associated with depression in US adults, national health and nutrition examination survey 2005–2010. *JAMA Otolaryngology – Head & Neck Surgery* 140 (4): 293–302.

Lindly, O.J., Nario-Redmond, M.R., and Noel, J.G. (2014). Creatively re-defining fat: identification predicts strategic responses to stigma, ingroup attitudes, and well-being. *Fat Studies* 3 (2): 179–195.

Linton, S. (1998). *Claiming Disability: Knowledge and Identity*. New York: New York University Press.

Little, D.L. (2010). Identity, efficacy, and disability rights movement recruitment. *Disability Studies Quarterly* 30 (1): 1–17.

Livingston, J.D. and Boyd, J.E. (2010). Correlates and consequences of internalized stigma for people living with mental illness: a systematic review and meta-analysis. *Social Science & Medicine* 71 (12): 2150–2161.

Major, B. and O'Brien, L.T. (2005). The social psychology of stigma. *Annual Review of Psychology* 56: 393–421.

Major, B., Quinton, W.J., and McCoy, S.K. (2002). Antecedents and consequences of attributions to discrimination: theoretical and empirical advances. In: *Advances in Experimental Social Psychology* (ed. M.P. Zanna), 251–330. San Diego, CA: Academic Press.

Major, B., Kaiser, C.R., and McCoy, S.K. (2003). It's not my fault: when and why attributions to prejudice protect self-esteem. *Personality and Social Psychology Bulletin* 29 (6): 772–781.

Marks, D. (1999). *Disability: Controversial Debates and Psychosocial Perspectives*. London: Routledge.

May, A.L. and Stone, C.A. (2014). An initial investigation into the role of stereotype threat in the test performance of college students with learning disabilities. *Journal of Postsecondary Education and Disability* 27 (1): 89–106.

McRuer, R. (2006). *Crip Theory: Cultural Signs of Queerness and Disability*. New York: New York University Press.

McVittie, C., Goodall, K.E., and McKinlay, A. (2008). Resisting having learning disabilities by managing relative abilities. *British Journal of Learning Disabilities* 36 (4): 256–262.

McWilliams, A. (2017). Deaf anxiety. Ai-Media. https://www.youtube.com/watch?v=YmlEq8JnBC0 (accessed 28 February 2019).

Mejias, N.J., Gill, C.J., and Shpigelman, C.N. (2014). Influence of a support group for young women with disabilities on sense of belonging. *Journal of Counseling Psychology* 61 (2): 208–220.

Molina, Y., Choi, S.W., Cella, D., and Rao, D. (2013). The stigma scale for chronic illnesses 8-item version (SSCI-8): development, validation and use across neurological conditions. *International Journal of Behavioral Medicine* 20 (3): 450–460.

Mummendey, A., Kessler, T., Klink, A., and Mielke, R. (1999). Strategies to cope with negative social identity: predictions by social identity theory and relative deprivation theory. *Journal of Personality and Social Psychology* 76 (2): 229–245.

Nario-Redmond, M.R. (2010). Cultural stereotypes of disabled and nondisabled men and women: consensus for global category representations and diagnostic domains. *British Journal of Social Psychology* 49 (3): 471–488.

Nario-Redmond, M.R. and Oleson, K.C. (2016). Disability group identification and disability-rights advocacy: contingencies among emerging and other adults. *Emerging Adulthood* 4 (3): 207–218.

Nario-Redmond, M.R., Noel, J.G., and Fern, E. (2013). Redefining disability, reimagining the self: disability identification predicts self-esteem and strategic responses to stigma. *Self and Identity* 12 (5): 468–488.

Nario-Redmond, M.R., Kemerling, A., and Silverman, A.M. (2019). Hostile, benevolent and ambivalent ableism: contemporary manifestations. *Journal of Social Issues*.

National Association to Advance Fat Acceptance. (2010). Health at every size (HAES). http://www.naafaonline.com/dev2/education/haes.html (accessed 26 February 2019).

Olkin, R. (1999). *What Psychotherapists Should Know about Disability*. New York: Guilford Press.

O'Toole, C.J. (2015). *Fading Scars: My Queer Disability History*. Fort Worth, TX: Autonomous Press.

Pascoe, E.A. and Richman, L.S. (2009). Perceived discrimination and health: a meta-analytic review. *Psychological Bulletin* 135 (4): 531–554.

Roberson, L., Deitch, E.A., Brief, A.P., and Block, C.J. (2003). Stereotype threat and feedback seeking in the workplace. *Journal of Vocational Behavior* 62 (1): 176–188.

Rosen, S., Mickler, S.E., and Collins, J.E. (1987). Reactions of would-be helpers whose offer of help is spurned. *Journal of Personality and Social Psychology* 53 (2): 288–297.

Rosenberg, M. (1979). *Conceiving the Self*. New York: Basic Books.

Rottenstein, A. T. (2013). Predicting disability self-identification: A mixed-methods approach. Doctoral dissertation. University of Michigan.

Rousso, H. (2013). *Don't Call Me Inspirational: A Disabled Feminist Talks Back*. Philadelphia: Temple University Press.

Rowe, J. M. (2011). The relationship between job satisfaction and disclosure of disability status of college students with disabilities. Master thesis. State University of New York.

Roy, A.W. and MacKay, G.F. (2002). Self-perception and locus of control in visually impaired college students with different types of vision loss. *Journal of Visual Impairment and Blindness* 96 (4): 254–266.

Schachter, S. (1959). *The Psychology of Affiliation: Experimental Studies of the Sources of Gregariousness*. Palo Alto, CA: Stanford University Press.

Schmader, T., Johns, M., and Forbes, C. (2008). An integrated process model of stereotype threat effects on performance. *Psychological Review* 115 (2): 336–356.

Schmitt, M.T., Branscombe, N.R., Postmes, T., and Garcia, A. (2014). The consequences of perceived discrimination for psychological well-being: a meta-analytic review. *Psychological Bulletin* 140 (4): 921–948.

Schneider, M.E., Major, B., Luhtanen, R., and Crocker, J. (1996). Social stigma and the potential costs of assumptive help. *Personality and Social Psychology Bulletin* 22 (2): 201–209.

Sedlovskaya, A., Purdie-Vaughns, V., Eibach, R.P. et al. (2013). Internalizing the closet: concealment heightens the cognitive distinction between public and private selves. *Journal of Personality and Social Psychology* 104 (4): 695–715.

Shakespeare, T. (1994). Cultural representation of disabled people: dustbins for disavowal? *Disability & Society* 9 (3): 283–299.

Shakespeare, T. (1996). Disability, identity, and difference. In: *Exploring the Divide* (ed. C. Barnes and C. Mercer), 94–113. Leeds: The Disability Press.

Shapiro, J.R. (2011). Different groups, different threats: a multi-threat approach to the experience of stereotype threats. *Personality and Social Psychology Bulletin* 37 (4): 464–480.

Shapiro, J.R. and Neuberg, S.L. (2007). From stereotype threat to stereotype threats: implications of a multi-threat framework for causes, moderators, mediators, consequences, and interventions. *Personality and Social Psychology Review* 11 (2): 107–130.

Sidanius, J. and Pratto, F. (1999). *Social Dominance: An Intergroup Theory of Social Hierarchy and Oppression*. Cambridge: Cambridge University Press.

Silverman, A.M. and Cohen, G.L. (2012). Correlates of well-being and employment among blind and partially sighted adults in the United States. Unpublished raw data.

Silverman, A.M. and Cohen, G.L. (2014). Stereotypes as stumbling-blocks: how coping with stereotype threat affects life outcomes for people with physical disabilities. *Personality and Social Psychology Bulletin* 40 (10): 1330–1340.

Silverman, A.M., Molton, I.R., Smith, A.E. et al. (2017). Solace in solidarity: disability friendship networks buffer well-being. *Rehabilitation Psychology* 62 (4): 525–533.

Solomon, A. (2012). *Far from the Tree: Parents, Children, and the Search for Identity*. New York: Scribner.

Sparrow, R. (2005). Defending deaf culture: the case of cochlear implants. *Journal of Political Philosophy* 13 (2): 135–152.

Spencer, S., Steele, C.M., and Quinn, D. (1999). Stereotype threat and women's math test performance. *Journal of Experimental Social Psychology* 35 (1): 4–28.

Steele, C.M. (1997). A threat in the air: how stereotypes shape intellectual identity and performance. *American Psychologist* 52 (6): 613–629.

Steele, C.M. (2010). *Whistling Vivaldi: How Stereotypes Affect Us and What We Can Do (Issues of Our Time)*. New York: Norton.

Steele, C.M. and Aronson, J. (1995). Stereotype threat and the intellectual test performance of African Americans. *Journal of Personality and Social Psychology* 69 (5): 797–811.

Steele, C.M., Spencer, S.J., and Aronson, J. (2002). Contending with group image: the psychology of stereotype and social identity threat. *Advances in Experimental Social Psychology* 34: 379–440.

Steffen, P.R., McNeilly, M., Anderson, N., and Sherwood, A. (2003). Effects of perceived racism and anger inhibition on ambulatory blood pressure in African Americans. *Psychosomatic Medicine* 65 (5): 746–750.

Stone, J. (2002). Battling doubt by avoiding practice: the effects of stereotype threat on self-handicapping among White athletes. *Personality and Social Psychology Bulletin* 28 (12): 1667–1678.

Stone, J., Perry, W., and Darley, J. (1997). "White men can't jump": evidence for the perceptual confirmation of racial stereotypes following a basketball game. *Basic and Applied Social Psychology* 19 (3): 291–306.

Swain, J. and French, S. (2000). Towards an affirmation model of disability. *Disability & Society* 15 (4): 569–582.

Tajfel, H. and Turner, J.C. (1979). An integrative theory of intergroup conflict. In: *The Social Psychology of Intergroup Relations* (ed. W.A. Austin and S. Worschel), 33–47. Monteray, CA: Brooks Cole.

Tajfel, H., Billig, M.G., Bundy, R.P., and Flament, C. (1971). Social categorization and intergroup behaviour. *European Journal of Social Psychology* 1 (2): 149–178.

Taylor, V.J. and Walton, G. (2011). Stereotype threat undermines academic learning. *Personality and Social Psychology Bulletin* 37 (8): 1055–1067.

TenBroek, J. (1951). The neurotic blind and the neurotic sighted: twin psychological fallacies. An address delivered at the annual convention of the National Federation of the Blind, Oklahoma City, OK (17 June).

Twenge, J. and Crocker, J. (2002). Race, ethnicity, and self-esteem: meta-analyses comparing Whites, Blacks, Hispanics, Asians, and Native Americans, including a commentary on Gray-Little & Hafdahl (2000). *Psychological Bulletin* 128 (3): 371–408.

Van der Beek, K.M., Bos, I., Middel, B., and Wynia, K. (2013). Experienced stigmatization reduced quality of life of patients with a neuromuscular disease: a cross-sectional study. *Clinical Rehabilitation* 27 (11): 1029–1038.

Van Zomeren, M., Postmes, T., and Spears, R. (2008). Toward an integrative social identity model of collective action: a quantitative research synthesis of three socio-psychological perspectives. *Psychological Bulletin* 134 (4): 504–535.

Wang, K., Silverman, A.M., Gwinn, J.D., and Dovidio, J. (2015). Independent or ungrateful? Consequences of confronting patronizing treatment for people with disabilities. *Group Processes & Intergroup Relations* 18 (4): 489–503.

Watkins, H. (2017). Disability Visibility Project. From Heather Watkins Facebook wall. https://www.facebook.com/groups/356870067786565 (accessed 26 February 2019).

Watson, N. (2002). Well, I know this is going to sound very strange to you, but I don't see myself as a disabled person: identity and disability. *Disability & Society* 17 (5): 509–527.

Wills, T.A. (1981). Downward comparison principles in social psychology. *Psychological Bulletin* 90 (2): 245–271.

Wolanin, T.R. and Steele, P.E. (2004). *Higher Education Opportunities for Students with Disabilities: A Primer for Policymakers*. Washington, DC: The Institute for Higher Education Policy.

Wolbring, G. (2008). Ableism, enhancement medicine and the techno door disabled. In: *Unnatural Selection: The Challenges of Engineering Tomorrow's People* (ed. P. Healey and S. Rayner). London: Earthscan.

Wolbring, G. (2009). What next for the human species? Human performance enhancement, ableism and pluralism. *Development Dialogue* 2: 141–161.

Wood, J.V. (1989). Theory and research concerning social comparisons of personal attributes. *Psychological Bulletin* 106 (2): 231–248.

Wood, C. (ed.) (2014). *Criptiques*. Minneapolis, MN: May Day Publishing.

Wright, S.C. (2001). Strategic collective action: social psychology and social change. In: *Blackwell Handbook of Social Psychology: Intergroup Processes* (ed. R. Brown and S. Gaertner), 409–430. Oxford: Blackwell.

Wright, S.C. and Taylor, D.M. (1998). Responding to tokenism: individual action in the face of collective injustice. *European Journal of Social Psychology* 28 (4): 647–667.

Yeager, D.S., Purdie-Vaughns, V., Garcia, J. et al. (2013). Breaking the cycle of mistrust: wise interventions to provide critical feedback across the racial divide. *Journal of Experimental Psychology: General* 143 (2): 804–824.

Zahl, P.A. (1950). *Modern Approaches to the Unseen Environment*. Princeton, NJ: Princeton University Press.

When Good Intentions Become Ableist ...

People frequently think they understand what I need better than I do ...
~ Person with a visible physical disability, 2015.

Sometimes, when I objected, the other person would act as if I was unreasonably angry when they were "only trying to help" or "doing what was best" for me ~Person with multiple disabilities, 2015.

Often when I am going through a door, and am pushing the door open (I walk with crutches), people grab the door to open it for me, which sometimes throws my balance off ~ Person with a visible physical disability, 2015.

People often commit benevolent forms of ableism unknowingly. However, while intentions may be good, the actions may still hurt. Giving unwanted help can make someone feel inferior. As a general rule, if someone needs help, they will ask.

Disability Rights advocate Dale DiLeo (2015) explains this further:

When Helping Hurts:

*When the helping is imposed or consent is granted
*When the helper has more power over the person they are helping or does not afford them the autonomous choice.

Strength in Numbers

As we learned in the chapter, disabled people are often widely dispersed and have fewer opportunities to interact with similar others. Feeling like the "only one" can increase stigmatization and the negative mental health effects of ableism. Below are some ways that disabled activists have created communities of activism, shared experiences, and support.

https://www.invisibledisabilityproject.org/

IDP (Invisible Disability Project) is an online community "devoted to building human connections and self-advocacy by dismantling shame and stigma. IDP affects change through public conversations and interactive online content with the goal of creating an informed, mutually supportive online community."
Check out: www.invisibledisabilityproject.org

http://nosmag.org/

NOS (Not Otherwise Specified) is a news and commentary source for thought and analysis about neurodiversity culture and representation. This is a great resource created by and for disabled people. Check out: nosmag.org

Ableism Takes a Toll on Mental Health

Discrimination can have lasting mental health effects, including increased risk of depression, anxiety, low self-esteem, suicidal ideation, and more. However, activists Alexia Kemerling and Artie McWilliams talk about how a lack of accommodations and acceptance can also impact mental health.

"**Deaf Anxiety**" **by Alexia Kemerling** is a watercolor painting of a woman with blue hearing aids and a somber expression. Circling her head are sayings representing anxiety like, "What if they think I'm ignoring them?" and "I can't say 'what' again – just smile and nod."

11.5% of people with hearing loss report experiencing depression. That's over twice the rate of depression among the hearing population – 5%. See study by Dr. Chuan Ming-Li et al. (2014) from the National institute on Deafness and Other Communication Disorders).

In her article "What I wish I knew about 'Deaf Anxiety'" Kemerling (2018) writes:

"It is not that I am ashamed of my hearing loss or my hearing aids … I think the challenge comes from years of training myself to pretend. It comes from living in a world that is often slow to accommodate and reluctant to understand. I put a lot of pressure on myself to single-handedly compensate for all the challenges my disability presents, rather than asking the world around me to be accommodating; and it is exhausting."

In the video "Deaf Anxiety" posted by Ai-Media, Arthur (Artie) McWilliams (2017) talks about the relationship of hearing loss and anxiety. He discusses the stress of having to constantly be on alert, the inability to relax, the feeling of always being watched, and the paranoia of missing out on something important.

Persevering in the Face of Ableism

Social creativity strategies for coping with ableism include re-evaluating disability as an asset or reclaiming certain labels as positive subcultural signifiers. Photographer Nina Lester (2017) explores this in her series, "Intersectionality."

Black and white photo of a woman sitting on a block next to a manual wheelchair. In the color version of this photo she is wearing a rainbow hat and shirt with rainbow writing – only these parts are in color.

"Creating art that celebrates who you are and those around you for who they are is liberating for the body, mind, and soul" says Lester, "This series about being aware of interconnectedness, and being proud of the many identities a person can have such as being a disabled lesbian woman like Ceara Nario-Redmond, featured in the photograph."

More resources that share the disability experience ~

Hash tags to follow on social media: #CheekyNotTragic #Disabilityisnormal #DisabledIsNotABadThing #DisabledFashion #SpoonieLife #CripplePunks #DisabledAndProud #ActuallyAutistic #CripTheVote @sitting_pretty

Books: *Criptiques* by Caitlin Wood (2014); *Don't Call Me Inspirational* by Harilyn Rousso (2013); *Fading Scars: My Queer Disability History* by Corbett O'Toole (2015).

For more recommendations about the disability experience see: http://www.nlcdd.org/resources-books-movies-disability.html

7

Interventions to Reduce Prejudice

> If prejudice were likened to a sickness, many laboratory interventions would be walk-in clinics, built to handle low-grade prejudices. (Paluck and Green 2009, p. 350)

Over the past 25 years, there have been numerous approaches to reducing prejudice toward people who experience disabilities. Most have focused on reducing bias or improving attitudes toward disabled people as a group or increasing the acceptance of particular group members. Far fewer have examined the factors contributing to support for disability rights, increased access, and a more equitable distribution of outcomes. In fact, prejudice reduction programs have not been in the service of challenging intergroup inequalities or group-based disparities. Instead, the field has been focused on interpersonal outcomes such as liking and tolerance, with an emphasis on changing the prejudiced perceiver (Dixon and Levine 2012). It has been assumed that once advantaged group members change their negative attitudes, they will stop discriminating and open the doors of opportunity to the passive disadvantaged – a critique described as part of the prejudice problematic (Wetherell 2012).

Consider how prejudice reduction is typically operationalized in terms of interpersonal liking, interaction comfort, and less stigmatizing attitudes. Fewer studies have investigated behavioral changes or the endorsement of legislative and other policy reforms, although some investigations have examined the proportion of cross-group friendships (Gerard and Miller 1975), preferences for interaction partners (Clore et al. 1978), and seating choices (Schofield 1979). A sample of measures commonly used is provided in Table 7.1 although interpersonal and intergroup indicators are often interchangeable depending on whether evaluating reactions toward individuals or groups.

Critiques of this field have acknowledged the limitations of work that prioritizes changing interpersonal attitudes without sufficiently validating whether attitude change has broader implications for intergroup status relations

Ableism: The Causes and Consequences of Disability Prejudice, First Edition.
Michelle R. Nario-Redmond.
© 2020 John Wiley & Sons, Inc. Published 2020 by John Wiley & Sons, Inc.

Table 7.1 Sample of prejudice reduction indicators.

Individual-level measures	Intergroup measures
Liking of target	Social distance preferences
Interest in target	Cross-group friendships
Target attractiveness	Support for minority rights
Stereotypic impressions of target	Support for integration policies
Stigmatizing attitudes of target	Volunteering for group advocacy
Interaction comfort ratings	Funding contributions to group issues
Behavioral intentions	Intergroup emotions (collective guilt)
Voluntary behavior change	Confrontation and ally behaviors

(Dixon and Levine 2012). When prejudice is most often defined in terms of individual attitudes and impressions, the broader structural forms of prejudice and discrimination remain unaddressed. Furthermore, interpersonal friendship alone is insufficient to change inequalities between groups, and at times may even impede awareness of disparities and support of social change. For example, when does liking an individual disabled person generalize to support for disability rights, and can improved attitudes ever *undermine* the recognition of discrimination or the promotion of fairness and justice – making challenges to inequality less likely?

The goal of the final two chapters is to summarize the expansive literatures on what works to reduce disability prejudice, promote understanding, and increase equality. Chapter 8 focuses on broader social change, collective action for disability rights, and advocacy. Chapter 7 summarizes convergent evidence on prejudice reduction and the robust evaluation of programs designed to address ableism or mitigate disability prejudice. This includes meta-analytic reviews of experimental and field studies that range from putting nondisabled people into "contact" with disabled peers to having them imagine or "feel" what disability is like through simulations that involve blindfolds, ear plugs, and the use of wheelchairs. Many of these interventions have produced mixed results, and some have actually worsened disability stigma.

Other studies have investigated disability awareness campaigns, or programs that aim to debunk stereotypic myths, confront bias, and alter the conceptualization of disability itself. Lessons from studies that alter the salience and framing of disability as a construct range from personalized approaches that promote a common identity or universalize disability as one, value-neutral, aspect of human variability (Mackelprang and Salsgiver 1999) to multicultural approaches and diversity training programs. Where possible, this section will synthesize the benefits and limitations of different program types, and compare the effectiveness of initiatives that minimize disability status compared to those that keep disability categorization salient. The interventions in this chapter are organized into three parts: direct and indirect contact approaches, categorical framing studies, and empathy or emotion-based programs.

Part I. Reducing Prejudice Through Direct and Indirect Contact

The most well researched areas in the field of prejudice reduction began with the simple and intuitive recognition that unless we interact with people from groups outside of our own, we are doomed to remain ignorant of our commonalities and misunderstandings (Allport 1954). In response to changing US political and social circumstances, researchers were inspired to examine the impacts of racial desegregation in the military (Brophy 1946), the integration of public housing (Wilner et al. 1952), the diversification of schools (Pettigrew 1971), and the mainstreaming of disabled children (Harper and Wacker 1985; Naor and Milgram 1980).

According to the contact hypothesis, it is not sufficient to simply expose other people to those from different groups – putting them in close proximity so they come into some form of contact with one another. Decades of research has now accumulated on what types of interactions and social conditions contribute to meaningful understanding and the promotion of positive attitudes – not only toward those with whom one has had contact, but toward other members of their group as well (Brown 2011). In general, there are five optimal contact conditions that facilitate positive intergroup relationships – when individuals from different groups have *(i) equal status, (ii) cooperative relationships, (iii) common goals, (iv) the support of institutional authorities, and (v) the potential to become friends.* To illustrate an "ideal" scenario, imagine two students, one disabled and one non-disabled, working on a collaborative class project. Although the former is from an advantaged group in society, in this classroom they have similar ranks – both are freshman and neither has an objective advantage over the other within the inclusive setting. Additionally, the project requires their cooperation and combined effort in order to attain a common goal or grade. Finally, the school endorses their collaboration, and the instructor is supportive and encourages frequent opportunities for the students to get to know each other personally. While hypothetical, this example illustrates the ingredients considered key to the development of positive attitudes through contact. Multiple studies show that it may not be necessary to meet all five of the ideal contact conditions to improve attitudes and reduce prejudice; some conditions may play a more critical role depending on the groups involved, the type of prejudice, and other social circumstances (Pettigrew and Tropp 2006).

Contact with disabled and other stigmatized groups has been studied in many formats, from institutional or group settings to one-on-one interactions at work, school, or in the community. Contact may be conceptualized as a first encounter or a repeated exchange (e.g. peer mentoring), as short in duration or over an extended period of time. Many have examined contact retrospectively, asking people to report on their previous experiences with stigmatized groups. Fewer have carefully manipulated the contact situation to investigate causal effects. Some researchers have investigated more direct forms of in-person contact, while others have focused on indirect exposures to outgroup members in the media, through storytelling, or even as imaginary friends (for reviews see Armstrong et al. 2017; MacMillan et al. 2014). Finally, some interventions have attempted to improve attitudes and interactions toward disability or disabled people in general while others have focused on contact with particular impairment groups.

Direct Contact: Lessons from Other Social Groups

Direct contact typically refers to face-to-face encounters in real time; however, the duration, degree, and nature of the interaction vary considerably across studies. The vast majority of research testing the contact hypothesis has focused on reducing racism and ethnic biases, but interventions to reduce sexism (Becker et al. 2014), anti-fat attitudes (Daníelsdóttir et al. 2010), and disability prejudice have proliferated as well (Armstrong et al. 2017; Couture and Penn 2003). In a recent review of what works to reduce prejudice through contact, Paluck and Green (2009) summarized both field and laboratory studies testing contact theory to isolate the most important factors involved in changing attitudes and other forms of bias across social groups. They specifically examined experimental studies to test causal influences by comparing people assigned to interact with either fellow ingroup or outgroup members while holding other influences constant.

One of the most famous of these studies was conducted in the American South during the 1960s. White college women (previously identified as racially prejudiced) were recruited to work on a month-long railroad management project under ideal contact conditions (e.g. equal status roles, intimate, cooperative, and supported interactions). They were randomly assigned to unexpectedly interact with either a Black or a White coworker on a variety of tasks (Cook 1971). When the one-month study concluded, Black coworkers were viewed as more attractive, likeable, and competent, and those who interacted with a Black coworker were more supportive of desegregation policies than those who interacted with a White coworker.

Although few and far between, subsequent real-world experiments have found that White college students randomly assigned Black roommates were more supportive of affirmative action policies three and a half years later compared to those assigned White roommates (Boisjoly et al. 2006). Similar results were demonstrated in a multi-week educational adventure study: One month after participating in an Outward Bound wilderness experience, White teenagers who traveled with ethnic minority peers (Black and Latino) reported increased tolerance toward both ethnic and sexual minorities compared to those who traveled with only White peers (see Paluck and Green 2009). Very few laboratory studies have been able to replicate these experiments under such realistic field conditions, and of those that have, few have met all of Allport's (1954) ideal contact conditions.

In a comprehensive review of over 500 direct contact interventions conducted between 1940 and 2000 in various school, residential, and other organizational settings, Pettigrew and Tropp (2006) calculated the overall strength of the relationship between face-to-face interactions and various measures of prejudice reduction. Using meta-analytic procedures, these authors computed correlations across over 700 samples from 38 different countries that measured both the degree of interaction and levels of prejudice toward several social groups.[1] This allowed them to discern whether contact interventions with race, sexuality, elderly, and disability groups were more or less effective. Effectiveness here is approximated as the *effect size* or the magnitude of the relationship between level of contact experienced and subsequent prejudice expressed toward interaction partners.

Their findings revealed that across race, disability, and other social groups, in 94% of the samples, intergroup contact was associated with reduced prejudice. In general, the greater the amount of contact experienced between groups, the less prejudice was demonstrated. Furthermore, the prejudice measures that focused on feelings toward outgroups (e.g. reduced anxiety or increased empathy) revealed stronger effects of contact than the measures related to knowledge or beliefs about outgroups (e.g. stereotype change). Interestingly, while the vast majority of studies tested interracial contact, the overall impact of interracial contact interventions was only average in terms of effect size. Contact interventions between heterosexuals and gay men or lesbians had the most substantial effects on prejudice reduction. Similarly, interventions that put people into contact with those who had physical disabilities produced larger than average effects, followed by those who experienced cognitive disabilities. By contrast, studies involving contact with older adults and those with psychiatric disabilities had smaller effect sizes than any of the other groups examined. Therefore, the effectiveness of cross-group contact appears to depend on the type of stigmatized group examined.

Direct Contact with Disabled People: Impairment-Specific Groups

Many studies have examined how contact affects prejudice toward particular impairment groups. Recently, LaBelle et al. (2013) found that those who reported having more contact with Deaf individuals on a regular basis expressed more positive attitudes toward Deaf people in general and less interaction anxiety. Moreover, the reason those most anxious about interacting with Deaf people had the most negative Deaf attitudes was due to their lack of previous contact with individuals from this group. That is, contact fully mediated the relationship between feelings of anxiety and negative attitudes about Deaf people.

Similarly, in a classroom intervention devoted to teaching students about stigma and mental "illnesses," those who engaged directly with individuals who experienced psychiatric conditions (e.g. major depression and schizophrenia) reported higher levels of interaction comfort two weeks after the intervention compared to before (Matteo and You 2012). More convincingly, a review of psychiatric disability contact interventions found substantial evidence for positive outcomes from studies that either retrospectively measured previous contact or prospectively manipulated the contact situation (Couture and Penn 2003).

The review concluded that retrospective studies consistently demonstrate that those who report more contact *in the past* with those who experience "severe mental illness" have much more accepting attitudes, fewer negative emotions, and prefer less social distance. Yet, retrospective studies cannot discern whether positive attitudes are the result of direct life experiences with members of the group, or whether people had more positive attitudes before ever interacting with the group. Therefore, studies that assess prejudice both before and after an experimental manipulation of contact are more valid assessment strategies. According to this review, prospective contact studies yield more discrepant findings: while most studies demonstrate reduced mental illness stigma following contact, some failed to alter attitudes for the better, particularly those that involved job training sessions (Couture and Penn 2003). The authors speculated that the lack of attitude change in job settings may be due to the involuntary nature of being required to participate in contact training on the job, which is not an ideal situation.

Finally, Seewooruttun and Scior (2014) reviewed the effectiveness of 17 contact interventions focused on improving attitudes toward people with intellectual disabilities. They found that enhanced attitudes and improved comfort ratings were related to opportunities for direct contact that continued over several months, were co-facilitated by people who experienced these conditions, and did not reinforce perceptions of dependency (see also Siperstein et al. 2007). Apparently, direct contact is more effective when group members are afforded a sustained, authoritative voice that promotes their status as equals instead of as stereotypical subordinates.

Indirect or Mediated Contact with Disabled People and Other Groups

Direct face-to-face encounters may not always be necessary to reduce prejudice. Indirect contact through documentary films, web-based presentations of social injustice, or photographs that contradict stereotypes produces similarly positive outcomes (Seewooruttun and Scior 2014). For example, a study of *mediated* contact, using celebrity news stories, found that readers exposed to minority personalities engaging in positive behavior reported less stereotypical perceptions and reduced prejudicial attitudes toward the group as a whole. In turn, these reduced prejudicial attitudes then increased support for minority rights (Ramasubramanian 2015). Earlier research found similar results using a storybook format to introduce children to fictional friendships between disabled and nondisabled kids. Specifically, Cameron and Rutland (2006) found increased positivity and interest in playing with disabled kids after a six-week story-based intervention compared to before.

Indirect contact does not even have to be observed to make a positive impact. Studies of *imagined* contact have shown that when people are simply asked to imagine meeting someone from a different social group, attitudes and behavioral intentions become more positive toward the entire outgroup (Crisp et al. 2009; Turner and West 2012). Some of these studies have asked people to imagine themselves positively interacting with an elderly stranger (Husnu and Crisp 2010), or a person with schizophrenia (West et al. 2011) – rehearsing what they might learn and feel. In another study, nondisabled children who imagined playing in the park with disabled peers were less likely to favor the nondisabled, rated disabled people as more competent, and were more interested in creating cross-disability friendships than those who did not imagine contact (Cameron et al. 2011).

Across ethnic, sexuality, age, weight, and disability groups, studies now confirm that mentally imagining such an interaction produces positive intergroup attitudes at both the explicit and the implicit levels (for a review see Crisp et al. 2009). Imagined contact also contributes to increased intentions for future contact (Husnu and Crisp 2010; Turner and West 2012). These studies have important implications particularly in contexts where opportunities for direct contact are less likely – for example among institutionalized populations or those segregated in group homes or isolated in prison.

Comparing Direct, Indirect, and Informational Forms of Disability Contact

Some researchers have compared direct and indirect contact interventions to assess the relative effectiveness of each (Hean and Dickinson 2005). A recent study compared the impact of a 45-minute semi-structured conversation that was either pre-recorded on audio or that occurred live between a paraplegic wheelchair user and a nondisabled participant as they strolled outside together (Galli et al. 2015). Results showed that implicit preferences for the able-bodied over those who used wheelchairs remained unchanged among people who simply listened to the pre-recorded conversation. Yet, for those who engaged in an in-person conversation with a legitimate wheelchair user, automatic preferences for able-bodied people were eliminated. Another study found that interaction comfort was increased among those who had the opportunity to directly interact with people who experienced psychiatric disabilities, but did not change in response to discussions or videos designed to challenge mental "illness" stigma (Matteo and You 2012).

In a review of 72 studies from 14 countries, face-to-face contact interventions were found to be more effective than studies that simply exposed participants to videos of people who experienced "serious mental illnesses" (Corrigan et al. 2012). Others have compared the effectiveness of interventions providing direct contact to those that varied the type of disability information provided (e.g. impairment limitations) during contact or independent of it. Specifically, in a review of 273 investigations, comparing over 640 effects, studies that provided a combination of contact and disability information resulted in more positive effects than studies that provided information alone (Shaver et al. 1989). In fact, information-only interventions had among the highest proportion of negative effects. That is, in 35% of these studies, disability attitudes worsened among those exposed to the information provided; yet the size and direction of attitude change effects varied widely across study formats. For example, attitudes toward disability and/ or disabled people were more likely to be negative in studies where the only information provided focused on the problems associated with disability, managing disabled children, or how to relate to "them" (disabled people) in social situations. By contrast, attitude changes were more positive in studies providing information on the similarities between disabled and nondisabled people or how capable and "nondisabled" people with disabilities appeared to be. Therefore, some have concluded that informational campaigns to improve attitudes using messages that emphasize group differences are not only ineffective, but may actually increase disability prejudice (Yuker 1994). This argument has been contested, however, and will be revisited in Part II of this chapter, on the framing of disability as a category.

Despite positive trends related to virtual forms of intergroup contact, several researchers have concluded that when it comes to prejudice reduction, direct forms of interaction that begin with interpersonal friendships continue to be among the most effective forms of prejudice reduction (Brown and Hewstone 2005). Nevertheless, direct contact can also contribute to increased intergroup anxieties among some people – at least in the short term (Stephan and Stephan 1985). For this reason, indirect contact has been suggested as a way to prepare and build confidence in advance of in-person interactions with unfamiliar groups. In this way, indirect contact may be deployed to reduce the stress and embarrassment that may drive avoidance of actual contact in the first place (Stathi et al. 2012).

Factors Moderating the Effects of Contact

Beyond indirect or mediated contact approaches, other conditions make a difference in whether or not contact interventions are more or less successful. These moderating factors include the social status of those targeted for contact, the context and goals of the interaction, and the frequency with which contact occurs. It should be noted that the vast majority of contact interventions have targeted the attitudes and behaviors of dominant group members. For example, how are nondisabled people affected by contact with disabled people? Of those that have investigated how contact affects the perceptions and attitudes of minority members, the effects of contact tend to be weaker (Lopez 2004; Molina and Wittig 2006; Tropp and Pettigrew 2005), which may reflect important interaction differences.

> I'm asking for everyone to hear what disabled people are saying. Hear us if we ask you to consider how the ways you convey stories about disability may be hurtful or harmful. Hear us when we say that we want you to speak with us, not for us. Voicing your experiences cannot, and should not ever, be at the expense of the perspectives of the disability community … We should all be in this together. (Ladau 2016)

As noted in Chapter 6 on how disabled people contend with prejudice, disadvantaged group members bring different expectations, motivations, and strategies to intergroup encounters. Minority members including disabled people may be suspicious of those with more power and privilege, even in situations where equal status relationships are intended (Yeager et al. 2013). Disabled people also tend to have more experience with the nondisabled than the nondisabled have with them. Therefore, disabled people may attend more to how others view them while nondisabled people may be more concerned with self-impressions to not embarrass or offend – although both are sensitive to the awkwardness common to many mixed-ability exchanges (see Chapter 5; Hebl and Kleck 2000).

Interdependent and Cooperative Contexts The effectiveness of contact interventions also depends on the particulars of the contact setting. Situations that foster competition for rewards instead of cooperation for a common goal can impede the benefits of contact (Pettigrew 1998). For example, outgroup interaction partners are considered more attractive when an interaction activity results in success compared to failure, particularly when one partner outperforms the other (Blanchard et al. 1975). Even in classroom settings designed to foster equal status among students, teachers can inadvertently privilege certain formats, learning styles, and abilities of some students more than others in ways that reinforce group differences.

By contrast, a cooperative learning context helps to facilitate equal status and mutuality in the service of a common goal using techniques like task interdependence (Slavin 1983). In an inclusive classroom, cooperative interdependence might the take the form of dividing project tasks between students in ways that harness each student's unique strengths and abilities. An activity could be managed in a way that fosters positive interactions where each student is in the position to help the other and bring an area of expertise to bear. Without each member's expertise, the mutual goal cannot be accomplished. In fact, achieving the project goal may not be as important as task *interdependence* in terms of explaining why cooperative learning programs are so effective at increasing attraction among partners (Roseth et al. 2008). Experimental studies on mixed-ability classrooms have noted the importance of cooperative learning goals to improving not only peer attraction but achievement as well. In one study, students with learning disabilities (LDs) were either assigned to work cooperatively with two to three nondisabled students where achievement depended on all the students working together toward a common goal, or were assigned to work independently on the same assignment. Findings showed that LD students in the cooperative groups were more likely to be chosen as friends, and were considered smarter and more valuable than LD students who worked independently; LD students in the cooperative groups also completed more of the assignments correctly (Armstrong et al. 1981).

Maras and Brown (1996) extended these findings in a longitudinal study where nondisabled children were randomly assigned either to a nonintegrated class or to an integrated weekly program where they worked in pairs with children with severe cognitive and physical disabilities on several cooperative activities. Over a three-month period, not only did the attitudes of nondisabled participants improve toward disabled peers, but they came to view disabled peer abilities as more similar to nondisabled peers. By contrast, the attitudes and ability ratings of children who did not participate in the program remained unchanged. Furthermore, at the beginning of the program, the nondisabled kids assumed that other kids with physical, learning, or hearing impairments all had the same running, hearing, and thinking abilities. That is, they tended to stereotype them as all the same. By the end of the integrated program, however, the nondisabled students developed more complex representations of those with disabilities – although they still used disability as an umbrella category. Finally, improved evaluations of disabled peers generalized to unknown children from *different* impairment groups that participants had never met. Specifically, when shown photographs of children who had Down syndrome, wore hearing aids, or used wheelchairs, the nondisabled kids who participated in the cooperative program wanted to play with them more than the control participants who had not participated in the program. The generalizability of these effects are unusual since most studies evaluating cooperative learning groups have focused on short-term effects and attraction to those directly involved in the interaction (Brown 2011).

Increasingly, cooperative interdependence is being discussed as a value espoused by disability studies scholars and advocates alike (Garland-Thomson 2012) who recognize that we all depend on each other for various human and material resources. Thus, employment and education settings that valorize independent achievement at the expense of collaboration, teamwork, and mutuality may inadvertently contribute to ongoing group conflict – especially in diverse contact settings.

Degree and Frequency of Contact Of all the factors studied as important to positive attitude change, one of the best predictors relates to the frequency of intergroup contact (Brown 2011). Contrary to fears of crime and declining property values associated with integrated communities and residential homes, people who live in neighborhoods with disabled residents develop more positive attitudes over time (Yuker 1994). Even those with friends who have friends from different social groups have less prejudice than people without friends who have cross-group friendships (Wright et al. 1997).

Convergent evidence has established that the more disabled friends people have, the longer these relationships have lasted, or the more people interact with those who experience disabilities, the more positive their attitudes are (MacMillan et al. 2014; Paluck and Green 2009). The degree of interpersonal closeness may be more important than the sheer number of disabled friends accumulated (Yuker 1994). Frequency of contact facilitates time spent engaging and self-disclosure, which have both been identified as critical to the development of cross-group friendships (Davies et al. 2011; Miller 2002). Another benefit of cross-group friendships is that they signal a new normative standard that works to reduce the presumption among majority members that minorities do not want to have contact with them or prefer to "keep to themselves" (Pfafferott and Brown 2006). Unfortunately, most contact interventions are staged for only brief periods of time (e.g. weeks or months), which may not be sufficient to alter the impression of those with particularly entrenched biases that have been years in the making (Hill and Augustinos 2001).

Research has also examined the bidirectional effects of contact, noting that not only does contact lead to reduced prejudice but the opposite may be true as well: less prejudiced people seek out more interaction with outgroups while more prejudiced people seek to avoid such contacts (Pettigrew 1998). More recent studies have concluded that this pattern is more likely when people get to choose with whom they want to interact, which is the case in many naturalistic settings. Therefore, while contact can certainly contribute to prejudice reduction, predispositions toward prejudice may explain why some groups continue to avoid others (Levin et al. 2003).

When Contact Backfires

Over the past 60 years, several reviews have synthesized the primary lessons learned about when intergroup contact works to reduce anxieties and improve attitudes and behavioral outcomes (e.g. Paluck and Green 2009; Pettigrew and Tropp 2006). We also know when intergroup contact is most likely to backfire, enflame hostilities, and undermine positive relations between groups (for reviews see: Brown 2011; Schofield and Eurich-Fulcer 2001). Conclusions from these reviews warn against the antagonism that can result when interaction activities are either (i) competitive, (ii) unequal, or (iii) reinforce group stereotypes. For example, when groups are entrenched in conflict, hurtle insults, or only experience each other in limited, stereotypical roles, prejudicial attitudes can easily worsen (Stephan and Stephan 1985).

Another common lament associated with many school-based interventions relates to the problem of "re-segregation" that often occurs following programs designed to increase intergroup interactions. That is, contact interventions are assumed to fail when majority (and minority) group members choose to return to their own ingroups during lunch, on the playground, and even in the classroom unless otherwise directed to integrate. It is worth noting that evidence of re-segregation of students has also been found in studies of "mainstreamed" disabled children (Armstrong et al. 1981; Goodman et al. 1972; Iano et al. 1974). Post-contact re-segregation may also be common in settings where some students are tracked into programs or "streamed by ability."

> After all these years of seeking, I am finding spaces where my big fat white femme whiskered aching buzzing zaftig hard-to-move one-legged strong and soft body can feel at home, can speak up when I am called to, and be quiet when I need to, for the sake of all of us. This is disability justice, in action, in process. And it is revolutionary. (Patty Berne as cited by Lamm 2015)

Importantly, efforts to seek members of one's own subcultural communities are not necessarily signs of failed intergroup contact. People are motivated simultaneously by needs for belonging and distinctiveness (Leonardelli et al. 2010), and may seek refuge and support from others who share a mutual understanding. Behavioral expressions of differences between multicultural groups are not necessarily signs of intolerance – especially when people recognize and respect that others do not all share the same social experiences and affiliation groups. Not everyone can be member of the Black caucus, just as not everyone can join the disabled student union – a point of contention for those who value assimilation into a common cultural melting pot. I return to this topic on the importance of belonging and distinctiveness in Part II of the chapter, on the power of categorization and framing.

How Contact Works: Stereotype Change as a Mediator of Prejudice Reduction

There are a few critical reasons why contact is effective at reducing prejudice (Pettigrew 1998). When people have contact with those from other groups, they are challenged to learn new things (and their emotional reactions, that is, fears, apprehensions, and empathetic, concerns change too – a topic described in Part III of this chapter). When people have meaningful contact with others, they begin to notice self-similarities and realize that not everyone in the outgroup is the same. They come to recognize that many outgroup members defy stereotypical expectations, and may appear downright counter-stereotypical. For example, when people have frequent contact with those who experience disability, they meet many competent, self-determined, sexual beings who occupy a variety of social roles – contrary to disability stereotypes that represent the group as incompetent, dependent, and asexual (Nario-Redmond 2010).

Therefore, one of the reasons why frequent contact improves understanding relates to opportunities for getting to know people and discovering them as individuals inconsistent with group expectations. As result of new knowledge, stereotypes do change (Rothbart and John 1985). To illustrate, Corrigan et al. (2001) found that after listening to a 10-minute recording about the life history of someone with a severe form of mental illness, participants recalled more positive information than negative information about his life, and were less likely to blame other people with psychiatric disabilities (depression and psychoses) for their conditions. These generalized findings, however, did not extend to those with physical or developmental disabilities or drug addictions.

In a more recent study, disabled people were viewed as more competent but no less warm after participants viewed a short (one-minute) video of another disabled person actively engaged in some kind of physical activity (e.g. downhill skiing, exercising, or transferring into a van). That is, the common stereotype that disabled people are more warm than competent was reversed, particularly among those who viewed the skiing video (Kittson et al. 2013). These experimental studies confirm that intergroup contact can causally produce more positive attitudes that generalize to the broader group (Paluck and Green 2009). That is, not only does contact improve attitudes toward people from outgroups with which one has interacted, with but it can transcend to new situations and toward other people from these groups that one has yet to meet. Indeed, when multiple studies are analyzed together, new knowledge about the outgroup emerges as a reliable mediator driving the positive relationship between contact and attitude change (Pettigrew and Tropp 2008).

However, knowledge about disability and disabled people is neither the only nor the most powerful explanatory variable involved in reducing prejudice through contact (Pettigrew and Tropp 2008). Beyond improving knowledge and reducing myths (Patterson and Witten 1987), contact also alters how people come to understand themselves and others in terms of their similarities and differences – their unique and shared group memberships (Gaertner and Dovidio 2000). In addition to updating knowledge and representations of ingroups and outgroups, one of most powerful ways that contact influences attitude change is through emotional channels (e.g. reducing feelings of anxiety and increasing empathy and other positive emotions) (Brown and Hewstone 2005).

The specific cognitive classifications and the emotional drivers of prejudice reduction are reviewed in Parts II and III of this chapter. First, I consider interventions that examine the impact of self–other categorizations or the framing of intergroup boundaries. Following this, I review the impact of emotion-inducing interventions as critical to explaining why direct and even imagined contact with others alters intergroup attitudes.

Part II. Categorical Framing Approaches

Beliefs that value harmony between groups, common ground, and unification have critically informed prejudice-reduction efforts, as have those that emphasize the importance of diversity, difference, and multiculturalism. Many lessons have accumulated on how the framing of a stigmatized status impacts attitudes toward outgroups; however, not all findings generalize to improved understanding, reduced prejudicial behaviors, and more equitable outcomes. So, which framing is most advantageous for these outcomes: one that diminishes the relevance of categories, that is "colorblind," or one that keeps category distinctions salient? When should disability status be highlighted as central, made neutral, or subordinated as part of some larger whole?

Previous chapters have described the prejudicial impacts of how disability is portrayed in language and in the media (Chapters 3 and 4). However, it's not only about whether the informational content is positive, negative, or focused on individual limitations. It's also about how disability is framed as a concept and a classification category. For example, disability can be framed as a personal characteristic that is either minimized or made centrally relevant. Disability is also group membership associated with stereotypes from which individuals can be liberated, and a group identity that impacts intergroup power and status relations. The way people think about themselves with respect to disability and disabled people as a group matters.

De-categorization and "Colorblind" Approaches

For many years it was assumed that interpersonal contact was effective at improving intergroup attitudes because people could get to know each other as individuals – distinct from their social groups and the stereotypical baggage that comes along with them. When interacting one on one, individuals are personalized, and similarities are discovered which can facilitate friendships divorced of categorical expectations. This "de-categorization" approach to prejudice reduction suggests that during contact, the boundaries between groups should be minimized or ignored – if not erased altogether. In this way, interactions can occur at the interpersonal level, diminishing the relevance of intergroup information, like group labels, viewed as problematic (Brewer and Gaertner 2001). Examples of the de-categorization approach in everyday conversation include statements such as: "I don't notice skin color because I only focus on the person"; *or* "I don't even think of you as a woman"; *or* "You are the least disabled person I know." Such statements seem to reflect a desire for acceptance of the person behind the demographic classifications of race, gender, and disability. Yet, because social group memberships are often important to people's identities or sense of self, such "personalizing" comments may come across as ignorant and insulting.

De-categorization strategies are consistent with colorblind ideologies that downplay the relevance of social group distinctions in an effort to be fair and avoid biases by treating people as equals (Rattan and Ambady 2013). Those who espouse colorblind racial ideologies reject the idea of White superiority, and believe everyone has the same opportunities to achieve (Neville et al. 2013). They believe that the colorblind approach will lead to more positive intergroup relationships (Ryan et al. 2007). The "colorblind" ideal is also consistent with the American notion of a "melting pot" that assumes that people should be judged on their own merits regardless of skin color, gender, class, or other demographics.

Studies testing the de-categorization approach to prejudice reduction have produced mixed results (Miller 2002). Some find that after personalized interactions with outgroup members, people express less prejudice and form more cross-group friendships (Pettigrew 1998). Similarly, in cooperative intergroup experiments, those who personalize outgroup members as individuals later demonstrate less bias favoring their own groups. In fact, most research finds that when intergroup bias does occur, it is driven primarily by preferential treatment toward the ingroup, and not necessarily by outgroup discrimination (Turner and Reynolds 2001). For example, when choosing between job candidates from different social groups, people usually favor the candidate who shares at least one of their group affiliations over candidates whose group memberships are unknown.

There is less evidence for a pattern of bias that discriminates or chooses *against* outgroup candidates compared to those whose group memberships are unknown (Hewstone et al. 2002). This suggests that revealing those memberships that are shared with others can sometimes be strategic, as discussed in the next sections on integrative and multicultural approaches.

Unfortunately, several studies have found that improved attitudes toward personalized outgroup members often fail to translate beyond those involved in the contact situation (Rothbart and John 1985; Wilder and Thompson 1980). Newly formed positive feelings are often limited to specific individuals, who may be seen as distinct or independent from their outgroups (Brown and Hewstone 2005). As a consequence, attitudes and liking may improve toward the specific people one interacts with, but unless recognized as part of the minority group, positive attitudes may not generalize to those yet to be encountered.

De-categorization approaches have also been criticized for ignoring important group status and value differences which may further restrict their effectiveness at reducing prejudice at the intergroup level. Both minority and majority groups have values and cultural traditions they seek to preserve or want appreciated as part of the multicultural landscape (Brown 2011). Because de-categorization (or colorblind) approaches fail to acknowledge group-based social disadvantages, they can worsen intergroup tensions through the denial of social inequalities and other economic and cultural differences that matter (Berry 1984).

Indeed, studies find that those who endorse colorblind beliefs are more likely to deny institutional racism and the societal factors that contribute to race disparities in the criminal justice system (Neville et al. 2013). College students scoring higher on colorblind beliefs also indicate that they are less bothered by social media images insulting to Black and Latino cultures (Tynes and Markoe 2010). Even children exposed to stories emphasizing colorblind beliefs are less likely to identify and report blatant acts of discrimination involving physical assault of a Black student by a White student (Apfelbaum et al. 2010).

Not surprisingly, *minority* members are less likely to endorse colorblind ideologies than those from majority groups, who are more likely to avoid discussing race in an effort to appear unbiased (Ryan et al. 2007). Furthermore, support for colorblind ideologies increases with age: White children under 10 ask more questions about race while those over 10 actively avoid mentioning race in tasks requiring the identification of ethnic groups (Apfelbaum et al. 2008). White students who attempt to appear colorblind (by avoiding the mention of race when interacting with a Black partner) also make less eye contact and are judged to be less friendly (Norton et al. 2006). Moreover, teachers with colorblind beliefs are less willing to accommodate culturally diverse students (Hachfeld et al. 2015). This may be why "mainstreaming" disabled students with nondisabled peers is not always seen as the ideal if disabled students' cultural identities become diluted or diminished. When it comes to promoting disability as a positive cultural identity, private schools designed to optimize educational and other outcomes for particular populations offer viable alternatives for some (Lawson 2001).

Convergent evidence finds that the endorsement of colorblind racial ideologies (which includes a denial of racial differences and a discomfort in discussing racial issues) is linked to both blatant and subtle expressions of racism, fear, anger, and aggression. In fact, the colorblind approach is conceived by some to be an ultra-contemporary form of racism used to justify the status quo (for a review see Neville et al. 2013). For these reasons, alternative framing approaches have been proposed that acknowledge the importance of social categories and group-relevant information – not only for their role in sustaining prejudice but for eliminating it as well.

Cross-Cutting, Integrative, and Universalizing Approaches

The integrative category models of prejudice reduction work to leverage the power of categorization (and ingroup favoritism) in creative ways. For example, the cross-cutting categorization approach involves making people from different groups aware that they share memberships in some subgroups but not others, making intergroup comparisons more complex in an effort to reduce bias (Brewer and Gaertner 2001). For example, disabled and nondisabled people may learn that some from each group are Democrats while others are Republicans and Independents. To date, reviews of research testing these integrative approaches have focused primary on ethnicity, region, and professional affinity groups (Paluck and Green 2009). Many studies document that favoritism toward one's own group can be reduced when people from different social groups find out that they share other group memberships in common (Crisp and Hewstone 1999; Hornsey and Hogg 2000, but see Vescio et al. 2004).

Similarly, the "re-categorization" approach (Gaertner and Dovidio 2000) encourages people from different groups to think of themselves as belonging to a broader, superordinate group that has certain characteristics or affiliations in common. For example, students of different ethnicities can unite under the common umbrella of their various school identities: "We may be different, but we're all Hiram College Terriers, psychology majors, or members of the soccer team." The common ingroup identity model proposes that prejudice can be redirected when people shift from an "us" versus "them" mentality to a "we" mentality (Gaertner and Dovidio 2000). According to this model, when self–other representations become part of a broader collective that encompasses former ingroup and outgroup distinctions, people come to view themselves (and others) as part of one common ingroup, which can result in less bias and more prosocial behavior.

Studies testing this approach have been successful in reducing intergroup bias in both lab and field studies with diverse groups of children, college students, merged corporations, and even step families (see Gaertner and Dovidio 2000 for a review). To help promote the notion of a common ingroup, some researchers have used external cues such as badges, matching shirts, or alternative seating arrangements to redraw intergroup boundaries in a way that signals unification

(Houlette et al. 2004; Nier et al. 2001). Much research supports the benefits of creating common or shared identity groups in order to redirect the power of ingroup favoritism to reduce prejudice.

Yet, the common ingroup identity approach is not without its problems (Dovidio et al. 2016). When superordinate groups become too inclusive, people feel their unique identities get lost in the crowd, leading them to seek new ways to distinguish themselves – as members of smaller social units or cliques, for example (Leonardelli et al. 2010). Similarly, when people are lumped into an overarching group that undermines the distinctiveness of other valued group memberships, feelings of identity threat can result in even more prejudice (Branscombe et al. 1999), and lower outgroup trust (Verkuyten 2011).

Colorblind, de-categorization, and re-categorization approaches have also been criticized as imposing assimilationist views or ideals that value conformity in line with the majority (Dovidio et al. 2009). Studies show that a common ingroup identity that implicitly reflects dominant group values is more appealing to members of the majority who may be more willing to accept minorities to the extent that they resemble majority standards (Dovidio et al. 2016). Examples of this universalizing sentiment appear in statements like: "America is a melting pot but everyone should speak English"; *and* "We are all disabled in some way or another." Inclusive identity approaches to intergroup harmony are also reflected in the resistance to expressions that promote multiculturalism: "I'm not saying 'Happy Holidays' at Christmastime"; *or* "There is no need for a disability culture if disability is just one aspect of human variation." Disability studies scholar Carol Gill (1994) questioned the framing of disability as a phenomenon that exists on a continuum, noting the dangers associated with nondisabled people appropriating disability as a way to connect with (or control) the disability community.

> I find it hard to embrace as brothers and sisters those folks who spend their whole lives comfortably in the nondisabled world without any mention of personal disability until a disabled person challenges their authority to speak for us. Then they justify their position of profit or leadership in a disability organization by trotting out their spectacles or trick knee or rheumatiz. "Actually, we're all disabled in some way, aren't we?" they ask. "No!" I say. If the only time you "walk the walk" of disability is when it's convenient for you and you even admit your disability has little impact on your life and no one regards you as disabled, give me a break – you ain't one of us! (p. 46)

Other disability activists and scholars have critiqued categorization schemes that position the term "ability status" as an inclusive classification alongside gender, nationality, race, and sexuality in organizational definitions of diversity (e.g. American Association of Colleges and Universities). This argument harkens to debates about those who want to avoid the term "disability" based on its presumed negativity, or seek to dress it up in euphemisms like *dis/ability* or *differently abled* (see Chapter 3). Instead, some promote the use of *disability status* as a way to signify current membership in a politically relevant constituency with legal protections (S. Linton, personal communication, May 2, 2017). Unlike race and gender, which appear to be more neutral classifications, there is no widely accepted umbrella term that covers those with and without impairments. Given that the default person is assumed to be White, male, and heterosexual, unless otherwise noted (Smith and Zarate 1992), the term disability status can help decenter presumptions of normalcy as descriptive of only nondisabled people. According to Linton, while one's disability status can change, category-salient framing assumes that one is either categorized as currently in the group or not. Thus, disability as a social category may or may not be permanent, but it is distinct from other more inclusive ability classifications like painting or juggling. Even the neurodiversity movement (which emphasizes the variability among people living on the autistic spectrum) distinguishes between those considered neuro-typical and those who qualify as neuro-diverse, recognizing the importance of retaining certain categorical distinctions (Runswick-Cole 2014).

Similar to continuums, some disability awareness campaigns are premised on the notion that improved understanding of disability issues can only be attained through universalizing strategies that consider impairments as value-neutral traits similar to height or hair color (e.g. Stiker 1999; Snow 2001). These are in contrast to universal design approaches that seek to accommodate a broader range of human variability than the average type in education and other environmental contexts (for reviews see Burgstahler 2015; Roberts et al. 2011). Few of these campaigns to raise awareness or improve understanding about the complexity of disability have been subject to empirical evaluation. Furthermore, few studies have investigated how alternative framing of intergroup boundaries is effective at reducing prejudice against outgroups (Vescio et al. 2004); and none have focused on disability or compared how alternative categorizations impact ableist attitudes and practices.

At times, universalizing approaches may be useful in reminding individuals of their shared objectives as part of the human family or to unite factions under an overarching organizational banner; but this common categorization is only part of the story, as people belong to many identity groups – only some of which are shared. Furthermore, some group memberships cannot be ignored because of their ongoing social relevance.

Multicultural Approaches to Diversity

In contrast to approaches that aim to dissolve social groups into broader classifications, more contemporary models of prejudice reduction emphasize techniques designed to keep intergroup boundaries salient and clear (Brewer and Gaertner 2001). Multicultural perspectives challenge the effectiveness of de-categorization and melting pot approaches that require minority groups to forget their differences and assimilate into the dominant culture to gain acceptance (Goldberg 1994). Instead, multiculturalism promotes the idea that cultural groups can co-exist without having to conform to majority expectations, and cross-group interactions are enhanced when we learn about other groups' social realities. Moreover, multicultural ideologies emphasize the importance of recognizing and valuing diverse social identities as central to improving intergroup relations and equality (Rosenthal and Levy 2010).

In an effort to increase the integration and productivity of employees and effective interactions with diverse consumers, diversity training initiatives have proliferated across organizational settings to promote multicultural ideals. According to a review by Pendry et al. (2007), "Little is known about the effectiveness of such initiatives … When it comes to strategies for tackling diversity issues, there is something of a divide between theory and practice" (p. 27). For this reason, diversity trainers and social psychologists have much potential to collaboratively advance the knowledge base, particularly in applied settings (see Ehrke et al. 2014; Paluck 2006). Some of the principles of multiculturalism have also been tested under more controlled experimental conditions.

The mutual intergroup differentiation model of prejudice reduction stresses the importance of recognizing the distinct social categories that comprise a diverse society (Brown and Hewstone 2005). The model proposes that positive intergroup relations depend on interactions structured in ways that acknowledge group strengths and highlight group memberships. Studies have tested this model across intergroup settings involving ethnic groups, immigrants, the elderly, gay people, and those with psychiatric conditions. Findings consistently demonstrate improved attitudes toward outgroup members when between-group distinctions remain clear (Brown 2011). Specifically, prejudice toward outgroups in general is reduced when individuals are identified as group members, and characterized as similar, typical, or otherwise representative of the outgroup.

In one of the few studies examining disability prejudice, Cameron and Rutland (2006) found that children's disability attitudes consistently improved over time only when storybook characters were clearly described in group membership terms as typical disabled or nondisabled kids. When the category boundaries between "ability groups" were minimized, and the stories focused more on the preferences and interests of individual characters, attitude change was not significant. Additionally, increased interest in playing with disabled kids was also observed when category boundaries were made salient *and* when storybook characters were personalized. Similarly, in a cooperative employment setting, nondisabled people reported feeling less anxious around colleagues with psychiatric conditions only when aware of their group membership during contact (Vezzali and Capozza 2011). Only when these group distinctions were clear, did the nondisabled employees express more empathy and less anxiety toward disabled people overall.

According to Hewstone et al. (2002), improved intergroup relationships require an appreciation of *both the similarities and the differences between groups* – the privileges, disadvantages, and diversity that characterize group life. Some mechanism that enables new positive associations to develop between interaction partners and their social group memberships also seems critical. Hewstone and colleagues argue that membership salience should be considered alongside the other five "ideal" contact conditions considered optimal for prejudice reduction: equal status, friendship potential, cooperative relationships, common goals, and the support of institutional authorities.

Critiques of the multicultural approach emphasize the dangers of isolationist attitudes and separatism. It was long assumed that conflict and increased prejudice would follow whenever group differences were accentuated (Schlesinger 1992). Even competition between disadvantaged groups operating separately to improve their circumstances was viewed as inevitable (Walzer 1994). Some argued that defining disability as a culture has also led to within-group divisions about who belongs and who does not (e.g. mental health conditions, obese, chronically ill) – with implications for who can make claims for accommodations and protection from discrimination (Gilson and Depoy 2000). Some argue that applying a multicultural lens to disability as an aspect of diversity fails to address its multiple determinants (Anastasiou et al. 2016). To illustrate, the Americans with Disabilities Act (ADA) requires that disabled people (as a protected class) must be allowed "in the door" for jobs or educational opportunities; once in, however, access to the supports and technologies best designed to meet their individual needs may still be lacking (Schriner and Scotch 2001). Thus, despite legal mandates to improve the integration of disabled people as a minority group, disparities remain across social institutions (Kessler Foundation 2015; Kraus 2017; Reingle-Gonzalez et al. 2016; Rowland et al. 2014).

> What benefits minority group members the most, a colorblind or multicultural ideology? Although extant research seems to suggest that expecting not to be treated differently based on group membership can be beneficial … There is more consensus in the data showing that a multicultural ideology benefits minorities. (Rattan and Ambady 2013, p. 18)

Comparing Multicultural and Colorblind Approaches: What Works When?

Some studies have directly compared the effectiveness of alternative framing strategies to examine when multicultural versus colorblind approaches are more or less effective at reducing stereotypes and/or prejudice. To illustrate, in a series of experiments White students were asked to review "leading scientific evidence," and then to reflect on how best to resolve conflicts between US ethnic groups (Wolsko et al. 2000). Those in the colorblind condition read that evidence suggests that intergroup harmony is best achieved when people recognize that "at our core we are all the same, that all men are created equal, and that we are first and foremost a nation of individuals." Those in the multicultural condition read that the evidence suggests intergroup harmony is best achieved "if we better appreciate our diversity, and recognize and accept each group's positive and negative qualities." Findings revealed that compared to controls, both colorblind and multicultural perspectives resulted in less ethnocentric prejudice (White ingroup positivity). However, those asked to consider the importance of diversity and group differences demonstrated *more awareness of stereotypes* – both positive and negative: they assumed more Black people are religious and have run-ins with police while more Whites grow up with unlimited opportunities and are given things without having to work for them. Those who reflected upon the value of a colorblind society may have assumed that ethnic differences should be avoided or suppressed.

A few studies have since replicated and extended these results (for reviews see Sasaki and Vorauer 2013; Rattan and Ambady 2013). Correll et al. (2008) found that compared to colorblind messages, multicultural messages reduce not only explicit but implicit racial biases (see also Richeson and Nussbaum 2004). Multicultural messages have also been found to increase liking toward minorities who are more stereotypical of their groups, whereas those exposed to a colorblind ideology prefer minorities who are less stereotypical (Gutierrez and Unzueta 2010). Exposure to different ideologies also affects interaction behavior and support for equality between groups. For example, multicultural approaches have led majority members to make more positive comments during interactions with minorities, while colorblind approaches tend to produce more negative feelings (Sasaki and Vorauer 2013). In one longitudinal study, White students who had a higher proportion of Black friends reported significant declines in their support of colorblind ideologies over a four-year period (Neville et al. 2013).

When majority members are primed with colorblind (versus multicultural) messages, they may be so focused on suppressing their intergroup thoughts and feelings that they act more nervous and uncomfortable during interactions (see Holoien and Shelton 2012). One consequence of interaction discomfort is that minority members report feeling less engaged at work when their White co-workers are more supportive of colorblind beliefs. By contrast, minorities feel more engaged the more their White co-workers support multiculturalism (Plaut et al. 2009). Personal support for multicultural ideals is also more likely in countries with policies and norms that endorse the value of cultural diversity over national unity (Guimond et al. 2013).

Moderating Influences on Diversity Ideologies

The effects of exposure to multicultural perspectives differ for those in the dominant majority (Karafantis et al. 2010), depending on how highly they identify as White. Morrison et al. (2010) found that exposure to multicultural (versus colorblind) ideology increased prejudice among those highly identified as White but it reduced prejudice among those less identified as White. Among highly identified Whites, multicultural ideologies can even backfire, leading to stronger preferences for social inequality (Morrison et al. 2010). Therefore, the multicultural approach has been described as more effective with people whose dominant group identities are not centrally defining (Sasaki and Vorauer 2013).

Generally, research finds that multiculturalism improves intergroup attitudes and behaviors in nonthreatening circumstances. That is, when people feel threatened, the positive effects of multiculturalism dissolve and may even reverse (Verkuyten 2009), particularly among highly prejudice people (Sasaki and Vorauer 2013). For example, when there was no conflict perceived between groups, both multicultural and colorblind strategies reduced prejudice; however, when minority students were portrayed as competing for a scarce resource (e.g. early registration for classes), colorblind approaches were more effective at suppressing explicit racial bias. Yet, when it comes to more implicit or automatic biases that are difficult to suppress, colorblind approaches are *not* more effective, and result in even more prejudice after a short delay (Correll et al. 2008). Such "rebound effects" are common to studies that require participants to actively suppress their true beliefs, which is difficult to sustain and may later result in the ironic return of negative feelings once this effort has been expended (Monteith et al. 1998).

In summary, while multicultural approaches may increase recognition of stereotypes (not all of which are inaccurate: e.g. Black people do have more run-ins with police, and more Whites grow up with wealth and privilege), they are clearly more effective at reducing prejudices, and contribute to smoother interactions and more support for minority rights. Although minority members tend to favor multicultural ideologies, studies show that Whites are more supportive of multicultural ideals when they are low prejudice to begin with, less highly identified as White, or made to feel that their European American identities are affirmed as part of a multicultural message (Morrison and Chung 2011). Colorblind approaches are more problematic for both majority and minority groups. They signal the irrelevance of social disparities and differences that derive from valued group memberships, and focus on preventing group-based thoughts and feelings that are often beyond an individual's control. According to multiple reviews, colorblind ideologies have more inconsistent effects that seem more effective in the short term. Furthermore, colorblind ideologies and superordinate identities may reduce recognition of structural inequalities, which can reduce motivation to take collective action for change (see Chapter 8). Future research is needed to test how differential framing of disability as a socially relevant category impacts prejudice, stereotyping, and support for more equitable relationships across groups. This work is especially needed in light of all the disability awareness training that occurs without evaluation of its impacts.

Part III. Empathy Inductions and Experiential Simulations

Some of the most popular interventions among school children and adults alike go beyond multicultural training or framing to create an emotional experience as a way to reduce prejudice. Many of these more emotionally arousing approaches have investigated the role of empathy – an other-oriented emotion considered critical to fostering prosocial attitudes and behaviors (Batson 2010). Among the more well-researched ways of inducing empathy are interventions that require people to actively consider another person's perspective. Some perspective-taking approaches have used photographs, audio recordings (Batson et al. 1997b), or written scenarios (Finlay and Stephan 2000) that ask participants to "imagine a day in the life" of someone from another social group (Galinsky and Moskowitz 2000). Other perspective-taking activities create a more direct experience using role-playing games that attempt to simulate what it is like to be old (Pacala et al. 2006), overweight (Rodriguez et al. 2016), or disabled (Nario-Redmond et al. 2017). For example, deafness is frequently simulated with ear plugs, low vision with blindfolds, and paralysis with wheelchairs and/or restraints that bind the legs and arms.

For many years, education and rehabilitation professionals have emphasized the value of such interactive role-playing experiences to improve attitudes and increase understanding (e.g. Burgstahler and Doe 2004; Dorn 1989). Unfortunately, disability simulations have only recently been subject to empirical scrutiny (Flower et al. 2007). There remains a strong assumption that as a teaching tool, role-playing deafness, blindness, and paralysis can accurately capture the disability experience through approximations of altered embodiment that are neither permanent nor complete (French 1996).

Perspective-Taking Interventions

Intuitively appealing, the primary assumption behind perspective-taking interventions is that prejudice involves a failure to imagine what it must be like to walk in the shoes of someone from another social group. To the extent that people can consider the perspective of outgroup others, understanding of their disadvantaged circumstances can be more fully informed. Therefore, perspective taking is considered one vehicle through which the power of empathy can be harnessed to cultivate more positive and compassionate attitudes and less distorted reactions toward stigmatized others. Such ideas have been around for many years, and emphasize that the development of empathetic concern is critical to motivating cooperative and altruistic actions (Batson 2010).

Empathetic concern can be conceptualized as either feeling *for* another person or feeling *as* another person does – although both may be triggered simultaneously, and researchers do not always distinguish between these alternative forms of empathy in practice. Identifying the specific antecedents and motivations for empathy is important because empathy has been shown to improve positive attitudes toward a variety of stigmatized groups – not only in the short term but over longer periods of time as well (see Batson 2010 and Davis and Begovic 2014 for reviews). Empathic concern can even help focus attention to the long-term welfare of those in need, thereby producing more responsive care (Sibicky et al. 1995).

Daniel Batson and colleagues have published numerous studies investigating the effects of imagining the perspective of others on empathetic responses, intergroup attitudes, and a willingness to help stigmatized groups including racial minorities, the elderly, drug addicts, and convicted murderers (Todd and Galinsky 2014). One experimental paradigm used to test these ideas presents participants with a "radio broadcast" or written scenario about a particular person in need (e.g. a surviving member of a family killed in a car accident). While all participants are exposed to the same information, only some are asked to carefully imagine what the disadvantaged person might be feeling about their experience, while others are asked to consider their story from a more detached or objective position (Batson 2010).

In one classic set of studies, attitudes toward the homeless as a group (and people living with AIDS) became more positive when people were first asked to imagine the circumstances of individuals from each group, compared to those who did not assume an insider's perspective (Batson et al. 1997b). Positive intergroup evaluations have also been found in studies of race-based perspective taking (Shih et al. 2009); and the beneficial effects of perspective taking seem to generalize across both explicit and implicit attitude measures (see Todd and Galinsky 2014 for a review). Critically, perspective-taking interventions not only affect the evaluation of outgroups, they also influence nonverbal reactions and other forms of prosocial behavior. Todd et al. (2011) found that White students who previously took the perspective of a Black man showed more interaction rapport (e.g. open body language and eye contact), and sat closer to another person presumed to be Black than non-perspective takers. Similarly, people were more willing to interact with homeless people after taking the perspective of another homeless person (Wang et al. 2014). In medical settings, patient satisfaction was higher with clinicians who had previously taken their perspective compared to those who followed standard exam procedures (Blatt et al. 2010); and nurses who take patient perspectives offer more comprehensive treatment options as well (Drwecki et al. 2011).

Perspective-taking interventions have also been associated with heightened recognition of intergroup inequalities and reduced denials of discrimination (Todd and Galinsky 2014). Specifically, taking the perspective of a racial minority (Black or Latino) increased perceptions of racial discrimination (Todd and Galinsky 2012) and support for affirmative-action policies to increase the representation of minorities in school admissions and employment. Furthermore, perspective taking strengthens the association and recognition of race-based oppression and White privilege (Todd et al. 2011). The extent to which perspective-taking interventions can be used to promote more egalitarian attitudes toward disabled people and support for intergroup equality and disability rights remains a subject for future research.

Mediators of Perspective-Taking Interventions Across studies, the positive effects of perspective taking on attitudes have been driven in large part by feelings of sympathy, compassion, and warmth. That is, indicators of empathy often mediate the relationship between perspective taking and helping behavior. For example, empathetic concern through perspective taking predicts both volunteer time and charitable donations (Bekkers 2010; Cialdini et al. 1997; Penner 2002). Some note that perspective taking not only stimulates empathy and compassion, but can also signal commonality with another person – suggesting that both emotional and cognitive mechanisms are important to prejudice reduction (Cialdini et al. 1997; Todd and Galinsky 2014).

An important caveat to the perspective-taking–empathy relationship is based on the extent to which one's perception of the self "overlaps" with the person whose circumstances are imagined (Myers et al. 2014). In fact, the very act of perspective taking may stimulate the mental merging of self and other, such that perceptions of self and the imagined other become mentally intertwined (Davis et al. 1996). This self–other merging can increase implicit associations and identification with an imagined other, resulting in more positive outgroup impressions (Todd et al. 2012). Self–other merging has also been linked to *self-stereotyping* or the inadvertent taking on of outgroup stereotypes oneself. Galinsky et al. (2008) found that when taking the perspective of an elderly man, people later considered themselves to be weaker and more dependent than those who did not take his perspective – and they behaved more stereotypically as well, choosing to cooperate more than compete. Similar results were found among White students who took the perspective of African Americans and other social groups.

A sense of social bonding and kinship are additional benefits associated with behaving similarly to members of stereotyped groups. "An elderly individual may appreciate a perspective taker walking more slowly down a hallway, but the same behavior could annoy a more energetic youth" (Galinsky et al. 2008, p. 417). Based on research reviewed in Chapter 6, elderly and disabled people may resent even unconsciously triggered actions that appear to patronize, infantilize, or presume helplessness and incompetence. If self-stereotyping is an automatic by-product of perspective-taking interventions, behavioral mimicry might appear to be phony, and perpetuate distrust, stigma by association, and personal distress.

Moderators of Perspective-Taking Interventions Critically, the emotional consequences associated with perspective taking can differ dramatically depending on whether one imagines what life is like for the other, or imagines oneself in the position of the other. This may seem like a trivial distinction, but across multiple studies emotional distress is much more likely when people are asked to imagine themselves in the place of a disadvantaged other (e.g. imagine your life as a paraplegic) as opposed to imagining what a disadvantaged other might be experiencing (imagine the life of this paraplegic person). Batson et al. (1997a) found that imagining how "someone else" feels about a traumatic accident, instead of imagining how "you yourself" would feel, produced more empathy for the individual imagined and less personal distress for the person taking her perspective. While both approaches produced empathy, imagining how *you yourself would feel* in the same situation resulted in more negative feelings such as being distressed, alarmed, troubled, and perturbed. The authors speculated that imagining yourself experiencing a traumatic event may elicit more self-oriented empathy and egotistical concerns. By contrast, imagining what a trauma is like for another person may elicit more other-oriented empathy and altruistic concerns.

Although not typically considered as an indicator of prejudice reduction, generosity as a form of procedural justice also depends on who is imagined as gaining or losing a preferential outcome. In studies on the fair distribution of limited resources, Batson et al. (2003) found that when one of two people start off with an unearned privilege that could be distributed more equally, imagining *oneself* as the disadvantaged other (*how would I want to be treated if I didn't have this privilege*) produced more generosity and fairer outcomes than not taking a perspective at all. By contrast, when a limited resource can only be assigned to one person, then imagining how *the other person would want to be treated* produced more generosity than imagining how *I would want to be treated* or not taking a perspective at all. Similarly, when it comes to charitable giving, imagining the perspective of the recipient elicits more donations and willingness to help compared to imagining oneself from the perspective of the donor (Hung and Wyer 2009). Thus, helping in the form of volunteer time and money seems most effectively encouraged when people are asked to focus on the other's perspective rather than their own.

In addition to perspective-taking focus, other conditions have been found to influence reactions, sometimes resulting in greater stereotyping and intergroup hostility. For example, taking the perspective of an elderly or overweight person can increase negative attitudes when targets are portrayed in highly stereotypic ways (Skorinko and Sinclair 2013). Some people are also reluctant to identify with outgroups that are intensely disliked (Paluck 2010) or threatening due to long-standing conflicts, or when resources are scarce (Pierce et al. 2013). Specific characteristics of the perspective taker also influence reactions. Those with higher self-esteem are more readily able to extend their positive self-views to embrace the perspectives of stigmatized others than those with low levels of self-worth (Galinsky and Ku 2004). Furthermore, some may be less motivated or capable of imagining the circumstances of others. For example, those more prejudiced to begin with (Sasaki and Vorauer 2013), who identify highly with their own ingroup (Tarrant et al. 2012), or who belong to powerful groups (Galinsky et al. 2006) may have little interest in lower status group perspectives. Assuming the perspective of a powerful majority may also be aversive to members of minority groups (Bruneau and Saxe 2012), illustrating the potential difficulties with encouraging perspective taking in the real world. Yet, when people believe that others have successfully taken their perspective, they too feel more similar to, and act more generously toward, those who can see things from their point of view (Goldstein et al. 2014). Finally, in addition to interventions designed to induce the temporary *state* of empathetic concern, others have examined the relationships between *trait* perspective taking (the dispositional tendency to adopt another's perspective), *trait* empathy (the dispositional tendency to feel compassion for others) (Cuff et al. 2016), prejudice, and dehumanization (Bruneau et al. 2018), although much evidence supports the importance of situational influences on the expression of these traits.

In summary, perspective-taking interventions produce complex outcomes. First, they can increase how warm and connected people feel toward members of outgroups while contributing to stereotypical self-perceptions and behaviors. Second, research suggests that imagining oneself in the place of others – rather than taking the other's perspective – is less effective at inducing empathy and assistance. Third, imagining *oneself* in the place of stigmatized others is not only threatening, but may also coincide with a desire for greater social distance. These findings have significant implications for other interventions that seek to provide first-person experiences of marginalized identities such as those with disabilities.

> To fully understand perspective taking as the dynamic process that it is, it is critically important that we get inside the minds not only of those walking in another's shoes but also of those standing by in their socks watching and reacting to the process as it occurs. (Goldstein et al. 2014, p. 958)

Interactive Disability, Aging, and Psychiatric Simulations

The distinction between traditional perspective-taking interventions and the limited evidence on disability simulations is that rather than just *imagining* the problems that people with disabilities confront, simulation activities require people *to personally experience* a manufactured version of conditions like blindness, deafness, and dyslexia. Disability simulations typically involve nondisabled people doing ordinary activities with alterations meant to mimic the assumed physical, sensory, and motor challenges disabled people face. For example, some disability simulations require participants to eat a meal or perform everyday tasks while blindfolded, wearing ear plugs, or maneuvering a hospital-style wheelchair with a focus on what *cannot* be done independently. Other simulations attempt to approximate age-related declines (Pacala et al. 2006) or psychiatric conditions like schizophrenia (Ando et al. 2011). For example, at conferences (e.g. the American Psychiatric Association; Wells 2008), an interactive demonstration used goggles and headphones to simulate a range of hallucinations.

Unlike perspective-taking interventions, interactive simulations involve the active appropriation or "taking on" of another group's physical or other characteristics. This form of perspective taking is built on the assumption that people cannot fully understand the circumstances facing disabled people *unless* they know first-hand how they seem to do what they do. Simulations of obesity have been portrayed in films like *Shallow Hal* or made-for-TV social experiments like *What Would You Do?* where actors put on a "fat suit" or prosthetic makeup used to enlarge their appearance. This idea is similar to John Howard Griffin's famous journalism project, *Black Like Me* (Griffin 1961), where he used melanin-depositing medication and tanning to darken his skin prior to visiting six

Southern states to experience the trials of being Black in America. Simulating the experience of any minority group is problematic, particularly when role-played in stereotypical terms, which can lead to greater stereotyping (Skorinko and Sinclair 2013).

Yet, simulation exercises are quite common to disability awareness programming in public and private schools, college campuses, medical programs, and professional training seminars (Lindsay and Edwards 2013). Practitioners of these "arresting educational techniques" swear by their popularity to engage students and stimulate discussion (Pacala et al. 2006), despite mounting criticisms from experts within the disability community warning of their unintended consequences (Blaser 2003; Brew-Parrish 2004; Lalvani and Broderick 2013). Surprisingly, few studies have evaluated the efficacy of these simulations across knowledge, attitudinal, and behavioral outcomes (Kiger 1992). Does the use of a wheelchair for an hour or even a day provide an accurate window into the liberation associated with mobility, the creativity involved in navigating environmental barriers, or the affirmation of one's humanity linked to accessible spaces?

Disability and Aging Simulations Research The stated goals behind the use of disability simulations are to grant nondisabled people an opportunity to improve their understanding and acceptance of people with disabilities. Despite these good intentions, little empirical evidence supports that disability simulations accomplish these goals (Kiger 1992). A systematic review of disability-awareness interventions for children found only four simulation studies between 1980 and 2011 with at least one measured outcome for evaluation (Lindsay and Edwards 2013). Only one of these studies was considered effective at increasing knowledge about barriers to accessibility, particularly for fifth and sixth graders. However, instead of simulating disability directly, that study used a virtual reality game where children vicariously simulated the navigation of obstacles from the purview of a wheelchair user (Pivik et al. 2002). Because the other three studies found mixed evidence, the authors concluded that "the data were inadequate to make a recommendation on the effectiveness of this type of intervention" (Lindsay and Edwards 2013, p. 642).

One of the earliest experimental studies of disability simulations compared undergraduates on a 25-minute campus tour while either playing the role of a wheelchair user, walking alone, or walking behind a wheelchair user to observe their experiences (Clore and Jeffery 1972). No differences were found between those who used the wheelchair personally and those who followed behind a wheelchair user. Both of these groups expressed more empathetic concern (and more anxiety) but more favorable attitudes toward disability issues compared to those who walked alone. In fact, those who walked alone were less supportive of spending student funds for disabled students four months later. However, neither the direct nor the vicarious experience with the wheelchair impacted students' willingness to meet with prospective students with disabilities – which may be related to their heightened levels of anxiety.

Flower et al. (2007) conducted a meta-analysis to evaluate the impact of 10 studies that simulated orthopedic, cognitive, visual, and hearing impairments: Not only did the simulations produce small attitude-change effects, 6 out of 17 results showed that attitudes changed for the worse following the simulation activities. Compared to interventions that used a combination of educational programming (e.g. videos and face-to-face contact with disabled people), direct simulations were the least effective. The authors concluded that while not necessarily harmful, the utility of disability simulations was not supported, and discontinuation was recommended.

In terms of age-related simulations, the Aging Game curricula – designed for medical students – simulates progressive dependency using arm slings for arthritis and disorienting instructions for cognitive decline. A review of the program found "two general categories of behavioral responses – withdrawal and aggression – that students invariably exhibit when participating in the simulation experience" (Pacala et al. 2006, p. 145). Unfortunately, less than half of the estimated 1500 students who participated in the Aging Game over a 10-year period completed the optional evaluations. Those who did, consistently rated the simulations as both interesting and educationally valuable. Therefore, even when the evidence suggests otherwise, simulations are often considered successful not only because they are entertaining, but because many are designed to instigate the frustration and fear assumed to characterize life with disability (French 1996).

A more recent review of studies that simulated the visual and/or auditory hallucinations associated with certain psychiatric disabilities found increased empathetic concern and increased negative emotions, physical distress, and ambivalent attitudes, as well as a greater desire to distance from those experiencing "mental illnesses" (Ando et al. 2011). Yet, participants (psychology, nursing, and medical students) assumed they had a better understanding of the insider's perspective, and considered psychiatric simulations to be acceptable educational tools. Some practitioners argue that when simulations are combined with an insider's personal account, positive changes can occur. For example, Galletly and Burton (2011) gave medical students the opportunity to listen to someone discuss his experiences with schizophrenia *before* they simulated auditory hallucinations as part of a workshop. Following this, attitudes improved but only among those who had the most negative attitudes toward mental illness at the outset. In other studies, where insider perspectives were not included, simulations of auditory hallucinations led to increased social rejection (Brown et al. 2010) and diminished empathetic responses – particularly among those with low empathy to begin with (Bunn and Terpstra 2009). Together these findings suggest that the impact of simulations may depend on other moderating variables including the type of impairment simulated and the frequency of contact with disabled people (MacMillan et al. 2014).

In an effort to test the moderating effects of impairment type and contact, my research team investigated the emotional, attitudinal, and behavioral consequences of simulating both single and multiple disabilities including sensory, reading, and mobility impairments. Our first field study capitalized on a campus-wide disability-awareness program arranged in the dining hall through residential education. Although we did not control the three activity stations, we were allowed to evaluate their impact by measuring student perceptions before and after the simulations. Specifically, we asked a group of students to complete baseline questions at the end of a psychology class, and then randomly assigned them to participate in one of the three standard simulations. Hearing impairment was simulated at one table where students were asked to wear foam ear plugs while attempting to read the lips of another student reading a short passage. To simulate a reading impairment, students were asked to read a short passage that had each word typed backwards, which is one of the most popular – though inaccurate – simulations of dyslexia across educational settings (Wadlington et al. 2008). Finally, to simulate mobility impairment, students were asked to get their meals using a hospital-style wheelchair. Post-test questions were then given immediately following the simulations.

Our findings revealed several negative consequences of single-impairment simulations that worsened depending on which simulation they completed. People experienced more anxiety, frustration, embarrassment, and confusion, especially after simulating mobility and reading disabilities, while feelings of hostility were highest following the simulation of dyslexia. Interestingly, these negative emotions occurred alongside heightened feelings of warmth – an indicator of empathetic concern – toward disabled people overall. In a follow-up experiment, we tested whether multiple simulations (e.g. low vision, hearing-impairment, and dyslexia) would produce similarly ambivalent emotions, and whether these depended on how much previous contact participants had with disabled people. Replicating previous results, a combination of simulation activities produced more hostility, embarrassment, and confusion. However, feelings of anxiety, depression, guilt, and frustration increased reliably only among those who interacted with disabled people the least (less than once per month). Those with more frequent interpersonal contact with disabled people did *not* experience increased negative emotions. Furthermore, while both of our experimental simulations produced heightened feelings of empathetic warmth toward people with disabilities, afterwards participants felt more vulnerable to becoming disabled themselves. That is, simulations not only failed to improve attitudes about interacting with disabled people across both studies, in Study 2 disability attitudes worsened, and people expressed more interaction discomfort and more pity toward disabled people as a group. Finally, in terms of translating into positive behavioral intentions, our simulation activities did not lead to more willingness to interview disabled students for a campus accessibility project (Nario-Redmond et al. 2017).

Disability Simulation Critiques In recent years, disability simulations have come under increasing scrutiny (Lalvani and Broderick 2013; Valle and Connor 2011). Criticisms emphasize that such portrayals of disability are inauthentic and misinform those required to perform them (Asch and McCarthy 2003). Disability simulations misattribute the source of disadvantage to individual impairments and personal deficits while ignoring environmental barriers and policies that discriminate against certain types of minds and bodies (Scullion 1996). Simulations focus almost exclusively on what a newly acquired impairment might be like – even though people realize they are playing a role that is neither real nor permanent (French 1996). Temporary simulations simply do not account for the diverse coping mechanisms that come from living long-term with a disability (Wright 1980). Instead they emphasize the absence of familiar embodiment (Wilson and Alcorn 1969). For example, people who have grown up Deaf have learned many creative ways to navigate without sound using other sensory cues and sign language. This is not something that can be simulated in a few minutes of having one's ears plugged, and demonstrates an ableist perspective that focuses on personal loss rather than the lived experience in a discriminatory world.

Disability simulations not only distort the reality of disability but reproduce stereotypes related to incompetence and dependency (Nario-Redmond 2010), especially when focused on personal limitations. Consistent with this idea, Silverman et al. (2015) found that those who participated in a blindness simulation judged blind people as less capable of working and living independently compared to non-simulating controls. Blindness simulators also anticipated that their own lives would remain limited – even after three years of imagined future blindness. In general, people are simply not very good at predicting how they will adjust to differing life circumstances (Riis et al. 2005). Disability simulations can also lead people to self-stereotype, as they report feeling more helpless and less competent after participating in simulations than before (Nario-Redmond et al. 2017).

To summarize, most disability simulations to date focus on how physical, learning, and psychiatric conditions affect individual functioning instead of making salient the socially created obstacles, inaccessible spaces, and practices that systematically exclude (but see Barney 2012; Pivik et al. 2002). Despite these shortcomings, simulations have sparked much interest in the topic of disability. While producing inconsistent results, simulation games may persist because they spark conversation or increase tolerance for ambiguity (Bredemeier and Greenblat 1981). People may also enjoy simulations because they fulfill their curiosity with a token experience of temporary distress that once relieved may instigate a sense of gratitude for current abilities. However, as demonstrated in the perspective-taking literature, imagining oneself in the position of a stigmatized other can produce distress and self-stereotyping when the self–other divide becomes blurred, or the situation is threatening (Batson et al. 1997a; Galinsky et al. 2008). Disability is a permeable group membership that anyone can join, and many will, at least temporarily. If simulating impairments heightens one's perceived vulnerability to disability – not to mention perceived helplessness and incompetence – feelings of alarm and a desire to avoid may follow. Evidence now exists for all of these reactions: emotional distress, the taking on of disability stereotypes, increased interaction discomfort, and little interest in working to improve environmental access (Nario-Redmond et al. 2017). When simulating impairments, people are not taking the perspective of a disabled person as much as they are imagining themselves as having a new disability. Under these imagine-self conditions, more self-oriented empathy and egotistical concerns trigger personal distress (Batson 2010). Given that the self-focused experience of simulating disability does not seem to encourage support for more equitable outcomes, future research should examine how shifting the focus to the discriminatory aspects of society might alter these results (Cairns and Nario-Redmond 2017). Research could also examine how perceptions of environmental accessibility depend on whether resources are presented as constrained (funds are limited or allocated only to exclusive groups) or unconstrained (accommodations are universal or not at the expense of others). One of the pioneers of rehabilitation psychology, Beatrice Wright (1980) warned that experiences that promote fear, aversion, and guilt often fail to contribute to constructive perspectives about disability. Evidence indicates that disability simulations are producing these exact outcomes.

Summarizing and Comparing Prejudice-Reduction Interventions

Lessons from the literatures reviewed in this chapter highlight a few key conclusions. Contact with other groups is vital to an expanded worldview that recognizes the complexity and humanity of unfamiliar others; however, interactions are most effective at reducing prejudice when on equal terms, cooperatively structured, supported, and extended over time. Meaningful contact enhances our knowledge base of intergroup similarities and differences – both of which are important to appreciate. Pretending to be colorblind when ongoing disparities persist is disingenuous to the varied experiences of the many cultural groups that co-exist across societies, which we don't have to appropriate or simulate in order to acknowledge. Multicultural approaches that are inclusive of majority and minority identities and values are also quite promising, particularly as societies are becoming more diverse. Although threatening to some, the ability to listen to others' perspectives, to cultivate empathetic concern for another's well-being, is far more effective at reducing prejudice and increasing prosocial behaviors when egocentric concerns are not competing. It may be difficult to maintain a sense of personal agency or self-protective boundaries when empathizing with others' pain as we are social creatures that need to connect, relate, and express curiosity about the unfamiliar. However, we don't have to personally mimic others' identities to bear witness to their circumstances. Specifically, disability, age, and other embodied simulations have unintended consequences that misrepresent others' lives instead of increasing respect and understanding; perhaps future research will investigate how to better harness role-playing activities in ways that draw attention to the social and environmental factors that foster ongoing inequalities.

Very few studies have attempted to compare the relative effectiveness of the interventions and strategies designed to reduce prejudice. One exception, however, is a recent investigation that compared 17 distinct interventions with a sample of over 17 000 people using techniques designed to control for differences in setting, samples, and procedures (Lai et al. 2014). Using a contest approach, researchers invited teams to submit prejudice-reduction interventions that targeted implicit racial preferences of the White majority. Their meta-analytic findings revealed that among the most reliably effective interventions were *not* those that attempted to induce emotions, train people to feel empathy through perspective taking, or create a common human identity. Instead, the most potent interventions were those that exposed participants to vivid counter-stereotypical examples of ethnic minorities, followed by those that repeatedly associated positive information with this outgroup, and those that primed a multicultural mindset. A separate comparative study found that exposure to multicultural beliefs strengthens motivation to engage in intergroup perspective taking, and reciprocally, taking another group's perspective also increases positivity toward multiculturalism (Todd and Galinsky 2012).

Consistent with multicultural approaches that recognize both commonalities and differences between groups, interventions that facilitate positive experiences with outgroups in isolation may be less effective than those that recognize some negativity (or unearned privileges) associated with the ingroup. For example, a future study might compare the effectiveness of engaging meaningfully with disabled students, artists, and professionals who are highly inconsistent with stereotypical expectations in the same context as nondisabled people who reveal their own group incongruities, biases, or other limitations.

More large-scale comparative studies are critical to differentiating the relative usefulness of anti-prejudice interventions. It is also important to recognize that the effectiveness of interventions to reduce racism may not fully generalize to other groups like disabled people for whom different sources of prejudice may operate in distinct ways. Still, the few comparative studies that have been conducted all converge to conclude that the most effective interventions are those that incorporate multiple strategies and mechanisms for change.

In his concluding chapter on reducing prejudice, Rupert Brown, the author of *Prejudice: It's Social Psychology*, notes: "It would be foolish to pretend that any one academic discipline has a monopoly on wisdom when it comes to unravelling a phenomenon as complex and as deeply enmeshed in historical, economic and political forces as is prejudice. Indeed, it is my view that it is quite likely that the world's long-standing conflicts and their associated prejudices will first require some radical socio-political transformation before any intergroup contact, be it direct or extended, is even remotely conceivable" (2011, p. 279).

The final chapter of this volume is devoted to sharing some of the lessons learned on the radical socio-political transformation that has emerged since the inception of the disability rights movement – work that draws attention to the recognition of discrimination as intergroup injustice, and the impact of individual and collective actions that challenge the status quo.

Note

1 Most of the samples in this meta-analysis focused on interracial contact interventions (N = 362 samples), followed by samples of contact with physically disabled (N = 93), psychiatric (N = 66), elderly (N = 54), LGBT (N = 42), and cognitive impairment (N = 40) groups.

References

Allport, G.W. (1954). *The Nature of Prejudice*. Cambridge, MA: Addison-Wesley.

Anastasiou, D., Kauffman, J.M., and Michail, D. (2016). Disability in multicultural theory: conceptual and social justice issues. *Journal of Disability Policy Studies* 27 (1): 3–12.

Ando, S., Clement, S., Barley, E.A., and Thornicroft, G. (2011). The simulation of hallucinations to reduce the stigma of schizophrenia: a systematic review. *Schizophrenia Research* 133 (1): 8–16.

Apfelbaum, E.P., Pauker, K., Ambady, N. et al. (2008). Learning (not) to talk about race: when older children underperform in social categorization. *Developmental Psychology* 44 (5): 1513–1518.

Apfelbaum, E.P., Pauker, K., Sommers, S.R., and Ambady, N. (2010). In blind pursuit of racial equality? *Psychological Science* 21 (11): 1587–1592.

Armstrong, B., Johnson, D.W., and Balow, B. (1981). Effects of cooperative vs individualistic learning experiences on interpersonal attraction between learning-disabled and normal-progress elementary school students. *Contemporary Educational Psychology* 6 (2): 102–109.

Armstrong, M., Morris, C., Abraham, C., and Tarrant, M. (2017). Interventions utilizing contact with people with disabilities to improve children's attitudes toward disability: a systematic review and meta-analysis. *Disability Health Journal* 10 (1): 11–22.

Asch, A. and McCarthy, H. (2003). Infusing disability issues into the psychology curriculum. In: *Teaching Gender and Multicultural Awareness: Resources for the Psychology Classroom* (ed. P. Bronstein and K. Quina), 253–269. Washington, DC: American Psychological Association.

Barney, K.W. (2012). Disability simulations: using the social model of disability to update an experiential educational practice. *SCHOLE: A Journal of Leisure Studies and Recreation Education* 27 (1): 1–11.

Batson, C.D. (2010). Empathy-induced altruistic motivation. In: *Prosocial Motives, Emotions, and Behavior: The Better Angels of Our Nature* (ed. M.E. Mikulincer and P.R. Shaver), 15–34. Washington, DC: American Psychological Association.

Batson, C.D., Early, S., and Salvarani, G. (1997a). Perspective taking: imagining how another feels versus imagining how you would feel. *Personality and Social Psychology Bulletin* 23 (7): 751–758.

Batson, C.D., Polycarpou, M.P., Harmon-Jones, E. et al. (1997b). Empathy and attitudes: can feeling for a member of a stigmatized group improve feelings toward the group? *Journal of Personality and Social Psychology* 72 (1): 105–118.

Batson, C.D., Lishner, D.A., Carpenter, A., and Sampat, B. (2003). "…As you would have them do unto you": does imagining yourself in other's place stimulate moral action? *Personality and Social Psychology Bulletin* 29 (9): 1190–1201.

Becker, J.C., Zawadzki, M.J., and Shields, S.A. (2014). Confronting and reducing sexism: a call for research intervention. *Journal of Social Issues* 70 (4): 603–614.

Bekkers, R. (2010). Who gives what and when? A scenario study of intentions to give time and money. *Social Science Research* 39 (3): 369–381.

Berry, J.W. (1984). Multicultural policy in Canada: a social psychological analysis. *Canadian Journal of Behavioral Science* 16 (4): 353–370.

Blanchard, F.A., Weigel, R.H., and Cook, S.W. (1975). The effect of relative competence of group members upon interpersonal attraction in cooperating interracial groups. *Journal of Personality and Social Psychology* 32 (3): 519–530.

Blaser, A. (2003). Awareness days: some alternatives to simulation exercises. *Ragged Edge Online* (September/October). http://www.raggededgemagazine.com/0903/0903ft1.html (accessed 22 February 2019).

Blatt, B., LeLacheur, S., Galinsky, A.D. et al. (2010). Does perspective-taking increase patient satisfaction in medical encounters? *Academic Medicine* 85 (9): 1445–1452.

Boisjoly, J., Duncan, G.J., Kremer, M. et al. (2006). Empathy or antipathy? The impact of diversity. *American Economic Review* 96 (5): 1890–1905.

Branscombe, N.R., Schmitt, M.T., and Harvey, R.D. (1999). Perceiving pervasive discrimination among African Americans: implications for group identification and well-being. *Journal of Personality and Social Psychology* 77 (1): 135–149.

Bredemeier, M.E. and Greenblat, C.S. (1981). The educational effectiveness of simulation games: a synthesis of findings. *Simulation & Gaming* 12 (3): 307–332.

Brewer, M.B. and Gaertner, S.L. (2001). Toward the reduction of prejudice: intergroup contact and social categorization. In: *Blackwell Handbook of Social Psychology: Intergroup Processes* (ed. R. Brown and S.L. Gaertner), 451–474. Oxford: Blackwell.

Brew-Parrish, V. (2004). The wrong message – still. *Ragged Edge Online* (9 August). http://www.raggededgemagazine.com/focus/wrongmessage04.html (accessed 22 February 2019).

Brophy, I.N. (1946). The luxury of anti-negro prejudice. *Public Opinion Quarterly* 9 (4): 456–466.

Brown, R. (2011). *Prejudice: Its Social Psychology*. Malden, MA: Wiley Blackwell.

Brown, K. (2016). Disabled people of color struggle to be heard. The Establishment. Retrieved from: https://medium.com/the-establishment/disabled-people-of-color-struggle-to-be-heard-b6c7ea5af4b4 (accessed 1 March, 2019).

Brown, R. and Hewstone, M. (2005). An integrative theory of intergroup contact. *Advances in Experimental Social Psychology* 37: 255–343.

Brown, S.A., Evans, Y., Espenschade, K., and O'Connor, M. (2010). An examination of two brief stigma reduction strategies: filmed personal contact and hallucination simulations. *Community Mental Health Journal* 46 (5): 494–499.

Bruneau, E.G. and Saxe, R.R. (2012). The power of being heard: the benefits of "perspective giving" in the context of intergroup conflict. *Journal of Experimental Psychology* 48 (4): 855–866.

Bruneau, E.G., Kteily, N., and Laustsen, L. (2018). The unique effects of blatant dehumanization on attitudes and behavior towards Muslim refugees during the European "refugee crisis" across four countries. *European Journal of Social Psychology* 48 (5): 645–662.

Bunn, W. and Terpstra, J. (2009). Cultivating empathy for the mentally ill using simulated auditory hallucinations. *Academic Psychiatry* 33 (6): 457–460.

Burgstahler, S.E. (2015). *Universal Design in Higher Education: From Principles to Practice*, 2e. Cambridge, MA: Harvard Education Press.

Burgstahler, S.E. and Doe, T. (2004). Disability-related simulations: if, when, and how to use them in professional development. *Review of Disability Studies: An International Journal* 1 (2): 8–18.

Cairns, Z., and Nario-Redmond, M. R. (2017). Enhancing support for social change in advantaged groups using disability simulations. Undergraduate thesis. Hiram College.

Cameron, L. and Rutland, A. (2006). Extended contact through story reading in school: reducing children's prejudice toward the disabled. *Journal of Social Issues* 62 (3): 469–488.

Cameron, L., Rutland, A., Turner, R. et al. (2011). "Changing attitudes with a little imagination": imagined contact effects on a young children's intergroup bias. *Annals of Psychology* 27 (3): 708–717.

Cialdini, R.B., Brown, S.L., Lewis, B.P. et al. (1997). Reinterpreting the empathy–altruism relationship: when one into one equals oneness. *Journal of Personality and Social Psychology* 73 (3): 481–494.

Clore, G.L. and Jeffery, K.M. (1972). Emotional role playing, attitude change, and attraction toward a disabled person. *Journal of Personality and Social Psychology* 23 (1): 105–111.

Clore, G.L., Bray, R.M., Itkin, S.M., and Murphy, P. (1978). Interracial attitudes and behavior at a summer camp. *Journal of Personality and Social Psychology* 36 (2): 107–116.

Cook, S.W. (1971). *The Effect of Unintended Interracial Contact Upon Racial Interaction and Attitude Change*. Washington DC: Education Resources in Information Center, US Department of Health, Education & Welfare.

Correll, J., Park, B., and Smith, J.A. (2008). Colorblind and multicultural prejudice reduction strategies in high-conflict situations. *Group Processes & Intergroup Relations* 11 (4): 471–491.

Corrigan, P.W., River, L.P., Lundin, R.K. et al. (2001). Three strategies for changing attributions about severe mental illness. *Schizophrenia Bulletin* 27 (2): 187–195.

Corrigan, P.W., Morris, S.B., Michaels, P.J. et al. (2012). Challenging the public stigma of mental illness: a meta-analysis of outcome studies. *Psychiatric Services* 63 (10): 963–973.

Couture, S. and Penn, D. (2003). Interpersonal contact and the stigma of mental illness: a review of the literature. *Journal of Mental Health* 12 (3): 291–305.

Crisp, R.J. and Hewstone, M. (1999). Differential evaluation of crossed category groups: patterns, processes, and reducing intergroup bias. *Group Processes & Intergroup Relations* 2 (4): 303–333.

Crisp, R.J., Stathi, S., Turner, R.N., and Husnu, S. (2009). Imagined intergroup contact: theory, paradigm and practice. *Social and Personality Psychology Compass* 3 (1): 1–18.

Cuff, B.M., Brown, S.J., Taylor, L., and Howat, D.J. (2016). Empathy: a review of the concept. *Emotion Review* 8 (2): 144–153.

Daníelsdóttir, S., O'Brien, K.S., and Ciao, A. (2010). Anti-fat prejudice reduction: a review of published studies. *Obesity Facts: The European Journal of Obesity* 3 (1): 47–58.

Davies, K., Tropp, L.R., Aron, A. et al. (2011). Cross-group friendships and intergroup attitudes: a meta-analytic review. *Personality and Social Psychology Review* 15 (4): 332–351.

Davis, M.H. and Begovic, E. (2014). Empathy-related interventions. In: *The Wiley Blackwell Handbook of Positive Psychological Interventions* (ed. A.C. Parks and S.M. Schueller), 111–134. Malden, MA: Wiley Blackwell.

Davis, M.H., Conklin, L., Smith, A., and Luce, C. (1996). Effect of perspective taking on the cognitive representation of persons: a merging of self and other. *Journal of Personality and Social Psychology* 70 (4): 713–726.

Dixon, J. and Levine, M. (2012). *Beyond Prejudice: Extending the Social Psychology of Conflict, Inequality and Social Change*. Cambridge: Cambridge University Press.

Dorn, D.S. (1989). Simulation games: one more tool on the pedagogical shelf. *Teaching Sociology* 17 (1): 1–18.

Dovidio, J.F., Gaertner, S.L., and Saguy, T. (2009). Commonality and the complexity of "we": social attitudes and social change. *Personality and Social Psychology Review* 13 (1): 3–20.

Dovidio, J.F., Gaertner, S.L., Ufkes, E.G. et al. (2016). Included but invisible? Subtle bias, common identity and the darker side of "we.". *Social Issues and Policy Review* 10 (1): 6–46.

Drwecki, B.B., Moore, C.F., Ward, S.E., and Prkachin, K.M. (2011). Reducing racial disparities in pain treatment: the role of empathy and perspective taking. *Pain* 152 (5): 1001–1006.

Ehrke, F., Berthold, A., and Steffens, M.C. (2014). How diversity training can change attitudes: increasing perceived complexity of superordinate groups to improve intergroup relations. *Journal of Experimental Social Psychology* 53: 193–206.

Finlay, K.A. and Stephan, W.G. (2000). Improving intergroup relations: the effects of empathy on racial attitudes. *Journal of Applied Social Psychology* 30 (8): 1720–1737.

Flower, A., Burns, M.K., and Bottsford-Miller, N.A. (2007). Meta-analysis of disability simulation research. *Remedial and Special Education* 28 (2): 72–79.

French, S. (1996). Simulation exercises in disability awareness training: a critique. In: *Beyond Disability: Towards an Enabling Society* (ed. G. Hales), 114–123. Thousand Oaks, CA: Sage.

Gaertner, S.L. and Dovidio, J.F. (2000). *Reducing Intergroup Bias: The Common Intergroup Identity Model*. Philadelphia, PA: Psychology Press.

Galinsky, A.D. and Ku, G. (2004). The effects of perspective-taking prejudice: the moderating role of self-evaluation. *Personality and Social Psychology Bulletin* 30 (5): 594–604.

Galinsky, A.D. and Moskowitz, G.B. (2000). Perspective-taking: decreasing stereotype expression, stereotype accessibility, and in-group favoritism. *Journal of Personality and Social Psychology* 78 (4): 708–724.

Galinsky, A.D., Magee, J.C., Inesi, M.E., and Gruenfeld, D.H. (2006). Power and perspectives not taken. *Psychological Science* 17 (12): 1068–1074.

Galinsky, A.D., Wang, C.S., and Ku, G. (2008). Perspective-takers behave more stereotypically. *Journal of Personality and Social Psychology* 95 (2): 404–419.

Galletly, C. and Burton, C. (2011). Improving medical student attitudes towards people with schizophrenia. *Australian & New Zealand Journal of Psychiatry* 45 (6): 473–476.

Galli, G., Lenggenhager, B., Scivoltetto, G. et al. (2015). Don't look at my wheelchair! The plasticity of longlasting prejudice. *Medical Education* 49 (12): 1239–1247.

Garland-Thomson, R. (2012). New conversations in disability studies. *Disability Studies Quarterly* 32 (4): http://dsq-sds.org/article/view/3362/3183 (accessed 22 February 2019).

Gerard, H.B. and Miller, N. (1975). *School Desegregation: A Long-Range Study*. New York: Plenum Press.

Gill, C.J. (1994). Questioning continuum. In: *The Ragged Edge: The Disability Experience from the Pages of the First Fifteen Years of "The Disability Rag"* (ed. B. Shaw), 42–49. Louisville, KY: The Advocado Press.

Gilson, S.F. and Depoy, E. (2000). Multiculturalism and disability: a critical perspective. *Disability & Society* 15 (2): 207–218.

Goldberg, D.T. (1994). *Multiculturalism: A Critical Reader*. Malden, MA: Blackwell.

Goldstein, N.J., Vezich, S., and Shapiro, J.R. (2014). Perceived perspective taking: when others walk in our shoes. *Journal of Personality and Social Psychology* 106 (6): 941–960.

Goodman, H., Gottlieb, J., and Harrison, R. (1972). Social acceptance of EMRs integrated into a nongraded elementary school. *American Journal of Mental Deficiency* 76 (4): 412–417.

Griffin, J.H. (1961). *Black Like Me*. Boston, MA: Houghton Mifflin.

Guimond, S., Crisp, R.J., De Oliveira, P. et al. (2013). Diversity policy, social dominance, and intergroup relations: predicting prejudice in changing social and political contexts. *Journal of Personality and Social Psychology* 104 (6): 941–958.

Gutierrez, A.S. and Unzueta, M.M. (2010). The effect of interethnic ideologies on the likability of stereotypic vs. counterstereotypic minority targets. *Journal of Experimental Social Psychology* 46 (5): 775–784.

Hachfeld, A., Hahn, A., Schroeder, S. et al. (2015). Should teachers be colorblind? How multicultural and egalitarian beliefs differentially relate to aspects of teachers' professional competence for teaching in diverse classrooms. *Teaching and Teaching Education* 48: 44–55.

Harper, D.C. and Wacker, D.P. (1985). Children's attitudes toward disabled peers and the effects of mainstreaming. *Academic Psychology Bulletin* 7: 87–98.

Hean, S. and Dickinson, C. (2005). The Contact Hypothesis: an exploration of its further potential in interprofessional education. *Journal of Interprofessional Care* 19 (5): 480–491.

Hebl, M.E. and Kleck, R.E. (2000). The social consequences of physical disability. In: *The Social Psychology of Stigma* (ed. T.F. Heatherton, R.E. Kleck, M. Hebl and J. Hull), 419–436. New York: Guilford Press.

Hewstone, M., Rubin, M., and Willis, H. (2002). Intergroup bias. *Annual Review of Psychology* 53: 575–604.

Hill, M.E. and Augustinos, M. (2001). Stereotype change and prejudice reduction: short- and long-term evaluation of a cross-cultural awareness programme. *Journal of Community & Applied Social Psychology* 11 (4): 243–262.

Holoien, D.S. and Shelton, J. (2012). You deplete me: the cognitive costs of colorblindness on ethnic minorities. *Journal of Experimental Social Psychology* 48 (2): 562–565.

Hornsey, M.J. and Hogg, M.A. (2000). Assimilation and diversity: an integrative model of subgroup relations. *Personality and Social Psychology Review* 4 (2): 143–156.

Houlette, M., Gaertner, S.L., Johnson, K.M. et al. (2004). Developing a more inclusive social identity: an elementary school intervention. *Journal of Social Issues* 60 (1): 35–56.

Hung, I.W. and Wyer, R.S. (2009). Differences in perspective and the influence of charitable appeals: when imagining oneself as the victim is not beneficial. *Journal of Marketing Research* 26 (3): 421–234.

Husnu, S. and Crisp, R.J. (2010). Elaboration enhances the imagined contact effect. *Journal of Experimental Social Psychology* 46 (6): 943–950.

Iano, R., Ayers, D., Heller, H. et al. (1974). Sociometric status of retarded children in an integrated program. *Exceptional Children* 40 (1): 267–271.

Karafantis, D.M., Pierre-Louis, J., and Lewandowski, G.W. (2010). A comparison of the multicultural and colorblind perspectives on the intergroup attitudes of college students. *Journal of Human Behavior in the Social Environment* 20 (5): 688–710.

Kessler Foundation. (2015). National Employment and Disability Survey: Report of Main Findings. https://kesslerfoundation.org/kfsurvey15 (accessed 22 February 2019).

Kiger, G. (1992). Disability simulations: logical, methodological and ethical issues. *Disability, Handicap & Society* 7 (1): 71–78.

Kittson, K., Gainforth, H.L., Edwards, J. et al. (2013). The effect of video observation on warmth and competence ratings of individuals with a disability. *Psychology of Sport and Exercise* 14 (6): 847–851.

Kraus, L. (2017). *2016 Disability Statistics Annual Report*. Durham, NH: University of New Hampshire.

LaBelle, S., Booth-Butterfield, M., and Rittenour, C.E. (2013). Attitudes towards profoundly hearing impaired and deaf individuals: links with intergroup anxiety, social dominance orientation, and contact. *Western Journal of Communication* 77 (4): 489–506.

Ladau, E. (2016). The Mighty question: who should speak for the disability community? Words I Wheel By. http://wordsiwheelby.com/2016/01/the-mighty-question (accessed 22 Feburary 2019).

Lai, C.K., Marini, M., Lehr, S.A. et al. (2014). Reducing implicit racial preferences: II. Intervention effectiveness across time. *Journal of Experimental Psychology: General* 143 (4): 1765–1785.

Lalvani, P. and Broderick, A.A. (2013). Institutionalized ableism and the misguided "Disability Awareness Day": transformative pedagogies for teacher education. *Equity & Excellence in Education* 46 (4): 468–483.

Lamm, N. (2015). This is disability justice. The Body Is Not an Apology. https://thebodyisnotanapology.com/magazine/this-is-disability-justice (accessed 22 February 2019).

Lawson, J. (2001). Disability as a cultural identity. *International Studies in Sociology of Education* 11 (3): 201–222.

Leonardelli, G.J., Pickett, C.L., and Brewer, M.B. (2010). Optimal distinctiveness theory: a framework for social identity, social cognition, and intergroup relations. *Advances in Experimental Social Psychology* 43: 63–113.

Levin, S., van Laar, C., and Sidanius, J. (2003). The effects of ingroup and outgroup friendships on ethnic attitudes in college: a longitudinal study. *Group Processes & Intergroup Relations* 6 (1): 76–92.

Lindsay, S. and Edwards, A. (2013). A systematic review of disability interventions for children and youth. *Disability and Rehabilitation* 35 (8): 623–646.

Lopez, G.E. (2004). Interethnic contact, curriculum, and attitudes in the first year of college. *Journal of Social Issues* 60 (1): 75–94.

Mackelprang, R.W. and Salsgiver, R.O. (1999). *Disability: A Diversity Model Approach in Human Service Practice*. Pacific Grover, CA: Brooks/Cole.

MacMillan, M., Tarrant, M., Abraham, C., and Morris, C. (2014). The association between children's contact with people with disabilities and their attitudes towards disability: a systematic review. *Developmental Medicine & Child Neurology* 56 (6): 529–546.

Maras, P. and Brown, R. (1996). Effects of contact on children's attitudes toward disability: a longitudinal study. *Journal of Applied Social Psychology* 26 (23): 2113–2134.

Matteo, E.K. and You, D. (2012). Reducing mental illness stigma in the classroom. *Teaching of Psychology* 39 (2): 121–124.

McGlensey, M. (2016). 11 people with autism explain what stimming feels like. The Mighty. https://themighty.com/2016/01/what-stimming-feels-like-for-people-with-autism/ (accessed 1 March, 2019).

Miller, N. (2002). Personalization and promise of contact theory. *Journal of Social Issues* 58 (2): 387–410.

Molina, L.E. and Wittig, M.A. (2006). Relative importance of contact conditions in explaining prejudice reduction in a classroom context: separate but equal? *Journal of Social Issues* 62 (3): 489–509.

Monteith, M.J., Sherman, J.W., and Devine, P.G. (1998). Suppression as a stereotype control strategy. *Personality and Social Psychology Review* 2 (1): 63–82.

Morrison, K.R. and Chung, A.H. (2011). "White" or "European American"? Self-identifying labels influence majority group members' interethnic attitudes. *Journal of Experimental Social Psychology* 47 (1): 165–170.

Morrison, K.R., Plaut, V.C., and Ybarra, O. (2010). Predicting whether multiculturalism positively or negatively influences white Americans' intergroup attitudes: the role of ethnic identification. *Personality and Social Psychology Bulletin* 36 (12): 1628–1661.

Myers, M.W., Laurent, S.M., and Hodges, S.D. (2014). Perspective taking instructions and self-other overlap: different motives for helping. *Motivation and Emotions* 38 (2): 224–234.

Naor, M. and Milgram, R.M. (1980). Two preservice strategies for preparing regular class teachers for mainstreaming. *Exceptional Children* 47 (2): 126–129.

Nario-Redmond, M.R. (2010). Cultural stereotypes of disabled and non-disabled men and women: consensus for global category representations and diagnostic domains. *British Journal of Social Psychology* 49 (3): 471–488.

Nario-Redmond, M.R., Gospondinov, D., and Cobb, A. (2017). Crip for a day: the unintended negative consequences of disability simulations. *Rehabilitation Psychology* 62 (3): 324–333.

Neville, H.A., Awad, G.H., Brooks, J.E. et al. (2013). Colorblind racial ideology: theory, training, and measurement implications in psychology. *American Psychologist* 68 (6): 455–466.

Nier, J.A., Gaertner, S.L., Dovidio, J.F. et al. (2001). Changing interracial evaluations and behavior: the effects of a common group identity. *Group Processes & Intergroup Relations* 4 (4): 299–316.

Norton, M.I., Sommers, S.R., Apfelbaum, E.P. et al. (2006). Color blindness and interracial interaction: playing the political correctness game. *Psychological Science* 17 (1): 949–953.

Pacala, J.T., Boult, C., and Hepburn, K. (2006). Ten years' experience conducting the Aging Game workshop: was it worth it? *Journal of the American Geriatrics Society* 54 (1): 144–149.

Paluck, E.L. (2006). Diversity training and intergroup contact: a call to action research. *Journal of Social Issues* 62 (3): 577–595.

Paluck, E.L. (2010). Peer pressure against prejudice: a high school field experiment examining social network change. *Journal of Experimental Social Psychology* 47 (2): 350–358.

Paluck, E.L. and Green, D.P. (2009). Prejudice reduction: what works? A review and assessment of research and practice. *Annual Review of Psychology* 60: 339–367.

Patterson, J.B. and Witten, B.J. (1987). Disabling language and attitudes toward persons with disabilities. *Rehabilitation Psychology* 32 (4): 245–248.

Pendry, L.F., Driscoll, D.M., and Field, S.C. (2007). Diversity training: putting theory into practice. *Journal of Occupational and Organizational Psychology* 80 (1): 27–50.

Penner, L.A. (2002). Dispositional and organizational influences on sustained volunteerism: an interactionist perspective. *Journal of Social Issues* 58 (3): 447–467.

Pettigrew, T.F. (1971). Attitudes on race and housing: a social psychological view. In: *Segregation in Residential Areas: Papers on Racial and Socioeconomic Factors in Choice of Housing*, vol. 4 (ed. H. Hawley and V.P. Rock), 21–84. Washington, DC: National Academies Press.

Pettigrew, T.F. (1998). Intergroup contact theory. *Annual Review of Psychology* 49: 65–85.

Pettigrew, T.F. and Tropp, L.R. (2006). A meta-analytic test of intergroup contact theory. *Journal of Personality and Social Psychology* 90 (5): 751–783.

Pettigrew, T.F. and Tropp, L.R. (2008). How does intergroup contact reduce prejudice? Meta-analytic tests of three mediators. *European Journal of Social Psychology* 38 (6): 922–934.

Pfafferott, I. and Brown, R. (2006). Acculturation preferences of majority and minority adolescents in Germany in the context of society and family. *International Journal of Intercultural Relations* 30 (6): 703–717.

Pierce, J., Kilduff, G.J., Galinsky, A.D., and Sivanathan, N. (2013). From glue to gasoline: how competition turns perspective takers unethical. *Psychological Science* 24 (10): 1986–1994.

Pivik, J., McComas, J., Macfarlane, I., and Laflamme, M. (2002). Using virtual reality to teach disability awareness. *Journal of Educational Computing Research* 26 (2): 203–218.

Plaut, V.C., Thomas, K., and Goren, M. (2009). Is multiculturalism or color blindness better for minorities? *Psychological Science* 20 (4): 444–446.

Ramasubramanian, S. (2015). Using celebrity news stories to effectively reduce racial/ ethnic prejudice. *Journal of Social Issues* 71 (1): 123–138.

Rattan, A. and Ambady, N. (2013). Diversity ideologies and intergroup relations: an examination of colorblindness and multiculturalism. *European Journal of Social Psychology* 43 (1): 12–21.

Reingle-Gonzalez, J.M., Cannell, M.B., Jetelina, K.K., and Froehlich-Grobe, K. (2016). Disproportionate prevalence rate of prisoners with disabilities: evidence from a nationally representative sample. *Journal of Disability Policy Studies* 27 (2): 106–115.

Richeson, J.A. and Nussbaum, R.J. (2004). The impact of multiculturalism versus colorblindness on racial bias. *Journal of Experimental Social Psychology* 40 (3): 417–423.

Riis, J., Loewenstein, G., Baron, J. et al. (2005). Ignorance of hedonic adaptation to hemodialysis: a study using ecological momentary assessment. *Journal of Experimental Psychology: General* 134 (1): 3–9.

Roberts, K.D., Park, H.J., Brown, S., and Cook, B. (2011). Universal design for instruction in postsecondary education: a systematic review of empirically based articles. *Journal of Postsecondary Education and Disability* 24 (1): 5–15.

Rodriguez, A.I., Heldreth, C.M., and Tomiyama, A.J. (2016). Putting on weight stigma: a randomized study of the effects of wearing a fat suit on eating, well-being, and cortisol. *Obesity* 24 (9): 1892–1898.

Rosenthal, L. and Levy, S.R. (2010). The colorblind, multicultural, and polycultural ideological approaches to improving intergroup attitudes and relations. *Social Issues and Policy Review* 4 (1): 215–246.

Roseth, C.J., Johnson, D.W., and Johnson, R.T. (2008). Promoting early adolescents' achievement and peer relationships: the effects of cooperative, competitive, and individualistic goal structures. *Psychological Bulletin* 134 (2): 223–246.

Rothbart, M. and John, O.P. (1985). Social categorization and behavioral episodes: a cognitive analysis of the effects of intergroup contact. *Journal of Social Issues* 41 (3): 81–104.

Rowland, M., Peterson-Besse, J., Dobbertin, K. et al. (2014). Health outcome disparities among subgroups of people with disabilities: a scoping review. *Disability and Health Journal* 7 (2): 136–150.

Runswick-Cole, K. (2014). "Us" and "them": the limits and possibilities of a "politics of neurodiversity" in neoliberal times. *Disability & Society* 29 (7): 1117–1129.

Ryan, C.S., Hunt, J.S., Weible, J.A. et al. (2007). Multicultural and colorblind ideology, stereotypes, and ethnocentrism among Black and White Americans. *Group Processes & Intergroup Relations* 10 (4): 617–637.

Sasaki, S.J. and Vorauer, J.D. (2013). Ignoring versus exploring differences between groups: effects of salient color-blindness and multiculturalism on intergroup attitudes and behavior. *Social and Personality Psychology Compass* 7 (4): 246–259.

Schlesinger, A.M. (1992). *The Disuniting of America: Reflections on a Multicultural Society*. New York: Norton.

Schofield, J.W. (1979). The impact of positively structured contact on intergroup behavior: does it last under adverse conditions? *Social Psychology Quarterly* 42 (3): 280–284.

Schofield, J.W. and Eurich-Fulcer, R. (2001). When and how school desegregation improves intergroup relations. In: *Blackwell Handbook of Social Psychology* (ed. R. Brown and S. Gaertner), 475–494. Malden, MA: Blackwell.

Schriner, K. and Scotch, R.K. (2001). Disability and institutional change: a human variation perspective on overcoming oppression. *Journal of Disability Policy Studies* 12 (2): 100–106.

Scullion, P. (1996). "Quasidisabilty" experiences using simulation. *British Journal of Therapy and Rehabilitation* 3 (9): 498–502.

Seewooruttun, L. and Scior, K. (2014). Interventions aimed at increasing the knowledge and improving attitudes towards people with intellectual disabilities among lay people. *Research in Developmental Disabilities* 35 (12): 3482–3495.

Shaver, J.P., Curtis, C.K., Jesunthadas, J., and Strong, C.J. (1989). The modification of attitudes toward persons with disabilities: is there a best way? *International Journal of Special Education* 4 (1): 33–57.

Shih, M., Wang, E., Trahan Bucher, A., and Stotzer, R. (2009). Perspective taking: reducing prejudice towards general outgroups and specific individuals. *Group Processes & Intergroup Relations* 12 (5): 565–577.

Sibicky, M.E., Schroeder, D.A., and Dovidio, J.F. (1995). Empathy and helping: considering the consequences of intervention. *Basic and Applied Social Psychology* 16 (4): 435–453.

Silverman, A.M., Gwinn, J.D., and Van Boven, L. (2015). Stumbling in their shoes: disability simulations reduce judged capabilities of disabled people. *Social Psychological and Personality Science* 6 (4): 464–471.

Siperstein, G.N., Norins, J., and Mohler, A. (2007). Social acceptance and attitude change. In: *Handbook of Intellectual and Developmental Disabilities* (ed. J.W. Jacobson, J.A. Mulick and J. Rojahn). Boston, MA: Springer.

Skorinko, J.L. and Sinclair, S.A. (2013). Perspective taking can increase stereotyping: the role of apparent stereotype confirmation. *Journal of Experimental Social Psychology* 49 (1): 10–18.

Slavin, R.E. (1983). When does cooperative learning increase student achievement? *Psychological Bulletin* 94 (3): 429–445.

Smith, S. E. (2017). How to make your social justice events accessible to the disability community. Rooted in Rights. https://rootedinrights.org/how-to-make-your-social-justice-events-accessible-to-the-disability-community-a-checklist/ (accessed 1 March, 2019).

Smith, E.R. and Zarate, M.A. (1992). Exemplar-based model of social judgement. *Psychological Review* 99 (1): 3–21.

Snow, K. (2001). *Disability Is Natural: Revolutionary Common Sense for Raising Successful Children with Disabilities*. Woodland Park, CO: Braveheart Press.

Stathi, S., Tsantila, K., and Crisp, R.J. (2012). Imagined intergroup contact can combat mental health stigma by reducing anxiety, avoidance and negative stereotyping. *The Journal of Social Psychology* 152 (6): 746–757.

Stephan, W.G. and Stephan, C.W. (1985). Intergroup anxiety. *Journal of Social Issues* 41 (3): 157–175.

Stiker, H.J. (1999). *A History of Disability*. Ann Arbor, MI: University of Michigan Press.

Tarrant, M., Calitri, R., and Weston, D. (2012). Social identification structures the effects of perspective taking. *Psychological Science* 23 (9): 973–978.

Thompson, V. (2016). Black Disabled Woman Syllabus. Ramp Your Voice! http://rampyourvoice.com/2016/05/05/black-disabled-woman-syllabus-compilation/ (accessed 1 March, 2019).

Todd, A.R. and Galinsky, A.D. (2012). The reciprocal link between multiculturalism and perspective-taking: how ideological and self-regulatory approaches to manage diversity reinforce each other. *Journal of Experimental Social Psychology* 48 (6): 1394–1398.

Todd, A.R. and Galinsky, A.D. (2014). Perspective-taking as a strategy for improving intergroup relations: evidence, mechanisms and qualifications. *Social and Personality Psychology Compass* 8 (7): 347–387.

Todd, A.R., Bodenhausen, G.V., Richeson, J.A., and Galinsky, A.D. (2011). Perspective taking combats automatic expressions of racial bias. *Journal of Personality and Social Psychology* 100 (6): 1027–1042.

Todd, A.R., Bodenhausen, G.V., and Galinsky, A.D. (2012). Perspective taking combats the denial of intergroup discrimination. *Journal of Experimental Social Psychology* 48 (3): 738–745.

Tropp, L.R. and Pettigrew, T.F. (2005). Relationships between intergroup contact and prejudice among minority and majority status groups. *Psychological Science* 16 (12): 951–957.

Turner, J.C. and Reynolds, K.J. (2001). The social identity perspective in intergroup relations: theories, themes, and controversies. In: *Blackwell Handbook of Social Psychology: Intergroup Relation* (ed. R. Brown and S. Gaertner), 133–152. Malden, MA: Blackwell.

Turner, R.N. and West, K. (2012). Behavioral consequences of imagined intergroup contact with stigmatized outgroups. *Group Processes & Intergroup Relations* 15 (2): 193–202.

Tynes, B.M. and Markoe, S.L. (2010). The role of color-blind racial attitudes in reactions to racial discrimination on social network sites. *Journal of Diversity in Higher Education* 3 (1): 1–13.

Valle, J.W. and Connor, D.J. (2011). *Rethinking Disability: A Disability Studies Approach to Inclusive Practices*. New York: McGraw-Hill.

Verkuyten, M. (2009). Support for multiculturalism and minority rights: the role of national identification and outgroup threat. *Social Justice Research* 22 (1): 31–52.

Verkuyten, M. (2011). Assimilation ideology and outgroup attitudes among ethnic majority members. *Group Processes & Intergroup Relations* 14 (6): 789–806.

Vescio, T.K., Judd, C.M., and Kwan, V.S.Y. (2004). The crossed-categorization hypothesis: evidence of reductions in the strength of categorization, but not intergroup bias. *Journal of Experimental Social Psychology* 40 (4): 478–496.

Vezzali, L. and Capozza, D. (2011). Reducing explicit and implicit prejudice toward disabled colleagues: effects of contact and membership salience in the workplace. *Life Span and Disability* 14 (2): 139–162.

Wadlington, E., Elliot, C., and Kirylo, J. (2008). The dyslexia simulation: impact and implications. *Literacy Research and Instruction* 47 (4): 264–272.

Walzer, M. (1994). Multiculturalism and individualism. *Dissent* 41: 185–191.

Wang, C.S., Kenneth, T., Ku, G., and Galinsky, A.D. (2014). Perspective-taking increases willingness to engage in intergroup contact. *PLoS One* 9 (1): e85681.

Wells, J. (2008). MINDSTORM: Experiencing the world of schizophrenia. CNBC (2 May). https://www.cnbc.com/id/24425378 (accessed 22 February 2019).

West, K., Holmes, E., and Hewstone, M. (2011). Enhancing imagined contact to reduce prejudice against people with schizophrenia. *Group Processes & Intergroup Relations* 14 (3): 407–428.

Wetherell, M. (2012). *Affect and Emotion: A New Social Science Understanding.* Los Angeles, CA: Sage.

Wilder, D.A. and Thompson, J.E. (1980). Intergroup contact with independent manipulations on in-group and out-group interaction. *Journal of Personality and Social Psychology* 38 (4): 589–603.

Wilner, D.M., Walkley, R.P., and Cook, S.W. (1952). Residential proximity and intergroup relations in public housing projects. *Journal of Social Issues* 8 (1): 45–69.

Wilson, E.D. and Alcorn, D. (1969). Disability simulation and development of attitudes toward the exceptional. *The Journal of Special Education* 3 (3): 303–307.

Wolsko, C., Park, B., Judd, C.M., and Wittenbrink, B. (2000). Framing interethnic ideology: effects of multicultural and color-blind perspectives on judgments of groups and individuals. *Journal of Personality and Social Psychology* 78 (4): 635–654.

Wright, B. (1980). Developing constructive views of life with a disability. *Rehabilitation Literature* 41 (11–12): 274–279.

Wright, S.C., Aron, A., McLaughlin-Volpe, T., and Ropp, S.A. (1997). The extended contact effect: knowledge of cross-group friendships and prejudice. *Journal of Personality and Social Psychology* 73 (1): 73–90.

Yeager, D.S., Purdie-Vaughns, V., Garcia, J. et al. (2013). Breaking the cycle of mistrust: wise interventions to provide critical feedback across the racial divide. *Journal of Experimental Psychology: General* 143 (2): 804–824.

Yuker, H.E. (1994). Variables that influence attitudes toward people with disabilities: conclusions from the data. *Journal of Social Behavior and Personality* 9 (5): 3–22.

Zaikowski, C. (2016). Six ways your social justice might be ableist. Everyday Feminism. https://everydayfeminism.com/2016/09/social-justice-activism-ableist/ (accessed 1 March, 2019).

Intersectional Identity and Inclusive Activism

Disabled people of color are underrepresented both within the disability rights movement and in the media. Disabled people of color also face barriers to health care and housing, and police violence; and disabled children of color are more likely to be expelled from school, and sent to juvenile detention. *Disability justice is about fighting against prejudice and advocating for disabled people of color and other minority groups.* Below are a few intersectional activism resources.

> "If your disability activism isn't inclusive, it isn't activism," Keah Brown (2016)

#GetWokeADA26 is a project led by Vilissa Thompson and Alice Wong that draws attention to how the Americans with Disabilities Act (ADA) fails to address issues faced by disabled people of color. **Learn more:** http://rampyourvoice.com/2016/07/26/getwokeada26-disabled-people-color-speak-part-1/

Sins Invalid, is a performance project led by disabled people of color that celebrates diverse abilities, queer, gender-variant artists, and other marginalized communities. **Learn more:** sinsinvalid.org

Black Disabled Woman Syllabus: A Compilation

Vilissa Thompson, LMSW, is a Black disability advocate and the creator of Ramp Your Voice, an online social justice platform. It offers many resources including the Black Disabled Woman Syllabus (Thompson 2016) – check this out to learn about feminism and Black disability experiences.

Reducing Prejudice: Alternatives to Simulations

As discussed in the chapter, simulations that claim to help people understand what it feels like to be disabled can promote ableism and harmful stereotypes. Here are some alternative ways to learn about disability:

Change Your Perspective

Rather than concentrating on someone's impairment as the source of a challenge, take a look at the surrounding circumstances. Navigating a city in a wheelchair would not be as difficult if sidewalks were well maintained and ramps were just as common as stairs. A visually impaired student would not need to request accommodations weeks in advance if academic institutions and curricula were required to adhere to accessible design standards. The real challenges disabled people face are often the result of environmental, political, and social barriers.

Listen to Insider Voices

The best way to gain insight to another person's experience is not to try to live that experience for a day, but rather to listen to what they say. For example, articles in The Mighty, a national disability/health blog, like "11 People with Autism Explain What Stimming Feels Like" (McGlensey 2016), can help people understand diverse experiences. Reading books, blog posts, and articles by disabled writers can also increase understanding about disability – but always keep in mind that there is no singular "disability experience" because everyone is different!

Be Conscious of Accessibility

Check out AXSMap, an app to increase awareness about accessibility and support for accessible businesses!

This app is comparable to Yelp but the reviews focus on accessibility. **Learn more** here axsmap.com

https://www.axsmap.com/

Interview with Alice Wong

> Alice Wong is a disabled, Asian American activist. She is the founder and director of the Disability Visibility Project (disabilityvisibilityproject.com), and is a part of Disabled Writers (www.disabledwriters.com) and #CripTheVote.

https://disabilityvisibilityproject.com/

Q. Can you provide some concrete suggestions on how to encourage more visibility of disability issues? "… the really simple question when people write about a particular community is to ask whether disabled people are represented. We're everywhere and should appear in all kinds of coverage. Even with coverage of disabled people, I see way too many white people rather than disabled people of color."

Q. How can other activists or advocacy groups become more intersectional when promoting disability issues? "Seek out the disabled people who are part of your communities – we're everywhere but many are still reluctant or uninterested in identifying as disabled. If activists and community leaders talk about disability and embrace the diversity of disabled people, it might encourage people to be open."

Q. In a recent article on the representations of disabled people in stock photography, S. E. Smith said *"Disabled people being happy are unusual. Disabled people engaged in collective activity in a mixed disabled/nondisabled group are rare. Disabled people shopping for fun? Unusual."* What can be done to counteract this? "I recently saw Getty Images partner with an organization called MuslimGirl.com to promote realistic images of Muslim girls and women. I'd LOVE for them to have a similar partnership with the Disability Visibility Project or another disability organization …"

Q. What do we need to know to organize effective groups grounded in solidarity with disabled people? Can major shifts in government occur without protest? "People can definitely create change in our government without protesting. Being engaged at the local level is one example – people with disabilities can volunteer, attend public meetings, write letters, start conversations online or in person. Having more disabled people in public service is another way to shift the current political situation. This can be in the form of people running, working in government, or being appointed to serve on various commissions, agencies, and other positions." Lester, N. (30 April 2017) Personal interview with Alice Wong, Disability Visibility Project.

Recommendations for Activist and Allies

Avoid Ableism in Your Activism

1. When organizing an event make sure it is accessible to those with mobility, sensory, or other impairments.
   - Can people get around; are there interpreters for those who use sign language?
   - Are presentations captioned and audio described?
   - Will service dogs be accommodated?
   - Is the event scent free?

2. Don't ignore and/or invalidate people with less visible impairments, or those who choose not to participate.
3. Avoid enforcing the use of academic jargon: **"Just because someone doesn't completely understand your words, doesn't mean they aren't as oppressed or revolutionary as you."**

Learn more: "Six Ways Your Social Justice Activism Might Be Ableist," by Carolyn Zaikowski (2016); "How to Make Your Social Justice Events Accessible to the Disability Community: A Checklist," by S. E. Smith (2017).

Some hashtags to follow:
#DisabilityTooWhite
#DisabilityAwareness
#Diversability
#DifferentNotLess
#WhaaatMoments
#CripTheVote

https://www.reclapress.com/books/naomi-ortiz/

Naomi Ortiz is a Disabled, Mestiza (Indigenous/White) woman. She is a poet, writer, activist, and visual artist. Her book *Sustaining Spirit* contains short reflective essays and poetry and teaches activists how to change the world without losing themselves. **Learn more** from this intersectional work at: www.naomiortiz.com/

8

Beyond Contact: Promoting Social Change and Disability Justice

There is no place in our society for prejudice of any kind, yet it was not that long ago when Americans with disabilities were often not given equal rights and opportunities. Whether the cause was ignorance or indifference, it was not acceptable. We can all take pride in how much the ADA has accomplished, which is evident every time you attend a sporting event, ride the subway, or go to work. Yet, there is always more to be done, which is why it's good not only to celebrate our successes, but to look forward at what still must be done. (Statement from Former President George H.W. Bush on the Anniversary of the Americans with Disabilities Act – July 24. The White House: Office of the Press Secretary 2009)

The ADA offered millions of people the opportunity to earn a living and help support their families. But we all know too many people with disabilities are still unemployed – even though they can work, even though they want to work, even though they have so much to contribute. In some cases, it's a lack of access to skills training. In some cases, it's an employer that can't see all that these candidates for a job have to offer. Maybe sometimes people doubt their own self-worth after experiencing a lifetime of discouragement and expectations that were too low. Whatever the reason, we've got to do better – our country cannot let all that incredible talent go to waste. We've got to tear down barriers externally, but we also have to tear down barriers internally. That's our responsibility as Americans and it's our responsibility as fellow human beings. (Remarks by Former President Barack Obama on the Anniversary of the Americans with Disabilities Act – July 20. The White House: Office of the Press Secretary 2015)

Many still recall a time prior to the 1990 passage of the Americans with Disabilities Act (ADA) when access options taken for granted in the United States today were not yet in place: ramps and elevators instead of only stairs, wider restrooms and automatic doors, curb cuts, flashing lights and beeping sounds at crosswalks, and software that enlarges fonts, captions dialogue, and converts media into sounds, images, touchable formats, and other languages. Many of these advances that now benefit disabled and nondisabled people alike were made possible because of the actions of those who fought for changes in policy and practice – people who participated in the movement for disability rights.

Although this history of accomplishments is detailed elsewhere (Barnartt and Scotch 2001; Stroman 2003), the disability rights movement (DRM) was essential to forging the kind of social change that made more equitable contact between disabled and nondisabled people possible. Yet, to date, few students are exposed to the history of the DRM, its leaders, or other human rights milestones in primary, secondary, or higher education contexts. Some are working to change this (Carson 2013; Reynolds 2017; Steinborn 2017), and to leverage the many voices of those living with disability.

Historically, prejudice-reduction research has failed to incorporate the voices and perspectives of those who are the targets of prejudice – in this case, disabled people themselves (cf. Makas 1988; Wright and Lubensky 2009). Furthermore, as acknowledged in Chapter 7, most prejudice-reduction research has presumed the necessity of *cooperative* and conciliatory strategies as essential to attitude change, improved understanding, and cross-group friendships. Far less work has investigated whether such cooperative approaches contribute to broader social changes like reducing inequalities and increasing the civil rights of disadvantaged groups. To address these limitations, this final chapter is devoted to work on the relevance of intergroup *conflict*, the recognition of discrimination as injustice, and the impact of collective actions that confront prejudice and challenge the status quo.

Beginning with a brief review of the DRM in the United States and actions that altered the normative landscape, this section describes research on how individual and collective actions have been leveraged to create social and societal change. Specifically, I discuss the factors that motivate and inhibit engagement in actions designed to confront discrimination. Following this is a summary of the key factors involved in disability-directed advocacy among disabled people and their allies, and suggestions for next steps in transforming society through research and activism. Not all disability advocacy is directed toward improving outcomes for the group; therefore, distinctions are made between collective activism for disability rights, and advocacy for and by disabled people on a range of issues affecting their participation – although these can overlap.

> People with disabilities are an integral part of society, and as such, should not be segregated, isolated, or subjected to the effects of discrimination. (Young 2010, p. xv)

The Disability Rights Movement Actions and Accomplishments

As noted in Chapter 1, before legislative changes like the ADA in 1990, many disabled people were isolated from view, prohibited from attending movies and community events, blocked from public transportation, restricted from working, or warehoused in segregated facilities (Greene 2013). In order to address their marginalized treatment, disabled people created a social movement that traces its roots to the 1960s (Charlton 1998; Winter 2003). The following highlights some of the key challenges and accomplishments of the DRM from its humble beginnings in the 1960s through the present day. Consistent with White's (2010) theorizing, the early goals of the DRM involved raising awareness of civil rights violations and educating the public that disabled people constituted a disadvantaged minority group that deserved legal protection against discrimination. In contrast to traditional disability advocacy models (described below), the DRM asserted the leadership of people with disabilities to represent their common concerns; nondisabled allies in partnership with disabled professionals played important roles as well (e.g. Disability Rights and Education Defense Fund; White 2010).

Among the earliest and most visible of the disability rights leaders was Ed Roberts, a polio survivor and power wheelchair user who required an "iron lung" to support his breathing 18 hours a day (White 2010). In 1962, when Ed was denied admission to the University of California, Berkeley (UCB), he took action – first as an individual by alerting news organizations of the UCB decision. Later that year, he was admitted, along with several other students with disabilities (known as the "Rolling Quads") who resided in a separate wing of the university's hospital. For a history of DRM leaders, see the Paul K. Longmore Institute on Disability. Following graduation, Roberts was instrumental in organizing the first Center for Independent Living (CIL) in the United States (Meneghello and Russon 2008). CILs emphasized self-determination and autonomous decision making with minimal overreach from medical professionals (Winter 2003). According to movement activist James Charlton, author of the seminal book *Nothing About Us Without Us: Disability Oppression and Empowerment*, self-determination asserts that:

> We are able to take responsibility for our own lives, and we do not need or want [others] to manage our affairs; we best understand what is best for us; we demand control of our own organizations and programs and influence over the government funding, public policy and the economic enterprises that directly affect us. (1998, p. 128)

Central to the philosophy of independent living is the empowerment of disabled people as experts on the services they need, as in control over their life choices, and as fully integrated into all facets of society (White 2010). Importantly, independence is not considered synonymous with productivity, employment, or doing things alone without support. Instead, contributions by disabled people can be voluntary, through paid work, or through interdependent networks – what matters is that disabled people are consulted in all matters involving their lives, from grooming and dating decisions to housing, employment, and future living arrangements (Smith 2001).

Key actions of the DRM included a series of nonviolent protests in the late 1970s staged across nine US cities from Seattle to Boston and Dallas to Atlanta, demanding the signing of regulations to enforce Section 504 of the Rehabilitation Act (Barnartt and Scotch 2001). This was the first general disability rights law in the United States to prohibit organizations that get federal funds from discriminating against people based on disability status. The 504 protests took the form of sit-ins where disabled people converged to occupy key government offices for up to several days, making speeches and chanting (e.g. "We shall not be moved!" "What do we want? Human rights! When do we want them? Now! Sign 504!"). These protests were backed by members of other social movements, including the Farm Workers Union and the Black Panther Party (Patient No More n.d.; Young 2010). In one case, disabled people remained in the San Francisco Office of Housing, Education, and Welfare for 25 days in a row – until the 504 regulations became law (Meneghello and Russon 2008).

According to disability rights scholars, this victory energized the DRM to work for a national law that prohibited discrimination in public facilities and businesses, and required reasonable accommodations so more disabled people could contribute as citizens (Barnartt and Scotch 2001). Over the next 15 years, members of the disability community recruited people from across impairment categories to build coalitions, develop agendas, lobby politicians, and organize public demonstrations that sometimes resulted in arrest and imprisonment.

Other acts of civil disobedience in response to inaccessible mass transit systems were staged by disability rights activists in the 1980s fighting under the banner of ADAPT (Americans with Disabilities for Accessible Public Transportation). Before the ADA, accessible public transportation was virtually nonexistent despite being taxpayer supported (White 2010). To draw media attention to this issue, ADAPT activists chained themselves in wheelchairs to city buses at the national convention of public transit operators. They proclaimed that while Black people fought against being assigned to the back of the bus, disabled people wanted to get on the bus (White 2010). Eventually, accessible transportation was included as a civil right under the ADA.

Following success in making public transportation accessible, ADAPT has gone on to fight for the right of disabled people to obtain personal care services in their own homes, which is far more cost-effective than being condemned to living in a nursing home (Dickson and Blahovec 2016). This battle is still in progress: The Disability Integration Act of 2017 was recently introduced to Congress as a mechanism to shift long-term care funding away from institutionalized placements, prohibiting insurance companies from denying disabled individuals the right to live in their own communities (Dickson and Blahovec 2016).

Another legislative victory came with the passage of the Individuals with Disabilities Education Act or IDEA (1990, amended and reauthorized in 2004), which expanded the right to a free public education to children with disabilities in "the least restrictive environment" (Department of Education n.d.). Prior to the amended IDEA 2004, disabled students were being "mainstreamed" but not fully included in the public schools – spending much of the day in special education or therapy classes segregated from their peers without disabilities.

One of the most significant and comprehensive accomplishments of the DRM in the United States has been the passage of the ADA of 1990. "The ADA is a civil rights law that prohibits discrimination against individuals with disabilities in all areas of public life, including jobs, schools, transportation, and all public and private places that are open to the general public" (ADA National Network 2017). The ADA provides for civil rights protections to individuals with disabilities similar to those provided on the basis of race, color, sex, national origin, age, and religion. It establishes a guarantee for people with disabilities to have equal opportunities for employment, transportation, state and local government services, public accommodations, and telecommunications.

Similarly, the Psychiatric Survivors (Ex-Mental Patients) Movement has fought to promote self-help, mutual-support recovery options, and patient rights (e.g. against forced treatments/involuntary commitment) (Chamberlin 1978). As a consequence, in 1999, the Supreme Court ruled in *Olmstead vs. L.C.* (Ginsburg and Supreme Court of the United States 1998) that undue institutionalization of people with mental disabilities qualifies as discrimination under the ADA. Another victory came in 2003, when the US President's Freedom Commission on Mental Health provided for a national consumer-driven and recovery-oriented continuum of community care. This was the same year that hunger strikes and protests at the American Psychiatric Association Convention took place (McLean 2003; Stroman 2003). Today disability rights activism continues to focus on a number of issues, from the right to life support (see Chapter 3 Activist pages) to the growth of the Visitability Movement (e.g. Concrete Change) working for basic access in newly constructed homes: homes with at least one step-free entry, a first-floor bathroom, and wider interior doors making it possible for anyone to visit (Wadsley 2008).

> We just can't always be talking about new policies when we have a lot of exemplary policies, but we don't have exemplary implementation and enforcement. (O'Day and Goldstein 2005, p. 245)

The Evolution of the Disability Rights Movement

Consistent with other civil rights movements, the DRM developed in phases (Winter 2003). The movement actually incorporated activism from three distinct reform efforts: those working toward deinstitutionalization, independent living, and civil rights (Greene 2013). In the beginning, the DRM needed to redefine the problem of disability as one of clearly *recognizable discrimination*. To do so, activists mounted a direct challenge to discredit the dominant biomedical model view of disability as a tragic, internal condition of sick people dependent on healthcare professionals. In place of this, they promoted a socio-political alternative of disability as a disadvantaged social status. According to Winter (2003), the DRM was instrumental in shifting the ideological debate away from an emphasis on impairments as a personal problem (and stigma as an interpersonal dilemma) to a discussion about oppression, dehumanization, and discrimination against a class of citizens systematically denied access to resources that affected their economic, educational, and political lives (Barnartt and Scotch 2001). This civil rights framing was critical to overcoming arguments that justified costs for disability services on the basis of improved rehabilitation outcomes like walking upright. Access and accommodations are also less likely to be viewed as welfare benefits when framed as rights needed to exercise the role of citizen (Greene 2013).

Second, the DRM needed to build consensus across diverse constituencies that the appropriate strategy to combat barriers to full citizenship required group-based collective actions. Collective actions are broadly described as the intentional activities taken by people who share a common group membership for the purpose of benefiting the overall group (Louis 2009). These actions can be in coordination with others, but collective action does not require physical interaction between people in close proximity. Individual group members can act alone on behalf of the collective through voting, contacting public officials, and serving as political representatives. Furthermore, collective actions can be pre-planned or spontaneous; some are disruptive (e.g. boycotts or protests) while others are more routine (e.g. forming unions, petitioning). Thus, while some movement factions may have been more focused on consumer services, independent living, or deinstitutionalization, all could unite as members of a disadvantaged collective using the language and tools of other civil rights movements (Winter 2003).

A third phase of the movement for disability rights is reflected in reactions to the aftermath of newly enacted laws and policies, including member responses to unresolved enforcement issues, and backlash from those seeking a return to the status quo. For example, in 2000, the National Council on Disability found that every state in the United States was out of compliance with the IDEA. As a consequence, many families were required to file formal complaints to access their educational rights to a free public education in the least restrictive environment (Winter 2003).

Since the signing of the ADA in 1990, there have been a number of criticisms of the law, primarily related to its lack of enforcement (Schwochau and Blanck 2000; Stein 2004). People seem to forget that just because a law passes doesn't mean it will be followed or that violations will be prosecuted. New laws require coordination across dozens of regulatory agencies at federal, state, and local levels. Some agencies are needed to provide technical assistance to implement regulations, others are charged with enforcing compliance or investigating complaints. There is even a new science of implementation that promotes the application of evidence-based practices to study the factors that influence and impede behavior change (Durlak and DuPre 2008). Critics note that the ADA has suffered from both a lack of proactive enforcement and minimal compliance monitoring (Winter 2003). Particularly when agencies are underfunded, reports of noncompliance often go uninvestigated. Finally, even when allegations of discrimination resulted in the filing of an ADA lawsuit, most of these lawsuits failed as judgments often hinged on the ambiguity of key definitions (Bruyère et al. 2010; Colker 1999).

For example, what qualifies as a "reasonable accommodation for those charged with integrating disabled students and employees?" What does it mean to have "a substantial limitation" in a "major life activity"?

In response to several court rulings to address these and other implementation problems undermining the effectiveness of the ADA, in 2009, the Americans with Disabilities Act Amendments Act was passed. Since these amendments have been in place, more cases against discriminatory practices have been successfully litigated. These more recent victories include several judgments finding in favor of students with disabilities whose rights under the ADA were violated in higher education contexts. For example, one university was cited for refusing to remove multiple barriers to accessing academic programs and other public event facilities, including inaccessible paths of travel, ramps, entrances, classrooms, and bathrooms. The plaintiff documented that she could not access the restroom at the site of her master's program, and reported:

> "Feelings of humiliation, embarrassment and indignity" when her catheter bag overflowed, often in public, leaving her to sit in her own urine, while waiting for a ride home to change her clothes … She was required to "sit at a contorted and uncomfortable angle in order to use classroom desks" because they weren't tall enough to accommodate her wheelchair. "It is especially difficult for her when she needs to use a computer, because she cannot slide under the desk to reach the computer keyboard." (Grossman and Colker 2015, p. 26)

It has now been almost 30 years since the passage of the ADA, and compliance is still an issue. Yet, legal scholars acknowledge several key achievements of the DRM: altering the legislative landscape; making possible increased integration and access to more public spaces; and growing independent living and disability rights organizations – consistent with empowerment objectives (Charlton 1998; Shapiro 1993). Not only did the DRM influence policies, but legal and policy changes contributed to the growth of national advocacy groups as well (Scotch 1988). Ongoing recruitment of new DRM members nevertheless remains a significant challenge (Barnartt and Scotch 2001). For example, recent research across US and international samples finds that compared to adults over 30, younger adults under 30 are more likely to be involved in organizations advocating for disability rights although they tend to affiliate less with other disabled people (Nario-Redmond and Oleson 2016).

Thus while the DRM continues to promote a socio-political model that frames ableism as among the most disabling features of the disability experience, in the social and psychological sciences, this approach is only now gaining traction (Dirth and Branscombe 2018; Dunn and Andrews 2015; Goodley and Lawthom 2006; Olkin and Pledger 2003). Most psychologists remain preoccupied with impairment-based variables, stigma, and interpersonal forms of prejudice that reflect a medicalized understanding of disability – ignoring rich investigative opportunities to extend intergroup relations, social identity, and collective action research to disabled people as the nation's largest minority group (Balcazar and Suarez-Balcazar 2016). In the next sections, I review the relevance of recent theoretical and empirical advancements in the psychology of collective action.

> I have seen people who make polite speeches and write letters finally become so frustrated that they are willing to take an activist stance … I think in general activism is predicated on two things. One is the perception of need, urgency or pain. The other is a perception that a solution is possible, that power is available and can be harnessed. The absence of these are like a disease in an activist organization. (McColl and Boyce 2003, p. 386)

Collective Action Precursors and Tactics

Organizing a movement and taking political action to affect social change requires much more than the witnessing or experiencing of unfair, exclusionary treatment. Several factors must converge to motivate collective action on behalf of the group, and there are many barriers along the way. Based on research across several social groups, collective action intentions depend on perceptions of injustice, the strength of identification with the group, the collective efficacy of members, and other variables related to expectations about advancement and potential for change (Klandermans 1997; van Zomeren et al. 2008).

> There may be times when we are powerless to prevent injustice, but there must never be a time when we fail to protest. (Elie Wiesel, writer, Nobel laureate 1986)

Perceptions of Injustice and Common Fate Collective action for social change only emerges in response to perceived inequalities when people compare how their ingroup is treated relative to more privileged outgroups (Wright and Baray 2010). Unless group members perceive that their marginalized position is unjust or illegitimate, they may simply accept their lower status position as deserved on the basis of their personal circumstances or limitations (Ellemers 1993; Jetten et al. 2013). Therefore, the *recognition* of status inequality or discrimination at the hands of unjust agents is an important first step toward collective action for change. This is consistent with disability movement scholars who have argued that identifying with disability as an inclusive group membership may first require the recognition of disability prejudice (Scotch 1988). This recognition relates to the idea that what binds disabled people together is not the sum of their individual impairments but their common experiences with stigma, misrepresentation, and discrimination. Research on how this appraisal process occurs within disability groups is sorely lacking, although some CILs actively work to transform their clients from passive individuals who accept their treatment, into future activists required to demonstrate awareness of disability oppression and recognize ableist practices before seeking independent living (Little 2010).

> CIL staff presented a diagnostic frame in which the difficulties experienced by impaired people were the result of injustices imposed by societal barriers and attitudes ... Staff repeatedly explained that disability is a consequence of environmental and attitudinal barriers rather than functional loss. (Little 2010)

This paradigm shift is not exclusive to CILs. Even at the annual meetings of impairment-specific organizations focused on medical advancements and family concerns, disabled people have opportunities to come together to share their stories and strategies for coping and responding to ableism. A sense of common fate can also be facilitated through discussions and exposure to news about the struggles of fellow disabled people. In this way, those living alone or in remote areas can cultivate a sense that the rejection they experience is not unique – that others with disabilities both similar and different from theirs have common experiences with staring, exclusion, and invalidation (Putnam 2005). Through increased awareness of these common experiences with rejection, objectification, and the like, what may have felt personally threatening before may come to be interpreted as instances of disability prejudice or ableism. This shifting awareness that the problems one confronts are neither unique nor attributable to the self but to a discriminating society is key to motivating a sense of belonging to something broader than one's own impairment community, and to laying the groundwork for collective action (Hahn 1985). That is, to stimulate a sense of disability consciousness, a new cross-impairment disability identity was critical to the emerging DRM – though perhaps not sufficient to mobilize action for change (Anspach 1979).

> Disability exists in every sector of society: in immigrant communities, in prisons, in religious and spiritual communities, among veterans and homeless folks, among children and elders and everyone in between... Liberation can't happen alone; we have to reach toward one another. Whether online, in our bedrooms and living rooms, in letters passing through prison guards' hands, or in the streets, we are part of a growing movement. (Lamm, 2015)

Ingroup Identification Action on behalf of one's ingroup requires not only self-categorization or an awareness of one's belonging to the group, but a strong sense of the *importance* of that membership to one's self-definition (Wright and Baray 2010; Simon and Klandermans 2001). This collective sense of identity takes time to develop. It is not necessarily something people learn during socialization, particularly disabled people who often grow up in nondisabled families (Little 2010). Only recently has research shown that those most likely to support collective action and participate in political activism are those who strongly identify as disabled (Nario-Redmond and Oleson 2016; Nario-Redmond et al. 2013) – consistent with a large body of research on other minority groups. In fact, it is the highly identified members of disadvantaged groups who want to talk most about power differences, and are most motivated to change group-based power inequalities (Saguy et al. 2008).

Group commitment and feelings of solidarity can also be enhanced whenever a collective identity is made salient or figures prominently in a given context (Abrams and Hogg 2010). For example, as people learn about gatherings of "the disability community" (including events that celebrate disability arts and culture), social identities may become more prominent in memory, and may even take on new meaning for those who previously viewed disability as but one of many self-descriptive traits. Another by-product of identity salience is increased conformity to ingroup norms and goals which can also facilitate loyalty and consensus building – both useful to collective action endeavors (Ellemers et al. 2002). Over time, with increased involvement in disability community issues, disability can become a centrally important, politicized identity to be deployed in the service of the group.

Collective Efficacy and Change Beliefs Other prerequisites for collective action relate to beliefs about advancement and social change. If people believe that upward mobility or social advancement is possible without collective action, why bother? It is only when advancement in status or access to the advantaged group appears to be systematically blocked that challenges through collective action seem warranted (Tajfel and Turner 1979). The belief that one's group is being obstructed from improving its position through legitimate channels (e.g. merit-based promotions) also contributes to stronger perceptions of injustice and collective identification (van Zomeren et al. 2008; Wright 2010).

In addition to beliefs about rigid intergroup boundaries that block advancement, people must also believe that system change through collective action is truly *possible* before they will engage in the kinds of strategies used by other social movements (Snow and Benford 1988). Without an expectation that their collective actions can be effective, people may concede defeat or revert to beliefs that justify their disadvantaged status (e.g. I'll never get promoted so I might as well take whatever charity I can get). Collective actions may also need to be somewhat *successful* in order to sustain member involvement (Drury and Reicher 2009; Louis 2009). However, even simple participation in collective actions can contribute to feelings of empowerment and beliefs that the status quo can be disrupted. Taking collective action on behalf of one's group is particularly motivating when it gives people the opportunity to directly affirm their group's distinct identity (Jetten et al. 2004; Stürmer and Simon 2004), or express group emotions like anger and outrage over injustice (Iyer et al. 2007).

On the other hand, collective actions (e.g. riots, class action lawsuits) that reduce perceptions of stability about "the way things are," can be threatening to majority members who may become defensive and vilify those who blame their circumstances on a discriminating society (Eliezer and Major 2012; Louis 2009). For example, instead of blaming businesses that haven't complied with the ADA's anti-discrimination legislation for the past 28 years, the media sometimes villainizes disabled people for pursuing litigation against businesses for failing to comply with the accessibility provisions of the ADA (e.g. Bekhour 2016; Grimoldby 2016; Secret 2012).

> Effective social change is achieved when collective actors pick a target that can change and that is responsive to the costs or benefits offered by the collective action ... New issues, newly formed organizations, new increases in the frequency or magnitude of collective action events: all these are expected to lead to policy change. (Louis 2009, p. 735)

Collective Action Tactics: What Works? Collective action can take many forms, although most research in this tradition emphasizes the actions of disadvantaged actors, and presumes that conflict between groups is essential to exposing, resisting, and remedying intergroup inequalities (Wright and Baray 2010). Some forms of collective action for change are considered more "routine" because they conform to existing rules or follow established conflict resolution procedures. Examples include filing complaints, lobbying public officials for policy changes, or boycotting an organization's goods. By contrast, "disruptive" collective actions more directly challenge existing hierarchical arrangements or deliberately violate established rules. These include protests, riots, and acts of civil (and uncivil) disobedience against organizations that discriminate. Such disruptive tactics tend to be more effective for disadvantaged groups who have already met with resistance when trying to influence change from within a bureaucracy that privileges the advantaged (Louis 2009). Disruptive collective actions are also more likely to be effective when they produce negative publicity about organizations that discriminate, or impact such organizations' profits, assuming that the business is in a position to rectify the problem (Luders 2006).

Civil rights movements are particularly successful when novel actions target local and more consumer-oriented groups. Recent litigation through class action lawsuits fighting pervasive disability discrimination illustrates another way collective action campaigns have leveraged organizational change when more routine approaches fail (Grossman and Colker 2015). These efforts have also been more successful following better enforcement via the 2009 amendments to the ADA. According to Burnstein (2006), policy changes in the United States are much more likely when public opinion supports the issues and the issues are highly salient. In fact, collective action operating through public opinion is a strong predictor of policy change (Louis 2009). Therefore, social movements should leverage their collective activities in ways that bring the most visibility to the issues they seek to change. A recent example of this relates to the successful blocking of the vote to repeal the US Affordable Health Care Act in July of 2017 on the heels of national news coverage of disabled people organizing "die-ins" – putting their bodies on the line and holding vigils in Senate buildings where some were ultimately hauled out of their wheelchairs and arrested (Wanshel 2017). "They unfurled banners that declared: 'Capping

Medicaid = Death 4 Disabled.' The protests were so bold, so effective, that congressional leaders were shaken" (Nichols 2017). Such coordinated actions are by no means easy to accomplish, and can come at much physical, emotional, and financial expense.

Barriers and Caveats to Collective Action In addition to personal costs, anything that can undermine the recognition of discrimination, a strong disadvantaged group identity, or beliefs about the impossibility of advancement without a fight can reduce collective action intentions. For example, campaigns designed to convince people that: the system is fair the way it is; that upward mobility is possible regardless of group membership; or that the benefits of harmony with well-intentioned others outweigh the need for conflict, can all serve as barriers to collective action (see Techakesari et al. 2017). With respect to those fighting for disability rights, barriers related to transportation and structural inaccessibility complicate the coordination of actions between individuals if disconnected from powerful networks or geographically isolated from one another (Scotch 1988). Building consensus can be difficult across diverse constituencies with varying agendas that may not be organized under the same banner of disability (e.g. those with psychiatric conditions, chronic illnesses, etc.). Furthermore, for some, identifying as an activist for disability rights poses risks to safety and well-being, the loss of needed services, and victimization by those in positions of authority who provision resources and care – especially of those in institutionalized settings.

Research on collective actions that fail to achieve social change also warns that when discrimination is widely practiced and therefore normative, it can be made to seem acceptable (Louis 2009). For example, some college students may assume that wheelchair users are not interested in visiting places that cannot be accessed via elevator or ramp if this is the way things have always been. Some may even assume that change is unnecessary if disabled students are uncommon or otherwise invisible. Furthermore, if change seems highly unlikely due to narratives about limited institutional resources, collective action can also be undermined (Louis 2009). These beliefs about the difficulties of change are different than beliefs that discount the need for collective action by assuring people that upward mobility is possible without it. That is, people are not going to mobilize for change if they think they can advance through their own efforts or network connections. In fact, when individual opportunities for advancement are presented to people, militancy for change among activists is reduced (Wright et al. 1990). This is why social movement messaging must make group-based disadvantage clear from the outset, noting that enduring inequalities exist that block access and deny opportunities for advancement simply because of one's group membership.

> Norms change over time, in part as the result of successive challenges which produce new balances of power, reflected in new structures of rules. (Piven and Cloward 1991, p. 440)

Changing the Normative Landscape Through Confrontation: Allies in the Fight for Change

According to Crandall et al. (2013), as disadvantaged groups raise awareness about the injustice of discrimination, public perceptions about the acceptability of prejudice toward them become more variable. Specifically, when groups make progress toward improving their status, they enter a "normative window" marked by changing social expectations and a lack of consensus about what constitutes bias and unfair treatment. During times of normative change, social movement leaders have a unique window within which to sway public opinion with new information (e.g. the Disability Visibility Project) and novel collective actions.

But what about the actions of those who are not directly affected by what some consider to be "minority concerns" – those who are not the direct targets of discrimination? Such individuals are sometimes called "non-targets" or "bystanders" of prejudice – but they are also potential advocates and allies in the fight for social change. Research is now emerging on the factors that contribute to majority group involvement in actions that confront prejudicial treatment to defend minority rights and improve egalitarian outcomes (Droogendyk et al. 2016; Techakesari et al. 2017). Some of this work focuses on the use of confrontation strategies as a means to prejudice reduction (Drury and Kaiser 2014).

> Indeed, confrontations represent a "grassroots" endeavor for social change in which any individual person has the potential to influence and improve others and perhaps society in general. (Czopp and Ashburn-Nardo 2012, p. 177)

> By witnessing confrontation, people come to see that behaviors they might otherwise see as benign are actually harmful. Just as believing that prejudice is socially acceptable can lead to more public displays of prejudice. (Drury 2013, p. 3)

Confronting Others to Reduce Prejudice: What Works?

Confrontation is the voluntary act of expressing disapproval toward those who perpetuate the prejudicial treatment of others (Kaiser and Miller 2004). As opposed to remaining a silent bystander, those who confront prejudicial comments and behaviors can do so verbally or through other forms of communication with the intention of preventing perpetrators from committing future acts of bias (Shelton et al. 2006). For example, when overhearing someone say, "That's so retarded," people are increasingly speaking up to raise awareness of the harmful and dehumanizing implications of this term as a form of hate speech. There is even a campaign encouraging people to pledge to "Spread the Word to End the Word" (Palumbo n.d.). Opportunities to practice effective confrontation strategies offer another promising avenue for educating those who may want to rebuke prejudicial comments but need guidance on how to respond appropriately in the moment (Bozeman 2015; Paluck 2011). For example, some confrontation trainings encourage students to track prejudicial encounters, and offer strategies to role-play effective responses with questions designed to get perpetrators thinking, such as: "I'm surprised to hear you say that because I've always thought of you as someone who is very open-minded" (Plous 2000, p. 1999). In a study evaluating the effects of confrontation practice, Lawson et al. (2010) found that students who practiced confronting others' prejudices for a week increased their ability to generate effective responses compared to those who had not practiced confrontations.

To date, experimental research on the effectiveness of various confrontation techniques has focused primarily on reducing sexism (Becker et al. 2014), racism (Czopp et al. 2006), antisemitism, and heterosexism (Hyers 2007). Across several studies, findings reveal that confronting prejudice can reduce subsequent stereotyping – not only among perpetrators (e.g. Czopp et al. 2006), but also among those who observe the confrontation (Rasinski and Czopp 2010); for reviews see (Czopp and Ashburn-Nardo 2012; Becker et al. 2014). Confrontation seems to reduce prejudice through several mechanisms, including the arousal of self-criticism, guilt, and discomfort in those who are confronted, which results in less future bias (Czopp et al. 2006), lasting up to several weeks (Hillard 2011). When confronted, some perpetrators of prejudice become motivated to repair the damage of their prior offenses through apologies and other compensatory gestures like smiling (Mallett and Wagner 2011). This evidence suggests that confrontation can instigate an internal motivation for curbing future prejudicial expressions. However, it can also instigate anger and backlash, especially from those who are less internally motivated, or who resent having to conform to external factions pressuring them to appear "politically correct" (Plant and Devine 2001). Interestingly, when those who are confronted respond with hostility, they are also viewed as more prejudiced compared to those who apologize.

> As social norms change some people find themselves discrepant from the moving standard of tolerance. It is the people who are behind the times, who fail to adapt easily to shifting standards of decency, whose intolerance of groups reflects patterns of yesterday, that we label, "prejudiced." (Crandall et al. 2013, p. 63)

Although less is known about the most optimal forms of anti-prejudice confrontation, research has found that people are more likely to take confronters (those who speak up) seriously when they do not belong to the disadvantaged group in question. For example, confrontations toward those who stereotype Blacks as less intelligent than Whites are more persuasive (Czopp and Monteith 2003), and are more likely to be accepted as valid, when made by a White compared to a Black confronter (Gulker et al. 2013). Similarly, compared to women, male allies who confronted the sexist remarks of another man were judged more positively, and considered more legitimate (Drury and Kaiser 2014). Apparently, non-target group confronters are thought to be less self-interested, and are therefore more convincing than disadvantaged group members who stand to benefit directly from reduced levels of prejudice. Generally speaking, people are more receptive to criticism from members of their own ingroups compared to outgroups (Hornsey et al. 2002), and are more likely to change their beliefs in the direction of agreement with non-target confronters (Monteith and Mark 2005). The enhanced credibility of non-target ingroup allies could also be related to the authority associated with their dominant or advantaged group status.

The Role of Allies in Challenging Prejudice and Creating New Normative Standards

Although research on disability allies is in its infancy (Brown and Ostrove 2013; Ostrove et al. 2009), descriptions about the characteristics of nondisabled allies converge to define them as people who "seem devoid of disability prejudice but who know and despise it when they see it," and "make the effort to learn who their disabled associates are in their full glory and their full ordinariness"; in short, allies are "the ones who 'get it'" (Gill 2001, p. 368). Allies who choose to confront also tend to be those who are more optimistic, communal, and activist identified. They are often respected and admired more when they choose to confront blatant prejudice compared to those who remain silent (Dickter et al. 2012).

> The increased effectiveness of public confrontations may be the result of their ability to increase the salience of social norms that promote nonprejudiced responding. When people are provided with consensus information that most other people hold less prejudiced beliefs than them, they respond by changing their own racial beliefs in the corresponding direction. (Czopp and Asburn-Nardo 2012, p. 187)

More recently, research has found that when it comes to confronting sexism, a male ally's public confrontation made the perpetrator appear more sexist than when he was confronted in private (Gervais and Hillard 2014). This same study found that compared to a male ally's more accusatory (direct) public confrontations, less accusatory (indirect) confrontations were also considered more persuasive. This is consistent with other research on the benefits of nonaggressive, low-threat confrontations (Becker and Barreto 2014). In general, people seem more accepting and receptive to changing behavior when confrontations emphasize principles of fairness, integrity, and equal treatment for all (Czopp et al. 2006). However, Drury (2013) found that when framed as part of the "greater good," highlighting the cross-group benefits of improved collaboration, productivity, and idea exchange, confrontations to reduce prejudice were taken just as seriously whether delivered by targets of prejudice or their allies.

There are, of course, barriers to taking a stand by confronting others' prejudicial comments and discriminatory actions. Confrontations should be less likely when prejudice is dismissed as "just a joke" (Ford et al. 2008). In general, people must first recognize the inciting event as discriminatory, be willing to take responsibility for intervening, and come up with an appropriate response after appraising the consequences (Asburn-Nardo et al. 2008). This may be why confronting prejudice seems to be more of the exception than the rule (Bozeman 2015).

Confrontation is also less likely when people fear others will view them as antagonistic troublemakers and retaliate against them (Czopp and Monteith 2003), or when the perpetrators of prejudice occupy positions of power over others' future financial prospects (Asburn-Nardo et al. 2014; Gervais and Hillard 2014; Shelton and Stewart 2004). These results have important implications for the recruitment of dominant group allies to campaign against prejudice perpetuated by members of their own high status groups. Strong, supportive allies can even increase the collective action intentions of some disadvantaged group members (Techakesari et al. 2017).

Because confrontation strategies are externally focused, like peer pressure and ostracism, they have the potential to more broadly encourage conformity to new standards of acceptable behavior. For example, Blanchard and her colleagues (1994) found that simply *overhearing* arguments against racism led White participants to more strongly condemn racism compared to those who did not overhear anti-racist arguments. Moreover, failure to confront public expressions of prejudice increased support for the status quo, perpetuating bias (Gulker et al. 2013). People assume that when others are silent in response to overt expressions of prejudice, there is implicit agreement about the acceptability of these remarks, which increases support for prejudice, and for the person who expresses it (Rasinski et al. 2013).

> Where you see wrong or inequality or injustice, speak out, because this is your country. This is your democracy. Make it. Protect it. Pass it on. (Thurgood Marshall 2003, p.276)

When one influential ally demonstrates how prejudice can be effectively confronted, others in their peer network may follow to adopt similar attitudes, especially if they think a majority will no longer tolerate such bias (Stangor et al. 2003). Therefore, confrontation is an important tool of social influence for changing attitudes and behavior toward disadvantaged groups, particularly as advantaged group members come to recognize the legitimacy of a group's claims of discrimination (Iyer et al. 2007). A sense of collective guilt (Wohl et al. 2006) can also stimulate moral outrage and the desire to rectify inequalities among some members of the advantaged majority (Nickerson and Louis 2008), particularly those who value egalitarianism (Wright and Taylor 1998).

Group norms play an important role in shaping what people consider worthy of collective action efforts. People often weigh the costs and benefits associated with contesting discriminatory treatment, getting out to support fellow activists, or sacrificing time to advocate for change as an ally to disadvantaged groups (see Drury and Reicher 2009; Louis et al. 2005). Yet when people do converge to challenge prejudice and social inequalities, what was considered normative can and does change. Disability advocacy has undergone tremendous shifts in recent years as disabled people are increasingly taking control to articulate their priority concerns and an agenda for the future.

Organizations change from activist to non-activist, or from non-activist to activist. They move in both directions, and it has something to do with the people that are in them, and the causes that animate them. (McColl and Boyce 2003, p. 385)

Disability and Disability-Directed Advocacy

Based on interviews with members of 23 disability advocacy organizations involved in multiple policy change efforts between 1981 and 2001, McColl and Boyce (2003) developed a descriptive framework that distinguishes between tactics that are more collaborative and those that are more confrontational since both surface in response to changes in the economic and political landscape. According to their key informants, activism for disability rights will always be a dynamic process.

The history of advocacy on behalf of people with disabilities has been fraught with tensions and competing agendas about how to best advance the interests of the group and its members (Dirth and Nario-Redmond 2019). Furthermore, their remains much confusion on the relationship between *disability advocacy* and *disability rights activism*, contributing to a lack of precision in the field. Disability advocacy covers a much broader set of issues than activism for social change, which aligns more closely with disability *rights* advocacy. Furthermore, disability advocacy has been conducted primarily *on behalf of* people with disabilities, even in organizations that support clients' self-determination (e.g. Autism Speaks). In general, disability advocacy describes any effort directed at improving the quality of life for people with disabilities drawing on scientific and legal arguments to press for action on issues ranging from access to assistive technologies and affordable healthcare to job training and protection against physical and sexual abuse (National Council on Disability 2001).

Advocates for disadvantaged populations can target their work either at the level of the individual (e.g. peer to peer, family, and self-advocacy), or at the level of the group through collective advocacy efforts (e.g. lobbying government; community organizing; Neufeld 1991). Unfortunately, much of the history of disability advocacy has been about eliminating or remediating individual impairments or training people with disabilities to approximate nondisabled ways of being (McPhail and Freeman 2005). For example, charity-driven advocacy has relied on telethons (e.g. Muscular Dystrophy Association, MDA), walk-a-thons, and benefit concerts to raise funds (e.g. Autism Speaks). These more "ameliorative approaches" tend to focus on curative treatments and services to "normalize" disabled people's appearances – like teaching paralyzed clients to walk upright with walkers and crutches, or training deaf people to lip read and vocalize speech – regardless of the impracticality, energy consumption, or pain associated with such endeavors (Longmore and Umansky 2001).

However good passivity and the creation of dependency may be for the careers of service providers, it is bad news for disabled people and the public purse ... There are a number of ways in which dependency is created through the delivery of professional-ized services. The kinds of services that are available – notably residential and day care facilities with their institutionalized regimes, their failure to involve disabled people meaningfully in the running of such facilities, the transportation of users in specialized transport and the rigidity of the routine activities which take place therein – all serve to institutionalize disabled people and create dependency. (Barton 2005, p. 13)

Because traditional disability advocacy organizations have prioritized access to consumer goods and services like the use adaptive equipment and community transitions (McColl and Boyce 2003), these organizations have been dominated by nondisabled providers with authority over the educational, employment, and rehabilitation needs of "their" disabled clients (e.g. the National Down Syndrome Society and the American Council for the Blind; Longmore and Umansky 2001). Fewer disability advocacy groups have emphasized the importance of more "transformative approaches" to addressing ableism and inequality, or to challeng-ing human rights violations (White 2010). This is changing somewhat as disabled people push back against being used as objects of pity to raise charitable dona-tions (e.g. Jerry's Orphans; Johnson 1994) or to justify assisted suicide (e.g. Not Dead Yet; Barnartt 2008). Some of these are considered single-issue advocacy organizations even if they represent multiple impairment groups. Organizations that represent the broader disability community on a *range* of issues are less com-mon (e.g. National Organization on Disability).

According to Barnartt et al. (2001), disability advocacy organizations that have a group-focused mission are known as *disability-directed* organizations for change. For example, the Disability Rights Network advocates for specific causes like ensuring accountability in healthcare or providing accessible housing, but also promotes a more general human rights agenda that documents abuse across settings in addition to political disenfranchisement and institutionalized ableism. Other group-advocacy organizations promote acceptance training to teach toler-ance, or may lobby for inclusion opportunities without necessarily confronting the structural inequalities and policy barriers that impede their goals (McColl and Boyce 2003). It should be noted, however, that many disability advocacy groups provide important social support, material resources, and educational outreach services even while some perpetuate dependency, misinformation, and ableist practices (Dirth and Nario-Redmond 2019).

Evidence-based scholarship on advocacy aimed at prejudice reduction and improving the disadvantaged status of disabled people as a group is only begin-ning to emerge. This is despite the fact that cross-impairment advocacy groups have been around since the mid-1970s campaigning for policy changes that ben-efit disabled people as a broad constituency (e.g. the American Coalition of Citizens with Disabilities; Disabled in Action). More importantly, many cross-impairment advocacy groups involve disabled people in leadership and decision-making roles – some more successfully than others (Foster-Fishman et al. 2007). For example, frustration with contemporary US policy debates (ADA violations and affordable healthcare) has reinvigorated the call for direct action and civil disobedience (see American Association of People with Disabilities).

> In effect, controversy and attention developed only when a person with a disability challenged the traditional power structures that maintained professionals as the controlling agents and people with disabilities as voiceless objects to be controlled in an environment that malnourished both the body and the soul. (Kliewer and Drake 1998, p. 106)

A key distinction to keep in mind when evaluating this work is the extent to which the advocacy is *for* disabled people, *with* disabled people, and/or *by* disabled people – consistent with the rallying cry that mobilized the disability rights movement: *Nothing About Us Without Us* (Charlton 1998). A socio-political model of advocacy reflects the philosophy that disabled people are the experts when it comes to representing their concerns. This does not mean there is no place in such organizations for nondisabled allies; however, central to the mission of these groups is the privileging of those who experience disability directly as equal partners if not leaders in the advocacy process (Barnartt et al. 2001).

Precursors to Effective Disability-Directed Advocacy

Research evaluating the success of advocacy groups in meeting their policy goals has been both limited and controversial. Some argue that success is achieved only when disability issues become routinely represented as part of an organization's "normal" policy process (e.g. through standing committees or advisory councils), thus eliminating the need for further advocacy. Others evaluate success based on the attainment of specific policy goals and objectives (Crichton and Jongbloed 1998; McColl and Boyce 2003).

Empowering individuals to engage in advocacy that is by and for disabled people requires strategic investment. Under-resourcing for professional development contributes to less proactive and coordinated approaches (Dirth and Nario-Redmond 2019). To address this issue, many disability-directed advocacy groups work to build capacity within the disability community by developing skills in grant writing, public speaking, and court testimony in addition to providing networking experience at the local and national levels (Little 2010). These endeavors are challenging against a backdrop of ableism, poverty, and ongoing disparities in education and employment (Erickson et al. 2015; Harpur 2014; O'Day and Goldstein 2005), even within organizations dedicated to disability-directed advocacy. One qualitative study found that despite having equal representation of disabled people, organizational effectiveness was compromised when members were perceived to lack supervisory and management experience (e.g. conflict negotiation, cultural competence) and other practical skills (e.g. leadership, collaboration, and technical prowess; Radermacher et al. 2010). If people with disabilities remain underrepresented in higher education contexts, where such skills are often acquired, disabled people will continue to remain in short supply. Self-advocacy skills are also significant predictors of effective disability advocacy work (Wilson-Kovacs et al. 2008).

Other studies demonstrate the importance of material resources for productive disability advocacy. Unpaid volunteers, understaffing, time-limited grant funding, and the costs associated with planning inclusive meetings that include sign language interpretation, audio description, and other accessibility provisions can add additional costs, particularly when participation from diverse constituents is prioritized. Without distinctive and strategic goals for the future, many organizations struggle to compete with for-profit professional organizations that may have more paternalistic agendas, or fail to empower those they seek to represent (McColl and Boyce 2003). As noted in the sections on effective contact and diversity training interventions, unless institutional authorities promote an atmosphere of equality that values diverse opinions, efforts to change organizations from within, or to leverage underrepresented voices, will not be as successful (Radermacher et al. 2010).

Disability-Directed Advocacy: An Agenda for the Future

Over a decade ago, O'Day and Goldstein (2005) identified some of the top advocacy priorities for the twenty-first century, many of which have become even more urgent today. Based on input from national disability advocacy leaders and policy researchers (88% of whom experienced a variety of impairments), more work was needed on the *impact of poverty* which cuts across several advocacy issues, and on the *interrelationships between advocacy issues* that cannot be solved in isolation. For example, job opportunities should not be competing against income support programs that create disincentives to working: people will not seek employment if having a job means losing their independent living or eligibility for life-sustaining supports. Following these two unifying themes, advocacy leaders agreed that among the top priorities for advocacy were *affordable healthcare, long-term care options, the removal of persistent employment barriers, access to assistive technologies,* and the *enforcement of existing civil rights legislation.* Additional advocacy priorities have highlighted the importance of *more interdependent* (vs independent) *approaches to work, school, and community living* (Barnes 2003). Others have championed the need for *more effective transitioning of disabled high school students to fair pay community living or internship programs, and more sustainable accommodations for college students with disabilities* that incorporate co-curricular programming, recruitment, and retention plans (Balcazar and Suarez-Balcazar 2016). Students often come to college unprepared to self-advocate, and many colleges fail to provide such training opportunities (Gil 2007; Keys et al. 2014). Yet, self-advocacy in higher education directly contributes to educational achievement and well-being (Adams and Proctor 2010; Daly-Cano et al. 2015; Getzel and Thoma 2008; Murray et al. 2014). Furthermore, college students with disabilities who know how to advocate for themselves on campus (and in the classroom) are more likely to develop a collective consciousness as members of the disability community poised to take action for change (Kimball et al. 2016).

Another priority domain of disability-directed advocacy has focused on *increasing the political participation of people with disabilities* as change agents of the future. For example, some organizations have missions to increase voter registration and turnout, develop legislative agendas that prioritize disability concerns, and increase the election and appointment of disabled people to public offices and other positions of power (Barnartt et al. 2001). Building capacity for a more inclusive cross-disability community requires representation from emerging constituencies that have not been as involved in disability rights politics, including the intersectional voices of those with several marginalized identities, particularly people of color, those with lower incomes, and sexual, language, and other minorities (e.g. immigrant, Deaf, and speech impairments).

The most far-reaching priority for those who claim to advocate for the inclusion and quality of life of people with disabilities relates to the *implementation of the global initiative known as the United Nations Convention on the Rights of Persons with Disabilities (UNCRPD)* (Mittler 2015). So far, 175 international governments have ratified the CRPD, solidifying their commitment to abide by international laws to realize disability rights on a global scale. This commitment requires sustained and coordinated advocacy to translate policy into practice; increase public awareness; develop mechanisms for data collection and collaboration with the scientific community; and monitor progress to ensure accountability across all sectors of civil society.

> The CRPD is not merely the latest in a long line of UN declarations, but a potential catalyst for a radical reappraisal of policy and practice among governments and organizations of persons with disabilities (disabled persons' organizations (DPOs)) and by service planners and providers, members of professional and voluntary organizations, the research community, and by society at large. (Mittler 2015, p. 79)

In order to build momentum for advocacy that (i) aligns with a socio-political orientation of disability, (ii) emphasizes the unification of disparate groups through inclusive practices, and (iii) prioritizes transformational approaches to reduce ableist practices, some have leveraged the benefits of cross-organization coalition building.

Building Coalitions

Effective coalition building requires a shared vision about priority advocacy issues and frequent communication about how different organizations can each contribute to common goals instead of pulling in different directions and competing for the same limited funds. This is complicated when advocacy efforts are fragmented or when groups have differing priorities. Some may be more concerned about enforcing nondiscrimination laws while others seek to extend legal protections to those with less recognized impairments (e.g. multiple chemical sensitivity, gender "dysphoria," auto-immune conditions, and addictions) (Brown 2000). Another barrier to effective coalition building relates to the ableism of organizations reticent to build coalitions with others for fear of stigma by association (Gerber 2009). For example, as early as the 1950s the Paralyzed Veterans of America successfully lobbied for accessible bathrooms and parking spaces, but were reluctant to align with the broader disability rights movement (Scotch 1988). Similar rifts have been documented within some factions of the Deaf community unwilling to unite under the banner of disability, and between those who advocate for research on autism prevention and those dedicated to promoting neurodiversity (Ne'eman 2010).

Despite these difficulties, many disability-directed advocacy groups have formed effective coalitions to mobilize on a number of fronts. For example, the Center for Advanced Communications Policy has developed a collaborative network to better coordinate disability and technology policy (Baker et al. 2008). Rehabilitation Research and Training Centers (RRTCs) around the country also work collaboratively with independent living groups to advance the inclusion of disabled people from diverse cultures, economic statuses, and emerging impairment groups (e.g. multiple chemical sensitivity, chronic illness, and auto-immune conditions; Balcazar and Suarez-Balcazar 2016; White 2010). Similarly, the Ford Foundation, recently infused its strategic plan with a disability rights agenda aimed at disrupting inequality (Dickson and Blahovec 2016). Globally, Inclusion International has over 200 member societies actively working toward implementation of the treaty for global disability rights UNCRPD among other issues; they continue to seek partnership with universities, research centers, and individuals.

In summary, effective disability advocacy incorporates the expertise and experience of disabled people while building capacity for members to engage in planning, management, and implementation of objectives. Organizations must provide structure for efficient resource allocation, and assess progress toward measurable objectives while promoting autonomy, leadership development, and access to decision making. For a more complete discussion of an agenda for critical disability advocacy and its generative potential for anti-ableism research see Dirth and Nario-Redmond (2019).

> Framing disability advocacy according to a sociopolitical model is consonant with the Disability Rights Movement's history of self-determination, its capacity to unite people with disparate impairments under the shared experience of social disadvantage, and its generative potential for future advocacy work. (Dirth and Nario-Redmond 2019, p. 356)

Conclusions, Implications, and Recommendations

In an effort to generate a few conclusions, speculations, and recommendations for next steps, this synopsis responds to the five queries offered in the first chapter of this book.

- What does ableism look like? What are its common manifestations?
- What are the causes of ableism against disabled people, and how are these perpetuated?
- How do disabled people respond to ableism, and how do responses affect well-being?
- What works to reduce ableism, promote understanding, and increase equality?
- What research questions remain unanswered for a future research agenda?

What Does Ableism Look like?

Disability prejudice is multifaceted and evolving. Much more than a unitary negative attitude, ableism can be benevolent, paternalistic, ambivalent, and hostile; it can be expressed unintentionally or deliberately in individual beliefs, emotions, behaviors, and institutional practices that result in the prejudicial treatment of people on the basis of disability. While much of the traditional scientific literature concluded that disability attitudes were predominantly explicit and negative, historic changes in the legislative landscape have revealed new manifestations of ableism that include sympathetic, envious, exploitive, and still brutal forms of discrimination that reflect how ableism continues to change over time. The following suggests when these different forms seem most likely to emerge.

Benevolent or Indulgent Ableism When asked to explicitly evaluate others' achievements (e.g. applications, transcripts, contributions), people consistently exaggerate the favorability of people with disabilities over those without – even when the credentials of both groups are equivalent. This "positivity" bias does not necessarily equate to truly positive appraisals. Normative pressures that dictate charitable kindness, along with the sense of astonishment that comes from having low expectations for the group, both seem to be operating, especially toward those not held responsible for their disability status. Moreover, the tendency to admire those perceived to have "overcome" their limitations by daring to appear in public, go to college, date, or play a sport has evolved into a modern form of ableism known as inspiration porn. Inspiration porn describes the portrayal of disabled people, often in the media, as objects of amazement and wonder as a way to motivate those without disabilities to get a move on and aspire for self-improvement. The criticism is not that disabled people are never deserving of respect and admiration, but when ordinary activities of daily living are portrayed as heroic, and disabled people are used to motivate appreciation for those with more privileged lives, objectification and misunderstanding prevails. Furthermore, when those admired as brave and heroic are used to shame other disabled people, the message is that with enough effort, *anyone* can get ahead (get out of bed, walk, talk, see, and hear) *if* they really want to – so they must not be working hard enough. More dangerously, people may infer that if some people can overcome, so should everybody else, suggesting there is no need for legal protection against discrimination or the removal of environmental barriers. As a result, accommodations and other services may be denied to those who fail to overcome. These well-intentioned compliments, and the deferential posturing that occurs alongside nervous nonverbal behaviors, contribute to the awkwardness of "mixed-ability interactions" that so often communicate confusion and mistrust. As a consequence, both disabled and nondisabled people may approach such interactions with caution, and still misinterpret one another when "admiring" intentions result in intrusive inquiries and overcompensation that makes neither party feel particularly understood.

Paternalistic or Condescending Ableism Beyond the benevolent expressions of sympathy lurk the more ambivalent or mixed forms of prejudice that appear with much more regularity than purely positive or negative ableism. Contemporary theories explain how certain groups – stereotyped as incompetent and warm – elicit feelings of pity and behaviors that infantilize, overprotect, and take control over those considered to be society's legitimate dependents (e.g. children, the elderly, women, people with disabilities) – as long as they don't violate the role expectations of a submissive and cooperative subordinate. In contrast to genuine compassion, pity and other "fatherly" prejudices are by nature condescending and dismissive. Paternalistic prejudice works to maintain the inferior status of its targets because it only appears prosocial; yet, many fail to recognize its harmfulness to the integrity, autonomy, and authority of disabled subjects, which perpetuates the problem. Consequences of paternalistic ableism include the justification of forced medication, institutionalization, and the sheltered regulation of disabled lives "for their own good." In addition, because pity involves both tenderness and distress (e.g. guilt), disabled people are often exploited as objects of suffering to raise charitable funds, and are generally neglected when organizations fail to plan for their arrival or dismiss their requests for access deemed unnecessary by authorities. No one wants to hire or befriend someone they pity. Pity leads to the chronic mistaking of disabled identities as tragic and suffering instead of satisfying and worthwhile.

Envious and Resentful Ableism A second form of ambivalent prejudice reflects a mixture of begrudging admiration, jealousy, resentment, and bitterness toward groups stereotyped as competent but cold because they occupy positions of relative (or increasing) power. Disabled people have been viewed as capable of competing for the resources available to higher status groups. Those who are the targets of envious and resentful prejudices may have previously been among the lower status, less legitimate groups whose social circumstances have since improved, or threaten to surpass those who currently occupy positions of dominance. As disabled people are increasingly being recognized as the largest minority group in the United States, their public visibility has substantially improved, and they have made important gains as a constituency working to advance human rights. Ableism in the form of backlash against disability rights protections has resulted. For example, recent headlines depict disabled people as manipulative scammers for filing lawsuits against businesses that have failed to comply with the ADA, or as imposters if they don't appear disabled enough because they can walk for limited distances without a mobility device. As a consequence, disabled people struggle to justify their need for accommodations in school and at work, especially when these are described as "special needs" or "privileges" instead of civil rights.

Several minority groups (e.g. Jews, Asians, the nouveau rich) have been targets of envious prejudices following their upward social mobility and "encroachment" into established roles, cultural traditions, and leadership positions. This is especially the case for groups not so easily absorbed into the American melting pot who – instead of assimilating – are viewed as diversifying, complicating, or supplanting the status quo. Those in positions of power do not necessarily yield it without a fight, and may actively work to prevent their "invasion" by lashing out against policies that protect certain groups, blaming them for societal problems they did not create. Historically, disabled people were among the first rounded up by the Nazis for extermination, and like the Jews were scapegoated as responsible for the degeneration of society, attributed to their genetic inferiority. Social Darwinist practices have evolved into a new eugenics which still aims to improve the human species using genetic technologies to eradicate disability if not before birth then afterwards through euthanasia, assisted suicide, and other "merciful" practices designed to eliminate those considered defective or causing burdensome, unnecessary suffering.

Derisive, Disdainful, or Contemptuous Ableism Ableism also emerges as negative prejudice expressed in the form of shaming language, disgusted looks, and defensive or hostile behaviors directed toward those considered the illegitimate dependents of society (e.g. immigrants, homeless, scroungers). These groups are thought to compete with dominant worldviews refusing to conform to the rules of a civilized society. They are the groups stereotyped as incompetent but cold; they incite feelings of dread and disgust which are then used to justify their public banishment, containment, and elimination in order to keep them from "contaminating" others. Internment camps, ethnic cleansings, and the 2016 massacre of disabled people in Japan are all extreme examples of contemptuous prejudice. This form of ableism can also be found in rising hate crimes, including the murder, rape, and torture of disabled people – particularly those with more noticeable conditions or behaviors. Remember, disgust is not only aroused toward those assumed to be contagious with disease, but also toward people who violate moral imperatives like those who cheat or leech from the resources intended for the more "deserving."

Ableism in the form of degradation, humiliation, and hostile punishment is often rationalized as necessary to defend against those who threaten to erode the current social order – particularly those whose human status can be questioned because they fail to walk upright, leak human waste, or seem bereft of language, rationality, or self-reflection. When confronted with people who remind us of our animalistic natures, some recoil and work to reaffirm their supreme status by denying the humanity of others. By restraining, caging, or otherwise taming disabled people who "refuse" to become normalized, non-disabled people are able to sustain the belief that they are superior to those deemed less than human. This begs the question of whether a promising avenue for future research involves cultivating an appreciation of our essential creatureliness as a pathway toward humanizing others: recognizing the self as an equal member of the animal family. Alternatively, to the extent that technologies for human enhancement (e.g. memory implants, bionic limbs, animal organ transplants) become more available, perhaps some people will come to identify as part of a superordinate or transhuman class of cyborgs: part human, part animal, and part machine.

What Are the Causes of Ableism, and How Are These Perpetuated?

Ableism reflects some common cognitive and motivational roots shaped by the unique histories of disabled people, in addition to contemporary contexts, and individual differences that impact its expression, justification, and potential for change. Among the more "distal" origins of ableism are those that refer to the predisposing factors that set the stage for prejudicial reactions; "proximal" origins are those thought have a more direct impact on prejudicial outcomes – although these factors often interact and are mutually influential. In biology, distal explanations for behavior refer to universal traits and mechanisms considered evolutionary adaptations because they contributed to the reproductive potential of a species, while proximal explanations refer to the physiology or more immediate environment of the animal. In sociology, distal explanations refer to the remote social structures and institutions within which people live their lives as compared to the more proximal influences of home or family relationships. As a social psychologist, I have borrowed the language of both disciplines to help explain the origins of ableism, and to capture explanations that operate as universal preconditions, and those more directly tied to the people involved, and the contexts preceding a prejudicial reaction. While many sources of disability prejudice operate below the level of awareness, the more distal sources may also be less available to conscious awareness or less accessible to introspection, which has implications for intentionality and change. In psychology, the study of prejudice also reflects a functional perspective that considers the various needs that human beliefs, emotions, and behaviors can serve: from those that benefited survival, safety, and belonging to those people use to make sense of the world and their place in it.

Evolutionary Origins of Ableism Some needs are very basic to survival, and involve self-protection from a variety of dangerous threats. From an evolutionary perspective, it would have been adaptive for species to develop mechanisms like a wariness of the unknown (e.g. strangers from competing groups), and a sensitivity to cues associated with disease and contamination (e.g. poisonous foods; infectious sores). Those who were better at avoiding dangers would be more likely to survive into adulthood to mate, resulting in a more vigilant population over time – highly sensitive to the detection of distinct threats. Over many years of evolutionary history, this disease-avoidance mechanism may have become over-reactive to a variety of clues that signaled vulnerability to disease. Therefore, some argue that disgust, distancing, and avoidance reactions to disabled people are due, in part, to an evolved capacity that automatically triggers the disease-avoidance mechanism whenever people are confronted by those who cough, spasm, smell, limp, slump, or have an irregular pace, uneven eyes, or missing limbs – conditions that also correspond to some of the world's deadliest infections.

Evidence for this often false-alarm, contagion-fear account of disability prejudice comes from studies of people who consistently maintain a greater distance from those with noncontagious conditions like facial disfigurements, birthmarks, burns, and amputations, in addition to less visible conditions like epilepsy, cancer, and mental illness. People even express disgust and avoid objects *touched* by those with chronic conditions and disabilities, particularly the more severe and transmittable they are perceived to be. Critically, avoidant forms of prejudice are more common during first encounters with unfamiliar disabled people, in settings that make disease more salient, and among perceivers who are particularly germaphobic. By contrast, those who regularly encounter friends and family with disabilities do not demonstrate the same distancing behaviors, and are actually less concerned about disease than others. In fact, opportunities to witness or gaze upon disabled people before meeting them tend to reduce interpersonal avoidance. Therefore, evolutionary sources of ableism are also perpetuated (and can be disrupted) by social influences, including learned beliefs and imagined alternatives. That is, these reactions are neither inevitable nor context independent.

Thus, while disabled people have a long history of being quarantined in institutions, cast away, and shunned from communal events, avoidance behaviors are not universally distributed across cultures or other animal species. Some forms of disability prejudice even seem to contradict the disease-avoidance account, like the more sympathetic forms of caregiving, impositions of help, and behaviors that suggest curiosity and interest (e.g. invasive questions about one's sexuality and toileting habits). Finally, the high incidence of rape and sexual assault of people with disabilities also seems to be driven more by existential anxiety and dehumanizing ideologies than by fears of contagion.

Existential Origins of Ableism The universal need for self-protection extends beyond a drive for physical safety. People also need psychological security, and are wired to develop cognitive mechanisms that protect us from threats to our needs for belonging and purpose in life, bodily integrity, and self-worth. Many of the psychological defenses (e.g. denial, repression, and projection of fears; rationalization of inappropriate behaviors) are central to the origins and operation of prejudice because they allow people to unconsciously distort reality in order to avoid the thoughts, feelings, and behaviors considered too threatening to accept. Disability prejudice has long been considered a response to unwanted fears of death, the meaninglessness of life (social death), and the body's vulnerability to damage and decline. Unlike many stigmatized groups, disability is a category that anyone can join. Most people prefer not to think about this by denying the possibility, identifying as invincible, or rationalizing how disability only happens to those who deserve it. Yet, the open enrollment nature of disability suggests that like death, disability is more a question of when, not if. Those who survive to age 75 can expect to live with disability for at least 10 years. If people were less threatened by this fact, perhaps they could better prepare for these eventualities. Most do not.

Thus, according to existential accounts of disability prejudice, another reason people ignore, avoid, mock, and even attack disabled people is because they serve as unwanted reminders of the indefinite frailties of life, and our vulnerability to decline, dismemberment, and deterioration. The problem with existential approaches to ableism is that they have not been well tested to identify when these different reactions are more likely to occur. However, ample evidence supports that reminders of death strongly contribute to the denigration, condemnation, and ridicule of many outgroups, including disabled people – the presence of whom can provoke death-related thoughts, particularly those with more permanent (versus temporary) impairments. Cross-cultural studies confirm that making people think about their own death not only increases prejudice, but reduces compassion toward same-sex peers with disabilities. Those with low self-worth respond even more prejudicially when considering their own death. Thoughts of death lead people to express more disgust over bodily fluids like mucus, urine, and feces, and to prefer stories that emphasize how humans are unique from other animals. Furthermore, people are more likely to dehumanize others in places where they experience disgust (e.g. hospitals, nursing homes) as disgust seems to inhibit the brain's ability to perceive others' humanity. Believing that humans are superior to animals is a strong predictor of several intergroup prejudices; and people with mental illnesses, developmental and other disabilities are thought to possess among the fewest uniquely human characteristics. What remains unclear is when threats of death and/or disability are more likely to trigger hostile, mixed, or benevolent forms of ableism depending on particular beliefs, existential concerns, and other opportunities afforded by the interaction context.

Ideological Origins that Perpetuate Ableism How belief systems are propagated, publicized, and confirmed through socialization and other communication practices constitutes another source of ableism. For example, in Western cultures, the values of freedom, personal control, independence, and equality may be questioned when people observe how these can be compromised by disability, lost when imprisoned, or replaced by alternatives that apply elsewhere. People need to make sense of inconsistencies, and justification ideologies provide handy explanations for why some people get treated differently than others, who is deserving of certain outcomes, and what happens to those that violate societal standards. Expressions of disability prejudice that deploy these ideologies, therefore, provide one way for people to validate the importance of their values and beliefs which require frequent affirmation to sustain.

Throughout history, dehumanizing treatments have evolved along with ideologies that justified the denial of humanity to those considered an affront to the human form. Some people can't seem to tolerate those who threaten their identity as human beings, so instead of acknowledging their humanity, they characterize them subhuman. This makes it easier to impose (and ignore) the abuse of disabled people who are victimized at much higher rates than those without disabilities. Violent disability hate crimes have included the smearing of feces and the dumping of urine on victims as some kind of testament to their animalistic natures.

Dehumanizing actions that seek to tame, punish, or incarcerate disabled people have been well documented. Even in school settings, the imposition of restraints and the seclusion of disabled students are justified as protection from self-harm or harm to others, without the critical input of the students themselves or their families – who may not be aware of school practices. By characterizing others as unfeeling, less than human machines, institutions have justified the denial of pain relief and other basic comforts in a variety of "care" facilities. Today, not only do anti-disability hate groups have an increased presence on the internet, hate incidents have also increased since the election of Donald Trump. "Whenever a vulnerable group is given national attention – whether the attention is positive or negative – people who are biased against the group may lash out" (Middlebrook 2017). Curiously, many of these crimes have escaped prosecution, and they are rarely reported in the media. It's hard to track hate crimes in states without anti-hate crime legislation, when reporting is voluntary, or when victims feel too unsafe to report.

Ideologies related to the origins of disability also impact how ableism is expressed. Those who understand disability to be a biomedical condition expect people to pursue treatments to cure, correct, or eliminate their impairments, which undermines support for services like sign language interpretation and personal care attendants, especially for conditions assumed to be reversible. Ideologies about meritocracy and political conservativism also work together in ways that resist change, and those who believe in the value of social dominance most strongly oppose the full inclusion of disabled people who they view as competing for scarce resources. In general, people are less willing to support assistance for those they believe to be responsible for disability onset, which is affected by how disability is discussed. Increasingly, news outlets have been held to account for reinforcing narratives that either pathologize disabled people as tragic, or objectify them supercrips (and their friends as saints). To the extent that we continue to describe access to community living and supports as "special needs," people are less able to recognize them as human rights.

Disability studies scholarship has also raised awareness by interrogating ideologies that portray disabled people as subverting traditional values associated with compulsory independence, paid productivity, and a "just" world – where bad things only happen to those who deserve it, can handle it, or haven't done enough to overcome it. We know surprisingly little about how to most effectively shift the public narrative about the social determinants of disability. Those who are younger and the more educated are more likely to have learned how disability is created by policies and practices that violate the civil rights of a large minority group whenever decision makers fail to take them into account when planning events, upgrading facilities, and recruiting personnel. If this work is to transform the debate into one that changes policies instead of fixing people, more need to be exposed to its curriculum from an early age.

Stereotypical Origins that Perpetuate Ableism Consensually shared stereotypes also develop to explain, predict, and prescribe why some groups more frequently occupy certain roles but not others. Cross-impairment stereotypes are among the more immediate sources of ableism that can produce infantilizing insults, low performance expectations, and neglectful actions based on assumed dependence, incompetence, and asexuality, among other traits ascribed to this group. These stereotypes are portrayed across a variety of media, and communicated from an early age through children's books, jokes, and everyday conversations. Whether people believe them to be true or not, disability stereotypes are often engrained in memory, and filter what information people consider when evaluating others and making decisions. This can result in biased diagnoses and unfair service eligibility decisions in healthcare settings. Disability stereotypes can also become self-fulfilling: disabled people are, in fact, less likely to graduate from college, be hired, marry, or become parents. Doctors have been known to forget to screen disabled patients for sexually transmitted diseases (STDs) and pregnancy, and still encourage their celibacy and sterilization. Furthermore, sexual health and fertility services remain inadequate for adults with disabilities, and those who are parents experience heightened scrutiny since disability status is still grounds for the legal termination of parenting rights in over 30 states.

While global disability stereotypes are remarkably consistent, sometimes effects depend on impairment type. For example, some with intellectual disabilities are assumed to be promiscuous or hypersexual degenerates, unable to control their animalistic tendencies, while those on the autistic spectrum are assumed to be violent or "machine-like" savants. Even when unaware of implicit beliefs, people still automatically associate disability with childlike tendencies; those with psychiatric disabilities trigger unconscious thoughts of danger and unpredictability as well. Such stereotypic expectations have important implications, especially given the differential punishment and incarceration of those assumed to be dangerous criminals. Many are surprised to learn that one out of three people incarcerated in federal and state prisons has documented disabilities – over three times the rate of disability in the general population. Perhaps there is a reason that many disability groups are stereotyped as vulnerable and angry.

Disability stereotypes are also deployed to help nondisabled people fulfill their need for self-esteem. For example, the importance of health, beauty, and intelligence are often considered essential to quality living. As a consequence, disabled people have become a convenient scapegoat for nondisabled people to project those characteristics they would rather not acknowledge in themselves. Conveniently, when disabled people are stereotyped as helpless and incompetent, those without disabilities can think of themselves as helpful and competent, which feels good. Of course, the need to preserve a positive identity can be accomplished without stereotypes and prejudice through personal and group achievements and prosocial actions, but disability stereotypes continue to be used to shore up the boundaries between good and evil, human and animal, self and other.

How Do Disabled People Respond to Ableism; How Do Responses Affect Well-Being?

When confronted with social rejection, hostility, condescension, and humiliation, people may react in the short term with sadness, fear, anger, frustration, and/or shame. Over time, however, pervasive experiences with prejudice and discrimination have many negative consequences, not only for the health and achievement of individuals, but for the broader society. Pervasive prejudice is an ongoing stressor that can make people sick, hyper-vigilant to rejection, paranoid, and suicidal; it can ruin relationships, preclude partnerships, and deny opportunities for advancement and societal progress, thereby underutilizing its talent pool. In some cases, prejudice results in violence, war, and mass extermination; but it can also provide the impetus for large-scale social change and more egalitarian outcomes. All of these eventualities apply when it comes to the impacts of disability prejudice.

Although target reactions to ableism vary widely, certain patterns can be discerned depending on: whether an outcome/action is attributed to prejudice; how much one identifies as disabled; and other factors like who's involved, what's at stake, and what could happen next. For example, when approached by a stranger who says, "You're so inspirational for attending this event," one disabled person might take this as a compliment while another may notice that this only happens when the service dog is present, so they consider it patronizing. A recently disabled person may be more likely to ignore the comment, but someone highly identified as a disability rights activist may try to educate the stranger or express sarcasm: "If you think my being here is inspiring, wait until you see me fly this dog." What happens next depends on a host of factors: is the stranger a future employer, are they grabbing the dog or carrying a weapon; is the disabled person fatigued or motivated to respond; do they think a response will make any difference, and how will they feel as a consequence?

Whether disabled or not, people need to feel good about themselves, to have a sense of belonging, and to exercise control over their environment. For those who belong to stigmatized groups, these needs are often thwarted by others who harbor misinformed beliefs, betray their fears with expressions of disgust, and engage in discriminatory practices. Research has identified a framework of strategies that disabled people can use in an effort to protect themselves from ableist threats to their health, well-being, and overall livelihood. Among the more common strategies are those that help people avoid situations where they expect to be devalued or treated prejudicially. This is not always possible as ableism is ubiquitous, though people can't always predict when and where it will show up. Therefore, other strategies used to cope with prejudice include those that address it head on by either confronting bias, challenging how disability is conceptualized, and/or engaging in collective actions for change. People may also prefer some strategies more than others, and switch between different strategies over the life course.

Social Mobility Strategies According to the social identity perspective, among the paths of least resistance for responding to prejudicial treatment is to escape it – if possible – to mobilize away from a disadvantaged status and into a higher status alternative. Research has documented a number of individual coping strategies used to accomplish just this. At the most basic level of social mobility, some simply deny their disability status: they avoid diagnostic labels, refuse to self-categorize, and present as nondisabled. This strategy is more common among those with less identifiable conditions. Some may not even know they have particular impairments if family members do not tell them or prevent their diagnostic testing to avoid stigma by association. Others escape through curative solutions like limb lengthening for short stature, liposuction for fat, prosthetic limbs for amputations, or plastic surgery to remove the visible markers of Down syndrome and other "irregularities." An entire tragic persons' industry exists within the allied medical professions to help those with disabilities escape their "abnormalities" – if not by curing them, then through therapies that minimize disability characteristics like: medicating psychiatric symptoms, training away autistic behaviors, or implanting devices to correct for hearing loss and low vision. For some, disability status is minimized because it is just not among the most salient or important identities a person currently claims; therefore, when confronted with ableist speech or bias, some simply ignore it, or may not even label it prejudicial. Others work hard to overcome their perceived "limitations" by practicing more "typical" behaviors, speech, and walking patterns – often declining assistive technologies that might otherwise give them away.

To illustrate, when my daughter was young, daily physical therapy was prescribed so she could walk upright with crutches, thereby avoiding the "dreaded" wheelchair – she opted for the latter. As a freshman, a former student of mine insisted on staying up all hours of the night to compensate for dyslexia by reading printed texts and writing out her papers longhand instead of requesting accommodations like an audio book or a spell checker. There are many ways to deliberately conceal disability, which is *not* the same as nondisclosure: some people have less visible conditions that they simply don't reveal to every stranger, but this doesn't necessarily mean they want to detach themselves from their disability status. What distinguishes social mobility tactics from other ways of coping with prejudice is that they typically describe intentionally deployed efforts to psychologically, if not physically, distance oneself away from a stigmatized status, and toward a higher status alternative. In general, people are much more likely to distance themselves from disability to the extent that they are less identified with the group, and more invested in the way things are. This includes those with less apparent or more temporary conditions; those who consider disability less important to self-definition; and those who believe that the existing system treats people as they deserve to be treated.

Consequences of Social Mobility Strategies There are several practical benefits to deploying some of the individualistic strategies designed to distance the self from ableism. Passing as nondisabled can protect people from job and other forms of discrimination that limit economic opportunities. Choosing to disclose disability is risky because ableist stereotypes can bias the evaluation of candidates seeking to be admitted, hired, and promoted. Deciding if, and when, to disclose disability information, which may be irrelevant in some situations, also offers disabled people a sense of control over their self-presentation. Minimizing the importance of disability can also protect self-esteem as long as people have not internalized a pathologized view of their impairment as a personal failure, which can result in self-loathing, social withdrawal, and a sense of hopelessness about the future. When prejudice is internalized, people tend to blame themselves for their disadvantaged circumstances and are less likely to notice discrimination. They are also more susceptible to stress and unhealthy coping behaviors, including substance abuse and poor wellness management.

Even the strategic use of medical therapies to normalize appearances *can be* beneficial, and may improve functioning in compliance with typical ways of learning, moving, and being in the world. Recall that the ideologies of meritocracy, rugged individualism, and hard work reinforce beliefs that people should do everything they can to overcome perceived limitations; therefore, it's not surprising that many attempt to overcome disability. For those who grew up as the only disabled person in the family, school, or neighborhood, social mobility strategies may be the only tactics they've been taught: "No one has to know; You are totally normal; We don't even think of you as disabled; This is just temporary; We can fix this; Disability doesn't define you; You can overcome anything."

However, these individualistic strategies can come at significant costs. For example, the use of crutches is time-consuming and exhausting, impeding activities that involve the hands, which are often busy gripping the crutch handles to avoid falling. Expensive surgeries, bionic implants, and high-tech stair-climbing devices are neither affordable nor appropriate for many people with disabilities.

Similarly, while the strategy of practicing to overcome impairment limitations may improve certain skills and produce a sense of accomplishment, overcoming can also compromise achievement – especially when failure to disclose disability precludes qualifying for accommodations needed to demonstrate competencies. Unlike in primary schools, which are required to accommodate students with disabilities, in college and in the workplace, in order to qualify for sign language interpretation, large print, flex time, and other accommodations, people must first disclose their disabilities to the appropriate personnel. For example, blind students can be extremely successful when provided with materials they can read using the capacities of hearing and touch – otherwise they may not be able to access the curriculum.

As an undergraduate professor, I have witnessed several students who received disability services in high school but failed to request these in college until they were on the brink of failure. Actively concealing one's disability status can also be psychologically damaging and produce feelings of inauthenticity, discomfort about deceiving others, and anxiety about being discovered. Finally, even when social mobility strategies protect individuals from interpersonal prejudice in the short term, these strategies do nothing to address ableism in society or to improve the material circumstances of disabled people as a group. Conceivably, these strategies may even reinforce the idea that disability is something to be avoided, concealed, diminished, or overcome. Those who choose to defect from the group may perpetuate the notion that ableism isn't a widespread problem since it isn't a problem for them.

Social Creativity and Social Change Strategies Sometimes escaping or distancing oneself from disability status is not desirable, and sometimes it's impossible (e.g. for those with more noticeable conditions). An alternative set of strategies is available to help people respond to ableism by changing the way people think about disability instead of changing people with disabilities. To illustrate, some choose to compare themselves to other impairment groups in ways that make them look or feel better: "I may be blind but at least I can hear"; or "I may be deaf but at least I can see." This kind of social comparison seems quite common among those newly adjusting to acquired disabilities; however, considering others as "worse off" than oneself turns disability groups against each other, which undermines the solidarity needed to build cross-impairment coalitions. Another socially creative comparison simply diminishes the importance of former ways of doing things while promoting areas of strength: "I don't need to see the rain when I can hear the raindrops and smell it in the air"; or "I love to retreat from noise pollution by turning off my hearing aids"; or "Because I can't feel my arms, I can get full tattoo sleeves without any pain." The strategy of reframing disability as an asset is similar to the reclaiming of previously offensive terms like cripple and madness as signifiers of pride and a new cultural identity: King Gimp, Born Freak, Mad Pride, Queer Crip are all examples of social creativity gaining traction through popular media, music, films, and blog posts.

Another group-level strategy relates to affiliating with other members of the disability community, which provides a sense of belonging and mentorship for how to best navigate ableist attitudes and practices. Increasingly, disabled people have access to various in-person and online communities run by fellow disabled people that go beyond self-help, friendship, and dating sites. Many of these disability wisdom, humor, news, and educational forums are referenced in the activist pages throughout this book, including those that curate personal stories, disability arts and cultural events, community access information, and legal advocacy for disability rights. Finally, some choose to address ableism by way of collective action for social change, either with others or as individuals taking action on behalf of the group. These activities include raising awareness about the sociopolitical determinants of disability, educating others about how to confront ableism, volunteering or becoming politically active by voting, litigating ADA violations, petitioning officials, boycotting businesses that discriminate, and running for office. Those most likely to take the road less traveled, conceptualize disability as valued status, and support social change tend to be those more identifiable with the group, who are less invested in the way things are, including: people with more visible or permanent conditions; those who consider disability as a central aspect of the self; and those who consider the system to be unjust. Whether or not they engage in collective actions to advance disability rights may depend on whether they consider these strategies to be successful at changing the status quo.

Consequences of Social Creativity and Social Change Strategies Instead of escaping disability as a way to maintain positive self-regard, social creativity and social change strategies can improve the way disability is conceptualized, and the way disabled people are treated as a group. These strategies go beyond protecting people from experiencing prejudice to improving outcomes for the community as a whole. For this reason, the group-level strategies have the potential to make people feel good about themselves, not only as individuals but as members of a group – a group that is worthwhile and gaining in status. The advantages of social creativity strategies include feelings of pride and empowerment that come when one's group is recognized as valuable, portrayed respectfully, and celebrated for its historic and contemporary achievements. Those who claim disability as a group identity have strong feelings of self-worth and a recognition that misfortune is not inevitable nor due to impairment; instead they view disadvantage as deriving directly from unfair practices that discriminate against disabled people. That is, the more people identify as members of the disability community, the more they become sensitized to injustice on the basis of disability, and the more willing they are to affiliate with other disabled people and to become involved in disability rights organizations.

Affiliation with the disability community can go a long way toward developing more awareness about how to effectively educate others about different forms of ableism, and the advantages of identifying as disabled people. These advantages include improved mood and well-being from spending time with similar others who provide a sense of belonging and validate the legitimacy of experiences because they've been there too. Affiliating with similar others who share an understanding of what it's like to be accused of faking, or not working hard enough to overcome, can be a watershed for those otherwise isolated, particularly people with less apparent conditions. Without connections to disabled peers, those with more visible conditions (who are often the targets of unwanted help) may assume they need to gratefully accept others' good intentions even when this makes them feel inferior. They may not know how to decline impositions of help they didn't ask for, or how to confront others about condescending speech or infantilizing actions. Some may fear hurting others' feelings for rejecting their help, or worse, provoking their anger and violence.

To be clear, confronting others' prejudicial actions can backfire: those who harbor both benevolent and hostile feelings toward disable people have retaliated when their offers to "help" or "protect" have been rebuffed. They can lash out in that moment or decline to assist others who request help in the future. Actively promoting oneself as disabled may also threaten those who harbor feelings of animosity or disbelief when disabled people share that they do not want to be prayed for or cured, or that they are proud of their disability identity. When disabled people assert themselves as capable and competent but their accomplishments are attributed to "special privileges" or "unfair advantages," envious forms of ableism may be incited, contributing to hate crimes like the obstruction of accessible parking spaces, or damage to assistive equipment. Disabled people who engage in protests, file complaints, or bring lawsuits against civil rights violations have risked public disparagement, arrest, and bodily harm, not to mention the loss of social services for "talking back." Personal care attendants can quit or refuse to assist their clients who confront them, and policy disincentives still exist that penalize those who work too many hours by eliminating their independent living benefits – a form of institutionalized backlash. Not only have disabled people been punished for "complaining," but for years they have been rewarded for their compliance and complacency by charitable organizations and other authorities appointed as protectors of their "best interests." Some social scientists, educators, and practitioners have been among the most zealous when it comes to putting their disciplines to work to improve public attitudes about disability.

What Works to Reduce Ableism, Promote Understanding, and Increase Equality?

Most scientific efforts to reduce prejudice have assumed that prejudiced people can change their attitudes provided they have positive encounters with disabled people, empathize with them, or witness them in nonstereotypical roles. We now know that disability attitudes do improve, the more engaged contact one has with disabled people, and the longer these relationships last – as long as interactions are cooperative, and both parties appear as equals, working toward common, institutionally supported goals. That is, the vast majority of studies show that interpersonal contact does reduce feelings of prejudice and anxiety toward those involved in the interaction, at least for a limited time. The extent to which these "positive feelings" spill over to new disabled people depends on whether a connection has been made between the people one has met and the broader category of disability. For example, a positive experience with a few amazing disabled students may not generalize to the group if those students didn't disclose the fact that they were, in fact, members of the disability community. Unfortunately, much of this work ignores the existing structural and intergroup context, and whether disabled peers are positioned as inferior, role restricted, or misrepresented in media in ways that reinforce stereotypical assumptions. Furthermore, friendly interactions with a particular disabled person do not guarantee support for disability rights or equal opportunities. Just because someone likes a few disabled people, doesn't mean they are interested in becoming an ally, challenging discriminatory policies, or promoting access. This is why we need to be much clearer about what we mean by improved understanding, prejudice reduction, and support for social change.

Because human beings are intensely curious, several intervention efforts have tried to capitalize on the interest people have in feeling what it must be like to experience disability using simulations of blindness, deafness, and physical, learning, and psychiatric conditions. By and large, these simulations do not work; most promote the idea that disability is a personal deficit while ignoring the impact of environmental barriers and policies that discriminate. Attempts to mimic the emotions and behaviors of another person are problematic because simulations distort reality, perpetuate misinformation, and reproduce stereotypes related to incompetence and dependency. Those who are curious about the experiences of disabled people should talk to friends and family with disabilities, and check out the activist pages of this book that highlight various personal accounts. Remember that people don't have to appropriate another's skin color, sexuality, age, body size, or form to genuinely empathize with what people tell you in person, in books, and online about their most pressing cares and concerns.

Interestingly, much research supports the benefits of interventions that encourage people to bear witness to other group perspectives, which not only reduces bias but can increase empathetic understanding and prosocial intentions. Perspective-taking interventions can increase recognition of social inequalities, reduce the denial of discrimination, and increase support for equal rights. The problem with any intervention that blurs the boundary between a nondisabled self and a disabled other is that distress (and a desire to escape) may result due to the fact that disability is a category anyone can join. One does not need to vicariously take on another persons' pain to bear witness to their experiences. In fact, it can be downright off-putting when people insist they know exactly what another person is going through, and then proceed to take over the conversation instead of genuinely listening.

From the many educational campaigns and diversity programs designed to raise awareness about disability, those that focus on personalizing the individual have been criticized for ignoring the reality of intergroup disparities and cultural identities. People who support these de-categorization approaches are also less willing to accommodate group differences, and fail to notice discrimination. Other universalizing approaches promote awareness of the variability of sensory, learning, endurance, mobility, and engagement capacities as a way to circumvent jealousy for solutions that apply more narrowly to some mythical average, or to those who must first qualify on the basis of a legitimate disability diagnosis. However, educational interventions seem most effective when disability is framed as part of the multicultural landscape, and people are encouraged to discuss both their similarities *and* their unique and divergent experiences. Over time, those with more cross-group friendships increasingly support multicultural approaches as well.

In comparative studies, while de-categorization approaches can increase friendships and improve attitudes toward individuals, approaches that prioritize interpersonal liking often fail to translate beyond the interaction context. Specifically, the more personalized or colorblind approaches produce more inconsistent, short-lived, and sometimes negative results while multicultural approaches increase positivity, even toward stereotypical group members. Among the few studies that have compared the effectiveness of anti-prejudice interventions, friendly face-to-face contact still appears to be among the most effective. When direct interaction is not possible, indirect contact through exposure to positive media examples or even imagined interactions with disabled people not only reduces stereotypes but increases friendship potential. One implication of this finding is that for individuals who are isolated from diverse disabled people (or anxious about these encounters), indirect exposure to disability culture is one way to cultivate understanding under conditions of low stress and minimal embarrassment. For example, listening to disabled people's stories and observing their lives in a variety of contexts can broaden the knowledge base about the variability of disabled people in ways that facilitate more direct forms of interaction in the future. This is consistent with recent comparative studies on the effectiveness of interventions to reduce racism: the most potent anti-racism techniques were those that exposed people to vivid counter-stereotypical examples of ethnic minorities, followed by those that repeatedly associated positive information with the group, and those that primed a multicultural mindset.

Finally, interventions can be interspersed to foster maximum effectiveness in ways that capitalize on the benefits of each approach. For example, new friendships can be seeded through a process that is more personal and individualizing. Once interpersonally acquainted, a recognition of group identities and socio-cultural differences may be important to facilitate the transfer of positive evaluations to new members of the disability community. While disabled people should not be impelled to acknowledge their conditions, an awareness of disability as an intergroup topic may very well be important for stereotype change to establish how disabled and nondisabled representatives complexify their broader categories in memory.

This volume has emphasized the intergroup dynamics of social identities that effect personal and interpersonal prejudices, stereotypic expectations, and discriminatory actions. However, ableism goes beyond intergroup psychologies as it impacts family and other organizational relationships, institutional practices, and policies. One of the most contentious debates in the field has revolved around how to go from improving intergroup attitudes to increasing support for social change and promoting equality. It's one thing to get people to like those they've interacted with, but liking does not necessarily translate into an appreciation of cultural heritage or histories of oppression. Advancing the civil rights of disabled people did not happen because prejudiced people participated in interventions to improve their attitudes. Changes to the legislative landscape and access to the built environment were hard fought through collective actions and other forms of resistance to bigotry and injustice. Most large-scale social changes have required disadvantaged groups and their allies to directly confront both interpersonal and institutionalized discrimination because dominant groups do not part well with their privileges, nor do they welcome the redistribution of resources or opportunities considered to be "theirs." The problem with this assumption is that human rights are not for the dominant group to give to those of lesser status. Civil rights are not about waiting for reformers to carry out interventions or to invite the inclusion of more minorities to the table. Disabled people have had to become active participants in the change process.

Drawing on the perspectives of disability rights activists and the history of other social movements, it is clear that sometimes intergroup cooperation isn't enough to alter long-standing and systemic forms of ableism. Sometimes confrontation and challenge to the status quo is required to shift the policies and structures that make interaction opportunities possible, or to establish new standards for acceptable behavior and fair practice. When people express ableist beliefs or actions, they can be effectively confronted. Confrontation makes salient the unacceptability of prejudice and can arouse self-criticism among perpetrators in ways that motivate change. Confrontations create an awareness of discrepancies between how people want to be perceived and how they actually come across as racist, sexist, homophobic – prejudicial. Confrontation can even motivate a sense of collective guilt or moral outrage in those who value egalitarian beliefs, who may seek opportunities to repair the damage they have done. Confrontation also stimulates an internal motivation to curb future expressions of prejudice, especially when people are not just conforming to be politically correct.

Much evidence suggests that public, less accusatory approaches to confront prejudice, particularly when delivered by allies from the dominant majority, may be among the most persuasive forms of confrontation. Allies are often members of an advantaged group with the power to influence peers that admire them; they are also viewed as having less to gain from putting others in their place than members of the disadvantaged group. This suggests that more work on recruiting strongly supportive allies may be beneficial, as their credibility can influence others who might otherwise remain silent when prejudice is observed.

Witnessing confrontation can also encourage collective action intentions among members of disadvantaged groups who may feel emboldened to respond or complain when others pave the way. Increasingly, disabled people are voicing their discontent toward those who fail to address them personally, who impose unwanted help, or who speak in condescending tones while making decisions without their input. Confronting prejudice in a way that highlights the "greater good" associated with more equitable outcomes also has the potential to encourage conformity to new norms that condemn bias. Social movement leaders and their allies can create a unique window within which to sway public opinion about human rights that go beyond minority concerns. For example, grassroots efforts that work to increase recognition of the harmful effects of prejudice can teach others to speak up and practice anti-prejudice responses in ways that positively impact perpetrators and complacent bystanders.

Consistent with a transformative approach to social change, disability-directed advocacy insists on the recruitment, capacity building, and leadership of disabled people, and moves beyond advocacy aimed at helping people cope with stigma, ameliorate their symptoms, or normalize their appearances. Goals for the future include well-funded campaigns to advance rights-based advocacy skills and opportunities for political participation, like getting the disability vote out, and electing disabled people to public office. Coalitions of disabled and transgendered people, senior citizens, and those with other chronic conditions can better influence policies that affect their groups, which may be currently divided and competing for limited funds. If united for equality of opportunity, these constituencies would make up a major voting block that together could prioritize strategies for more inclusive and flexible healthcare and housing options, and more effective responses to hate crimes, police brutality, incarceration biases, and civil rights violations.

What Research Questions Remain Unanswered for a Future Research Agenda?

What the public currently considers to be prejudicial evolves with the times, just as language, media memes, and humor evolve to shine a light on certain hypocrisies of ignorance, neglect, and impositions that may be less tolerated or more contentiously debated. That is, the normative window of change is opening to the reconsideration of what *should* qualify as ableism: what insults, what harms, what failures of policy are now being called into question as ableist, but used to be considered acceptable or business as usual? Just a few short years ago, social psychologists were not asking questions about ableism because we were guided by faulty assumptions about impairment as the primary cause of disabling conditions; we also failed to recognize disabled people as a minority group subject to many of the same prejudices and stereotypes as other groups. While diverse, disabled people are still very much the targets of intergroup cognitive and motivational processes. What's exciting is that we can now bring more social scientific theory and intergroup methodologies to bear to better understand the complexity of ableist phenomena, and to provide more nuanced solutions.

Future research informed by disability studies and extending the stereotype content model and social identity theory seem particularly promising as certain predictions based on other minority groups may require contingent interpretations unique to disability and the history of disability rights. The appendix of this book includes many of the research questions generated throughout the chapters, but there are many more. While an intergroup perspective seems long overdue in explaining the power and identity dynamics at play with disability prejudice, even this perspective may have its boundary conditions or unintended consequences. We must continue to check our assumptions, not only about disability and ableism, but about how we study these concepts, which tends to shift between cooperative and competitive approaches. Perhaps we need to examine the intersections of cooperation and conflict within the same studies or paradigms. When it comes to how to best address, abolish, or redirect prejudices that have multiple origins, meet different needs, and manifest as distinctly different expressions depending on context, motives, and individual differences, we need to be clear about our goals. Are we interested in the formation of cross-group friendships, support for event accessibility, the designation of more integrated (or exclusive) spaces, the boycotting of businesses that discriminate, the promoting of accurate media representations, or the reduction of income, employment, and educational disparities? We also need to explicate the connections between large-scale educational campaigns, anti-prejudice interventions, and the work of disabled people and their allies in changing institutional practices, bringing about legal reforms, and securing policies to better monitor hate crimes and human rights violations.

An intergroup perspective can more fully account for the psychological tendency to dichotomize and discriminate on the basis of group memberships into which we self-categorize or not. But at some point this approach may need to be supplemented with other, more universalized understandings of human variation. Some things cannot be legislated, and may be better addressed through more informal channels, media exposure, economic sanctions, and universally designed solutions. The term ableism itself is one that can apply to anyone impacted by ability-related discrimination if denied rights based on their physical, mental, and sensory differences. One of the original drafters of the bill that became the ADA argued that disability was never meant to suggest categorical certainty, and that a central misconception is that there are:

> Two distinct groups in society – those with disabilities and those without – and that it's possible to have a list of all those who have disabilities ... That's simply not reality ... People vary across a whole spectrum of infinitely small gradations of ability with regard to any given function ... The importance of any functional skill varies immensely according to the situation ... What makes anyone "eligible" for protection under the ADA is the same thing makes any of us "eligible" for protection under the laws against age discrimination, or gender discrimination: We're "eligible" to use the law once we run into discrimination. (The Disabilities Act covers all of us 1999)

We also need to bring an analysis of disability to our work, whatever that work may be. For those in academic positions, contemporary pedagogy emphasizes the importance of having difficult dialogues with our students and fellow colleagues; we shouldn't be afraid of productive discomfort when it comes to intergroup relations and discussions of privilege, ability, disability, and our creaturely vulnerabilities. We need to infuse the curriculum with disability studies scholarship and first-hand accounts of disabled people with a variety of experiences from early childhood onward to provide the next generation with contemporary examples of disability culture, movement leaders, artists, and historic figures.

Extending Maria Palacios's (2017) poem "Naming Ableism," that opened this volume, I hope that each of you will consider the following as you go about your daily lives to meet, greet, and commune with others: Instead of assuming that your audience does not include disabled people, plan for inclusion and multiple ways of participating. Instead of fearing embarrassment and avoiding others, try, approach, listen, and converse: so you make some mistakes, it's OK. Instead of ignoring or staring, acknowledge your fellow human beings. Instead of imposing unwanted help, ask first, help may not be desired, and don't hesitate to ask what others can do for you. Consider becoming an ally. Instead of suspecting fraud, give people the benefit of the doubt: most impairments are not visible, and benefits are notoriously difficult to qualify for. Instead of saying you'd rather be dead than disabled, know that disabled people can and do live quality lives, and that most of us have friends and family living with multiple impairments. Instead of praising children for doing things "all by themselves," praise them for working together, for collaborating. Instead of yanking children away from an oncoming person with a disability, allow them to express curiosity, but respect those who prefer not to share; instead of praying for a cure, pray for humility and understanding. Instead of refusing to touch or taste the unfamiliar, expand your palate: take a bite from the bounty that is the human condition.

References

Abrams, D. and Hogg, M.A. (2010). Social identity and self-categorization. In: *The SAGE Handbook of Prejudice, Stereotyping and Discrimination* (ed. J.F. Dovidio, M. Hewstone, P. Glick and V.M. Esses), 179–193. Thousand Oaks, CA: Sage.

ADA National Network. (2017). What is the Americans with Disabilities Act (ADA)? https://adata.org/learn-about-ada (accessed 23 February 2019).

Adams, K.S. and Proctor, B.E. (2010). Adaptation to college for students with and without disabilities: group differences and predictors. *Journal of Postsecondary Education and Disability* 22 (3): 166–184.

Alland, S., Barokka, K., and Sluman, D. (eds.) (2017). *Stairs and Whispers: D/deaf and Disabled Poets Write Back*. Rugby: Nine Arches Press.

Anspach, R.P. (1979). From stigma to identity politics: political activism among the physically disabled and former mental patients. *Social Science of Medicine* 13: 765–773.

Ashburn-Nardo, L., Morris, K.A., and Goodwin, S.A. (2008). The Confronting Prejudiced Responses (CPR) model: applying CPR in organizations. *Academy of Management Learning & Education* 7 (3): 332–342.

Ashburn-Nardo, L., Blanchar, J.C., Petersson, J. et al. (2014). Do you say something when it's your boss? The role of perpetrator power in prejudice confrontation. *Journal of Social Issues* 70 (4): 615–636.

Baker, P. M., Dickson, A. C., and Moon, N. W. (2008). Collaborative policy networks: coordinating disability and technology policy. Center for Advanced Communications Policy (CACP), Wireless RERC, Workplace Accommodations RERC, Atlanta, GA. CACP Working Paper, 1(08).

Balcazar, F.E. and Suarez-Balcazar, Y. (2016). On becoming scholars and activists for disability rights. *American Journal of Community Psychology* 58 (3–4): 251–258.

Barnartt, S.N. (2008). Social movement diffusion? The case of disability protests in the US and Canada. *Disability Studies Quarterly* 28 (1): http://dsq-sds.org/announcement (accessed 23 February 2019).

Barnartt, S.N. and Scotch, R.K. (2001). *Disability Protests: Contentious Politics 1970–1999*. Washington DC: Gallaudet University Press.

Barnartt, S.N., Schriner, K., and Scotch, R.K. (2001). Advocacy and political action. In: *Handbook of Disability Studies* (ed. G.L. Albrecht, K.D. Seelman and M. Bury), 430–467. London: Sage.

Barnes, C. (2003). Independent living, politics and implications. Independent Living Institute. https://www.independentliving.org/docs6/barnes2003.html (accessed 27 February 2019).

Barokka, K. (2016). *Indigenous Species*. Sheffield: Tilted Axis Press CIC.

Barton, L. (2005). *Disability and Dependency*. London: Routledge.

Becker, J. and Barreto, M. (2014). Ways to go: men's and women's support for aggressive and nonaggressive confrontation of sexism as a function of gender identification. *Journal of Social Issues* 70 (4): 668–686.

Becker, J.C., Zawadzki, M.J., and Shields, S.A. (2014). Confronting and reducing sexism: a call for research on intervention. *Journal of Social Issues* 70 (4): 603–614.

Bekhour, D. (2016). Anderson Cooper: What were you thinking? *Medium* (7 December). https://medium.com/@OptimisticGrin/anderson-cooper-what-were-you-thinking-425fa6a9932a (accessed 23 February 2019).

Blanchard, F.A., Crandall, C.S., Brigham, J.C. et al. (1994). Condemning and condoning racism: a social context approach to interracial settings. *Journal of Applied Psychology* 79 (6): 993–997.

Bozeman, R. (2015). Bystander confronting of anti-Black racism: effects of belonging affirmation and confrontation training. Master thesis. Loyola University Chicago. Paper 2886. http://ecommons.luc.edu/luc_theses/2886 (accessed 23 February 2019).

Brown, K.T. and Ostrove, J.M. (2013). What does it mean to be an ally? The perception of allies from the perspective of people of color. *Journal of Applied Social Psychology* 43 (11): 2211–2222.

Brown, S. (2000). *Freedom of Movement: Independent Living History and Philosophy*. Houston, TX: Independent Living Research Utilization https://www.ilru.org/sites/default/files/freedom_of_movement.pdf (accessed 27 February 2019).

Bruyère, S.M., von Schrader, S., Coduti, W., and Bjelland, M. (2010). United States employment disability discrimination charges: implications for disability management practice. *International Journal of Disability Management* 5 (2): 48–58.

Burstein, P. (2006). Why estimates of the impact of public opinion on public policy are too high: empirical and theoretical implications. *Social Forces* 84: 2273–2290.

Carson, D.P. (2013). *Ed Roberts: Father of Disability Rights*. Indianapolis, IN: Dog Ear Publishing.

Chamberlin, J. (1978). *On Our Own: Patient-Controlled Alternatives to the Mental Health System*. New York: McGraw-Hill.

Charlton, J.I. (1998). *Nothing About Us Without Us: Disability Oppression and Empowerment*. Berkley, CA: University of California Press.

Colker, R. (1999). The Americans with Disabilities Act: a windfall of defendants. *Harvard Civil Rights-Civil Liberties Law Review* 34: 99–162.

Crandall, C.S., Ferguson, M.A., and Bahns, A.J. (2013). When we see prejudice: the normative window and social change. In: *Stereotyping and Prejudice* (ed. C. Stangor and C.S. Crandall), 53–69. New York: Psychology Press.

Crichton, A. and Jongbloed, L. (1998). *Disability and Social Policy in Canada*. Toronto: Captus Press.

Czopp, A.M. and Monteith, M.J. (2003). Confronting prejudice (literally): reactions to confrontations of racial and gender bias. *Personality and Social Psychology Bulletin* 29 (4): 532–544.

Czopp, A.M., Monteith, M.J., and Mark, A.Y. (2006). Standing up for a change: reducing bias through interpersonal confrontation. *Journal of Personality and Social Psychology* 90 (5): 784–803.

Czopp, A.M. and Ashburn-Nardo, L. (2012). Interpersonal confrontations of prejudice. In: *The Psychology of Prejudice: Interdisciplinary Perspectives on Contemporary Issues* (ed. D.W. Russell and C.A. Russell), 175–201. Hauppauge, NY: Nova Science Publishers.

Daly-Cano, M., Vaccaro, A., and Newman, B. (2015). College student narratives about learning and using self-advocacy skills. *Journal of Postsecondary Education and Disability* 28 (2): 213–227.

Department of Education. (n.d.). IDEA: Individuals with Disabilities Act. https://sites.ed.gov/idea (accessed 23 February 2019).

Dickson, J. and Blahovec, S. (2016). Ford Foundation and supporting the Disability Rights Movement: we've only just begun. *Responsive Philanthropy* https://www.ncrp.org/wp-content/uploads/2016/12/RP_Fall16-120516-Dickson-Blahovec.pdf (accessed 23 February 2019).

Dickter, C.L., Kittel, J.A., and Gyurovski, I.I. (2012). Perceptions of non-target confronters in response to racist and heterosexist remarks. *European Journal of Social Psychology* 42 (1): 112–119.

Dirth, T.P. and Branscombe, N.R. (2018). Disability models affect disability policy support through awareness of structural discrimination. *Journal of Social Issues* 73 (2): 413–442.

Dirth, T.P. and Nario-Redmond, M.R. (2019). Disability advocacy for a new era: leveraging social psychology and a sociopolitical approach to change. In: *Understanding the Experience of Disability: Perspectives from Social and Rehabilitation Psychology*, Academy of Rehabilitation Psychology Series (ed. D.S. Dunn). New York: Oxford University Press.

Droogendyk, L., Louis, W.R., and Wright, S.C. (2016). Renewed promise for positive cross-group contact: the role of supportive contact in empowering collective action. *Canadian Journal of Behavioural Science/Revue Canadienne Des Sciences Du Comportement* 48 (4): 317–327.

Drury, B. J. (2013). Confronting for the greater good: are confrontations that address the broad benefits of prejudice reduction taken seriously? Doctoral dissertation. University of Washington.

Drury, B.J. and Kaiser, C.R. (2014). Allies against sexism: the role of men in confronting sexism. *Journal of Social Issues* 70 (4): 637–652.

Drury, J. and Reicher, S. (2009). Collective psychological empowerment as a model of social change: researching crowds and power. *Journal of Social Issues* 65 (4): 707–725.

Dunn, D.S. and Andrews, E.E. (2015). Person-first and identity-first language: developing psychologists' cultural competence using disability language. *American Psychologist* 70 (3): 255–264.

Durlak, J.A. and DuPre, E.P. (2008). Implementation matters: a review of research on the influence of implementation on program outcomes and the factors affecting implementation. *American Journal of Community Psychology* 41 (3–4): 327–350.

Eliezer, D. and Major, B. (2012). It's not your fault: the social costs of claiming discrimination on behalf of someone else. *Group Processes & Intergroup Relations* 15 (4): 487–502.

Ellemers, N. (1993). The influence of socio-structural variables on identity management strategies. *European Review of Social Psychology* 4 (1): 27–57.

Ellemers, N., Spears, R., and Doosje, B. (2002). Self and social identity. *Annual Review of Psychology* 53 (1): 161–186.

Erickson, W., Lee, C., and von Schrader, S. (2015). *Disability Statistics from the 2013 American Community Survey (ACS)*. Ithaca, NY: Cornell University Employment and Disability Institute (EDI) www.disabilitystatistics.org (accessed 23 February 2019).

Ford, T.E., Boxer, C.F., Armstrong, J. et al. (2008). More than "just a joke": the prejudice-releasing function of sexist humor. *Personality and Social Psychology Bulletin* 34 (2): 159–170.

Foster-Fishman, P., Jimenez, T., Valenti, M., and Kelley, T. (2007). Building the next generation of leaders in the disabilities movement. *Disability & Society* 22 (4): 341–356.

Gerber, D. (2009). Creating group identity: disabled veterans and American government. *OAH Magazine of History* 23 (3): 23–28.

Gervais, S.J. and Hillard, A.L. (2014). Confronting sexism as persuasion: effects of a confrontation's recipient, source, message, and context. *Journal of Social Issues* 70 (4): 653–667.

Getzel, E.E. and Thoma, C.A. (2008). Experiences of college students with disabilities and the importance of self-determination in higher education settings. *Career Development for Exceptional Individuals* 31 (2): 77–84.

Gil, L.A. (2007). Bridging the transition gap from high school to college: preparing students with disabilities for a successful postsecondary experience. *Teaching Exceptional Children* 40 (2): 12–15.

Gill, C.J. (2001). Divided understandings: the social experience of disability. In: *Handbook of Disability Studies* (ed. G.L. Albrecht, K.D. Seelman and M. Bury), 351–372. London: Sage.

Ginsburg, R. B. and Supreme Court of the United States. (1998). US Reports: *Olmstead v. L.C.*, 527 U.S. 581.

Goodley, D. and Lawthom, R. (2006). Disability studies and psychology: new allies? In: *Disability and Psychology: Critical Introductions and Reflections* (ed. D. Goodley and R. Lawthom), 1–18. New York: Palgrave Macmillan.

Greene, K.R. (2013). Disability rights movement (United States). In: *The Wiley-Blackwell Encyclopedia of Social and Political Movements* (ed. D.A. Snow, D. della Porta, B. Klandermans and D. McAdam), 360–364. Hoboken, NJ: Wiley Blackwell.

Grimoldby, S.N. (2016). Easy access: Chicago shops large & small latest targets of growing trend of ADA Title III accessibility lawsuits. *CookCountyRecord* https://cookcountyrecord. com/stories/510708140-easy-access-chicago-shops-large-small-latest-targets-of-growing-trend-of-ada-title-iii-accessibility-lawsuits (accessed 23 February 2019).

Grossman, P.D. and Colker, R. (2015). *The Law of Disability Discrimination for Higher Education Professionals: 2015 Update. Court Decisions, Settlements, and Guidance.* Durham, NC: Carolina Academic Press https://cap-press.com/pdf/Grossman Disability2015Supp.pdf (accessed 23 February 2019).

Gulker, J.E., Mark, A.Y., and Monteith, M.J. (2013). Confronting prejudice: the who, what, and why of confrontation effectiveness. *Social Influence* 8 (4): 280–293.

Hahn, H.D. (1985). Toward a politics of disability: definitions, disciplines, & policies. *The Social Science Journal* 22 (4): 87–105.

Harpur, P. (2014). Naming, blaming and claiming ableism: the lived experiences of lawyers and advocates with disabilities. *Disability & Society* 29 (8): 1234–1247.

Hillard, A. L. (2011). Why confronting sexism works: applying persuasion theories to confronting sexism. Doctoral dissertation. University of Nebraska-Lincoln. ProQuest Dissertation and Theses database (Publication No. AAT 3465862).

Hornsey, M.J., Oppes, T., and Svensson, A. (2002). "It's OK if we say it, but you can't": responses to intergroup and intragroup criticism. *European Journal of Social Psychology* 32 (3): 293–307.

Hyers, L.L. (2007). Resisting prejudice every day: exploring women's assertive responses to anti-Black racism, anti-Semitism, heterosexism, and sexism. *Sex Roles* 56 (1): 1–12.

Iyer, A., Schmader, T., and Lickel, B. (2007). Why individuals protest the perceived transgressions of their country: the role of anger, shame, and guilt. *Personality and Social Psychology Bulletin* 33 (4): 572–587.

Jetten, J., Spears, R., and Postmes, T. (2004). Intergroup distinctiveness and differentiation: a meta-analytic integration. *Journal of Personality and Social Psychology* 86 (6): 862–879.

Jetten, J., Iyer, A., Branscombe, N.R., and Zhang, A. (2013). How the disadvantaged appraise group-based exclusion: the path from legitimacy to illegitimacy. *European Review of Social Psychology* 24 (1): 194–224.

Johnson, M. (1994). A test of wills: Jerry Lewis, Jerry's Orphans, and the telethon. In: *The Ragged Edge: The Disability Experience from the Pages of the First Fifteen Years of the Disability Rag* (ed. B. Shaw), 125–136. Louisville, KY: The Avocado Press.

Kaiser, C.R. and Miller, C.T. (2004). A stress and coping perspective on confronting abstract sexism. *Psychology of Women Quarterly* 28 (2): 168–178.

Keys, C.B., McMahon, S.D., and Viola, J.J. (2014). Including students with disabilities in urban public schools: community psychology theory and research. *Journal of Prevention & Intervention in the Community* 42 (1): 1–6.

Kimball, E.W., Moore, A., Vaccaro, A. et al. (2016). College students with disabilities redefine activism: self-advocacy, storytelling, and collective action. *Journal of Diversity in Higher Education* 9 (3): 245–260.

Klandermans, B. (1997). *The Social Psychology of Protest.* Oxford: Blackwell.

Kliewer, C. and Drake, S. (1998). Disability, eugenics, and the current ideology of segregation: a modern moral tale. *Disability & Society* 13 (1): 95–111.

Lamm, N. (2015). This is disability justice. *The Body is Not an Apology* https://thebody isnotanapology.com/magazine/this-is-disability-justice/ (accessed 27 May 2019).

Lawson, T., McDonough, T., and Bodle, J. (2010). Confronting prejudiced comments: effectiveness of a role-playing exercise. *Teaching of Psychology* 37 (4): 257–261.

Little, D.L. (2010). Identity, efficacy, and disability rights movement recruitment. *Disability Studies Quarterly* 30 (1): 1–17. http://dsq-sds.org/article/view/1013/1226 (accessed 27 February 2019).

Longmore, P.K. and Umansky, L. (2001). *The New Disability History: American Perspectives*. New York: New York University Press.

Louis, W.R. (2009). Collective action – and then what? *Journal of Social Issues* 65 (4): 727–748.

Louis, W.R., Taylor, D.M., and Douglas, R.L. (2005). Normative influence and rational conflict decisions: group norms and cost-benefit analyses for intergroup behavior. *Group Processes & Intergroup Relations* 8 (4): 355–374.

Luders, J. (2006). The economics of movement success: business responses to civil rights mobilization. *American Journal of Sociology* 111 (4): 963–998.

Makas, E. (1988). Positive attitudes toward disabled people: disabled and nondisabled persons' perspectives. *Journal of Social Issues* 44 (1): 49–61.

Mallett, R.K. and Wagner, D.E. (2011). The unexpectedly positive consequences of confronting sexism. *Journal of Experimental Social Psychology* 47 (1): 215–220.

Marshall, T. (2003). *Supreme Justice: Speeches and Writings*. Philadelphia: University of Pennsylvania Press.

McColl, M.A. and Boyce, W. (2003). Disability advocacy organizations: a descriptive framework. *Disability and Rehabilitation* 25 (8): 380–392.

McLean, J. (2003). Employees with long term illnesses or disabilities in the UK social services workforce. *Disability & Society* 18 (1): 51–70.

McPhail, J.C. and Freeman, J.G. (2005). Beyond prejudice: thinking toward genuine inclusion. *Learning Disabilities Research & Practice* 20 (4): 254–267.

Meneghello, R. and Russon, H. (2008). Creating a movement: the first 18 years of the ADA. *Momentum* 1 (4): 21–25.

Middlebrook, H. (2017). The fascinating, if unreliable, history of hate crime tracking in the US. *Cable News Network* https://www.cnn.com/2017/01/05/health/hate-crimes-tracking-history-fbi/index.html (accessed 23 February 2019).

Mittler, P. (2015). The UN convention on the rights of persons with disabilities: implementing a paradigm shift. *Journal of Policy and Practice in Intellectual Disabilities* 12 (2): 79–89.

Monteith, M.J. and Mark, A.Y. (2005). Changing one's prejudiced ways: awareness, affect, and self-regulation. *European Review of Social Psychology* 16 (1): 113–154.

Murray, C., Lombardi, A., and Kosty, D. (2014). Profiling adjustment among postsecondary students with disabilities: a person-centered approach. *Journal of Diversity in Higher Education* 7 (1): 31–44.

Nario-Redmond, M.R. and Oleson, K.C. (2016). Disability group identification and disability-rights advocacy: contingencies among emerging and other adults. *Emerging Adulthood* 4 (3): 207–218.

Nario-Redmond, M.R., Noel, J.G., and Fern, E. (2013). Redefining disability, re-imagining the self: disability identification predicts self-esteem and strategic responses to stigma. *Self and Identity* 12 (5): 468–488.

National Council on Disability. (2001). *The Accessible Future*. Washington, DC: National Council on Disability https://ncd.gov/publications/2001/June_2001 (accessed 23 February 2019).

Ne'eman, A. (2010). The future (and the past) of autism advocacy, or why the ASA's magazine, *The Advocate*, wouldn't publish this piece. *Disability Studies Quarterly* 30 (1): http://www.dsq-sds.org/article/view/1059/1244 (accessed 23 February 2019).

Neufeld, G. (1991). Advocacy: applications in the early years of childhood. In: *Early Intervention Studies for Young Children with Special Needs* (ed. D. Mitchell and R. Brown), 192–210. London: Chapman Hall.

Nichols, J. (2017). Disability-rights activists are the real heroes of the health-care fight. *The Nation* (28 July). https://www.thenation.com/article/disability-rights-activists-are-the-real-heroes-of-the-health-care-fight/ (accessed 27 February 2019).

Nickerson, A.M. and Louis, W.R. (2008). Nationality versus humanity? Personality, identity, and norms in relation to attitudes toward asylum seekers. *Journal of Applied Social Psychology* 38 (3): 796–817.

O'Day, B. and Goldstein, M. (2005). Advocacy issues and strategies for the 21st century: key informant interviews. *Journal of Disability Policy Studies* 15 (4): 240–250.

Olkin, R. and Pledger, C. (2003). Can disability studies and psychology join hands? *American Psychologist* 58 (4): 296–304.

Ostrove, J.M., Cole, E.R., and Oliva, G.A. (2009). Toward a feminist liberation psychology of alliances. *Feminism & Psychology* 19 (3): 381–386.

Palacios, M. G. (2017). "Naming Ableism". CripStory. https://cripstory.wordpress.com/2017/04/01/naming-ableism (accessed 23 February 2019).

Paluck, E.L. (2011). Peer pressure against prejudice: a high school field experiment examining social network change. *Journal of Experimental Social Psychology* 47 (2): 350–358.

Palumbo, S. (n.d.). Spread the word: inclusion. Special Olympics. https://www.specialolympics.org/stories/news/spread-the-word-inclusion (accessed 27 February 2019).

Patient No More. (n.d.). April 1977: day by day. Longmore Institute of Disability. http://longmoreinstitute.sfsu.edu/patient-no-more/april-1977-day-day (accessed 23 February 2019).

Piven, F.F. and Cloward, R.A. (1991). Collective protest: a critique of resource mobilization theory. *International Journal of Politics, Culture and Society* 4 (4): 435–458.

Plant, E.A. and Devine, P.G. (2001). Responses to other-imposed pro-Black pressure: acceptance or backlash? *Journal of Experimental Social Psychology* 37 (6): 486–501.

Plous, S. (2000). Responding to overt displays of prejudice: a role-playing exercise. *Teaching of Psychology* 27 (3): 198–200.

Putnam, M. (2005). Conceptualizing disability: developing a framework for political disability identity. *Journal of Disability Policy Studies* 16 (3): 188–198.

Radermacher, H., Sonn, C., Keys, C., and Duckett, P. (2010). Disability and participation: it's about us but still without us! *Journal of Community & Applied Social Psychology* 20 (5): 333–346.

Raff, J. (2017). Why Americans with disabilities fear medicaid cuts. *The Atlantic* (10 July). https://www.theatlantic.com/politics/archive/2017/07/why-disabled-american-fear-medicaid-cuts/533085/ (accessed 1 March 2019).

Rasinski, H.M. and Czopp, A.M. (2010). The effect of target status on witnesses' reactions to confrontations of bias. *Basic and Applied Social Psychology* 32 (1): 8–16.

Rasinski, H.M., Geers, A.L., and Czopp, A.M. (2013). "I guess what he said wasn't that bad": dissonance in nonconfronting targets of prejudice. *Personality and Social Psychology Bulletin* 39 (7): 856–869.

Reynolds, J.M. (2017). "I'd rather be dead than disabled" – the ableist conflation and the meanings of disability. *Review of Communication* 17 (3): 149–163.

Saguy, T., Dovidio, J.F., and Pratto, F. (2008). Beyond contact: intergroup contact in the context of power relations. *Personality and Social Psychology Bulletin* 43 (3): 432–445.

Schwochau, S. and Blanck, P.D. (2000). The economics of the Americans with Disabilities Act, part III: does the ADA disable the disabled? *Berkeley Journal of Employment and Labor Law* 21 (1): 271–313.

Scotch, R.K. (1988). Disability as the basis for a social movement: advocacy and the politics of definition. *Journal of Social Issues* 44 (1): 159–172.

Secret, M. (2012). Disabilities act prompts flood of suits some cite as unfair. *The New York Times* (17 April). https://www.cnbc.com/id/47072996 (accessed 23 February 2019).

Shapiro, J.P. (1993). *No Pity*. New York: Times Books.

Shelton, J.N. and Stewart, R.S. (2004). Confronting perpetrators of prejudice: the inhibitory effects of social costs. *Psychology of Women Quarterly* 28 (3): 215–223.

Shelton, J.N., Richeson, J.A., Salvatore, J. et al. (2006). Silence is not golden: the intrapersonal consequences of not confronting prejudice. In: *Stigma and Group Inequality: Social Psychological Perspectives* (ed. S. Levin and C. Van Laar), 65–81. Mahwah, NJ: Lawrence Erlbaum.

Simon, B. and Klandermans, B. (2001). Politicized collective identity: a social psychological analysis. *American Psychologist* 56 (4): 319–331.

Smith, S.R. (2001). Distorted ideals: the "Problem of Dependency" and the mythology of independent living. *Social Theory and Practice* 27 (4): 579–598.

Snow, D.A. and Benford, R.D. (1988). Ideology, frame resonance, and participant mobilization. *International Social Movement Research* 1 (1): 197–217.

Stangor, C., Swim, J.K., Sechrist, G.B. et al. (2003). Ask, answer, and announce: the three stages in perceiving and responding to discrimination. *European Review of Social Psychology* 14 (1): 277–311.

Stein, M.A. (2004). Same struggle, different difference: ADA accommodations as antidiscrimination. *University of Pennsylvania Law Review* 153 (2): 579–673.

Steinborn, M. L. (2017). Reimagining ability, reimagining America: teaching disability in United States history classes. Master's Projects and Capstones, 504. https://repository.usfca.edu/capstone/504 (accessed 23 February 2019).

Stroman, D.F. (2003). *The Disability Rights Movement: From Deinstitutionalization to Self-Determination*. Lanham, MD: University Press of America.

Stürmer, S. and Simon, B. (2004). The role of collective identification in social movement participation: a panel study in the context of the German gay movement. *Personality and Social Psychology Bulletin* 30 (3): 263–277.

Tajfel, H. and Turner, J.C. (1979). An integrative theory of intergroup conflict. In: *The Social Psychology of Intergroup Relations* (ed. W.A. Austin and S. Worschel), 33–47. Monteray, CA: Brooks Cole.

Techakesari, P., Droogendyk, L., Wright, S.C. et al. (2017). Supportive contact and LGBT collective action: the moderating role of membership in specific groups. *Peace and Conflict: Journal of Peace Psychology* 23 (3): 307–316.

The White House: Office of the Press Secretary. (2009). Statement from former president George H. W. Bush on the anniversary of the Americans with Disabilities Act. Press release (24 July). https://obamawhitehouse.archives.gov/the-press-office/statement-former-president-george-hw-bush-anniversary-americans-with-disabilities-a (accessed 23 February 2019).

The Disabilities Act covers all of us (1999). Interview with Robert L. Burgdorf, Jr. The Ragged Edge Online. http://www.raggededgemagazine.com/extra/edgextraburgdorf. htm (accessed 27 February 2019).

The White House: Office of the Press Secretary. (2015). Remarks by the president on the Americans with Disabilities Act. Press release (20 July). https://obamawhitehouse. archives.gov/the-press-office/2015/07/20/remarks-president-americans-disabilities- act (accessed 23 February 2019).

Wadsley, P. (2008). Beyond the ADA: Eleanor Smith is fighting for access at home. *Momentum* 1 (4): 27–28.

Wanshel, E. (2017). Protestors with disabilities deserve the credit for saving Obamacare. *Huffington Post* (28 July). https://www.huffpost.com/entry/activists-disabilities- adapt-healthcare-bill_n_597b5508e4b02a4ebb751e2e (accessed 27 February 2019).

White, G.W. (2010). Ableism. In: *Community Psychology: In Pursuit of Liberation and Well- Being* (ed. G. Nelson and I. Prilleltensky), 431–452. New York: Palgrave Macmillan.

Wiesel, E. (1986). Hope, Despair and Memory. Nobel Lecture (11 December). https:// www.nobelprize.org/prizes/peace/1986/wiesel/lecture/ (accessed 23 February 2019).

Wilson-Kovacs, D., Ryan, M.K., Haslam, S.A., and Rabinovich, A. (2008). "Just because you can get a wheelchair in the building doesn't necessarily mean that you can still par- ticipate": barriers to the career advancement of disabled professionals. *Disability & Society* 23 (7): 705–717.

Winter, J.A. (2003). The development of the disability rights movement as the social problem solver. *Disability Studies Quarterly* 23 (1): 33–61.

Wohl, M.J., Branscombe, N.R., and Klar, Y. (2006). Collective guilt: emotional reactions when one's group has done wrong or been wronged. *European Review of Social Psychology* 17 (1): 1–37.

Wright, S.C. (2010). Collective action and social change. In: *Handbook of Prejudice, Stereotyping, and Discrimination* (ed. J.F. Dovidio, M. Hewstone, P. Glick and V.M. Esses), 577–596. Thousand Oaks, CA: Sage.

Wright, S.C. and Baray, G. (2010). Models of social change in social psychology: collective action or prejudice reduction? Conflict or harmony? In: *Beyond Prejudice: Extending the Social Psychology of Conflict, Inequality and Social Change* (ed. J. Dixon and M. Levine), 225–244. Cambridge: Cambridge University Press.

Wright, S.C. and Lubensky, M.E. (2009). The struggle for social equality: collective action versus prejudice reduction. In: *Intergroup Misunderstandings: Impact of Divergent Social Realities* (ed. S. Demoulin, J.-P. Leyens and J.F. Dovidio), 291–310. New York: Psychology Press.

Wright, S.C. and Taylor, D.M. (1998). Responding to tokenism: individual action in the face of collective injustice. *European Journal of Social Psychology* 28 (4): 647–667.

Wright, S.C., Taylor, D.M., and Moghaddam, F.M. (1990). Responding to membership in a disadvantaged group: from acceptance to collective protest. *Journal of Personality and Social Psychology* 58 (6): 994–1003.

Young, J. M. (2010). Equality of Opportunity: The Making of the Americans with Disabilities Act. Report of the National Council on Disabilities. https://files.eric.ed. gov/fulltext/ED512697.pdf (accessed 23 February 2019).

van Zomeren, M., Postmes, T., and Spears, R. (2008). Toward an integrative social identity model of collective action: a quantitative research synthesis of three socio-psychological perspectives. *Psychological Bulletin* 134 (4): 504–535.

Four Disabled Activists You Should Know

Khairani Barokka is a disabled Indonesian writer, poet, performer, and artist. She is passionate about accessibility; her poetry-art book *Indigenous Species* (2016) includes both Braille and text. She is the co-editor of the anthology *Stairs and Whispers: D/deaf and Disabled Poets Write Back* (Alland et al. 2017). For more see: khairanibarokka.com

http://www.khairanibarokka.com/

Finn Gardiner is a Black trans and autistic queer activist. Finn works at the Lurie Institute for Disability Policy at Brandeis University and the Autistic Self Advocacy Network. His work involves translating academic research into policy briefs to help advance disability rights. He is passionate about increasing inclusion for disabled and LGBTQ people. See: expectedly.org/new/welcome/

http://expectedly.org/new/welcome/

Dior Vargas is a Latina mental health Activist. She created the People of Color and Mental Illness Photo project to increase the visibility and representation of mental illness among people of color. Follow her current projects and discover resources on mental illness at: diorvargas.com/about

http://diorvargas.com/booking/

Ayman Eckford is a White, neuro-diverse, disability justice and queer activist. Born in Ukraine, Ayman now lives in Russia. Their numerous disability justice projects are the "Autistic initiative for civil rights," the first Russian group created by and for autistic people; "Neurodiversity in Russia," a web project; and "Intersection," a website focused on queer-autistic people.

https://www.facebook.com/people/
Ayman-Eckford/100011356041821

Disability Activism in Higher Education

Disabled students are frequently unrepresented in higher education and despite the Americans with Disabilities Act (ADA) protections, continue to face barriers in receiving necessary accommodations. This is a brief guide for disabled students and disability rights advocates in higher education.

1. **Know Your Rights.** Title III of the ADA covers the rights of disabled students. Both private and public postsecondary schools that receive federal funds are required to make their programs accessible. This legislation is available for viewing on www.ada.gov
2. **Find Your Campus Allies.** Every college should have a Disability Services office and website. This is where you can request accommodations or specific materials. Often documentation of disability (Individualized Education Program (IEP) or medical forms) is required. Find out who the ADA Compliance Officer is on your campus to share your concerns or complaints.
3. **Utilize Outside Resources.** The National Center for College Students with Disabilities (NCCSD) and the Association on Higher Education and Disability (AHEAD) are two federally funded organizations that offer many resources for disabled students.
4. **Stronger Together.** You are not alone. If your college already has a club or student union for disabled students, join! If not, don't be afraid to start one. The resources above offer suggestions on how to do so.
5. **Be Persistent.** If you feel disabled students' needs are not being met, raise your concerns to the administration and the student body. Your voice matters.

Notable Disability Advocacy Groups

Concrete Change: Visitability. This international network, active since the 1980s, has been devoted to ensuring newly built homes are accessible – with at least one zero-step entrance, wider door frames, and a first-floor bathroom. Imagine not being able to visit your best friend's house or attend a family reunion: universal accessible housing is vital for the inclusion of disabled people. This group focuses on implementing change through policy and law. **Learn more:** www.visitability.org

The **National Black Disability Coalition** examines the intersections of race and disability, with goals that promote unity, equity, and opportunity for and among Black people with disabilities. Their website offers educational

NATIONAL BLACK DISABILITY COALITION
http://www.blackdisability.org/

resources, inclusion toolkits, and a history of Black disabled people. **Learn more**: http://blackdisability.org/.

http://www.pacer.org/about/

Parent Advocacy Coalition for Educational Rights is an online resource to help students, parents, and teachers better understand disability rights. Resources are especially useful for navigating IEP's and school accommodations.

Learn more: www.pacer.org

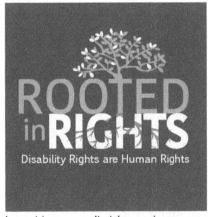

https://www.rootedinrights.org/

Rooted in Rights is a national disability advocacy group. Check their website for tools and information about voting and disability justice.

Learn more: rootedinrights.org

US Disability Rights: Then and Now

Then...

1950–1959: Healthcare costs connected to disability covered by Social Security

1962: Ed Roberts wins lawsuit against UC Berkeley drawing attention to accessibility

1964: Civil Rights Act outlaws racial discrimination, sets stage for ADA

1973: Rehabilitation Act addresses discrimination of disabled people; Section 504 requires accessibility in federally funded programs

1978: Americans Disabled for Public Transit (ADAPT) is founded

1996: Not Dead Yet is founded to oppose euthanasia laws

2002: Help America Vote Act improves access to polls

2012: Patient Protection and Affordable Care Act prohibits insurance companies from denying claims based on "pre-existing conditions" and expands healthcare coverage. More of this timeline at: https://rootedinrights.org/history-of-disability-rights-interactive-timeline-text-only/

> Feel like you missed out on disability history in school? **Read:** Maya L. Steinborn (2017) *Reimagining Ability, Reimagining America: Teaching Disability in United States History Classes.*
>
> **Also check out:** Diana Pastora Carson (2013) *Ed Roberts: Father of Disability Rights.*

Now...

A Victory: In July, 2017, a bill was introduced that would reduce the Medicaid budget by 35%. For disabled people, whose participation as active members of society often depends on healthcare services, this bill was especially threatening. Disabled activists protested outside of Senator McConnell's office: 43 protestors were arrested, some dragged from their wheelchairs. The protests earned national media coverage (Raff 2017), and effectively stopped the bill from passing, protecting health care!

Policy in Progress: The Disability Integration Act of 2017 seeks to protect the civil rights of disabled people by providing them with at-home care instead of institutionalized care. The bill, supported by ADAPT, was introduced by Senator Schumer (D-NY) and Congressman Sensenbrenner (R-Wis.). Learn more: www.disabilityintegrationact.org/

Appendix: Summary of Future Research Questions

Chapter 2: The Evolutionary and Existential Origins of Ableism

Do fears of contagion, as distinct from other fears developed over time, predict specific forms of ableism?

What are some alternative responses to ostracism and avoidance that eliminate the costly exclusion of valued members and concerns about stigma by association?

How might we reduce disease-avoidance behaviors by thinking critically about the irrationality of overgeneralized fears of contagious and noncontagious targets?

When are contagion fears mitigated? Does perceived cleanliness buffer anxieties?

When made to feel personally vulnerable, under what circumstances will particular types of people express different forms of disability prejudice?

Given that studies have tested reactions to same-sex disabled peers after manipulating mortality salience, what would be the reaction to opposite-sex disabled peers?

What are the parameters of viewing humans as superior to animals: are certain characteristics considered essential to quality of life used to justify decisions about sterilization, abortion, physician-assisted suicide, or life-sustaining treatments on the basis of disability?

Does perceiver power moderate animalistic forms of dehumanization and the perception of disabled people as threatening the importance of human superiority?

Ableism: The Causes and Consequences of Disability Prejudice, First Edition.
Michelle R. Nario-Redmond.
© 2020 John Wiley & Sons, Inc. Published 2020 by John Wiley & Sons, Inc.

Do schizophrenics, autistics, or people who use certain assistive technologies experience more objectifying forms of dehumanization that assume them to be unfeeling machines (e.g. denial of pain medication, stealing or destruction of equipment, or assault with prosthetic devices?)

Chapter 3: Justifying Ableism: Ideologies and Language

What are some of the factors that influence when people shift between alternative explanations or models for understanding disability?

What individual differences moderate who will be most receptive and resistant to interventions that reframe disability as discrimination against a minority group?

What are the dynamics involved in changing the "normative window" – the process by which ideas and language shift from being considered acceptable to being widely recognized as ableist?

What forms of disability humor (e.g. making salient societal ignorance) exacerbate or reduce disability prejudice?

How does the framing of disability as a minority group membership impact prejudice, stereotyping, and support for more equitable intergroup relationships?

What other modern-day justification ideologies perpetuate ableist beliefs?

Chapter 4: Cultural and Impairment-Specific Stereotypes

To what extent do individuals personally endorse cultural stereotypes about disability, and what conditions contribute to their use and modification?

When are people more likely to express prejudice or bias toward disabled people who violate stereotypic expectations compared to those who appear more stereotype consistent?

What are the boundary conditions of competency standards and other stereotypic evaluations of disabled people, and to what extent do biased judgments depend on the judgment context?

How much impact do cultural stereotypes about disability have on hiring and performance evaluations, college admissions, and support service determinations?

Are eligibility determinations for limited funding opportunities (e.g. accessible technologies and scholarships) contingent on perceptions of disabled people as cooperative dependents, interdependent, or independent agents?

If portrayed as "fighting" for access to limited resources, or as qualified for high-status positions, to what extent will perceptions of the group's warmth diminish and/or perceptions of competence improve?

What are the mechanisms involved in stereotype change as it pertains to individual impairments and more globalized beliefs about disabled people as a group?

To what extent do deeply engrained automatic biases change in response to updated representations of disabled people as a group, or information about their changed social circumstances?

As a result of the recent campaigns designed to raise awareness about parental rights of disabled people, to what extent have perceptions of disabled mothers and fathers changed?

Chapter 5: Hostile, Ambivalent, and Paternalistic Attitudes and Interactions

If some disabled people are less easily categorized or appear less stereotypical, how will attitudes depend more on context and behavior?

Are certain rights more likely to be denied when group membership is less obvious, and which forms of prejudice are more common when disability stereotypes are activated?

Are accusations of faking one's disability and victim blaming more common among those with less well-established conditions that have yet to be medically legitimized?

How are ambivalent attitudes toward disabled people used to justify inequalities?

When do ambivalent disability attitudes shift from benevolent to hostile and vice versa?

How do the manifestations of ambivalent ableism depend on impairment type and severity?

How does the manifestation of ambivalent ableism depend on specific threats aroused in others: fear of contamination, competition for scarce resources, or perceptions of fakery?

When perceivers describe how disabled people inspire them, what are they inspired to do?

When do inspirational feelings translate into action for disability rights?

When do disabled people perceive inquiries about disability to be legitimate as compared to offensive or objectifying?

What are some examples of how implicit disability attitudes are enacted behaviorally during interactions with others?

When first primed with disability imagery or stereotypes before meeting with peers, disabled or not, how are interactions affected?

When do automatic associations manifest as behavioral avoidance, rejection, unwanted helping, or aggression?

What other implicit measures could be developed that operate through speech forms like conversational contradictions that can shape policy decisions?

When are self-fulfilling effects most likely to undermine mixed-ability interactions with negative consequences for employment, educational, and other outcomes?

When do healthcare professionals respond with more compassion toward those who gratefully submit to the sick role, while withholding care as punishment from those who refuse to comply or get well?

Chapter 6: Contending with Ableism from Internalized Ableism to Collective Action

If those who experience discriminatory injustice are more likely to participate in collective action in support of disability rights, under what conditions might disabled people perceive their group's status as illegitimate yet changeable?

How have disability stereotypes changed as disabled people make collective gains through social activism, legislative reforms, and the penetration of disability arts and culture into the social imagination?

Under what conditions might disability identity threat or stereotype threat be triggered?

What types of institutional programs and policies can counteract social identity threats for disabled people, and affirm a positive sense of belonging among those more isolated from the disability community, the history of the disability rights, and the contemporary figures working for increased disability visibility?

What are some of the consequences of social mobility strategies for disabled people? When will those who escape disability to advance individually work on behalf of those still disabled by society, and when will they neglect former ingroup members or even sabotage their progress?

What are some of the personal and group consequences of dis-identification from disability status given the growing influence of alternate identifications, transhumanism, and human enhancement?

Chapter 7: Interventions to Reduce Prejudice

When does liking an individual disabled person generalize to support for disability rights; can improved attitudes ever undermine the recognition of discrimination or the promotion of fairness and justice, making challenges to inequality less likely?

When does interdependent or cooperative intergroup contact generalize to other disabled people not involved in the contact situation, and for how long?

Are interventions that facilitate positive experiences with outgroups in isolation less effective than those that recognize some negativity (or unearned privileges) associated with the ingroup?

How might engaging meaningfully with disabled students, artists, and professionals who are highly inconsistent with stereotypical expectations in the same context as nondisabled people who reveal their own ingroup inconsistencies and limitations improve intergroup relations?

How effective are anti-prejudice initiatives that minimize disability status as compared to those that keep disability categorization salient?

How effective are universalizing strategies that equate impairments as value neutral traits at reducing ableism or improving support for disability rights?

Similarly, when are universal design approaches that minimize disability status to accommodate a broader range of human variability most beneficial compared to other framing strategies that keep disability salient?

How do perceptions of environmental accessibility depend on whether resources are presented as constrained (funds are limited or allocated only to exclusive groups) or unconstrained (accommodations are universal or not at the expense of others)?

When multicultural initiatives are put into practice, how effective are they in promoting disability as an aspect of diversity? Are there barriers to this conceptualization of disability as a cultural group?

When does exposure to multicultural beliefs strengthen motivation to engage in intergroup perspective taking, and when does taking another group's perspective increase positivity toward multiculturalism?

To what extent can perspective-taking interventions be used to promote more egalitarian attitudes toward disabled people, and/or support for intergroup equality and disability rights?

If simulating impairments heightens one's perceived vulnerability to disability – not to mention perceived helplessness and incompetence – do feelings of alarm and a desire to avoid necessarily follow?

When do interventions that promote fear, aversion, and guilt often fail to contribute to constructive perspectives about disability?

If simulating disability fails to encourage support for more equitable outcomes, how might shifting the focus of simulations to the discriminatory aspects of society alter results?

How might other role-playing activities, besides simulating the experience of different impairments, be used to draw attention to the social and environmental factors that foster ongoing inequalities?

If self-stereotyping is an automatic by-product of perspective-taking interventions, when might this produce personal distress, or perpetuate distrust and stigma by association?

Chapter 8: Beyond Contact: Promoting Social Change and Disability Justice

What are the most effective recruitment strategies to increase the membership of the disability rights movement as a way to unite people with disparate impairments under the shared experience of social disadvantage?

Is the strategy of teaching independent living clients how to demonstrate awareness of disability discrimination necessary and/or sufficient to the development of an activist identity?

How do disabled people appraise the pervasive discrimination, their common fate with other disabled people, the permeability of intergroup boundaries, and the likelihood of collective action success?

What best predicts political participation for disability rights, and how does identification as an ally or an activist develop as a part of this process?

To what extent is confrontation of ableist expressions useful at exposing, resisting, and remedying intergroup inequalities?

When are cooperative as compared to competitive or confrontational approaches most effective at increasing the recognition of disability discrimination?

What factors contribute to majority group involvement in actions that confront prejudicial treatment to defend minority rights and improve egalitarian outcomes?

What are the most optimal forms of anti-ableist confrontation in different circumstances? For example, when should public vs. private, assertive vs. indirect, target vs. ally confrontations be most persuasive in altering what is considered acceptable?

What makes for an effective disability rights ally?

How should successful advocacy be defined? How do we build common ground between disadvantaged groups for effective cross-impairment coalitions?

What are the most effective strategies for shifting appraisals that attribute the problems of inaccessibility to the environment instead of to the person with a disability.

What are the most effective strategies for identifying the benefits of the Americans with Disabilities Act (ADA) litigation, and shifting interpretations from that of "burdening businesses" to making progress toward the implementation of civil rights.

When are disruptive compared to more routine forms of collective action most effective in exposing, resisting, and remedying intergroup inequalities?

What is the impact of disability-infused curricula on student outcomes and perceptions?

Index

Ableism: The Causes and Consequences of Disability Prejudice, First Edition.
Michelle R. Nario-Redmond.
© 2020 John Wiley & Sons, Inc. Published 2020 by John Wiley & Sons, Inc.

CPSIA information can be obtained
at www.ICGtesting.com
Printed in the USA
JSHW010238160822
29328JS00006B/68

9 781119 142072